ENGLISH LAW
DICTIONARY

ENGLISH
LAW
DICTIONARY

P. H. Collin

PETER COLLIN PUBLISHING

First published in Great Britain 1986
by Peter Collin Publishing Ltd
31 Teddington Park, Teddington, Middlesex

Reprinted 1987 (*twice*)

© P. H. Collin 1986

ISBN 0 948549 01 7

Computer Typeset in Helvetica, Times and Ehrhardt by SB Datagraphics,
Colchester

Printed by Richard Clay Ltd, Bungay, Suffolk

PREFACE

This dictionary provides the user with the basic vocabulary used in British and American law. The subject matter covers criminal, civil, commercial and international law, dealing with situations as different as the solicitor's office, the courtroom, and the prison. The level of languages ranges from the very formal (including many Latin terms) to prison slang.

The 6,000 main words and phrases are explained in simple English using a limited vocabulary of 500 words over and above those words which actually appear in the dictionary as main words. Very many examples are given to show the words and phrases used in context, and many of the more difficult phrases are also defined in clear and simple English. Words which pose particular grammatical problems have short grammar notes attached, giving irregular verb forms and plurals, together with notes on constructions and the differences between British and American usage. Many words also have comments of a more general nature, referring to the judicial system, or to particular points of law. At the back of the book a supplement gives information in tabular form about legal systems, writs, judgments, conveyances, wills and other legal documents. We are particularly grateful to the Office for Official Publications, acting on behalf of the institutions of the European Communities, to Her Majesty's Stationery Office, and to the Solicitors' Law Stationery Society Plc for giving permission to reproduce copyright documents in the supplement.

We would also like to thank many people who helped in the compilation and checking of this dictionary, in particular Stephen Baister who brought his trained legal mind to bear on the printouts and provided many valuable expert comments as well as drafting the supplements; Derek Beattie and Françoise Collin, who read and checked all the proofs, providing many suggestions and corrections; and Peter Cartwright who designed the cover.

Aa

A *first letter of the alphabet* **category "A" prisoners** = prisoners who are dangerous, and would be a danger to the public if they escaped from prison; **Schedule A** = schedule to the Finance Acts under which tax is charged on income from land *or* buildings; **Table A** = model articles of association of a limited company set out in the Companies Act, 1985; **"A" shares** = ordinary shares with limited voting rights

◇ **A1** *adjective* **(a)** best; **we sell only goods in A1 condition (b) ship which is A1 at Lloyd's** = ship which is in best condition according to Lloyd's Register

A.B.A. = AMERICAN BAR ASSOCIATION

abandon *verb* **(a)** to give up *or* not to continue; **to abandon an action** = to give up a court case **(b)** to leave (something *or* a person); **he abandoned his family and went abroad; the crew abandoned the sinking ship**

◇ **abandonment** *noun* act of giving something up voluntarily (such as the right to a property); **abandonment of a claim** = giving up a claim in a civil action

COMMENT: abandoning a child under two years old is a notifiable offence

abate *verb* **(a)** to remove *or* stop a nuisance **(b)** (i) to reduce (a legacy); (ii) (*of a legacy*) to be reduced (because there is not enough money in the estate to pay in full)

◇ **abatement** *noun* **(a)** removal *or* stopping of a nuisance; **noise abatement** = stopping someone who is making an unpleasant loud noise; **a noise abatement notice was served on the club (b)** reducing a legacy *or* legacies, where the deceased person has not left enough money to pay them all in full

◇ **abator** *noun* person who abates a nuisance

abduct *verb* to take (someone, especially a woman *or* child) away by force; **the bank manager was abducted at gunpoint; the robbers abducted the heiress and held her to ransom**

◇ **abduction** *noun* notifiable offence of taking someone (especially a woman *or* child) away by force

◇ **abductor** *noun* person who takes someone away by force

abet *verb* to encourage someone to commit a crime; **aiding and abetting** = offence of helping and encouraging someone to commit a crime
NOTE: **abetting - abetted**

abeyance *noun* **(a) this law is in abeyance** = this law in not being enforced at the present time **(b)** situation where there is no owner of a piece of land
NOTE: no plural

ABH = ACTUAL BODILY HARM

abide by *verb* to obey (an order *or* a rule); **he promised to abide by the decision of the court; she did not abide by the terms of the agreement**

ab initio *Latin phrase meaning* "from the beginning"

abjure *verb* US to swear not to bear allegiance to another country

◇ **abjuration** *noun* act of abjuring

abnormal *adjective* not normal *or* not usual

abode *noun* residence *or* place where someone lives; **right of abode** = right to live in a country

abolish *verb* to cancel *or* to remove (a law *or* a rule); **the Chancellor of the Exchequer refused to ask Parliament to abolish the tax**

on alcohol; **the Senate voted to abolish the death penalty**

◇ **abolition** *noun* act of abolishing; **to campaign for the abolition of the death penalty**

abortion *noun* ending of a pregnancy before the natural term

> COMMENT: illegal abortion is a notifiable offence

abrogate *verb* to end (a law *or* a treaty)

◇ **abrogation** *noun* ending (of a law *or* a treaty)

abscond *verb* to go away without permission *or* not to return to the court after being released on bail *or* to escape from prison; **he was charged with absconding from lawful custody**

absence *noun* not being at a meeting *or* hearing; **in the absence of** = when someone is not there; **in the absence of the chairman, his deputy took the chair; the trial took place in the absence of the defendant; she was sentenced to death in her absence; leave of absence** = being allowed to be absent from work; *see also* IN ABSENTIA

◇ **absent** *adjective* not at a meeting *or* hearing

◇ **absentee** *noun* person who is not able to attend a meeting *or* hearing

absolute *adjective* complete *or* total; **absolute discharge** = letting a convicted person go free without any punishment; **absolute monopoly** = situation where only one producer or supplier produces or supplies something; **absolute privilege** = privilege which protects a person from being sued for defamation (such as an MP speaking in the House of Commons, a judge making a statement in judicial proceedings); *see also* DECREE, FORECLOSURE

abstain *verb* to refrain from doing something (especially voting); **sixty MPs abstained in the vote on capital punishment**

◇ **abstention** *noun* **(a)** refraining from doing something (especially voting); **the motion was carried by 200 votes to 150, with 60 abstentions (b)** *US* situation where a

federal court refuses to hear a case and passes it to a state court

abstract 1 *noun* short form of a report *or* document; **to make an abstract of the deeds of a property; abstract of title** = summary of the details of the ownership of a property which has not been registered **2** *verb* to make a summary

abuse 1 *noun* **(a)** using something wrongly; **abuse of power** = using legal powers in an illegal *or* harmful way; **abuse of process** = suing someone in bad faith *or* without proper justification *or* for malicious reasons; **drug abuse** = being mentally and physically dependent on taking a drug regularly **(b)** rude *or* insulting words; **the prisoner shouted abuse at the judge (c)** bad treatment (usually sexual) of a person; **child abuse** *or* **sexual abuse of children** (NOTE: no plural for (b) or (c)) **2** *verb* **(a)** to use something wrongly; **to abuse one's authority** = to use authority in an illegal *or* harmful way **(b)** to say rude words to (someone); **he abused the police before being taken to the cells (c)** to treat someone badly (usually in a sexual way); **he had abused small children**

abut (on) *verb* (*of a piece of land*) to touch another property
NOTE: **abutting - abutted**

ACAS = ADVISORY CONCILIATION AND ARBITRATION SERVICE

ACC = ASSISTANT CHIEF CONSTABLE

accept *verb* **(a)** to take something which is being offered **(b)** to say "yes" *or* to agree to something; **she accepted the offer of a job in Australia; he accepted £200 for the car; to accept an offer conditionally** = to accept provided that certain conditions apply

◇ **acceptable** *adjective* which can be accepted; **the offer is not acceptable to both parties**

◇ **acceptance** *noun* one of the main conditions of a contract, where one party agrees to what is proposed by the other party; **acceptance of an offer** = agreeing to an offer (and therefore entering into a contract); **we have his letter of acceptance** = we have received a letter from him accepting the offer; *see note at* CONTRACT

◇ **accepting house** *noun* firm which accepts bills of exchange (i.e. promises to pay them) and is paid a commission for this

◊ **acceptor** *noun* person who accepts an offer

access 1 *noun* **(a)** right of the owner of a piece of land to use a public road which is next to the land; **he complained that he was being denied access to the main road (b)** to **have access to something** = to be able to obtain *or* reach something; **to gain access to something** = to reach *or* to get hold of something; **access to the courts should be open to all citizens; the burglar gained access through the window (c)** right of a child to see a parent regularly *or* of a parent or grandparent to see a child regularly, where the child is in the care of someone else (NOTE: no plural) **2** *verb* to call up (data) which is stored in a computer

◊ **accession** *noun* joining something *or* taking up a position; **accession to the throne** = becoming King *or* Queen; **Treaty of Accession** = treaty whereby the UK joined the EEC

◊ **accessory** *noun* person who helps *or* advises someone who is committing a crime; **accessory after the fact** = person who helps a criminal after the crime has been committed; **accessory before the fact** = person who helps a criminal before the crime is committed

accident *noun* something unpleasant which happens by chance (such as the crash of a plane); **industrial accident** = accident which takes place at work; **accident insurance** = insurance which will pay when an accident takes place

◊ **accidental** *adjective* which happens by accident; **a case of accidental death**

accommodation *noun* **(a)** money lent for a short time **(b)** something done to help someone; **to reach an accommodation with creditors** = ·to agree terms for settlement; **accommodation address** = address used for receiving messages but which is not the real address of the company; **accommodation bill** = bill of exchange where the person signing is helping someone to raise a loan; **accommodation maker** = person who signs a promissory note for no fee, but who expects to lend the creditor money

accompany *verb* to go with; **they sent a formal letter of complaint, accompanied by an invoice**
NOTE: accompanied **by** something

accomplice *noun* person who helps another to commit a crime

accord and satisfaction *noun* payment by a debtor of (part of) a debt *or* the performing by a debtor of some act or service which is accepted by the creditor in full settlement, so that the debtor can no longer be sued

accordance *noun* **in accordance with** = in agreement with *or* according to; **in accordance with your instructions we have deposited the money in your current account; I am submitting the claim for damages in accordance with the advice of our legal advisers**

◊ **according to** *preposition* as someone says *or* writes; **according to the witness, the accused carried the body on the back seat of his car; the payments were made according to the maintenance order**

◊ **accordingly** *adverb* in agreement with what has been decided; **we have received your letter and have altered the contract accordingly**

account 1 *noun* **(a)** invoice *or* record of money paid *or* owed; **please send me your account *or* a detailed *or* an itemized account; accounts payable** = money owed to creditors; **accounts receivable** = money owed by debtors; **action for an account** = court action to establish how much money is owed by one party to another **(b)** (*in a shop*) arrangement which a customer has with the shop to buy goods and pay for them at a later date (usually the end of the month) **(c)** customer who does a large amount of business with a firm and has a credit account with that firm **(d)** the **accounts of a business *or* a company's accounts** = detailed record of a company's financial affairs **(e) bank account *or* US banking account** = arrangement to keep money in a bank **(f)** (*Stock Exchange*) period of credit (usually fourteen days) at the end of which all people who have traded must pay for shares bought **(g)** notice *or* attention; **to take account of the age of the accused *or* to take the accused's age into account when passing sentence** = to pass a certain sentence because the accused is very old *or* very young **2** *verb* **to account for** = to explain and record a money deal; **to account for a loss** *or* **a discrepancy**

◊ **accountable** *adjective* (person) who has to explain what has taken place *or* who is responsible for something; **if money is lost, the person at the cash desk is held accountable; the group leader will be held accountable for the actions of the group**

◊ **accountability** *noun* being accountable *or* responsible

◊ **accountant** *noun* person trained in keeping *or* drawing up accounts *or* arranging systems of accounts; **Chartered Accountant** = accountant who has passed the professional examinations and is a member of the Institute of Chartered Accountants

◊ **accounting** *noun* preparing the accounts of a business; **false accounting** = notifiable offence of changing *or* destroying *or* hiding financial records for money

accredited *adjective* (agent) who is appointed by a company to act on its behalf

accrual *noun* slow increase by addition; **accrual of interest** = automatic addition of interest to capital

◊ **accrue** *verb* (*of interest* or *dividends*) to increase and be due for payment at a later date

accumulate *verb* to grow larger by adding

accuse *verb* to say that someone has committed a crime *or* to charge someone with a crime; **she was accused of stealing £25 from her boss; he was accused of murder; of what has she been accused?** *or* **what has she been accused of?**
NOTE: you accuse someone **of** a crime

◊ **accusation** *noun* act of saying that someone has committed a crime

◊ **accused** *noun* **the accused** = person *or* persons charged with a crime; **all the accused pleaded not guilty; the police brought the accused into the court**
NOTE: can be singular or plural: **the six accused all pleaded guilty**

acknowledge *verb* (a) to accept that something is true; **acknowledged and agreed** = words written on an agreement

to show that it has been read and approved (b) to confirm that (a letter) has been received; **to acknowledge service** = to confirm that a legal document (such as a writ) has been received

◊ **acknowledgement** *noun* act of acknowledging; **acknowledgement of service** = document whereby a defendant confirms that a writ *or* a legal document has been received and that he intends to defend the case

acquire *verb* to buy *or* to obtain

◊ **acquisition** *noun* (i) thing bought; (ii) act of obtaining *or* buying something; **the acquisition of Smith & Sons by Jones Ltd** = the takeover of Smith & Sons

acquit *verb* to set a person free because he has been found not guilty; **he was acquitted of the crime; the court acquitted two of the accused**
NOTE: **acquitting - acquitted** Note also that you acquit someone **of** a crime

◊ **acquittal** *noun* act of acquitting someone of a crime; **after his acquittal he left the court smiling**

act 1 *noun* (a) statute which has been approved by a law-making body (in Great Britain, by Parliament); **Act of Parliament** = decision which has been approved by Parliament and so becomes law; **Companies Act** = British Act which rules how companies should do their business; **Finance Act** = annual Act of the British Parliament which gives the government power to raise taxes as proposed in the budget (NOTE: use **under** when referring to an Act of Parliament: **a creditor seeking a receiving order under the Bankruptcy Act; she does not qualify under section 2 of the 1979 Act**)

COMMENT: before an Act becomes law, it is presented to Parliament in the form of a Bill. See notes at BILL

(b) **act of God** = natural disaster which you do not expect to happen, and which cannot be avoided (such as a storm *or* a flood)

COMMENT: acts of God are usually not covered by an insurance policy

2 *verb* (a) to work; **to act as an agent for an American company; to act for someone** *or* **to act on someone's behalf** (b) to do something; **the lawyers are acting on our**

instructions; **to act on a letter** = to do what a letter asks to be done

action *noun* **(a)** thing which has been done; **to take action** = to do something **(b) court action** = civil case in a law court where a person sues another person; **letter before action** = letter written by a lawyer to give a party the chance to pay his client before he sues; **action in personam** = court case in which one party claims that the other should do some act *or* should pay damages; **action in rem** = court case in which one party claims property *or* goods in the possession of the other; **action in tort** = case brought by a plaintiff who alleges he has suffered damage *or* harm caused by the defendant; **to take legal action** = to begin a legal case (such as to instruct a solicitor *or* to sue someone); **action for damages; action for libel** *or* **libel action; to bring an action for damages against someone; chose in action** = personal right which can be enforced or claimed as if it were a property (such as a patent *or* copyright); **civil action** = case brought by a person *or* company (the plaintiff) against someone who is alleged to have harmed them (the defendant); *US* **class action** = legal action brought on behalf of a group of people; **criminal action** = case brought usually by the state against someone who is charged with a crime; **personal action** = (i) legal action brought by a person himself; (ii) common law term for an action against a person arising out of a contract *or* tort

◇ **actionable** *adjective* (writing *or* speech *or* act) which could provide the grounds for bringing an action against someone; **torts which are actionable per se** = torts which are in themselves sufficient grounds for bringing an action without the need to prove that damage has been suffered

◇ **active** *adjective* working *or* busy; **active partner** = partner who works in the firm

◇ **actively** *adverb* in a busy way

◇ **activity** *noun* being active

actual *adjective* real; **actual bodily harm (ABH)** = assault which causes injury to the victim; **actual loss** *or* **damage** = real loss *or* damage which can be shown to have been suffered; **actual notice** = real knowledge which someone has of something;

actual value = real value of something if sold on the open market

actuary *noun* person employed by an insurance company to calculate premiums

◇ **actuarial** *adjective* calculated by an actuary; **the premiums are worked out according to actuarial calculations; actuarial tables** = lists showing how long people of certain ages are likely to live, used to calculate life assurance premiums

actus reus *Latin phrase meaning* "guilty act": act which is forbidden by the criminal law, one of the two elements of a crime; *compare* MENS REA. *See note at* CRIME

addict *noun* **drug addict** = person who is physically and mentally dependent on taking drugs regularly

◇ **addicted** *adjective* **addicted to alcohol** *or* **drugs** = being unable to live without taking alcohol *or* drugs regularly

◇ **addiction** *noun* **drug addiction** = being mentally and physically dependent on taking a drug regularly

address 1 *noun* details of number, street and town where an office is or where a person lives; **address for service** = address where court documents (such as pleadings) can be sent to a party in a case **2** *verb* **(a)** to write the details of an address on an envelope, etc.; **an incorrectly addressed package (b)** to speak to; **the defendant asked permission to address the court**

adduce *verb* to bring before the court; **to adduce evidence** = to bring evidence before a court

adeem *verb* to remove a legacy from a will because it no longer exists

◇ **ademption** *noun* removing a legacy from a will, because the item concerned no longer exists

adequate *adjective* large enough; **to operate without adequate cover** = to act without being protected by insurance; **he made adequate provision for his wife** = in his will he left his wife enough money to live on

ad hoc *Latin phrase meaning* "for this particular purpose"; **an ad hoc committee** = a committee set up to study a particular problem; *see also* STANDING

ad idem *Latin phrase meaning* "in agreement"

adjoin *verb* (*of a property*) to touch another property; **the developers acquired the old post office and two adjoining properties; the fire spread to the adjoining property**

adjourn *verb* to stop a meeting for a period *or* to put off a legal hearing to a later date; **to adjourn a meeting; the chairman adjourned the tribunal until three o'clock; the meeting adjourned at midday; the appeal was adjourned for affidavits to be obtained; the hearing was adjourned sine die** = the hearing was adjourned without saying when it would meet again

◊ **adjournment** *noun* act of adjourning; **the adjournment lasted two hours; the defendant has applied for an adjournment; adjournment debate** = debate in the House of Commons on a motion to adjourn the sitting

adjudicate *verb* to give a judgment between two parties in law; to decide a legal problem; **to adjudicate a claim; to adjudicate in a dispute; magistrates may be paid expenses when adjudicating; he was adjudicated bankrupt** = he was declared legally bankrupt

◊ **adjudication** *noun* act of giving a judgment *or* of deciding a legal problem; **adjudication order** *or* **adjudication of bankruptcy** = order by a court making someone bankrupt; **adjudication tribunal** = group which adjudicates in industrial disputes

◊ **adjudicator** *noun* person who gives a decision on a problem; **an adjudicator in an industrial dispute**

adjust *verb* to change something to fit new conditions, especially to calculate and settle an insurance claim

◊ **adjuster** *noun* person who calculates losses for an insurance company; **average adjuster** *or* **loss adjuster** = person who calculates how much is due to the insured when he makes a claim under his policy

◊ **adjustment** *noun* act of adjusting; slight change; **average adjustment** = calculation of the share of cost of damage or loss of a ship

◊ **adjustor** *noun* = ADJUSTER

ad litem *Latin phrase meaning* "referring to the case at law"; **guardian ad litem** = person who acts on behalf of a minor who is a defendant in a court case

administer *verb* (a) **to administer justice** = to provide justice; **to administer an oath** = to make someone swear an oath (b) to organize *or* to manage; **he administers a large pension fund** (c) to give someone a medicine *or* a drug; **she was accused of administering a poison to the old lady**

◊ **administration** *noun* (a) organization *or* control *or* management, especially the management of the affairs of someone who has died; **letters of administration** = document given by a court to allow someone to deal with the estate of a person who has died without leaving a will *or* where the executor appointed under the will cannot act (NOTE: not used in the singular) **administration bond** = oath sworn by an administrator that he will pay the state twice the value of the estate being administered, if it is not administered in accordance with the law; **administration order** = order by a court, appointing someone to administer the estate of someone who is not able to meet the obligations of a court order (b) government; **the Act became law under the previous administration; she was Minister of Education in the last administration**

◊ **administrative** *adjective* referring to administration; **administrative law** = laws which regulate how government organizations affect the lives and property of individuals; **administrative tribunal** = tribunal which decides in cases where government regulations affect and harm the lives and property of individuals

◊ **administrator** *noun* (a) person who arranges the work of other employees in a business so that the business functions well (b) person appointed by a court to represent a person who has died without making a will or without naming executors, and who is recognized in law as able to manage the estate

◊ **administratrix** *noun* woman appointed by a court to administer the estate of a person who has died

Admiralty *noun* British government office which in charge of the Navy; **Admiralty Court** = court which decides in disputes involving ships; **Admiralty law** =

law relating to ships and sailors, and actions at sea

admit *verb* **(a)** to allow someone to go in; **children are not admitted to the bank; old age pensioners are admitted at half price (b)** to allow someone to practise as a solicitor; **he was admitted in 1978 (c)** to allow evidence to be used in court; **the court agreed to admit the photographs as evidence (d)** to agree that an allegation is correct *or* to say that something really happened; **he admitted his mistake** *or* **his liability; she admitted having stolen the car; he admitted to being in the house when the murder took place**
NOTE: **admitted - admitting.** Note also that you admit **to** something, or admit **having done** something

◊ **admissibility** *noun* being admissible; **the court will decide on the admissibility of the evidence**

◊ **admissible** *adjective* (evidence) which a court will admit *or* will allow to be used; **the documents were not considered relevant to the case and were therefore not admissible**

◊ **admission** *noun* **(a)** allowing someone to go in; **there is a £1 admission charge; admission is free on presentation of this card; free admission on Sundays (b)** making a statement that you agree that certain facts are correct *or* saying that something really happened

adopt *verb* **(a)** to become the legal parent of a child who was born to other parents **(b)** to agree to (something) *or* to accept (something) so that it becomes law; **to adopt a resolution; the proposals were adopted unanimously**

◊ **adoption** *noun* **(a)** act of becoming the legal parent of a child which is not your own; **adoption order** = order by a court which legally transfers the rights of the natural parents to the adoptive parents; **adoption proceedings** = court action to adopt someone **(b)** act of agreeing to something so that it becomes legal; **he moved the adoption of the resolution**

◊ **adoptive** *adjective* **adoptive child** = child who has been adopted; **adoptive parent** = person who has adopted a child

COMMENT: if a child's parents divorce, or if one parent dies, the child may be adopted by a step-father or step-mother

adult *noun* person who is eighteen years old *or* who has reached majority

adultery *noun* sexual intercourse by consent between a married person and someone of the opposite sex who is not that person's spouse; **his wife accused him of committing adultery with Miss X**
NOTE: no plural

◊ **adulterous** *adjective* referring to adultery; **he had an adulterous relationship with Miss X**

ad valorem *Latin phrase meaning* "according to value"; **ad valorem duty** *or* **ad valorem tax** = tax calculated according to the value of the goods taxed

advance 1 *noun* **(a)** money paid as a loan *or* as a part of a payment which is to be completed later; **a cash advance; to receive an advance from the bank; an advance on account; to make an advance of £100 to someone (b) in advance** = early *or* before something happens; **to pay in advance; freight payable in advance (c)** early; **advance booking; advance payment; you must give seven days' advance notice of withdrawals from the account 2** *verb* **(a)** to lend (money); **the bank advanced him £10,000 against the security of his house (b)** to increase; **prices generally advanced on the stock market (c)** to make something happen earlier; **the date of the hearing has been advanced to May 10th**

advantage *noun* something useful which may help you to be successful; **to learn something to your advantage** = to hear news which is helpful to you, especially to hear that you have been left a legacy; **obtaining a pecuniary advantage by deception** = offence of deceiving someone so as to derive a financial benefit

adversary *noun* opponent *or* the other side (in a court case)

adverse *adjective* contrary *or* which goes against one party; **adverse possession** = occupation of property (such as by squatters) contrary to the rights of the real owner; **adverse witness** = hostile witness *or* witness called by a party, whose evidence goes unexpectedly against that party and who can then be cross-examined by his own side as if he were giving evidence for the other side

advert *verb* to refer to; **this case was not adverted to in** *Smith* v. *Jones Machines Ltd*

advice *noun* **(a) advice note** = written notice to a customer giving details of goods ordered and shipped but not yet delivered; **as per advice** = according to what is written on the advice note **(b)** opinion as to what action should be taken; **to take legal advice** = to ask a lawyer to advise about a problem in law; **counsel's advice** = opinion of a barrister about a case; **we sent the documents to the police on the advice of the solicitor** *or* **we took the solicitor's advice and sent the documents to the police**

advise *verb* **(a)** to tell someone what has happened; **we are advised that the shipment will arrive next week (b)** to suggest to someone what should be done; **we are advised to take the shipping company to court; the solicitor advised us to send the documents to the police**

◇ **advise against** *verb* to suggest that something should not be done; **the bank manager advised against closing the account; our lawyers have advised against suing the landlord**

◇ **adviser** *or* **advisor** *noun* person who suggests what should be done; **he is consulting the company's legal adviser; financial adviser** = person *or* company which gives advice on financial problems for a fee

◇ **advisory** *adjective* as an adviser; **he is acting in an advisory capacity; an advisory board** = a group of advisers; *GB* **the Advisory Conciliation and Arbitration Service (ACAS)** = government body which assists in settling industrial and employment disputes

advocacy *noun* (i) skill of pleading a case orally before a court; (ii) support for a cause; **his advocacy of the right of illegal immigrants to remain in the country**

advocate **1** *noun* (*in Scotland*) barrister; *US* lawyer; **Faculty of Advocates** = legal body to which Scottish barristers belong; **Judge Advocate-General** = lawyer

appointed by the state to advise on all legal matters concerning the army

◇ **Advocate General** *noun* **(a)** one of the two Law Officers for Scotland **(b)** (*in the European Court of Justice*) officer of the court who summarizes and presents a case to the judges to assist them in coming to a decision

advowson *noun* right to nominate a person to be a parish priest

affair *noun* **(a)** business *or* dealings; **are you involved in the copyright affair? his affairs were so difficult to understand that the lawyers had to ask accountants for advice (b)** adulterous relationship *or* sexual relationship where one party (or both parties) is married to someone else; **to have an affair with someone** = to commit adultery

affect *verb* to change *or* to have a bad effect on (something); **the new government regulations do not affect us; the company's sales in the Far East were seriously affected by the embargo**

◇ **affection** *noun* love (for another person); *see also* ALIENATION

affidavit *noun* written statement which is signed and sworn before a solicitor and which can then be used as evidence in court hearings

affiliation *noun* **affiliation order** = court order which makes the father of an illegitimate child pay for the child's maintenance; **affiliation proceedings** = court case to order the father of an illegitimate child to provide for the child's maintenance

affirm *verb* **(a)** to state that you will tell the truth, but without swearing an oath **(b)** to confirm that something is correct

◇ **affirmation** *noun* statement in court that you will say the truth, though this is not sworn on oath

◇ **affirmative** *adjective* meaning "yes"; **the answer was in the affirmative** = the answer was "yes"

affray *noun* public fight which frightens other people

COMMENT: a person is guilty of affray if he uses or threatens to use unlawful violence towards another, and his conduct is such that a reasonable person who happened to be present might fear for his safety

aforementioned *adjective* which has been mentioned earlier; **the aforementioned company**

aforesaid *adjective* said earlier; **as aforesaid** = as was stated earlier

aforethought *adjective* **with malice aforethought** = with the intention of committing a crime (especially murder)

a fortiori *Latin phrase meaning* "for a stronger reason"; **if the witness was present at the scene of the crime, then a fortiori he must have heard the shot**

against *preposition* **(a) against the law** = which breaks the law; **lighting fires in the street is against the law; the company went against the law by sending dangerous goods through the post (b)** relating to *or* part of; **to pay an advance against next month's salary; the bank advanced him £10,000 against the security of his house**

agency *noun* **(a)** (i) arrangement where one person *or* company acts on behalf of another person in contractual matters; (ii) office *or* job of representing another company in an area; **they signed an agency agreement *or* an agency contract (b)** branch of government; **the Atomic Energy Agency; a counter-intelligence agency**

agenda *noun* list of things to be discussed at a meeting; **the committee meeting agenda *or* the agenda of the committee meeting; after two hours we were still discussing the first item on the agenda; the Secretary put finance at the top of the agenda**

agent *noun* **(a)** person who represents a company *or* another person in matters relating to contracts; **land agent** = person who manages a farm *or* large area of land for someone **(b)** person in charge of an agency; **advertising agent; estate agent; travel agent; commission agent** = agent who is paid by commission, not by fee **(c)** person who works for a government agency, especially in secret; **secret agent** =

person who tries to find out information in secret about other countries *or* other governments *or* other armed forces

◊ **agent provocateur** *French words meaning* "agent who provokes": person who provokes others to commit a crime (often by taking part in it himself) in order to find out who is not reliable *or* in order to have his victim arrested

aggravation *noun* something (usually the carrying of a weapon) which makes a crime more serious

◊ **aggravated** *adjective* made worse; **aggravated assault** = assault causing serious injury *or* carried out in connection with another serious crime; **aggravated burglary** = burglary where guns *or* other weapons are used; **aggravated damages** = damages awarded by a court against a defendant who has behaved maliciously *or* wilfully

aggrieved *adjective* (party) who has been damaged *or* harmed by a defendant's actions

AGM = ANNUAL GENERAL MEETING

agree *verb* **(a)** to approve; **the figures were agreed between the two parties; terms of the contract are still to be agreed (b)** to say "yes" *or* to accept; **it has been agreed that the lease will run for twenty-five years; after some discussion he agreed to our plan; the bank will never agree to lend the company £250,000 (c) to agree to do something** = to say that you will do something
NOTE: you agree **to** or **on** a plan or agree **to do** something

◊ **agree with** *verb* **(a)** to say that your opinions are the same as someone else's **(b)** to be the same as; **the witness' statement does not agree with that of the accused**

◊ **agreed** *adjective* which has been accepted by everyone; **an agreed amount; on agreed terms *or* on terms which have been agreed upon**

◊ **agreement** *noun* document setting out the contractual terms agreed between two parties *or* contract between two parties where one party makes an offer, and the other party accepts it; **written agreement; unwritten *or* verbal agreement; to draw up *or* to draft an agreement; to break an agreement; to sign an agreement; to witness an agreement; an agreement has** been reached *or* concluded *or* come to; to reach an agreement *or* to come to an agreement on prices *or* salaries; an international agreement on trade; collective wage agreement; an agency agreement; a marketing agreement; blanket agreement = agreement which covers many different items; exclusive agreement = agreement where a company is appointed sole agent for a product in a market; shareholders' agreement = agreement showing the rights of shareholders in a company; agreement in principle = agreement with the basic conditions of a proposal; gentleman's agreement = verbal agreement between two parties who trust each other

COMMENT: a gentleman's agreement is not usually enforceable by law

aid 1 *noun* help; **Legal Aid** = British government scheme whereby a person with very little money can have legal representation and advice paid for by the state; **to pray in aid** = to rely on something when pleading a case; **I pray in aid the Statute of Frauds in support of the defendant's case 2** *verb* to help; **to aid and abet** = to help and encourage someone to commit a crime

◊ **aiding and abetting** *noun* offence of helping and encouraging someone to commit a crime

a. k. a. = ALSO KNOWN AS

al. *see* ET AL.

alarm *noun* device which gives a warning, usually by ringing a bell; **as he put his hand through the window he set off an alarm bell; burglar alarm** = bell which is set to ring when someone tries to break into a house *or* shop; **fire alarm** = bell which is set to sound if it detects fire

aleatory *adjective* not certain *or* which carries a risk; **aleatory contract** = bargain (such as a wager) where what is done by one party depends on something happening which is not certain to happen

alia *see* ET ALIA, INTER ALIA

alias 1 *noun* name which you take to hide your real name; **the confidence trickster used several aliases 2** *adverb* otherwise

known as *or* using the name of; **John Smith, alias Reginald Jones**

alibi *noun* plea that a person charged with a crime was somewhere else when the crime was committed

alien *noun* person who is not a citizen of a country; (*in the UK*) person who is not a UK citizen, not a citizen of a Commonwealth country and not a citizen of the Republic of Ireland

alienation *noun* the transfer of property (usually land) to someone else; **alienation of affection** = making one of the partners in a marriage stop loving the other

alimony *noun* money which a court orders a husband to pay regularly to his separated *or* divorced wife; **alimony pending suit *or* pendente lite** = money paid by a husband to his wife while their divorce case is being prepared; *see also* PALIMONY (NOTE: no plural; in GB English is usually referred to as **maintenance**)

COMMENT: can occasionally be applied to a wife who is ordered to support her divorced husband

all *adjective & pronoun* everything *or* everyone; **all the witnesses say they saw the accused with the can of petrol; all the evidence suggests that it was a gang of three people who held up the bank; on all fours with** = exactly similar to; **this case is on all fours with** *Donoghue* v. *Stevenson*

◊ **All England Law Reports (All E.R.)** *plural noun* reports of cases in the higher courts

◊ **all-in** *adjective* including everything

allege *verb* to state (usually in evidence) that something has happened *or* is true; **the prosecution alleged that the accused was in the house when the crime was committed**

◊ **allegation** *noun* statement (usually in evidence) that something has happened *or* is true

allegiance *noun* obedience to the State *or* the Crown; **oath of allegiance** = oath which is sworn to put the person under the orders *or* rules of a country *or* an army, etc.; **he swore an oath of allegiance to the new president**

All E. R. = ALL ENGLAND LAW REPORTS

allocate *verb* to divide (something) in various ways and share it out

◇ **allocation** *noun* (a) dividing a sum of money in various ways; **allocation of funds to research into crime** (b) **share allocation** *or* **allocation of shares** = spreading a small number of shares among a large number of people who have applied for them

◇ **allocatur** *Latin word meaning* "it is allowed": court document confirming the amount of costs to be paid by one party to another after a court action

allot *verb* to share out; **to allot shares** = to give a certain number of shares to people who have applied for them
NOTE: allotting - allotted

◇ **allotment** *noun* (a) sharing out funds by giving money to various departments (b) giving some shares in a new company to people who have applied to buy them

allow *verb* (a) to say that someone can do something; **the law does not allow you to drive on the wrong side of the road; begging is not allowed in the station; visitors are not allowed into the prisoners' cells** (b) to give (someone) time *or* a privilege; **the court adjourned to allow the prosecution time to find the missing witness; you are allowed thirty days to pay the fine** (c) to agree *or* to accept legally; **to allow a claim** *or* **an appeal**

◇ **allow for** *verb* to give a discount for *or* to add an extra sum to cover something; **delivery is not allowed for** = delivery charges are not included; **allow twenty-eight days for delivery** = calculate that delivery will take at least 28 days

◇ **allowable** *adjective* legally accepted; **allowable expenses** = expenses which can be claimed against tax

◇ **allowance** *noun* (a) money which is given for a special reason; **travel allowance** *or* **travelling allowance; foreign currency allowance; cost-of-living allowance** = addition to normal salary to cover increases in the cost of living (b) **personal allowances** = part of a person's income which is not taxed; **allowances against tax** *or* **tax allowances; wife's earned income allowance** = tax allowance to be set against money earned by the wife of the main taxpayer (c) proportion of money

removed; **to make an allowance for legal expenses** *or* **an allowance for exchange loss**

alphabet *noun* the 26 letters used to make words

◇ **alphabetical order** *noun* arrangement of records (such as files, index cards) in the order of the letters of the alphabet (A,B,C,D, etc.); **the names of the accused were read out in alphabetical order**

alter *verb* to change; **to alter the terms of a contract; he has altered his will six times in the last ten years**

◇ **alteram** *see* AUDI

◇ **alteration** *noun* change which has been made; **we made some alterations to the terms of a contract**

alternative 1 *noun* thing which can be done instead of another 2 *adjective* other *or* which can take the place of something; **to find someone alternative employment** = to find someone another job

a.m. *or* **ante meridiem** *Latin phrase meaning* "in the morning" *or* "before 12 midday"; **the flight leaves at 9.20 a.m.; telephone calls before 6 a.m. are charged at the cheap rate**

ambiguous *adjective* (words) which can mean two or more things *or* which can be misleading; **the wording of the clause is ambiguous and needs clarification**

◇ **ambiguity** *noun* (a) being ambiguous (b) words which are ambiguous; **latent ambiguity** = words in a contract which can mean two or more things, but which do not appear to be misleading at first sight

amend *verb* to change *or* correct; **please amend your copy of the contract accordingly**

◇ **amendment** *noun* (a) change made in a document; **to propose an amendment to the draft agreement; to make amendments to a contract** (b) change proposed to a Bill which is being discussed in Parliament

◇ **amends** *plural noun* **to make amends** = to do something to compensate for damage *or* harm done; **offer of amends** = offer (by a libeller) to write an apology

American Bar Association *noun* association of lawyers practising in the USA

amicus curiae *Latin phrase meaning* "friend of the court": lawyer who does not represent a party in a case but who is called upon to address the court to help clear up a difficult legal point *or* to explain something which is in the public interest

amnesty 1 *noun* pardon, often for political crimes, given to several people at the same time; **general amnesty** = pardon granted to all prisoners **2** *verb* to grant convicted persons a pardon; **they were amnestied by the president**

anarchy *noun* lack of law and order, because the government has lost control; **when the president was assassinated, the country fell into anarchy**
NOTE: no plural

◊ **anarchical** *adjective* with no law or order; **the anarchical state of the country districts**

ancestor *noun* person living many years ago from whom someone is descended; **common ancestor** = person from whom two or more people are descended; **Mr Smith and the Queen have a common ancestor in King Henry VIII**

ancient lights *plural noun* claim by the owner of a property that he has the right to enjoy light in his windows, which light must not be blocked by a neighbour's buildings

ancillary *adjective* which gives help *or* support; **ancillary relief** = financial provision *or* adjustment of property rights ordered by a court for a spouse or child in divorce proceedings

animus *noun* intention; **animus cancellandi** = the intention to cancel; **animus furandi** = the intention to steal; **animus manendi** = the intention to stay (in a place); **animus revocandi** = the intention to revoke (a will)
NOTE: when used to mean "with the intention of", use **animo: animo revocandi** = with the intention of revoking a will

annexe *or* *US* **annex 1** *noun* document added *or* attached to a contract **2** *verb* to attach (a document)

announce *verb* to tell something to the public; **the foreman of the jury announced their verdict**

◊ **announcement** *noun* telling something in public; **the chairman made an announcement about the takeover bid**

annual *adjective* for one year; **Annual General Meeting** = meeting of the shareholders of a company which takes place once a year to approve the accounts; **annual return** = form to be completed by each company once a year, giving details of the directors and the financial state of the company; **on an annual basis** = each year

◊ **annually** *adverb* each year; **the figures are revised annually**

annuity *noun* money paid each year to a person, usually as the result of an investment; **he has a government annuity** *or* **an annuity from the government; to buy** *or* **to take out an annuity**

◊ **annuitant** *noun* person who receives an annuity

annul *verb* (i) to cancel *or* to stop something having any legal effect; (ii) to declare that something never existed *or* that something never had legal effect; **the contract was annulled by the court; their marriage has been annulled**
NOTE: **annulling - annulled**

◊ **annullable** *adjective* which can be cancelled

◊ **annulling 1** *adjective* which cancels; **annulling clause 2** *noun* act of cancelling; **the annulling of a contract**

◊ **annulment** *noun* act of cancelling; **annulment of adjudication** = cancelling of an order making someone bankrupt; **annulment of marriage** = ending of a marriage, by saying that it never existed

annum *see* PER ANNUM

answer 1 *noun* (a) reply *or* letter or conversation coming after someone else has written or spoken; **I am writing in answer to your letter of October 6th; my letter got no answer** *or* **there was no answer to my letter; I tried to phone his office but there was no answer** (b) formal reply to an allegation made in court, especially defence made by a respondent to a divorce petition **2** *verb* (a) to speak *or* write after someone has spoken or written to you; **to answer a letter** = to write a letter in reply to a letter which you have received; **to answer the telephone** = to lift the telephone when it rings and listen to what the caller is saying (b) to reply formally to an allegation made in court; **to answer charges**

= to plead guilty *or* not guilty to a charge; **the judge ruled there was no case to answer** = the judge ruled that the prosecution *or* the plaintiff had not shown that the accused *or* the defendant had done anything wrong

◊ **answerable** *adjective* having to explain why actions have been taken *or* being responsible for one's actions; **he is answerable to the Police Commissioner for the conduct of the officers in his force; she refused to be held answerable for the consequences of the police committee's decision**
NOTE: you are answerable **to** someone **for** an action

ante *Latin adverb meaning* "which has taken place earlier" *or* "before"; **status quo ante** = the situation as it was before

antecedents *plural noun* details of the background of a convicted person given to a court before sentence is passed

antedate *verb* to put an earlier date on a document; **the invoice was antedated to January 1st**

anti- *prefix* against; **an anti-drug campaign; the anti-terrorist squad**

◊ **anti-trust** *adjective* which attacks monopolies and encourages competition; **anti-trust laws** *or* **legislation**

anticipation *noun* doing something before it is due to be done

◊ **anticipatory** *adjective* done before it is due; **anticipatory breach** = refusal by a party to a contract to perform his obligations under the contract at a time before they were due to be performed

Anton Piller order *noun* order by a court in a civil case allowing a party to inspect and remove a defendant's documents, especially where the defendant might destroy evidence

COMMENT: called after the case of *Anton Piller K.G.* v. *Manufacturing Processes Ltd*

AOB = ANY OTHER BUSINESS

apologize *verb* to say you are sorry; **to apologize for the delay in answering; she apologized for being late; he apologized to the court for the absence of the chief witness**

◊ **apology** *noun* saying you are sorry; **to write a letter of apology; I enclose a cheque for £10 with apologies for the delay in answering your letter; the writer of the libel was ordered to print a full apology**

a posteriori *Latin phrase meaning* "from what has been concluded afterwards"; **a posteriori argument** = argument based on observation

apparent *adjective* which can be seen; **apparent defect** = defect which can be easily seen; **heir apparent** = heir who will certainly inherit if a person dies before him

appeal 1 *noun* asking a higher court to change a decision of a lower court *or* asking a government department to change a decision; **the appeal from the court order** *or* **the appeal against the planning decision will be heard next month; he lost his appeal for damages against the company; she won her case on appeal** = her case was lost in the first court, but the appeal court said that she was right; **appeal against conviction** = asking a higher court to change the decision of a lower court that a person is guilty; **appeal against sentence** = asking a higher court to reduce a sentence imposed by a lower court; **Appeal Court** *or* **Court of Appeal** = civil or criminal court to which a person may go to ask for a sentence to be changed and of which the decisions are binding on the High Court and lower courts; **Lord of Appeal in Ordinary** = one of the eleven lords who sits as a member of the House of Lords when it acts as a Court of Appeal **2** *verb* to ask a government department to change its decision *or* a high law court to change a sentence; **the company appealed against the decision of the planning officers; he has appealed to the Supreme Court** (NOTE: you appeal **to** a court or **against** a decision; an appeal is **heard** and **allowed** or **dismissed**)

COMMENT: in English law, in the majority of cases decisions of lower courts and of the High Court can be appealed to the Court of Appeal. The Court of Appeal is divided into the Civil Division and the Criminal Division. The Civil Division hears appeals from the County Court and the High Court; the Criminal Division hears appeals from the Crown Court. From the Court of Appeal, appeal lies to the House of Lords. When the remedies available under English law are exhausted, it is in certain cases possible to appeal to the European Court of Justice. For many countries (especially Commonwealth countries) appeals may be heard from the highest court of these countries by the Privy Council

appear *verb* (a) to seem; **the witness appeared to have difficulty in remembering what had happened** (b) to come to court to stand trial (c) to come to court to represent a client; **Mr A. Clark QC is appearing on behalf of the defendant**

◊ **appearance** *noun* act of coming to court to defend *or* prosecute a case; **to enter an appearance** = to register with a court that a defendant intends to defend an action; **entry of appearance** = lodging by the defendant of a document in court to confirm his intention to defend an action

appellant *noun* person who appeals *or* who goes to a higher court to ask it to change a decision *or* a sentence imposed by a lower court

appellate *adjective* referring to appeal; **appellate jurisdiction** = jurisdiction of the House of Lords to hear appeals

appendix *noun* additional text at the end of a document; **the markets covered by the agency agreement are listed in the Appendix; see Appendix B for the clear-up rates of notifiable offences**
NOTE: plural is **appendices**

apply *verb* (a) to ask for something, usually in writing; **to apply for a job; to apply for shares; to apply in writing; to apply in person; my client wishes to apply for Legal Aid; he applied for judicial review** *or* **for compensation** *or* **for an adjournment; to apply to the Court** = to ask the court to make an order; **he applied to the Court for an injunction** to affect *or* to touch; **this clause applies only to deals outside the EEC; the legal precedent applies to cases where the parents of the child are divorced**

◊ **applicant** *noun* person who applies for something; **applicant for a job** *or* **job applicant; there were thousands of applicants for shares in the new company**

◊ **application** *noun* (a) asking for something, usually in writing; **application for shares; shares payable on application; application for a job** *or* **job application; application form** = form to be filled in when applying; **to fill in an application (form) for a job** *or* **a job application (form); letter of application** = letter in which someone applies for a job *or* applies for shares in a new company (b) act of asking the Court to make an order; **his application for an injunction was refused; solicitors acting for the wife made an application for a maintenance order**

appoint *verb* to choose someone for a job; **to appoint James Smith to the post of manager; the government has appointed a QC to head the inquiry; the court appointed a receiver**
NOTE: you appoint a person **to** a job or **to do** a job

◊ **appointee** *noun* person who is appointed to a job

◊ **appointment** *noun* (a) arrangement to meet; **to make** *or* **to fix an appointment for two o'clock; to make an appointment with someone for two o'clock; he was late for his appointment; she had to cancel her appointment; appointments book** = desk diary in which appointments are noted (b) being appointed to a job; **on his appointment as magistrate** = when he was made a magistrate; **letter of appointment** = letter in which someone is appointed to a job (c) job; **legal appointments vacant** = list in a newspaper of legal jobs which are vacant

apportion *verb* to share out (property *or* rights *or* liabilities) in proportion; **costs are apportioned according to planned revenue**

◊ **apportionment** *noun* sharing out of (property *or* rights *or* liabilities)

appraise *verb* to make an estimate of the value of something

◊ **appraiser** *noun* person who appraises something

appreciate *verb* (a) to notice how good something is; **a judge always appreciates a well-documented case** (b) to increase in value; **property values have appreciated by 20% over the last two years**

◊ **appreciation** *noun* **(a)** increase in value **(b)** act of valuing something highly; **in appreciation of** = to show how much something is valued

apprehend *verb formal* **(a)** to understand; **I apprehend that you say your client has a reference (b)** to arrest; **the suspect was apprehended at the scene of the crime**

◊ **apprehension** *noun formal* arrest (of a person)

approach 1 *noun* **(a)** getting in touch with someone with a proposal; **the company has had an approach from an Australian consortium (b)** method of dealing with something; **he has a professional approach to his work** 2 *verb* **(a)** to get in touch with someone with a proposal; **he approached the bank with a request for a loan; the company was approached by an American publisher with the suggestion of a merger (b)** to come closer *or* to bring closer; **the offer does not approach the figure my client seeks**

appropriate 1 *adjective* suitable *or* which fits; **is a fine an appropriate punishment for sex offences?** 2 *verb* to take control of (something) for one's own use; **the town council appropriated the land to build the new municipal offices**

◊ **appropriation** *noun* allocating of money for a particular purpose; **appropriations committee** = committee which examines government expenditure

approve *verb* **(a) to approve of** = to think something is good **(b)** to agree to something officially; **to approve the terms of a contract; the proposal was approved by the board; the motion was approved by the committee**

◊ **approval** *noun* **(a)** agreement; **to submit a budget for approval; certificate of approval** = document showing that an item has been approved officially **(b) on approval** = sale where the buyer pays for goods only if they are satisfactory

◊ **approved school** *noun* old name for a school for young delinquents

appurtenant *adjective* connected to *or* belonging to

◊ **appurtenances** *plural noun* land *or* buildings attached to *or* belonging to a property

a priori *Latin phrase meaning* "from the first"; **a priori argument** = reasoning based on ideas *or* assumptions, not on real examples

arbitrate *verb* to settle a dispute between parties by referring it to an arbitrator instead of going to court (usually used in building *or* shipping *or* employment disputes); **to arbitrate in a dispute**

◊ **arbitration** *noun* settling of a dispute by an outside person *or* persons, chosen by both sides; **to submit a dispute to arbitration; to refer a question to arbitration; to take a dispute to arbitration; to go to arbitration; arbitration agreement** = agreement by two parties to submit a dispute to arbitration; **arbitration award** = ruling given by an arbitrator; **arbitration board** *or* **arbitration tribunal** = group which arbitrates; **industrial arbitration tribunal** = court which decides in industrial disputes; **to accept the ruling of the arbitration board**
NOTE: no plural

◊ **arbitrator** *noun* person not concerned with a dispute who is chosen by both sides to try to settle it; **industrial arbitrator; to accept** *or* **to reject the arbitrator's ruling**

argue *verb* **(a)** to discuss something about which there is disagreement; **they argued over** *or* **about the price; counsel spent hours arguing about the precise meaning of the clause; the union officials argued among themselves over the best way to deal with the ultimatum from the management (b)** to give reasons for something; **prosecuting counsel argued that the accused should be given exemplary sentences; the police solicitor argued against granting bail**
NOTE: you argue **with** someone **about** *or* **over** something

◊ **argument** *noun* **(a)** discussing something without agreeing; **they got into an argument with the judge over the relevance of the documents to the case; he sacked his solicitor after an argument over costs (b)** (speech giving) reasons for something; **the judge found the defence arguments difficult to follow; counsel presented the argument for the prosecution; the Court of Appeal was concerned that the judge at first instance**

had delivered judgment without proper argument
NOTE: can be used without **the**

arise *verb* to happen *or* to come as a result; **the situation has arisen because neither party is capable of paying the costs of the case; the problem arises from the difficulty in understanding the VAT regulations; matters arising** = section in an agenda, where problems *or* questions which refer to items in the minutes of the previous meeting can be discussed
NOTE: **arising - arose - arisen**

arm's length *noun* **at arm's length** = not closely connected *or* dealt with in an official and not a personal way; **the directors were required to deal with the receiver at arm's length**

armourer *noun slang* criminal who supplies guns to other criminals

arraign *verb* to make the accused person appear in the court and to read the indictment to him
◊ **arraignment** *noun* reading of the indictment to the accused and hearing his plea

arrange *verb* **(a)** to put in order; **the office is arranged as an open-plan area with small separate rooms for meetings; the files are arranged in alphabetical order; arrange the documents in order of their dates (b)** to organize; **the hearing was arranged for April; we arranged to have the meeting in their offices; she arranged for a car to meet him at the airport**
NOTE: you arrange **for** someone to do something or you arrange **for** something to be done
◊ **arrangement** *noun* **(a)** way in which something is organized; **the company secretary is making all the arrangements for the AGM (b)** settling of a financial dispute, especially by proposing a plan for repaying creditors; **to come to an arrangement with the creditors; deed of arrangement** = agreement made between a debtor and his creditors whereby the creditors accept an agreed sum in settlement of their claim rather than make the debtor bankrupt; **scheme of arrangement** = agreement between a company and its creditors whereby the creditors accept an agreed sum in settlement of their claim rather than force the company into insolvency

arrears *plural noun* money which is owed, but which has not been paid at the right time; **to allow the payments to fall into arrears; in arrears** = owing money which should have been paid earlier; **the payments are six months in arrears; he is six weeks in arrears with his rent**

arrest 1 *noun* **(a)** act of taking and keeping someone legally, so that he can be kept in custody and charged with a crime; **a warrant is out for his arrest** = a magistrate has signed a warrant, giving the police the power to arrest someone for a crime; **under arrest** = kept and held by the police; **six of the gang are in the police station under arrest; citizen's arrest** = right of a private person to arrest without a warrant someone who he suspects has committed a crime; **house arrest** = being ordered by a court to stay in your own house and not to leave it; **the opposition leader has been under house arrest for six months; summary arrest** = arrest without a warrant **(b) arrest of judgment** = situation where a judgment is held back because there appears to be an error in the documentation 2 *verb* **(a)** to hold someone legally so as to keep him in custody and charge him with a crime; **two of the strikers were arrested; the constable stopped the car and arrested the driver (b)** to seize a ship *or* its cargo
◊ **arrestable offence** *noun* crime for which someone can be arrested without a warrant (usually an offence which carries a penalty of at least five years' imprisonment)
◊ **arrest warrant** *noun* warrant signed by a magistrate which gives the police the power to arrest someone for a crime

COMMENT: any citizen may arrest a person who is committing a serious offence, though members of the police force have wider powers, in particular the power to arrest persons on suspicion of a serious crime or in cases where an arrest warrant has been granted. Generally a policeman is not entitled to arrest someone without a warrant if the person does not know or is not told the reason for his arrest

arson *noun* notifiable offence of setting fire to property; **he was charged with arson;**

during the riot there were ten cases of looting and two of arson; **the police who are investigating the fire suspect arson; an arson attack on a house** = setting fire to a house
NOTE: no plural

◊ **arsonist** *noun* person who commits arson

article *noun* (**a**) product *or* thing for sale; **a black market in imported articles of clothing** (**b**) section of a legal agreement; **see article 8 of the contract** (**c**) **articles of association** *or* *US* **articles of incorporation** = document which regulates the way in which a company's affairs are managed; **articles of partnership** = document which sets up the legal conditions of a partnership; **he is a director appointed under the articles of the company; this procedure is not allowed under the articles of association of the company** (**d**) **articles** = time when a clerk is working in a solicitor's office learning the law; **articles of indenture** = contract by which a trainee craftsman works for a master for some years to learn a trade; **to serve articles** = to work in a solicitor's office to learn the law

◊ **articled** *adjective* **articled clerk** = clerk who is bound by contract to work in a solicitor's office for some years to learn the law

artificial person *noun* body (such as a company) which is a person in the eyes of the law

aside *adverb* to one side *or* out of the way; **to put aside** *or* **to set aside** = to say that something no longer applies; **the appeal court set aside the earlier judgment**

ask *verb* (**a**) to put a question to someone; **prosecuting counsel asked the accused to explain why the can of petrol was in his car** (**b**) to tell someone to do something; **the police officers asked the marchers to go home; she asked her secretary to fetch a file from the managing director's office; the customs officials asked him to open his case; the judge asked the witness to write the name on a piece of paper**

◊ **ask for** *verb* (**a**) to say that you want *or* need something; **he asked for the file on 1984 debtors; counsel asked for more time to consult with his colleagues; there is a man on the phone asking for Mr Smith; to ask for bail to be granted** = to ask a court to

allow a prisoner to be remanded on bail (**b**) to put a price on something for sale; **they are asking £24,000 for the car**

assassin *noun* murderer of a public figure

◊ **assassinate** *verb* to murder (a public figure)

◊ **assassination** *noun* murder of a public figure

assault 1 *noun* crime *or* tort of acting in such a way that someone is afraid he will be attacked and hurt; **he was sent to prison for assault; the number of cases of assault** *or* **the number of assaults on policemen is increasing;** *see also* BATTERY (NOTE: as a crime *or* tort, assault has no plural; when it has a plural this means "cases of assault") 2 *verb* to attack someone; **she was assaulted by two muggers**

COMMENT: assault should be distinguished from battery, in that assault is the threat of violence, whereas battery is actual violence. However, because the two are so closely connected, the term "assault" is frequently used as a general term for violence to a person. "Aggravated assault" is assault causing serious injury or carried out in connection with another serious crime. The term "common assault" is frequently used for any assault which is not an aggravated assault

assay *noun* test (especially of gold *or* silver) to see if a metal is of the right quality; **assay mark** = hallmark *or* mark put on gold or silver items to show that the metal is of correct quality

assemble *verb* (**a**) to put something together from various parts; **the police are still assembling all the evidence** (**b**) to come together *or* to gather; **the crowd assembled in front of the police station**

◊ **assembly** *noun* coming together in a group; **the Assembly of the EEC** = the European Parliament; **freedom of assembly** = being able to meet as a group without being afraid of prosecution; **unlawful assembly** = notifiable offence when a number of people come together to commit a breach of the peace or any other crime

assent *noun* agreement to something; **Royal Assent** = formal passing of a Bill into law to become an Act of Parliament

assert *verb* to state in a strong way *or* to insist; **he asserted that the damage suffered was extremely serious**

◇ **assertion** *noun* strong statement; **counsel made a series of assertions which were disputed by the witness**

assess *verb* to calculate the value of something, especially for tax *or* insurance purposes; **to assess damages at £1,000; to assess a property for the purposes of insurance**

◇ **assessment** *noun* calculation of value; **assessment of damages; assessment of property; tax assessment**

◇ **assessor** *noun* expert who can help a judge in a particularly difficult case

asset *noun* thing which belongs to company or person, and which has a value; **he has an excess of assets over liabilities; her assets are only £640 as against liabilities of £24,000; concealment of assets** = hiding assets so that creditors do not know that they exist; **capital assets** *or* **fixed assets** = property *or* machinery which a company owns and uses; **current assets** = assets used by a company in its ordinary work (such as materials, finished goods, cash); **fictitious assets** = assets which do not really exist, but are entered as assets to balance the accounts; **frozen assets** = assets of a company which cannot be sold because someone has a claim against them; **intangible assets** = assets which have a value, but which cannot be seen (such as goodwill *or* a patent *or* a trademark); **liquid assets** = cash, or bills which can be quickly converted into cash; **personal assets** = moveable assets which belong to a person; **tangible assets** = assets which are solid (such as furniture *or* jewels *or* cash); **asset value** = value of a company calculated by adding together all its assets

assign *verb* (a) to give *or* transfer; **to assign a right to someone; to assign shares to someone; to assign a debt to someone** (b) to give someone a piece of work to do; **he was assigned the job of checking the numbers of stolen cars; three detectives have been assigned to the case**

◇ **assignee** *noun* person who receives something which has been assigned

◇ **assignment** *noun* (a) legal transfer of a property *or* of a right; **assignment of a patent *or* of a copyright; assignment of a lease; deed of assignment** = agreement which legally transfers a property from a debtor to a creditor (b) document whereby something is assigned (c) particular job of work; **we have put six constables on that particular assignment**

◇ **assignor** *noun* person who assigns something to someone

◇ **assigns** *plural noun* people to whom property has been assigned; **his heirs and assigns** = people who have inherited his property and had it transferred to them

assist *verb* to help; **the accused had to be assisted into the dock; assisted person** = person who is receiving Legal Aid

◇ **assistance** *noun* help; **litigants who receive assistance under the Legal Aid scheme; financial assistance** = help in the form of money

Assizes *or* **Assize Courts** *plural noun* old name for what is now the Crown Court

associate **1** *adjective* joined together with something; **associate company** = company which is partly owned *or* controlled by another; **associate director** = director who attends board meetings, but does not enjoy the full powers of a director **2** *noun* person who works in the same business as someone; **in his testimony he named six associates; associate of the Crown Office** = official who is responsible for the clerical and administrative work of a court **3** *verb* to mix with *or* to meet (people); **she associated with criminals** = she was frequently in the company of criminals

◇ **associated** *adjective* joined to *or* controlled by; **Smith Ltd and its associated company, Jones Brothers**

◇ **association** *noun* (a) group of people *or* of companies with the same interest; **trade association; employers' association; freedom of association** = being able to join together in a group with other people without being afraid of prosecution; **guilt by association** = presumption that a person is guilty because of his connection with a guilty person (b) **articles of association** = document which regulates the way in which a company's affairs are managed (such as the appointment of directors and rights of shareholders); **memorandum of association** = document setting up a limited company, giving details of its aims, the way it is financed and its registered office **(c)** (*in prison*) time when prisoners can move about and meet other prisoners

assume *verb* **(a)** to believe something without any proof; **everyone assumed he was guilty (b)** to take; **to assume all risks; he has assumed responsibility for marketing**
◇ **assumption** *noun* taking; **assumption of risks** = situation where someone sees that risks exist but still takes the risks

assure *verb* to insure *or* to have a contract with a company where if regular payments are made, the company will pay compensation if you die *or* suffer harm or damage; **the assured** = person whose interests are assured *or* who is entitled to the benefit in an insurance policy
◇ **assurance** *noun* insurance *or* agreement that in return for regular payments, one party will pay another party compensation for loss of life
◇ **assurer** *or* **assuror** *noun* insurer *or* company which insures

> COMMENT: **assure** and **assurance** are used in Britain for insurance policies relating to something which will certainly happen (such as death or the end of a given period of time); for other types of policy use **insure** and **insurance**

asylum *noun* **(a)** hospital for person who are mentally ill **(b)** safe place; **to ask for political asylum** = to ask to be allowed to remain in a foreign country because it would be dangerous to return to the home country for political reasons

at issue *see* ISSUE

attach *verb* **(a)** to fasten *or* to join; **I am attaching a copy of my previous letter; attached is a copy of my letter of June 24th (b)** to arrest (a person *or* a property)
◇ **attachment** *noun* **(a)** holding a debtor's property to prevent it from being sold until debts are paid; **attachment of earnings** = legal power to take money from a person's salary to pay money,

which is owed, to the courts; **attachment of earnings order** = court order to make an employer pay part of an employee's salary to the court to pay off debts **(b) warrant of attachment** = warrant which authorizes the bailiff to arrest a person in contempt of court

attack 1 *verb* **(a)** to try to hurt *or* harm someone; **the security guard was attacked by three men carrying guns (b)** to criticize; **MPs attacked the government for not spending enough money on the police 2** *noun* **(a)** act of trying to hurt *or* harm someone; **there has been an increase in attacks on police** *or* **in terrorist attacks on planes (b)** criticism; **the newspaper published an attack on the government** NOTE: you attack someone, but make an attack on someone
◇ **attacker** *noun* person who attacks; **she recognized her attacker and gave his description to the police**

attainder *noun* **bill of attainder** = obsolete way of punishing a person legally without holding a trial, by passing a law to convict and sentence him

attempt 1 *noun* **(a)** trying to do something; **the company made an attempt to break into the American market; the takeover attempt was turned down by the board; all his attempts to get a job have failed (b)** trying to do something illegal *or* to commit an offence

> COMMENT: attempt is a crime even if the attempted offence has not been committed

2 *verb* to try; **the solicitor attempted to have the charge dropped; he was accused of attempting to contact a member of the jury; attempted murder** = notifiable offence of trying to murder someone

attend *verb* to be present at; **the witnesses were subpoenaed to attend the trial**
◇ **attend to** *verb* to give careful thought to (something) and deal with it; **the managing director will attend to your complaint personally**
◇ **attendance** *noun* being present; **attendance centre** = place where a young person may be sent by a court to take part in various types of sport or do hard work as a punishment

◇ **attention** *noun* careful thought; **for the attention of the Managing Director; your orders will have our best attention**

attest *verb* to sign (a document such as a will) in the presence of a witness who also signs as evidence that the signature is real

◇ **attestation** *noun* signing a document (such as a will) in the presence of a witness to show that the signature is genuine; **attestation clause** = clause showing that the signature of the person signing a legal document has been witnessed

COMMENT: the attestation clause is usually written: "signed sealed and delivered by ... in the presence of ..."

attorn *verb* to transfer

◇ **attorney** *noun* **(a)** person who is legally allowed to act on behalf of someone else; **letter of attorney** = document showing that someone has power of attorney; **power of attorney** = official power giving someone the right to act on someone else's behalf in legal matters; **his solicitor was granted power of attorney (b)** *US* lawyer

◇ **Attorney-General** *noun* *GB* one of the Law Officers, a Member of Parliament, who prosecutes for the Crown in certain cases, advises government departments on legal problems and decides if major criminal offences should be tried; *US* minister of legal affairs in a state or federal government

COMMENT: in the US Federal Government, the Attorney-General is in charge of the Department of Justice

attribute *verb* to suggest that something came from a source; **remarks attributed to the Chief Constable**

◇ **attributable** *adjective* which can be attributed

auction **1** *noun* selling of goods where people offer bids, and the item is sold to the person who makes the highest offer; **to put something up for auction** = to offer an item for sale at an auction **2** *verb* to sell to the person who makes the highest offer; **the factory was closed and the machinery was auctioned off**

◇ **auctioneer** *noun* person who conducts an auction

audi alteram partem *Latin phrase meaning* "hear the other side": a rule in natural justice that everyone has the right to speak in his own defence and to have the case against him explained to him

audience *noun* right to speak to a court, which can be used by the parties in the case or their legal representatives; **a barrister has right of audience in any court in England and Wales**

audit **1** *noun* examination of the books and accounts of a company; **to carry out an annual audit; external audit** *or* **independent audit** = audit carried out by an independent auditor; **general audit** = examining of all the books and accounts of a company; **internal audit** = audit carried out by a department inside the company **2** *verb* to examine the books and accounts of a company; **to audit the accounts; the books have not yet been audited**

◇ **auditor** *noun* person who audits; **the AGM appoints the company's auditors; Comptroller and Auditor General** = official whose duty is to examine the accounts of ministries and government departments; **external auditor** = independent person who audits the company's accounts; **internal auditor** = member of staff who audits a company's accounts

authenticate *verb* to show that something is true

authority *noun* **(a)** official power given to someone to do something; **he has no authority to act on our behalf; she was acting on the authority of the court; on whose authority was the charge brought? (b) local authority** = section of elected government which runs a small area of a country; **a court can give directions to a local authority; a decision of the local authority pursuant to the powers and duties imposed upon it by the statutory code; the Bill aims at giving protection to children in the care of a local authority (c) the authorities** = the government *or* those who are in control

authorize *verb* **(a)** to give official permission for something to be done; **to authorize payment of £10,000 (b)** to give someone the authority to do something; **to authorize someone to act on your behalf**

◊ **authorization** *noun* **(a)** official permission *or* power to do something; **do you have authorization for this expenditure? he has no authorization to act on our behalf** **(b)** document showing that someone has official permission to do something; **he showed the bank his authorization to inspect the contents of the safe**

◊ **authorized** *adjective* permitted; **authorized capital** = amount of capital which a company is allowed to have, according to its memorandum of association; **authorized dealer** = person *or* company (such as a bank) which is allowed to buy and sell foreign currency

automatic *adjective* which works *or* takes place without any special action *or* instruction; **there is an automatic increase in salaries on January 1st**

◊ **automatically** *adverb* working without a person giving instructions; **unpaid fines are automatically increased by 15%**

◊ **automatism** *noun* defence to a criminal charge whereby the accused states he acted involuntarily

autopsy *noun* examination of a dead person to see what was the cause of death

autrefois acquit *French phrase meaning* "previously acquitted": plea that an accused person has already been acquitted of the crime with which he is charged

◊ **autrefois convict** *French phrase meaning* "previously convicted": plea that an accused person has already been convicted of the crime with which he is charged

available *adjective* which can be used *or* which is ready to be used; **the right of self-defence is only available against unlawful attack**

aver *verb* to make a statement *or* an allegation in pleadings
NOTE: averring - averred

◊ **averment** *noun* statement *or* allegation made in pleadings

average **1** *noun* **(a)** number calculated by adding together several figures and dividing by the number of figures added; **the average for the last three months** *or* **the**
last three months' average; sales average *or* average of sales; on an average** = in general; **on an average, £15 worth of goods are stolen every day** **(b)** sharing of the cost of damage or loss of a ship between the insurers and the owners; **average adjuster** = person who calculates how much is due to the insured when he makes a claim under his policy; **general average** = sharing of the cost of the lost goods by all parties to an insurance; **particular average** = situation where part of a shipment is lost or damaged and the insurance costs are borne by the owner of the lost goods and not shared among all the owners of the shipment **2** *adjective* **(a)** middle (figure); **average cost of expenses per employee; the average figures for the last three months; the average increase in prices** **(b)** not very good; **the company's performance has been only average; he is an average worker** **3** *verb* to produce as an average figure; **price increases have averaged 10% per annum; days lost through sickness have averaged twenty-two over the last four years**

◊ **averager** *noun* person who buys the same share at various times and at various prices to give an average price

avoid *verb* to try not to do something; **the company is trying to avoid bankruptcy; my aim is to avoid paying too much tax; we want to avoid direct competition with Smith Ltd; to avoid creditors** = to make sure that creditors cannot find you so as not to pay them
NOTE: you avoid something or someone or avoid **doing** something

◊ **avoidance** *noun* **(a)** trying not to do something; **avoidance of an agreement** *or* **of a contract; tax avoidance** = trying (legally) to pay as little tax as possible; *see also* EVASION **(b)** confession to a charge, but suggesting it should be cancelled

await *verb* to wait for; **we are awaiting the decision of the planning department; they are awaiting a decision of the court; the solicitor is awaiting our instructions**

award **1** *noun* decision which settles a dispute; **an award by an industrial tribunal; the arbitrator's award was set aside on appeal; arbitration award** = ruling given by an arbitrator **2** *verb* to decide the amount of money to be given to someone; **to award someone a salary increase; to award damages; the judge awarded costs to**

the defendant; **to award a contract to a company** = to decide that a company will have the contract to do work for you

Bb

B *second letter of the alphabet* **category "B" prisoners** = less dangerous prisoners, who still have to be guarded carefully to prevent them from escaping; **Schedule B** = schedule to the Finance Acts under which tax is charged on income from woodlands; **Table B** = model memorandum of association of a limited company set out in the Companies Act, 1985; **"B" shares** = ordinary shares with special voting rights

back 1 *noun* opposite side to the front; **the conditions of sale are printed on the back of the invoice; please endorse the cheque on the back 2** *adjective* referring to the past; **back interest** = interest not yet paid; **back rent** = rent owed; **back taxes** = taxes which have not been paid; **back wages** *or* **back pay** = wages which are owed to a worker **3** *adverb* as things were before; **he will pay back the money in monthly instalments; the store sent back the cheque because the date was wrong; he went back on his promise not to see the girl 4** *verb* **(a) to back someone** = to help someone financially **(b) to back a bill** = (i) to sign a bill promising to pay it if the person it is addressed to is not able to do so; (ii) to support a Bill in Parliament

◊ **backdate** *verb* to put an earlier date on a cheque *or* an invoice; **backdate your invoice to April 1st; the pay increase is backdated to January 1st**

◊ **backer** *noun* **backer of a bill** = person who backs a bill

◊ **background** *noun* **(a)** past work *or* experience *or* family connections; **the accused is from a good background; can you tell us something of the girl's family background? (b)** past details; **he explained the background to the claim; the court asked for details of the background to the case; I know the contractual situation as it** stands now, but can you fill in the background details?

◊ **backsheet** *noun* last sheet of paper in a legal document which, when folded, becomes the outside sheet and carries the endorsement

bad *adjective* not good; **bad debt** = debt which will never be paid; **in bad faith** = dishonestly

bail 1 *noun* releasing an arrested person from custody after payment has been made to a court as guarantee that the person will return to face trial; **to stand bail of £3,000 for someone; he was granted bail on his own recognizance of £1,000; the police opposed bail on the grounds that the accused might try to leave the country; police bail** = bail granted by the police; **he was remanded on bail of £3,000** = he was released on payment of £3,000 as a guarantee that he would return to the court to face trial; **to jump bail** = not to appear in court after having been released on bail; **bail bond** = signed document which is given to the court as security for payment of a judgment (NOTE: no plural) **2** *verb* **to bail someone out** = to pay a debt on behalf of someone; **she paid £3,000 to bail him out**

◊ **bailee** *noun* person who receives property by way of bailment

◊ **bailment** *noun* transfer of goods by someone (the bailor) to someone (the bailee) who then holds them until they have to be returned to the bailor (as when leaving a coat in a cloakroom *or* at the cleaner's)

◊ **bailor** *noun* person who transfers property by way of bailment

Bailey *see* OLD BAILEY

bailiff *noun* **(a)** *GB* person employed by the court, whose responsibility is to see that documents (such as summonses) are served, and that court orders are obeyed; **the court ordered the bailiffs to seize his property because he had not paid his fine (b)** *US* deputy to a sheriff

balance 1 *noun* **(a)** amount in an account which makes the total debits and credits equal; **credit balance** = balance in an account showing that more money has been received than is owed; **debit balance** = balance in an account showing that more money is owed than has been received **(b)** rest of an amount owed; **you can pay £100 deposit and the balance within sixty days (c) bank balance** = state of an account at a bank at a particular time **(d) balance of mind** = good mental state; **disturbed balance of mind** = state of mind when someone is temporarily incapable of rational action (as because of illness *or* depression); **the verdict of the coroner's court was suicide while the balance of mind was disturbed 2** *verb* **(a)** to calculate the amount needed to make the two sides of an account equal; **I have finished balancing the accounts for March (b)** to plan a budget so that expenditure and income are equal

◊ **balance sheet** *noun* statement of the financial position of a company at a particular time, such as the end of the financial year or the end of a quarter; **the company balance sheet for 1984 shows a substantial loss; the accountant has prepared the balance sheet for the first half-year**

ballot 1 *noun* **(a)** election where people vote for someone by marking a cross on a paper with a list of names; **ballot paper** = paper on which the voter marks a cross to show for whom he wants to vote; **ballot box** = sealed box into which ballot papers are put; **postal ballot** = election where the voters send their ballot papers by post; **secret ballot** = election where the voters vote in secret **(b)** selecting by taking papers out of a box; **the share issue was oversubscribed, so there was a ballot for the shares 2** *verb* to take a vote by ballot; **the union is balloting for the post of president**

◊ **ballot-rigging** *noun* illegal arranging of the votes in a ballot, so that a particular candidate *or* party wins

ban 1 *noun* order which forbids someone from doing something *or* which makes an act against the law; **a government ban on the sale of weapons; a ban on the copying of computer software; to impose a ban on smoking** = to make an order which forbids smoking; **to lift the ban on smoking** = to allow people to smoke **2** *verb* to forbid something *or* to make something illegal; **the government has banned the sale of alcohol; the sale of pirated records has been banned**
NOTE: **banning - banned**

bandit *noun* person who robs people in lonely country areas; **after the coup groups of bandits came down from the mountains to attack police stations**

◊ **banditry** *noun* act of robbing people
NOTE: no plural

banish *verb* to send (someone) to live a long distance away (usually out of the country, or to a distant part of the country) as a punishment; **he was banished for ten years**

◊ **banishment** *noun* being banished
NOTE: no plural

bank 1 *noun* business which holds money for its clients, which lends money at interest, and trades generally in money; **central bank** = main government-controlled bank in a country, which controls the financial affairs of the country by fixing main interest rates, issuing currency and controlling the foreign exchange rate; **clearing bank** = bank which clears cheques by transferring money from the payer's account to another account **2** *verb* to deposit money into a bank or to have an account with a bank

◊ **bankable** *adjective* (paper) which a bank will accept as security for a loan

◊ **bank account** *noun* account which a customer has with a bank, where the customer can deposit and withdraw money

◊ **bank draft** *noun* cheque payable by a bank

◊ **banker** *noun* person who carries on the business of a bank; **banker's draft** = cheque payable by a bank

◊ **bank holiday** *noun* a weekday which is a public holiday when the banks are closed; **Easter Monday is a bank holiday**

◊ **bank note** *or* **banknote** *noun* piece of printed paper money
NOTE: US English is **bill**

◊ **bank statement** *noun* document showing payments into and out of a bank account

bankrupt 1 *adjective & noun* (person) who has been declared by a court not to be capable of paying his debts and whose affairs are put into the hands of a trustee; **he was adjudicated *or* declared bankrupt; a bankrupt property developer; he went bankrupt after two years in business; certificated bankrupt** = bankrupt who has been discharged from bankruptcy with a certificate to show he was not at fault;

discharged bankrupt = person who has been released from being bankrupt; **undischarged bankrupt** = person who has been declared bankrupt and has not been released from that state **2** *verb* to make someone become bankrupt; **the recession bankrupted my father**

COMMENT: a bankrupt cannot serve as a Member of Parliament, a Justice of the Peace, a director of a limited company, and cannot sign a contract or borrow money

◇ **bankruptcy** *noun* state of being bankrupt; **the recession has caused thousands of bankruptcies; bankruptcy notice** = notice warning someone that he faces bankruptcy if he fails to pay money which he owes; **bankruptcy petition** = petition to the Court asking for an order making someone bankrupt; **bankruptcy proceedings** = court case to make someone bankrupt; **adjudication of bankruptcy** *or* **declaration of bankruptcy** = legal order making someone bankrupt; **criminal bankruptcy** = bankruptcy of a criminal in the Crown Court as a result of crimes of which he has been convicted; **discharge in bankruptcy** = being released from bankruptcy; **to file a petition in bankruptcy** = to apply to the Court to be made bankrupt *or* to ask for someone else to be made bankrupt

◇ **Bankruptcy Court** *noun* court which deals with bankruptcies

banns *plural noun* declaration in church that a couple intend to get married; **to publish the banns of marriage between Anne Smith and John Jones**

bar 1 *noun* **(a)** place where you can buy and drink alcohol; **the solicitors for the plaintiffs met in the bar of the hotel (b)** small shop; **snack bar** = small restaurant where you can get simple meals **(c)** thing which stops you doing something; **government legislation is a bar to foreign trade (d) the Bar** = (i) the profession of barrister; (ii) all barristers *or* lawyers; **to be called to the bar** = to pass examinations and fulfil certain requirements to become a barrister; **the Bar Council** = the ruling body of English and Welsh barristers; **the American Bar Association** = the ruling body of American lawyers **(e)** rails in a court, behind which the lawyers and public have to stand or sit; **prisoner at the**

bar = prisoner being tried in court *or* the accused **2** *verb* to forbid something *or* to make something illegal; **he was barred from attending the meeting; the police commissioner barred the use of firearms**

barely *adverb* almost not; **there is barely enough money left to pay the staff; she barely had time to call her lawyer**

bargain 1 *noun* **(a)** agreement between two parties (such as when one sells and the other buys something) **(b)** thing which is cheaper than usual; **bargain hunter** = person who looks for cheap deals **(c)** sale of one lot of shares on the Stock Exchange; **bargains done** = number of deals made on the Stock Exchange during a day **2** *verb* to discuss a price for something; **you will have to bargain with the dealer if you want a discount; they spent two hours bargaining about *or* over the discount**

◇ **bargaining** *noun* act of discussing a price, usually wage increases for workers; **(free) collective bargaining** = negotiations between employers and workers' representatives over wages and conditions; **bargaining power** = strength of one person or group when discussing prices *or* wage settlements; **bargaining position** = statement of position by one group during negotiations; **plea bargaining** = arrangement where the accused pleads guilty to some charges and the prosecution drop other charges *or* ask for a lighter sentence

baron *noun* *slang* prisoner who has power over other prisoners because he sells tobacco and runs other rackets in a prison

barrier *noun* thing which stops someone from doing something, especially sending goods from one place to another; **customs barriers** *or* **tariff barriers** = customs duty intended to make trade more difficult; **to impose trade barriers on certain goods** = to restrict the import of certain goods by charging high duty; **to lift trade barriers from imports** = to remove restrictions on imports

barrister *noun* lawyer (especially in England) who can plead *or* argue a case in one of the higher courts

COMMENT: in England and Wales, a barrister is a member of one of the Inns of Court; he has passed examinations and spent one year in pupillage before being called to the bar. Barristers have right of audience in all courts in England and Wales. Note also that barristers are instructed only by solicitors and never by members of the public. A barrister or a group of barristers is referred to as "counsel"

base 1 *noun* **(a)** lowest or first position; **base year** = first year of an index, against which later years' changes are measured **(b)** place where a company has its main office or factory *or* place where a businessman has his office; **the company has its base in London and branches in all European countries; he has an office in Madrid which he uses as a base while he is travelling in Southern Europe** 2 *verb* **(a)** to start to calculate *or* to negotiate from a position; **we based our calculations on last year's turnover; based on** = calculating from **(b)** to set up a company *or* a person in a place; **the European manager is based in our London office; our foreign branch is based in the Bahamas; a London-based sales executive**

basic 1 *adjective* **(a)** normal; **basic pay** *or* **basic salary** *or* **basic wage** = normal salary without extra payments; **basic rate tax** = lowest rate of income tax **(b)** most important; **basic commodities** = ordinary farm produce, produced in large quantities (such as corn, rice, sugar) **(c)** simple *or* from which everything starts; **he has a basic knowledge of the market; to work at the cash desk, you need a basic qualification in maths**
◊ **basics** *plural noun* simple and important facts; **to get back to basics** = to start discussing the basic facts again
◊ **basically** *adverb* seen from the point from which everything starts
◊ **BASIC** *noun* = BEGINNER'S ALL-PURPOSE SYMBOLIC INSTRUCTION CODE simple language for writing computer programs

basis *noun* **(a)** point *or* number from which calculations are made; **we have calculated the turnover on the basis of a 6% price increase (b)** general terms of agreement *or* general principles on which something is decided; **on a short-term *or* long-term basis** = for a short *or* long period; **he has been appointed on a short-term basis; we have three people working on a freelance basis**

bastard *noun* illegitimate child *or* child born to an unmarried mother

batter *verb* to hit someone *or* something hard; **the dead man had been battered to death with a hammer; police were battering on the door of the flat; battered child *or* battered wife** = child who is frequently beaten by one of its parents *or* wife who is frequently beaten by her husband
◊ **battery** *noun* crime *or* tort of using force against another person
NOTE: no plural *Compare* ASSAULT

battle *noun* fight; **courtroom battles** = arguments between lawyers in court

beak *noun* *slang* magistrate

bear *verb* **(a)** to pay (costs); **the company bore the legal costs of both parties (b)** to **bear on** *or* **to have a bearing on** = to refer to *or* to have an effect on; **the decision of the court bears on *or* has a bearing on future cases where immigration procedures are disputed**
NOTE: **bearing - bore - borne**
◊ **bearer** *noun* person who holds a cheque *or* certificate; **the cheque is payable to bearer** = is paid to the person who holds it, not to any particular name written on it
◊ **bearer bond** *noun* bond which is payable to the bearer and does not have a name written on it
◊ **bearer cheque** *noun* cheque which entitles the person who has it to be paid

beat 1 *noun* area which a policeman patrols regularly; **the constable on the beat** = the ordinary policeman on foot patrol 2 *verb* **(a)** to hit; **the prisoners were beaten with sticks; the warders beat the prisoner to make him confess (b)** to win in a fight against someone; **they have beaten their competitors into second place in the computer market (c)** to **beat a ban** = to do something which is going to be forbidden by doing it rapidly before the ban is enforced
NOTE: **beating - beat - has beaten**

beforehand *adverb* in advance; **the terms of the payment will be agreed beforehand**

begin *verb* to start; **the case began with the reading of the indictment; the auditors' report began with a description of the general principles adopted**
NOTE: **beginning - began - begun**

behalf *noun* **on behalf of** = acting for (someone *or* a company); **I am writing on behalf of the minority shareholders; she is acting on my behalf; solicitors acting on behalf of the American company**

behead *verb* to cut off someone's head; **the accused was found guilty of treason and beheaded**

believe *verb* to think that something is true; **we believe he has offered to buy 25% of the shares; the chairman is believed to be in South America on business**

belli *see* CASUS BELLI

bellman *noun* *slang* criminal who specializes in stopping alarm signals

belong *verb* **(a) to belong to** = to be the property of; **the company belongs to an old American banking family; the patent belongs to the inventor's son (b) to belong with** = to be part of (a group); **those documents belong with the sales reports**

bench *noun* place where judges *or* magistrates sit in court; **bench of magistrates** = group of magistrates in an area; **he is on the bench** = he is a magistrate; **bench warrant** = warrant issued by a court for the arrest of an accused person who has not appeared to answer charges; **Queen's Bench Division** = one of the main divisions of the High Court; **Masters of the Bench** = senior members of an Inn of Court

◊ **Bencher** *noun* one of the senior members of an Inn of Court

benefactor *noun* person who gives property or money to others, especially in a will

◊ **benefactress** *noun* woman who leaves property or money to others, especially in her will

beneficial *adjective* **beneficial interest** = interest of the beneficiary of a property *or* shares *or* trust, which allows someone to occupy or receive rent from a property, while the property is owned by a trustee; **beneficial occupier** = person who occupies a property but does not own it; **beneficial owner** = true *or* ultimate owner (whose interest may be concealed by a nominee); **beneficial use** = right to use *or* occupy *or* receive rent from a property which is owned by a trustee

◊ **beneficiary** *noun* **(a)** person who is left property in a will; **the main beneficiaries of the will are the deceased's family (b)** person whose property is administered by a trustee

COMMENT: in a trust, the trustee is the legal owner of the property, while the beneficiary is the equitable owner who receives the real benefit of the trust

benefit 1 *noun* **(a)** money *or* advantage gained from something; **the estate was left to the benefit of the owner's grandsons (b)** payments which are made to someone under a national or private insurance scheme; **she receives £20 a week as unemployment benefit; the sickness benefit is paid monthly; the insurance office sends out benefit cheques each week; death benefit** = money paid to the family of someone who dies in an accident at work **2** *verb* **to benefit from** *or* **by something** = to be improved by something *or* to gain more money because of something

bent *adjective* *slang* corrupt *or* stolen *or* illegal; **bent copper** = corrupt policeman; **bent job** = illegal deal

bequeath *verb* to leave (property, but not freehold land) to someone in a will; **he bequeathed his shares to his daughter**

◊ **bequest** *noun* giving of property, money, etc. (but not freehold land) to someone in a will; **he made several bequests to his staff**

COMMENT: freehold land given in a will is a **devise**

BES = BUSINESS EXPANSION SCHEME

best 1 *adjective* very good; **best evidence** = original document used as evidence (as opposed to a copy) **2** *noun* very good effort; **the lawyers did their best, but the jury was not convinced by the evidence**

bet 1 *noun* amount deposited when you risk money on the result of a race *or* of a game 2 *verb* to risk money on the result of something; **he bet £100 on the result of the election; I bet you £25 the accused will get off with a fine; betting duty *or* tax** = tax levied on betting on horses, dogs, etc.

betray *verb* to give away a secret; **he betrayed the secret to the enemy; to betray one's country *or* a friend** = to give away one's country's *or* friend's secrets to an enemy

◊ **betrayal** *noun* **betrayal of trust** = acting against something with which you have been entrusted

beware *verb* to be careful; **beware of imitations** = be careful not to buy cheap low-quality items which are made to look like more expensive items

beyond *preposition* further than; **it is beyond question that** = it is certain that; **beyond reasonable doubt** = almost certain proof needed to convict a person in a criminal case

bi- *prefix* twice; **bi-monthly** = (i) twice a month; (ii) every two months *or* six times a year; **bi-annually** = twice a year

◊ **bicameralism** *noun* system of government where there are two houses of parliament, one senior to the other

bias *noun* leaning towards *or* favouring one party in a case; **likelihood of bias** = possibility that bias will occur because of a connection between a member of the court and a party in the case

◊ **biased** *adjective* (judge *or* juror) who favours one of the parties in a case

bid 1 *noun* **(a)** offer to buy something at a certain price (especially at an auction); **to make a bid for something** = to offer to buy something; **to put in a bid for something *or* to enter a bid for something** = to offer to buy something **(b)** offer to do some work at a certain price; **he made the lowest bid for the job;** *US* offer to sell something at a certain price; **they asked for bids for the supply of spare parts (c) takeover bid** = offer to buy all or a majority of shares in a company so as to control it; **to make a takeover bid for a company** = to offer to buy a majority of the shares in a company; **to withdraw a takeover bid** = to say that

you no longer offer to buy the majority of the shares in a company 2 *verb* (*at an auction*) **to bid for something** = to offer to buy something; **he bid £1,000 for the jewels** = he offered to pay £1,000 for the jewels NOTE: **bidding - bid**

◊ **bidder** *noun* person who makes a bid; **the lot was sold to the highest bidder** = to the person who has offered the most money

bigamy *noun* notifiable offence of going through a ceremony of marriage to someone when you are still married to someone else; *see also* MONOGAMY, POLYGAMY NOTE: no plural

◊ **bigamist** *noun* person who is married to two people at the same time

◊ **bigamous** *adjective* referring to bigamy; **they went through a bigamous marriage ceremony**

bilateral *adjective* (agreement) between two parties *or* countries; **the minister signed a bilateral trade agreement**

bilking *noun* offence of removing goods without paying for them *or* of refusing to pay a bill

bill 1 *noun* **(a)** written list of charges to be paid; **the salesman wrote out the bill; does the bill include VAT? the bill is made out to Smith Ltd; the builder sent in his bill; he left the country without paying his bills; to foot the bill** = to pay the costs **(b)** list of charges in a restaurant; **can I have the bill please? the bill comes to £20 including service; does the bill include service? the waiter has added 10% to the bill for service (c)** written paper promising to pay money; **bill of exchange** = document which orders one person to pay another person a sum of money **(d) bill of health** = document given to the master of a ship showing that the ship is free of disease; **bill of indictment** = (i) draft of an indictment which is examined by the court, and when signed becomes an indictment; (ii) *US* list of charges given to a grand jury, asking them to indict the accused; **bill of lading** = list of goods being shipped, which the shipper gives to the person sending the goods to show that the goods have been loaded **(e)** *US* piece of paper money **(f) bill of sale** = (i) document which the seller gives to the buyer to show that the sale has taken place; (ii) document given to a lender by a borrower to show that the lender owns the property as security for the loan **(g)** draft of a new law which will be discussed in Parliament; **the house is discussing the Noise Prevention Bill; the Finance Bill had its second reading yesterday; Private Member's Bill** = Bill which is drafted and proposed by an ordinary Member of Parliament, not by a government minister; **Private Bill** = Bill relating to a particular person *or* corporation *or* institution; **Public Bill** = ordinary Bill relating to a matter applying to the public in general, introduced by a government minister **(h)** *US* **Bill of Rights** = those sections (the first ten amendments) of the constitution of the United States which refer to the rights and privileges of the individual **2** *verb* to present a bill to someone so that it can be paid; **the builders billed him for the repairs to his neighbour's house**

COMMENT: a Bill passes through the following stages in Parliament: **First Reading, Second Reading, Committee Stage, Report Stage** and **Third Reading.**
The Bill goes through these stages first in the House of Commons and then in the House of Lords. When all the stages have been passed the Bill is given the Royal Assent and becomes law as an Act of Parliament.
In the USA, a Bill is introduced either in the House or in the Senate, passes through **Committee Stage** with public hearings, then to general debate in the full House. The Bill is debated section by section in **Second Reading** and after being passed by both House and Senate is engrossed and sent to the President as a **joint resolution** for signature (or veto)

bind *verb* to tie *or* to attach (someone) so that he has to do something; **the company is bound by its articles of association; he does not consider himself bound by the agreement which was signed by his predecessor; High Court judges are bound by the decisions of the House of Lords**

◊ **binder** *noun* **(a)** stiff cardboard cover for papers; **ring binder** = cover with rings

in it which fit into special holes made in sheets of paper **(b)** *US* temporary agreement for insurance sent before the insurance policy is issued
NOTE: the British English for this is **cover note**

◊ **binding** *adjective* which legally forces someone to do something; **this document is legally binding or it is a legally binding document; the agreement is binding on all parties** = all parties signing it must do what is agreed; **binding precedent** = decision of a higher court which has to be followed by a judge in a lower court

◊ **bind over** *verb* **(a)** *GB* to make someone promise to behave well and not commit another offence *or* to return to court at a later date to face charges; **he was bound over (to keep the peace or to be of good behaviour) for six months (b)** *US* to order a defendant to be kept in custody while a criminal case is being prepared

◊ **bind-over order** *noun* court order which binds someone over; **the applicant sought judicial review to quash the bind-over order**

birth *noun* being born; **he is British by birth** = he has British nationality because his parents are British; **date and place of birth** = day of the year when someone was born and the town where he was born; **birth certificate** = document giving details of a person's date and place of birth; **concealment of birth** = offence of hiding the fact that a child has been born

black 1 *adjective* **(a) black market** = buying and selling goods in a way which is not allowed by law; **there is a lucrative black market in spare parts for cars; you can buy gold coins on the black market; they lived well on black-market goods; to pay black market prices** = to pay high prices to get items which are not easily available; **black marketeer** = person who sells goods on the black market **(b) black economy** = work which is paid for in cash *or* goods, and therefore not declared to the tax authorities **2** *verb* to forbid trading in certain goods or with certain suppliers; **three firms were blacked by the government; the union has blacked a shipping firm**

◊ **blackleg** *noun* worker who goes on working when there is a strike

◊ **black list** *noun* list of goods *or* people *or* companies which have been blacked

◊ **blacklist** *verb* to put goods *or* people *or* a company on a black list; **his firm was blacklisted by the government**

◊ **Black Maria** *noun informal* van used by the police to take prisoners from one place to another

blackmail 1 *noun* notifiable offence of getting money from someone, by threatening to make public facts about him which he does not want revealed *or* by threatening violence; **he was charged with blackmail; they got £25,000 from the managing director by blackmail; she was sent to prison for blackmail**
NOTE: no plural
2 *verb* to threaten someone that you will make public facts about him *or* to do violence to him unless he pays you money; **he was blackmailed by his former secretary**

◊ **blackmailer** *noun* person who blackmails someone

blag *noun slang* robbery by an armed gang

blame 1 *noun* saying that someone has done something wrong *or* that someone is responsible; **the sales staff got the blame for the poor sales figures 2** *verb* to say that someone has done something wrong *or* is responsible for a mistake; **the magistrate blamed the social services for not reporting the case quickly; the lack of fire equipment was blamed by the coroner for the deaths**

◊ **blameworthy** *adjective* which is likely to attract blame *or* to be blamed

blanche *see* CARTE

blank 1 *adjective* with nothing written; **a blank cheque** = a cheque with the amount of money and the payee left blank, but signed by the drawer **2** *noun* space on a form which has to be completed

blanket *noun* thick woollen cover for a bed; **blanket agreement** = agreement which covers many items; **blanket insurance policy** = policy covering several items; **blanket refusal** = refusal to accept many different items

blasphemy *noun* formerly the crime of ridiculing *or* denying God *or* the Christian religion in a scandalous way

◊ **blaspheme** *verb* to ridicule *or* deny God *or* the Christian religion

block 1 *noun* **(a)** series of items grouped together; **he bought a block of 6,000 shares; block booking** = booking of several seats *or* rooms at the same time; **the company has a block booking for twenty seats on the plane *or* for ten rooms at the hotel; block vote** = casting of a large number of votes at the same time (such as of trade union members) by a person who has been delegated by the holders of the votes to vote for them in this way **(b)** series of buildings forming a square with streets on all sides; **a block of offices *or* an office block** = a large building which contains only offices **(c)** building in a prison; **H-block** = building in a prison built with a central section and two end wings, forming the shape of the letter H; **hospital block** = section of a prison which contains the hospital **(d) block capitals *or* block letters** = capital letters (as A,B,C); **write your name and address in block letters 2** *verb* to stop something taking place; **he used his casting vote to block the motion; the planning committee blocked the plan to build a motorway through the middle of the town; blocked currency** = currency which cannot be taken out of a country because of exchange controls

blockade 1 *noun* act of preventing goods *or* people going into or out of a place; **the government brought in goods by air to beat the blockade; the enemy lifted the blockade of the port for two months to let emergency supplies in 2** *verb* to prevent goods *or* food *or* people going into or coming out of a place; **the town was blockaded by the enemy navy**

blood *noun* red liquid in the body; **blood relationship** = relationship between people who have a common ancestor; **blood sample** = small amount of blood taken from someone for a blood test (such as to establish the alcohol level in the blood); **blood test *or* blood grouping test** = test to establish the paternity of a child

blotter *noun US* book in which arrests are recorded at a police station

blue bag *noun* blue bag in which a junior barrister carries his gown; *see also* RED BAG

◊ **Blue Book** *noun* official report of a Royal Commission

◊ **blue laws** *plural noun* *US* laws relating to what can *or* cannot be done on a Sunday

board 1 *noun* **board of directors** = group of directors elected by the shareholders to run a company; **the bank has two representatives on the board; he sits on the board as a representative of the bank; two directors were removed from the board at the AGM; board meeting** = meeting of the directors of a company **(b)** group of people who run a trust *or* a society; **advisory board** = group of advisors; **editorial board** = group of editors; **parole board** = group of people who advise the Home Secretary if a prisoner should be released on parole before the end of his sentence; **board of visitors** = group of people appointed by the Home Secretary to visit and inspect the conditions in prisons 2 *verb* to go on to a ship *or* plane *or* train; **customs officials boarded the ship in the harbour**

◊ **boarding card** *or* **boarding pass** *noun* card given to passengers who have checked in for a flight *or* voyage to allow them to board the plane *or* ship

bobby *noun* *informal* *GB* policeman

bodily *adverb* to the body; **actual bodily harm (ABH)** = really hitting and hurting someone; **grievous bodily harm (GBH)** = crime of causing serious injury to someone

bodyguard *noun* person who protects someone; **the minister was followed by his three bodyguards**

bona fides *or* **bona fide** *Latin phrase* meaning "good faith" *or* "in good faith"; **he acted bona fide; the respondent was not acting bona fides; a bona fide offer** = an offer which is made honestly *or* which can be trusted

bona vacantia *noun* property with no owner *or* which does not have an obvious owner and which usually passes to the Crown

bond *noun* **(a)** contract document promising to repay money borrowed by a company *or* by the government; **government bonds** *or* **treasury bonds (b)** contract document promising to repay money borrowed by a person; **bearer bond** = bond which is payable to the bearer and does not have a name written on it; **debenture bond** = certificate showing that a debenture has been issued; **mortgage bond** = certificate showing that a mortgage exists and that the property is security for it **(c)** signed legal document which binds one or more parties to do *or* not to do something; **bail bond** = signed document which is given to the court as security for payment of a judgment; **goods (held) in bond** = goods held by the customs until duty has been paid; **entry of goods under bond** = bringing goods into a country in bond; **to take goods out of bond** = to pay duty on goods so that they can be released by the customs

◊ **bonded** *adjective* held in bond; **bonded goods** = goods which are held by the customs under a bond until duty has been paid; **bonded warehouse** = warehouse where goods are stored in bond until duty is paid

◊ **bondholder** *noun* person who holds government bonds

◊ **bondsman** *noun* person who has stood surety for another person

book 1 *noun* **(a)** set of sheets of paper attached together; **a company's books** = the financial records of a company; **book value** = value of a company's assets as shown in the company accounts **(b)** phone **book** *or* **telephone book** = book which lists names of people or companies with their addresses and telephone numbers **(c) to bring someone to book** = to find a suspect and charge him with a crime 2 *verb* **(a)** to order *or* to reserve something; **to book a room in a hotel** *or* **a table at a restaurant** *or* **a ticket on a plane; I booked a table for 7.45; he booked a ticket through to Cairo; to book someone into a hotel** *or* **onto a flight** =. to order a room *or* a plane ticket for someone **(b)** *informal* to charge someone with a crime; **he was booked for driving on the wrong side of the road**

◊ **booking** *noun* act of ordering a room *or* a seat

bootleg *adjective* illicit (alcohol)

◊ **bootlegger** *noun* person who makes *or* supplies illicit alcohol

◊ **bootlegging** *noun* **a)** making illicit alcohol **(b)** making illegal records *or* tapes from live concerts

borough *noun* town which has been incorporated; **borough council** = representatives elected to run a borough

borrow *verb* **(a)** to take money from someone for a time, possibly paying interest for it, and repaying it at the end of the period; **he borrowed £1,000 from the bank; the company had to borrow heavily to repay its debts; they borrowed £25,000 against the security of the factory (b)** *slang* to steal
◇ **borrower** *noun* person who borrows; **borrowers from the bank pay 12% interest**
◇ **borrowing** *noun* **(a)** action of borrowing money; **the new factory was financed by bank borrowing; borrowing power =** amount of money which a company can borrow **(b) borrowings =** money borrowed; **the company's borrowings have doubled; bank borrowings =** loans made by banks

borstal *noun* formerly a centre where a young offender was sent for training if he had committed a crime which would normally be punishable by a prison sentence

boss *noun* head of a Mafia family *or* criminal gang

bottleneck *noun* position when activity is slowed down because one section of the operation cannot cope with the amount of work; **there are serious bottlenecks in the divorce courts**

bottomry *noun* mortgage of a ship *or* cargo; **bottomry bond =** bond which secures a ship *or* cargo against a loan NOTE: no plural

bounce *verb* *slang* (*of a cheque*) to be returned to the person who has tried to cash it, because there is not enough money in the payer's account to pay it; **he paid for the car with a cheque that bounced**

bound *see* BIND, DUTY

boundary (line) *noun* line marking the edge of a piece of land owned by someone; **the boundary dispute dragged through the courts for years**
◇ **Boundary Commission** *noun* committee which examines the area and population of constituencies for the House of Commons and recommends changes to make each Member of Parliament represent similar numbers of people

bounty *noun* (i) government subsidy made to help an industry; (ii) payment made by government to someone who has saved lives *or* found treasure

box *noun* **(a)** container; **the goods were sent in thin cardboard boxes; the drugs were hidden in boxes of office stationery; envelopes come in boxes of two hundred =** packed two hundred to a box; **box file =** file (for papers) made like a box **(b) witness box =** place in a courtroom where the witnesses give evidence (NOTE: American English is **witness stand) (c) box number =** reference number used in a post office or an advertisement to avoid giving an address; **please reply to Box No. 209; our address is: P.O. Box 74209, Edinburgh**

boycott 1 *noun* refusal to buy *or* to deal in goods from a certain country *or* company, used as a punishment; **the union organized a boycott against *or* of imported cars 2** *verb* to refuse to buy *or* to deal in goods from a certain country *or* company, as a punishment; **the company's products have been boycotted by the main department stores; we are boycotting all imports from that country; the management has boycotted the meeting =** has refused to attend the meeting

bracelets *plural noun* *slang* handcuffs

bracket 1 *noun* group of items *or* people of a certain type taken together; **income bracket *or* tax bracket =** level of income where a certain percentage tax applies **2** *verb* **to bracket together =** to treat several items together in the same way

branch 1 *noun* **(a)** local office of a bank or large business; local shop of a large chain of shops; **the bank *or* the store has branches in most towns in the south of the country; the insurance company has closed its branches in South America; he is the manager of our local branch of Lloyds bank; we have decided to open a branch office in Chicago; the manager of our branch in Lagos *or* of our Lagos branch; branch manager =** manager of a branch **(b)** part *or* separate section (of the law); **the Law of Contract and the Law of Tort are branches of civil law 2** *verb* **to branch out =** to start a new (but usually related) type of business;

from dealing in stolen bicycles, the gang branched out into car theft

brand 1 *noun* make of product, which can be recognized by a name *or* by a design **2** *verb* to mark with a special mark

◊ **branded** *adjective* branded goods = goods sold under brand names

breach *noun* (a) failure to carry out the terms of an agreement; **in breach of** = failing to do something which was agreed; **the defendant is in breach of his statutory duty; breach of contract** = failing to do something which is in a contract; **the company is in breach of contract** = the company has failed to carry out what was agreed in the contract; **breach of promise** = formerly, complaint in court that someone had promised to marry the plaintiff and then had not done so; **breach of trust** = failure to act properly on the part of a trustee in regard to a trust; **breach of warranty** = supplying goods which do not meet the standards of the warranty applied to them **(b)** failure to obey the law; **the soldier was charged with a serious breach of discipline; breach of the peace** = creating a disturbance which is likely to annoy *or* frighten people

break 1 *noun* short space of time, when you can rest; **the court adjourned for a ten-minute break 2** *verb* **(a)** to do something which is against the law; **if you hit a policeman you will be breaking the law; he is breaking the law by selling goods on Sunday; the company broke section 26 of the Companies Act (b)** to fail to carry out the duties of a contract; **the company has broken the contract** *or* **the agreement; to break an engagement to do something** = not to do what has been agreed **(c)** to cancel (a contract); **the company is hoping to be able to break the contract**
NOTE: breaking - broke - broken

◊ **breakages** *plural noun* breaking of items; **customers are expected to pay for breakages**

◊ **break down** *verb* **(a)** to stop working because of mechanical failure; **the two-way radio has broken down; what do you do when your squad car breaks down? (b)** to stop; **negotiations broke down after six hours; their marriage broke down and they separated (c)** to show all the items in a total list; **we broke the crime figures down into crimes against the person and crimes against**

property; **can you break down this invoice into spare parts and labour?**

◊ **breakdown** *noun* **(a)** stopping work because of mechanical failure; **we cannot communicate with our squad car because of the breakdown of the radio link (b)** stopping work *or* discussion; **a breakdown in wage negotiations; she petitioned for divorce on account of the breakdown of their marriage; irretrievable breakdown of a marriage** = situation where the two spouses can no longer live together, where the marriage cannot be saved and therefore divorce proceedings can be started **(c)** showing details item by item; **give me a breakdown of the latest clear-up figures**

◊ **break in** *verb* to go into a building by force in order to steal; **burglars broke in through a window at the back of the house**

◊ **break-in** *noun* *informal* crime of breaking into a house; **there have been three break-ins in our street in one week**

◊ **breaking and entering** *noun* crime of going into a building by force and stealing things; **he was charged with breaking and entering;** *see also* HOUSEBREAKING

◊ **break into** *verb* to go into (a building) by force to steal things; **their house was broken into while they were on holiday; looters broke into the supermarket**

◊ **break off** *verb* to stop; **we broke off the discussion at midnight; management broke off negotiations with the union**

◊ **break up** *verb* **(a)** to split something large into small sections; **the company was broken up and separate divisions sold off (b)** to come to an end *or* to make something come to an end; **the meeting broke up at 12.30; the police broke up the protest meeting**

breath *noun* air which a person takes into his body to live; **breath test** = test where a person's breath is sampled to establish the amount of alcohol he has drunk

◊ **breathalyse** *verb* to test someone's breath using a breathalyser

◊ **breathalyser** *noun* device for testing the amount of alcohol a person has drunk by testing his breath

bribe 1 *noun* money offered corruptly to someone to get him to do something to help you; **the police sergeant was dismissed for taking bribes 2** *verb* to give someone money corruptly to get him to help you; **he bribed the police sergeant to get the charges dropped**

◊ **bribery** *noun* crime of paying someone money corruptly to get him to do something to help you; **bribery in the security warehouse is impossible to stamp out**
NOTE: no plural

bridewell *noun slang* cells in a police station

bridging loan *noun* short term loan to help someone buy a new house when he has not yet sold his old one

bridleway *noun* path used by people on horseback

brief 1 *noun* (a) details of a client's case, prepared by his solicitor and given to the barrister who is going to argue the case in court (b) *slang* lawyer *or* barrister 2 *verb* to explain something to someone in detail; **the superintendent briefed the press on the progress of the investigation; to brief a barrister** = to give a barrister all the details of the case which he will argue in court

◊ **briefcase** *noun* case with a handle for carrying papers and documents; **he put all the files into his briefcase**

◊ **briefing** *noun* telling someone details; **all the detectives on the case attended a briefing given by the commander**

bring *verb* to come to a place with someone *or* something; **he brought his documents with him; the solicitor brought his secretary to take notes of the meeting; to bring a lawsuit** *or* **proceedings against someone** = to sue someone
NOTE: **bringing - brought**

◊ **bring forward** *verb* to make earlier; **to bring forward the date of repayment; the date of the hearing has been brought forward to March**

◊ **bring in** *verb* to decide a verdict; **the jury brought in a verdict of not guilty**

◊ **bring up** *verb* to refer to something for the first time; **the chairman brought up the question of corruption in the police force**

broker *noun* person who buys *or* sells on behalf of others; **insurance broker** = person who sells insurance to clients

brothel *noun* house where sexual intercourse is offered for money

budget *noun* (a) plan of expected spending and income (usually for one year); **to draw up a budget; we have agreed the budgets for next year (b) the Budget** = the annual plan of taxes and government spending proposed by a finance minister; **the minister put forward a budget aimed at slowing down the economy; to balance the budget** = to plan income and expenditure so that they balance; **the president is planning for a balanced budget**

◊ **budgetary** *adjective* referring to a budget; **budgetary policy** = policy of planning income and expenditure; **budgetary control** = keeping check on spending; **budgetary requirements** = spending or income required to meet the expected budget

◊ **budgeting** *noun* preparing of budgets to help plan expenditure and income

bug 1 *noun* small device which can record conversations secretly and send them to a secret radio receiver; **the cleaners planted a bug under the lawyer's desk** 2 *verb* to place a secret device in a place so that conversations can be heard and recorded secretly; **the agents bugged the President's office; bugging device** = bug; **police found a bugging device under the lawyer's desk**

buggery *noun* notifiable offence of sexual intercourse with animals *or* rectal intercourse with man or woman

building society *noun* *GB* financial institution which accepts and pays interest on deposits and lends money to people who are buying property

bumping *noun* *US* situation were a senior employee takes the place of a junior (in a restaurant *or* in a job)

bunco *noun slang* swindle *or* cheating someone out of money (usually at cards)

burden of proof *noun* duty to prove that something which has been alleged in court is right; **to discharge a burden of proof** = to prove something which has been alleged in court; **the burden of proof is on the prosecution** = the prosecution must prove that what it alleges is true

bureau *noun* office which specializes; **computer bureau** = office which offers to do work on its computers for companies which do not own their own computers; **employment bureau** = office which finds jobs for people; **information bureau** = office which gives information; *US* **Federal Bureau of Investigation (FBI)** = American government office, a section of the Department of Justice, which investigates crimes against federal law and subversive acts in the USA
NOTE: the plural is **bureaux**

burglar *noun* person who steals (or tries to steal) goods from property *or* who enters property intending to commit a crime; **burglar alarm** = bell which is set to ring when someone tries to break into a house *or* shop; **as he put his hand through the window he set off the burglar alarm**

◇ **burglarize** *verb US informal* to steal things from (a building *or* a household)

◇ **burglary** *noun* crime of going into a building (usually by force) and stealing things; **he was charged with burglary; there has been a series of burglaries in our street; aggravated burglary** = burglary where guns or other offensive weapons are carried or used

◇ **burgle** *verb* to steal things from (a building *or* a household); **the school was burgled when the caretaker was on holiday**

burn *verb* to destroy by fire; **the chief accountant burned the documents before the police arrived**
NOTE: **burning - burned** *or* **burnt**

◇ **burn down** *verb* to destroy completely in a fire

business *noun* **(a)** work in buying or selling; **on business** = on commercial work **(b)** commercial company; **he owns a small car repair business; she runs a business from her home; he set up in business as an insurance broker; Business Expansion Scheme (BES)** = government scheme to encourage investment by making money invested for some years in a new company to be free of tax; **business hours** = time (usually 9 a.m. to 5 p.m.) when a business is open; **business name** = name under which a firm *or* company trades **(c)** affairs discussed; **the main business of the meeting was finished by 3 p.m.; any other business**

(AOB) = item at the end of an agenda, where any matter can be raised
NOTE: no plural for meanings (a) and (c); (b) has the plural **businesses**

busy *adjective* occupied in doing something *or* in working; **the police were kept busy dealing with the crowds; the court has a busy schedule; the line is busy** = the telephone line is being used

buy **1** *verb* to get something by paying money; **he bought 10,000 shares; the company has been bought by its leading supplier; to buy wholesale and sell retail; to buy forward** = to buy foreign currency before you need it, in order to be sure of the exchange rate (NOTE: **buying - bought**) **2** *noun* **good buy** *or* **bad buy** = thing bought which is *or* is not worth the money paid for it; **that watch was a good buy; this car was a bad buy**

◇ **buy back** *verb* to buy something which you have sold; **he sold the shop last year and is now trying to buy it back**

◇ **buyer** *noun* **(a)** person who buys **(b)** person who buys a certain type of goods wholesale, which are then stocked by a large store; **head buyer** = most important buyer in a store

by-election *noun* election for Parliament *or* for a council during a term of office (because of the death *or* retirement of the person first elected)

bylaw *or* **byelaw** *or* **by-law** *or* **byelaw** *noun* rule *or* law made by a local authority *or* public body and not by central government; **the bylaws forbid playing ball in the public gardens; according to the local bylaws, noise must be limited in the town centre**

COMMENT: bylaws must be made by bodies which have been authorized by Parliament, before they can become legally effective

Cc

C *third letter of the alphabet* **category "C" prisoners** = prisoners who are not likely to try to escape, but who cannot be kept in open prisons; **Schedule C** = schedule to the Finance Acts under which tax is charged on profits from government stock; **Table C** = model memorandum and articles of association set out in the Companies Act 1985 for a company limited by guarantee having no share capital

cabinet *noun* **(a)** piece of furniture for storing records or for display; **last year's correspondence is in the bottom drawer of the filing cabinet (b)** committee formed of the most important members of the government, chosen by the Prime Minister or President to be in charge of the main government departments; **Cabinet Office** = section of the British Civil Service which works for the Prime Minister and the Cabinet

cadaver *noun US* dead body
NOTE: GB English is **corpse**

cadet *noun* trainee police officer; **he has entered the police cadet college; she joined the police force as a cadet**

calculate *verb* **(a)** to find the answer to a problem using numbers; **the bank clerk calculated the rate of exchange for the dollar (b)** to estimate; **he calculated that they had six minutes left to escape before the police patrol would arrive**

◇ **calculating** *adjective* (person) who plans clever schemes in a careful way; **the judge called the prisoner a cool calculating villain**

◇ **calculation** *noun* answer to a problem in mathematics; **I made some rough calculations on the back of an envelope; according to my calculations, the detection rate has increased by 20% over the last six months**

◇ **calculator** *noun* electronic machine which works out the answers to problems in mathematics

calendar *noun* **(a)** book *or* set of sheets of paper showing the days and months in a year, often attached to pictures; **calendar month** = a whole month as on a calendar, from the 1st to the 30th or 31st; **calendar year** = year from the 1st January to 31st December **(b)** *US* list of Bills for consideration by the House of Representatives *or* the Senate

call **1** *noun* **(a)** conversation on the telephone; **local call** = call to a number on the same exchange; **trunk call** *or* **long-distance call** = call to a number in a different zone *or* area; **overseas call** *or* **international call** = call to another country; **person-to-person call** = call where you ask the operator to connect you with a named person **(b)** (i) demand for repayment of a loan by a lender; (ii) demand by a company to pay for shares; **money at call** *or* **money on call** *or* **call money** = money loaned for which repayment can be demanded without notice; **call option** = option to buy shares at a certain price **(c)** (i) admission of a barrister to the bar; (ii) number of years a barrister has practised at the bar; **he is ten years' call** = he has been practising for ten years **(d)** visit, **the salesmen make six calls a day; business call** = visit to talk to someone on business **2** *verb* **(a)** to telephone to someone; **I shall call you at your office tomorrow (b)** to admit someone to the bar to practise as a barrister; **he was called (to the bar) in 1980**

◇ **call box** *noun* outdoor telephone kiosk

◇ **called** *adjective* named *or* with a certain name; **a property called "High Trees"**

◇ **caller** *noun* **(a)** person who telephones **(b)** person who visits

◇ **call in** *verb* **(a)** to visit; **the sales representative called in twice last week (b)** to ask someone to come to help; **the local police decided to call in the CID to help in the murder hunt (c)** to ask for plans to be sent to the ministry for examination; **the minister has called in the plans for the new supermarket (d)** to ask for a debt to be paid

◇ **call off** *verb* to ask for something not to take place; **the search for the missing children has been called off**

◇ **call on** *verb* **(a)** to visit someone; **the probation officers call on their clients twice a month (b)** to ask someone to do something; **the minister called on community leaders to help prevent street crime**

camera *see* BICAMERALISM, IN CAMERA

campaign 1 *noun* planned method of working; **the police have launched a campaign against drunken drivers** 2 *verb* to try to change something by writing about it *or* by organizing protest meetings *or* by lobbying Members of Parliament; **they are campaigning for the abolition of the death penalty *or* they are campaigning against the death penalty; he is campaigning for a revision of the Official Secrets Act**

cancel *verb* **(a)** to stop something which has been agreed *or* planned; **to cancel an appointment** *or* **a meeting; to cancel a contract (b) to cancel a cheque** = to stop payment of a cheque which you have signed
NOTE: GB English is **cancelling - cancelled** but US English **canceling - canceled**

◊ **cancellandi** *see* ANIMUS

◊ **cancellation** *noun* stopping something which has been agreed *or* planned; **cancellation of an appointment; cancellation of an agreement; cancellation clause** = clause in a contract which states the terms on which the contract may be cancelled

candidate *noun* person who applies for a job *or* person who puts himself forward for election; **there are six candidates for the post of security guard; we interviewed ten candidates for the post; all the candidates in the election appeared on television; which candidate are you voting for?**

canon law *noun* law applied by the church to priests; also formerly to other members of the church in cases of marriage, legitimacy and personal property

canvass *verb* to visit people to ask them to buy goods *or* to vote *or* to say what they think

◊ **canvasser** *noun* person who canvasses

◊ **canvassing** *noun* action of asking people to buy goods *or* to vote *or* to say what they think

capable *adjective* **(a) capable of** = able *or* clever enough to do something; **she is capable of very fast typing speeds; he is capable of very complicated frauds (b)**

efficient *or* (person) who works well; **she is a very capable divorce barrister**

capacity *noun* **(a)** amount which can be produced *or* amount of work which can be done **(b)** amount of space; **storage capacity** = space available for storing goods *or* information **(c)** ability; **he has a particular capacity for business (d)** ability to enter into a legal contract, one of the essential elements of a contract; **person of full age and capacity** = person who is over eighteen years of age and of sound mind, and therefore able to enter into a contract **(e) in his capacity as chairman** = acting as chairman; **speaking in an official capacity** = speaking officially

capax *see* DOLI

capita *see* PER CAPITA

capital 1 *noun* **(a)** money, property and assets used in a business; **capital gains** = money made by selling a fixed asset *or* by selling shares at a profit; **capital gains tax** = tax paid on capital gains; **capital transfer tax** = tax paid on the transfer of capital *or* assets from one person to another **(b) capital letters** *or* **block capitals** = letters written as A, B, C, D, etc., and not a, b, c, d; **write your name in block capitals at the top of the form** (NOTE: no plural for (a)) **2** *adjective* **capital crime** *or* **offence** = crime for which the punishment is death; **capital punishment** = punishment of a criminal by execution

COMMENT: in the UK the only capital crime is now treason

◊ **capitalization** *noun* **market capitalization** = value of a company calculated by multiplying the price of its shares on the Stock Exchange by the number of shares issued

caption *noun* formal heading of an indictment *or* affidavit or other court document

captive *adjective* prisoner, especially a soldier captured in war

◊ **captivity** *noun* being held captive; **the guerillas were held in captivity for three months**
NOTE: no plural

capture *verb* to take *or* to get control of something; **the castle was captured by the**

enemy; the opposition captured six seats in the general election

care *noun* **(a)** act of looking after someone; **the children were put in the care of the social services department; care and control** = responsibility for day-to-day decisions relating to the welfare of a child; *compare* CUSTODY; **child in care** = child who has been put into the care of the local social services department; **care order** = order from a juvenile court, putting a child into the care of a local authority; **care proceedings** = action in court to put a child into the care of someone **(b)** making sure that someone is not harmed; **duty of care** = duty which everyone has not to act negligently; **driving without due care and attention** = driving a car in a careless way, so that other people are in danger

◇ **careless** *adjective* without paying attention to other people; **careless driving** = driving without due care and attention

◇ **carelessly** *adverb* in a careless way

◇ **care of** *phrase* (*in an address*) words to show that the person lives at the address, but only as a visitor; **Herr Schmidt, care of Mr W Brown**

caretaker *noun* person whose job is to look after property; **caretaker Prime Minister** *or* **caretaker chairman** = Prime Minister *or* chairman who occupies the office temporarily until a newly elected *or* appointed official arrives

carry *verb* **(a)** to take from one place to another; **to carry goods; the train was carrying a consignment of cars; carrying offensive weapons** = offence of holding a weapon or something (such as a bottle) which could be used as a weapon **(b)** to vote to approve; **the motion was carried** = the motion was accepted after a vote **(c)** to be punishable by; **the offence carries a maximum sentence of two years' imprisonment**

◇ **carriage** *noun* act of carrying goods from one place to another; **carriage charges; carriage by air**
NOTE: no plural

◇ **carriageway** *noun* way where the public have a right to go in vehicles

◇ **carrier** *noun* person *or* company which takes goods from one place to another; **common carrier** = firm which carries goods *or* passengers, which cannot

normally refuse to do so, and which can be used by anyone; **private carrier** = firm which carries goods *or* passengers, but which is not contractually bound to offer the service to anyone; **carrier's lien** = right of a carrier to hold goods until he has been paid for carrying them

◇ **carry off** *verb* to steal *or* to kidnap; **the looters carried off all the stock of television sets**

◇ **carry out** *verb* to do a job which has been assigned; **the police carried out the raid with great speed; the bailiffs had to carry out the order of the court and seize the woman's property**

carte blanche *French phrase meaning* "white card": permission given by someone to another person, allowing him to do anything *or* to act in any way; **he has carte blanche to act on behalf of the company** *or* **the company has given him carte blanche to act on its behalf**

case 1 *noun* **(a)** suitcase *or* box with a handle for carrying clothes and personal belongings when travelling; **the customs made him open his case; she had a small case which she carried onto the plane** **(b)** (i) cardboard or wooden box for packing and carrying goods; (ii) box containing twelve bottles of alcohol; **a packing case** = large wooden box for carrying items which can be easily broken **(c)** possible crime and its investigation by the police; **we have three detectives working on the case; the police are treating the case as murder** *or* **are treating it as a murder case; we had six cases of looting during the night** **(d)** court case = legal action *or* trial; **the case is being heard next week** = the case is coming to court; **case law** = law as established by precedents, that is by the decisions of courts in earlier cases **(e)** arguments *or* facts put forward by one side in legal proceedings; **defence counsel put his case; there is a strong case against the accused; case stated** = statement of the facts of a case which has been heard in a lower court, drawn up so that a higher court can decide on an appeal; **he appealed by way of case stated; the Appeal Court dismissed the appeal by way of case stated; the case rests** = all the arguments for one side have been put forward; **no case to answer** = submission by the defence (after the prosecution has put its case) that the case should be dismissed 2 *verb slang* **to**

case the joint = to look at a building carefully before deciding how to break into it

> COMMENT: a case is referred to by the names of the parties, the date and the reference source where details of it can be found: *Smith* v. *Jones* [1985] 2 *W.L.R. 250* This shows that the case involved Smith as plaintiff and Jones as defendant, it was heard in 1985, and is reported in the second volume of the Weekly Law Reports for that year on page 250

cast *verb* to cast a vote = to vote; **the number of votes cast in the election was 125,458; under proportional representation, the number of seats occupied by each party is related to the number of votes cast for that party; casting vote** = vote used by the chairman in a case where the votes for and against a proposal are equal; **the chairman has a casting vote; he used his casting vote to block the motion**
NOTE: **casting - cast - has cast**

casual *adjective* **(a)** not permanent *or* not regular; **casual labour** = workers who are hired for a short period; **casual work** = work where the workers are hired for a short period; **casual labourer** *or* **casual worker** = worker who can be hired for a short period **(b)** not formal; **he appeared in court wearing casual clothes**

casus belli *Latin phrase meaning* "case for war": reason which is used to justify a declaration of war

category *noun* type *or* sort of item; **the theft comes into the category of petty crime; category "A" prisoners** = prisoners who are dangerous, and would be a danger to the public if they escaped from prison; **category "B" prisoners** = less dangerous prisoners, who still have to be guarded carefully to prevent them from escaping; **category "C" prisoners** = prisoners who are not likely to try to escape, but who cannot be kept in open prisons; **category "D" prisoners** = reliable prisoners who can be kept in open prisons

cater for *verb* to deal with *or* to provide for; **the police station has to cater for every type of crime**

causa *see* DONATIO

cause 1 *noun* **(a)** thing which makes something happen; **cause of action** = reason why a case is brought to court; **challenge for cause** *or* **without cause** = objection to a proposed juror, stating *or* not stating the reasons for the objection; **contributory causes** = causes which help something to take place; **the report listed bad community relations as one of the contributory causes to the riot; to show cause** = to give a reason for something; **the judgment debtor was given fourteen days in which to show cause why the charging order should not be made absolute (b)** legal proceedings; **cause list** = list of cases which are to be heard by a court; **matrimonial causes** = cases referring to the rights of partners in a marriage **2** *verb* to make something happen; **the recession caused hundreds of bankruptcies**

caution 1 *noun* **(a)** warning from a policeman, telling someone not to repeat a minor crime; **the boys were let off with a caution (b)** warning by a police officer, that someone will be charged with a crime, and that what he says will be used in evidence; **he typed his confession under caution (c)** document lodged at the Land Registry to prevent land *or* property being sold without notice to the cautioner (NOTE: in meaning (b) and (c) can be used without the or **a: to lodge caution**) **2** *verb* **(a)** to warn (someone) that what he has done is wrong and should not be repeated; **the policeman cautioned the boys after the he caught them stealing fruit (b)** to warn (someone) that he will be charged with a crime, and that what he says will be used as evidence at his trial; **the accused was arrested by the detectives and cautioned**

> COMMENT: the person who is cautioned has the right not to answer any question put to him

◊ **cautioner** *noun* person who lodges caution at the Land Registry

caveat *noun* warning; **to enter a caveat** = to warn legally that you have an interest in a case, and that no steps can be taken without notice to you (especially warning to a probate court not to grant probate)

◊ **caveat emptor** *Latin phrase meaning* "let the buyer beware": phrase meaning that the buyer is himself responsible for checking that what he buys is in good order

◊ **caveator** *noun* person who warns the court not to give probate without asking his consent

CB (*in the armed forces*) = CONFINED TO BARRACKS

CC = CHIEF CONSTABLE

cell *noun* small room in a prison *or* police station where a criminal can be kept locked up; **she was put in a small cell for the night; he shares a cell with two other prisoners; condemned cell** = cell where a prisoner is kept who has been condemned to death
NOTE: often used in the plural, meaning the cells in a police station: **he spent the night in the cells**

◊ **cellmate** *noun* person who shares a prison cell with someone else

censor 1 *noun* official whose job is to say whether books *or* films *or* TV programmes, etc., are acceptable and can be published or shown to the public; **the film was cut *or* was banned *or* was passed by the censor 2** *verb* to say that a book *or* film *or* TV programme, etc. cannot be shown or published because it is not considered right to do so; **all press reports are censored by the government; the news of the riots was censored; the TV report has been censored and only parts of it can be shown**

◊ **censorship** *noun* act of censoring; **TV reporters complained of government censorship; the government has imposed strict press censorship *or* censorship of the press**
NOTE: no plural

censure 1 *noun* vote of censure *or* censure vote = vote which criticizes someone, especially a vote in parliament which criticizes the government; **the meeting passed a vote of censure on the minister 2** *verb* to criticize; **the opposition put forward a motion to censure the government**

central *adjective* organized at one main point; **central office** = main office which

controls all smaller offices; **Central Criminal Court** = the Crown Court sitting in London (= THE OLD BAILEY)

◊ **centralization** *noun* organization of everything from a central point

◊ **centralize** *verb* to organize from a central point; **the gathering of all criminal records has been centralized in the police headquarters**

◊ **centre** *noun* (a) business centre = part of a town where the main banks, shops and offices are (b) important town; **an industrial centre; the centre for the shoe industry** (c) office; **Job Centre** = government office which lists jobs which are vacant; **Law Centre** = local office (mainly in London) with full-time staff who advise and represent clients free of charge; **Legal Aid Centre** = local office giving advice to clients with legal problems, giving advice on obtaining Legal Aid and recommending clients to solicitors

certain *adjective* (a) sure; **the superintendent is certain that the head of the gang is still at large** (b) a certain = one particular; **a certain number *or* a certain quantity** = some

◊ **certainty** *noun* thing which is certain

certificate *noun* official document which shows that something is true; **clearance certificate** = document showing that goods have been passed by customs; **fire certificate** = document from the municipal fire department to say that a building is properly protected against fire; **land certificate** = document which shows who owns a piece of land, and whether there are any charges on it; **practising certificate** = certificate from the Law Society allowing someone to work as a solicitor; **share certificate** = document proving that you own shares; **certificate of approval** = document showing that an item has been officially approved; **certificate of deposit** = document from a bank showing that money has been deposited; **certificate of incorporation** = document showing that a company has been officially registered; **certificate of judgment** = official document showing a decision of a court; **certificate of origin** = document showing where goods were made *or* produced; **certificate of registration** = document showing that an item has been registered;

certificate of registry = document showing that a ship has been officially registered

◊ **certificated** *adjective* **certificated bankrupt** = bankrupt who has been discharged from bankruptcy with a certificate to show that he was not at fault

certify *verb* to make an official declaration in writing; **I certify that this is a true copy; the document is certified as a true copy; certified accountant** = accountant who has passed the professional examinations and is a member of the Association of Certified Accountants; **certified cheque** *or* *US* **certified check** = cheque which a bank says is good and will be paid out of money put aside from the bank account; **certified copy** = copy which is certified as being the same as the original

certiorari *Latin word meaning* "to be informed"; **order of certiorari** = order which transfers a case from a lower court to the High Court for investigation into its legality; **he applied for judicial review by way of certiorari; the court ordered certiorari following judicial review, quashing the order made by the juvenile court**

cessate grant *noun* special grant of probate made because of the incapacity of an executor *or* grant made to renew a grant which has expired

cession *noun* giving up property to someone (especially a creditor)

CGT = CAPITAL GAINS TAX

chair 1 *noun* (a) piece of furniture for sitting on; **electric chair** *or* **the chair** = chair attached to a powerful electric current, used in the USA for executing criminals (b) position of the chairman, presiding over a meeting; **to be in the chair; she was voted into the chair; Mr Jones took the chair** = Mr Jones presided over the meeting; **to address the chair** = in a meeting, to speak to the chairman and not to the rest of the people at the meeting 2 *verb* to preside over a meeting; **the meeting was chaired by Mrs Smith**

◊ **chairman** *noun* (a) person who is in charge of a meeting; **chairman of the magistrates** *or* **of the bench; Mr Howard was chairman** *or* **acted as chairman; Mr Chairman** *or* **Madam Chairman** = way of speaking to the chairman (b) person who presides over the board meetings of a company; **the chairman of the board** *or* **the company chairman**

◊ **chairmanship** *noun* being a chairman; **the committee met under the chairmanship of Mr Jones** = Mr Jones chaired the meeting of the committee

◊ **chairperson** *noun* person who is in charge of a meeting

◊ **chairwoman** *noun* woman who is in charge of a meeting

challenge 1 *noun* act of objecting to a decision, and asking it to be set aside; **challenge for cause** *or* **challenge without cause** = objecting to a juror, stating *or* not stating the reason for the objection; **peremptory challenge** = challenge without cause 2 *verb* to object to *or* to refuse to accept (a juror *or* evidence); **to challenge a sentence passed by magistrates by appeal to the Crown Court**

Chamber of Commerce *noun* group of local businessmen who meet to discuss problems which they have in common, and to promote business in the town

◊ **chambers** *plural noun* (a) offices of barristers (b) office of a judge; **the judge heard the case in chambers** = in his private rooms, without the public being present and not in open court

champerty *noun* financial help given to a person starting a proceedings against a party, where the person giving help has a share in the damages to be recovered
NOTE: no plural

chance (a) being possible; **is there any chance of the hearing taking place before the summer?** (b) opportunity to do something; **the prosecuting counsel seized his chance and asked the witness to repeat the conversation which he had had with the accused**

Chancellor *noun* (a) (*in the United Kingdom*) **Chancellor of the Exchequer** = chief finance minister in the government; **the Lord Chancellor** = chief minister of justice

> COMMENT: the Lord Chancellor is a member of the Cabinet; he presides over debates in the House of Lords; he is the head of the judicial system and advises on the appointment of judges

(b) *US* judge who presides over a court of equity

Chancery *noun* **the Chancery Bar** = barristers who specialize in the Chancery Division; **Chancery Court** = formerly the court presided over by the Lord Chancellor, which established case law *or* equity; **Chancery Division** = one of the three divisions of the High Court, dealing with wills, partnerships and companies, taxation, bankruptcies, etc.

channel *noun* way in which information or goods are passed from one place to another; **to go through the official channels** = to deal with government officials (especially when making a request); **to open up new channels of communication** = new ways of communicating with someone

chaos *noun* disorder *or* disorderly state; **after the coup the country was in chaos; chaos reigned in the centre of the town until the police and fire engines arrived**

◇ **chaotic** *adjective* in a disorderly state; **the situation was chaotic until the police arrived to control the traffic**

chapter *noun* official term for an Act of Parliament

character *noun* general qualities of a person which make him different from others; **he is a man of good character** = he is an honest *or* hard-working *or* decent man; **to give someone a character reference** = to say that someone has good qualities; **to introduce character evidence** = to produce witnesses to say that a person is of good *or* bad character

charge 1 *noun* **(a)** money which must be paid *or* price of a service; **to make no charge for delivery; to make a small charge for rental; there is no charge for service** *or* **no charge is made for service; admission charge** *or* **entry charge** = price to be paid before going into an exhibition, etc.; **scale of charges** = list showing various prices; **free of charge** = free *or* with no payment to be made; **solicitors' charges** = payments to be made to solicitors for work done on behalf of clients **(b) charge on land** *or* **charge over property** = mortgage *or* liability on a property which has been used as security for a loan; **fixed charge** = charge over a particular asset *or* property; **floating charge** = charge over changing assets of a

business; **charge by way of legal mortgage** = way of borrowing money on the security of a property, where the mortgagor signs a deed which gives the mortgagee an interest in the property **(c)** official statement in a court accusing someone of having committed a crime; **he appeared in court on a charge of embezzling** *or* **on an embezzlement charge; the clerk of the court read out the charges; charge sheet** = document listing the charges which a magistrate will hear *or* listing the charges against the accused together with details of the crime committed; **to answer charges** = to appear in court to plead guilty *or* not guilty to a charge; **the charges against him were withdrawn** *or* **dropped** = the prosecution decided not to continue with the trial; **to press charges against someone** = to say formally that someone has committed a crime; **he was very angry when his neighbour's son set fire to his car, but decided not to press charges; holding charge** = minor charge brought against someone so that he can be held in custody while more serious charges are being prepared **(d)** instructions given by the judge to the jury, summing up the evidence and giving advice on the points of law which have to be considered **2** *verb* **(a)** to ask someone to pay for services; to ask for money to be paid; **to charge £5 for delivery; how much does he charge?; he charges £6 an hour** = he asks to be paid £6 for an hour's work **(b)** (*in a court*) to accuse someone formally of having committed a crime; **he was charged with embezzling his clients' money; they were charged with murder**
NOTE: you charge someone **with** a crime

◇ **chargee** *noun* person who holds a charge over a property

◇ **charging order** *noun* court order made in favour of a judgment creditor granting him a charge over a debtor's property

charity *noun* body which aims not to make money, but to benefit the general public by helping the poor *or* by promoting education or religion *or* by doing other useful work; **the Charity Commissioners** = body which governs charities and sees that they follow the law and use their funds for the purposes intended

◇ **charitable trust** *or* *US* **charitable corporation** *noun* trust which benefits the public as a whole, which promotes education or religion *or* which helps the poor *or* or which does other useful work

chart *noun* diagram showing information as a series of lines *or* blocks, etc.; **flow chart** = diagram showing the arrangement of various work processes in a series; **organization chart** = diagram showing how a company *or* an office is organized

charter **1** *noun* **(a)** document from the Crown establishing a town *or* a corporation *or* a university *or* a company; **bank charter** = official government document allowing the establishment of a bank **(b)** hiring transport for a special purpose; **charter flight** = flight in an aircraft which has been hired for that purpose; **charter plane** = plane which has been chartered; **boat on charter to Mr Smith** = boat which Mr Smith has hired for a voyage **2** *verb* to hire for a special purpose; **to charter a plane** *or* **a boat** *or* **a bus**

◇ **chartered** *adjective* **(a) chartered accountant** = accountant who has passed the professional examinations and is a member of the Institute of Chartered Accountants **(b)** (company) which has been set up by royal charter, and not registered as a company **(c) chartered ship** *or* **bus** *or* **plane** = ship *or* bus *or* plane which has been hired for a special purpose

◇ **charterer** *noun* person who hires a ship, etc., for a special purpose

◇ **chartering** *noun* act of hiring for a special purpose

◇ **charterparty** *noun* contract where the owner of a ship charters his ship to someone for carrying goods

chattel mortgage *noun* *US* mortgage using personal property as security

◇ **chattels** *plural noun* **goods and chattels** = moveable property (but not freehold real estate); **chattels real** = leaseholds; **chattels personal** = any property that is not real property; **incorporeal chattels** = intangible properties (such as patents *or* copyrights)

cheat **1** *noun* person who tricks someone so that he loses money *or* property **2** *verb* to trick someone so that he loses money *or* property; **he cheated the Income Tax out of**

thousands of pounds; **she was accused of cheating clients who came to ask her for advice**
NOTE: you cheat someone **out of** money

check **1** *noun* **(a)** sudden stop; **to put a check on the sale of firearms** = to stop some firearms being sold **(b) check sample** = sample to be used to see if a consignment is acceptable **(c)** investigation *or* examination; **the auditors carried out checks on the petty cash book; a routine check of the fire equipment; baggage check** = examination of passengers' baggage to see if it contains bombs **(d)** *US* = CHEQUE **2** *verb* **(a)** to stop *or* to delay; **to check the entry of contraband into the country (b)** to examine *or* to investigate; **to check that an invoice is correct; to check and sign for goods; he checked the computer printout against the invoices** = he examined the printout and the invoices to see if the figures were the same **(c)** *US* to mark with a sign to show that something is correct

◇ **checking** *noun* examination *or* investigation; **the inspectors found some defects during their checking of the building**

cheque *noun* order to a bank to pay money from your account to the person whose name is written on it; **cheque account** = bank account which allows the customer to write cheques; **crossed cheque** = cheque with two lines across it showing that it can only be deposited at a bank and not exchanged for cash; **open** *or* **uncrossed cheque** = cheque which can be exchanged for cash anywhere; **blank cheque** = cheque with the amount of money and the payee left blank, but signed by the drawer; **traveller's cheques** = cheques used by a traveller which can be exchanged for cash in a foreign country **(b) to endorse a cheque** = to sign a cheque on the back to make it payable to someone else; **to make out a cheque to someone** = to write out a cheque to someone; **to pay by cheque** = to pay by writing a cheque, and not by using cash *or* a credit card; **to pay a cheque into your account** = to deposit a cheque; **to dishonour a cheque** *or* *informal* **to bounce a cheque** = to refuse to pay a cheque because there is not enough money in the account to pay it; **the bank referred the cheque to the drawer** = returned the cheque to the person who wrote it because there was not enough money in the account to pay it; **to**

sign a cheque = to sign on the front of a cheque to show that you authorize the bank to pay the money from your account; **to stop a cheque** = to ask a bank not to pay a cheque which you have written

chief *adjective* **(a)** most important; **he is the chief accountant of an industrial group;** *GB* **Lord Chief Justice** = chief judge of the Queen's Bench Division of the High Court who is also a member of the Court of Appeal; *US* **Chief Justice** = main judge in a court; **Chief Constable** = person in charge of a police force; **Assistant Chief Constable** *or* **Deputy Chief Constable** = ranks in the police force below Chief Constable; **Chief Inspector** *or* **Chief Superintendent** = ranks in the police force above Inspector *or* Superintendent **(b) in chief** = in person; **examination in chief** = examining of a witness by counsel for his side

child *noun* person under ' the age of majority; **child destruction** = notifiable offence of a killing an unborn child capable of being born alive; **child stealing** = notifiable offence of taking away a child from its parents *or* guardian

> COMMENT: In Great Britain a child does not have full legal status until the age of eighteen. A contract is not binding on a child, and a child cannot own land, cannot make a will, cannot vote, cannot drive a car (under the age of seventeen). A child cannot marry before the age of sixteen. A child who is less than ten years old is not considered capable of committing a crime; a child between ten and fourteen years of age may be considered capable to committing a crime if there is evidence of malice or knowledge.

chose *French word meaning* "item" *or* "thing"; **chose in action** = personal right which can be enforced or claimed as if it were property (such as a patent *or* copyright *or* debt *or* cheque); **chose in possession** = physical thing which can be owned (such as a piece of furniture)

Christmas Day *noun* 25th December, one of the four quarter days when rent is payable on land

chronic *adjective* permanently bad

chronological order *noun* arrangement of records (files, invoices, etc.) in order of their dates

c.i.f. = COST, INSURANCE, FREIGHT contract for the sale of goods where the seller arranges the export licence, loading, carriage, and insurance and provides a bill of lading, and the purchaser pays on delivery of documents and pays duties and the unloading

circuit *noun* one of six divisions of England and Wales for legal purposes; **he is a judge on the Welsh Circuit; circuit judge** = judge in the Crown Court or a County Court

> COMMENT: the six circuits are: Northern, North-Eastern, Midland and Oxford, Wales and Chester, South-Eastern, and Western

circular 1 *adjective* (letter) sent to many people; **circular letter of credit** = letter of credit sent to all branches of the bank which issues it **2** *noun* leaflet *or* letter sent to many people; **they sent out a circular offering a 10% discount**

◇ **circularize** *verb* to send a circular to; **the committee has agreed to circularize the members; they circularized all their customers with a new list of prices**

◇ **circulate** *verb* to send information to; **they circulated a new list of prices to all their customers**

◇ **circulating** *adjective* which is moving about freely

◇ **circulation** *noun* **(a)** movement; **the company is trying to improve the circulation of information between departments; circulation of capital** = movement of capital from one investment to another; **free circulation of goods** = movement of goods from one country to another without import quotas or other restrictions **(b) to put money into circulation** = to issue new notes to business and the public; **the amount of money in circulation increased more than had been expected (c)** (*of newspapers*) number of copies sold; **a circulation battle** = competition between two newspapers to try to sell more copies in the same market

circumstances *plural noun* situation as it is when something happens; **the police**

inspector described the circumstances leading to the riot; *see also* EXTENUATING

◇ **circumstantial** *adjective* which allows someone to infer facts; **circumstantial evidence** = evidence which suggests that something happened, but does not give firm proof of it

cite *verb* **(a)** to summon someone to appear in court **(b)** to quote *or* to refer to something; **the judge cited several previous cases in his summing up**

◇ **citation** *noun* **(a)** official request asking someone to appear in court (NOTE: used mainly in the Scottish and US courts) **(b)** quotation of a legal case *or* authority *or* precedent

citizen *noun* **(a)** person who lives in a city **(b)** person who has the nationality of a certain country; **he is a French citizen by birth; Citizens' Advice Bureau** = office where people can go to get free advice on legal and administrative problems; **citizen's arrest** = arrest of a suspected criminal by an ordinary citizen without a warrant

◇ **citizenship** *noun* state of being a citizen of a country

city *noun* **(a)** large town; **the largest cities in Europe are linked by hourly flights; capital city** = main town in a country, where the government and parliament are situated **(b) the City** = old centre of London, where banks and large companies have their main offices; **the London financial centre**

civil *adjective* referring to the rights and duties of private persons *or* corporate bodies (as opposed to criminal, military or ecclesiastical); **civil action** = court case brought by a person *or* a company (the plaintiff) against someone who is alleged to have done them wrong (the defendant); **civil disorder** = riots *or* fighting in public places; **civil law** = laws relating to people's rights and agreements between individuals (as opposed to criminal law); **civil liberties** = freedom to act within the law (liberty of the press, liberty of the individual, etc.); **civil rights** = rights and privileges of each individual person according to the law; **civil strife** = trouble where gangs of people fight each other, usually over matters of principle; **civil war** = situation in a country where the nation is divided into two or more sections which fight each other

◇ **civil service** *noun* organization which administers a country; **he has a job in the civil service; you have to pass an examination to get a job in the civil service** *or* **to get a civil service job**

◇ **civil servant** *noun* person who works in the civil service

CJ = CHIEF JUSTICE

claim **1** *noun* **(a)** (i) assertion of a legal right; (ii) document used in the County Court to start a legal action; **particulars of claim** = County Court pleading setting out the plaintiff's claim **(b)** statement that someone has a right to property held by another person; **legal claim to something** = statement that you think you own something legally; **he has no legal claim to the property** *or* **to the car** **(c)** asking for money; **wage claim** = asking for an increase in wages; **the union put in a 6% wage claim** = the union asked for a 6% increase in wages for its members; **she put in a claim for £250,000 damages against the driver of the other car** **(d) insurance claim** = asking an insurance company to pay for damages *or* for loss; **no claims bonus** = reduction of premiums to be paid because no claims have been made against the insurance policy; **to put in a claim** = to ask the insurance company officially to pay for damage *or* loss; **claim form** = form which has to be completed when making an insurance claim; **she put in a claim for repairs to the car; he filled in the claim form and sent it to the insurance company; to settle a claim** = to agree to pay what is asked for **(e) small claim** = claim for less than £500 in the County Court; **small claims court** = court which deals with disputes over small amounts of money **2** *verb* **(a)** to state a grievance in court **(b)** to ask for money; **he claimed £100,000 damages against the cleaning firm; she claimed for repairs to the car against her insurance (c)** to say that you have a right to property held by someone else; **he is claiming possession of the house; no one claimed the umbrella found in my office (d)** to state that something is a fact; **he claims he never received the goods; she claims that the shares are her property (e)** *slang* (i) to attack someone in prison; (ii) to arrest someone

◇ **claimant** *noun* person who claims; **rightful claimant** = person who has a legal claim to something

◇ **claim back** *verb* to ask for money to be paid back

clandestine *adjective* secret *or* hidden

clarify *verb* to make something clear *or* easy to understand; **the opposition asked the minister to clarify his statement**

◇ **clarification** *noun* making something clear *or* easy to understand; **the wording of the clause is ambiguous and needs clarification**

class 1 *noun* category *or* group into which things are classified; **first-class** = top quality *or* most expensive; **Class F charge** = charge on a property registered by a spouse who is not an owner, claiming the right to live in the property; **class gift** = gift to a defined group of people; *US* **class action** *or* **class suit** = legal action brought on behalf of a group of people **2** *verb* to put into a category *or* to classify; **the magazine was classed as an obscene publication**

classify *verb* to put into classes *or* categories; **classified directory** = book which lists businesses grouped under various headings (such as computer shops, newsagents, hairdressers); **classified information** = information which is secret and can be told only to certain people

◇ **classification** *noun* way of putting into classes

clause *noun* section of a contract *or* of a constitution; **there are ten clauses in the contract; according to clause six, payment will not be due until next year; exclusion clause** = clause in an insurance policy *or* contract which says which items are not covered by the policy *or* gives details of circumstances where the insurance company will refuse to pay; **forfeit clause** = clause in a contract which says that goods *or* a deposit will be forfeited if the contract is not obeyed; **liability clause** = clause in the articles of association of a company which states that the liability of its members is limited; **penalty clause** = clause which lists the penalties which will be imposed if the terms of the contract are not fulfilled; **termination clause** = clause which explains how and when a contract can be terminated

claw back *verb* (i) to take back money which has been allocated; (ii) (*of the Inland Revenue*) to take back tax relief which was previously granted; **income tax claws back 25% of pensions paid out by the government; of the £1m allocated to the development of the system, the government clawed back £100,000 in taxes**

◇ **clawback** *noun* (i) money taken back; (ii) loss of tax relief previously granted

clean hands *plural noun* **the plaintiff must have clean hands** = the plaintiff cannot claim successfully if his motives or actions are dishonest *or* if he has not discharged his own obligations to the defendant

COMMENT: from the maxim: "he who comes to equity must come with clean hands"

clear 1 *adjective* **(a)** easily understood; **he made it clear that he wanted the manager to resign; there was no clear evidence *or* clear proof that he was in the house at the time of the murder (b) clear profit** = profit after all expenses have been paid; **we made $6,000 clear profit on the sale; to have a clear title to something** = to have a right to something with no limitations *or* charges **(c)** free *or* total period of time; **three clear days** = three whole working days; **allow three clear days for the cheque to be paid into your account 2** *verb* **(a)** to sell cheaply in order to get rid of stock **(b) to clear goods through the customs** = to have all documentation passed by the customs so that goods can leave the country **(c) to clear 10% *or* $5,000 on the deal** = to make 10% *or* $5,000 clear profit; **we cleared only our expenses** = the sales revenue paid only for the costs and expenses without making any profit **(d) to clear a cheque** = to pass a cheque through the banking system, so that the money is transferred from the payer's account to another account; **the cheque took ten days to clear *or* the bank took ten days to clear the cheque (e) to clear someone of charges** = to find that someone is not guilty of the charges against him; **he was cleared of all charges *or* he was cleared on all counts**

◇ **clearance** *noun* **customs clearance** = act of clearing goods through the customs; **clearance certificate** = document which shows that goods have been passed by customs

◇ **clearing** *noun* **(a) clearing of goods through the customs** = passing of goods through the customs **(b) clearing of a debt** = paying all of a debt **(c)** clearing **bank** = bank which clears cheques, one of the major British High Street banks; **clearing house** = central office where clearing banks exchange cheques

◇ **clear up** *verb* to solve a crime *or* to discover who has committed a crime and arrest him; **half the crimes committed are never cleared up; clear-up rate** = number of crimes solved, as a percentage of all crimes committed

COMMENT: clear up can be divided into two categories: **primary clear up,** when a crime is solved by arresting the suspect, and **secondary clear up,** where a person charged with one crime then confesses to another which had not previously been solved

clemency *noun* pardon *or* mercy; **as an act of clemency, the president granted an amnesty to all political prisoners**
NOTE: no plural

clerical *adjective* **(a)** (work) done in an office *or* done by a clerk; **clerical error** = mistake made in an office; **clerical staff** = staff of an office; **clerical work** = paperwork done in an office; **clerical worker** = person who works in an office **(b)** referring to the church

clerk *noun* **(a)** person who works in an office; **accounts clerk; sales clerk; wages clerk; articled clerk** = trainee who is bound by a contract to work in a solicitor's office for some years to learn the law; **chief clerk** *or* **head clerk** = most important clerk; **Clerk of the House (of Commons** *or* **of Lords)** = head of the administrative staff which runs the House of Commons *or* House of Lords; **clerk to the justices** = official of a magistrates' court (a qualified lawyer) who advises the magistrates on legal questions; **the functions of a justices' clerk include giving advice about law, practice and procedure; the clerk advised the magistrates that the case had to be passed to the Crown Court for trial**

◇ **clerkess** *noun* (*in Scotland*) woman clerk

◇ **clerkship** *noun* US time when a student lawyer is working in the office of a lawyer before being admitted to the bar

clever *adjective* intelligent *or* able to learn quickly; **he is very clever at spotting a bargain; clever shareholders have made a lot of money on the deal**

client *noun* **(a)** person who pays for a service carried out by a professional person (such as an accountant *or* a solicitor) **(b)** person who is represented by a lawyer; **the solicitor paid the fine on behalf of his client**

◇ **clientele** *noun* all the clients of a business; all the customers of a shop
NOTE: no plural

clinch *verb* to settle (a business deal) *or* to come to an agreement; **he offered an extra 5% to clinch the deal; they need approval from the board before they can clinch the deal**

close **1** *noun* end; **at the close of the day's trading the shares had fallen 20%** **2** *adjective* **close to** = very near *or* almost; **the company was close to bankruptcy; we are close to solving the crime** **3** *verb* **(a)** to stop doing business for the day; **the office closes at 5.30; we close early on Saturdays** **(b) to close the accounts** = to come to the end of an accounting period and make up the profit and loss account **(c) to close an account** = (i) to stop supplying a customer on credit; (ii) to take all the money out of a bank account and stop the account **(d) the shares closed at $15** = at the end of the day's trading the price of the shares was $15

◇ **close company** *or* US **close(d) corporation** *noun* privately owned company where the public may own a small number of shares

◇ **closed** *adjective* **(a)** shut *or* not open *or* not doing business; **the office is closed on Mondays; all the banks are closed on the National Day** **(b)** restricted to a few people; **closed shop** = system where a company agrees to employ only union members in certain jobs; **a closed shop agreement; the union is asking the management to agree to a closed shop; closed market** = market where a supplier deals only with one agent and does not supply any others direct; **they signed a closed market agreement with an American company; closed session** = meeting which is not open to the public or to journalists; **the town council met in closed session to discuss staff problems in the Education Department; the public gallery was cleared when the meeting went into closed session**

◊ **close down** *verb* to shut a shop *or* factory for a long period or for ever; **the company is closing down its London office; the strike closed down the railway system**

◊ **closing** 1 *adjective* (a) final *or* coming at the end; **closing speeches** = final speeches for prosecution and defence at the end of a trial (b) at the end of an accounting period 2 *noun* (a) shutting of a shop *or* being shut; **Sunday closing** = not opening a shop on Sundays; **closing time** = time when a shop or office stops work; **early closing day** = weekday (usually Wednesday or Thursday) when many shops close in the afternoon (b) **closing of an account** = act of stopping supply to a customer on credit

◊ **closure** *noun* (a) act of closing (b) (*in the House of Commons*) **closure motion** = proposal to end a debate

clue *noun* thing which helps someone solve a crime; **the police have searched the room for clues; the police have several clues to the identity of the murdered**

Cmnd = COMMAND PAPERS

c/o = CARE OF

Co = COMPANY **J. Smith & Co Ltd**

co- *prefix* working *or* acting together; **co-creditor** = person who is a creditor of the same company as you are; **co-defendant** = person who appears in a case with another defendant; **co-director** = person who is a director of the same company as you; **co-insurance** = insurance policy where the risk is shared among several insurers

c.o.d. = CASH ON DELIVERY, *US* COLLECT ON DELIVERY

code 1 *noun* (a) official set of laws *or* regulations; **the Highway Code** = rules which govern the behaviour of people and vehicles using roads; **the penal code** = set of laws governing crime and its punishment; **failure to observe the code** does not render anyone liable to proceedings (b) set of laws of a country; *US* **the Louisiana Code** = laws of the state of Louisiana; **Code Napoleon** = civil laws of France (introduced by Napoleon) (c) set of semi-official rules; **code of conduct** = informal (sometimes written) rules by which a group of people work; **code of practice** = (i) rules to be followed when applying a law; (ii) rules drawn up by an association which the members must follow when doing business; **the Code of Practice on Picketing has been issued by the Secretary of State** (d) system of signs *or* numbers *or* letters which mean something; **the spy sent his message in code; area code** = numbers which indicate an area for telephoning; **machine-readable codes** = sets of signs or letters (such as bar codes *or* post codes) which can be read by computers; **post code** *or* *US* **zip code** = letters and numbers used to indicate a town *or* street in an address on an envelope 2 *verb* to write (a message) using secret signs; **we received coded instructions from our agent in New York**

◊ **coding** *noun* act of putting a code on something; **the coding of invoices**

codicil *noun* document executed in the same way as a will, making additions *or* changes to an existing will

codify *verb* to put (laws) together to form a code

◊ **codification** *noun* (a) putting all laws together into a formal legal code (b) bringing together all statutes and case law relating to a certain issue, to make a single Act of Parliament; *see also* CONSOLIDATION

coercion *noun* forcing someone by pressure to commit a crime *or* do some act
NOTE: no plural

cohabit *verb* (*of a man and a woman*) to live together as man and wife

◊ **cohabitation** *noun* living together as man and wife (whether married or not)

◊ **cohabiter** *or* **cohabitee** *noun* person who lives with another person of the opposite sex without being married

coin *noun* piece of metal money; **he gave me two 10-cent coins in my change; I need some 10p coins for the telephone**

◊ **coinage** *noun* system of metal money used in a country

NOTE: no plural

collaborate *verb* to work together; **to collaborate with a French firm on building a bridge; they collaborated on the new aircraft**

◇ **collaboration** *noun* working together; **their collaboration on the development of the computer system was very profitable**

collateral *adjective & noun* **(a)** (security) used to provide a guarantee for a loan; **collateral security; collateral contract =** contract which induces a person to enter into a more important contract **(b) collateral issue =** issue which arises from a plea in a criminal court

collation *noun* comparing a copy with the original to see if it is perfect

colleague *noun* person who works with someone else; **counsel asked for more time to consult his colleagues**

collect 1 *verb* **(a)** to make someone pay money which is owed; **to collect a debt =** to go a. d make someone pay a debt **(b)** to take goods away from a place; **we have to collect the stock from the warehouse; can you collect my letters from the typing pool?; letters are collected twice a day =** the post office workers take them from the letter box to the post office so that they can be sent off 2 *adverb & adjective US* (phone call) where the person receiving the call agrees to pay for it; **to make a collect call; he called his office collect**

◇ **collecting** *noun* **collecting agency =** agency which collects money owed to other companies for a commission

◇ **collection** *noun* **(a)** getting money together *or* making someone pay money which is owed; **debt collection =** collecting money which is owed; **debt collection agency =** company which collects debts for other companies for a commission; **bills for collection =** bills where payment is due **(b)** fetching of goods; **the stock is in the warehouse awaiting collection; collection charges** *or* **collection rates =** charge for collecting something; **to hand something in for collection =** to leave something for someone to come and collect **(c) collections =** money which has been collected **(d)** taking of letters from a letter box or mail room to the post office to be

sent off; **there are six collections a day from the letter box**

◇ **collective** *adjective* working together; **(free) collective bargaining =** negotiations about wages and working conditions between management and workers' representatives; **collective ownership =** ownership of a business by the workers who work in it; **collective responsibility =** doctrine that all members of a group (such as the British cabinet) are responsible together for the actions of the group; **they signed a collective wage agreement =** an agreement was signed between management and the trade union about wages

◇ **collector** *noun* person who makes people pay money which is owed; **collector of taxes** *or* **tax collector; debt collector**

college *noun* **(a)** place where people can study after they have left school; **business college** *or* **commercial college =** college which teaches general business methods; **correspondence college =** college where the teaching is done by mail (sending work to the students who then return it to be marked); **secretarial college =** college which teaches shorthand, typing and word-processing **(b) electoral college =** group of people elected by larger groups to vote on their behalf in an election

collision *noun* crash *or* accident between vehicles; **six people were injured in the collision**

collusion *noun* illicit co-operation between people *or* agreement between parties in order to cheat another party *or* in order to defraud another party of a right; **he was suspected of (acting in) collusion with the owner of the property**
NOTE: no plural

◇ **collusive action** *noun* action which is taken in collusion with another party

column *noun* list of figures one written underneath the other; **debit column** *or* **credit column =** lists of figures in accounts, showing money paid to others *or* owed by others

comfort *noun* **letter of comfort** *or* **comfort letter =** letter supporting someone who is trying to get a loan *or* letter which reassures someone on a particular point

comity (of nations) *noun* custom whereby the courts of one country acknowledge and apply the laws of another country in certain cases

command 1 *noun* order; **by Royal Command** = by order of the Queen *or* King; **Command papers** = papers (such as White papers *or* Green Papers *or* reports of Royal Commissions) which are presented to Parliament by the government **2** *verb* to order someone to do something; **the judge commanded that the public gallery should be cleared; the President commanded the Chief of Police to arrest the Members of Parliament**

commander *noun* high rank in the Metropolitan Police force (equivalent to Assistant Chief Constable)

commence *verb* to begin; **the proceedings commenced with the swearing-in of witnesses; the police inspector commenced the questioning of the suspect**

◊ **commencement** *noun* beginning; **date of commencement** = date when an Act of Parliament takes effect

comment 1 *noun* remark *or* spoken *or* written opinion; **the judge made a comment on the evidence presented by the defence; the newspaper has some short comments about the trial; fair comment** = remark which is honestly made on a matter of public interest and so is not defamatory **2** *verb* to remark *or* to express an opinion; **the judge commented on the lack of evidence; the newspapers commented on the result of the trial**

◊ **commentary** *noun* (i) textbook which comments on the law; (ii) brief notes which comment on the main points of a judgment

commerce *noun* business *or* buying and selling of goods and services; **Chamber of Commerce** = group of local businessmen who meet to discuss problems which they have in common and to promote business in their town

◊ **commercial 1** *adjective* **(a)** referring to business; **commercial college** = college which teaches business studies; **commercial course** = course where business skills are studied; **Commercial Court** = court in the Queen's Bench Division which hears cases relating to business

disputes; **commercial directory** = book which lists all the businesses and business people in a town; **commercial law** = laws regarding business **(b)** profitable: **not a commercial proposition** = not likely to make a profit

◊ **commercialization** *noun* making something into a business enterprise

◊ **commercialize** *verb* to make something into a business

◊ **commercially** *adverb* in a business way; **not commercially viable** = not likely to make a profit

commission *noun* **(a)** official order to someone, giving him authority and explaining what his duties are; **he has a commission in the armed forces** = he is an officer in the armed forces **(b)** payment (usually a percentage of turnover) made to an agent; **he has an agent's commission of 15% of sales (c)** group of people officially appointed to examine some problem; **the government has appointed a commission of inquiry to look into the problems of prison overcrowding; he is the chairman of the government commission on football violence; Commission of the European Community** = main executive body of the EC, made up of members of each state; **Law Commission** = permanent committee which reviews English law and recommends changes to it; **Royal Commission** = group of people specially appointed by a minister to examine and report on a major problem

◊ **commissioner** *noun* member of an official commission; person who has an official commission; member of the Commission of the European Community; **the Commissioners of Inland Revenue** = the Board of Inland Revenue; **commissioner for oaths** = solicitor appointed by the Lord Chancellor to administer affidavits which may be used in court; **commissioner of police** *or* **police commissioner** = highest rank in a police force; **Metropolitan Police Commissioner** = head of the Metropolitan Police in London

commit *verb* **(a)** to send (someone) to prison *or* to a court; **he was committed for trial in the Central Criminal Court; the magistrates committed her for trial at the Crown Court (b)** to carry out (a crime); **the gang committed six robberies before they were caught**

NOTE: **committing - committed**

◇ **commitment** *noun* **(a)** order for sending someone to prison **(b)** commitments = obligations *or* things which have to be done; **to honour one's commitments** = to do what one is obliged to do; **financial commitments** = money which is owed *or* debts which have to be paid

◇ **committal** *noun* sending someone to a court *or* to prison; **committal order** = order sending someone to prison for contempt of court; **committal proceedings** = preliminary hearing of a case before the magistrates' court, to decide if it is serious enough to be tried before a jury in a higher court; **committal for trial** = sending someone to be tried in a higher court following committal proceedings in a magistrates' court; **committal for sentence** = sending someone who has been convicted in a magistrates court to be sentenced in a higher court; **committal warrant** = order sending someone to serve a prison sentence

committee *noun* **(a)** official group of people who organize or plan for a larger group; **to be a member of a committee** *or* **to sit on a committee; he was elected to the committee of the staff club; the new plans have to be approved by the committee members; to chair a committee** = to be the chairman of a committee; **he is the chairman of the planning committee; she is the secretary of the finance committee (b)** (*in the House of Commons*) **Committee Stage** = one of the stages in the discussion of a Bill, where each clause is examined in detail; **select committee** = special committee of the House of Commons (with members representing various political parties) which examines the work of a ministry; **standing committee** = permanent committee which examines Bills not sent to other committees; **Committee of the Whole House** = the House of Commons acting as a committee to examine the clauses of a Bill; **Committee of Privileges** = special committee of the House of Commons which examines cases of breach of privilege; **Public Accounts Committee** = committee of the House of Commons which examines the spending of each ministry and department; **Committee of Ways and Means** = committee of the whole House of Commons which considers a Supply Bill (i.e. a Bill relating to public finance)

commodity *noun* thing sold in very large quantities, especially raw materials and food such as metals or corn; **primary** *or* **basic commodities** = farm produce grown in large quantities, such as corn, rice, cotton; **commodity market** *or* **commodity exchange** = place where people buy and sell commodities; **commodity futures** = trading in commodities for delivery at a later date; **silver rose 5% on the commodity futures market yesterday; commodity trader** = person whose business is buying and selling commodities

common **1** *noun* land on which anyone can walk, and may have the right to keep animals, pick wood, etc. (NOTE: now usually used in place names such as **Clapham Common**) **2** *adjective* **(a)** which happens very often; **putting the carbon paper in the wrong way round is a common mistake; being caught by the customs is very common these days (b)** referring to *or* belonging to several different people or to everyone; **common assault** = crime *or* tort of acting in such a way that another person is afraid he will be attacked and hurt; **common carrier** = firm which carries goods *or* passengers, which cannot normally refuse to do so and which can be used by anyone; **common land** = land on which anyone can walk and may have the right to keep animals, pick wood, etc.; **common nuisance** = criminal act which causes harm *or* danger to members of the public in general *or* to their rights; **common ownership** = ownership of a company *or* a property by a group of people who each own a part; **common pricing** = illegal fixing of prices by several businesses so that they all charge the same price; **common seal** = seal which a corporation must possess, and which is used to seal official papers **(c) in common** = together; **ownership in common** = COMMON OWNERSHIP **tenancy in common** = situation where two or more persons jointly lease a property and each can leave his interest to his heirs when he dies *Compare* JOINT TENANCY

◇ **common law** *noun* **(a)** law as laid down in decisions of courts, rather than by statute **(b)** general system of laws which

formerly were the only laws existing in England, and which in some cases have been superseded by statute
NOTE: you say **at common law** when referring to something happening according to the principles of common law

◇ **common-law** *adjective* according to the old unwritten system of law; **common-law marriage** = situation where two people live together as husband and wife without being married; **common-law wife** = woman who is living with a man as his wife, although they have not been legally married

◇ **Common Market** *noun* **the European Common Market** = the European Community *or* organization which joins several European countries for the purposes of trade; **the Common Market finance ministers** = the finance ministers of all the Common Market countries meeting as a group

◇ **Commons** *plural noun* = HOUSE OF COMMONS **the Commons voted against the Bill; the majority of the Commons are in favour of law reform**

◇ **Common Serjeant** *noun* senior barrister who sits as a judge in the City of London and acts as adviser to the City of London Corporation

◇ **Commonwealth** *noun* **the Commonwealth** = association of independent countries which were once ruled by the UK

commorientes *plural noun* people who die at the same time (as a husband and wife who die in an accident)

> COMMENT: the law assumes that the younger person has died after the older one

communicate *verb* to pass information to someone; **the members of the jury must not communicate with the witnesses**

◇ **communication** *noun* **(a)** passing of information; **to enter into communication with someone** = to start discussing something with someone, usually in writing; **we have entered into communication with the relevant government department (b)** official message; **we have had a communication from the local tax inspector; privileged communication** = letter which could be libellous, but which is protected by privilege (such as a letter from a client to his lawyer) **(c) communications** = being

able to contact people *or* to pass messages; **after the flood all communications with the outside world were broken**

community *noun* **(a)** group of people living or working in the same place; **the local business community** = the business people living and working in the area; **community home** = house which belongs to a local authority, where children in care can be kept; **community policing** = way of policing a section of a town, whereby the people in the area and the local police force act together to prevent crime and disorder; **community service** = working on behalf of the local community; **community service order** = punishment where a criminal is sentenced to do unpaid work in the local community **(b) the European (Economic) Community** = the Common Market; **Community legislation** = regulations *or* directives issued by the EC Council of Ministers *or* the EC Commission; **the Community ministers** = the ministers of member states of the Common Market **(c)** (*in the USA, Canada, France and many other countries*) **community property** = situation where the husband and wife jointly own any property which they acquire during the course of their marriage

commute *verb* **(a)** to travel to work from home each day; **he commutes from the country to his office in the centre of town (b)** to change a right into cash **(c)** to reduce a harsh sentence to a lesser one; **the death sentence was commuted to life imprisonment**

◇ **commutation** *noun* reducing a harsh sentence to a lesser one

◇ **commuter** *noun* person who commutes to work; **he lives in the commuter belt** = area of country where the commuters live round a town; **commuter train** = train which commuters take in the morning and evening

compact *noun* agreement

company *noun* **(a)** business *or* group of people organized to buy, sell or provide a service **(b)** group of people organized to buy or sell or provide a service which has been legally incorporated, and so is a legal entity separate from its individual members; **to put a company into liquidation** = to close a company by selling its assets to pay its creditors; **to set up a company** =

to start a company legally; **associate company** = company which is partly owned by another company; **close company** = privately owned company where the public may own a small number of shares; **family company** = company where most of the shares are owned by members of the same family; **holding company** = company which exists only to own shares in subsidiary companies; **joint-stock company** = company whose shares are held by many people; **limited (liability) company** = company where a shareholder is responsible for repaying the company's debts only to the face value of the shares he owns; **listed company** = company whose shares can be bought or sold on the Stock Exchange; **parent company** = company which owns more than half of another company's shares; **private (limited) company** = company with a small number of shareholders, whose shares are not traded on the Stock Exchange; **public limited company (plc)** = company whose shares can be bought on the Stock Exchange; **subsidiary company** = company which is owned by a parent company **(c) finance company** = company which provides money for hire-purchase; **insurance company** = company whose business is insurance; **shipping company** = company whose business is in carrying goods by sea; **a tractor** or **aircraft** or **chocolate company** = company which makes tractors or aircraft or chocolate **(d) company director** = person appointed by the shareholders to run a company; **company law** = laws which refer to the way companies may work; **company member** = shareholder in a company; **company secretary** = person responsible for the company's legal and financial affairs; **the Companies Act** = Act of the British parliament which states the legal limits within which a company may do business; **Registrar of Companies** = official who keeps a record of all incorporated companies, the details of their directors and financial state; **register of companies** or **companies' register** = list of companies showing details of their directors and registered addresses; **Companies House** = office which keeps details of incorporated companies **(e)** organization in the City of London which does mainly charitable work, and is derived from one of the former trade associations; **the Drapers' Company; the Grocers' Company**

compare *verb* to look at several things to see how they differ; **the finance director compared the figures for the first and second quarters; the detective compared the finger-prints on the bottle and those on the knife**

◊ **compare with** *verb* to put two things together to see how they differ; **compared with that of some major cities, our crime rate is quite low**

◊ **comparable** *adjective* which can be compared; **the two crimes are not comparable; which is the nearest company comparable to this one in size?** = which company is of a roughly similar size and can be compared with this one?

◊ **comparison** *noun* way of comparing; **sales are down in comparison with those of last year; there is no comparison between export and home sales** = export and home sales are so different they cannot be compared

◊ **comparative** *adjective* which compares one thing with another; **comparative law** = study which compares the legal systems of different countries

compel *verb* to force (someone) to do something; **the Act compels all drivers to have adequate insurance**
NOTE: **compelling - compelled**

◊ **compellable** *adjective* (person) who can be forced to do something; **a compellable witness**

◊ **compellability** *noun* being compellable

compensate *verb* to pay for damage done; **to compensate a manager for loss of commission**

◊ **compensation** *noun* **(a)** payment made by someone to cover the cost of damage or hardship which he has caused; **unlimited compensation may be awarded in the Crown Court; compensation for damage** = payment for damage done; **compensation for loss of office** = payment to a director who is asked to leave a company before his contract ends; **compensation for loss of earnings** = payment to someone who has stopped earning money or who is not able to earn money; **compensation fund** = special fund set up by the Law Society to compensate clients for loss suffered because of the actions of solicitors; **compensation order** = order made by a criminal court to compel a criminal to pay money to his victim **(b)** *US* salary *or* payment made to someone for work which he has done; **compensation package =** salary, pension and other benefits offered with a job

◊ **compensatory** *adjective* **compensatory damages =** damages which compensate for loss *or* harm suffered

compete *verb* **to compete with someone** *or* **with a company =** to try to do better than another person *or* another company; **the gangs were competing for control of the drugs market**

◊ **competition** *noun* competing with another company *or* trying to do better than another company; **free competition =** being free to compete without government interference; **unfair competition =** trying to do better than another company by bringing cheap foreign products into the country *or* by making incorrect criticisms of the other company's products

◊ **competitor** *noun* person *or* company which competes; **two German firms are our main competitors; the contract of employment forbids members of staff from leaving to go to work for competitors**

competence *or* **competency** *noun* **(a)** state of a witness who is permitted to give evidence **(b) the case falls within the competence of the court =** the court is legally able to deal with the case

◊ **competent** *adjective* **(a)** able to do something; efficient; **she is a competent secretary** *or* **a competent manager (b)** legally able to do something; **the court is not competent to deal with this case =** the court is not legally able to deal with the case

complain *verb* to say that something is no good *or* does not work properly; **the office is so cold the staff have started complaining; she complained about the service; they are complaining that our prices are too high; if you want to complain, write to the manager**

◊ **complainant** *noun* person who makes a complaint *or* who starts proceedings against someone

◊ **complaint** *noun* **(a)** statement that you feel something is wrong; **when making a complaint, always quote the reference number; she sent her letter of complaint to the managing director; to make** *or* **lodge a complaint against someone =** to write and send an official complaint to someone's superior; **complaints procedure =** agreed way for workers to make complaints to the management about working conditions; **Police Complaints Committee =** group of people who investigate complaints made by members of the public against the police **(b)** document signed to start proceedings in a Magistrates' Court **(c)** statement of the case made by the plaintiff at the beginning of a civil action

complete 1 *adjective* whole *or* with nothing missing; **the order is complete and ready for sending; the order should be delivered only if it is complete** 2 *verb* **(a)** to finish; **the factory completed the order in two weeks; how long will it take you to complete the job? (b) to complete a conveyance =** to convey a property to a purchaser, when the purchaser pays the purchase price and the vendor hands over the signed conveyance and the deeds of the property

◊ **completely** *adverb* all *or* totally; **the cargo was completely ruined by water; the warehouse was completely destroyed by fire**

◊ **completion** *noun* act of finishing something; **completion date =** date when something will be finished; **completion of a conveyance =** last stage in the sale of a property when the solicitors for the two parties meet, when the purchaser pays and the vendor passes the conveyance and the deeds to the purchaser; **completion statement =** statement of account from a solicitor to a client showing all the costs of the sale *or* purchase of a property

complex 1 *noun* series of large buildings; **a large industrial complex** 2 *adjective* with many different parts; **a complex system of import controls; the regulations governing immigration are very complex**

compliance *noun* agreement to do what is ordered; **the documents have been drawn up in compliance with the provisions of the Act; declaration of compliance =** declaration made by a person forming a limited company, that the requirements of the Companies' Act have been met

◊ **compliant** *adjective* which agrees with something; **not compliant with =** not in agreement with; **the settlement is not compliant with the earlier order of the court**

complicated *adjective* with many different parts *or* sections which make things difficult to understand; **the VAT rules are very complicated; the judge warned the jury that the case was a complicated one and might last several weeks**

comply *verb* **to comply with** = to obey; **the company has complied with the court order; she refused to comply with the injunction**

composition *noun* agreement between a debtor and creditors to settle a debt immediately by repaying only part of it

compos mentis *Latin phrase meaning* "of sound mind" *or* "sane"

compound 1 *adjective* **compound interest** = interest which is added to the capital and then itself earns interest **2** *verb* **(a)** to agree with creditors to settle a debt by paying part of what is owed **(b) to compound an offence** = to agree (in return for payment) not to prosecute someone who has committed an offence

comprehensive *adjective* which includes everything; **comprehensive insurance** = insurance policy which covers you against a large number of possible risks

compromise 1 *noun* agreement between two sides, where each side gives way a little in order to reach a settlement; **management offered £5 an hour, the union asked for £9, and a compromise of £7.50 was reached; after some discussion a compromise solution was reached 2** *verb* **(a)** to reach an agreement by giving way a little; **he asked £15 for it, I offered £7 and we compromised on £10 (b)** to involve someone in something which makes his reputation less good; **the minister was compromised in the bribery case**

comptroller *noun* person in charge, especially referring to accounts; **Comptroller and Auditor General** = official whose duty is to examine the accounts of ministries and government departments

compulsory *adjective* which is forced *or* ordered; **compulsory liquidation** *or* **compulsory winding up** = liquidation which is ordered by a court; **compulsory purchase** = buying of a property by the local council *or* the government even if the owner does not want to sell; **compulsory purchase order** = official order from the local council *or* from the government ordering an owner to sell his property; **compulsory winding up order** = order from a court saying that a company must be wound up

computer *noun* electronic machine which calculates *or* stores information and processes it automatically; **computer bureau** = office which offers to do work on its computers for companies which do not have their own computers; **computer error** = mistake made by a computer; **computer file** = section of information on a computer (such as a list of addresses *or* customer accounts); **computer fraud** = fraud committed by using computer files (such as in a bank); **computer language** = system of signs, letters and words used to instruct a computer; **computer program** = instructions to a computer, telling it to do a particular piece of work

◊ **computerize** *verb* to change from a manual system to one using computers; **the police criminal records have been completely computerized**

con 1 *noun* **(a)** *informal* trick done to try to get money from someone; **trying to get us to pay him for ten hours' overtime was just a con (b)** *slang* (i) convict *or* prisoner; (ii) conviction **2** *verb* *informal* to trick someone to try to get money; **they conned the bank into lending them £25,000 with no security; he conned the finance company out of £100,000**
NOTE: **con - conning - conned** Note also you con someone **into** doing something

conceal *verb* to hide; **he was accused of concealing information; the accused had a gun concealed under his coat**

◊ **concealment** *noun* hiding for criminal purposes; **concealment of assets** = hiding assets so that creditors do not know they exist; **concealment of birth** = notifiable offence of hiding the fact that a child has been born

concede *verb* to admit (that the opposing party is right); **counsel conceded that his client owed the money; the witness conceded under questioning that he had never been near the house; to concede defeat** = to admit that you have lost

concern 1 *noun* **(a)** business *or* company; **his business is a going concern** = the company is working (and making a profit); **sold as a going concern** = sold as an actively trading company **(b)** state of being worried about a problem; **the management showed no concern at all for the workers' safety 2** *verb* to deal with *or* to be connected with; **the court is not concerned with the value of the items stolen; the report does not concern itself with the impartiality of the judge; he has been asked to give evidence to the commission of inquiry concerning the breakdown of law and order; the contract was drawn up with the agreement of all parties concerned**

concert party *noun* two or more people who act together in secret to take over a company

concession *noun* **(a)** right to use someone else's property for business purposes; **mining concession** = right to dig a mine on a piece of land **(b)** right to be the only seller of a product in a place; **she runs a jewellery concession in a department store (c)** allowance; **tax concession** = allowing less tax to be paid **(d)** admission

◊ **concessionnaire** *noun* person who has the right to be the only seller of a product in a place

◊ **concessionary** *adjective* **concessionary fare** = reduced fare for certain types of passenger (such as employees of the transport company)

conciliation *noun* bringing together the parties in a dispute so that the dispute can be settled; **the Conciliation Service** = ADVISORY, CONCILIATION AND ARBITRATION SERVICE

conclude *verb* **(a)** to complete successfully; **to conclude an agreement with someone (b)** to believe from evidence; **the police concluded that the thief had got into the building through the main entrance**

◊ **conclusion** *noun* **(a)** believing *or* deciding from evidence; **the police have come to the conclusion *or* have reached the conclusion that the bomb was set off by radio control (b)** final completion; **the conclusion of the defence counsel's address; in conclusion** = finally *or* at the end; **in conclusion, the judge thanked the jury for their long and patient service**

◊ **conclusive** *adjective* which proves something; **the fingerprints on the gun were conclusive evidence that the accused was guilty**

◊ **conclusively** *adverb* in a way which proves a fact; **the evidence of the eye witness proved conclusively that the accused was in the town at the time the robbery was committed**

concur *verb* to agree; **Smith LJ dismissed the appeal, Jones and White LJJ concurring**

◊ **concurrence** *noun* agreement; **in concurrence with the other judges, Smith LJ dismissed the appeal**

concurrent *adjective* taking place at the same time; **concurrent sentence** = sentence which takes place at the same time as another; **he was given two concurrent jail sentences of six months**

◊ **concurrently** *adverb* taking place at the same time; **he was sentenced to two periods of two years in prison, the sentences to run concurrently;** *see also* CONSECUTIVE, CONSECUTIVELY

condemn *verb* **(a)** to sentence someone to suffer punishment; **the prisoners were condemned to death; condemned cell** = cell where a prisoner is kept who has been sentenced to death **(b)** to say that a house is not fit for people to live in

◊ **condemnation** *noun* **(a)** sentencing of someone to a certain punishment **(b)** forfeiting a piece of property when it has been legally seized

condition *noun* **(a)** term of a contract *or* duty which has to be carried out as part of a contract *or* something which has to be agreed before a contract becomes valid; **conditions of employment *or* conditions of service** = terms of a contract of employment; **conditions of sale** = agreed ways in which a sale takes place (such as discounts *or* credit terms); **on condition that** = provided that; **they were granted the lease on condition that they paid the legal costs; condition precedent** = condition which says that a right will not be granted until something is done; **condition subsequent** = condition which says that a contract will be modified *or* annulled if something is not done **(b)** general state; **item sold in good condition; what was the condition of the car when it was sold?**

◊ **conditional** *adjective* provided that certain things take place *or* (agreement) which is dependent on something; **to give a conditional acceptance** = to accept, provided that certain things happen *or* certain terms apply; **the offer is conditional on the board's acceptance** = provided the board accepts; **he made a conditional offer** = he offered to buy, provided that certain terms applied; **conditional discharge** = allowing a prisoner to be set free, with no punishment, provided that he does not commit a crime for a period of time

◊ **conditionally** *adverb* provided certain things take place; **to accept an offer conditionally** = to accept provided certain conditions are fulfilled

condominium *noun* US system of ownership, where a person owns an apartment in a building, together with a share of the land and common parts (stairs, roof, etc.)

condone *verb* to forgive (criminal behaviour); **the court cannot condone your treatment of your children**

◊ **condonation** *noun* the forgiving by one spouse of the acts of the other (especially forgiving adultery)

conducive *adjective* which is likely to produce; **the threat of strike action is not conducive to an easy solution to the dispute**

conduct 1 *noun* (a) way of behaving; **he was arrested for disorderly conduct in the street; code of conduct** = informal (sometimes written) rules by which a group of people work (b) bad way of behaving; **she divorced her husband because of his conduct; conduct conducive to a breach of the peace** = way of behaving (using rude or threatening language in speech or writing) which seems likely to cause a breach of the peace 2 *verb* to carry on; **to conduct discussions *or* negotiations; the chairman conducted the proceedings very efficiently**

confer *verb* (a) to give power *or* responsibility to someone; **the discretionary powers conferred on the tribunal by statute** (b) to discuss; **the Chief Constable conferred with the Superintendent in charge of the case**

conference *noun* meeting of a group of people to discuss something; **the Police Federation is holding its annual conference this week; conference proceedings** = written report of what has been discussed at a conference; **press conference** = meeting where reporters from newspaper and TV are invited to hear news of a police investigation *or* the result of a court case, etc.

confess *verb* to admit that you have committed a crime; **after six hours' questioning by the police the accused man confessed**

◊ **confession** *noun* (i) admitting that you have committed a crime; (ii) document in which you admit that you have committed a crime; **the police sergeant asked him to sign his confession; the accused typed his own confession statement; the confession was not admitted in court, because the accused claimed it had been extorted**

confidence *noun* (a) feeling sure *or* being certain *or* having trust in (someone); **the sales teams do not have much confidence in their manager; the board has total confidence in the managing director; confidence vote *or* vote of no confidence** = vote to show that a person *or* group is *or* is not trusted; **he proposed a vote of confidence in the government; the chairman resigned after the motion of no confidence was passed at the AGM** (b) trusting someone with a secret; **breach of confidence** = betraying a secret which someone has told you; **in confidence** = in secret; **I will show you the report in confidence**

◊ **confidence trick** *or* US **confidence game** *noun* business deal where someone gains another person's confidence and then tricks him

◊ **confidence trickster** *or* US **confidence man** *noun* person who carries out confidence tricks on people

◊ **confident** *adjective* certain *or* sure; **I am confident the turnover will increase rapidly; are you confident the sales team is capable of handling this product?**

◊ **confidential** *adjective* secret *or* not to be told or shown to other people; **he sent a confidential report to the chairman; please mark the letter "Private and Confidential"**

◊ **confidentiality** *noun* being secret; **he broke the confidentiality of the discussions**

= he told someone about the secret discussions
NOTE: no plural

confine *verb* to keep (a criminal) in a room or area; **confined to barracks** = (soldier) who is sentenced to stay in the barracks for a set period of time and not to go outside

◇ **confinement** *noun* being kept in a place as a punishment; **solitary confinement** = being kept alone in a cell, without being able to speak to other prisoners; **he was kept in solitary confinement for a week**
NOTE: no plural

confirm *verb* to say that something is certain *or* is correct; **the Court of Appeal has confirmed the judge's decision; his secretary phoned to confirm the hotel room** *or* **the ticket** *or* **the agreement** *or* **the booking; to confirm someone in a job** = to say that someone is now permanently in the job

◇ **confirmation** *noun* **(a)** being certain; **confirmation of a booking** = checking that a booking is certain **(b)** document which confirms something; **he received confirmation from the bank that the deeds had been deposited**

confiscate *verb* to take away private property into the possession of the state; **the court ordered the drugs to be confiscated**

◇ **confiscation** *noun* act of confiscating

conflict **1** *noun* **conflict of interest** = situation where a person may profit personally from decisions which he takes in his official capacity *or* may not be able to act properly because of some other person or matter with which he is connected; **Conflict of Laws** = section in a country's legal statutes which deals with disputes between that country's laws and those of another country **2** *verb* not to agree; **the evidence of the wife conflicts with that of her husband; the UK legislation conflicts with the directives of the EEC; conflicting evidence** = evidence from different witnesses which does not agree; **the jury has to decide who to believe among a mass of conflicting evidence**

conform *verb* to act in accordance with something; **the proposed Bill conforms to the recommendations of the Royal Commission**

◇ **conformance** *noun* acting in accordance with a rule; **in conformance with the directives of the Commission; he was criticized for non-conformance with the regulations**

◇ **conformity** *noun* **in conformity with** = agreeing with; **he has acted in conformity with the regulations**

Congress *noun* elected federal legislative body of the USA (formed of the House of Representatives and the Senate)

◇ **Congressional** *adjective* referring to Congress; **a Congressional subcommittee**

◇ **Congressman** *noun* member of the House of Representatives

conjugal *adjective* referring to marriage; **conjugal rights** = rights of a husband and wife in relation to each other

conman *noun informal* = CONFIDENCE TRICKSTER

connect *verb* **(a)** to link *or* to join; **the company is connected to the government because the chairman's father is a minister; connected persons** = people who are closely related to *or* have a close business association with a certain company director

◇ **connection** *noun* link *or* something which joins; **is there a connection between the loss of the documents and the death of the lawyer?; in connection with** = referring to; **the police want to interview the man in connection with burglaries committed last November**

connive *verb* **to connive at something** = to shut one's eyes to wrongdoing *or* know that a crime is being committed, but not to report it

◇ **connivance** *noun* shutting one's eyes to wrongdoing *or* knowing that a crime is being committed, but not reporting it; **with the connivance of the customs officers, he managed to bring the goods into the country**

consecutive *adjective* which follows; **consecutive sentences** = two or more sentences which follow one after the other

◇ **consecutively** *adverb* which follows; **he was sentence to two periods of two years in jail, the sentences to run consecutively;** *see also* CONCURRENT, CONCURRENTLY

consensus *noun* general agreement; **there was a consensus between all parties as to the next steps to be taken; in the absence of a consensus, no decisions could be reached; consensus politics** = way of ruling a country, where the main political parties agree in general on policy

◇ **consensus ad idem** *Latin phrase meaning* "agreement to this same thing": real agreement to a contract by both parties

◇ **consensual** *adjective* which happens by agreement; **consensual acts** = sexual acts which both parties agree should take place

consent 1 *noun* agreeing that something should happen; **he borrowed the car without the owner's consent; the age of consent** = sixteen years old (when a girl can agree to have sexual intercourse); **consent order** = court order that someone must not do something without the agreement of another party **2** *verb* to agree that something should be done; **the judge consented to the request of the prosecution counsel**

consider *verb* **(a)** to think seriously about something; **to consider the terms of a contract** = to examine and discuss if the terms are acceptable; **the judge asked the jury to consider their verdict** = he asked the jury to discuss the evidence they had heard and decide if the accused was guilty or not **(b)** to believe; **he is considered to be one of the leading divorce lawyers; the law on libel is considered too lenient**

◇ **consideration** *noun* **(a)** serious thought; **we are giving consideration to moving the head office to Scotland; to take something into consideration** = to think about something when deciding what to do; **to ask for other offences to be taken into consideration** = to confess to other offences after being accused *or* convicted of one offence, so that the sentence can cover all of them; **the accused admitted six other offences, and asked for them to be taken into consideration; having taken the age of the accused into consideration, the court has decided to give him a suspended sentence (b)** the price (but not necessarily money) paid by one person in exchange for the other person promising to do something, an essential element in the formation of a contract; **for a small consideration** = for a small fee *or* payment; **executed**

consideration = consideration where one party has made a promise in exchange for which the other party has done something for him; **executory consideration** = consideration where one party makes a promise in exchange for a counter-promise from the other party

considerable *adjective* quite large; **we sell considerable quantities of our products to Africa; they lost a considerable amount of money on the commodity market**

◇ **considerably** *adverb* quite a lot; **crime figures are considerably higher than they were last year**

consign *verb* to consign goods to someone = to send goods to someone for him to use or to sell for you

◇ **consignation** *noun* act of consigning

◇ **consignee** *noun* person who receives goods from someone for his own use or to sell for the person who sends them

◇ **consignment** *noun* **(a)** sending of goods to someone who will hold them for you and sell them on your behalf; **consignment note** = note saying that goods have been sent; **goods on consignment** = goods kept for another company to be sold on their behalf for a commission **(b)** certain quantity of goods sent for sale; **a consignment of goods has arrived; we are expecting a consignment of cars from Japan**

◇ **consignor** *noun* person who consigns goods to someone

> COMMENT: the goods remain the property of the consignor until the consignee sells them

consist of *verb* to be formed of; **the Magistrates' Court consists normally of three justices; a delegation consisting of all the heads of department concerned**

consistent *adjective* which does not contradict *or* which agrees with; **the sentence is consistent with government policy on the treatment of young offenders**

consolidate *verb* to bring several Acts of Parliament together into one act; to hear several sets of proceedings together; **the judge ordered the actions to be consolidated**

◇ **Consolidating Act** *noun* Act of Parliament which brings together several previous Acts which relate to the same subject; *see also* CODIFICATION

◇ **consolidation** *noun* (i) bringing together various Acts of Parliament which deal with one subject into one single Act; (ii) procedure whereby several sets of proceedings are heard together by the court

consortium *noun* (a) group of different companies which work together on one project (b) right of a husband and wife to the love and support of the other

conspire *verb* to agree with another person *or* other people to commit a crime *or* tort

◇ **conspiracy** *noun* agreeing with another person *or* other people to commit a crime *or* tort

COMMENT: conspiracy to commit a crime is itself a crime

constable *noun* **police constable** *or* **woman police constable** = lowest rank of police officer; **the sergeant and six constables searched the premises** NOTE: constable can be used to address a policeman; also used with a name: **Constable Smith**; it is usually abbreviated to PC or WPC

constituency *noun* area of a country which is represented by a Member of Parliament; **he represents one of the northern constituencies**

constitute *verb* to make *or* to form; **the documents constitute primary evidence; this Act constitutes a major change in government policy; conduct tending to interfere with the course of justice constitutes contempt of court**

constitution *noun* (a) (usually written) laws under which a country is ruled; **the freedom of the individual is guaranteed by the country's constitution; the new president asked the assembly to draft a new constitution** (b) written rules *or* regulations of a society *or* association *or* club; **under the society's constitution, the chairman is elected for a two-year period; payments to officers of the association are not allowed by the constitution**

◇ **constitutional** *adjective* (a) referring to a country's constitution; **censorship of the press is not constitutional; constitutional law** = laws under which a country is ruled *or* laws relating to government and its function; **constitutional lawyer** = lawyer who specializes in constitutional law *or* in drafting or interpreting constitutions; **constitutional right** = right which is guaranteed by a constitution (b) according to a constitution; **the re-election of the chairman for a second term is not constitutional**

construct *verb* to build; **the company has tendered for the contract to construct the new airport**

◇ **construction** *noun* (a) building; **construction company** = company which specializes in building; **under construction** = being built; **the airport is under construction** (b) interpreting the meaning of words; **to put a construction on words** = to suggest a meaning for words which is not immediately obvious

◇ **constructive** *adjective* which helps in the making of something; **she made some constructive suggestions for improving management-worker relations; we had a constructive proposal from a shipping company in Italy; constructive dismissal** = situation when a worker leaves his job voluntarily but because of pressure from the management; **constructive knowledge** = knowledge of a fact *or* matter which the law says a person has, whether or not that person actually has it; **constructive notice** = knowledge which the law says a person has of something (whether or not the person actually has it) because certain information is available to him if he makes reasonable inquiry; **constructive trust** = trust arising by reason of a person's behaviour

construe *verb* to interpret the meaning of words *or* of a document; **the court construed the words to mean that there was a contract between the parties; written opinion is not admissible as evidence for the purposes of construing a deed of settlement**

consult *verb* to ask an expert for advice; **he consulted his solicitor about the letter**

◇ **consultancy** *noun* act of giving specialist advice; **a consultancy firm; he offers a consultancy service**

◊ **consultant** *noun* specialist who gives advice; **engineering consultant; management consultant; tax consultant**

◊ **consultation** *noun* meeting between a client and his professional adviser, such as between a QC (and often a junior barrister) and a solicitor and clients

◊ **consulting** *adjective* person who gives specialist advice; **consulting engineer**

consumer *noun* person *or* company which buys and uses goods and services; **gas consumers are protesting at the increase in prices; the factory is a heavy consumer of water; consumer council** = group representing the interests of consumers; **consumer credit** = provision of loans by finance companies to help people buy goods; **consumer goods** = goods bought by the general public and not by businesses; **consumer legislation** = laws which give rights to people who buy goods *or* who pay for services; **consumer protection** = protecting consumers from unfair *or* illegal business practices

consummation *noun* having sexual intercourse for the first time after the marriage ceremony

consumption *noun* buying or using goods or services; **a car with low petrol consumption; the factory has a heavy consumption of coal**

contact 1 *noun* (a) person you know *or* person you can ask for help or advice; **he has many contacts in the city; who is your contact in the Ministry?** (b) act of getting in touch with someone; **I have lost contact with them** = I do not communicate with them any longer; **he put me in contact with a good lawyer** = he told me how to get in touch with a good lawyer 2 *verb* to get in touch with someone *or* to communicate with someone; **he tried to contact his office by phone; can you contact the solicitors representing the vendors?**

contain *verb* to hold something inside; **the contract contains some clauses which are open to misinterpretation; some of the instructions contained in the will are quite impossible to carry out**

contemnor *noun* person who commits a contempt of court

contempt *noun* being rude *or* showing lack of respect to a court *or* Parliament; **to be in contempt** = to have shown disrespect to a court, especially by disobeying a court order; **contempt of court** = being rude to a court, as by bad behaviour in court, or by refusing to carry out a court order; **at common law, conduct tending to interfere with the course of justice in particular legal proceedings constitutes criminal contempt; contempt of Parliament** *or* **contempt of the House** = conduct which may bring the authority of Parliament into disrepute; **to purge one's contempt** = to apologize *or* to do something to show that you are sorry for the lack of respect shown

content *noun* the ideas inside a letter, etc.; **the content of the letter** = the real meaning of the letter

◊ **contents** *plural noun* things contained *or* what is inside something; **the contents of the bottle poured out onto the floor; the customs officials inspected the contents of the box; the contents of the letter** = the words written in the letter

contentious *adjective & noun* (legal business) where there is a dispute

contest 1 *noun* competition, especially in an election 2 *verb* (a) to argue that a decision *or* a ruling is wrong; **I wish to contest the statement made by the witness** (b) to fight (an election); **the seat is being contested by five candidates; contested takeover** = takeover where the directors of the company being bought do not recommend the bid and try to fight it

context *noun* other words which surround a word or phrase; general situation in which something happens; **the words can only be understood in the context of the phrase in which they occur; the action of the police has to be seen in the context of the riots against the government**

contingency *noun* possible state of emergency when decisions will have to be taken quickly; **contingency fund** *or* **contingency reserve** = money set aside in case it is needed urgently; **contingency plan** = plan which will be put into action if something happens which is expected to happen

◊ **contingent** *adjective* **contingent expenses** = expenses which will be incurred only if something happens; *US* **contingent fee** = fee paid to a lawyer which is a proportion of the damages recovered in the case; **contingent policy** = policy which pays out only if something happens (as if the person named in the policy dies before the person due to benefit)

continue *verb* to go on doing something *or* to do something which you were doing earlier

◇ **continual** *adjective* which happens again and again

◇ **continually** *adverb* again and again

◇ **continuation** *noun* act of continuing

◇ **continuous** *adjective* with no end *or* with no breaks; **to be in continuous employment** = to work for a period of time (possibly for several different employers) with no time when you are not employed; **continuous feed** = device which feeds continuous stationery into a printer; **continuous stationery** = paper made as one long sheet, used in computer printers

◇ **continuously** *adverb* without stopping; **the meeting discussed the problem of budgets continuously for five hours**

contra 1 *preposition* against *or* differing **2** *noun* **contra account** = account which offsets another account; **contra entry** = entry made in the opposite side of an account to make an earlier entry worthless (i.e. a debit against a credit); **per contra** *or* **as per contra** = words showing that a contra entry has been made **3** *verb* **to contra an entry** = to enter a similar amount in the opposite side of an account

◇ **contra proferentem** *Latin phrase meaning* "against the one making the point": rule that an ambiguity in a document is construed against the party who drafted it

contraband *noun* **contraband (goods)** = goods brought into or taken out of a country illegally, without paying customs duty

contract 1 *noun* **(a)** legal agreement between two or more parties; **to draw up a contract; to draft a contract; to sign a contract; the contract is binding on both parties** = both parties signing the contract must do what is agreed; **under contract** = bound by the terms of a contract; **the firm is under contract to deliver the goods by November; to void a contract** = to make a contract invalid; **contract of service** *or* of **employment** = contract between management and employee showing all conditions of work; **service contract** = contract between a company and a director *or* employee showing all conditions of work; **exchange of contracts** = point in the conveyance of a property when the solicitors for the buyer and seller hand over the contract of sale which then becomes binding **(b) contract law** *or* **law of contract** = laws relating to agreements; **by private contract** = by private legal agreement; **contract note** = note showing that shares have been bought or sold but not yet paid for **(c) contract for services** = agreement for supply of a service or goods; **contract for the supply of spare parts; to enter into a contract to supply spare parts; to sign a contract for £10,000 worth of spare parts; to put work out to contract** = to decide that work should be done by another company on a contract, rather than employing members of staff to do it; **to award a contract to a company** *or* **to place a contract with a company** = to decide that a company shall have the contract to do work for you; **to tender for a contract** = to put forward an estimate of cost for work to be carried out under contract; **conditions of contract** *or* **contract conditions; breach of contract** = breaking the terms of a contract; **the company is in breach of contract** = the company has failed to do what was agreed in the contract; **contract work** = work done according to a written agreement **(d)** *slang* agreement to kill someone for a payment; **there is a contract out for him** = someone has offered money for him to be killed

COMMENT: a contract is an agreement between two or more parties to create legal obligations between them. Some contracts are made "under seal", i.e. they are signed and sealed by the parties; most contracts are made orally or in writing. The essential elements of a contract are: (a) that an offer made by one party should be accepted by the other; (b) consideration; (c) the intention to create legal relations. The terms of a contract may be express or implied. A breach of contract by one party entitles the other party to sue for damages or in some cases to seek specific performance

2 *verb* to agree to do some work by contract; **to contract to supply spare parts** *or* **to contract for the supply of spare parts; the supply of spare parts was contracted out to Smith Ltd** = Smith Ltd was given the contract for supplying spare parts; **to contract out of an agreement** = to withdraw from an agreement with written permission of the other party

◊ **contracting** *adjective* **contracting party** = person or company which signs a contract

◊ **contractor** *noun* person who enters into a contract, especially a person *or* company which does work according to a written agreement

◊ **contractual** *adjective* according to a contract; **contractual liability** = legal responsibility for something as stated in a contract; **to fulfil your contractual obligations** = to do what you have agreed to do in a contract; **he is under no contractual obligation to buy** = he has signed no agreement to buy

◊ **contractually** *adverb* according to a contract; **the company is contractually bound to pay his expenses**

contradict *verb* not to agree with *or* to say exactly the opposite; **the statement contradicts the report in the newspapers; the witness contradicted himself several times**

◊ **contradiction** *noun* statement which contradicts; **the witness' evidence was a mass of contradictions; there is a contradiction between the Minister's statement in the House of Commons and the reports published in the newspapers**

◊ **contradictory** *adjective* which does not agree; **a mass of contradictory evidence**

contrary *noun* opposite instructions; **failing instructions to the contrary** = unless different instructions are given; **on the contrary** = quite the opposite; **counsel was not annoyed with the witness - on the contrary, he praised her**

contravene *verb* to break *or* to go against (rules, regulations); **the workshop has contravened the employment regulations; the fire department can close a** restaurant if it contravenes the safety regulations

◊ **contravention** *noun* act of breaking a regulation; **in contravention of** = which contravenes; **the restaurant is in contravention of the safety regulations; the management of the cinema locked the fire exits in contravention of the fire regulations**

contribute *verb* **(a)** to give money *or* to add to money; **to contribute 10% of the profits; he contributed to the pension fund for ten years (b) to contribute to** = to help something; **the public response to the request for information contributed to the capture of the gang**

◊ **contribution** *noun* money paid to add to a sum; **employer's contribution** = money paid by an employer towards a worker's pension; **National Insurance contributions** = money paid each month by a worker and the company to the National Insurance; **pension contributions** = money paid by a company or worker into a pension fund

◊ **contributor** *noun* **contributor of capital** = person who contributes capital

◊ **contributory** **1** *adjective* **contributory pension plan** *or* **scheme** = pension plan where the employee has to contribute a percentage of salary; **contributory causes** = causes which help something to take place; **contributory factor** = something which contributes to a result; **contributory negligence** = negligence partly caused by the plaintiff and partly by the defendant, which results in harm done to the plaintiff **2** *noun* shareholder who is liable in respect of partly paid shares to a company being wound up

con trick *noun* *informal* = CONFIDENCE TRICK

control **1** *noun* **(a)** power *or* being able to direct something; **the company is under the control of three shareholders; the family lost control of its business; to gain control of a business** = to buy more than 50% of the shares so that you can direct the business; **to lose control of a business** = to find that you have less than 50% of the shares in a company, and so are not longer able to direct it; **control test** = test to decide if someone is an employee or is self-employed (used for purposes of tax assessment) **(b)** restricting *or* checking something *or* making sure that something is kept in check; **under control** = kept in check; **out of control** = not kept in check **(c) exchange controls** = government restrictions on changing the local currency into foreign currency; **the government imposed exchange controls to stop the rush to buy dollars; price controls** = legal measures to prevent prices rising too fast; **rent controls** = government regulation of rents charged by landlords **(d) control systems** = systems used to check that a computer system is working correctly **2** *verb* **(a) to control a business** = to direct a business; **the business is controlled by a company based in Luxembourg; the company is controlled by the majority shareholder (b)** to make sure that something is kept in check *or* is not allowed to develop; **the government is fighting to control inflation** *or* **to control the rise in the cost of living**

◊ **controlled** *adjective* ruled *or* kept in check; **government-controlled** = ruled by a government; **controlled economy** = economy where most business activity is directed by orders from the government

◊ **controller** *noun* **(a)** person who controls (especially the finances of a company) **(b)** *US* chief accountant in a company

◊ **controlling** *adjective* **to have a controlling interest in a company** = to own more than 50% of the shares so that you can direct how the company is run

convene *verb* to ask people to come together; **to convene a meeting of shareholders**

convenience *noun* **at your earliest convenience** = as soon as you find it possible; **ship sailing under a flag of convenience** = ship flying the flag of a country which may have no ships of its own but allows ships of other countries to be registered in its ports

◊ **convenient** *adjective* suitable *or* handy; **a bank draft is a convenient way of sending money abroad; is 9.30 a.m. a convenient time for the meeting?**

convenor *noun* person who convenes a meeting, especially a trade unionist who organizes union meetings

convention *noun* **(a)** general way in which something is usually done, though not enforced by law; **it is the convention for** American lawyers to designate themselves "Esquire" **(b)** international treaty; **the Geneva Convention on Human Rights**

conversion *noun* tort of dealing with a person's property in a way which is not consistent with that person's rights over it; **conversion of funds** = using money which does not belong to you for a purpose for which it is not supposed to be used

◊ **convert** *verb* **(a)** to change property into another form (as into cash) **(b)** to change money of one country for money of another; **we converted our pounds into Swiss francs; to convert funds to one's own use** = to use someone else's money for yourself

◊ **convertible** *adjective* which can be changed into something else (such as cash); **convertible loan stock** = money which can be exchanged for shares at a later date

convey *verb* to carry goods from one place to another; **to convey a property to a purchaser** = to pass the ownership of the property to the purchaser

◊ **conveyance** *noun* legal document which transfers the ownership of land from the seller to the buyer; **fraudulent conveyance** = putting a property into someone else's possession to avoid it being seized to pay creditors

◊ **conveyancer** *noun* person who draws up a conveyance

◊ **conveyancing** *noun* (i) drawing up the document which legally transfers a property from a seller to a buyer; (ii) law and procedure relating to the purchase and sale of property; **do-it-yourself conveyancing** = drawing up a legal conveyance without the help of a lawyer

convict 1 *noun* person who is kept in prison as a punishment for a crime; **convict settlement** = prison camp where convicts are sent **2** *verb* **to convict someone of a crime** = to find that someone is guilty of a crime; **he was convicted of manslaughter and sent to prison; convicted criminal** = criminal who has been found guilty and sentenced

◊ **conviction** *noun* **(a)** being sure that something is true; **it is his conviction that the plaintiff has brought the case maliciously (b)** finding that a person accused of a crime is guilty; **he has had ten** convictions for burglary; *compare* SENTENCE

convince *verb* to make someone believe something is true; **counsel tried to convince the jury that the accused was not guilty; he convinced the owner of the shop that the building needed painting; the two conmen convinced the woman that they were plainclothes policemen**

cooling off period *or US* **cooling time** *noun* (i) during an industrial dispute, a period when negotiations have to be carried on and no action can be taken by either side; (ii) period when a person is allowed to think about something which he has agreed to buy on hire-purchase and possibly change his mind

co-operate *verb* to work together; **the governments are co-operating in the fight against piracy; the two firms have co-operated on planning the computer system**

◇ **co-operation** *noun* working together; **the work was completed ahead of schedule with the co-operation of the whole staff**

◇ **co-operative** **1** *adjective* willing to work together; **the staff have not been co-operative over the management's reorganization plan; co-operative society =** society where the customers and workers are partners and share the profits **2** *noun* business run by a group of workers who are the owners and who share the profits; **industrial co-operative; to set up a workers' co-operative**

co-opt *verb* **to co-opt someone onto a committee =** to ask someone to join a committee without being elected

co-owner *noun* person who owns something jointly with another person or persons; **the two sisters are co-owners of the property**

◇ **co-ownership** *noun* **(a)** arrangement where two or more persons own a property **(b)** arrangement where partners *or* workers have shares in a company

cop **1** *noun informal* **(a)** policeman **(b)** arrest; **it's a fair cop =** you have caught me **2** *verb slang* to get *or* to receive; **to cop a plea =** to plead guilty to a lesser charge and so hope the court will give a shorter sentence to save the time of a full trial

co-partner *noun* person who is a partner in a business with another person

◇ **co-partnership** *noun* arrangement where partners *or* workers have shares in the company

cope *verb* to deal with; **the judges have difficulty in coping with all the divorce cases; how can the police cope with inner city violence when they do not have enough staff?**

copper *noun GB informal* policeman

◇ **copper-bottomed** *adjective* (guarantee) which cannot possibly be broken

co-property *noun* ownership of property by two or more people together

◇ **co-proprietor** *noun* person who owns a property with another person or several other people

copy **1** *noun* **(a)** document which looks the same as another; **carbon copy =** copy made with carbon paper; **certified copy =** document which is certified as being exactly the same in content as the original; **file copy =** copy of a document which is filed in an office for reference **(b)** document; **fair copy** *or* **final copy =** document which is written or typed with no changes or mistakes; **hard copy =** printout of a text which is on a computer *or* printed copy of something which is on microfilm; **rough copy =** draft of a document which, it is expected, will have changes made to it before it is complete; **top copy =** first or top sheet of a document which is typed with carbon copies **(c)** a book *or* a newspaper; **have you kept yesterday's copy of "The Times"? I read it in the office copy of "Fortune"; where is my copy of the telephone directory? 2** *verb* to make a second document which is like the first; **he copied the company report at night and took it home**

◇ **copier** *or* **copying machine** *noun* machine which makes copies of documents

copyright **1** *noun* legal right (lasting for fifty years after the death of an artist whose work has been published) which a writer *or* film maker *or* musician has in his own work allowing him not to have it copied without the payment of royalties; **Copyright Act =** Act of Parliament making copyright legal, and controlling the copying of copyright material; **copyright law** = laws concerning the protection of copyright; **work which is out of copyright** = work by a writer, etc., who has been dead for fifty years, and which anyone can publish; **work still in copyright** = work by a living writer, or by a writer who has not been dead for fifty years; **infringement of copyright** *or* **copyright infringement** = act of illegally copying a work which is in copyright; **copyright notice** = note in a book showing who owns the copyright and the date of ownership; **copyright owner** = person who owns the copyright in a work **2** *verb* to confirm the copyright of a written work by printing a copyright notice and publishing the work **3** *adjective* covered by the laws of copyright; **it is illegal to take copies of a copyright work**

◊ **copyrighted** *adjective* in copyright

cordon 1 *noun* **a police cordon** = barriers and policemen put round an area to prevent anyone getting near it **2** *verb* **to cordon off** = to put barriers and policemen round (an area) so that no one can get near it; **the street was cordoned off after the bomb was discovered**

co-respondent *noun* party to divorce proceedings who has committed adultery with another person; *see also* CORRESPONDENT

coroner *noun* public official (either a doctor or a lawyer) who investigates sudden violent deaths and also treasure trove; **coroner's court** = court presided over by a coroner; **coroner's inquest** = inquest carried out by a coroner into a death *or* case of treasure trove

> COMMENT: coroners investigate deaths which are violent or unexpected, deaths which may be murder *or* manslaughter, deaths of prisoners and deaths involving the police

corporal punishment *noun* punishing a criminal by whipping him

corporate *adjective* referring to a company; **corporate personality** = legal status of a company, so that it can be treated as a person; **corporate planning** =

planning the future work of a whole company; **corporate profits** = profits of a corporation

◊ **corporation** *noun* **(a)** legal body (such as a limited company *or* town council) which has been incorporated; *US* company which is incorporated in the United States **(b)** generally, any large company; **finance corporation** = company which provides money for hire purchase

corporeal hereditaments *plural noun* rights of property which physically exist, such as houses and furniture

corpse *noun* *GB* body of a dead person
NOTE: US English is **cadaver**

corpus *noun* body (of laws); *see also* HABEAS CORPUS
NOTE: plural is **corpora**

◊ **corpus delicti** *Latin phrase meaning* "the body of the crime": the real proof that a crime has been committed

◊ **corpus legis** *Latin phrase meaning* "body of laws": books containing Roman civil law

correct 1 *adjective* accurate *or* right; **the published accounts do not give a correct picture of the company's financial position 2** *verb* to remove mistakes from something; **the secretary will have to correct all these typing errors before you send the contract**

◊ **correction** *noun* act of making something correct; change which makes something correct; **he made some corrections to the draft contract**

◊ **corrective** *adjective* which punishes (a criminal) in such a way that he becomes a better person; **he was sent to the detention centre for corrective training**

correspond *verb* **(a)** **to correspond with someone** = to write letters to someone **(b)** **to correspond with something** = to fit *or* to match something

◊ **correspondence** *noun* letters which are exchanged; **business correspondence** = letters concerned with a business; **to be in correspondence with someone** = to write letters to someone and receive letters back
NOTE: no plural

◊ **correspondent** *noun* **(a)** person who writes letters **(b)** journalist who writes articles for a newspaper on specialist subjects; **a financial correspondent;** "**The Times**" **legal correspondent;** **he is the Paris correspondent of the "Telegraph**"; *see also* CO-RESPONDENT

corrigendum *noun* correction *or* word which has been corrected
NOTE: plural is **corrigenda**

corroborate *verb* to prove evidence which has already been given; **the witness corroborated the accused's alibi, saying that at the time of the murder he had seen him in Brighton**

◇ **corroboration** *noun* evidence which confirms and supports other evidence; **the witness was unable to provide corroboration of what he had told the police**

◇ **corroborative** *adjective* which corroborates; **the letter provides corroborative evidence, showing that the accused did know that the victim lived alone**

corrupt 1 *adjective* (person, especially an official) who takes bribes 2 *verb* **to corrupt someone's morals** = to make someone willing to commit a crime *or* to act against normal standards of behaviour

◇ **corruption** *noun* paying money *or* giving a favour to someone (usually an official) so that he does what you want; **the government is keen to stamp out corruption in the police force; bribery and corruption are difficult to control**
NOTE: no plural

◇ **corruptly** *adverb* in a corrupt way; **he corruptly offered the officer money to get the charges dropped**

Cosa Nostra = MAFIA

cosh 1 *noun* heavy stick for hitting people 2 *verb* to hit someone with a stick; **the burglars coshed the shopkeeper and stole money from the till**

cost 1 *noun* (a) amount of money which has to be paid for something; **computer costs are falling each year; we cannot afford the cost of two telephones; to cover costs** = to produce enough money in sales to pay for the costs of production (b) **costs** = expenses involved in a court case, which can be awarded by the judge to the party which wins (so that the losing side pays the expenses of both sides); **the judge awarded costs to the defendant; costs of the case will**

be borne by the prosecution; **the court awarded the plaintiff £2,000 in damages, with costs; to pay costs** = to pay the expenses of a court case; **costs order** = court order requiring someone to pay costs; **fixed costs** = set amount of money to which a plaintiff is entitled in legal proceedings; **taxed costs** = varying amount of costs which can be awarded in legal proceedings 2 *verb* (a) to have a price; **how much does the machine cost? rent of the room will cost £50 a day** (b) **to cost a product** = to calculate how much money will be needed to make a product, and so work out its selling price

◇ **cost of living** *noun* money which has to be paid for food, heating, rent etc.; **to allow for the cost of living in salaries; cost-of-living allowance** = addition to normal salary to cover increases in the cost of living; **cost-of-living increase** = increase in salary to allow it to keep up with the increased cost of living; **cost-of-living index** = way of measuring the cost of living which is shown as a percentage increase on the figure for the previous year

coterminous *adjective* (two things) which terminate at the same time; **the leases are coterminous**

council *noun* (a) official group chosen to run something *or* to advise on a problem; **consumer council** = group representing the interests of consumers; **borough council** *or* **town council** = representatives elected to run a town; **Council of Ministers** = body made up of the foreign ministers of the member states of the EEC; **Security Council** = permanent ruling body of the United Nations (b) = PRIVY COUNCIL; **Order in Council** = legislation made by the Queen in Council, which is allowed by an Act of Parliament and does not have to be ratified by Parliament

◇ **councillor** *noun* member of a council, especially member of a town council; *see also* PRIVY COUNCILLOR

counsel *noun* barrister (or barristers) acting for one of the parties in a legal action; **defence counsel; prosecution counsel; the plaintiff appeared in court with his solicitor and two counsel; counsel's advice** *or* **opinion** = written opinion of a barrister about a case; **leading counsel** = main barrister (usually a QC) in a team appearing for one side in a case; **Queen's**

Counsel = senior British lawyer appointed to the rank of Queen's Counsel by the Lord Chancellor
NOTE: **Queen's Counsel** is usually abbreviated to **QC.** Note that there is no plural for counsel which is always used in the singular whether it refers to one barrister or several, and it is never used with the article **the** or **a.** On the other hand the abbreviation QC can have a plural: **two QCs represented the defendant**

◇ **counsellor** *noun* *US* lawyer *or* person who gives legal advice

count 1 *noun* separate charge against an accused person read out in court in the indictment; **he was found guilty on all four counts** 2 *verb* **(a)** to add figures together to make a total; **he counted up the sales for the six months to December** **(b)** to include; **did the defence count the accused's theft of money from the till as part of the total theft?**

◇ **count on** *verb* **(a)** to expect something to happen; **the defence seems to be counting on winning the sympathy of the jury** **(b)** to rely on someone *or* something; **you can count on Mr Jones, he is an excellent solicitor**

counter 1 *noun* long flat surface in a shop for displaying and selling goods; **over the counter** = legally; **goods sold over the counter** = retail sales of goods in shops; **over-the-counter market (OTC)** = legal selling of shares which are not listed in the official Stock Exchange list; **under the counter** = illegally; **under-the-counter sales** = black market sales 2 *adverb* counter to = against *or* opposite; **the decision of the court runs counter to the advice of the clerk to the justices**

counter- *prefix* against

◇ **counterclaim** 1 *noun* **(a)** claim in a court by a defendant against the plaintiff who has already brought in a claim against him **(b)** claim for damages made in reply to a previous claim; **Jones claimed £25,000 in damages against Smith, and Smith entered a counterclaim of £50,000 for loss of office** 2 *verb* to put in a counterclaim; **Jones claimed £25,000 in damages and Smith counterclaimed £50,000 for loss of office**

◇ **counterfeit** 1 *adjective* false *or* imitation (money); **he was charged with passing counterfeit notes in shops** 2 *verb* to make imitation money

◇ **counterfeiting** *noun* crime of making imitation money

◇ **counter-intelligence** *noun* organization of secret agents whose job is to work against the secret agents of another country; **the offices were bugged by counter-intelligence agents**

◇ **countermand** *verb* to countermand an order = to say that an order must not be carried out

◇ **counteroffer** *noun* offer made in reply to another offer

◇ **counterpart** *noun* **(a)** copy of a lease **(b)** person who has a similar job in another company; **John is my counterpart in Smith's** = he has a similar post at Smith's as I have here

◇ **counter-promise** *noun* promise made in reply to a promise

◇ **countersign** *verb* to sign a document which has already been signed by someone else; **the payment has to be countersigned by the mortgagor**

country *noun* land which is an entity and governs itself; **the contract covers sales in the countries of the Common Market; some African countries export oil; country of origin** = country where the goods have been produced or made

county *noun* one of the administrative divisions of a country; **county council** = group of people elected to run a county; **County Court** = one of the types of court set up in England and Wales which hears local civil cases; **County Court Rules** = book of procedural rules for County Courts; *see also* GREEN BOOK

COMMENT: the County Court hears most civil cases up to a value of £5,000

coup (d'état) *noun* rapid revolution which removes one government and replaces it by another; **after the coup, groups of students attacked the police stations**

course *noun* **(a)** in the course of = during *or* while something is happening; **in the course of the hearing, several new allegations were made by the defendant** **(b)** series of lessons; **he is taking a management course; she has finished her secretarial course; the company has paid for her to attend a course for trainee sales managers**

(c) course of action = action which has been taken *or* which can be taken; **what is the best course of action the defendant should take?**; **in the course of employment** = done as part of the work of the person concerned **(d) of course** = naturally; **of course the company is interested in profits; are you willing to go on a sales trip to Australia? - of course!**

court *noun* **(a) court of law** *or* **law court** = place where a trial is held; **the law courts are in the centre of the town; she works in the law courts as an usher; court action** *or* **court case** = legal action or trial; **to take someone to court** = to start legal proceedings against someone; **in court** = present during a trial; **the defendant was in court for three hours; in open court** = in a courtroom with members of the public present; **a settlement was reached out of court** *or* **the two parties reached an out-of-court settlement** = the dispute was settled between the two parties privately without continuing the court case; **contempt of court** = being rude to a court, as by bad behaviour in the courtroom or by refusing to carry out a court order; **court order** = legal order made by a court, telling someone to do *or* not to do something; **the court made an order for maintenance** *or* **made a maintenance order; he refused to obey the court order and was sent to prison for contempt (b) Criminal Court** *or* **Civil Court** = court where criminal *or* civil cases are heard; **Court of Appeal** *or* **Appeal Court** = civil *or* criminal court to which a person may go to ask for an award *or* a sentence to be changed; **court of first instance** = court where a case is heard first; **Court of Protection** = court which administers the property of people suffering from a disability; **High Court (of Justice)** = main civil court in England and Wales; **International Court of Justice** = the court of the United Nations, which sits in the Hague, Netherlands; **magistrates' court** = court presided over by magistrates; **Supreme Court (of Judicature)** = (i) highest court in England and Wales (except for the House of Lords), formed of the High Court and the Court of Appeal; (ii) highest federal court in the USA; (*in Scotland*) **Court of Session** = highest civil court in Scotland **(c)** the judges *or* magistrates in a court; **the court will retire for thirty minutes**

◊ **court-martial 1** *noun* **(a)** court which tries someone serving in the armed forces for offences against military discipline **(b)** trial of someone serving in the armed forces by the armed forces authorities; **the court-martial was held in the army headquarters; he was found guilty by the court-martial and sentenced to imprisonment** (NOTE: plural is **courts-martial**) **2** *verb* to try someone who is serving in the armed forces

NOTE: **court-martialled**

◊ **courtroom** *noun* room where a judge listens to a trial

COMMENT: in England and Wales the main courts are:
the Magistrates' Court: petty crime; adoption; affiliation; maintenance and domestic violence; licensing;
the County Court: most civil actions up to a value of £5,000;
the High Court: most civil claims where the value exceeds £5,000;
the Crown Court: major crime;
the Court of Appeal: appeals from lower courts;
the House of Lords: the highest court of appeal in the country;
the Privy Council: appeals on certain matters from England and Wales, and appeals from certain Commonwealth countries;
the European Court of Justice: appeals where EEC legislation is involved.
Other courts include
Industrial tribunals: employment disputes;
courts-martial: military matters

covenant 1 *noun* agreement *or* undertaking to do something or not to do something, contained in a deed *or* contract; **he signed a covenant against underletting the premises; deed of covenant** = official signed agreement to do something (such as to pay someone a sum of money each year); **covenant to repair** = agreement by a landlord *or* tenant to keep a rented property in good repair; **restrictive covenant** = clause in a contract which prevents someone from doing something

> COMMENT: examples of restrictive covenants could be a clause in a contract of employment which prevents the employee from going to work for a competitor, or a clause in a contract for the sale of a property which prevents the purchaser from altering the building

2 *verb* to agree to pay a sum of money each year by contract; **to covenant to pay £10 per annum to a charity**

> COMMENT: there is a tax advantage to the recipient of covenanted money; a charity pays no tax, so it can reclaim tax at the standard rate on the money covenanted

cover 1 *noun* **(a) insurance cover =** protection guaranteed by an insurance policy; **do you have cover against theft?; to operate without adequate cover =** without being protected by insurance; **to ask for additional cover =** to ask the insurance company to increase the amount for which you are insured; **full cover =** insurance against all types of risk; **cover note =** letter from an insurance company giving basic details of an insurance policy and confirming that the policy exists **(b)** security to guarantee a loan; **do you have sufficient cover for this loan? (c) to send something under separate cover =** in a separate envelope; **to send a document under plain cover =** in an ordinary envelope with no company name printed on it **2** *verb* **(a)** to deal with *or* to refer to something completely; **the agreement covers all agencies; the newspapers have covered the murder trial; the fraud case has been covered by the consumer protection legislation (b) to cover a risk =** to be protected by insurance against a risk; **to be fully covered =** to have insurance against all risks; **the insurance covers fire, theft and loss of work (c)** to have enough money to pay; to ask for security against a loan which you are making; **the damage was covered by the insurance =** the insurance company paid for the damage; **to cover a position =** to have enough money to be able to pay for a forward purchase **(d)** to earn enough money to pay for costs, expenses, etc.; **we do not make enough sales to cover the expense of running the shop; we hope to reach the point soon when sales will cover all costs; the dividend is covered four**

times = profits are four times the dividend paid out

◊ **coverage** *noun* **(a) press coverage** *or* **media coverage =** reports about something in the newspapers *or* on TV, etc.; **the company had good media coverage for the launch of its new model (b)** *US* protection guaranteed by insurance; **do you have coverage against fire damage?**

◊ **covering** *adjective* **covering letter** *or* **covering note =** letter or note sent with documents to say why you are sending them

covert *adjective* hidden *or* secret; **covert action =** action which is secret (such as spying); *see also* FEME COVERT

◊ **coverture** *noun* state of being married (of a woman)

cracksman *noun* *slang* criminal who specializes in breaking safes

create *verb* to make something new; **by acquiring small unprofitable companies he soon created a large trading group; the government scheme aims at creating new jobs for young people**

◊ **creation** *noun* making; **job creation scheme =** government-backed scheme to make work for the unemployed

credere *see* DEL CREDERE

credit 1 *noun* **(a)** time given to a debtor before he has to pay; **to give someone six months' credit; to sell on good credit terms; credit account =** account which a customer has with a shop which allows him to buy goods and pay for them later; **credit agency** *or* *US* **credit bureau =** company which reports on the ability of customers to pay their debts and shows whether they should be allowed credit; **credit bank =** bank which lends money; **credit card =** plastic card which allows the owner to borrow money, and to buy goods without paying for them immediately; **credit facilities =** arrangement with a bank or supplier to have credit so as to buy goods; **letter of credit =** letter from a bank, allowing someone credit and promising to repay at a later date; **irrevocable letter of credit =** letter of credit which cannot be cancelled; **credit limit =** fixed amount which is the most a customer can owe; **credit rating =** amount which a credit agency feels a customer should be allowed to borrow; **to buy on credit** = without paying immediately **(b)** money received by a person *or* company and recorded in the accounts; **to enter £100 to someone's credit; to pay in £100 to the credit of Mr Smith; debit and credit** = money which a company owes and which it is entitled to receive; **credit side** = right side of accounts which records money received **2** *verb* to put money into someone's account; to note money received in an account; **to credit an account with £100** *or* **to credit £100 to an account**

◇ **creditor** *noun* person who is owed money; **creditors' meeting** = meeting of all persons to whom a company in receivership owes money; **judgment creditor** = person who has been given a court order making a debtor pay a debt; **preferential creditor** = creditor who must be paid first if a company is in liquidation; **secured** *or* **unsecured creditor** = creditor who holds *or* does not hold a mortgage *or* charge against the debtor's property as security for the loan

crime *noun* **(a)** act which is against the law and which is punishable by law; **there has been a 50% increase in crimes of violence (b)** illegal acts in general; **crime is on the increase; there has been an increase in violent crime; crime rate** = number of crimes committed, shown as a percentage of the total population; **crime wave** = sudden increase in crime NOTE: no plural for (b)

COMMENT: a crime is an illegal act which may result in prosecution and punishment by the state if the accused is convicted. Generally, in order to be convicted of a crime, the accused must be shown to have committed an unlawful act **(actus reus)** with a criminal state of mind **(mens rea)**.
The main types of crime are:
1. crimes against the person: murder; manslaughter; assault, battery, wounding; grievous bodily harm; abduction;
2. crimes against property: theft; robbery; burglary; obtaining property *or* services *or* pecuniary advantage by deception; blackmail; handling stolen goods; going equipped

to steal; criminal damage; possessing something with intent to damage *or* destroy property; forgery;
3. sexual offences: rape; buggery; bigamy; indecency;
4. political offences: treason; terrorism; sedition; breach of the Official Secrets Act;
5. offences against justice: assisting an offender; conspiracy; perjury; contempt of court; perverting the course of justice;
6. public order offences: obstruction of the police; unlawful assembly; obscenity; possessing weapons; misuse of drugs; breach of the peace;
7. road traffic offences: careless *or* reckless driving; drunken driving; driving without a licence *or* insurance.
Most minor crime is tried before the Magistrates' Courts; more serious crime is tried at the Crown Court which has greater powers to sentence offenders. Most crimes are prosecuted by the police or the Crown Prosecutors, though private prosecutions brought by individuals are possible

criminal 1 *adjective* **(a)** illegal; **misappropriation of funds is a criminal act; criminal offence** = action which is against the law **(b)** referring to crime; **criminal action** = court case brought by the state against someone who is charged with a crime; **criminal bankruptcy** = bankruptcy of a criminal in the Crown Court as a result of crimes of which he has been convicted; **criminal court** = court (such as a Crown Court) which hears criminal cases; **criminal damage** = notifiable offence of causing serious damage; **criminal law** = laws relating to acts committed against the laws of the land, and which are punished by the state; **criminal libel** = serious libel which might cause a breach of the peace; **criminal negligence** = acting recklessly with the result that harm is done to other people; **the criminal population** = all people who have committed crimes; **criminal record** = note of previous crimes for which someone has been convicted; **the accused had no criminal record; he has a criminal record going back to the time when he was still at school; age of criminal responsibility** =

age at which a person is considered to be capable of committing a crime

> COMMENT: the age of criminal responsibility is ten years. Children under ten years old cannot be charged with a crime

2 *noun* person who has committed a crime *or* person who often commits crimes; **the police have contacted known criminals to get leads on the gangland murder; a hardened criminal** = a person who has committed many crimes

◊ **Criminal Injuries Compensation Board** *noun* committee which administers the awarding of compensation to victims of crime

criminology *noun* academic study of crime
NOTE: no plural

criterion *noun* standard by which something can be judged; **using the criterion of the ratio of cases solved to cases reported, the police force is becoming more efficient**
NOTE: plural is **criteria**

criticize *verb* to say that something *or* someone is wrong *or* is working badly, etc.; **the judge criticized the police for their handling of the rape case**

◊ **criticism** *noun* words showing that you consider that someone *or* something is wrong; **the judge made some criticisms of the way in which the police handled the case**

crook *noun* *slang* criminal *or* person who has committed a crime, especially involving deceit

cross *verb* **(a)** to go across; **Concorde takes only three hours to cross the Atlantic; to get to the bank, you turn left and cross the street at the post office (b) to cross a cheque** = to write two lines across a cheque to show that it has to be paid into a bank; **crossed cheque** = cheque with two lines across it to show that it can only be deposited at a bank and not exchanged for cash

◊ **cross off** *verb* to remove something from a list; **he crossed my name off his list; you can cross him off our mailing list**

◊ **cross out** *verb* to put a line through something which has been written; **she crossed out £250 and put in £500**

cross-examine *verb* to question witnesses called by the other side in a case, in the hope that you can destroy their evidence

◊ **cross-examination** *noun* questioning witnesses called by the other side in a case

Crown *noun* *GB* **(a) the Crown** = the King *or* Queen as representing the State; **Mr Smith is appearing for the Crown; the Crown submitted that the maximum sentence should be applied in this case; the Crown case** *or* **the case for the Crown was that the defendants were guilty of espionage**
NOTE: in legal reports, the Crown is referred to as **Rex** *or* **Regina** (abbreviated to **R.**) depending on whether there is a King or Queen reigning at the time: **the case of** *R*. v. *Smith Limited* **(b) associate of the Crown Office** = official who is responsible for the clerical and administrative work of a court; **Crown Lands** *or* **Crown property** = land *or* property belonging to the King *or* Queen; **Crown copyright** = copyright in government publications

◊ **Crown Court** *noun* court, above the level of the magistrates' courts, which has centres all over England and Wales and which hears criminal cases

> COMMENT: a Crown Court is formed of a circuit judge and jury, and hears major criminal cases

◊ **Crown privilege** *noun* right of the Crown *or* the government not to have to produce documents to a court by reason of the interest of the state

◊ **Crown prosecutor** *noun* official of the Director of Public Prosecution's department who is responsible for prosecuting criminals in a local area

cruelty *noun* **(a)** hurting a person *or* animal **(b)** acting harshly to a spouse
NOTE: no plural

CTT = CAPITAL TRANSFER TAX

culpable *adjective* which is likely to attract blame; **culpable homicide** = murder *or* manslaughter; **culpable negligence** = negligence which is so bad that it amounts to an offence

◊ **culpability** *noun* being culpable
NOTE: no plural

culprit *noun* person who is responsible for a crime *or* for something which has gone wrong

curiam *see* PER CURIAM

currency *noun* money in coins and notes which is used in a particular country; **blocked currency** = money which cannot be taken out of a country because of exchange controls; **foreign currency** = currency of another country; **free currency** = currency which a government allows to be bought or sold without restriction; **hard currency** = currency of a country which has a strong economy and which can be changed into other currencies easily; **legal currency** = money which is legally used in a country; **soft currency** = currency of a country with a weak economy, which is cheap to buy and difficult to exchange for other currencies

current *adjective* referring to the present time; **current account** = ordinary account in a bank into which money can be deposited and on which cheques can be drawn; **current liabilities** = debts which a company has to pay within the next accounting period
◊ **currently** *adverb* at the present time; **six murders which are currently being investigated**

curriculum vitae *noun* summary of a person's life story showing details of education and work experience; **candidates should send a letter of application with a curriculum vitae to the administrative office**
NOTE: the US English is **résumé**

curtilage *noun* land round a house

custody *noun* (a) being kept in prison *or* in a cell; **the young men were kept in police custody overnight; remanded in custody** = remanded to be kept in prison until the trial starts (b) right and duty of a parent to keep and bring up a child after a divorce; **custody of the children was awarded to the mother; the court granted the mother custody of both children**
NOTE: no plural
◊ **custodial** *adjective* **custodial establishment** *or* **institution** = prison *or* other institution where criminals are kept; **custodial sentence** = sentence which involves sending someone to prison

◊ **custodian** *noun* person who guards a museum or public building

custom *noun* (a) unwritten law which lays down how things are usually done and have been done since time immemorial; **it is the custom that everyone stands up when the magistrates enter the courtroom; local custom** = way in which things are usually done in a particular place; **the customs of the trade** = general way of working in a trade (b) use of a shop by regular shoppers; **to lose someone's custom** = to do something which makes a regular customer go to another shop

◊ **customs** *or* **Customs and Excise** *plural noun* the government department which organizes the collection of taxes on imports; office of this department at a port *or* airport; **to go through the customs** = to pass through the area of a port or airport where customs officials examine goods; **he was stopped by the customs; her car was searched by the customs; customs barrier** = customs duty intended to prevent imports; **customs clearance** = act of clearing goods through the customs; **customs declaration** = statement showing goods being imported on which duty will have to be paid; **customs union** = agreement between several countries that goods can travel between them without paying duty, while goods from other countries have to pay special duties

cut 1 *noun* (a) sudden lowering of a price *or* salary *or* numbers of jobs; **price cuts** *or* **cuts in prices; salary cuts** *or* **cuts in salaries** (b) share in a payment; **he introduces new customers and gets a cut of the salesman's commission 2** *verb* (a) to lower suddenly; **we are cutting prices on all our models; to cut (back) production** = to reduce the quantity of products made (b) to stop *or* to reduce the number of something; **to cut jobs** = to reduce the number of jobs by making people redundant
◊ **cut in on** *verb* **to cut someone in on** = to offer someone part of the profits of a deal

CV *noun* = CURRICULUM VITAE **please apply in writing, enclosing a current CV**

cycle *noun* period of time when something leaves its original position and then returns to it

◊ **cyclical** *adjective* which happens in cycles; **cyclical factors** = way in which a trade cycle affects businesses

cy-près *adjective & adverb* as near as possible; **cy-près doctrine** = rule that if a charity cannot apply its funds to the purposes for which they were intended, a court can apply the funds to a purpose which is as close as possible to the original intention

Dd

D *fourth letter of the alphabet* **category "D" prisoners** = reliable prisoners who can be kept in open prisons; **Schedule D** = schedule to the Finance Acts under which tax is charged on income from trades, professions, interest and other earnings which do not come from employment; **Table D** = model memorandum and articles of association of a public company with share capital limited by guarantee, set out in the Companies Act, 1985

DA *US* = DISTRICT ATTORNEY

dabs *plural noun slang* fingerprints

damage 1 *noun* **(a)** harm done to things; **fire damage** = damage caused by a fire; **malicious damage** = deliberate and intentional harming of property; **storm damage** = damage caused by a storm; **to suffer damage** = to be harmed; **to cause damage** = to harm something; **causing criminal damage** = notifiable offence where serious damage is caused; **damage feasant** = situation where the animals of one person damage the property of another person (NOTE: no plural) **(b) damages** = money claimed by a plaintiff from a defendant as compensation for harm done; **to claim £1,000 in damages; to be liable for** *or* **in damages; to pay £25,000 in damages; to bring an action for damages against someone** = to take someone to court and claim damages; **aggravated damages** = damages awarded by court against a defendant who has behaved maliciously *or* wilfully; **compensatory**

damages = damages which compensate for the loss *or* harm suffered; **exemplary damages** = damages which punish the defendant for the loss *or* harm caused to the plaintiff *or* heavy damages awarded to show that the court feels the defendant has behaved badly towards the plaintiff; **general damages** = damages awarded by court to compensate for a loss which cannot be calculated (such as an injury); **measure of damages** = calculation of how much money a court should order one party to pay another to compensate for a tort *or* breach; **mitigation of damages** = reduction in the extent of damages awarded; **nominal damages** = very small amount of damages, awarded to show that the loss *or* harm suffered was technical rather than actual; **special damages** = damages awarded by court to compensate for a loss which can be calculated (such as the expense of repairing something)
NOTE: damages are noted at the end of a report on a case as: *Special damages: £100 General damages: £2,500*
2 *verb* to harm; **the storm damaged the cargo; stock which has been damaged by water; he alleged that the newspaper article was damaging to the company's reputation**

◊ **damaged** *adjective* which has suffered damage *or* which has been harmed; **fire-damaged goods** = goods harmed in a fire

danger *noun* **(a)** possibility of being harmed *or* killed; **there is danger to the workers in using old machinery (b)** likelihood *or* possibility; **there is no danger of the case being heard early** = it is not likely that the case will be heard early; **in danger of** = which may easily happen; **he is in danger to being in contempt of court**

◊ **danger money** *noun* extra money paid to workers in dangerous jobs; **the workers have stopped work and asked for danger money**

◊ **dangerous** *adjective* which can be harmful; **dangerous drugs** = drugs which may be harmful to people who take them, and so can be prohibited from import and general sales; **dangerous job** = job where the workers may be killed or hurt; **dangerous weapon** = weapon which can hurt someone

data *noun* information (letters *or* figures) which is available on computer; **data bank** *or* **bank of data** = store of information in a

computer; **data processing** = selecting and examining data in a computer to produce special information; **data protection** = protecting information (such as records about private people) in a computer from being copied or used wrongly
NOTE: **data** is usually singular: **the data is easily available**

◊ **database** *noun* store of information in a large computer; **the police maintain a database of fingerprints**

date 1 *noun* (a) number of day, month and year; **date of commencement** = date when an Act of Parliament takes effect; **date stamp** = rubber stamp for marking the date on letters received; **date of receipt** = date when something is received (b) **at an early date** = very soon; **up to date** = current *or* recent *or* modern; **to bring something up to date** = to add the latest information to something; **to keep something up to date** = to keep adding information to something so that it is always up to date (c) **to date** = up to now; **interest to date** = interest up to the present time 2 *verb* to put a date on a document; **the cheque was dated March 24th; he forgot to date the cheque**

◊ **dated** *adjective* with a date written on it; **the murderer's letter was dated June 15th**

day *noun* (a) period of 24 hours; **there are thirty days in June; the first day of the month is a public holiday; three clear days** = three whole working days; **to give ten clear days' notice; allow four clear days for the cheque to be paid into the account; early day motion** = motion proposed in the House of Commons for discussion at an early date (usually used to introduce the particular point of view of the MP proposing the motion, without necessarily going to a full debate) (b) period of work during a 24 hour day; **the trial lasted ten days**

◊ **day-to-day** *adjective* ordinary *or* which goes on all the time; **the clerk organizes the day-to-day running of the courts**

◊ **day training centre** *noun* centre where young offenders attend courses as a condition of being on probation

DC = DETECTIVE CONSTABLE

DCC = DEPUTY CHIEF CONSTABLE

dead *adjective* (a) not alive; **six people were dead as a result of the accident; we inherited the house from my dead grandfather** (b) not working; **dead account** = account which is no longer used; **dead letter** = regulation which is no longer valid; **this law has become a dead letter; dead loss** = total loss; **the car was written off as a dead loss**

◊ **deadline** *noun* date by which something has to be done; **to meet a deadline** = to finish something in time; **to miss a deadline** = not to finish something in time

◊ **deadlock** 1 *noun* point where two sides in a dispute cannot agree; **to break a deadlock** = to find a way to start discussions again 2 *verb* to be unable to agree to continue discussing; **talks have been deadlocked for ten days** = after ten days the talks have not produced any agreement

deal 1 *noun* (a) business agreement *or* affair *or* contract; **to arrange a deal *or* to set up a deal *or* to do a deal; to sign a deal; to call off a deal** = to stop an agreement; **package deal** = agreement where several different items are agreed at the same time (b) **a great deal *or* a good deal of something** = a large quantity of something; **he has made a good deal of money on the stock market; counsel wasted a great deal of time cross-examining the dead man's father** 2 *verb* **to deal with** = to be busy with *or* to have to do with; **Crown Courts do not deal with civil cases**

◊ **dealer** *noun* person who buys and sells; **a wine dealer *or* a foreign exchange dealer**

◊ **dealing** *noun* (a) buying and selling on the Stock Exchange; **fair dealing** = (i) legal trade *or* legal buying and selling of shares; (ii) legal quoting of small sections of a copyright work; **foreign exchange dealing** = buying and selling foreign currencies; **forward dealings** = buying or selling commodities forward; **insider dealing** = illegal buying or selling of shares, such as by staff of a company who have secret information about the company's plans (b) buying and selling goods; **to have dealings with someone** = to do business with someone

dear *adjective* (a) expensive *or* costing a lot of money; **property is very dear in this area; dear money** = money which has to be borrowed at a high rate of interest (b) way of starting a letter; **Dear Sir** *or* **Dear Madam** = addressing a man or woman whom you do not know, or addressing a company; **Dear Sirs** = addressing a firm; **Dear Mr Smith** *or* **Dear Mrs Smith** *or* **Dear Miss Smith** = addressing a man or woman whom you know; **Dear James** *or* **Dear Julia** = addressing a friend *or* a person you do business with

death *noun* act of dying; **death benefit** = insurance benefit paid to the family of someone who dies in an accident at work; **death certificate** = official certificate signed by a doctor, stating that a person has died and giving details of the person; **death grant** = state grant to the family of a person who has died, which is supposed to contribute to the funeral expenses; **death in service** = insurance benefit *or* pension paid when someone dies while employed by a company; **death penalty** = sentence of a criminal to be executed; *US* **death duty** *or* **death tax** = tax paid on the property left by a dead person; **presumption of death** = situation where a person has not been seen for seven years and is presumed to be legally dead

debate 1 *noun* discussion leading to a vote, especially the discussion of a motion in Parliament; **several MPs criticized the government in** *or* **during the debate on the Finance Bill; the Bill passed its Second Reading after a short debate; the debate continued until 3 a.m.** 2 *verb* to discuss a proposal, especially in Parliament; **the MPs are still debating the Data Protection Bill**

debenture *noun* document whereby a company acknowledges it owes a debt, and gives the company's assets as security; **mortgage debenture** = debenture where the lender can be repaid by selling the company's property; **debenture issue** *or* **issue of debentures** = borrowing money against the security of the company's assets; **debenture bond** = certificate showing that a debenture has been issued; **debenture capital** *or* **debenture stock** = capital borrowed by a company, using its fixed assets as security; **debenture holder** = person who holds a debenture for money lent; **debenture register** *or* **register of debentures** = list of debenture holders of a company

debit 1 *noun* money which a company owes; **debit and credit** = money which a company owes and money it is entitled to receive; **debit column** = left-hand column in accounts showing the money paid or owed to others; **debit entry** = entry on the debit side of an account; **debit side** = left-hand side of an account showing the money paid or owed to others; **debit note** = note showing that a customer owes money; **direct debit** = system where a customer allows a company to charge costs to his bank account automatically and where the amount charged can be increased or decreased automatically, the customer being informed of the change by letter; *compare* STANDING ORDER 2 *verb* **to debit an account** = to charge an account with a cost; **his account was debited with the sum of £25**

◇ **debitable** *adjective* which can be debited

debt *noun* (a) money owed for goods or services; **the company stopped trading with debts of over £1 million; to be in debt** = to owe money; **to get into debt** = to start to borrow more money than you can pay back; **to be out of debt** = not to owe money any more; **to pay back a debt** = to pay all the money owed; **to pay off a debt** = to finish paying money owed; **to service a debt** = to pay interest on a debt; **bad debt** = money owed which will never be paid back; **debt collection** *or* **collecting** = collecting money which is owed; **debt collection agency** *or* **collecting agency** = company which collects debts for other companies for a commission; **debt collector** = person who collects debts; **debt factor** = person who buys debts at a discount and enforces them for himself *or* person who enforces debts for a commission

◇ **debtor** *noun* person who owes money; **debtor side** = debit side of an account; **debtor nation** = country whose foreign debts are larger than money owed to it by other countries; **judgment debtor** = person who has been ordered by a court to pay a debt

decapitate *verb* to cut off someone's head

◇ **decapitation** *noun* act of cutting off someone's head; **he was sentenced to death by decapitation**
NOTE: no plural

decease *noun* (*formal*) death; **on his decease all his property will go to his widow**

◊ **deceased** *adjective & noun* (person) who has died; **the deceased left all his property to his widow; she inherited the estate of a deceased aunt**

deceive *verb* to trick (someone) *or* to make someone think something is true when it is not

◊ **deceit** *or* **deception** *noun* making a wrong statement to someone in order to trick him into paying money *or* in order to make him do something which will harm him; **she obtained £10,000 by deception; obtaining a pecuniary advantage by deception** = crime of tricking someone into handing over money; **obtaining property by deception** = tricking someone into handing over possession of property

◊ **deceiver** *noun* person who deceives

◊ **deceptive** *adjective* which deceives

decent *adjective* which does not shock other people *or* which is accepted by society in general; **this book should be banned - it will shock any decent citizen**

◊ **decency** *noun* being decent; **the film shocked public decency**

decide *verb* (a) to give a judgment in a civil case; **the judge decided in favour of the plaintiff** (b) to make up your mind to do something; **we have decided to take our neighbours to court; the tribunal decided against awarding any damages**

◊ **decided case** *noun* case where a court has decided, and where that decision then becomes a precedent

◊ **decidendi** *see* RATIO

◊ **deciding** *adjective* **deciding factor** = most important factor which influences a decision

◊ **decision** *noun* (a) judgment in a civil court; **the decision of the House of Lords is final** = there is no appeal against a decision of the House of Lords (b) making up one's mind to do something; **to come to a decision** *or* **to reach a decision; decision making** = act of coming to a decision; **the decision-making processes** = ways in which decisions are reached; **decision maker** = person who has to decide

◊ **decisis** *see* STARE DECISIS

declare *verb* to make an official statement *or* to announce to the public; **to declare someone bankrupt; to declare a dividend of 10%; to declare goods to the customs** = to state that you are importing goods which are liable to duty; **to declare an interest** = to state in public that you own shares in a company being investigated *or* that you are related to someone who can benefit from your contacts, etc.

◊ **declared** *adjective* which has been made public or officially stated; **declared value** = value of goods entered on a customs declaration

◊ **declaration** *noun* official statement; **declaration of association** = statement in the articles of association of a company, saying that the members have agreed to form the company and buy shares in it; **declaration of bankruptcy** = official statement that someone is bankrupt; **declaration of income** = statement declaring income to the tax office; **customs declaration** = statement declaring goods brought into a country on which customs duty may be paid; **statutory declaration** = (i) statement made to the Registrar of Companies that a company has complied with certain legal conditions; (ii) statement made, signed and witnessed for official purposes; **VAT declaration** = statement declaring VAT income to the VAT office

◊ **declaratory judgment** *noun* judgment where a court states what the legal position of the various parties is

decline 1 *noun* slow fall; **the decline in the value of the franc; a decline in buying power; the last year has seen a decline in real wages** 2 *verb* to refuse to do something; **the witness declined to take the oath**

decontrol *verb* to stop *or* remove controls from something; **to decontrol the price of petrol** = to stop controlling the price of petrol so that a free market price can be reached
NOTE: **decontrolled - decontrolling**

decrease *verb* to make smaller *or* to become smaller; **the government proposes to decrease the rate of VAT**

decree 1 *noun* (a) order made by a head of state, but which is not passed by a parliament; **to govern by decree** = to rule a country by issuing orders without having them debated and voted in a parliament

(b) decree nisi = order from a court which ends a marriage for the time being, and becomes final when decree absolute is pronounced; **decree absolute** = order from a court which ends a marriage finally **2** *verb* to make an order; **the President decreed that June 1st should be a National Holiday**

deduce *verb* to conclude *or* to come to a decision based on observing something; **from his clothes, we can deduce that the victim was a rich man**

◊ **deducing title** *noun* proving (by the vendor) of his title to the property being sold

deduct *verb* to remove money from a total; **to deduct £3 from the price; to deduct a sum for expenses; to deduct 5% from salaries; tax deducted at source** = tax which is removed from a salary, interest payment or dividend payment on shares before the money is paid

◊ **deductible** *adjective* which can be deducted; **tax-deductible** = which can be deducted from an income before tax is paid; **these expenses are not tax-deductible** = tax has to be paid on these expenses

◊ **deduction** *noun* **(a)** conclusion which is reached by observing something; **by deduction, the detective came to the conclusion that the dead person has not been murdered (b)** removing of money from a total *or* money removed from a total; **net salary is salary after deduction of tax and social security contributions; deductions from salary** *or* **salary deductions** *or* **deductions at source** = money which a company removes from salaries to give to the government as tax, national insurance contributions, etc.; **tax deductions** = (i) money removed from a salary to pay tax; (ii); *US* business expenses which can be claimed against tax

deed *noun* legal document which has been signed, sealed and delivered by the person making it; **deed of arrangement** = agreement made between a debtor and his creditors whereby the creditors accept an agreed sum in settlement of their claim rather than make the debtor bankrupt; **deed of assignment** = agreement which legally transfers a property from a debtor to a creditor; **deed of covenant** = signed legal agreement to do something (such as to pay someone a sum of money every

year); **deed of partnership** = agreement which sets up a partnership; **deed of transfer** = agreement which transfers the ownership of shares; **title deeds** = document showing who owns a property; **we have deposited the deeds of the house in the bank**

◊ **deed poll** *noun* document made under seal, to which there is only one party; **to change one's name by deed poll** = to sign a legal document by which you change your name

deem *verb* to believe *or* to consider; **the judge deemed it necessary to order the court to be cleared; if no payment is made, the party shall be deemed to have defaulted**

de facto *Latin phrase meaning* "in fact": as a matter of fact, even though the legal title may not be certain; **he is the de facto owner of the property;** *see also* DE JURE

defalcation *noun* illegal use of money by someone who is not the owner but who has been trusted to look after it

defame *verb* to say *or* write things about the character of someone so as to damage his reputation

◊ **defamation** *noun* **defamation of character** = act of ruining someone's reputation by maliciously saying *or* writing things about him

> COMMENT: defamation is a tort and may be libel (if it is in a permanent form, such as printed matter) or slander (if it is spoken)

◊ **defamatory** *adjective* **defamatory statement** = statement which is made to defame someone's character

default 1 *noun* failure to carry out the terms of a contract, especially failure to pay back a debt; **in default of payment** = if no payment is made; **the company is in default** = the company has failed to carry out the terms of the contract; **by default** = because no one else will act; **he was elected by default** = he was elected because all the other candidates withdrew *or* because there were no other candidates; **judgment by default** *or* **default judgment** = judgment against a defendant who fails to defend his case; **default action** = County Court action to get back money owed; **default summons** = County Court summons to someone to pay what is owed **2** *verb* to fail to carry out the terms of a contract, especially to fail to pay back a debt; **to default on payments** = not to make payments which are due under the terms of a contract

◇ **defaulter** *noun* person who defaults

defeasance *noun* clause (in a collateral deed) which says that a contract *or* bond *or* recognizance will be revoked if something happens *or* if some act is performed

defeat 1 *noun* failure to get a majority in a vote; **the minister offered to resign after the defeat of the motion in the House of Commons** 2 *verb* **(a)** to beat someone *or* something in a vote; **the bill was defeated in the Lords by 52 to 64; the government was defeated in a vote on law and order (b)** to revoke *or* to render invalid (an agreement *or* a contract *or* a bond)

defect 1 *noun* something which is wrong *or* which stops a machine from working properly 2 *verb* (*of a spy* or *agent* or *government employee*) to leave your country and go to work for an enemy country

◇ **defective** *adjective* **(a)** faulty *or* not working properly; **the machine broke down because of a defective cooling system (b)** not legally valid; **his title to the property is defective**

defence *or* US **defense** *noun* **(a)** protecting someone *or* something against attack; **the merchant bank is organizing the company's defence against the takeover bid (b)** (i) party in a legal case which is sued by the plaintiff; (ii) party in a criminal case which is being prosecuted; (iii) lawyers representing a party being sued *or* prosecuted; **defence counsel** = lawyer who represents the defendant *or* the accused **(c)** arguments used when fighting a case; **his defence was that he did not know the property was stolen; to file a defence** = to state that you wish to defend a case, and outline the reasons for doing so **(d)** document *or* a pleading setting out the defendant's case; *compare* PROSECUTION

◇ **defend** *verb* **(a)** to fight to protect someone *or* something which is being attacked; **the company is defending itself against the takeover bid (b)** to speak on behalf of someone who has been charged with a crime; **he hired the best lawyers to defend him against the tax authorities; to**

defend an action = to appear in court to state your case when accused of something

◇ **defendant** *noun* (i) person who is sued in a civil case; (ii) person who is accused of a crime in a criminal case; *compare* PLAINTIFF

defer *verb* to put back to a later date *or* to postpone; **to defer judgment; the decision has been deferred until the next meeting** NOTE: **deferring - deferred**

◇ **deferment** *noun* postponement *or* putting back to a later date; **deferment of payment; deferment of a decision; deferment of sentence** = putting back the sentencing of a convicted criminal until a later date to see how he behaves

◇ **deferred** *adjective* put back to a later date; **deferred creditor** = person who is owed money by a bankrupt but who is paid only after all other creditors; **deferred payment** = payment for goods by instalments over a long period; **deferred stock** *or* **shares** = shares which receive a dividend after all other dividends have been paid

define *verb* to say clearly what a word *or* phrase means; **immigrant persons as defined in Appendix 3; the judge asked counsel to define what he meant by "incapable"**

deforce *verb* to take wrongfully and hold land which belongs to someone else

◇ **deforcement** *noun* wrongful taking and holding of another person's land

defraud *verb* to trick someone so as to obtain money illegally; **he defrauded the Inland Revenue of thousands of pounds** NOTE: you defraud someone **of** something

defray *verb* to provide money to pay (costs); **the company agreed to defray the costs of the prosecution**

degree *noun* **(a)** level *or* measure of a relationship; **prohibited degrees** = relationships which make it illegal for a man and woman to marry (such as father and daughter) **(b)** *US* system for classifying murders; **first degree murder** = premeditated and deliberate murder; **second degree murder** = murder without premeditation

COMMENT: in the US, the penalty
for first degree murder can be death

de jure *Latin phrase meaning* "by law": as
a matter of law, where the legal title is
clear; **he is the de jure owner of the property;**
see also DE FACTO

delay 1 *noun* time when someone *or*
something is later than planned; **there was
a delay of thirty minutes before the hearing
started *or* the hearing started after a thirty
minute delay 2** *verb* to be late; to make
someone late; **judgment was delayed while
the magistrates asked for advice**

del credere agent *noun* agent who
receives a high commission because he
guarantees payment by customers to his
principal

delegate 1 *noun* person who elected by
others to put their case at a meeting; **the
management refused to meet the trade union
delegates 2** *verb* to pass authority or
responsibility to someone else; **delegated
legislation** = orders, which have the power
of Acts of Parliament, but which are
passed by a minister to whom Parliament
has delegated its authority

◇ **delegation** *noun* **(a)** group of delegates; **a Chinese trade delegation; the
management met a union delegation (b)** act
of passing authority or responsibility to
someone else
NOTE: no plural for (b)

◇ **delegatus non potest delegare**
Latin phrase meaning "the delegate cannot
delegate to someone else"

delete *verb* to remove words in a document; **the court ordered the newspaper to
delete all references to the divorce case; the
lawyers have deleted clause two from the
contract**

deliberate 1 *adjective* done on purpose;
**the police suggest that the letter was a
deliberate attempt to encourage disorder 2**
verb to consider *or* to discuss a problem;
**the committee deliberated for several hours
before reaching a decision**

◇ **deliberately** *adverb* on purpose *or*
done intentionally; **he was accused of
deliberately setting fire to the shop**

◇ **deliberations** *plural noun* discussions; **the result of the committee's
deliberations was passed to the newspapers**

delicti *see* CORPUS

delicto *see* IN FLAGRANTE DELICTO

delinquency *noun* the act of committing
crime, usually minor crime

◇ **delinquent** *noun* **a juvenile delinquent**
or US **a delinquent** = young criminal who
commits minor crimes, especially crimes
against property

deliver *verb* to transport goods to a
customer; **goods delivered free *or* free
delivered goods** = goods carried to the
customer's address at a price which includes transport costs; **goods delivered on
board** = goods carried free to the ship or
plane but not to the customer's warehouse

◇ **delivery** *noun* **(a) delivery of goods** =
transport of goods to a customer's address;
delivery note = list of goods being delivered, given to the customer with the goods;
delivery order = instructions given by the
customer to the person holding his goods,
to tell him to deliver them; **recorded
delivery** = mail service where the letters
are signed for by the person receiving
them; **cash on delivery** = payment in cash
when the goods are delivered; **to take
delivery of goods** = to accept goods when
they are delivered **(b)** goods being delivered; **we take in three deliveries a day; there
were four items missing in the last delivery
(c)** transfer of a bill of exchange **(d)**
formal act whereby a deed becomes effective; **deeds take effect only from the time of
delivery**

demand 1 *noun* **(a)** asking for
payment; **payable on demand** = which
must be paid when payment is asked for;
demand bill = bill of exchange which must
be paid when payment is asked for; **final
demand** = last reminder from a supplier,
after which he will sue for payment; **letter
of demand** = letter issued by a party *or*
lawyer demanding payment before taking
legal action **(b)** need for goods at a certain
price; **supply and demand** = amount of a
product which is available at a certain
price and the amount which is wanted by
customers at that price; **law of supply and
demand** = general rule that the amount of
a product which is available is related to

the needs of possible customers **2** *verb* to ask for something and expect to get it; **they were accused of demanding payment with threats**

◊ **demanding with menaces** *noun* crime of demanding money by threatening someone

de minimis non curat lex *Latin phrase meaning* "the law does not deal with trivial things"

demise *noun* **(a)** death; **on his demise the estate passed to his daughter** (NOTE: no plural) **(b)** granting of property on a lease; **demise charter** = charter of a ship without the crew

demonstrate *verb* **(a)** to show; **the police demonstrated how the bomb was planted; counsel was able to demonstrate how it was impossible for the accused to climb through the window (b)** to make a public protest about something; **crowds of students were demonstrating against the government**

◊ **demonstration** *noun* act of demonstrating; **police broke up the student demonstration**

◊ **demonstrative legacy** *noun* gift in a will which is ordered to be paid out of a special account

◊ **demonstrator** *noun* person who demonstrates

demur **1** *noun* objection; **counsel made no demur to the proposal 2** *verb* **(a)** not to agree; **counsel stated that there was no case to answer, but the judge demurred (b)** to make a formal objection that the facts as alleged are not sufficient to warrant the civil action
NOTE: demurring - demurred

◊ **demurrage** *noun* money paid to the owner of a cargo when a ship is delayed in a port
NOTE: no plural

◊ **demurrer** *noun* plea that although the facts of the case are correct, they are not sufficient to warrant the action

denomination *noun* unit of money (on a coin *or* stamp *or* banknote); **small denomination banknotes; coins of all denominations**

de novo *Latin phrase meaning* "starting again"

deny *verb* **(a)** not to allow something; **he was denied the right to see his lawyer (b)** to say that you have not done something; **he denied being in the house at the time of the murder**
NOTE: you deny someone something or deny doing *or* having done something

◊ **denial** *noun* **(a)** act of not allowing something; **denial of human rights** = refusing someone a right which is generally accepted as fair; **denial of justice** = situation where justice appears not to have been done **(b)** act of stating that you have not done something; **in spite of his denials he was found guilty**

depart *verb* **(a)** to leave; **the plane departs at 11.15 (b) to depart from normal practice** = to act in a different way from the normal practice

◊ **department** *noun* **(a)** specialized section of a large company; **complaints department; legal department; accounts department** = section which deals with money paid or received; **head of department** *or* **department head** *or* **department manager** = person in charge of a department **(b)** section of a large store selling one type of product; **furniture department** = department in a large store which sells furniture **(c) Department of State** = major section of the British government headed by a Secretary of State; **the Department of Trade and Industry; the Department of Education and Science**

departure *noun* **(a)** going away; **the plane's departure was delayed by two hours (b)** new type of business; **selling records will be a departure for the local bookshop (c) departure from** = thing which is different from what happened before; **this forms a departure from established practice; any departure from the terms and conditions of the contract must be advised in writing**

depend *verb* **(a) to depend on** = to need someone *or* something to exist; **the company depends on efficient service from its suppliers; we depend on government grants to pay the salary bill (b)** to happen because of something; **the success of the anti-drug campaign will depend on the attitude of the public; depending on** = happening as a result of something;

depending on the circumstances, the accused may receive a fine or be sent to prison

◇ **dependant** *noun* person who is supported financially by someone else; **he has to provide for his family and dependants out of a very small salary**

◇ **dependent** *adjective* (person) who is supported financially by someone else; **tax relief is allowed for dependent relatives**

deponent *noun* person who makes a statement under oath *or* by affidavit

deport *verb* to send (someone) away from a country; **the illegal immigrants were deported**

◇ **deportation** *noun* sending of someone away from a country; **the convicts were sentenced to deportation; deportation order** = official order to send someone away from a country; **the minister signed the deportation order**
NOTE: no plural

depose *verb* **(a)** to state under oath **(b)** to remove (a king) from the throne

◇ **deposition** *noun* written statement of evidence of a witness

deposit 1 *noun* **(a)** money placed in a bank for safe keeping or to earn interest; **certificate of deposit** = certificate from a bank to show that money has been deposited; **deposit account** = bank account which pays interest but on which notice has to be given to withdraw money; **licensed deposit-taker** = business (such as a bank) which takes deposits from individuals and lends the money to others **(b) safe deposit** = bank safe where you can leave jewellery or documents; **safe deposit box** = small box which you can rent, in which you can keep jewellery or documents in a bank's safe **(c)** money given in advance so that the thing which you want to buy will not be sold to someone else; **to leave £10 as deposit; to forfeit a deposit** = to lose a deposit because you have decided not to but the item **(d)** money paid by a candidate when nominated for an election, which is forfeited if the candidate does not win enough votes; **he polled only 25 votes and lost his deposit** 2 *verb* **(a)** to put documents somewhere for safe keeping; **we have deposited the deeds of the house with the bank; he deposited his will with his solicitor (b)** to put money into a bank

account; **to deposit £100 in a current account**

◇ **depositary** *noun* *US* person *or* company with whom money or documents can be deposited

◇ **depositor** *noun* person who deposits money in a bank

◇ **depository** *noun* **(a) furniture depository** = warehouse where you can store household furniture **(b)** person or company with whom money or documents can be deposited

deprave *verb* to make someone's character bad; **TV programmes which may deprave the minds of children who watch them**

deprive *verb* **to deprive someone of something** = to remove something from someone *or* not to allow someone to have something; **the prisoners were deprived of contact with their families; the new Bill deprives aliens of the right to appeal**

dept = DEPARTMENT

deputy *noun* **(a)** person who takes the place of a higher official *or* who assists a higher official; **to act as deputy for someone *or* to act as someone's deputy (b)** *US* person who acts for *or* assists a sheriff

◇ **deputize** *verb* **to deputize for someone** = to take the place of someone who is absent

deregulation *noun* reducing government control over an industry; **the deregulation of the airlines**

derelict *noun* abandoned floating boat

◇ **dereliction of duty** *noun* failure to do what you ought to do; **he was found guilty of gross dereliction of duty**

derive *verb* **(a)** to come from; **this law derives from *or* is derived from the former Roman law of property (b)** to obtain; **he derived financial benefit from the transaction**

derogate *verb* **to derogate from something which has been agreed** = to act to prevent something which has been agreed from being fully implemented

◇ **derogation** *noun* act of avoiding *or* destroying something; **derogation of responsibility** = avoiding doing a duty

descended from *adjective* having a person as an ancestor; **he is descended from William I**

◊ **descendant** *noun* person who is descended from an ancestor; **his wife is a descendant of King Charles I**

◊ **descent** *noun* family ties of inheritance between parents and children; **he is British by descent** *or* **he is of British descent** = one (or both) of his parents is British; **lineal descent** = direct descent from parent to child

describe *verb* to say what someone *or* something is like; **she described her attacker to the police; he described the judge as a silly old man**

◊ **description** *noun* words which show what something is like; **the police circulated a description of the missing boy** *or* **of the wanted man; false description of contents** = wrongly stating the contents of a packet to trick customers into buying it; **trade description** = description of a product to attract customers; *GB* **Trade Descriptions Act** = Act of Parliament which limits the way in which products can be described so as to protect consumers from wrong descriptions made by the makers

desert *verb* **(a)** to leave the armed forces without permission; **he deserted and went to live in South America (b)** to leave a family *or* spouse; **the two children have been deserted by their father**

◊ **deserter** *noun* person who has left the armed forces without permission

◊ **desertion** *noun* **(a)** leaving the armed forces without permission **(b)** leaving one's spouse; **he divorced his wife because of her desertion**

designate **1** *adjective* person who has been appointed to a job but who has not yet started work; **the chairman designate** (NOTE: always follows a noun) **2** *verb* to name *or* to appoint officially; **the area was designated a National Park**

destruction *noun* action of killing someone *or* ending something completely; **the destruction of the evidence in the fire at the police station made it difficult to prosecute; child destruction** = notifiable offence of killing an unborn child capable of being born alive

detail 1 *noun* small part of a description; **in detail** = giving many particulars; **the contract lists all the markets in detail 2** *verb* **(a)** to list in detail; **the document details the arrangements for maintenance payments; the terms of the licence are detailed in the contract (b)** to tell someone to do something; **six officers were detailed to search the premises**

◊ **detailed** *adjective* in detail; **detailed account** = account which lists every item

detain *verb* to hold a person so that he cannot leave; **the suspects were detained by the police for questioning**

◊ **detainee** *noun* person who has been detained

◊ **detainer** *noun* act of holding a person

detect *verb* to notice *or* to discover (something which is hidden or difficult to see); **the machine can detect explosives**

◊ **detection** *noun* discovering something, especially discovering who has committed a crime *or* how a crime has been committed; **detection rate** = number of crimes which are solved, as a percentage of all crimes

◊ **detective** *noun* person, usually a policeman, who tries to solve a crime; **private detective** = person who for a fee will try to solve mysteries *or* to find missing people *or* will keep watch on someone; **detective agency** = office which hires out the services of private detectives

COMMENT: the ranks of detectives in the British Police Force are Detective Constable, Detective Sergeant, Detective Inspector, Detective Chief Inspector, Detective Superintendent, and Detective Chief Superintendent

detention *noun* **(a)** keeping someone so that he cannot escape; **the suspects were placed in detention; detention centre** = place where young offenders (aged between 14 and 21) can be kept for corrective training, instead of being sent to prison, if they are convicted of crimes which would normally carry a sentence of three months' imprisonment or more; **detention order** = court order asking for someone to be kept in detention **(b)** wrongfully holding goods which belong to someone else

deter *verb* to make someone not eager to do something; **it is hoped that long jail sentences will deter others from smuggling drugs**
NOTE: **deterring - deterred.** Note also that you deter someone **from** doing something

◇ **deterrence** *noun* idea that the harsh punishment of one criminal will deter other people from committing crimes

◇ **deterrent** 1 *noun* punishment which will deter people from committing crimes; **a long prison sentence will act as a deterrent to other possible criminals** 2 *adjective* **deterrent sentence** = harsh sentence which the judge hopes will deter other people from committing crimes

determine *verb* (a) to fix *or* to arrange *or* to decide; **to determine prices *or* quantities; the conditions of the contract are still to be determined** (b) to bring to an end; **the tenancy was determined by a notice to quit**

detinue *noun* tort of wrongfully holding goods which belong to someone else; **action in detinue** = action formerly brought to regain possession of goods which were wrongfully held by someone

detriment *noun* damage *or* harm; **without detriment to his claim** = without harming his claim; **his action was to the detriment of the plaintiff** = his action harmed the plaintiff

◇ **detrimental** *adjective* which may harm; **action detrimental to the maintenance of public order**

develop *verb* (a) to plan and produce; **to develop a new product** (b) to plan and build an area; **to develop an industrial estate**

◇ **developer** *noun* **a property developer** = person who plans and builds a group of new houses *or* new factories

◇ **development** *noun* (a) planning the production of a new product *or* new town; **industrial development** = planning and building of new industries in special areas; **development area *or* development zone** = area which has been given special help from a government to encourage businesses and factories to be set up there (b) change which has taken place; **the case represents a new development in the law of libel**

deviate *verb* **to deviate from a course of action** = to do something different *or* to act in a different way

device *noun* small useful machine; way of doing something; **a device to avoid paying tax *or* a tax-saving device**

devil 1 *noun* barrister to whom another barrister passes work because he is too busy 2 *verb* to pass instruction to another barrister because you are too busy to deal with the case yourself; **to devil for someone** = to do unpleasant *or* boring work for someone

devise 1 *noun* giving freehold land to someone in a will 2 *verb* to give freehold property to someone in a will

COMMENT: giving of other types of property is a **bequest**

◇ **devisee** *noun* person who receives freehold property in a will

diary *noun* book in which you can write notes or appointments for each day of the week and record events which have taken place

dictate *verb* to say something to someone who then writes down your words; **dictating machine** = machine which records what someone dictates, which a secretary can play back and then type out the text

◇ **dictation** *noun* act of dictating; **to take dictation** = to write down what someone is saying; **dictation speed** = number of words per minute which a secretary can write down in shorthand

dictum *noun* saying *or* statement made by a judge; **obiter dicta** = part of a judgment which does not form an essential part of it; *see also* RATIO DECIDENDI
NOTE: plural is **dicta**

differ *verb* not to agree with; **one of the appeal judges differed from the others; I beg to differ** = I want to say that I do not agree

◇ **difference** *noun* way in which two things are not the same

◇ **different** *adjective* not the same

digest *noun* book which collects summaries of court decisions together, used for reference purposes by lawyers

dilatory *adjective* too slow; **dilatory motion** = motion in the House of Commons to delay the debate on a proposal

diminish *verb* to get *or* to make smaller; **diminished responsibility** *or* *US* **diminished capacity** = mental state of a criminal (inherited *or* caused by illness or injury) which means that he cannot be held responsible for a crime which he has committed

DInsp = DETECTIVE INSPECTOR

dip *noun* *slang* pickpocket

diplomat *or* **diplomatist** *noun* person (such as an ambassador) who is the official representative of his country in another country

◊ **diplomatic** *adjective* referring to diplomats; **diplomatic immunity** = not being subject to the laws of the country in which you are living, because you are a diplomat; **he claimed diplomatic immunity to avoid being arrested; to grant someone diplomatic status** = to give someone the rights of a diplomat

direct 1 *verb* to order *or* to give an order to (someone); **the judge directed the jury to acquit all the defendants; the Crown Court directed the justices to rehear the case 2** *adjective* straight *or* with no interference; **direct debit** = system where a customer allows a company to charge costs to his bank account automatically and where the amount charged can be increased or decreased automatically, the customer being informed of the change by letter; **direct evidence** = first hand evidence, such as the testimony of an eye witness or the production of original documents; **direct examination** = asking a witness questions (by lawyers for his side) so that he gives oral evidence in court; **direct mail** = selling a product by sending advertising material by post to possible buyers; **direct selling** = selling a product direct to the customer without going through a shop; **direct taxation** = tax, such as income tax, which is paid direct to the government **3** *adverb* straight *or* with no third party involved; **we pay income tax direct to the** government; the fine is paid direct to the court

◊ **direction** *noun* (a) way in which something is going; **the new evidence changed the direction of the hearing** (b) organizing *or* managing; **he took over the direction of a large bank** (c) **directions** = (i) order which explains how something should be done; (ii) instructions from a judge to a jury; (iii) orders given by a judge concerning the general way of proceeding with a case; **the court is not able to give directions to the local authority**

◊ **directive** *noun* order *or* command to someone to do something (especially order from the Council *or* Commission of the European Community); **the Commission issued a directive on food prices**

◊ **directly** *adverb* (a) immediately; **the summons was served directly after the magistrate had signed the warrant** (b) in a straight way; **the Metropolitan Police Commissioner is directly responsible to the Home Secretary**

◊ **director** *noun* (a) person appointed by the shareholders to manage a company; **managing director** = the most senior executive director in a company; **chairman and managing director** = managing director who is also chairman of the board of directors; **board of directors** = all the directors of a company; **directors' report** = annual report from the board of directors to the shareholders; **executive director** = director who actually works full-time in the company; **non-executive director** = director who attends board meetings and gives advice, but does not work full-time for the company; **outside director** = director who is not employed by the company (b) person who is in charge of a programme of work, an official institute, etc.; **he is the director of a government institute; she was appointed director of the charity; Director-General of Fair Trading** = official in charge of the Office of Fair Trading, dealing with consumers and the law

◊ **directorate** *noun* group of directors
◊ **Director of Public Prosecutions (DPP)** *noun* government official in charge of a group of lawyers (working under the Attorney-General), who prosecutes in important cases and advises other government departments if prosecutions should be started; **the papers in the fraud**

case have been sent to the Director of Public Prosecutions

◇ **directorship** *noun* post of director; he was offered a directorship with Smith Ltd

directory *noun* list of people *or* businesses with information about their addresses and telephone numbers; **classified directory** = list of businesses grouped under various headings, such as computer shops or newsagents; **commercial directory** *or* **trade directory** = book which lists all the businesses and business people in a town; **street directory** = (i) list of people living in a street; (ii) map of a town which lists all the streets in alphabetical order in an index; **telephone directory** = book which lists all people and businesses who have telephones, in alphabetical order with their phone numbers

disability *noun* (a) being unable to use one's body properly (as because you are blind *or* cannot walk, etc.) (b) lack of legal capacity to act in one's own right (such as because of one's age *or* mental state); **person under a disability** = person who is not capable to taking legal action for himself

◇ **disabled person** *noun* person who is physically handicapped in some way (such as being blind or not capable of walking)

disadvantage *noun* something which makes you less successful; **it is a disadvantage for a tax lawyer not to have studied to be an accountant; to be at a disadvantage** = to be in a more awkward position (than another person); **not having studied law puts him at a disadvantage**

disagree *verb* not to agree; **the jury disagreed and were not able to return a verdict** = there were not enough jurors who were in agreement to be able to form even a majority verdict

◇ **disagreement** *noun* not agreeing; **there was disagreement among the MPs about how the police should deal with terrorist attacks**

disallow *verb* to reject *or* not to accept; **the judge disallowed the defence evidence; he claimed £2000 for fire damage, but the claim was disallowed**

disapprove *verb* to show doubt about (a decision made by a lower court), but not to reverse *or* overrule it; **the Appeal Court disapproved the County Court decision; to disapprove of something** = to show that you do not approve of something *or* that you do not think something is good; **the judge openly disapproves of juries**

◇ **disapproval** *noun* act of disapproving a decision made by a lower court

disbar *verb* to stop a barrister from practising
NOTE: **disbarring - disbarred**

disburse *verb* to pay money
◇ **disbursement** *noun* payment of money

discharge 1 *noun* (a) ending of a contract by performing all the conditions of the contract *or* by releasing a party from the terms of the contract *or* by being in breach of contract; **discharge by agreement** = situation where both parties agree to end a contract; **discharge by performance** = situation where the terms of a contract have been fulfilled; **discharge in *or* of bankruptcy** = order of a court to release someone from bankruptcy (b) payment of debt; **in full discharge of a debt** = paying a debt completely *or* paying less than the total amount owed, by agreement; **final discharge** = final payment of what is left of a debt (c) release from prison *or* from military service; **absolute discharge** = letting an offender go free without any punishment; **conditional discharge** = allowing an offender to be set free without any immediate punishment on condition that he does not commit an offence during the following period (d) **in discharge of his duties as director** = carrying out his duties as director 2 *verb* (a) to let (someone) go free; **the prisoners were discharged by the judge; the judge discharged the jury** = the judge told the jury that they were no longer needed (b) **to discharge a bankrupt** = to release someone from bankruptcy (as when a person has paid his debts) (c) **to discharge a debt *or* to discharge one's liabilities** = to pay a debt *or* one's liabilities in full (d) to dismiss *or* to sack; **to discharge an employee**

discipline *verb* to punish (an official); **the clerk was disciplined for leaking the report to the newspapers**

◊ **disciplinary** *adjective* **disciplinary procedure** = way of warning a worker officially that he is breaking rules *or* that he is working badly; **to take disciplinary action against someone** = to punish someone

disclaim *verb* to refuse to admit; **he disclaimed all knowledge of the bomb; the management disclaims all responsibility for customers' property**

◊ **disclaimer** *noun* **(a)** legal refusal to accept responsibility *or* to accept a right **(b)** clause in a contract where a party disclaims responsibility for something

disclose *verb* to tell details; **the bank has no right to disclose details of my account to the tax office**

◊ **disclosure** *noun* act of telling details *or* of publishing a secret; **the disclosure of the takeover bid raised the price of the shares; the defendant's case was made stronger by the disclosure that the plaintiff was an undischarged bankrupt**

discount *noun* percentage by which a full price is reduced by the seller to a buyer; **we give a 30% discount for large orders; he buys stock at a discount and sells at full price to the public**

discover *verb* to find something new; **the auditors discovered some errors in the accounts**

◊ **discovery** *noun* disclosure of each party's documents to the other before a hearing starts in the civil courts (usually done by preparing a list of documents)

discredit *verb* to show that a person is not reliable; **the prosecution counsel tried to discredit the defence witnesses**

discrepancy *noun* difference between two sets of figures; **there is a discrepancy between the crime figures released by the Home Office and those of the Metropolitan Police Force**

discretion *noun* being able to decide correctly what should be done; **magistrates have a discretion to allow an accused person to change his election from a summary trial to a jury trial; the judge refused the application, on the ground that he had a judicial discretion to examine inadmissible evidence; to exercise one's discretion** = to decide which of several possible ways to act; **the court exercised its discretion** = the court decided what should be done; **I leave it to your discretion** = I leave it for you to decide what to do; **at the discretion of someone** = if someone decides; **membership is at the discretion of the committee; sentencing is at the discretion of the judge; the granting of an injunction is at the discretion of the court**

◊ **discretionary** *adjective* which can be done if someone wants; **the minister's discretionary powers** = powers which the minister could use if he thought he should do so; **the tribunal has wide discretionary power** = the tribunal can decide on many different courses of action; **discretionary trust** = trust where the trustees decide how to invest the income and when and how much income should be paid to the beneficiaries

discrimination *noun* treating people in different ways because of class, religion, race, language, colour or sex; **sexual discrimination** *or* **sex discrimination** *or* **discrimination on grounds of sex** = treating men and women in different ways

discuss *verb* to talk about a problem; **they spent two hours discussing the details of the contract; the lawyers discussed the possibility of an acquittal**

◊ **discussion** *noun* talking about a problem; **after some discussion the magistrates agreed to an adjournment**

disenfranchise *or* **disfranchise** *verb* to take away someone's right to vote; **the company has tried to disenfranchise the ordinary shareholders**

disguise 1 *noun* change of clothes *or* hair style, etc., which makes someone difficult to recognize; **the spy crossed the border in disguise 2** *verb* to disguise yourself as someone = to change your clothes and appearance so as to look like someone else; **he entered the country disguised as a policeman**

dishonest *adjective* not honest *or* trying to deceive; **the public has been warned to look out for dishonest shopkeepers; he assisted the trustees to commit a dishonest breach of trust**

◇ **dishonestly** *adverb* in a deceiving way; **he was accused of dishonestly acquiring the jewels**

dishonour 1 *verb* to refuse to pay a cheque *or* bill of exchange because there is not enough money in the account to pay it; **the bank dishonoured his cheque** 2 *noun* act of dishonouring a cheque; **the dishonour of the cheque brought her business to a stop; notice of dishonour** = letter *or* document warning a person to pay a cheque or risk being sued

disinherit *verb* to make a will which prevents someone from inheriting; **he was disinherited by his father**

disk *noun* round flat object, used to store information in computers; **floppy disk** = small disk for storing information for a computer; **hard disk** = solid disk which will store a large amount of computer information in a sealed case; **disk drive** = part of a computer which makes a disk turn round in order to read it or store information on it

◇ **diskette** *noun* very small floppy disk

dismiss *verb* **(a) to dismiss an employee** = to remove an employee from a job; **he was dismissed for being late (b)** to refuse to accept; **the court dismissed the appeal** *or* **the application** *or* **the action; the justices dismissed the witness' evidence out of hand**

◇ **dismissal** *noun* removal of an employee from a job; **dismissal procedure** = correct way of dismissing an employee, following the rules in the contract of employment; **constructive dismissal** = situation where an employee leaves his job voluntarily but because of pressure from the management; **unfair dismissal** = removing someone from a job for reasons which are not fair; **wrongful dismissal** = removing someone from a job for a reason which does not justify dismissal and which is in breach of the contract of employment

COMMENT: an employee can complain of unfair dismissal to an industrial tribunal, or of wrongful dismissal to the County Court

disobey *verb* not to obey; **the husband disobeyed the court order to pay maintenance to his children**

◇ **disobedience** *noun* not obeying; **the prisoners were put in solitary confinement as punishment for their disobedience of the governor's orders; civil disobedience** = disobeying orders by civil authorities (such as the police) as an act of protest; **the group planned a campaign of civil disobedience as a protest against restrictions on immigrants** NOTE: no plural

disorder *noun* lack of order *or* of control; **civil disorder** *or* **public disorder** *or* **public disorders** = riots *or* disturbances *or* fighting in the streets; **mental disorder** = sickness of the mind

◇ **disorderly** *adjective* badly behaved *or* wild; **he was charged with disorderly conduct** *or* **with being drunk and disorderly; keeping a disorderly house** = being the proprietor *or* manager of a brothel

dispense *verb* **(a)** to give out (justice) **(b) to dispense with something** = not to use *or* to do without something; **the chairman of the tribunal dispensed with the formality of taking minutes; the accused decided to dispense with the services of a lawyer**

◇ **dispensation** *noun* **(a)** act of giving out justice **(b)** special permission to do something which is normally not allowed or is against the law

display *verb* to show; **all cars must display a valid parking permit**

dispose *verb* **to dispose of** = to get rid of *or* to sell cheaply; **to dispose of excess stock; to dispose of one's business**

◇ **disposable** *adjective* **(a)** which can be used and then thrown away **(b) disposable income** = income left after tax and national insurance have been deducted

◇ **disposal** *noun* sale; **disposal of securities** *or* **of property; lease** *or* **business for disposal** = lease *or* business for sale

◇ **disposition** *noun* act of passing property (land *or* goods) to another person, especially in a will; **to make testamentary dispositions**

dispossess *verb* to deprive someone wrongfully of his possession of land

◇ **dispossession** *noun* act of wrongfully depriving someone of possession of land

dispute 1 *noun* disagreement *or* argument; **industrial disputes** *or* **labour disputes** = arguments between management and workers; **to adjudicate** *or* **to mediate in a dispute** = to try to settle a dispute between other parties 2 *verb* to argue against something; **the defendant disputed the claim** = the defendant argued that the claim was not correct; **she disputed the policeman's version of events** = she said that the policeman's story of what had happened was wrong

disqualify *verb* to make (someone) not able to do something; **being a judge disqualifies you from being a Member of Parliament; after the accident he was fined £1000 and disqualified from driving for two years; he was convicted for driving a motor vehicle while disqualified**

◊ **disqualification** *noun* **(a)** being disqualified from driving a car **(b)** **disqualification from office** = rule which forces a director to be removed from a directorship if he does not fulfil certain conditions

disrepute *noun* bad reputation; **to bring something into disrepute** = to give something a bad reputation; **he was accused of bringing the club into disrepute by his bad behaviour**

disrespect *noun* lack of respect; **he was accused of showing disrespect to the judge**

disseisin *noun* dispossession *or* wrongfully depriving someone of possession of land

dissemination *noun* act of passing information *or* slanderous or libellous statements to other members of the public

dissent 1 *noun* not agreeing; **the opposition showed its dissent by voting against the Bill** 2 *verb* not to agree with someone; **one of the appeal judges dissented; dissenting judgment** = judgment of a judge, showing that he disagrees with other judges in a case which has been heard by several judges

dissolve *verb* to bring to an end; **to dissolve a marriage** *or* **a partnership** *or* **a company; to dissolve Parliament** = to end a session of Parliament, and so force a general election

◊ **dissolution** *noun* ending (of a partnership *or* a marriage); **dissolution of Parliament** = ending of a Parliament, so forcing a general election

distinction *noun* difference between two things; **the judge made no distinction between the parties; I see no distinction between the two claims**

◊ **distinguish** *verb* to state the difference between two things; **to distinguish a case** = to point to differences between a case and a previously decided case so as not to be bound by the precedent NOTE: you distinguish one thing **from** another, or you distinguish **between** two things

distrain *verb* to seize (goods) to pay for debts

◊ **distress** *noun* taking someone's goods to pay for debts; **distress sale** = selling of someone's goods to pay his debts

distribute *verb* to share out *or* to give out (to various people); **the money in the estate is to be distributed among the members of the deceased's family**

◊ **distribution** *noun* sharing out property in an estate; **distribution of assets** = sharing the assets of a company among the shareholders

district *noun* section of a town *or* of a country

◊ **district attorney** *noun* *US* (i) prosecuting attorney in a federal district; (ii) state prosecuting attorney

◊ **district court** *noun* *US* court in a federal district

disturb *verb* **to disturb the peace** = to make a noise which annoys people in the area

◊ **disturbance** *noun* noise *or* movement of people which annoys other people; **street disturbances forced the government to resign; he was accused of making a disturbance in the public library**

divide *verb* **(a)** to cut into separate sections; **England and Wales are divided into six court circuits; the two companies agreed to divide the market between them** **(b)** (*in the House of Commons*) to vote; **the House divided at 10.30**

dividend *noun* payment to shareholders of a proportion of a company's profits;

final dividend = dividend paid at the end of a year; **interim dividend** = dividend paid at the end of a half-year

division *noun* **(a)** main section of something large, especially the separate sections of the High Court (the Queen's Bench Division, the Family Division and the Chancery Division) or the separate sections of the Appeal Court (Civil Division and Criminal Division) **(b)** company which is part of a large group; **Smith's is now a division of the Brown group of companies (c) to have a division of opinion** = to disagree **(d)** vote in the House of Commons; **in the division on the Law and Order Bill, the government had a comfortable majority**
◇ **divisional** *adjective* referring to a division; **divisional court** = one of courts of the High Court; **divisional judge** = judge in a division of the High Court

divorce 1 *noun* legal ending of a marriage; **divorce petition** = official request to a court to end a marriage; **she was granted a divorce on the grounds of unreasonable behaviour by her husband** 2 *verb* to stop being married (to someone); **he divorced his wife and married his secretary**
◇ **Divorce Registry** *noun* court which deals with divorce cases in London

COMMENT: under English law, the only basis of divorce is the irretrievable breakdown of marriage. This is proved by one of five grounds: (a) adultery; (b) unreasonable behaviour; (c) one of the parties has deserted the other for a period of two years; (d) the parties have lived apart for two years and agree to a divorce; (e) the parties have lived apart for five years. In the context of divorce proceedings the court has wide powers to make orders regarding custody and care and control of children, and ancillary relief. Divorce proceedings are normally dealt with by the County Court, or in London at the Divorce Registry. Where divorce proceedings are defended, they are transferred to the High Court, but this is rare and most divorce cases are now conducted by

what is called the "special procedure"

divulge *verb* to tell a secret; **he refused to divulge any information about his bank account; she divulged that she had been with the accused on the evening of the murder**

dock 1 *noun* **(a)** part of a court where an accused prisoner stands; **the prisoner in the dock** = the prisoner who is being tried for a crime; **dock brief** = former system where an accused person could choose a barrister from those present in court to represent him for a small fee **(b)** harbour *or* place where ships can load or unload; **the docks** = part of a town where the harbour is; **dock dues** = money paid by a ship going into or out of a dock, used to keep the dock in good repair 2 *verb* **(a)** to go into dock; **the ship docked at 17.00 (b)** to remove money from someone's wages; **we will have to dock his pay if he is late for work again; he had £20 docked from his pay for being late**

docket *noun* **(a)** list of contents of a package which is being sent **(b)** *US* list of cases for trial

doctrine *noun* general principle of law; *US* **the Monroe Doctrine** = the principle that the USA has an interest in preventing outside interference in the internal affairs of other American states

document *noun* paper with writing on it; **deeds, contracts and wills are all legal documents; list of documents** = list prepared by parties in a civil action giving discovery of documents relevant to the action
◇ **documentary** *adjective* in the form of documents; **documentary evidence; documentary proof**
◇ **documentation** *noun* all documents referring to something; **please send me the complete documentation concerning the sale** NOTE: no plural

doli capax *or* **doli incapax** *Latin phrases meaning* "capable of crime" *or* "incapable of crime"

COMMENT: children under ten years of age are doli incapax and cannot be prosecuted for criminal offences; children aged between 10 and 14 are presumed to be doli incapax but the presumption can be reversed if there is evidence of malice or knowledge

domain *noun* area of responsibility; **public domain** = land *or* property *or* information which belongs to and is available to the public; **work which is in the public domain** = work which is no longer in copyright

Domesday Book *noun* record made for King William I in 1086, which recorded lands in England and their owners and inhabitants for tax purposes

domestic *adjective* (a) referring to a family; **domestic premises** = house *or* flat, etc., used for private accommodation; **domestic proceedings** = court case which involves a man and his wife, or parents and children (b) referring to the market of the country where a business is situated; **domestic consumption** = consumption on the home market; **domestic market** = market in the country where a company is based; **domestic production** = production of goods in the home country

domicile 1 *noun* country where someone is deemed to live permanently *or* where a company's office is registered (especially for tax purposes); **domicile of origin** = domicile which a person has from birth (usually the domicile of the father); **domicile of choice** = country where someone has chosen to live, which is not the domicile of origin 2 *verb* **he is domiciled in Denmark** = he lives in Denmark officially; **bills domiciled in France** = bills of exchange which have to be paid in France

dominant tenement *noun* land which has been granted an easement over another property

COMMENT: the grantor of the easement is the **servient tenement**

donatio mortis causa *Latin phrase meaning* "gift because of death": transfer of property made when death is imminent

◇ **donation** *noun* gift (especially to a charity)

◇ **donee** *noun* person who receives a gift from a donor

◇ **donor** *noun* person who gives property to another

dormant *adjective* not active; **dormant account** = bank account which is not used; **dormant partner** = SLEEPING PARTNER

double 1 *adjective* (a) twice as large *or* two times the size; **double taxation** = taxing the same income twice; **double taxation agreement** *or* **treaty** = agreement between two countries that a person living in one country shall not be taxed in both countries on the income earned in the other country (b) which happens twice; **in double figures** = with two figures *or* 10 to 99; **inflation is in double figures; we have had double-figure inflation for some years; double jeopardy** = right of a citizen not to be tried twice for the same crime 2 *verb* to become twice as big; to make something twice as big

doubt *noun* not being sure that something is correct; **beyond reasonable doubt** *or US* **beyond a reasonable doubt** = proof needed to convict a person in a criminal case

down *adverb & preposition* in a lower position *or* to a lower position; **the crime rate is gradually coming down; the price of petrol has gone down; to pay money down** = to make a deposit

◇ **downgrade** *verb* to reduce the importance of someone *or* of a job; **his job was downgraded in the company reorganization**

dowry *noun* money *or* property brought by a wife to her husband when she marries him

DPP = DIRECTOR OF PUBLIC PROSECUTIONS

draft 1 *noun* (a) order for money to be paid by a bank; **to make a draft on a bank** = to ask a bank to pay money for you; **bank draft** *or* **banker's draft** = cheque payable by a bank; **sight draft** = bill of exchange which is payable when it is presented (b) first rough plan *or* document which has not been finished; **draft of**

a contract *or* draft contract; **he drew up the draft agreement on the back of an envelope; the first draft of the contract was corrected by the managing director; the draft Bill is with the House of Commons lawyers; rough draft** = plan of a document which may have changes made to it before it is complete **2** *verb* to make a first rough plan of a document; **to draft a contract *or* a document *or* a bill; the contract is still being drafted *or* is still in the drafting stage**

◊ **drafter** *noun* person who makes a draft

◊ **drafting** *noun* act of preparing the draft of a document; **the drafting of the contract took six weeks; the drafting stage of a parliamentary Bill**

◊ **draftsman** *noun* person who drafts documents; **costs draftsman** = person who draws up a bill of costs for taxation; **parliamentary draftsman** = lawyer who drafts Bills going before Parliament

draw *verb* **(a)** to take money away; **to draw money out of an account; to draw a salary** = to have a salary paid by a company **(b)** to write a cheque; **to draw a cheque on a bank; he paid the invoice with a cheque drawn on an Egyptian bank**

◊ **drawee** *noun* person *or* bank asked to make a payment by a drawer

◊ **drawer** *noun* person who writes a cheque *or* a bill asking a drawee to pay money to a payee; **the bank returned the cheque to drawer** = the bank could not pay the cheque because the person who wrote his did not have enough money in his account to pay it; *see also* RD

◊ **drawings** *plural noun* money taken out of a partnership by a partner as his salary

◊ **draw up** *verb* to write a legal document; **to draw up a contract *or* an agreement; to draw up a company's articles of association**

drive **1** *noun* **(a)** energetic way of working; **economy drive** = vigorous effort to save money or materials; **the government has launched a drive against tax evaders (b)** part of a machine which makes other parts work; **disk drive** = part of a computer which makes the disk turn round in order to store information on it **2** *verb* **(a)** to make a car *or* lorry, etc. go in a certain direction; **he was driving to work when he heard the news on the car radio; she**

drives a company car; **careless driving *or* driving without due care and attention** = offence of driving in such a way that other people and property may be harmed; **drunken driving** = offence of driving a car when under the influence of alcohol; **reckless driving** = offence of driving a car in a wild way where the driver does not think that he is causing a risk to other people **(b) he drives a hard bargain** = he is a difficult negotiator
NOTE: **driving - drove - driven**

drop **1** *noun* **(a)** fall; **drop in sales; sales show a drop of 10%; a drop in prices (b) drop shipment** = delivery of a large order from the factory direct to a customer's shop or warehouse without going through an agent or wholesaler **2** *verb* **(a)** to fall; **sales have dropped by 10% *or* have dropped 10%; the pound dropped three points against the dollar (b)** to stop a case; **the prosecution dropped all charges against the accused; the plaintiff decided to drop the case against his neighbour**
NOTE: **dropping - dropped**

◊ **drop ship** *verb* to deliver a large order direct to a customer

drug *noun* medicine, especially substances which can be harmful if taken regularly; **dangerous drugs** = drugs which may be harmful to people who take them, and so can be prohibited from import and general sale; **drug addiction** = being mentally and physically dependent on taking a drug regularly; **the Drug Squad** = section of the police force which investigates crime related to drugs; **drug trafficking** = buying and selling drugs illegally

drunk *adjective* incapable because of having drunk too much alcohol; **drunk and disorderly** = incapable and behaving in a wild way because of having drunk too much alcohol

◊ **drunkard** *noun* person who is frequently drunk; *see also* HABITUAL

DSgt = DETECTIVE SERGEANT

dual *adjective* referring to two things; **person of dual nationality *or* person who has dual nationality** = person who is a citizen of two countries

dud *adjective & noun informal* false *or* not good (coin or banknote); **the £50 note was a dud; dud cheque** = cheque which the bank refuses to pay because the person writing it has not enough money in his account to pay it

due *adjective* **(a)** owed; **to fall due** *or* **to become due** = to be ready for payment; **bill due on May 1st** = bill which has to be paid on May 1st; **balance due to us** = amount owed to us which should be paid **(b)** expected to arrive; **the plane is due to arrive at 10.30** *or* **is due at 10.30 (c)** proper *or* as is right; **in due form** = written in the correct legal form; **receipt in due form; contract drawn up in due form; driving without due care and attention** = offence of driving in such a way that other people and property may be harmed; **after due consideration of the problem** = after thinking seriously about the problem; **the due process of the law** = the formal work of a fair legal action **(d) due to** = caused by; **supplies have been delayed due to a strike at the warehouse; the company continues to pay the wages of staff who are absent due to illness**

◊ **dues** *plural noun* **(a) dock dues** *or* **port dues** *or* **harbour dues** = payment which a ship makes to the harbour authorities for the right to use the harbour **(b)** orders taken but not supplied until new stock arrives

duly *adverb* **(a)** properly; **duly authorized representative (b)** as was expected; **we duly received his letter of 21st October**

dungeon *noun* underground prison (often in a castle)

duplicate 1 *noun* copy; **he sent me the duplicate of the contract; duplicate receipt** *or* **duplicate of a receipt** = copy of a receipt; **in duplicate** = with a copy; **receipt in duplicate** = two copies of a receipt; **to print an invoice in duplicate** 2 *verb* **(a)** (*of entry in accounts*) **to duplicate with another entry** = to repeat another entry *or* to be the same as another entry **(b) to duplicate a letter** = to make a copy of a letter

◊ **duplicating** *noun* copying; **duplicating machine** = machine which makes copies of documents; **duplicating paper** = special paper to be used in a duplicating machine

◊ **duplication** *noun* copying of documents; **duplication of work** = work which is done twice without being necessary

◊ **duplicator** *noun* machine which makes copies of documents

duress *noun* force *or* illegal threat to use force on someone to make him do something; **duress provides no defence to a charge of murder; under duress** = being forced to do something; **they alleged they had committed the crime under duress from another defendant; he signed the confession under duress** = he signed the confession because he was threatened
NOTE: no plural

duty *noun* **(a)** work which a person has to do; **it is the duty of every citizen to serve on a jury if called; the government has a duty to protect the citizens from criminals; duty of care** = duty which every citizen has not to act negligently **(b)** official work which you have to do in a job; **to be on duty** = to be doing official work at a special time; **night duty** = work done at night; **PC Smith is on night duty this week; point duty** = work of a policeman *or* traffic warden to direct the traffic at crossroads; **duty sergeant** = police sergeant who is on duty at a particular time; **duty solicitor** = solicitor who is on duty at a magistrates' court and can be contacted at any time by a party who is appearing in that court *or* by a party who has been taken to a police station under arrest *or* for questioning **(c)** tax which has to be paid; **to take the duty off alcohol; to put a duty on cigarettes; ad valorem duty** = duty calculated on the sales value of the goods; **customs duty** *or* **import duty** = tax on goods imported into a country; **excise duty** = tax on the sale of goods (such as alcohol and petrol) which are produced in the country *or* on imports where the duty was not paid on entry into the country; **goods which are liable to duty** = goods on which customs or excise tax has to be paid; **duty-paid goods** = goods where the duty has been paid; **stamp duty** = tax on legal documents (such as the conveyance of a property to a new owner); **estate duty** *or* *US* **death duty** = tax paid on the property left by a dead person

◊ **duty bound** *adjective* bound to do something because it is your duty; **witnesses under oath are duty bound to tell the truth**

◊ **duty-free** *adjective & adverb* sold with no duty to be paid; **he bought a duty-free watch at the airport** *or* **he bought the watch duty-free; duty-free shop** = shop at an airport *or* on a ship where goods can be bought without paying duty

◊ **dutiable** *adjective* **dutiable goods** *or* **dutiable items** = goods on which a customs or excise duty has to be paid

dwelling *noun* place where someone lives (such as a house *or* flat); **the tax on dwellings has been raised**

Ee

E *fifth letter of the alphabet* **Schedule E** = schedule to the Finance Acts under which tax is charged on wages, salaries and pensions; **E list** = list of the names of prisoners who frequently try to escape from prison; **Table E** = model memorandum and articles of association of an unlimited company with share capital set out in the Companies Act

e. & o.e. = ERRORS AND OMISSIONS EXCEPTED

early *adjective & adverb* **(a)** before the usual time; **early closing day** = weekday, usually Wednesday or Thursday, when most shops in a town close in the afternoon; **at your earliest convenience** = as soon as you find it possible; **at an early date** = very soon; **early day motion** = motion proposed in the House of Commons for discussion at an early date (usually used to introduce a particular point of view without necessarily going to a full debate) **(b)** at the beginning of a period of time; **he took an early flight to Paris; we hope for an early resumption of negotiations** = we hope negotiations will start again soon

earmark *verb* to reserve for a special purpose; **to earmark funds for a project; the grant is earmarked for computer systems development**

earn *verb* **(a)** to be paid money for working; **to earn £150 a week; our agent in Paris certainly does not earn his commission; wife's earned income allowance** = tax allowance to be set against money earned by the wife of the main taxpayer **(b)** to produce interest *or* dividends; **what level of dividend do these shares earn? account which earns interest at 10%**

◊ **earnings** *plural noun* money which someone receives for work done; **attachment of earnings** = legal power to take money from a person's salary to pay money which is owed to the courts *or* to a judgment creditor; *see also* GARNISHEE ORDER

earnest *noun* money paid as a down payment to show one's serious intention to proceed with a contract; **he deposited £1,000 with the solicitor as earnest of his intention to purchase**

easement *noun* right which someone has to use land belonging to someone else (such as for a path)

Easter *noun* one of the four sittings of the Law Courts; one of the four law terms

easy *adjective* not difficult; **easy terms** = credit terms which are not difficult to accept *or* instalments which are easy to pay; **the loan is repayable in easy payments** = with very small sums paid back regularly

◊ **easily** *adverb* **(a)** without any difficulty; **the motion was passed by the Commons easily (b)** much *or* a lot; **he is easily the most important international criminal to have been arrested this year; the firm is easily the biggest in the market; this is easily the largest consignment of drugs we have seized**

EC = EUROPEAN COMMUNITY

ecclesiastical *adjective* referring to the church; **ecclesiastical court** = court which hears matters referring to the church

economy *noun* **(a)** being careful not to waste money *or* materials; **an economy measure** = action to try to save money *or* materials; **economies of scale** = making a product more cheaply by producing it *or* buying it in large quantities **(b)** financial state of a country *or* the way in which a country makes and uses its money; **black economy** = work which is paid for in cash *or* goods but not declared to the tax authorities; **free market economy** = system where the government does not interfere in business activity in any way

◊ **economic** *adjective* referring to economy; **economic sanctions** = restrictions on trade with a country in order to influence its political situation *or* in order to make its government change its policy

edict *noun* public announcement of a law

editor *noun* (i) person in charge of a newspaper or a section of a newspaper; (ii) person who is responsible for a reference book; (iii) person who checks the work of a writer; **the city editor** = business *or* finance editor of a British newspaper

◊ **editorial** 1 *adjective* referring to an editor; **editorial board** = group of editors (on a newspaper, etc.) 2 *noun* main article in a newspaper, written by the editor

EEC = EUROPEAN ECONOMIC COMMUNITY **EEC ministers met today in Brussels; the USA is increasing its trade with the EEC**

effect 1 *noun* (a) result; **terms of a contract which take effect** *or* **come into effect from January 1st** = terms which start to operate on January 1st; **prices are increased 10% with effect from January 1st** = new prices will apply from January 1st; **to remain in effect** = to continue to be applied (b) meaning; **clause to the effect that** = clause which means that; **we have made provision to this effect** = we have put into the contract terms which will make this work (c) **personal effects** = personal belongings 2 *verb* to carry out; **to effect a payment** = to make a payment; **to effect customs clearance** = to clear something through customs; **to effect a settlement between two parties** = to bring two parties together and make them agree to a settlement

◊ **effective** *adjective* which works well *or* which gives the correct result; **the police are trying to find an effective means of dealing with young offenders; effective date** = date on which a rule *or* a contract starts to be applied; **clause effective as from January 1st** = clause which starts to be applied on January 1st

efficient *adjective* working well; **an efficient secretary; the efficient policing of city centres**

◊ **efficiently** *adverb* which works well; **the police coped efficiently with the crowds of protesters**

e.g. = for example *or* such as; **the contract is valid in some countries (e.g. France and Belgium) but not in others**

EGM = EXTRAORDINARY GENERAL MEETING

eject *verb* to make (someone) leave a property which he is occupying illegally

◊ **ejection** *noun* action of making someone leave a property which he is occupying illegally

◊ **ejectment** *noun* **action of ejectment** = court action to force someone to leave a property which he is occupying illegally

COMMENT: ejection of someone who is legally occupying a property is an **ouster**

ejusdem generis *or* **eiusdem generis** *Latin phrase meaning* "of the same kind": a rule of legal interpretation, that when a word or phrase follows two or more other words or phrases, it is construed to be of the same type as the words or phrases which precede it

COMMENT: in the phrase **houses, flats and other buildings** other buildings can mean only other dwellings, and would not include, for example, a church

elapse *verb* (*of time*) to pass; **six weeks elapsed before the court order was put into effect; we must allow sufficient time to elapse before making a complaint**

elect *verb* (a) to choose someone by a vote; **to elect the officers of an association; she was elected president** (b) to choose to do something; **he elected to stand trial by jury**

◊ **-elect** *suffix* person who has been elected but has not yet started the term of office; **she is the president-elect**
NOTE: the plural is **presidents-elect**

◊ **election** *noun* (a) act of electing; **general election** = choosing of a Parliament by all the voters in a country (b) act of choosing; **his election as president of the society; the accused made his election for jury trial;** *see also* BY-ELECTION

◊ **elector** *noun* person who votes *or* is eligible to vote in an election; **register of electors** = official list of names and addresses of people living in a certain area who are eligible to vote in local or national elections

◇ **electoral** *adjective* referring to an election; **electoral roll** = REGISTER OF ELECTORS; **electoral college** = group of people elected by a larger group to vote on their behalf in an election

COMMENT: the President of the USA is elected by an electoral college made up of people elected by the states of the USA

◇ **electorate** *noun* all electors taken as a group

electric chair *noun* chair attached to a powerful electric current, used in some states of the USA for executing criminals

eleemosynary *adjective* referring to charity

element *noun* basic part; **the elements of a settlement**

eligible *adjective* person who can be chosen; **she is eligible for re-election**

◇ **eligibility** *noun* being eligible; **the chairman questioned her eligibility to stand for re-election**

embargo **1** *noun* government order which stops a type of trade; **to lay** *or* **put an embargo on trade with a country** = to say that trade with a country must not take place; **to lift an embargo** = to allow trade to start again; **to be under an embargo** = to be forbidden (NOTE: plural is **embargoes**) **2** *verb* to stop trade *or* not to allow trade; **the government has embargoed trade with the Eastern countries**

embark *verb* **(a)** to go on a ship; **the passengers embarked at Southampton (b) to embark on** = to start; **the company has embarked on a development programme**

◇ **embarkation** *noun* going on to a ship or plane; **port of embarkation** = port at which you get on to a ship; **embarkation card** = card given to passengers getting on to a plane or ship

embezzle *verb* to use illegally *or* steal money which is not yours, or which you are looking after for someone; **he was sent to prison for six months for embezzling his clients' money**

◇ **embezzlement** *noun* act of embezzling; **he was sent to prison for six months for embezzlement**
NOTE: no plural

◇ **embezzler** *noun* person who embezzles

emblements *plural noun* vegetable products which come from farming

embracery *noun* offence of corruptly seeking to influence jurors

emergency *noun* dangerous situation where decisions have to be taken quickly; **the government declared a state of emergency** = the government decided that the situation was so dangerous that the police *or* army had to run the country; **to take emergency measures** = to take action rapidly to stop a serious state of affairs developing; **emergency powers** = special powers granted by law to a minister to deal with an emergency; **emergency reserves** = ready cash held in case it is needed suddenly

emigrate *verb* to go to another country to live permanently

◇ **emigration** *noun* leaving a country to go to live permanently in another country

◇ **emigrant** *noun* person who emigrates

empanel *verb* **to empanel a jury** = to choose and swear in jurors
NOTE: **empanelling - empanelled**

employ *verb* to give someone regular paid work; **to employ twenty staff** = to have twenty people working for you; **to employ twenty new staff** = to give work to twenty people who did not work for you before

◇ **employed 1** *adjective* **(a)** in regular paid work; **he is not gainfully employed** = he has no regular paid work; **self-employed** = working for yourself; **he worked in a bank for ten years but now is self-employed (b)** (money) used profitably; **return against capital employed 2** *plural noun* people who are working; **the employers and the employed; the self-employed** = people who work for themselves

◇ **employee** *noun* worker *or* person employed by someone; **employees of the firm are eligible to join a profit-sharing scheme; relations between management and employees have improved; the company has decided to take on new employees**

◊ **employer** *noun* person *or* company which has employees and pays them; **employers' organization** *or* **association** = group of employers with similar interests; **employer's contribution** = money paid by an employer towards an employee's pension

◊ **employment** *noun* contractual relationship between an employer and his employees; **conditions of employment** = terms of a contract whereby someone is employed; **contract of employment** *or* **employment contract** = contract between an employer and an employee showing all the conditions of work; **security of employment** = feeling by a worker that he has the right to keep his job until he retires; **employment office** *or* **bureau** *or* **agency** = office which finds jobs for people; **Employment Appeal Tribunal** = court which hears appeals from industrial tribunals

empower *verb* to give someone the power to do something; **the agent is empowered to sell the property; she was empowered by the company to sign the contract; a constable is empowered to arrest a person whom he suspects of having committed an offence**

emptor *see* CAVEAT

enable *verb* to make it possible for something to happen; **enabling legislation** *or* **statute** = Act of Parliament which gives a minister the power to put other legislation into effect

enact *verb* to make (a law)

◊ **enactment** *noun* (i) making a law; (ii) an Act of Parliament

enclose *verb* to put something inside an envelope with a letter; **to enclose an invoice with a letter; I am enclosing a copy of the contract; a letter enclosing two cheques; please find the cheque enclosed herewith**

◊ **enclosure** *noun* document enclosed with a letter

encourage *verb* to help someone to do something *or* to help something to happen; **the probation service encourages ex-offenders to settle in new jobs; leaving windows open only encourages burglars; some people believe that lenient sentences encourage crime**

encroachment *noun* illegally taking over someone's property little by little

encumbrance *noun* liability (such as a mortgage *or* charge) which is attached usually to a property or land

endanger *verb* to put someone in danger of being killed *or* hurt; **endangering railway passengers** *or* **endangering life at sea** *or* **criminal damage endangering life** = notifiable offences where human life is put at risk

endorse *verb* (a) to agree with; **the court endorsed counsel's view** (b) to endorse a bill *or* a cheque = to sign a bill *or* a cheque on the back to make it payable to someone else (c) to make a note on a driving licence that the holder has been convicted of a traffic offence (d) to write a summary of the contents of a legal document on the outside of the folded document

◊ **endorsee** *noun* person in whose favour a bill *or* a cheque is endorsed

◊ **endorsement** *noun* (a) act of endorsing; signature on a document which endorses it; summary of a legal document noted on the outside of the folded document (b) note on an insurance policy which adds conditions to the policy (c) note on a driving licence to show that the holder has been convicted of a traffic offence

◊ **endorser** *noun* person who endorses a bill *or* cheque

endowment *noun* giving money to provide a regular income; **endowment assurance** *or* **endowment policy** = assurance policy where a sum of money is paid to the insured person on a certain date, or to his heirs if he dies; **endowment mortgage** = mortgage backed by an endowment policy

enforce *verb* to make sure something is done *or* is obeyed; **to enforce the terms of a contract; to enforce a debt** = to make sure a debt is paid

◊ **enforceable** *adjective* which can be enforced

◊ **enforcement** *noun* making sure that something is obeyed; **enforcement of the terms of a contract; law enforcement** = making sure that a law is obeyed; **law**

enforcement officers = members of the police force, the Drug Squad, etc.
NOTE: no plural

enfranchise *verb* to give (someone) the right to vote

◇ **enfranchisement** *noun* action of giving someone a vote; **leasehold enfranchisement** = right of a leaseholder to buy the freehold of the property which he is leasing

engage *verb* **(a)** to engage someone to do something = to bind someone contractually to do something; **the contract engages the company to purchase minimum annual quantities of goods (b)** to employ; **we have engaged the best commercial lawyer to represent us (c) to be engaged in** = to be busy with; **he is engaged in work on computers; the company is engaged in trade with Africa**

◇ **engaged** *adjective* busy (telephone); **you cannot speak to the manager - his line is engaged**

◇ **engagement** *noun* **(a)** agreement to do something; **to break an engagement to do something** = not to do what you have legally agreed to do **(b) engagements** = arrangements to meet people; **I have no engagements for the rest of the day; she noted the appointment in her engagements diary**

engross *verb* to draw up a legal document in its final form ready for signature; *US* **engrossed Bill** = Bill which has been passed by both House and Senate, and is written out in its final form with all amendments for the President's signature

◇ **engrossment** *noun* (i) drawing up of a legal document in its final form; (ii) legal document in its final form; **engrossment paper** = thick heavy paper on which court documents are engrossed

enjoyment *noun* **quiet enjoyment of land** = right of an occupier to occupy a property under a tenancy without anyone interfering with that right

enquire = INQUIRE

◇ **enquiry** = INQUIRY

ensuing *adjective* which follows; **in the ensuing argument, the defendant hit the plaintiff with a bottle**

entail 1 *noun* interest in land where the land is given to another person and the heirs of his body, but reverts to the donor when the donee and his heirs have all died **2** *verb* to involve; **itemizing the sales figures will entail about ten days' work**

enter *verb* **(a)** to go in; **they all stood up when the judges entered the courtroom; the company has spent millions trying to enter the do-it-yourself market (b)** to write; **to enter a name on a list; the clerk entered the objection in the records; the defendant entered defence of justification; to enter appearance** = to register with a court that a defendant intends to defend an action; **to enter a bid for something** = to offer (usually in writing) to buy something; **to enter a caveat** = to warn legally that you have an interest in a case or a grant of probate, and that no steps can be taken without notice to you; **to enter judgment for someone** = to make a legal judgment on someone's behalf; **judgment was entered for the plaintiff; the plaintiff entered judgment** = the plaintiff took judgment (usually because the defendant failed to defend an action) **(c) to enter into** = (i) to begin to do something; (ii) to agree to do something; **to enter into relations with someone; to enter into negotiations with a foreign government; to enter into a partnership with a friend; to enter into an agreement** *or* **a contract**

◇ **entering** *noun* act of writing items in a record

enterprise *noun* **(a)** system of carrying on a business; **free enterprise** = system of business free from government interference; **enterprise zone** = area of a country, where the government offers special subsidies to firms to encourage them to set up businesses **(b)** business which is carried on; **she runs a mail order enterprise**

entertain *verb* **(a)** to offer meals *or* hotel accommodation *or* theatre tickets, etc. to business visitors **(b)** to be ready to consider a proposal; **the judge will not entertain any proposal from the prosecution to delay the start of the hearing**

entice *verb* to try to persuade someone to do something (by offering money); **they tried to entice the managers to join the new company**

◊ **enticement** *noun* trying to persuade someone to do something (especially trying to persuade a worker to leave his job *or* a wife to leave her husband)

entitle *verb* to give (someone) the right to something; **he is entitled to four weeks' holiday** = he has the right to take four weeks' holiday

◊ **entitlement** *noun* right *or* thing to which you are entitled; **holiday entitlement** = number of days' paid holiday which a worker has the right to take; **pension entitlement** = amount of pension which someone has the right to receive when he retires

entity *noun* thing which exists in law; **his private company is a separate entity**

entrust *verb* to entrust someone with something *or* to entrust something to someone = to give someone the responsibility for looking after something

entry *noun* **(a)** act of going into a building *or* onto land; **there is no right of entry through this door (b)** written information entered in a record; **the sergeant copied the entries into the report (b) entry of appearance** = lodging by the defendant of a document in court to confirm his intention to defend an action; **entry of judgment** = recording the judgment of a court in the official records

equal 1 *adjective* exactly the same; **male and female workers have equal pay; Equal Opportunities Commission** = official committee set up to make sure that men and women have equal chances of employment and to remove discrimination between the sexes; **equal opportunities programme** = programme to avoid discrimination in employment (NOTE: in US English this is **affirmative action program**) **2** *verb* to be the same as; **production this month has equalled our best month ever** NOTE: **equalling - equalled** but US English is **equaling - equaled**

◊ **equalize** *verb* to make equal; **to equalize dividends**

◊ **equalization** *noun* *GB* **Exchange Equalization Account** = account with the Bank of England used by the government when buying or selling foreign currency to influence the exchange rate for the pound

◊ **equally** *adverb* in the same way; **costs will be shared equally between the two parties**

equitable *adjective* fair and just *or* referring to equity; **equitable jurisdiction** = power of a court to enforce a person's rights; **equitable lien** = right of someone to hold property (which legally he does not own) until the owner pays money due; **equitable mortgage** = mortgage which does not give the mortgagee a legal estate in the land mortgaged

equity *noun* **(a)** fair system of laws *or* system of British law which developed in parallel with the common law to make the common law fairer, summarized in the maxim "equity does not suffer a wrong to be without a remedy"; **equity of redemption** = right of a mortgagor to redeem the estate by paying off the principal and interest **(b)** right to receive dividends as part of the profit of a company in which you own shares **(c)** shareholders' equity *or* equity capital = amount of a company's capital which is owned by shareholders
NOTE: no plural

◊ **equities** *plural noun* ordinary shares

equivalence *noun* being equivalent

◊ **equivalent** *adjective* to be equivalent to = to have the same value as *or* to be the same as; **the total dividend paid is equivalent to one quarter of the total profits**

equivocal *adjective* not certain *or* ambiguous; **the court took the view that the defendant's plea was equivocal**

error *noun* mistake; **he made an error in calculating the total; the secretary must have made a typing error; clerical error** = mistake made in an office; **computer error** = mistake made by a computer; **errors and omissions excepted (e. & o.e.)** = words written on an invoice to show that the company has no responsibility for mistakes in the invoice

escalate *verb* to increase at a constant rate

◊ **escalation** *noun* **escalation of prices** = constant increase in prices; **escalation clause** = ESCALATOR CLAUSE

◊ **escalator clause** *noun* clause in a contract allowing for regular price increases because of increased costs

escape 1 *noun* getting away from a difficult situation; **escape clause** = clause in a contract which allows one of the parties to avoid carrying out the terms of the contract under certain conditions 2 *verb* to get away from (a prison); **three prisoners escaped by climbing over the wall**

escrow *noun* deed which the parties to it deliver to an independent person who hands it over only when certain conditions have been fulfilled; **in escrow** = held in safe keeping by a third party; **document held in escrow** = document given to a third party to keep and to pass on to someone when, for example, money has been paid; *US* **escrow account** = account where money is held in escrow until a contract is signed *or* until goods are delivered, etc. NOTE: no plural

espionage *noun* spying; **industrial espionage** = trying to find out the secrets of a competitor's work or products, usually by illegal means NOTE: no plural

esquire *noun* (a) *GB* title written after the name of a man, in an address; **letter addressed to J. Smith, Esq.** NOTE: you can use **Mr** before a name, or **Esq.** after it; both are titles, but **Esq.** is more formal and suggests that the man is more important. **Esq.** is used by lawyers, bank managers, etc., when writing to clients (b) *US* title given to an American lawyer

essential *adjective* very important; **it is essential that all the facts of the case should be presented as clearly as possible; mens rea is one of the essential elements of a crime**

establish *verb* (a) to set up *or* to make *or* to open; **the company has established a branch in Australia; the business was established in Scotland in 1823; established post** = permanent post in the civil service or similar organization; **to establish oneself in business** = to become successful in a new business (b) to decide what is correct *or* what is fact; **the police are trying to establish his movements on the night of the murder; it is an established fact that the car could not have been used because it was out of petrol**

◊ **establishment** *noun* (a) commercial business; **he runs an important printing establishment (b)** (*in the EEC*) **right of establishment** = right of an EEC citizen to live and work in any EEC country (c) number of people working in a company; **establishment charges** = cost of people and property, in a company's accounts; **to be on the establishment** = to be a full-time employee; **office with an establishment of fifteen** = office with a permanent staff of fifteen

estate *noun* (a) interest in *or* right to hold and occupy land (b) **real estate** = property (land *or* buildings); **estate agency** = office which arranges for the sale of property; **estate agent** = person in charge of an estate agency (c) **industrial estate** *or* **trading estate** = area of land near a town specially for factories and warehouses (d) property left by a dead person; **his estate was valued at £100,000** *or* **he left estate valued at £100,000; estate duty** *or* *US* **estate tax** = tax on property left by a person now dead

estimate 1 *noun* (a) calculation of probable cost *or* size *or* time of something; **rough estimate** = very approximate calculation; **at a conservative estimate** = calculation which probably underestimates the final figure; **the crime rate has risen by at least 20% in the last year, and that is a conservative estimate; these figures are only an estimate** = these are not the final accurate figures; **estimates of expenditure** = calculation of future expenditure prepared for each government department by the minister (b) calculation of how much something is likely to cost in the future, given to a client so as to get him to make an order; **before we can give the grant we must have an estimate of the total costs involved; to ask a builder for an estimate for building the warehouse; to put in an estimate** = to give someone a written calculation of the probable costs of carrying out a job 2 *verb* (a) to calculate the probable cost *or* size *or* time of something; **to estimate that it will cost £1m** *or* **to estimate costs at £1m** (b) **to estimate for a job** = to state in writing the future costs of carrying out a piece of work so that a client can make an order

◊ **estimation** *noun* judgment; **in my estimation, he is the best commercial lawyer in town**

◊ **estimator** *noun* person whose job is to calculate estimates for the carrying out of work

estoppel *noun* rule of evidence whereby someone is prevented from denying *or* asserting a fact in legal proceedings; **estoppel of** *or* **by record** = rule that a person cannot reopen a matter which has already been decided by a court; **estoppel by deed** = rule that a person cannot deny having done something which is recorded in a deed; **estoppel by conduct** *or* **in pais** = rule that no one can deny things which he has done *or* failed to do which have had an effect on other persons' actions if that person has acted in a way which relied on the others' behaviour; *see also* PROMISSORY

estovers *plural noun* wood and timber taken from land

estreat *verb* to get a copy of a record of bail or a fine awarded by a court; **estreated recognizance** = recognizance which is forfeited because the person making it has not come to court

et al. *or* **et alia** *Latin phrase meaning* "and others" *or* "and other things"

etc. *or* **etcetera** and so on; **the import duty is to be paid on expensive items including cars, watches, etc.**

etiquette *noun* rules governing the way people should behave, such as the way in which a solicitor *or* barrister behaves towards clients in court

et seq. *or* **et sequenter** *Latin phrase meaning* "and the following"

Euro- *prefix* referring to Europe or the European Community

◊ **European** *adjective* referring to Europe; **the European (Economic) Community** = the Common Market; **European Community Law** = law created by the European Community and enforceable in EC states; **European Court of Justice** = court responsible for settling disputes relating to European Community Law; **European Court of Human Rights** = court considering the rights of citizens of states which are parties to the European Convention for the Protection of Human Rights; **the European Monetary System** = system of controlled exchange rates between some member countries of the Common Market; **the European Parliament** = parliament of delegates elected in each member country of the EEC

euthanasia *noun* mercy killing *or* killing of a sick person to put an end to his suffering
NOTE: no plural

evade *verb* to try to avoid something; **to evade tax** = to try illegally to avoid paying tax

evaluate *verb* to calculate a value; **to evaluate costs**

◊ **evaluation** *noun* calculation of value; **job evaluation** = examining different jobs within a company to see what skills and qualifications are needed to carry them out with a view to establishing appropriate salaries

evasion *noun* avoiding; **tax evasion** = illegally trying not to pay tax; *see also* AVOIDANCE

◊ **evasive** *adjective* which tries to avoid; **to give evasive answers** = to try to avoid answering questions directly

event *noun* thing which has happened; **the police are trying to piece together the events of the previous evening; the newspaper reports covered the events following the football match; in the event of** *or* **in the event that** = if something should happen; **in the event of a disagreement** *or* **in the event that the parties fail to agree, the case will be submitted to arbitration**

evict *verb* to force (someone) to leave a property; **all the tenants were evicted by the new landlords**

◊ **eviction** *noun* forcing someone to leave a property

evidence **1** *noun* written or spoken statement of facts which helps to prove something at a trial; **all the evidence points to arson; circumstantial evidence** = evidence which suggests that something must have happened, but does not give firm proof of it; **direct evidence** = first-hand evidence, such as the testimony of an eye witness *or* the production of original documents; **documentary evidence** = evidence in the form of documents; **the**

secretary gave evidence against her former employer = the secretary was a witness, and her statement suggested that her former employer was guilty; **to plant evidence** = to put items at the scene of a crime after the crime has taken place, so that a person is incriminated and can be arrested; **rule of evidence** = rule established by law which determines the type of evidence which a court will consider and how such evidence must be given; **to turn Queen's evidence** *or* *US* **to turn state's evidence** = to confess to a crime and then act as witness against the other criminals involved, in the hope of getting a lighter sentence (NOTE: no plural; to refer to a single item say **a piece of evidence**) **2** *verb* to show; **the lack of good will, as evidenced by the defendant's behaviour in the witness stand**

ex *preposition & prefix* **(a)** out of *or* from; **price ex warehouse** = price for a product which is to be collected from the factory or from an agent's warehouse and so does not include delivery; **price ex works** *or* **ex factory** = price not including transport from the maker's factory **(b) share quoted ex dividend** = share price not including the right to receive the next dividend **(c)** former *or* formerly; **Mr Smith, the ex-chairman of the company; she claimed maintenance from her ex-husband (d) ex-directory number** = telephone number which is not printed in the list of people having telephone numbers

examine *verb* to look at someone *or* something very carefully to see if it can be accepted; **the customs officials asked to examine the inside of the car; the police are examining the papers from the managing director's safe; examining justice** *or* **magistrate** = magistrate who hears a case when it is presented for the first time, and decides if there should be a prosecution

◇ **examination** *noun* **(a)** asking someone questions to find out facts, such as the questioning of a prisoner by a magistrate **(b) examination in chief** *or* *US* **direct examination** = asking a witness questions (by counsel for his side) to give oral evidence in court **(c)** looking at something very carefully to see if it is acceptable; **customs examination** = looking at goods *or* baggage by customs officials **(d)** test to see if someone has

passed a course; **he passed his law examinations; she came first in the final examination for the course; he failed his examination and so had to leave his job;** *see also* CROSS-EXAMINE, CROSS-EXAMINATION

◇ **examiner** *noun* person who conducts a test

example *noun* **(a)** thing chosen to show something; **these sentences are a good example of the harshness of the military tribunals; new laws on computer copying provide an example of how the law changes to keep in step with new inventions; for example (e.g.)** = to show one thing out of many; **the government took steps to control drugs, and, for example, increased the numbers of policemen in the Drug Squad (b)** thing which shows how something ought to be; **to set an example to someone** = to show someone how to behave; **the police ought to set an example to the community; the rioters were sentenced to periods of imprisonment as an example to others; to make an example of someone** = to punish someone harshly so that others will be warned not to do the same

exceed *verb* to be more than; **to exceed one's powers** = to act in a way which one is not legally entitled to do; **the judge exceeded his powers in criticizing the court of appeal; he was arrested for exceeding the speed limit** = he was arrested for driving faster than was permitted; **he has exceeded his credit limit** = he has borrowed more money than he is allowed to do

excellent *adjective* very good; **the accused is a person of excellent character**

except *preposition & conjunction* not including; **VAT is levied on all goods and services except books, newspapers and children's clothes; sales are rising in all markets except the Far East; the rule applies in all cases, except where otherwise stated**

◇ **excepted** *adverb* not including; **errors and omissions excepted** = note on an invoice to show that the company has no responsibility for mistakes in the invoice; **excepted persons** = types of workers listed in an insurance policy as not being covered by the insurance

◇ **exception** *noun* **(a)** thing which is not included with others; **all the accused were acquitted with the exception of Jones** who was sent to prison for three months **(b)** objection raised to the ruling of a judge; **to take exception to something** = to object to something *or* to protest against something; **counsel for the defence took exception to the witness' remarks; he has taken exception to the reports of the trial in the newspapers**

◊ **exceptional** *adjective* not usual *or* different; **exceptional items** = items in a balance sheet which do not appear there each year; **exceptional needs payment** = payment made by the social services to a claimant who has a particular urgent need (such as for clothes)

excess *noun* **(a)** amount which is more than what is allowed; **excess alcohol in the blood** = more alcohol in the blood than a driver is permitted to have; **excess fare** = extra fare to be paid (such as for travelling first class with a second class ticket); **excess of jurisdiction** = case where a judge or magistrate has exceeded his powers; **excess profits** = profits which are more than is considered to be normal; **in excess = above *or* more than; quantities in excess of twenty-five kilos (b)** amount to be paid by the insured as part of any claim made under the terms of an insurance policy; **he has to pay a £50 excess, and the damage amounted to over £1,000**

◊ **excessive** *adjective* too large; **we found the bill for costs excessive and applied to have it reduced; the driver had an excessive amount of alcohol in his blood**

exchange 1 *noun* **(a)** giving of one thing for another; **part exchange** = giving an old product as part of the payment for a new one; **exchange of contracts** = point in the conveyance of a property when the solicitors for the buyer and the seller hand over the contract which then becomes binding **(b) foreign exchange** = (i) exchanging the money of one country for that of another; (ii) money of another country; **foreign exchange broker** = person who buys and sells foreign currency on behalf of other people; **foreign exchange market** = dealings in foreign currencies; **rate of exchange** *or* **exchange rate** = price at which one currency is exchanged for another; **exchange controls** = government instructions on changing the local currency for foreign currency; **the government had to impose exchange controls to stop the rush to buy dollars;** *GB* **Exchange Equalization Account** = account with the Bank

of England used by the government when buying or selling foreign currency to influence the exchange rate for the pound **(c) bill of exchange** = document ordering the person to whom it is directed to pay a person money on demand *or* at a certain date **(d) Stock Exchange** = place where stocks and shares are bought and sold; **commodity exchange** = place where commodities are bought and sold 2 *verb* **(a) to exchange an article for another** = to give one thing in place of something else **(b) to exchange contracts** = to hand over a contract when buying or selling a property (done by both buyer and seller at the same time) **(c)** to change money of one country for money of another

◊ **exchangeable** *adjective* which can be exchanged

◊ **exchanger** *noun* person who buys and sells foreign currency

Exchequer *see* CHANCELLOR

excise 1 *noun* **(a) excise duty** *or* **tax** = tax on certain goods produced in a country (such as alcohol) **(b) Customs and Excise** *or* **Excise Department** = government department which deals with VAT and with taxes on imports and on products, such as alcohol, produced in the country 2 *verb* to cut out; **the chairman ordered the remarks to be excised from the official record**

◊ **exciseman** *noun* person who works in the Excise Department

exclude *verb* to keep out *or* not to include

◊ **excluding** *preposition* not including; **the regulations apply to members of the public, excluding those serving in the emergency services; not excluding** = including; **government servants, not excluding judges, are covered by the Bill**

◊ **exclusion** *noun* not including; **exclusion clause** = clause in a contract which limits the liability of a party, for example a clause in an insurance policy which says which items are not covered; **to the exclusion of** = not including *or* without including; **exclusion order** = court order in matrimonial proceedings which stops a wife *or* husband from going into the matrimonial home; **exc. ion zone** = area (usually an area of sea) near a country, which is forbidden to military forces of other countr...

◊ **exclusive** *adjective* **(a) exclusive agreement** = agreement where a person *or* firm is made sole agent for a product in a market; **exclusive licence** = licence where the licensee is the only person to be able to enjoy the licence; **exclusive right to market a product** = right to be the only person to market the product **(b) exclusive of** = not including

◊ **exclusivity** *noun* exclusive right to market a product

excuse 1 *noun* reason for doing something wrong *or* for omitting to do something; **what was his excuse for arriving late in court? the judge refused to accept the defendant's excuse**; *see also* IGNORANCE **2** *verb* **(a)** to forgive a small mistake **(b)** to allow someone not to do something; **he was excused jury service because he was deaf**

execute *verb* **(a)** to carry out (an order); to carry out (the terms of a contract); **executed consideration** = consideration where one party has made a promise in exchange for which the other party has done something for him **(b)** to kill someone who has been sentenced to death by a court; **he was executed by firing squad**

◊ **execution** *noun* **(a)** carrying out of a court order *or* of the terms of a contract; **stay of execution** = temporary stopping of a legal order; **the court granted the company a two-week stay of execution; warrant of execution** = warrant issued by a court which gives the bailiffs *or* sheriffs the power to seize goods from a debtor in order to pay his debts **(b)** killing of someone who has been sentenced to death by a court

◊ **executioner** *noun* person who executes people who have been sentenced to death

◊ **executive 1** *adjective* **(a)** which puts decisions into action; **executive committee** = committee which runs a society *or* a club; **executive director** = director who works full-time in the company; **executive powers** = right to put decisions into actions **(b)** *US* **executive order** = order by the president of the USA *or* of a state governor **2** *noun* **(a)** person in a business who takes decisions *or* manager *or* director; **chief executive** = executive director in charge of a company; **legal executive** = clerk in a solicitor's office who is not a solicitor and is not articled to become one,

but has passed the examinations of the Institute of Legal Executives **(b) the Executive** = (i) section of a government which puts into effect the laws passed by Parliament; (ii) *US* the president

executor *noun* someone who is appointed by a person making his will who will see that the terms of the will are carried out; **he was named executor of his brother's will**

◊ **executory** *adjective* which is still being carried out; **executory consideration** = consideration where one party makes a promise in exchange for a counter-promise from the other party

◊ **executrix** *noun* female executor

exemplary *adjective* which is so good that it serves as an example to others; **her conduct in the case was exemplary; exemplary damages** = damages which punish the defendant for loss or harm caused to the plaintiff *or* heavy damages which show that a court feels that the defendant has behaved badly towards the plaintiff; **exemplary sentence** = particularly harsh sentence which aims at deterring others from committing the same type of crime

exempt 1 *adjective* not covered by a law; not forced to obey a law; **exempt from tax** *or* **tax-exempt** = not required to pay tax; **exempt supplies** = sales of goods or services which are exempt from VAT **2** *verb* to free something from having tax paid on it or from having to pay tax; **non profit-making organizations are exempt(ed) from tax; food is exempt(ed) from sales tax; the government exempted trusts from tax**

◊ **exemption** *noun* act of exempting something from a contract *or* from a tax; **exemption clause** = clause in a contract exempting a party from certain liabilities; **exemption from tax** *or* **tax exemption** = being free from having to pay tax; **as a non profit-making organization you can claim tax exemption**

exercise 1 *noun* use (of a power); **a court can give directions to a local authority as to the exercise of its powers in relation to children in care; exercise of an option** = using an option *or* putting an option into action **2** *verb* to use *or* to put into practice; **to exercise one's discretion** = to decide which of several courses to take; **the magistrates exercised their discretion and**

let the accused off with a suspended sentence; **to exercise an option** = to put an option into action; **he exercised his option to acquire sole marketing rights for the product; not many shareholders exercised their option to buy the new issue of shares**

ex gratia *Latin phrase meaning* "as a favour"; **an ex gratia payment** = payment made as a gift, with no obligations

exhaust *verb* to wear out *or* to use up; **the appellant has exhausted all channels of appeal; the company has exhausted all its development budget**

exhibit *noun* object (such as a gun *or* coat *or* document) which is shown as evidence to a court

exile 1 *noun* **(a)** being sent to live in another country as a punishment; **the ten members of the opposition party were sent into exile** (NOTE: no plural) **(b)** person who has been sent to live in another country as a punishment **2** *verb* to send someone to live in another country as a punishment; **he was exiled for life; she was exiled to an island in the North Sea**

exist *verb* to be; **the right of way has existed since the early nineteenth century**

◊ **existence** *noun* being; **to come into existence** = to start to be; **the custom came into existence during the eighteenth century; immemorial existence** = before 1189, the date from which events are supposed to be remembered

ex officio *Latin phrase meaning* "because of an office held"; **the treasurer is ex officio a member *or* an ex officio member of the finance committee**

exonerate *verb* to say that someone who has been blamed, should not be blamed; **the judge exonerated the driver from all responsibility for the accident**

◊ **exoneration** *noun* act of exonerating

ex parte *Latin phrase meaning* "on behalf of"; **an ex parte application** = application made to a court where only one side is represented and no notice is given to the other side (often where the application is for an injunction); **the wife applied ex parte for an ouster order against her husband;** *see also* INTER PARTES

NOTE: in legal reports, abbreviated to **ex p** as in: *Williams* v. *Smith, ex p White* showing that White was the party which applied for the hearing to take place

expatriate 1 *noun* person who lives abroad; **there is a large expatriate community *or* a large community of expatriates in Geneva 2** *verb* to force someone to leave the country where he is living

◊ **expatriation** *noun* forcing someone to leave the country where he is living

expect *verb* to hope that something is going to happen; **we are expecting him to arrive at 10.45; they are expecting a cheque from their agent next week; the house was sold for more than the expected price**

◊ **expectancy** *or* **expectation** *noun* hope that you will succeed to a property; **expectation of life *or* life expectancy** = number of years a person is likely to live

expenditure *noun* amounts of money spent; **capital expenditure** = money spent on assets (such as property or machinery) NOTE: no plural

◊ **expense** *noun* **(a)** money spent; **at great expense** = having spent a lot of money **(b) expense account** = money which a businessman is allowed by his company to spend on travelling and entertaining clients in connection with his business

◊ **expenses** *plural noun* money paid for doing something; **all expenses paid** = with all costs paid by the company; **allowable expenses** = business expenses which are allowed against tax; **business expenses** = money spent on running a business, not on stock or assets; **entertainment expenses** = money spent on giving meals to business visitors; **fixed expenses** = money which is spent regularly (such as rent, electricity, telephone); **incidental expenses** = small amounts of money spent at various times, in addition to larger amounts; **legal expenses** = money spent on fees to lawyers; **overhead expenses *or* general expenses *or* running expenses** = money spent on the day-to-day costs of a business; **travelling expenses** = money spent on travelling and hotels for business purposes

experience 1 *noun* **(a)** having lived through various situations and therefore knowing how to make decisions; **he is a lawyer of considerable experience; she has a**

lot of experience of dealing with divorce cases; he gained most of his legal experience in the Far East **(b)** something one has lived through; **the accident was a terrible experience for her** NOTE: no plural for (a) **2** *verb* to live through a situation

◇ **experienced** *adjective* person who has lived through many situations and has learnt from them; **he is the most experienced negotiator I know; we have appointed a very experienced woman as sales director**

expert *noun* person who knows a lot about something; **an expert in the field of fingerprints** *or* **a fingerprints expert; the company asked a financial expert for advice** *or* **asked for expert financial advice; expert's report** = report written by an expert (usually for a court case); **expert witness** = witness who is a specialist in a subject and is asked to give his opinion on technical matters

◇ **expertise** *noun* specialist knowledge; **we hired Mr Smith because of his financial expertise** *or* **because of his expertise in the African market**
NOTE: no plural

expiration *noun* coming to an end; **expiration of an insurance policy; to repay before the expiration of the stated period; on expiration of the lease** = when the lease comes to an end
NOTE: no plural

◇ **expire** *verb* to come to an end; **the lease expires in 1987; his passport has expired** = his passport is no longer valid

◇ **expiry** *noun* coming to an end; **expiry of an insurance policy; expiry date** = date when something will end

explain *verb* to give reasons for something; **he explained to the customs officials that the two computers were presents from friends; can you explain to the jury how you came to be in the house on Thursday 13th July?**

◇ **explanation** *noun* reason for something; **the VAT inspector asked for an explanation of the invoices; he could give no explanation of how the drugs came to be in his suitcase**

◇ **explanatory** *noun* which explains; **read the explanatory notes before filling in the form**

explicit *adjective* which is clearly stated; **his explicit intention was to leave his house to his wife**

◇ **explicitly** *adverb* in a clear way; **the contract explicitly prohibits sale of the goods in Europe**

explore *verb* to examine carefully; **we are exploring the possibility of opening an office in London**

explosive *adjective & noun* (substance) which can blow up and damage property; **the car was full of explosives; an explosive device** = a bomb

export 1 *noun* sending of goods to a foreign country to be sold; **export licence** = permit which allows a company to send a certain type of product abroad to be sold **2** *verb* to send goods abroad to be sold; **most of the company's products are exported to the USA**

expose *verb* to show something which had previously been hidden; **the police investigation exposed corruption in the government; he was exposed as the boss of the gang of forgers**

◇ **exposure** *noun* act of showing something which was hidden; **the report's exposure of corruption in the police force; indecent exposure** = offence where a male person shows his sexual organs to a woman

ex post facto *Latin phrase meaning* "after the event"

express 1 *adjective* **(a)** rapid *or* very fast; **express letter; express delivery (b)** clearly shown in words; **the contract has an express condition forbidding sale in Africa; express term** = term in a contract which is clearly stated (as opposed to an implied term) **2** *verb* **(a)** to put into words *or* diagrams; **this chart shows crime in London expressed as a percentage of total crime in the UK (b)** to send very fast; **we expressed the order to the customer's warehouse**

◇ **expressly** *adverb* clearly in words; **the contract expressly forbids sales to the United States; the franchisee is expressly forbidden to sell goods other than those supplied by the franchisor**

expressio unius est exclusio alterius *Latin phrase meaning* "the mention that one thing is included implies that another thing is expressly excluded"

expunge *verb* to remove (from a record); **inadmissible hearsay evidence was expunged from the report**

extend *verb* (a) to make available *or* to give; **to extend credit to a customer** (b) to make longer; **to extend a contract for two years; the court extended the defendant's time for serving his defence by fourteen days; he was sentenced to five years imprisonment, extended; extended credit** = credit allowing the borrower a longer time to pay; **extended family** = group of related people, including distant relatives and close friends; **extended sentence** = sentence which is made longer than usual because the criminal is likely to repeat the offence

◊ **extension** *noun* (a) allowing longer time; **to get an extension of credit** = to get more time to pay back; **extension of a contract** = continuing the contract for a further period; **extension of time** = allowance by court to a party of more time in which to do something; **the defendant applied for an extension of time in which to serve her defence** (b) (*in an office*) individual telephone linked to the main switchboard; **can you get me extension 21? extension 21 is engaged; the legal department is on extension 53**

◊ **extensive** *adjective* very large *or* covering a wide area; **he has an extensive knowledge of drugs; she has extensive contacts in the underworld**

◊ **extent** *noun* amount *or* area covered by something; **they are assessing the extent of the damage after the fire; to a certain extent** = partly *or* not completely; **he was correct to a certain extent; the recommendations of the report were carried out to a certain extent**

extenuating circumstances *plural noun* factors which excuse a crime in some way

◊ **extenuation** *noun* **in extenuation of something** = in order to excuse something; **counsel pleaded the accused's age in extenuation of his actions**

extinction *noun* coming to an end; **the extinction of a legal right**

extinguishment *noun* act of cancelling a right *or* a power (especially the right to sue for non-payment once payment has been made)

extort *verb* to get money *or* promises *or* a confession from someone, by using threats; **he extorted £20,000 from local shopkeepers**

◊ **extortion** *noun* getting money by threats; **extortion racket** = racket to make money by threatening people NOTE: no plural

◊ **extortionate** *adjective* at very high cost *or* too much; **extortionate credit bargain** = transaction whereby money is lent at a very high rate of interest, thereby rendering the transaction illegal

◊ **extortionist** *noun* person who extorts money from people

extra- *prefix* outside

◊ **extra-territoriality** *noun* being outside the territory of the country where you are living, and so not subject to its laws (used of diplomats)

extract 1 *noun* printed document which is part of a larger document; **the solicitor sent an extract of the deeds** 2 *verb* to force someone to say something which he does not want to say; **the confession was extracted under torture; the magistrate extracted an admission from the witness that he had not seen the accident**

extradite *verb* to bring an arrested person from another country to your country because he is wanted for trial for a crime which he committed in your country; **he was arrested in France and extradited to stand trial in Germany**

◊ **extradition** *noun* bringing an arrested person from another country to be tried for a crime he committed in your country; **the USA requested the extradition of the leader of the drug gang; extradition treaty** = agreement between two countries that a person arrested in one country can be sent to the other to stand trial for a crime committed there

extraordinary *adjective* different from normal; **Extraordinary General Meeting (EGM)** = special meeting of shareholders *or* members of a club, etc., to discuss an important matter which cannot wait until the next Annual General Meeting;

extraordinary items = items in accounts which do not appear each year; **the auditors noted several extraordinary items in the accounts**

extrinsic evidence *noun* evidence used in the interpretation of a document which is not found in the document itself; *compare* INTRINSIC

eye witness *noun* person who saw something happen (such as an accident *or* a crime); **he gave an eye witness account of the bank hold-up**

Ff

F *sixth letter of the alphabet* **Class F charge** = charge on a property registered by a spouse who is not the owner, claiming a right to live in the property; **Schedule F** = schedule to the Finance Acts under which tax is charged on income from dividends

face 1 *noun* front part of something; **face value** = value written on a coin *or* share certificate *or* banknote 2 *verb* **to face a charge** = to appear in court and be charged with a crime; **he faces three charges relating to firearms**

facie *see* PRIMA FACIE

facsimile (copy) *noun* exact copy of a document

fact *noun* something which is true and real, especially something which has been proved by evidence in court; **the chairman of the tribunal asked to see all the facts on the income tax claim; in fact** *or* **in point of fact** = really; **matters of fact** = facts relevant to a case which is being tried at court; *see also* ACCESSORY

◊ **fact-finding** *adjective* looking for information; **a fact-finding delegation** = group of people who visit to search for information about a problem

facto *see* DE FACTO, IPSO FACTO

factor *noun* (a) thing which is important *or* which influences; **the rise in unemployment is an important factor in the increased crime rate; cyclical factors** = way in which a trade cycle affects businesses; **contributory factor** = something which contributes to a result; **deciding factor** = most important factor which influences a decision; **factors of production** = things needed to produce a product (land, labour and capital) (b) agent *or* person who buys or sells as an agent for another in exchange for a commission; **debt factor** = person who buys debts at a discount, and enforces them for himself *or* enforces them for a commission

◊ **factoring** *noun* selling debts to a debt factor

faculty *noun* special permission to do something, granted by a church (such as permission to get married without publishing banns)

◊ **Faculty of Advocates** *noun* legal body to which Scottish barristers belong

fail *verb* (a) not to do something which you were trying to do; **he failed to appear at the probation office; counsel failed to persuade the jury that his client was innocent** (b) to be unsuccessful commercially; **the company failed** = the company became insolvent

◊ **failing** 1 *noun* being weak *or* weakness; **the chairman has one failing - he goes to sleep at board meetings** 2 *preposition* if something does not happen; **failing instructions to the contrary** = unless different instructions are given; **failing prompt payment** = if the payment is not made on time; **failing that** = if that does not work; **try the company secretary, and failing that the chairman**

◊ **failure** *noun* (a) breaking down *or* stopping; **the failure of the negotiations** (b) not doing something which should be done; **his failure to comply with the court order; their failure to meet the deadline; her failure to pay a bill** (c) commercial failure = bankruptcy of a person *or* insolvency of a company; **he lost all his money in the bank failure**

fair 1 *noun* **trade fair** = large exhibition and meeting for advertising and selling a certain type of product 2 *adjective* (a) honest *or* correct; **fair comment** = remark which is honestly made on a matter of public interest and so is not defamatory; **fair dealing** = (i) legal buying and selling of shares; (ii) quoting small sections of a copyright work; **fair price** = good price for both buyer and seller; **fair trade** = international business system where countries agree not to charge import duties on certain items imported from their trading partners; **fair trading** *or* **fair dealing** = way of doing business which is reasonable and does not harm the consumer; **Office of Fair Trading** = British government department which protects consumers against unfair *or* illegal business; **fair wear and tear** = acceptable damage caused by normal use; **the insurance policy covers most damage, but not fair wear and tear to the machine (b) fair copy** = document which is written *or* typed with no corrections or mistakes

faith *noun* **to have faith in something** *or* **someone** = to believe that something *or* a person is good or will work well; **in good faith** = in an honest way; **he acted in good faith** *or* **in bad faith** = he acted honestly *or* dishonestly; **to buy something in good faith** = to buy something honestly *or* in the course of an honest transaction; **he bought the car in good faith, not knowing it had been stolen**

◊ **faithfully** *adverb* **yours faithfully** = used as an ending to a formal business letter not addressed to a named person

fake 1 *noun* forgery *or* copy made for criminal purposes; **the shipment came with fake documentation 2** *verb* to make an imitation for criminal purposes; **they faked a break-in to make the police believe the documents had been stolen**

fall *verb* to happen *or* to take place; **the national holiday falls on a Monday; the bill fell due** = the bill was due to be paid; **to fall outside** = not to be part of a list *or* not to be covered by a rule; **the case falls outside the jurisdiction of the court; to fall within** = to become part of a list *or* to be covered by a rule; **the newspaper report falls within the category of defamation; the case falls within the competence of the court**

false *adjective* not true *or* not correct; **to make a false entry in the record; false accounting** = notifiable offence of changing *or* destroying *or* hiding records for

money; **false imprisonment** = (i) tort of keeping someone imprisoned wrongfully; (ii) sending someone to prison for a wrong reason; **false pretences** = doing *or* saying something to cheat someone; **he was sent to prison for obtaining money by false pretences; false representation** = offence of making a wrong statement; **false weight** = weight on shop scales which is wrong and so cheats customers

◊ **falsehood** *noun* lie *or* incorrect statement; **injurious falsehood** *or* **malicious falsehood** = tort of making a wrong statement about someone so as to harm his reputation (usually in relation to his business *or* property)

◊ **falsify** *verb* to change something to make it wrong; **to falsify accounts** = to change *or* destroy a record

◊ **falsification** *noun* **falsification of accounts** = action of making false entries in a record *or* of destroying a record

family *noun* **(a)** group of people who are related (including husband, wife, mother, father, children); **extended family** = group of related people including distant relatives and close friends; **family company** = company where most of the shares are owned by members of the same family; **Family Division** = one of the three divisions of the High Court which deals with divorce cases and cases involving parents and children; **family law** = laws relating to families *or* to the rights and duties of the members of a family **(b)** *slang* group of organized Mafia gangsters, ruled by a boss or godfather

fatal *adjective* which causes a death; **he took a fatal dose of drugs; there were six fatal accidents in the first week of the year**

fault *noun* **(a)** being to blame for something which is wrong; **the witness said the accident was the fault of defective machinery; was it the fault of the police if the protest march developed into a riot? (b)** wrong working; **the technical staff are trying to correct a fault in the computer; we think there is a basic fault in the construction of the product**

◊ **faulty** *adjective* which does not work properly *or* which has not been done in the correct way; **the accident was caused by faulty brakes** *or* **by faulty repairs to the brakes**

favour *or* *US* **favor** 1 *noun* **(a) as a favour** = to help *or* to be kind to someone; **he asked the secretary for a loan as a favour (b) in favour of** = in agreement with *or* feeling that something is right; **most of the workers are in favour of shorter working hours; six members of the cabinet are in favour of the proposal, and three are against it** 2 *verb* to agree that something is right *or* to vote for something; **judges favour deterrent sentences for hooligans**

◊ **favourable** *adjective* which helps someone *or* which approves of something; **to buy on favourable terms** = to buy on terms which make it easier to pay

FBI = FEDERAL BUREAU OF INVESTIGATION

feasant *see* DAMAGE FEASANT

federal *adjective* referring to a system of government where a group of states are linked together in a federation; especially the central government of the United States; **federal court** *or* **federal laws** = court *or* laws of the USA, as opposed to state courts *or* state laws

◊ **Federal Bureau of Investigation (FBI)** *noun* section of the US Department of Justice, which investigates crimes against federal law and subversive acts in the USA

◊ **federation** *noun* group of societies *or* companies *or* organizations which have a central organization which represents them and looks after their common interests

fee *noun* **(a)** money paid for work carried out by a professional person (such as an accountant *or* a doctor *or* a lawyer); **we charge a small fee for our services; a barrister's fees;** *US* **contingent fee** = fee paid to a lawyer which is a proportion of the damages recovered in a case **(b)** money paid for something; **entrance fee** *or* **admission fee; registration fee (c) fee simple** = freehold ownership of land with no restrictions to it; **to hold an estate in fee simple; fee tail** = interest in land which is passed on to the owner's direct descendants, and which cannot be passed to anyone else

feed 1 *noun* device which puts paper into a printer *or* into a copying machine; **continuous feed** = device which feeds in continuous computer stationery into a printer; **sheet feed** = device which puts in one sheet at a time into a printer 2 *verb* to put information into a computer
NOTE: feeding - fed - has fed

felony *noun* old term for a serious crime; **to commit a felony**
NOTE: still used in **treason felony**

◊ **felonious** *adjective* criminal; **he carried out a felonious act**

feme covert *French phrase meaning* "married woman"

◊ **feme sole** *French phrase meaning* "unmarried woman"

fence 1 *noun* *informal* person who receives and sells stolen goods 2 *verb* to receive stolen goods to sell

fiat *noun* **(a)** agreement (as of the Attorney-General) to bring a prosecution **(b) fiat money** = coins or notes which are not worth much as paper or metal, but are said by the government to have a value

◊ **fiat justicia** *Latin phrase meaning* "let justice be done"

fiction *noun* **fiction of law** *or* **legal fiction** = assuming something to be true, even if it is not proved to be so (a procedural device by courts to get round problems caused by statute)

◊ **fictitious** *adjective* false *or* which does not exist; **fictitious assets** = assets which do not really exist, but are entered as assets to balance the accounts

fiddle 1 *noun* *informal* cheating; **it's all a fiddle; he's on the fiddle** = he is trying to cheat 2 *verb* *informal* to cheat; **he tried to fiddle his tax returns; the salesman was caught fiddling his expense account**

fide *see* BONA FIDE

fieri facias *Latin phrase meaning* "make it happen"; **writ of fieri facias** = court order to a sheriff telling him to seize the goods of a debtor against whom judgment has been made
NOTE: often abbreviated to **fi. fa.**

fiduciary *adjective & noun* (person) acting as trustee for someone else *or* being in a position of trust; **a company director owes a fiduciary duty to the company; he was**

acting in a fiduciary capacity = he was acting as a trustee

fi. fa. *see* FIERI FACIAS

figure *noun* (a) number *or* cost written in numbers; **he put a very low figure on the value of the lease** = he calculated the value of the lease as very low (b) **figures** = written numbers; **sales figures** = total sales; **to work out the figures** = to calculate; **his income from protection rackets runs into five figures** *or* **he has a five-figure income from protection rackets** = his income is more than £10,000; **in round figures** = not totally accurate, but correct to the nearest 10 or 100; **the number of prisoners in jail is 45,000 in round figures** (c) **figures** = results for a company; **the figures for last year** *or* **last year's figures**

file 1 *noun* (a) cardboard holder for documents, which can fit in the drawer of a filing cabinet; **put these letters in the unsolved cases file; look in the file marked "Scottish police forces"; box file** = cardboard box for holding documents (b) documents kept for reference; **the police keep a file of missing vehicles; look up her description in the missing persons' file; to place something on file** = to keep a record of something; **to keep someone's name on file** = to keep someone's name on a list for reference; **file copy** = copy of a document which is kept for reference in an office; **card file** = information kept on filing cards; **computer file** = section of information on a computer (such as a list of addresses *or* of customer accounts) (c) section of data on a computer (such as staff salaries, address list, customer accounts); **how can we protect our computer files?** 2 *verb* (a) **to file documents** = to put documents in order so that they can be found easily; **the correspondence is filed under "complaints"** (b) to make an official request; **to file a petition in bankruptcy** = to ask officially to be made bankrupt *or* to ask officially for someone else to be made bankrupt (c) to send a document to court; **the defence must be filed and served in seven days** = the defence must be sent to court and to the other party within seven days (d) to register something officially; **to file an application for a patent; to file a return to the tax office**

◊ **filing** *noun* (a) delivering a legal document to court (b) documents which have to be put in order; **there is a lot of filing to do at the end of the week; the manager looked through the week's filing to see what letters had been sent; filing basket** *or* **filing tray** = container kept on a desk for documents which have to be filed; **filing cabinet** = metal box with several drawers for keeping files; **filing card** = card with information written on it, used to classify information into the correct order; **filing clerk** = clerk who files documents; **filing system** = way of putting documents in order for reference

final *adjective* last *or* coming at the end of a period; **to pay the final instalment; to make the final payment; to put the final details on a document; final date for payment** = last date by which payment should be made; **final demand** = last reminder from a supplier, after which he will sue for payment; **final discharge** = last payment of what is left of a debt; **final dividend** = dividend paid at the end of the year; **final judgment** = judgment which is awarded at the end of an action after trial, as opposed to an interlocutory judgment

◊ **finally** *adverb* in the end; **the contract was finally signed yesterday; after ten hours of discussions, the House of Commons finally rose at two o'clock in the morning**

finance 1 *noun* money used by a company, club, etc.; **where will the authority find the finance to pay the higher salaries? he is the secretary of the local authority finance committee; Finance Act** = annual Act of Parliament which gives the government the power to raise taxes to spend as proposed in the Budget 2 *verb* to pay for something; **the new building must be financed by the local authority; a government-financed programme of prison construction**

◊ **financial** *adjective* referring to money *or* finance; **he has a financial interest in the company; financial assistance** = help in the form of money; **she receives financial assistance from the local authority; financial institution** = bank *or* other company which provides finance; **to make financial provision for someone** = to give someone money to live on

◊ **financially** *adverb* in the form of money; **he is financially involved in the property company; the company is financially very strong**

find *verb* (a) to get something which was not there before; **to find backing for a project** (b) to make a legal decision in court; **the tribunal found that both parties were at fault; the court found the accused guilty on all charges; the judge found for the defendant** = the judge decided that the defendant was right
NOTE: finding - found

◇ **findings** *noun* decision reached by a court; **the findings of a commission of enquiry** = the conclusions of the commission

fine 1 *noun* money paid as a punishment because something wrong has been done; **the court sentenced him to pay a £25,000 fine; we had to pay a £10 parking fine; the sentence for dangerous driving is a £1,000 fine or two months in prison** 2 *verb* to punish someone by making him pay money; **to fine someone £2,500 for obtaining money by false pretences**

fingerprint 1 *noun* mark left on a surface by fingers, from which a person may be identified; **they found his fingerprints on the murder weapon; the court heard evidence from a fingerprint expert; to take someone's fingerprints** = to take a copy of a person's fingerprints (by printing them with ink on a filing card) so that he can be identified in future 2 *verb* to take someone's fingerprints; **the police fingerprinted the suspect after charging him**

fire 1 *noun* (a) thing which burns; **the shipment was damaged in the fire on board the cargo boat; half the stock was destroyed in the warehouse fire; to catch fire** = to start to burn; **the papers in the waste paper basket caught fire; fire certificate** = certificate from the municipal fire department to say that a building is properly protected against fire; **fire damage** = damage caused by fire; **he claimed £250 for fire damage; fire-damaged goods** = goods which have been damaged in a fire; **fire door** = special door to prevent fire going from one part of a building to another; **fire escape** = door or stairs which allow staff to get out of a building which is on fire; **fire hazard** *or* **fire risk** = situation *or* goods which could start a fire; **that warehouse full of paper is a fire hazard; fire insurance** = insurance against damage by fire; **fire regulations** = local or national regulations which owners of buildings

used by the public have to obey in order to be granted a fire certificate (b) act of shooting; **the police opened fire on the crowd** = the police started to shoot at the crowd 2 *verb* (a) to shoot (with a gun); **he fired two shots at the crowd** (b) **to fire someone** = to dismiss someone from a job; **the new managing director fired half the sales force**

◇ **firearm** *noun* gun *or* other weapon used to shoot; **firearms certificate** = official document saying that someone has permission to own a gun

◇ **fireproof** *adjective* which cannot be damaged by fire; **we packed the papers in a fireproof safe; it is impossible to make the office completely fireproof**

◇ **fire-raiser** *noun* person who sets fire to property

◇ **fire-raising** *noun* setting fire to property on purpose; *see also* ARSON, ARSONIST

◇ **firing squad** *noun* group of soldiers who execute someone by shooting

firm 1 *noun* partnership *or* any other business which is not a company; **he is a partner in a law firm; a firm of accountants; an important publishing firm** (NOTE: firm is often used when referring to incorporated companies, but this is not correct) 2 *adjective* (a) which cannot be changed; **to make a firm offer for something; to place a firm offer for two aircraft; they are quoting a firm price of £1.22 per case** (b) not dropping in price, and possibly going to rise; **the pound was firmer on the foreign exchange markets; shares remained firm** 3 *verb* to remain at a price and seem likely to go up; **the shares firmed at £1.50**

◇ **firmness** *noun* remaining at a price *or* being likely to rise; **the firmness of the pound**

first *noun* person *or* thing which is there at the beginning *or* earlier than others; **our company was one of the first to sell into the European market; first quarter** = three months' period from January to the end of March; **first half** *or* **first half-year** = six months' period from January to the end of June; **first in first out** = (i) redundancy policy, where the people who have been working longest are the first to be made redundant; (ii) accounting policy where stock is valued at the price of the oldest purchases; **case of first impression** = case which raises points of law for which there are no precedents; **first offence** = committing an offence for the first time; **first offender** = person who has committed an offence for the first time; **First Reading** = formal introduction of a Bill into the House of Commons, after which it is printed

◊ **first-class** *adjective & noun* **(a)** top quality *or* most expensive; **he is a first-class accountant (b)** most expensive and comfortable type of travel *or* type of hotel; **to travel first-class; first-class travel provides the best service; a first-class ticket; to stay in first-class hotels; first-class mail** = (i) (in Britain) most expensive mail service, planned to be faster; (ii) (in the USA) mail service for letters and postcards; **a first-class letter should get to Scotland in a day**

◊ **first degree murder** *noun US* premeditated and deliberate murder

◊ **first instance** *noun* **court of first instance** = court in which a case is tried first

fiscal *adjective* referring to tax *or* to government revenue; **the government's fiscal policies; fiscal measures** = tax changes made by a government to improve the working of the economy; **fiscal year** = twelve-month period on which taxes are calculated (in the UK, April 6th to April 5th); **Procurator Fiscal** = Scottish law officer who decides whether an alleged criminal should be prosecuted

fit *adjective* physically *or* mentally able to do something; **the solicitor stated that his client was not fit to plead**

◊ **fitness** *noun* state of being of the necessary standard; **fitness for purpose** = implied contractual term that goods sold will be of the necessary standard to be used for the purpose for which they were bought

◊ **fittings** *see* FIXTURE

fix *verb* **(a)** to arrange *or* to agree; **to fix a budget; to fix a meeting for 3 p.m.; the date of the hearing has still to be fixed; the price of gold was fixed at $300; the punishment for drug offences has been fixed by Parliament (b)** to mend; **the maintenance staff are coming to fix the telephone; can you fix the copying machine?**

◊ **fixed** *adjective* permanent *or* which cannot be removed; **fixed assets** = property *or* machinery which a company owns

and uses; **fixed capital** = capital in the form of buildings and machinery; **fixed charge** = charge over a particular asset *or* property; (*see also* FLOATING CHARGE) **fixed costs** = (i) set amount of money to which a plaintiff is entitled in legal proceedings (as opposed to taxed costs); (ii) cost of producing a product, which does not increase with the amount of product made (such as rent); **fixed deposit** = deposit which pays a stated interest over a set period; **fixed expenses** = money which is spent regularly (such as rent, electricity, telephone); **fixed income** = income which does not change (such as from an annuity); **fixed-interest investments** = investments producing an interest which does not change; **fixed-price agreement** = agreement where a company provides a service *or* a product at a price which stays the same for the whole period of the agreement; **fixed scale of charges** = rate of charging which cannot be altered; **fixed term** = period which is fixed when a contract is signed and which cannot be changed afterwards

◊ **fixing** *noun* **(a)** arranging; **fixing of charges; fixing of a mortgage rate (b)** price **fixing** = illegal agreement between companies to charge the same price for competing products **(c) the London gold fixing** = system where the world price for gold is set each day in London

◊ **fixture** *noun* item in a property which is permanently attached to it (such as a sink or lavatory) and which passes to a new owner with the property itself; **fixtures and fittings** = objects in a property which are sold with the property (both those which cannot be removed and those which can)

flag *noun* piece of coloured cloth which is used to represent a country; **flag of convenience** = flag of a country which may have no ships of its own but allows ships of other countries to be registered in its ports; **to fly a flag** = to attach the flag in an obvious position to show that you belong to a certain country; **ship flying the British flag; ship flying a flag of convenience**

flagrant *adjective* clear and obvious; **a flagrant case of contempt of court; a flagrant violation of human rights**

◊ **flagrante** *see* IN FLAGRANTE DELICTO

flat 1 *adjective* **(a)** falling because of low demand; **the market was flat today (b)** fixed *or* not changing; **flat rate** = charge which always stays the same; **we pay a flat rate for electricity each quarter; he is paid a flat rate of £2 per thousand** 2 *noun* set of rooms for one family in a building with other sets of similar rooms; **he has a flat in the centre of town; she is buying a flat close to her office; company flat** = flat owned by a company and used by members of staff from time to time
NOTE: US English is **apartment**

floating charge *noun* a charge over the changing assets (such as debts or stock) of a business, as opposed to a fixed charge

flotsam *noun* rubbish floating in the water after a ship has been wrecked

flout *verb* to break *or* to go against (a rule *or* the law); **by selling alcohol to minors, the shop is deliberately flouting the law**

f.o.b. = FREE ON BOARD

follow *verb* to act in accordance with (a rule); **the court has followed the precedent set in the 1972 case**

◊ **follow up** *verb* to examine something further; **the police are following up several leads; to follow up an initiative** = to take action once someone else has decided to do something

foolscap *noun* large size of writing paper; **the letter was on six sheets of foolscap; a foolscap envelope** = large envelope which takes foolscap paper

forbear *verb* **to forbear from doing something** = not to do something which you intended to do; **he forbore from taking any further action**
NOTE: **forbearing - forbore - has forborne**

◊ **forbearance** *noun* not doing something which was intended
NOTE: no plural

forbid *verb* to tell someone not to do something *or* to say that something must not be done; **the contract forbids sale of the goods to the USA; the staff are forbidden to use the front entrance; the judge forbade any reference to the defendant in the media**
NOTE: **forbidding - forbade - has forbidden**

force 1 *noun* **(a)** strength; **to be in force** = to be operating *or* working; **the rules have been in force since 1946; to come into force** = to start to operate *or* work; **the new regulations will come into force on January 1st; the new regulations have the force of law** = they are the same as if they had been voted into law by parliament **(b)** group of people; **labour force** = all the workers in a company *or* in an area; **the management has made an increased offer to the labour force; we are opening a new factory in the Far East because of the cheap local labour force; police force** = group of policemen organized in an area; **members of several local police forces have collaborated in searching for the murderer (c) force majeure** = something which happens which is out of the control of the parties who have signed a contract (such as strike, war, storm) and which prevents the contract being fulfilled 2 *verb* to make someone do something; **competition has forced the company to lower its prices**

◊ **forced** *adjective* **forced sale** = sale which takes place because a court orders it *or* because it is the only way to avoid insolvency

◊ **forcible** *adjective* by force *or* using force; **forcible entry** = formerly, the criminal offence of entering a building *or* land and taking possession of it by force; **forcible feeding** = giving food by force to a prisoner on hunger strike

foreclose *verb* to take possession of a property because the owner cannot repay money which he has borrowed (using the property as security); **to foreclose on a mortgaged property**

◊ **foreclosure** *noun* act of foreclosing; **foreclosure order nisi** = court order which makes a mortgagor pay outstanding debts to a mortgagee within a certain period of time; **foreclosure order absolute** = court order giving the mortgagee full rights to the property

foreign *adjective* not belonging to one's own country; **foreign cars have flooded our market; we are increasing our trade with foreign countries; foreign currency** = money of another country; **foreign goods** = goods produced in other countries; **foreign investments** = money invested in other countries; **foreign trade** = trade with other countries

◊ **foreign exchange** *noun* exchanging the money of one country for that of another; **foreign exchange broker** *or* **dealer** = person who deals on the foreign exchange market; **foreign exchange dealing** = buying and selling foreign currencies; **the foreign exchange markets** = market where people buy and sell foreign currencies; **foreign exchange reserves** = foreign money held by a government to support its own currency and pay its debts; **foreign exchange transfer** = sending of money from one country to another

◊ **foreigner** *noun* person from another country

◊ **Foreign (and Commonwealth) Office** *noun* British government department dealing with relations with other countries

◊ **Foreign Secretary** *noun* British government minister in charge of relations with other countries

COMMENT: in most countries, the government department dealing with other countries is called the Foreign Ministry, with the Foreign Minister in charge. In the UK, these are the Foreign Office and Foreign Secretary; in the USA, they are the State Department and the Secretary of State

foreman of the jury *noun* person elected by the other jurors, who chairs the meetings of a jury, and pronounces the verdict in court afterwards

forensic *adjective* referring to courts *or* the law *or* pleading a case *or* punishing crime; **forensic medicine** = medical science concerned with solving crimes against people (such as autopsies of murdered people, taking blood samples from clothes); **forensic science** = science used in solving legal problems and criminal cases

foresee *verb* to imagine (correctly) what is going to happen in the future; **he did not foresee that his letter could be taken as a threat; the closure of the company was not foreseen by the staff**
NOTE: foreseeing - foresaw - has foreseen

◊ **foreseeability** *noun* ability of something to be foreseen; **foreseeability test** = test for calculating liability on the part of a person who should have foreseen the consequences of his action, especially in cases of negligence

◊ **foresight** *noun* seeing what effects an action will have in the future

forfeit 1 *noun* taking something away as a punishment; **forfeit clause** = clause in a contract which says that goods *or* a deposit will be taken away if the contract is not obeyed; **the goods were declared forfeit** = the court said that the goods had to be taken away from their owner 2 *verb* to have something taken away as a punishment; **to forfeit a deposit** = to lose a deposit which was left for an item because you have decided not to buy that item

◊ **forfeiture** *noun* act of forfeiting a property *or* a right; **forfeiture of shares** = losing the right to shares which a shareholder has not claimed

forge *verb* to copy money *or* a signature illegally *or* to make a document which looks like a real one; **he tried to enter the country with forged documents; she wanted to pay the bill with a forged £10 note**

◊ **forgery** *noun* **(a)** crime of making an illegal copy of a document *or* recording *or* banknote to use as if it were a real one; **he was sent to prison for forgery** **(b)** illegal copy; **the signature was proved to be a forgery**
NOTE: no plural for (a)

forget *verb* not to remember; **she forgot to put a stamp on the envelope; don't forget we're having lunch together tomorrow; he forgot to come to the hearing**
NOTE: forgetting - forgot - forgotten

fori *see* LEX FORI

form 1 *noun* **(a) form of words** = words correctly laid out for a legal document; **receipt in due form** = correctly written receipt **(b)** official printed paper with blank spaces which have to be filled in with information; **you have to fill in form A20; customs declaration form; a pad of order forms; application form** = form which has to be filled in to apply for something; **claim form** = form which has to be filled in when making an insurance claim 2 *verb* to start *or* to organize; **the brothers have formed a new company**

◊ **formation** *or* **forming** *noun* act of organizing; **the formation of a new company**

forma *see* PRO FORMA

formal *adjective* clearly and legally written; **to make a formal application; to send a formal order**

◇ **formality** *noun* formal procedure *or* thing which has to be done to obey the law or because it is the custom; **the chairman dispensed with the formality of reading the minutes; customs formalities** = declaration of goods by the shipper and examination of them by the customs

◇ **formally** *adverb* in a formal way; **we have formally applied for planning permission for the new shopping precinct**

formulate *verb* to put down *or* state clearly

forthwith *adverb* immediately

fortiori *see* A FORTIORI

forum *noun* court *or* place where matters are discussed; **the magistrates' court is not the appropriate forum for this application**

forward 1 *adjective* in advance *or* to be paid at a later date; **forward buying *or* buying forward** = buying shares *or* currency *or* commodities at today's price for delivery at a later date; **forward contract** = agreement to buy foreign currency *or* shares *or* commodities at a later date at a certain price; **forward market** = market for purchasing foreign currency *or* oil *or* commodities for delivery at a later date; **forward (exchange) rate** = rate for purchase of foreign currency at a fixed price for delivery at a later date; **forward sales** = sales for delivery at a later date **2** *adverb* **(a) to date an invoice forward** = to put a later date than the present one on an invoice; **carriage forward *or* freight forward** = deal where the customer pays for shipping the goods; **charges forward** = charges which will be paid by the customer **(b) to buy forward** = to buy foreign currency *or* gold *or* commodities before you need them, in order to be certain of the exchange rate; **to sell forward** = to sell foreign currency *or* gold *or* commodities for delivery at a later date **(c) balance brought forward *or* carried forward** = balance which is entered in an account at the end of a period *or* page and is then taken to be the starting point of the next period *or* page **3** *verb* **to forward something to someone** = to send something to someone; **please forward *or* to be forwarded** = words written on an envelope, asking the person receiving it to send it on to the person whose name is written on it

foster *verb* to look after and bring up (a child who is not your own); **foster child** = child brought up by people who are not its own parents; **foster home** = home where a foster child is brought up; **foster mother *or* foster father *or* fosterparent** = woman *or* man who looks after a child and brings it up

foul *adjective* **foul bill of lading** = bill of lading which says that the goods were in bad condition when received by the shipper

founder *noun* person who starts a company; **founder's shares** = shares issued to the founder of a company, which carry special rights

fours *see* ALL

frais *see* SANS FRAIS

frame *verb* *informal* to arrange for someone to appear to be guilty; **he has been framed** = he is innocent, but the situation has been arranged in such a way that he appears guilty

franchise 1 *noun* **(a)** right granted to someone to do something, especially the right to vote in local *or* general elections; **universal franchise** = right to vote which is given to all adult members of the population **(b)** licence to trade using a brand name and paying a royalty for it; **he has bought a printing franchise *or* a hot dog franchise** NOTE: no plural for (a) **2** *verb* to sell licences for people to trade using a brand name and paying a royalty; **his sandwich bar was so successful that he decided to franchise it**

◇ **franchisee** *noun* person who runs a franchise

◇ **franchiser** *noun* person who licenses a franchise

◇ **franchising** *noun* act of selling a licence to trade as a franchise; **he runs his sandwich chain as a franchising operation** NOTE: no plural

◇ **franchisor** *noun* = FRANCHISER

franco *adverb* free

frank *verb* to stamp the date and postage on a letter; **franking machine** = machine which marks the date and postage on letters so that the person sending them does not need to use stamps

fraud *noun* **(a)** harming someone (by obtaining property *or* money from him) after making him believe something which is not true; **he got possession of the property by fraud; he was accused of frauds relating to foreign currency; to obtain money by fraud** = to obtain money by saying or doing something to cheat someone; **Fraud Squad** = special police department which investigates frauds **(b)** act of deceiving someone in order to make money; **he was convicted of a series of frauds against insurance companies; computer fraud** = fraud committed by using computer files (as in a bank)

> COMMENT: frauds are divided into **fraud by a director** and other fraud

◊ **fraudulent** *adjective* not honest *or* aiming to cheat people; **fraudulent conveyance** = putting a property into someone else's possession to avoid it being seized to pay creditors; **fraudulent misrepresentation** = false statement made to trick someone *or* to persuade someone to enter into a contract; **fraudulent preference** = payment made by an insolvent company to a particular creditor in preference to other creditors; **fraudulent trading** = carrying on the business of a company, knowing that the company is insolvent

◊ **fraudulently** *adverb* not honestly; **goods imported fraudulently**

free 1 *adjective & adverb* **(a)** not costing any money; **he was given a free ticket to the exhibition; the price includes free delivery; goods are delivered free; price list sent free on request; free gift** = present given by a shop to a customer who buys a certain amount of goods; **free sample** = sample given free to advertise a product; **free trial** = testing of a machine with no payment involved; **to send a piece of equipment for two weeks' free trial; free of charge** = with no payment to be made; **free on board (f.o.b.)** = (i) international contract whereby the seller promises to deliver goods on board ship and notify the buyer

of delivery, and the buyer arranges freight, pays the shipping cost and takes the risk once the goods have passed onto the ship; (ii) *US* contract for sale whereby the price includes all the seller's costs until the goods are delivered to a certain place **(b)** not in prison; **to set someone free** = to let someone leave prison; **the crowd attacked the police station and set the three prisoners free (c)** with no restrictions; **free circulation of goods** = movement of goods from one country to another without import quotas or other restrictions; **free collective bargaining** = negotiations over wages and working conditions between the management and the workers' representatives without government interference; **free competition** = being free to compete without government interference; **free currency** = currency which is allowed by the government to be bought and sold without restriction; **free enterprise** = system of business with no interference from the government; **free market economy** = system where the government does not interfere in business activity in any way; **free movement of capital** = ability to transfer capital from one EEC country to another; **free port** *or* **free trade zone** = port *or* area where there are no customs duties; **free of tax** *or* **tax-free** = with no tax having to be paid; **interest-free credit** *or* **loan** = credit *or* loan where no interest is paid by the borrower; **free of duty** *or* **duty-free** = with no duty to be paid; **free trade** = system where goods can go from one country to another without any restrictions; **free trade area** = group of countries practising free trade **(d)** not busy *or* not occupied; **are there any tables free in the restaurant? the solicitor will be free in a few minutes; the hearing was delayed because there was no courtroom free** 2 *verb* to release someone from prison; **the new president freed all political prisoners**

◊ **freelance** *adjective, noun & adverb* independent worker who works for several different companies without being employed by any of them; **she is a freelance reporter for the local newspaper; he works freelance as an advertising agent**

◊ **freely** *adverb* with no restrictions; **money should circulate freely within the Common Market**

◊ **free pardon** *noun* pardon given to a convicted person where both the sentence and conviction are recorded as void

freedom *noun* (a) being free *or* not being held in custody; **the president gave the accused man his freedom** (b) being free to do something without restriction; **freedom of association** = being able to join together in a group with other people without being afraid of prosecution, provided that you do not break the law; **freedom of assembly *or* of meeting** = being able to meet as a group without being afraid of prosecution, provided that you do not break the law; **freedom of the press** = being able to write and publish in a newspaper what you wish without being afraid of prosecution, provided that you do not break the law; **freedom of speech** = being able to say what you want without being afraid of prosecution, provided that you do not break the law

freehold *noun* absolute right to hold land *or* property for an unlimited time without paying rent; **freehold property** = property which the owner holds in freehold

◇ **freeholder** *noun* person who holds a freehold property

freeze *verb* to order a person not to move money *or* not to sell assets; **the court ordered the company's bank account to be frozen; frozen assets** = assets of a company which cannot be sold because a person has a claim against them

freight *noun* cargo *or* goods which are carried by land *or* sea *or* air; **freight charges *or* freight rates** = money charged for carrying goods

French *noun* language spoken in France

COMMENT: French was used in England together with Latin as the language of the law courts for some centuries after the conquest by King William I. It still survives in some legal words and phrases, such as **chose, tort, oyez, puisne, autrefois convict, feme covert**

fresh pursuit *noun* chasing a thief, etc., to get back what he has stolen

friendly society *noun* group of people who pay regular contributions which are used to help members of the group when they retire, are ill or in financial difficulty

frisk *verb* to search someone by passing your hands over his clothes to see if he is carrying a weapon *or* a package

frivolous *adjective* **frivolous complaint *or* frivolous action** = complaint *or* action which is not brought for a serious reason

frolic *noun* **frolic of his own** = situation where an employee does damage outside the normal course of his employment, and for which his employer cannot be held responsible

frozen *see* FREEZE

frustrate *verb* to prevent something (especially the terms of a contract) being fulfilled

◇ **frustration** *noun* situation where the terms of a contract cannot possibly be fulfilled (as where the contract requires the use of something which then is destroyed)

fugitive *adjective & noun* (person) who is running away from justice; **fugitive offender** = person running away from the police who, if he is caught, is sent back to the place where the offence was committed

fulfil *verb* to do everything which is promised in a contract; **the company has fulfilled all the terms of the agreement**

full *adjective* (a) with as much inside it as possible; **prisoners have to share cells because the prisons are too full; the court has to deal with a full list of cases** (b) complete *or* including everything; **we are working at full capacity** = we are doing as much work as possible; **full costs** = all the costs of manufacturing a product, including both fixed and variable costs; **full cover** = insurance cover against all types of risk; **in full discharge of a debt** = paying a debt completely *or* paying less than the total amount owed by agreement; **the plaintiff accepted £500 in full and final settlement of his claim for £600, to avoid going to court; full title** = complete title of an Act of Parliament; **full trial** = properly organized trial according to the correct procedure (c) **in full** = completely; **give your full name and address *or* your name and address in full; he accepted all our conditions in full; full refund *or* refund paid in full; he got a full refund when he complained about the service; the clerk read**

out the charges in full; **full payment** *or* **payment in full** = paying all money owed

◇ **fully** *adverb* completely; **fully paid-up shares** = shares where the full face value has been paid; **fully paid-up capital** = all money paid for the issued capital shares

function 1 *noun* duty *or* job; **a management function** = one part of the duties of management, such as sales *or* financial planning; **the function of management** = the duties of being a manager 2 *verb* to work; **the advertising campaign is functioning smoothly; the new management does not seem to be functioning very well**

functus officio *Latin phrase meaning* "no longer having power *or* jurisdiction" (because the power has been exercised); **the justices' clerk asserted that the justices were functi officio**
NOTE: plural is **functi officio**

fundamental *adjective* basic *or* essential; **fundamental breach** = breach of an essential *or* basic term of a contract by one party, entitling the other party to treat the contract as terminated

fund *noun* (a) amount of money collected for a special purpose; **pension fund** = money which provides pensions for retired members of staff (b) **funds** = money available for a purpose; **conversion of funds** = using money which does not belong to you for a purpose for which it is not supposed to be used; **to convert funds to one's own use** = to use someone else's money for yourself

fungible goods *or* **fungibles** *plural noun* goods (such as seeds *or* coins) which are measured by weight *or* counted

furandi *see* ANIMUS

furnish *verb* (a) to supply *or* to provide; **he was asked to furnish the court with proof of his identity** (b) to put furniture into an office *or* room; **he furnished his office with secondhand chairs and desks; the company spent £10,000 on furnishing the chairman's office; furnished accommodation** = flat, house, etc., which is let with furniture in it

future 1 *adjective* referring to time to come *or* to something which has not yet happened; **future delivery** = delivery at a

later date; **future estate** = old term for the possession and enjoyment of an estate at some time in the future 2 *noun* time which has not yet happened; **try to be more careful in future; in future all reports must be sent to Australia by air**

◇ **futures** *plural noun* trading in shares *or* currencies *or* commodities for delivery at a later date

fuzz *noun slang* the police

Gg

gain 1 *noun* (a) increase *or* becoming larger; **gain in experience** = act of getting more experience (b) increase in profit *or* price *or* value; **to deal in stolen goods for gain** = to buy and sell stolen goods to make a profit; **capital gains** = money made by selling a fixed asset *or* by selling shares at a profit; **capital gains tax** = tax paid on capital gains 2 *verb* to get *or* to obtain; **he gained some useful experience working in a bank; to gain control of a business** = to buy more than 50% of the shares so that you can direct the business

◇ **gainful** *adjective* **gainful employment** = employment which pays money

◇ **gainfully** *adverb* **he is not gainfully employed** = he has no regular paid work

gallows *plural noun* wooden support from which criminals are executed by hanging

game *noun* (a) birds and animals which are hunted, especially for food; **game licence** = official permit which allows someone to sell game (b) **game of chance** = game (such as roulette) where the result depends on luck
NOTE: no plural for (a)

◇ **gaming** *noun* playing games of chance for money; **gaming licence** = official permit which allows someone *or* a club to organize games of chance

gang *noun* group of criminals working together; **a drugs gang; a gang of jewel thieves**

◇ **gangland** *noun* all gangs considered as a group; **a gangland murder** = murder of a gangster by another gangster

◇ **gangster** *noun* person who is a member of a gang of criminals; **the police shot six gangsters in the bank raid**

gaol 1 *noun GB* prison 2 *verb GB* to put someone in prison

◇ **gaoler** *noun GB* person who works in a prison *or* who is in charge of a prison; *for examples see* JAIL, JAILER

garnish *verb* to warn (a debtor) to pay his debts, not to the creditor, but to a creditor of the creditor who has a judgment

◇ **garnishee** *noun* person who owes money to a creditor and is ordered by a court to pay that money to a creditor of the creditor, and not to the creditor himself; **garnishee order** = court order, making a garnishee pay money to a judgment creditor

gas chamber *noun* room in which a convicted prisoner is executed by poisonous gas

COMMENT: used in some states in the USA

gather *verb* **(a)** to collect together *or* to put together; **he gathered his papers together before the meeting started; she has been gathering information on import controls from various sources (b)** to understand *or* to find out; **I gather he has left the office; did you gather who will be at the meeting?**

GATT = GENERAL AGREEMENT ON TARIFFS AND TRADE

gazump *verb* **he was gazumped** = his agreement to buy the house was cancelled because someone offered more money before exchange of contracts

◇ **gazumping** *noun* (*of a buyer*) offering more money for a house than another buyer has done, so as to be sure of buying it; (*of a seller*) removing the house from a sale which has been agreed, so as to accept a higher offer

GBH = GRIEVOUS BODILY HARM

general *adjective* **(a)** ordinary *or* not special; **general expenses** = all kinds of minor expenses *or* money spent on the day-to-day costs of running a business; **general manager** = manager in charge of the administration of a company; **general office** = main administrative office of a company **(b)** dealing with everything *or* with everybody; **general audit** = examining all the books and accounts of a company; **general average** = sharing of the cost of lost goods between all parties to an insurance; **general damages** = damages awarded by a court to compensate for an unquantifiable loss (such as an injury); **general election** = election of a parliament by all the voters in a country; **general lien** = holding goods or property until a debt has been paid; *compare also* PARTICULAR AVERAGE, PARTICULAR LIEN; **general meeting** = meeting of all the shareholders of a company; **general strike** = strike of all the workers in a country; **Annual General Meeting (AGM)** = meeting of all the shareholders *or* all the members of a club, which takes place once a year to approve the accounts; **Extraordinary General Meeting (EGM)** = special meeting of shareholders *or* members of a club to discuss an important matter which cannot wait until the next Annual General Meeting **(c) the General Agreement on Tariffs and Trade (GATT)** = international treaty which aims to try to reduce restrictions in trade between countries

◇ **generally** *adverb* normally *or* usually; **the office is generally closed between Christmas and the New Year; political crimes are generally dealt with more harshly in the military courts**

generation *noun* all people born at about the same time; members of the same family born at about the same time; **the jewels have been in our family for several generations** = the family has owned the jewels for many years; **generation gap** = age difference between one generation and another, usually making it difficult for them to understand each other

generous *adjective* (person) who is glad to give money; **the staff contributed a generous sum for the retirement present for the manager**

Geneva Convention(s) *noun* international treaties governing behaviour of countries at war; **the attacking army was accused of violating the Geneva Convention**

genocide *noun* killing of a whole race *or* religious group
NOTE: no plural

gentleman *noun* (a) "gentlemen" = (i) way of starting to talk to a group of men; (ii) *US* way of starting a letter to a firm; "ladies and gentlemen" = way of starting to talk to a group of women and men (b) man; **gentleman's agreement** *or* *US* **gentlemen's agreement** = verbal agreement between two parties who trust each other (not usually enforceable by law)

genuine *adjective* true *or* real; **this old table is genuine; a genuine leather purse; the genuine article** = real article, not an imitation; **genuine purchaser** = someone who is really interested in buying

◊ **genuineness** *noun* being real *or* not being an imitation

get *verb* (a) to receive; **we got a letter from the solicitor this morning; he got a £25 fine** *or* **a parking ticket** (b) to arrive at a place; **the shipment got to Canada six weeks late; she finally got to the courtroom at 10.30**
NOTE: getting - got - has got *or* *US* gotten

◊ **get back** *verb* to receive something which you had had before; **I got my money back after I had complained to the manager; he got his initial investment back in two months**

◊ **get off** *verb* not to be punished; **the boys got off with a reprimand from the magistrate**

◊ **get on** *verb* (a) to work *or* to manage; **how is the new secretary getting on?** (b) to succeed; **my son is getting on well - he has just been promoted**

◊ **get on with** *verb* (a) to be friendly *or* to work well with someone; **she does not get on with her new boss** (b) to go on doing work; **the staff got on with the work and finished the order on time**

◊ **get out** *verb* (a) to produce something (on time); **the Royal Commission got out the report in time for the meeting** (b) to sell an investment; **he didn't like the annual report, so he got out before the company became insolvent**

◊ **get round** *verb* to avoid; **we tried to get round the embargo by shipping from Canada; can you advise me how we can get round the quota system?**

get *or* **gett** *noun* divorce according to Jewish religious custom

gift 1 *noun* thing given to someone; **gift inter vivos** = present given by a living person to another living person; **free gift** = present given by a shop to a customer who buys a certain amount of goods

COMMENT: a gift is irrevocable

2 *verb* to give

gilt-edged securities *or* **gilts** *plural noun* British government securities (assumed to be a safe investment)

give *verb* (a) to pass something to someone as a gift; **the office gave him a clock when he retired** (b) to pass something to someone; **she gave the documents to the accountant; can you give me some information about the new computer system? do not give any details to the police** (c) to organize; **the company gave a party after they won their appeal**
NOTE: giving - gave - given

◊ **give away** *verb* to give something as a free present; **we are giving away a pocket calculator with each £10 of purchases**

◊ **giveaway** 1 *adjective* to sell at **giveaway prices** = to sell at very cheap prices 2 *noun* thing which is given as a free gift when another item is bought

◊ **give rise to** *verb* to be the cause of something; **the decision has given rise to complaints from the family of the defendant**

gloss *noun* interpretation *or* meaning given to a word or phrase

go *verb* (a) to move from one place to another; **the cheque went to your bank yesterday; the plane goes to Frankfurt, then to Rome; he is going to our Lagos office** (b) to be placed; **the date goes at the top of the letter**
NOTE: going - went - has gone

◊ **go back on** *verb* not to do what has been promised; **two months later they went back on the agreement**

◊ **going concern** *noun* business which is actively trading

◊ **going equipped for stealing** *noun* notifiable offence of carrying tools which could be used for burglary

◊ **go into** *verb* (a) to go into business = to start in business; **he went into business** selling cars; **she went into business in partnership with her son (b)** to examine carefully; **the bank wants to go into the details of the inter-company loans; the fraud squad is going into the facts behind the property deals**

◇ **go on** *verb* **(a)** to continue; **the staff went on working in spite of the fire; the chairman went on speaking for two hours (b)** to work with; **two fingerprints are all the police have to go on**

◇ **go to law** *verb* to start legal proceedings about something; **we went to law to try to regain our property**

godfather *noun slang* Mafia boss

good *adjective* **(a)** not bad; **a good buy =** excellent item which has been bought cheaply **(b) a good deal of =** a large quantity of; **we wasted a good deal of time discussing the arrangements for the AGM; the company had to pay a good deal of money for the building; a good many =** very many; **a good many staff members have joined the union**

◇ **good behaviour** *noun* behaving well *or* acting in a peaceful and lawful way; **the magistrates bound him over to be of good behaviour; she was sentenced to four years in prison, but was released early for good behaviour**
NOTE: no plural

◇ **good cause** *noun* reason which is accepted in law; **the court asked the accused to show good cause why he should not be sent to prison**
NOTE: not used with **the**

◇ **good consideration** *noun* proper consideration

◇ **good faith** *noun* general honesty; **in good faith =** in an honest way; **he acted in good faith =** he did it honestly; **to buy something in good faith =** to buy something honestly *or* in the course of an honest transaction; **he bought the car in good faith, not knowing that it had been stolen**

◇ **goods** *plural noun* **(a) goods and chattels =** moveable personal possessions; **household goods =** items which are used in the home **(b)** items which can be moved and are for sale; **goods (held) in bond =** imported goods held by the customs until duty is paid; **capital goods =** machinery, buildings and raw materials which are used to make other goods; **consumer goods =** goods bought by the general public and

not by businesses; **goods train =** train for carrying freight

◇ **good title** *noun* title to a property which gives the owner full rights of ownership

◇ **goodwill** *noun* good reputation of a business and its contacts with its customers (such as the name of the product which it sells *or* its popular appeal to customers); **he paid £10,000 for the goodwill of the shop and £4,000 for the stock**

govern *verb* **(a)** to rule a country; **the country is governed by a group of military leaders (b)** to rule *or* to be in authority; **the amount of damages is governed by the seriousness of the injuries suffered**

◇ **government** *noun* **(a)** organization which administers a country; **central government =** main organization dealing with the affairs of the whole country; **local government =** organizations dealing with the affairs of a small area of the country **(b)** coming from the government *or* referring to the government; **government intervention** *or* **intervention by the government; a government ban on the import of arms; a government investigation into organized crime; government officials prevented him leaving the country; government policy is outlined in the book; government regulations state that import duty has to be paid on expensive items; government contractor =** company which supplies goods or services to the government on contract

◇ **governmental** *adjective* referring to a government

◇ **governor** *noun* (i) person in charge of a prison; (ii) person representing the government as the official in charge of a colony; **a prison governor; the prisoners applied to the governor for parole**

gown *noun* long black item of clothing worn by a lawyer *or* judge, etc., over normal clothes when appearing in court; *see also* SILK

grace *noun* favour shown by granting a delay; **to give a creditor a period of grace** *or* **two weeks' grace =** to allow a creditor two weeks to pay

graft *noun informal* corruption of officials
NOTE: no plural

grand 1 *adjective* important; **grand plan = ** major plan; **grand total =** final total

made by adding several smaller totals **2** *noun* *informal* one thousand pounds *or* dollars; **they offered him fifty grand for the information**
NOTE: no plural

◇ **grand jury** *noun* *US* group of jurors (between twelve and twenty-four) who assemble as a preliminary to a trial to decide if an indictment should be issued to start criminal proceedings

◇ **grand larceny** *noun* *US* theft of goods valued at more than a certain price

grant **1** *noun* **(a)** act of giving something to someone (permanently *or* temporarily) by a written document, where the object itself cannot be transferred; **he made a grant of land to his son; grant of letters of administration** = giving of documents to administrators to enable them to administer the estate of a dead person who has not made a will; **grant of probate** = official document proving that a will is genuine, given to the executors so that they can act on the terms of the will **(b)** money given by the government to help pay for something; **the institute has a government grant to cover the cost of the development programme; the local authority has allocated grants towards the costs of the scheme; grant-aided scheme** = scheme which is backed by funds from the government; **death grant** = state grant to the family of a person who has died, which is supposed to contribute to the funeral expenses **2** *verb* to agree to give someone something *or* to agree to allow someone to do something; **to grant someone permission to build a house** *or* **to leave the country; the local authority granted the company an interest-free loan to start up the new factory; he was granted parole; the government granted an amnesty to all political prisoners**

◇ **grantee** *noun* person who is assigned an interest in a property *or* who receives a grant

◇ **grantor** *noun* person who assigns an interest in a property (especially to a lender) *or* who makes a grant

grass *slang* **1** *noun* criminal who gives information to the police about other criminals; *see also* SUPERGRASS **2** *verb* **to grass on someone** = to give information to the police about someone

grata *see* PERSONA

gratia *see* EX GRATIA

gratis *adverb* free *or* not costing anything *or* without paying anything; **we got into the exhibition gratis**

gratuitous *adjective* free *or* with no money being offered; **gratuitous promise** = promise which cannot be enforced because no money has been involved

gratuity *noun* tip *or* money given to someone who has helped you; **the staff are instructed not to accept gratuities**

Gray's Inn *noun* one of the four Inns of Court in London

great *adjective* large; **a great deal of** = very much; **he made a great deal of money on the Stock Exchange; there is a great deal of work to be done before the company can be made really profitable**

◇ **Great Seal** *noun* seal, kept by the Lord Chancellor, used for sealing important public documents on behalf of the Queen

Green Book *noun* the County Court Rules (book of procedural rules of county courts)

green card *noun* **(a)** special British insurance certificate to prove that a car is insured for travel abroad **(b)** work permit for a person going to live in the USA

green form *noun* form for giving free or subsidized legal advice to clients who are eligible for Legal Aid; **the green form scheme** = scheme where a solicitor will give advice to someone free of charge or at a subsidized rate, if the client has filled in the green form

Green Paper *noun* report from the British government on proposals for a new law to be discussed in Parliament

grievance *noun* complaint made by a trade union *or* an employee to the management; **grievance procedure** = agreed way of presenting complaints from a trade union *or* an employee to the management of a company

grievous bodily harm (GBH) *noun* crime of causing serious injury to someone

gross *adjective* **(a)** total *or* with no deductions; **gross domestic product** = annual value of goods sold and services paid for inside a country; **gross earnings** *or* **gross income** *or* **gross salary** = total earnings before tax and other deductions; **gross margin** = percentage difference between sales income and the cost of sales; **gross national product** = annual value of goods and services in a country including income from other countries; **gross profit** = profit calculated as sales income less the cost of the goods sold; **gross receipts** = total amount of money received before expenses are deducted; **gross weight** = weight of both the container and its contents **(b)** serious; **gross indecency** = crime entailing unlawful sexual contact between men or with a child; **gross negligence** = act showing very serious neglect of duty towards other people

ground *noun* **(a)** soil *or* earth; **ground landlord** = person *or* company which owns the freehold of a property which is then leased and subleased; **ground lease** = first lease on a freehold building; **ground rent** = rent paid by a lessee to the ground landlord **(b) grounds** = basic reasons; **does he have good grounds for complaint? there are no grounds on which we can be sued; what are the grounds for the claim for damages?** NOTE: (b) can be used in the singular if only one reason exists: **the judge refused the application on the ground that he had discretion to remove the hearsay evidence from the report**

group 1 *noun* **(a)** several things *or* people together; **a group of staff members has sent a memorandum to the chairman complaining about noise in the office (b)** several companies linked together in the same organization; **the group chairman** *or* **the chairman of the group; group turnover** *or* **turnover for the group; group results** = results of a group of companies taken together **2** *verb* **to group together** = to put several items together; **civil wrongs against persons and their property are grouped together under the heading "torts"**

guarantee 1 *noun* **(a)** document handed to a buyer of goods which promises that a machine will work properly *or* that an item is of good quality; **certificate of guarantee** *or* **guarantee certificate; the guarantee lasts for two years; the typewriter is sold with a two-year guarantee; the car is still under guarantee** = the car is still covered by the maker's certificate of guarantee

COMMENT: in English law, a guarantee must usually be in writing

(b) promise made by a person that he will do what someone else is obliged to do if that other person fails to do it **(c)** thing given as a security; **to leave share certificates as a guarantee**

COMMENT: the person making a guarantee is secondarily liable if the person who is primarily liable defaults. Compare INDEMNITY

2 *verb* to give a promise that something will happen; **to guarantee a debt** = to promise that you will pay a debt incurred by someone else if that person fails to pay it; **to guarantee an associated company** = to promise that an associate company will pay its debts; **to guarantee a bill of exchange** = to promise to pay a bill; **the product is guaranteed for twelve months** = the maker states that the product will work well for twelve months, and promises to mend it free of charge if it breaks down within that period

◊ **guarantor** *noun* person who gives a guarantee; **to stand guarantor for someone** = to promise to pay someone's debts

guard 1 *noun* **(a)** person whose job is to protect people *or* property; **there were three guards on duty at the door of the bank** *or* **three bank guards were on duty; the prisoner was shot by the guards as he tried to escape; security guard** = person whose job is to protect money *or* valuables *or* buildings against theft **(b)** state of being protected by a guard; **the prisoners were brought into the courtroom under armed guard 2** *verb* to protect someone *or* to prevent someone being harmed *or* to prevent someone escaping; **the building is guarded by a fence and ten guard dogs; the prisoners are guarded night and day**

◊ **guardian** *noun* person appointed by law to act on behalf of someone (such as a child) who cannot act on his own behalf; **guardian ad litem** = person who acts on behalf of a minor who is a defendant in a court case; *see also* NEXT FRIEND

◊ **guardianship** *noun* state of being a guardian; **guardianship order** = court order appointing a local authority to be the guardian of a child

guerilla *noun* armed person (not a regular soldier) who engages in unofficial war; **the train was attacked by guerillas; the appeal was made by a guerilla radio station**

guidelines *plural noun* unofficial suggestions from the government or some other body as to how something should be done; **the government has issued guidelines on increases in wages and prices; the Law Society has issued guidelines to its members on dealing with rape cases; the Secretary of State can issue guidelines for expenditure; the Lord Justice said he was not laying down guidelines for sentencing**

guillotine 1 *noun* **(a)** machine used in France for executing criminals by cutting off their heads **(b)** motion in the House of Commons to end a debate at a certain time 2 *verb* to execute someone by cutting his head off with a guillotine

guilt *noun* being guilty *or* state of having committed a crime or done some other legal wrong; **guilt by association** = presumption that a person is guilty because of his connection with another guilty person; **he admitted his guilt** = he admitted that he had committed the crime
NOTE: no plural

◊ **guilty** *adjective* (person) who has done something which is against the law; **he was found guilty of libel; the company was guilty of evading the VAT regulations; guilty knowledge** = MENS REA; (*of a judge or jury*) **to find someone guilty** *or* **to return a verdict of guilty** *or* **to return a guilty verdict** = to say at the end of the trial that the accused is guilty; (*of an accused person*) **to plead guilty** *or* **not guilty** = to say at the beginning of a trial that you did *or* did not commit the crime of which you are accused; **the accused pleaded not guilty to the charge of murder, but pleaded guilty to the lesser charge of manslaughter**

gun *noun* weapon used for shooting; **the police are not allowed to carry guns; they shouted to the robbers to drop their guns**

◊ **gun down** *verb* to kill someone with a gun; **he was gunned down in the street outside his office**
NOTE: **gunned - gunning**

◊ **gunman** *noun* man who carries and uses a gun; **the security van was held up by three gunmen**

◊ **gunpoint** *noun* **at gunpoint** = with a gun pointing at you; **he was forced at gunpoint to open the safe**

◊ **gunshot** *noun* result of shooting with a gun; **he died of gunshot wounds**

Hh

habeas corpus *Latin phrase meaning* "may you have the body": legal remedy against being wrongly imprisoned; **writ of habeas corpus** = writ to obtain the release of someone who has been unlawfully held in prison or in police custody, or to make the person holding him bring him to court to explain why he is being held

habendum *noun* section of a conveyance which gives details of how the property is to be assigned to the purchaser

habitual *adjective* (person) who does something frequently; **habitual criminal** *or* **habitual offender** = person who has been convicted of a similar crime at least twice before; **habitual drunkard** = person who drinks alcohol so frequently that he is almost always dangerous or incapable; **habitual residence** = (i) fact of living normally in a place; (ii) the place where someone normally lives

hallmark 1 *noun* mark put on gold *or* silver items to show that the metal is of the correct quality 2 *verb* to put a hallmark on a piece of gold *or* silver; **a hallmarked spoon**

hand *noun* **(a) to shake hands** = to hold someone's hand when meeting to show you are pleased to meet him *or* to show that an agreement has been reached; **to shake hands on a deal** = to shake hands to show that a deal has been agreed **(b) by hand** = using the hands, not a machine; **to send a letter by hand** = to ask someone to carry and deliver a letter personally, not sending it through the post **(c) in hand** = kept in reserve; **balance in hand** or **cash in hand** = cash held to pay small debts and running costs; **work in hand** = work which is in progress but not finished **(d) goods left on hand** = goods which have not been sold and are left with the retailer or producer **(e) out of hand** = immediately or without taking time to think; **the justices dismissed his evidence out of hand (f) to hand** = here or present; **I have the invoice to hand** = I have the invoice in front of me **(g) show of hands** = way of casting votes where people show how they vote by raising their hands; **the motion was carried on a show of hands (h) to change hands** = to be sold to a new owner; **the shop changed hands for £100,000 (i) note of hand** = document where someone promises to pay money at a stated time without conditions; **in witness whereof, I set my hand** = I sign as a witness

◊ **handcuffs** *plural noun* two metal rings chained together which are locked round the wrists of someone who is being arrested

◊ **handcuffed** *adjective* wearing handcuffs or attached with handcuffs; **the accused appeared in court handcuffed to two policemen**

◊ **hand down** *verb* **(a)** to pass (property) from one generation to another; **the house has been handed down from father to son since the nineteenth century (b) to hand down a verdict** = to announce a verdict

◊ **handgun** *noun* small gun which is carried in the hand; **the police found six handguns when they searched the car**

◊ **hand over** *verb* to pass something to someone; **she handed over the documents to the lawyer; he handed over to his deputy** = he passed his responsibilities to his deputy

◊ **hand up** *verb* to pass to someone who is in a higher place; **the exhibit was handed up to the judge**

◊ **handwriting** *noun* **(a)** writing done by hand; **send a letter of application in your own handwriting** = written by you with a pen, and not typed; **handwriting expert** = person who is able to identify a person by examining his handwriting **(b)** *slang* particular way of committing a crime which identifies a criminal

◊ **handwritten** *adjective* written by hand, not typed; **it is more professional to send in a typed rather than a handwritten letter of application**

handle *verb* **(a)** to deal with something or to organize something; **the courts had difficulty in handling all the cases; the fraud squad handles cases of business malpractice (b)** to sell or to trade in (a sort of product); **we do not handle foreign cars; they will not handle goods produced by other firms**

◊ **handling** *noun* moving something by hand or dealing with something; **handling charges** = money to be paid for packing and making invoices or for dealing with something in general or for moving goods from one place to another; **handling stolen goods** = notifiable offence of dealing with goods (receiving them or selling them) which you know to have been stolen

COMMENT: handling stolen goods is a more serious crime than theft, and the penalty can be higher

hang *verb* **(a)** to attach something to a hook, nail, etc.; **hang your coat on the hook behind the door; he hung his umbrella over the back of his chair (b)** to execute someone by hanging him by a rope round his neck *see also* HUNG
NOTE: **hanging - hung** for meaning (a) and **hanging - hanged** for meaning (b)

◊ **hanging** *noun* act of executing someone by hanging; **the hangings took place in front of the prison**

◊ **hangman** *noun* man who executes criminals by hanging them

Hansard *noun* official report of what is said and done in the House of Commons and the House of Lords

harass *verb* to worry or to bother someone, especially by continually checking on him or taking him into custody

◊ **harassment** *noun* action of harassing someone; **he complained of police harassment or of harassment by the police**
NOTE: no plural

harbour *verb* to give shelter and protection to (a criminal)

hard *adjective* **(a)** strong or not weak; **to take a hard line in trade union negotiations** = to refuse to accept any proposal from the other side **(b)** difficult; **a hard case** = a criminal or an addict who cannot be reformed **(c)** solid or real; **hard cash** = money in notes and coins which is ready at hand; **he paid out £100 in hard cash for the**

chair; **hard copy** = printout of a text which is on computer *or* printed copy of a document which is on microfilm; **hard disk** = computer disk which has a sealed case and can store large quantities of information **(d) hard bargain** = bargain with difficult terms; **to drive a hard bargain** = to be a difficult negotiator; **to strike a hard bargain** = to agree a deal where the terms are favourable to you **(e) hard currency** = currency of a country which has a strong economy and which can be changed into other currencies easily

◊ **hardened criminal** *noun* criminal who has committed many crimes and who will never go straight

◊ **hard labour** *noun* punishment of sending someone to prison to do hard manual labour there

◊ **hardship** *noun* difficulty in living (because of lack of money *or* house, etc.); **the court order may cause hardship to the family of the defendant; in hardship cases *or* in cases of hardship, the local authority may offer temporary accommodation** NOTE: no plural

harm 1 *noun* damage done to (someone); **the newspaper report has done a lot of harm to the firm's reputation** (NOTE: no plural) **2** *verb* to damage; **the news that the chairman has been arrested for fraud has harmed the company's reputation**

harsh *adjective* severe *or* which does not treat someone in a kind way; **the magistrate gave harsh sentences to the rioters; they complained of harsh treatment on the part of the warders**

◊ **harshly** *adverb* in a harsh way *or* not in a kind way; **the prisoners have complained that they are harshly treated in the military prisons**

◊ **harshness** *noun* being harsh; **the newspapers commented on the harshness of the sentence**

hatred *noun* violent dislike of someone *or* something; **his hatred of injustice *or* of inequality; racial hatred** = violent dislike of someone because of his race NOTE: no plural

hazard *noun* danger; **fire hazard** = situation *or* goods which could start a fire

head 1 *noun* **(a)** most important person; **head of department *or* department head** =

person in charge of a department **(b)** most important *or* main; **head clerk; head porter; head salesman; head waiter; head office** = main office, where the board of directors works and meets **(c)** top part *or* first part; **write the name of the company at the head of the list (d)** person; **allow £10 per head for expenses; representatives cost on average £25,000 per head per annum (e) heads of agreement** = draft agreement containing the most important points but not all the details; **head of damage** = item of damage in a pleading *or* claim **2** *verb* **(a)** to be the manager *or* to be the most important person; **to head a department; he is heading a government delegation to China (b)** to be first; **the list of cases to be heard is headed by two murder cases; the two largest oil companies head the list of stock market results**

◊ **headed** *adjective* **headed paper** = notepaper with the name of the company and its address printed on it

◊ **headhunt** *verb* to look for managers and offer them jobs in other companies; **he was headhunted** = he was approached by a headhunter and offered a new job

◊ **headhunter** *noun* person *or* company which looks for top managers and offers them jobs in other companies

◊ **heading** *noun* **(a)** words at the top of a piece of text, especially words at the beginning of a section of a statute; **items are listed under several headings; look at the figure under the heading "Costs 85-86" (b)** letter heading *or* heading on notepaper = name and address of a business, firm *or* company printed at the top of its notepaper

◊ **head lease** *noun* first lease given by a freeholder to a tenant

◊ **head licence** *noun* first licence given by the owner of a patent *or* copyright to someone who will use it

◊ **headnote** *noun* note at the beginning of a law report, giving a summary of the case

◊ **headquarters** *plural noun* main office; **police headquarters** = central office of a police force

hear *verb* **(a)** to sense a sound with the ears; **you can hear the printer in the next office; the traffic makes so much noise that I cannot hear my phone ringing (b)** to have a letter *or* a phone call from someone; **we**

have not heard from them for some time; we hope to hear from the lawyers within a few days **(c)** to listen to the arguments in a court case; **the judge heard the case in chambers; the case will be heard next month; the court has heard the evidence for the defence**
NOTE: hearing - heard

◊ **hearing** *noun* case which is being heard in court; **the hearing lasted ten days; hearing in camera** = court case which is heard in private with no member of the public present; **preliminary hearing** = court proceedings where the witnesses and the defendant are examined to see if there are sufficient grounds for the case to proceed *or* to try a specific issue rather than the whole case

◊ **hearsay evidence** *noun* evidence by a witness who has heard it from another source, but did not witness the acts himself

heavy 1 *adjective* harsh *or* not treating someone in a kind way; **the looters were given heavy jail sentences; he was sentenced to pay a heavy fine 2** *noun* *slang* strong man employed to frighten people

◊ **heavily** *adverb* **he had to borrow heavily to pay the fine** = he had to borrow a lot of money

heir *noun* person who receives *or* will receive property when someone dies; **his heirs split the estate between them; heirs and assigns** = people who have inherited property and had it transferred to them; **heir apparent** = heir who will certainly inherit if a person dies before him; **heir presumptive** = heir who will inherit if a person dies at this moment, but whose inheritance may be altered in the future

◊ **heiress** *noun* female heir

◊ **heirloom** *noun* piece of family property (such as silver *or* a painting *or* a jewel) which has been handed down for several generations; **the burglars stole some family heirlooms**

heist *noun* *slang* holdup

help 1 *noun* thing which makes it easy to do something; **she finds the computer a great help in writing letters; the company was set up with help from the government; counsel did not get much help from the witness 2** *verb* to make it easy for something to be done; **his evidence did not** help the case for the defendant; his case was not helped by the evidence of the expert witness; **to help police with their inquiries** = to be taken to the police station for questioning

henceforth *adverb* from this time on; **henceforth it will be more difficult to avoid customs examinations**

here- *prefix* this time *or* this point

◊ **hereafter** *adverb* from this time *or* point on

◊ **hereby** *adverb* in this way *or* by this letter; **we hereby revoke the agreement of January 1st 1982**

hereditament *noun* property, including land and buildings, which can be inherited; **corporeal hereditaments** = rights of property which physically exist, such as houses, furniture; **incorporeal hereditaments** = rights (such as patents *or* copyrights) which can form part of an estate and be inherited

hereditary *adjective* which is inherited *or* which is passed from one member of a family to another; **hereditary office** = official position which is inherited; **hereditary peer** = member of the House of Lords who has inherited his title

herein *adverb* in this document; **the conditions stated herein; see the reference herein above**

◊ **hereinafter** *adverb* stated later in this document; **the conditions hereinafter listed**

◊ **hereof** *adverb* of this; **in confirmation hereof we attach a bank statement** = to confirm this we attach a bank statement

◊ **hereto** *adverb* to this; **according to the schedule of payments attached hereto; as witness hereto** = as a witness of this fact; **the parties hereto** = the parties to this agreement

◊ **heretofore** *adverb* previously *or* earlier; **the parties heretofore acting as trustees**

◊ **hereunder** *adverb* under this heading *or* below this phrase; **see the documents listed hereunder**

◊ **herewith** *adverb* together with this letter; **please find the cheque enclosed herewith**

Her Majesty's pleasure *noun* **detention at** *or* **during Her Majesty's pleasure** = detention for an indefinite period, until the Home Secretary decides that a prisoner can be released

> COMMENT: used as a punishment for people under a disability and children who commit murder

hesitate *verb* not to be sure what to do next; **the jury is hesitating about its verdict; she hesitated for some time before answering the question**

hidden *adjective* which cannot be seen; **hidden asset** = asset which is valued in the company's accounts at much less than its true market value; **hidden reserves** = illegal reserves which are not declared in the company's balance sheet; **hidden defect in the program** = defect which was not noticed when a computer program was tested

high 1 *adjective* **(a)** tall; **the shelves are 30 cm high; the top of the table is 20 inches high; the door is not high enough to let us get the machines into the building; they are planning a 30-storey high office block (b)** large *or* not low; **highest bidder** = person who offers the most money at an auction; **high flier** = (i) person who is very successful *or* who is likely to get a very important job; (ii) share whose market price is rising rapidly; **high sales** = large amount of revenue produced by sales; **high taxation** = taxation which imposes large taxes on wages *or* profits; **high volume (of sales)** = large number of items sold **2** *adverb* **prices are running high** = prices are above their usual level **3** *noun* point where prices *or* sales are very large; **sales volume has reached an all-time high** = has reached the highest point at which it has ever been

◊ **High Court (of Justice)** *noun* main civil court in England and Wales

> COMMENT: in England and Wales, the High Court is divided into three divisions: the Queen's Bench, the Chancery and the Family Divisions; the Court hears most civil claims where the value exceeds £5,000

◊ **High Court of Justiciary** *noun* the supreme criminal court of Scotland

◊ **high seas** *plural noun* part of the sea which is further than three miles *or* five kilometres from a coast, and so is under international jurisdiction
NOTE: usually used with "the": **an accident on the high seas**

◊ **High Sheriff** *noun* senior representative appointed by the government in a county

◊ **highway** *noun* road *or* path with a right of way which anyone may use; **the Highway Code** = rules which govern the behaviour of people and vehicles using roads

> COMMENT: the Highway Code is not itself part of English law

hijack 1 *noun* act of taking control of a plane *or* ship *or* train *or* lorry which is moving; **the hijack was organized by a group of opponents to the government 2** *verb* to take control of a moving plane *or* ship *or* train *or* lorry, with passengers on board, by threatening the crew; **the plane was hijacked by six armed terrorists; the bandits hijacked the lorry and killed the driver**

◊ **hijacker** *noun* person who hijacks a vehicle

◊ **hijacking** *noun* act of taking control of a moving plane *or* ship *or* train *or* lorry by force; **the hijacking took place just after the plane took off; there have been six hijackings so far this year**

Hilary *noun* one of the four sittings of the law courts; one of the four law terms

hire 1 *noun* **(a)** paying money to rent a car *or* boat *or* piece of equipment for a time; **car hire firm** *or* **equipment hire firm** = company which owns cars *or* equipment and lends them to customers for a payment; **hire car** = car which has been rented **(b)** "**for hire**" = sign on a taxi showing it is empty **2** *verb* **(a) to hire staff** = to engage new staff to work for you; **we have hired the best lawyers to represent us; they hired a small company to paint the offices (b) to hire a car** *or* **a crane** = to pay money to use a car *or* a crane for a time **(c) to hire out cars** *or* **equipment** = to lend cars *or* equipment to customers who pay for their use

◊ **hired** *adjective* **a hired car** = car which has been rented; **hired killer** = person who will kill someone for a fee

◊ **hire purchase** *noun* system of buying something by paying a sum regularly each month until you own it completely; **to buy a refrigerator on hire purchase**; **to sign a hire-purchase agreement** = to sign a contract to pay for something by instalments; **hire-purchase company** = company which provides money for hire purchase
NOTE: the US English is **installment plan**

◊ **hirer** *noun* person who hires something

hit *verb* *slang* to kill

◊ **hit man** *noun* *slang* hired killer *or* person who will kill for a fee

hoard *verb* to buy and store food in case of need *or* to keep cash instead of investing it

◊ **hoarder** *noun* person who buys and stores food in case of need

◊ **hoarding** *noun* (a) **hoarding of supplies** = buying large quantities of food to keep in case of need (b) **advertisement hoarding** = large board for sticking advertisements

hoc *see* AD HOC

hold *verb* (a) to own *or* to keep *or* to possess; **he holds 10% of the company's shares; she holds the land under a lease from the property company** (b) to contain; **the tin holds twenty packets; each box holds 250 sheets of paper; a bag can hold twenty kilos of sugar** (c) to occupy land; **he holds fifty acres in South Scotland** (d) to make something happen; **to hold a meeting or a discussion; the hearings were held in camera; the receiver will hold an auction of the company's assets; the inquiry will be held in London in June** (e) to keep (someone) in custody; **the prisoners are being held in the police station; twenty people were held in the police raid; she was held for six days without being able to see her lawyer** (f) to decide *or* to make a judgment; **the court held that there was no case to answer; the appeal judge held that the defendant was not in breach of his statutory duty**
NOTE: holding - held

◊ **hold back** *verb* to wait *or* not to go forward; **he held back from signing the lease until he had checked the details** = he delayed signing the lease until he had

checked the details; **payment will be held back until the contract has been signed** = payment will not be made until the contract has been signed

◊ **holder** *noun* (a) person who owns *or* keeps something; **holders of government bonds** *or* **bondholders; holder of stock *or* of shares in a company; holder of an insurance policy** *or* **policy holder; she is a British passport holder** *or* **she is the holder of a British passport; credit card holder** = person who has a credit card; **debenture holder** = person who holds a debenture for money lent (b) person to whom a cheque is made payable and who has possession of it (c) person who is holding a bill of exchange *or* promissory note; **holder in due course** = person who takes a bill *or* promissory note *or* cheque before it becomes overdue *or* is dishonoured (d) thing which keeps something *or* which protects something; **card holder *or* message holder** = frame which protects a card *or* a message; **credit card holder** = plastic wallet for keeping credit cards

◊ **holding** *noun* group of shares owned; **he has sold all his holdings in the Far East; the company has holdings in German manufacturing companies; cross holdings** = situation where two companies own shares in each other in order to stop each from being taken over; **the two companies have protected themselves from takeover by a system of cross holdings**

◊ **holding charge** *noun* minor charge brought against someone so that he can be held in custody while more serious charges are being prepared

◊ **holding company** *noun* company which exists only to own shares in subsidiary companies

◊ **holding over** *noun* situation where a person who had a lease for a certain period continues to occupy the property after the end of the lease

◊ **hold out** *verb* (a) to behave in a way which misleads others; **he held himself out as a director of the company** = he behaved like a director (b) to hold out for = to ask for something and refuse to act until you get what you asked for; **he held out for a 50% discount; the union is holding out for a 10% wage increase**

◊ **hold over** *verb* (a) to postpone *or* to put back to a later date; **discussion of item 4 was held over until the next meeting** (b) to allow someone who has had a lease to continue to occupy the property after the lease has ended

◇ **hold to** *verb* not to allow something to change; **we will try to hold him to the contract** = we will try to stop him going against the contract; **the government hopes to hold wage increases to 5%** = the government hopes that wage increases will not be more than 5%

◇ **hold up** *verb* **(a)** to go into a bank *or* to stop a lorry, in order to steal money; **six gunmen held up the bank or the security van (b)** to stay at a high level; **share prices have held up well; sales held up during the tourist season (c)** to delay; **the shipment has been held up at the customs; payment will be held up until the contract has been signed; the strike will hold up delivery for some weeks**

◇ **holdup** *noun* act of holding up a bank, etc.; **the gang committed three armed holdups on the same day**

◇ **hold-up** *noun* delay; **the strike caused hold-ups in the shipment of goods**

holiday *noun* **(a)** bank holiday = weekday which is a public holiday when the banks are closed; **Easter Monday is a bank holiday; public holiday** = day when all workers rest and enjoy themselves instead of working; **statutory holiday** = holiday which is fixed by law **(b)** period when a worker does not work, but rests, goes away and enjoys himself; **to take a holiday** *or* **to go on holiday; when is the manager taking his holidays? my secretary is off on holiday tomorrow; he is away on holiday for two weeks; the job carries five weeks' holiday** = one of the conditions of the job is that you have five weeks' holiday; **the summer holidays** = holidays taken by the workers in the summer when the weather is good and children are not at school; **holiday entitlement** = number of days' paid holiday which a worker has the right to take; **holiday pay** = salary which is still paid during the holiday **(c) tax holiday** = period when a new business is exempted from paying tax

holograph *noun* document written by hand; **he left a holograph will**

home *noun* place where a person lives *or* country where a company is based; **home-produced products** = products which are not imported

◇ **Home Office** *noun* British government ministry dealing with internal affairs, including the police and prisons

◇ **Home Secretary** *noun* member of the British government, the minister in charge of the Home Office, dealing with law and order, the police and prisons

COMMENT: in most countries the government department dealing with the internal order of the country is called the Ministry of the Interior, with a Minister of the Interior in charge

◇ **homestead** *noun* US house and land where a family lives

COMMENT: a homestead cannot be the subject of a sale by court order

homicide *noun* **(a)** killing of a person (either accidental or illegal); **he was found guilty of homicide; the homicide rate has doubled in the last ten years; culpable homicide** = murder *or* manslaughter; **justifiable homicide** = killing of a person for an acceptable reason (such as in self-defence) **(b)** murder; **the Homicide Squad** = special section of the police force which investigates murders

COMMENT: homicide covers the crimes of murder, manslaughter and infanticide

◇ **homicidal** *adjective* (person) who is likely to commit murder

honest *adjective* truthful *or* saying what is right; **to play the honest broker** = to act for the parties in a negotiation to try to help them agree to a solution

◇ **honestly** *adverb* saying what is right *or* not cheating

◇ **honesty** *noun* being honest *or* telling the truth; **the court praised the witness for her honesty in informing the police of the crime**

honorarium *noun* money paid to a professional person, such as an accountant *or* a lawyer, which is less than a full fee

◇ **honorary** *adjective* person who is not paid a salary; **honorary secretary; honorary president; honorary member** = member of a club *or* group who does not have to pay a subscription

honour *verb* to accept and pay a cheque *or* bill of exchange; **to honour a debt** = to pay a debt because it is owed and is correct; **to honour a signature** = to pay something because the signature is correct

hoodlum *noun* *US* gangster

hooligan *noun* person who behaves violently in public; **the police put up barriers to prevent the football hooligans from damaging property**

hospital *noun* place where sick people can be kept and treated; **hospital order** = court order putting an insane offender in hospital instead of in prison

hostage *noun* person captured by an enemy *or* by criminals and kept until a ransom is paid; **he was taken hostage by the guerillas; the bandits took away the bank manager and kept him hostage; the terrorists released three hostages**

hostile *adjective* not friendly; **hostile witness** = witness called by a party, whose evidence goes unexpectedly against that party, and who can then be cross-examined by his own side as if he were giving evidence for the other side; **she was ruled a hostile witness by the judge**

hot *adjective* **(a)** very warm; **the staff complain that the office is too hot in the summer and too cold in the winter; the drinks machines sells coffee, tea and hot soup; switch off the machine if it gets too hot (b)** not safe *or* very bad; **to make things hot for someone** = to make it difficult for someone to work *or* to trade; **customs officials are making things hot for the drug smugglers; hot money** = money which is moved from country to country to get the best interest rates; **he is in the hot seat** = his job involves making many difficult decisions **(c)** *informal* stolen *or* illegal; **hot jewels; a hot car**

◊ **hot pursuit** *noun* right in international law to chase a ship into international waters *or* to chase suspected criminals across an international border into another country

hotchpot *noun* bringing together into one fund money to be distributed under a will

house *noun* **(a)** building in which someone lives; **house property** = private

houses, not shops, offices or factories; **house agent** = estate agent who deals in buying or selling houses **(b)** one of the two parts of the British Parliament; **the Houses of Parliament** = (i) the building where the British Parliament meets; (ii) the British Parliament **(c)** *US* **the House** = the House of Representatives

◊ **house arrest** *noun* being ordered by a court to stay in your house and not to leave it; **the opposition leader has been under house arrest for six years**

◊ **housebreaker** *noun* burglar *or* person who breaks into houses and steals things

◊ **housebreaking** *noun* burglary *or* entering a house and stealing things

◊ **household** *noun* people living in a house; **household effects** = furniture and other items used in a house, and moved with the owner when he moves house

◊ **householder** *noun* person who occupies a private house

◊ **House of Commons** *noun* lower house of the British Parliament, made up of about 650 elected members

◊ **House of Lords** *noun* upper house of the British Parliament made up of hereditary lords, life peers, leading judges and bishops; **Judicial Committee of the House of Lords** = highest court of appeal in both civil and criminal cases in England and Wales

COMMENT: as a court, the decisions of the House of Lords are binding on all other courts, and the only appeal from the House of Lords is to the European Court of Justice

◊ **House of Representatives** *noun* lower house of the Congress of the United States

◊ **house-to-house** *adjective* going from one house to the next (to ask people questions *or* to ask people to buy something *or* to vote for someone); **the police carried out a house-to-house search for the escaped prisoners**

human *adjective* referring to men and women; **human error** = mistake made by a person, not by a machine; **human rights** = rights of individual men and women to basic freedoms, such as freedom of association, freedom of speech

hung *adjective* with no majority; **hung jury** = jury which cannot arrive at a unanimous *or* majority verdict; **hung parliament** = parliament where no single party has enough votes to form a government; *see also* HANG

hunger strike *noun* protest (often by a prisoner), where the person refuses to eat until his demands have been met; **he went on hunger strike until the prison authorities allowed him to receive mail**

hunt 1 *noun* looking for something *or* someone; **the police have organized a hunt for the stolen gold** *or* **for the escaped prisoners** *or* **for the murder weapon; murder hunt** = search for a suspected murderer **2** *verb* to look for; **the police are hunting for clues to the murder**

hurdle *noun* thing which prevents something happening; **the defendant will have to overcome two hurdles if his appeal is to be successful**

hurry 1 *noun* doing things fast; **there is no hurry for the figures, we do not need them until next week; in a hurry** = very fast **2** *verb* to do something *or* to make something *or* to go very fast; **the government whips are trying to hurry the bill through the committee stages; the chairman does not want to be hurried into making a decision; the directors hurried into the meeting**

hurt *verb* to harm *or* to damage; **the criticism in the newspapers did not hurt our sales; sales of summer clothes were hurt by the bad weather; the company has not been hurt by the recession**

husband *noun* male spouse

hush money *noun* *informal* money paid to someone to stop him talking

hybrid offence *noun* offence which can be tried either by magistrates or by a judge and jury

Ii

ibid *or* **ibidem** *adverb* just the same *or* in the same place in a book

ID = IDENTITY; **ID card** = IDENTITY CARD

idem *pronoun* the same thing *or* the same person; **ad idem** = in agreement

identify *verb* to say who someone is *or* what something is; **she was able to identify her attacker; passengers were asked to identify their suitcases; the dead man was identified by his fingerprints**
◇ **identification** *noun* act of identifying someone *or* something; **proof of identification** = (i) proving that something is what the evidence says it is; (ii) proving that someone is who he says he is; **the policeman asked him for proof of identification; identification parade** = arranging for a group of people (including a suspect) to stand in line at a police station so that a witness can point out the criminal
◇ **identikit** *noun* method of making a picture of a criminal from descriptions given by witnesses, using pieces of photographs and drawings of different types of faces; **the police issued an identikit picture of the mugger**
◇ **identity** *noun* **(a)** who someone is; **he changed his identity** = he assumed a different name, changed his appearance, etc., (usually done to avoid being recognized); **he was asked for proof of identity** = he was asked to prove he really was the person he said he was; **identity card** *or* **ID card** *or* **identity disk** = card *or* disk carried to show who the holder is; **identity parade** = IDENTIFICATION PARADE; **case of mistaken identity** = situation where a person is wrongly thought to be someone else **(b)** being the same; **identity of parties** = situation where the parties in different actions are the same

i.e. that is; **the largest companies, i.e. Smith's and Brown's, show very good profits; the import restrictions apply to expensive items, i.e. items costing more than $2,500**

ignorance *noun* not knowing; **ignorance of the law is no excuse** = the fact that someone does not know that he has committed an offence does not make the offence any the less

ignorantia legis non *or* **neminem** *or* **haud excusat** *Latin phrase meaning* "ignorance of the law is not an excuse for anyone"

illegal *adjective* not legal *or* against criminal law; **the illegal carrying of arms; illegal immigrants are deported; illegal contract** = contract which cannot be enforced in law (such as a contract to commit a crime)
◊ **illegality** *noun* being illegal
◊ **illegally** *adverb* against the law; **he was accused of illegally bringing firearms into the country**

illegitimate *adjective* **(a)** against the law **(b)** (person) born to parents who are not married to each other
◊ **illegitimacy** *noun* being illegitimate
NOTE: no plural

illicit *adjective* not legal *or* not permitted; **illicit sale of alcohol; trade in illicit alcohol**

imitate *verb* to do what someone else does; **this new gang is imitating all the tricks of the famous Chinese gang of the 1930s**
◊ **imitation** *noun* thing which copies another; **beware of imitations** = be careful not to buy low quality goods which are made to look like other more expensive items

immediate *adjective* happening at once; **he wrote an immediate letter of complaint; the magistrate ordered her immediate release**
◊ **immediately** *adverb* at once; **as soon as she arrived in the country, she was immediately arrested by the airport police; as soon as he heard the news he immediately phoned his office; can you phone immediately you get the information?**

immemorial *adjective* so old it cannot be remembered; **immemorial existence** *or* **time immemorial** = before 1189, the date from which events are supposed to be remembered; **from time immemorial** = for so long that no one can remember when it started

immigrate *verb* to move to this country to live permanently
◊ **immigration** *noun* moving to this country to live permanently; **Immigration Laws** = legislation regarding immigration into a country
◊ **immigrant** *noun* person who moves to this country to live permanently; **illegal immigrant** = person who enters a country to live permanently without having the permission of the government to do so; *see also* EMIGRATE, EMIGRANT

immoral earnings *plural noun* money earned from prostitution; **living off immoral earnings** = offence of making a living from money obtained from prostitutes

immovable *adjective & noun* which cannot be moved; **immovable property** *or* **immovables** = land, and houses and other buildings on land

immunity *noun* protection against arrest *or* prosecution; **diplomatic immunity** = not being subject to the laws of the country in which you are living because of being a diplomat; **when he offered to give information to the police, he was granted immunity from prosecution** = he was told he would not be prosecuted; **judicial immunity** = safety from prosecution granted to judges when acting in a judicial capacity

COMMENT: immunity from prosecution is also granted to magistrates, counsel and witnesses as regards their statements in judicial proceedings. Families and servants of diplomats may be covered by diplomatic immunity

impanel = EMPANEL

impartial *adjective* not partial *or* not biased *or* not prejudiced; **a judgment must be impartial; to give someone a fair and impartial hearing**
◊ **impartiality** *noun* state of being impartial; **the newspapers doubted the impartiality of the judge**
◊ **impartially** *adverb* not showing any bias *or* favour towards someone; **the adjudicator has to decide impartially between the two parties**

impeach *verb* **(a)** formerly to charge a person with treason before Parliament **(b)** to charge a head of state with treason **(c)** *US* to discredit (a witness)

◇ **impeachment** *noun* charge of treason brought against a head of state

impending *adjective* which will happen soon; **the newspapers carried stories about the impending divorce case**

imperfect *adjective* not perfect; **sale of imperfect items; to check a shipment for imperfect products**

◇ **imperfection** *noun* part of an item which is not perfect; **to check a shipment for imperfections**

impersonal *adjective* without any personal touch *or* as if done by machines; **an impersonal style of management**

impersonate *verb* to pretend to be someone else; **he gained entrance to the house by impersonating a local authority inspector**

◇ **impersonation** *noun* pretending to be someone else; **he was charged with impersonation of a police officer**

implement **1** *noun* tool *or* instrument used to do some work; **he was hit on the head with a heavy implement 2** *verb* to put into action; **to implement an agreement** *or* **a decision**

◇ **implementation** *noun* putting into action; **the implementation of new rules**

implicit *adjective* implied *or* not clearly stated

imply *verb* to suggest (that something may be true); **counsel implied that the witness had not in fact seen the accident take place; do you wish to imply that the police acted improperly?**

◇ **implied** *adjective* which is presumed to exist *or* which can be established by circumstantial evidence; **implied contract** = agreement which is considered to be a contract, because the parties intended it to be a contract *or* because the law considers it to be a contract; **implied malice** = intention to commit grievous bodily harm on someone; **implied terms and conditions** = terms and conditions which are not written in a contract, but which are legally taken to be present in the contract; **implied trust** = trust which is implied by the intentions and actions of the parties

import **1** *noun* bringing foreign goods into a country to be sold; **the import of firearms is forbidden; import levy** = tax on imports, especially in the EEC a tax on imports of farm produce from outside the EEC; **import licence** = permit which allows a company to bring a certain type of product into a country **2** *verb* to bring foreign goods into a country

◇ **imports** *plural noun* goods brought into a country; **all imports must be declared to the customs**

importance *noun* having a value *or* mattering a lot; **the bank attaches great importance to the deal**

◇ **important** *adjective* which matters a lot; **he left a pile of important papers in the taxi; she has an important meeting at 10.30; he was promoted to a more important position**

importuning *noun* crime of asking someone to have sexual relations with you (for money)

impose *verb* to ask someone to pay a fine; to put a tax *or* a duty on goods; **the court imposed a fine of £100; to impose a tax on bicycles; they tried to impose a ban on smoking; the government imposed a special duty on oil; the customs have imposed a 10% tax increase on electrical items; the unions have asked the government to impose trade barriers on foreign cars**

◇ **imposition** *noun* putting a tax on goods or services

impossible *adjective* which cannot be done; **it is impossible for the police force to work harder than they are working already; getting skilled staff is becoming impossible; government regulations make it impossible for us to sell our computer parts**

◇ **impossibility of performance** *noun* situation where a party to a contract is unable to perform his part of the contract

impound *verb* to take something away and keep it until a tax is paid *or* until documents are checked to see if they are correct; **the customs impounded the whole cargo**

◇ **impounding** *noun* act of taking something and keeping it

impression *noun* effect which something *or* someone makes on a person; **counsel's speech made a strong impression on the jury; the judge got the impression that the witness worked in a bank; case of first impression** = case which raises points of law for which there are no precedents

imprison *verb* to put (someone) in prison; **he was imprisoned by the secret police for six months**
◇ **imprisonment** *noun* being put in prison; **the penalty for the first offence is a fine of £200 or six weeks' imprisonment; a term of imprisonment** = time which a prisoner has to spend in prison; **he was sentenced to the maximum term of imprisonment; false imprisonment** = (i) tort of keeping someone wrongly imprisoned; (ii) sending someone to prison for a wrong reason; **life imprisonment** = being put in prison for a long time (the penalty for murder)

COMMENT: life imprisonment is a term of many years, but not necessarily for the rest of the prisoner's life

improper *adjective* not correct *or* not as it should be
◇ **improperly** *adverb* not correctly; **the police constable's report was improperly made out; he was accused of acting improperly in going to see the prisoner's father**

impulse *noun* strong wish to do something; **irresistible impulse** = strong wish to do something which you cannot resist because of insanity

impunity *noun* **with impunity** = without punishment; **no one can flout the law with impunity**

impute *verb* to suggest; **to impute a motive to someone** = to suggest that someone had a certain motive in acting as he did
◇ **imputation** *noun* suggestion (that someone has done something wrong); **imputation of malice** = suggestion that someone acted out of malice

in absentia *adverb* in someone's absence; **she was tried and sentenced to death in absentia**

inadmissible *adjective* (evidence) which a court cannot admit

inalienable *adjective* (right) which cannot be taken away *or* transferred

Inc = INCORPORATED

in camera *adverb* in private *or* with no members of the public permitted to be present; **the case was heard in camera**

incapable *adjective* not able; **he was incapable of fulfilling the terms of the contract; a child is considered legally incapable of committing a crime; drunk and incapable** = offence of having drunk so much alcohol that you are not able to act normally
◇ **incapacity** *noun* not being legally able to do something; **the court had to act because of the incapacity of the trustees**

incapax *see* DOLI INCAPAX

incarcerate *verb* to put in prison; **he was incarcerated in a stone tower**
◇ **incarceration** *noun* imprisonment *or* act of putting a criminal in prison

incest *noun* notifiable offence of having sexual intercourse with a close relative (daughter, son, mother, father)

in chambers *adverb* in the office of a judge, and not in court; **the judge heard the application in chambers**

inchoate *adjective* started, but not complete; **inchoate instrument** = document which is not complete; **inchoate offences** = offences (such as incitement *or* attempt *or* conspiracy to commit a crime) which are offences even though the substantive offence may not have been committed

incidence *noun* how often something happens; **the incidence of cases of rape has increased over the last years; a high incidence of accidents relating to drunken drivers**

incident *noun* **1** thing which has happened (especially a crime *or* accident); **three incidents were reported when police vehicles were attacked by a crowd; incident**

room = special room in a police station to deal with a particular crime *or* accident **2** *adjective* **incident to something** = which depends on something else

◇ **incidental** *adjective* not important *or* depending on someone else; **incidental expenses** = small amounts of money spent at various times, in addition to larger amounts

incite *verb* to encourage *or* persuade *or* advise (someone) to commit a crime

◇ **incitement** *noun* crime of encouraging *or* persuading *or* advising someone to commit a crime; **incitement to racial hatred** = offence of encouraging (by words *or* actions *or* writing) people to attack others because of their race

◇ **inciter** *noun* person who incites someone to commit a crime

COMMENT: it is not necessary for a crime to have been committed for incitement to be proved

include *verb* to count something along with other things; **the charge includes VAT; the total comes to £1,000 including freight; the total is £140 not including insurance and freight; the account covers services up to and including the month of June; including, but not limited to** = counting this item, but not excluding other items

◇ **inclusive** *adjective* which counts something in with other things; **inclusive of tax** *or* **not inclusive of VAT; inclusive sum** *or* **inclusive charge** = charge which includes all costs; **the meeting runs from the 12th to the 16th inclusive** = it starts on the morning of the 12th and ends on the evening of the 16th

income *noun* money which a person receives as salary *or* dividend *or* interest; **income tax** = tax on a person's income

incompetent *adjective* **(a)** who cannot work well *or* who is not able to do something; **the sales manager is quite incompetent; the company has an incompetent sales director (b)** not legally able to do something; **he is incompetent to sign the contract**

◇ **incompetency** *noun* state of not being legally competent to do something

inconvenience 1 *noun* situation which someone finds awkward *or* difficult; **the protest march caused some inconvenience to the local shopkeepers 2** *verb* to make things difficult *or* awkward for someone

incorporate *verb* **(a)** to bring something in to form part of a main group *or* to make a document part of another document; **income from the 1984 acquisition is incorporated into the accounts; the list of markets is incorporated into the main contract (b)** to form a registered company; **a company incorporated in the USA; an incorporated company; J. Doe Incorporated**

◇ **incorporation** *noun* act of incorporating a company; **articles of incorporation** = document which regulates the way in which a company's affairs are managed; **certificate of incorporation** = certificate issued by the Registrar of Companies showing that a company has been officially incorporated and the date at which it came into existence

incorporeal *adjective* which is not physical *or* which cannot be touched; **incorporeal chattels** = properties like patents *or* copyrights; **incorporeal hereditaments** = rights (such as patents *or* copyrights) which can form part of an estate and be inherited

incorrect *adjective* wrong *or* not correct; **the minutes of the meeting were incorrect and had to be changed**

◇ **incorrectly** *adverb* wrongly *or* not correctly; **the indictment was incorrectly worded**

increase 1 *noun* **(a)** growth *or* becoming larger; **increase in tax** *or* **tax increase; increase in price** *or* **price increase; profits showed a 10% increase** *or* **an increase of 10% on last year; increase in the cost of living** = rise in the annual cost of living **(b)** higher salary; **increase in pay** *or* **pay increase; increase in salary** *or* **salary increase; the government hopes to hold salary increases to 3%; cost-of-living increase** = increase in salary to allow it keep up with the increased cost of living; **merit increase** = increase in pay given to a worker whose work is good **(c) on the increase** = growing larger *or* becoming more frequent; **stealing from shops is on the increase 2** *verb* **(a)** to grow bigger *or* higher; **to**

increase in price = to cost more; **to increase in size** *or* **in value** = to become larger *or* more valuable **(b) his salary was increased to £20,000** = he had a rise in salary to £20,000

◇ **increasing** *adjective* which is growing bigger; **increasing profits; the company has an increasing share of the market**

◇ **increasingly** *adverb* more and more; **the company has to depend increasingly on the home consumer market**

incriminate *verb* to show that a person has committed a criminal act; **he was incriminated by the recorded message he sent to the victim**

◇ **incriminating** *adjective* which shows that someone has committed a crime; **incriminating evidence was found in his car**

incumbent *adjective* **it is incumbent upon him** = he has to do this, because it is his duty; **it is incumbent upon justices to give some warning of their doubts about a case**

incumbrance = ENCUMBRANCE

incur *verb* to make yourself liable to; **to incur the risk of a penalty** = to make it possible that you risk paying a penalty; **to incur debts** *or* **costs** = to do something which means that you owe money *or* that you will have to pay costs; **the company has incurred heavy costs to implement the development programme** = the company has had to pay large sums of money
NOTE: **incurring - incurred**

incuriam *see* PER INCURIAM

indebted *adjective* owing money to someone; **to be indebted to a property company**

◇ **indebtedness** *noun* amount of money owed by someone; **state of indebtedness** = being in debt *or* owing money

indecent *adjective* rude *or* not decent *or* which an ordinary person would find shocking; **indecent assault** = crime of assaulting a person together with an indecent act or proposal; **indecent exposure** = offence where a male person shows his sexual organs to a woman

◇ **indecency** *noun* being indecent; (*of a man*) **to commit an act of gross indecency** = to have unlawful sexual contact with

another man *or* with a child
NOTE: no plural

indefeasible right *noun* right which cannot be made void

indefinite *adjective* not defined, especially with no stated end; **for an indefinite period of time** = for a period with no stated termination

indemnification *noun* payment for damage

◇ **indemnify** *verb* to pay for damage suffered; **to indemnify someone for a loss**

◇ **indemnity** *noun* (i) statement of liability to pay compensation for a loss *or* for a wrong in a transaction to which you are a party; (ii) (*in general*) compensation for a loss *or* a wrong; **he had to pay an indemnity of £100; letter of indemnity** = letter promising payment of compensation for a loss

> COMMENT: the person making an indemnity is primarily liable and can be sued by the person with whom he makes the transaction. Compare GUARANTEE

indent 1 *noun* **(a)** order placed for goods at a certain price (especially by a company which imports goods from overseas); **he put in an indent for a new stock of spare parts (b)** line of typing which starts several spaces from the left-hand margin **2** *verb* **(a) to indent for something** = to put in an order for something; **the department has indented for a new computer (b)** to start a line of typing several spaces from the left-hand margin; **indent the first line three spaces**

indenture 1 *noun* deed made between two or more parties; **indentures** *or* **articles of indenture** = contract by which a trainee craftsman works for a master for some years to learn a trade **2** *verb* to contract with an trainee who will work for some years to learn a trade; **he was indentured to a builder**

independent *adjective* free *or* not controlled by anyone; **independent company** = company which is not controlled by another company; **independent contractor** = person *or* company working independently, which is told what to do by a person *or* company giving a contract, but not how to do the work; **independent trader** *or* **independent shop** = shop which is owned by an individual proprietor, not by a chain

◊ **independently** *adverb* alone *or* without the help of anyone else; **the two detectives reached the same conclusion independently of each other**

index *noun* (a) list of items classified into groups or put into order; **we keep a card index of clients** (b) regular report which shows rises and falls in prices, etc.; **cost-of-living index** = way of measuring the cost of living shown as a percentage increase on the figure for the preceding period

indicate *verb* to show; **the latest figures indicate a fall in the crime rate**

◊ **indication** *noun* act of indicating; **he gave no indication that he was lying** = he did not show that he was lying

◊ **indicator** *noun* thing which indicates; **government economic indicators** = figures which show how the country's economy is going to perform in the short or long term

indict *verb* to charge (someone) with a crime; **he was indicted for murder**

◊ **indictable offence** *noun* formerly, a serious offence which could be tried in the Crown Court
NOTE: now called **notifiable offence**

◊ **indictment** *noun* written statement of the details of the crime with which someone is charged in the Crown Court; **the clerk to the justices read out the indictment; bill of indictment** = (i) draft of an indictment which is examined by the court and, when signed, becomes an indictment; (ii) *US* list of charges given to a grand jury, asking them to indict the accused

individual 1 *noun* single person; **he was approached by two individuals in white coats** 2 *adjective* referring to a single person; **the prisoners are kept in individual cells**

indorse *verb* to write something on the back of a document, especially to note details of a plaintiff's claim on a writ; **the writ was indorsed with details of the plaintiff's claim; he indorsed the cheque over to his solicitor** = he signed the cheque on the back so as to make it payable to his solicitor

◊ **indorsement** *noun* writing notes on a document, especially writing the details of a plaintiff's claim on a writ; **special indorsement** = full details of a claim involving money *or* land *or* goods which a plaintiff is trying to recover; *see also* ENDORSE, ENDORSEMENT

induce *verb* to help persuade someone to do something; **he was induced to steal the plans by an offer of a large amount of money**

◊ **inducement** *noun* thing which helps to persuade someone to do something; **they offered him a company car as an inducement to stay; inducement to break contract** = tort of persuading someone to break a contract he has entered into

industrial *adjective* relating to work; **industrial dispute** = argument between management and workers; **industrial property** = property owned by a company such as patents, trademarks, copyrights, etc.; **industrial tribunal** = court which decides in disputes between employers and employees or trade unions

in esse *Latin phrase meaning* "in being"

inevitable *adjective* (accident) which cannot be avoided even if you try to avoid it

infant *noun* person aged less than eighteen years
NOTE: this is an old term, now replaced by **minor**

◊ **infanticide** *noun* notifiable offence of killing a child, especially the killing of a child by its mother before it is twelve months old

infer *verb* to reach an opinion about something; **he inferred from the letter that the accused knew the murder victim; counsel inferred that the witness had not been present at the time of the accident**

inferior *adjective* not as good as others; **inferior products** *or* **products of inferior quality; inferior court** = lower court (such as a magistrates' court or County Court)

in flagrante delicto *Latin phrase meaning* "(caught) in the act of committing a crime"

inflation *noun* situation where prices rise to keep up with production costs; **rate of**

inflation or **inflation rate** = percentage increase in prices over the period of one year

influence 1 *noun* effect which is had on someone or something; **he was charged with driving under the influence of alcohol; the decision of the court was not influenced by the speech of the Prime Minister; we are suffering from the influence of a high exchange rate; undue influence** = pressure put on someone which prevents that person from acting independently **2** *verb* to have an effect on someone or something; **the court was influenced in its decision by the youth of the accused; the price of oil has influenced the price of industrial goods; he was accused of trying to influence the magistrates**

inform *verb* to tell someone officially; **I regret to inform you that your tender was not acceptable; we are pleased to inform you that your offer has been accepted; we have been informed by the Department of Trade that new tariffs are coming into force; to inform on someone** = to tell the police that someone has committed a crime

◇ **informant** *noun* person who informs or who gives information to someone; **is your informant reliable?**

◇ **information** *noun* (a) details which explain something; **have you any information on or about deposit accounts? I enclose this leaflet for your information; to disclose a piece of information; to answer a request for information; for further information, please write to Department 27; disclosure of confidential information** = telling someone information which should be secret (b) details of a crime given to a magistrate; **laying (an) information** = starting criminal proceedings in a magistrates' court by informing the magistrate of the offence; **the justices were ordered to rehear the information** (c) **information technology** = working with computer data; **information retrieval** = storing and then finding data in a computer (c) **information bureau** or **information office** = office which gives information to tourists or visitors; **information officer** = person whose job is to give information about a company or an organization or a government department to the public; person whose job is to give information to other departments in the same organization

NOTE: no plural: to indicate one item use **a piece of information**

◇ **informer** *noun* person who gives information to the police about a crime or about criminals

informal *adjective* not formal or not strictly official; **the head of the CID had an informal meeting with officers from Interpol**

in forma pauperis *Latin phrase meaning* "as a poor person"

> COMMENT: a term formerly used to allow a person who could prove that he had little money to bring an action even if he could not pay the costs of the case; now replaced by Legal Aid

infringe *verb* to break a law or a right; **to infringe a copyright** = to copy a copyright text illegally; **to infringe a patent** = to make a product which works in the same way as a patented product and not pay a royalty to the patent holder

◇ **infringement** *noun* breaking a law or a right; **infringement of copyright** or **copyright infringement** = act of illegally copying a work which is in copyright; **infringement of patent** or **patent infringement** = act of illegally using or making or selling an invention which is patented without the permission of the patent holder

inherit *verb* to succeed to an estate in realty; to acquire something from a person who has died; **when her father died she inherited the shop; he inherited £10,000 from his grandfather**

◇ **inheritance** *noun* property which is received from a dead person
NOTE: no plural

◇ **inheritor** *noun* person who receives something from a person who has died

initial 1 *adjective* first or starting; **initial capital** = capital which is used to start a business; **he started the business with an initial expenditure** or **initial investment of £500 2** *noun* **initials** = first letters of the words in a name; **what do the initials QC stand for? the chairman wrote his initials by each alteration in the contract he was signing 3** *verb* to write your initials on a document to show you have read it and approved; **to initial an amendment to a**

contract; please initial the agreement at the place marked with an X

initio *see* AB INITIO

injunction *noun* court order compelling someone to stop doing something *or* not to do something; **he got an injunction preventing the company from selling his car; the company applied for an injunction to stop their competitor from marketing a similar product; interim injunction** = injunction which prevents someone from doing something until a certain date; **interlocutory** *or* **temporary injunction** = injunction which is granted until a case comes to court; **prohibitory injunction** = injunction which prevents someone from doing an illegal act; *see also* MAREVA INJUNCTION

injure *verb* to hurt (someone); **two workers were injured in the fire**
◇ **injured party** *noun* party in a court case which has been harmed by another party
◇ **injurious** *adjective* which can cause an injury; **injurious falsehood** = tort of making a wrong statement about someone so as to affect his reputation
◇ **injury** *noun* hurt caused to a person; **injury benefit** = money paid to a worker who has been hurt at work; **industrial injuries** = injuries caused to workers at work; **personal injury** = injury to the body suffered by the victim of an accident

injustice *noun* lack of justice
NOTE: no plural

inland *adjective* **(a)** inside a country; **inland postage** = postage for a letter to another part of the country; **inland freight charges** = charges for carrying goods from one part of the country to another **(b)** the **Inland Revenue** = British government department dealing with income tax

in loco parentis *Latin phrase meaning* "in the place of a parent"; **the court is acting in loco parentis**

Inn *noun* the **Inns of Court** = four societies in London, of which the members are lawyers and who are called to the bar as barristers

COMMENT: the four societies are **Gray's Inn, Lincoln's Inn, Inner Temple and Middle Temple**

Inner Temple *see* INN

innocent *adjective* not guilty of a crime; **the accused was found to be innocent; in English law, the accused is presumed to be innocent until he is proved to be guilty**
◇ **innocence** *noun* being innocent *or* not being guilty; **he tried to establish his innocence**
NOTE: no plural

innuendo *noun* spoken words which are defamatory because they have a double meaning; **an apparently innocent statement may be defamatory if it contains an innuendo**

in personam *Latin phrase meaning* "against a person"; **action in personam** = action against an individual person; *see* IN REM

input **1** *noun* material *or* information put into something; **input tax** = VAT paid on goods or services bought **2** *verb* to put information into a computer
NOTE: **inputting - inputted**

inquest *noun* inquiry (by a coroner) into a death *or* into treasure trove

COMMENT: an inquest has to take place where death is violent or unexpected, where death could be murder *or* manslaughter, where a prisoner dies and when police are involved

inquire *verb* to ask questions about something; **he inquired if anything was wrong; she inquired about the rate of crimes solved; the commission is inquiring into corruption in the police force**
◇ **inquiry** *noun* official investigation; **there has been a government inquiry into the loss of the secret documents**

inquorate *adjective* without a quorum; **the meeting was declared inquorate and had to be abandoned**

in re *Latin phrase meaning* "concerning" *or* "in the case of"

in rem *Latin phrase meaning* "against a thing"; **action in rem** = action against a property, not a person; *see* IN PERSONAM

insane *adjective* mad *or* suffering from a state of mind which makes it impossible for you to know that you are doing wrong, and so you cannot be held responsible for your actions

◊ **insanity** *noun* being mad *or* not being sane
NOTE: no plural

COMMENT: where an accused is found to be insane, a verdict of "not guilty by reason of insanity" is returned and the accused is ordered to be detained at Her Majesty's pleasure

inside 1 *adjective & adverb* **(a)** in, especially in a company's office or building; **inside job** = crime which has been committed on a company's property by one of the employees of the company; **inside worker** = worker who works in the office or factory (not in the open air, not a salesman) **(b)** *slang* in prison 2 *preposition* in; **there was nothing inside the container; we have a contact inside our main competitor's production department who gives us very useful information**

◊ **insider** *noun* person who works in an organization and therefore knows its secrets; **insider dealing** *or* **insider trading** = illegal buying or selling of shares by staff of a company who have secret information about the company's plans

insist *verb* to state firmly *or* to demand; **he insisted on something being done** *or* **he insisted that something should be done to help the family of the plaintiff**

insolvent *adjective* not able to pay debts; **the company was declared insolvent**

◊ **insolvency** *noun* not being able to pay debts; **the company was in a state of insolvency** = it could not pay its debts
NOTE: no plural. **Insolvent** and **insolvency** are general terms, but are usually applied to companies; individuals are usually described as **bankrupt** once they have been declared so by a court

inspect *verb* to examine in detail; **to inspect a machine** *or* **a prison; to inspect the accounts of a company; to inspect products**

for defects = to look at products in detail to see if they have any defects

◊ **inspection** *noun* **(a)** close examination of something, especially the examination of the site of a crime by the judge and jury; **to make an inspection** *or* **to carry out an inspection of a machine** *or* **a new prison; inspection of a product for defects; to carry out a tour of inspection** = to visit various places *or* offices *or* factories to inspect them; **to issue an inspection order** = to order a defendant to allow a plaintiff to inspect documents, which the plaintiff thinks the defendant might want to destroy; **inspection stamp** = stamp placed on something to show it has been inspected **(b)** the examination of documents after discovery; **inspection was ordered to take place seven days after discovery**

◊ **inspector** *noun* **(a)** official who inspects; **inspector of factories** *or* **factory inspector** = government official who inspects factories to see if they are safely run; **inspector of taxes** *or* **tax inspector** = official of the Inland Revenue who examines tax returns and decides how much tax people should pay; **inspector of weights and measures** = government official who inspects weighing machines and goods sold in shops to see if the quantities and weights are correct **(b)** **(police) inspector** = rank in the police force above a sergeant and below chief inspector

◊ **inspectorate** *noun* all inspectors; **the factory inspectorate** = all inspectors of factories

inst = INSTANT; **your letter of the 6th inst** = your letter of the 6th of this month

instalment *noun* payment of part of the total purchase price *or* of part of the sum due; **he paid off his creditors in twelve instalments; you pay £25 down and twelve monthly instalments of £20**

◊ **installment plan** *noun* *US* system of buying something by paying a sum regularly each month until the purchase is completed
NOTE: GB English is **hire purchase**

instance *noun* particular example *or* case; **in this instance we will overlook the delay; court of the first instance** = court where a case is heard first

instant *adjective* **(a)** at this point; **our letter of the 6th instant** = our letter of the

6th of this current month; **the instant case** = the case now being considered by the court **(b)** immediately available; **instant credit**

institute 1 *noun* official organization; **research institute** = organization set up to do research **2** *verb* to start; **to institute proceedings against someone**

◊ **institution** *noun* **(a)** organization or society set up for a particular purpose; **financial institution** = bank or investment trust or insurance company whose work involves lending or investing large sums of money **(b)** building for a special purpose; **mental institution** = special hospital for patients suffering from mental disorders; **penal institution** = place (such as a prison) where convicted criminals are kept

◊ **institutional** *adjective* referring to a financial institution; **institutional buying** or **selling** = buying or selling shares by financial institutions; **institutional investors** = financial institutions who invest money in securities

instruct *verb* **(a)** to give an order to someone; **to instruct someone to do something** = to tell someone officially to do something; **he instructed the credit controller to take action (b)** to instruct a **solicitor** = to give information to a solicitor and to ask him to start legal proceedings on your behalf; (*of a solicitor*) **to instruct a barrister** = to give a barrister all the details of a case which he will plead in court

◊ **instructions** *plural noun* order which tells what should be done or how something is to be used, especially details of a case given by a client to a solicitor, or by a solicitor to a barrister; **he gave instructions to his stockbroker to sell the shares immediately; to await instructions** = to wait for someone to tell you what to do; **to issue instructions** = to tell everyone what to do; **in accordance with** or **according to instructions** = as the instructions show; **failing instructions to the contrary** = unless someone tells you to do the opposite; **forwarding instructions** or **shipping instructions** = details of how goods are to be shipped and delivered; *US* **instructions to the jury** = speech by a judge at the end of a trial where he reviews all the evidence and arguments and notes important points of

law for the benefit of the jury
NOTE: GB English is **summing up**

◊ **instructor** *noun* person who shows how something is to be done

instrument *noun* **(a)** tool or piece of equipment; **the technical staff have instruments to measure the output of electricity (b)** legal document; **inchoate instrument** = document which is not complete; **negotiable instrument** = document (such as a bill of exchange or a cheque) which can be exchanged for cash; **statutory instrument** = order (which has the force of law) made under authority granted by an Act of Parliament

insult *verb* to say rude things about someone; **insulting behaviour** = offence of acting (shouting or making rude signs) in a way which shows that you are insulting someone

insure *verb* to have a contract with a company where, if regular small payments are made, the company will pay compensation for loss, damage, injury or death; **to insure a house against fire; to insure someone's life; he was insured for £100,000; to insure baggage against loss; to insure against bad weather; to insure against loss of earnings; the life insured** = the person whose life is covered by a life assurance; **the sum insured** = the largest amount of money that an insurer will pay under an insurance

◊ **insurable** *adjective* which can be insured; **insurable interest** = interest which a person taking out an insurance policy must have in what is being insured

◊ **insurance** *noun* **(a)** agreement that in return for regular small payments, a company will pay compensation for loss or damage or injury or death; **to take out an insurance against fire** = to pay a premium, so that if a fire happens, compensation will be paid **(b) accident insurance** = insurance which will pay if an accident takes place; **car insurance** or **motor insurance** = insuring a car, the driver and passengers in case of accident; **legal expenses insurance** = insurance which will pay the costs of a court case; **life insurance** = situation which pays a sum of money when someone dies; **medical insurance** = insurance which pays the cost of medical treatment, especially when travelling abroad; **National Insurance** = state insurance which pays for medical care, hospitals, unemployment benefits, etc.; **term insurance** = life assurance which covers a person's life for a fixed period of time; **third-party insurance** = insurance which pays compensation if someone who is not the insured person incurs loss or injury; **whole-life insurance** = insurance where the insured person pays premiums for all his life and the insurance company pays a sum when he dies

◇ **insurer** *noun* company which insures NOTE: for life insurance, GB English prefers to use **assurance, assure, assurer**

intangible *adjective* which cannot be touched; **intangible assets** = assets which have a value, but which cannot be seen (such as goodwill *or* a patent *or* a trademark)

intellectual *adjective* belonging to the mind; **intellectual property** = ownership of something (a copyright *or* patent *or* design) which is intangible

intend *verb* to plan *or* to want to do something; **the company intends to sue for damages; we intend to offer jobs to 250 unemployed young people; intended murder** = murder which was planned in advance

◇ **intent** *noun* what is planned; **letter of intent** = letter which states what someone intends to do if a certain thing takes place; *see also* LOITERING

◇ **intention** *noun* (a) wanting *or* planning to do something; **he was accused of perjury with the intention of incriminating his employer** (b) knowing that something will happen as the result of an action (c) meaning of the words in a document such as a will (which may not be the same as what the maker of the document had actually written)

> COMMENT: intention to create a legal relationship is one of the essential elements of a contract

◇ **intentional** *adjective* which is intended; **an act of intentional cruelty**

◇ **intentionally** *adverb* on purpose *or* as intended; **he intentionally altered the date on the contract**

inter- *prefix* between; **inter-bank loan** = loan from one bank to another; **the inter-city rail services are good** = train services between cities are good; **inter-company**

dealings = dealings between two companies in the same group; **inter-company comparisons** = comparing the results of one company with those of another in the same product area

inter alia *Latin phrase meaning* "among other things"

intercourse *noun* **sexual intercourse** = sexual act between man and woman; **sexual intercourse with a girl under sixteen is an offence**

interdict *noun* (*in Scotland*) ban *or* written court order, telling someone not to do something

interest 1 *noun* (a) special attention; **the managing director takes no interest in the staff club; the police showed a lot of interest in the abandoned car** (b) payment made by a borrower for the use of money, calculated as a percentage of the capital borrowed; **simple interest** = interest calculated on the capital only, and not added to it; **compound interest** = interest which is added to the capital and then itself earns interest; **accrual of interest** = automatic addition of interest to capital; **accrued interest** = interest which is accumulating and is due for payment at a later date; **back interest** = interest which has not yet been paid; **fixed interest** = interest which is paid at a set rate; **high** *or* **low interest** = interest at a high or low percentage rate (c) money paid as income on investments or loans; **the bank pays 10% interest on deposits; to receive interest at 5%; the loan pays 5% interest; deposit which yields** *or* **gives** *or* **produces** *or* **bears 5% interest; account which earns interest at 10%** *or* **which earns 10% interest; interest-bearing deposits** = deposits which produce interest (d) percentage to be paid for borrowing; **interest charges** = cost of paying interest; **interest rate** *or* **rate of interest** = percentage charge for borrowing money; **interest-free credit** *or* **loan** = credit or loan where no interest is paid by the borrower; **the company gives its staff interest-free loans** (e) right *or* title to a property *or* money invested in a company *or* financial share in, and part control over, a company; **beneficial interest** = (i) interest of the beneficiary of a property *or* trust, which allows someone to occupy or receive rent from a property, while the property is owned by a trustee; (ii) situation where someone has an interest in shares even though the shares may be held in the name of another person; **conflict of interest** = situation where a person may profit personally from decisions which he takes in his official capacity *or* may not be able to act properly because of some other person or matter with which he is connected; **he has a controlling interest in the company** = he owns more than 50% of the shares and so can direct how the company is run; **life interest** = situation where someone benefits from a property as long as he is alive; **majority interest *or* minority interest** = situation where someone owns a majority *or* a minority of shares in a company; **he has a majority interest in a supermarket chain; to acquire a substantial interest in the company** = to buy a large number of shares in a company; **to declare *or* disclose an interest** = to state in public that you own shares in a company which is being investigated *or* that you are connected with someone who may benefit from your contacts **2** *verb* to attract someone's attention; **he tried to interest several companies in his new invention; interested in** = paying attention to; **the managing director is interested only in increasing profitability; interested party** = person *or* company with a financial interest in a company

◊ **interesting** *adjective* which attracts attention; **they made us a very interesting offer for the factory**

interfere *verb* to get involved *or* to try to change something which is not your concern; **to interfere with witnesses** = to try to get in touch with witnesses to influence their evidence

◊ **interference** *noun* the act of interfering; **the local authority complained of continual interference from the central government**

interim *adjective* temporary *or* not final; **interim dividend** = dividend paid at the end of a half-year; **interim injunction** = injunction which prevents someone from doing something until a certain date; **interim order** = order given which has effect while a case is still being heard; **interim payment** = part payment of a dividend *or* of money owed; **interim report** = report (from a commission) which is not final *or* financial report given at the end of

a half-year; **in the interim** = meanwhile *or* for the time being

interior *noun* what is inside; **Ministry of the Interior *or* Interior Ministry** = government department dealing with law and order, usually including the police

> COMMENT: in the UK, this ministry is called the Home Office

interlocutory *adjective* temporary *or* provisional *or* happening at a court hearing which takes place before full trial; **interlocutory injunction** = injunction which is granted for the period until a case comes to court; **interlocutory judgment** = judgment given during the course of an action before full trial (as opposed to a final judgment); **interlocutory matter** = subsidiary dispute which is dealt with before full trial; **interlocutory proceedings** = hearings that take place before the court before full trial

intermediary *noun* person who is the link between parties who do not agree or who are negotiating; **he refused to act as an intermediary between the two directors**

intern *verb* to put (someone) in prison *or* in a camp without trial (usually for political reasons)

◊ **internee** *noun* person who is interned

◊ **internment** *noun* being put in prison *or* in a camp without trial
NOTE: no plural

international *adjective* working between countries; **International Bar Association** = international lawyers' organization formed to promote international law; **international call** = telephone call to another country; **International Court of Justice** = the court of the United Nations, which sits in the Hague, Netherlands; **International Labour Organization** = section of the United Nations, an organization which tries to improve working conditions and workers' pay in member countries; **international law** = laws governing relations between countries

inter partes *Latin phrase meaning* "between the parties": case heard where both parties are represented; **the court's opinion was that the case should be heard**

inter partes as soon as possible; *see also* EX PARTE

interpleader *noun* court action started by a person who has property which is not his, but which is claimed by two or more people *or* by a person who may be sued by two different parties

Interpol *noun* international police organization whereby the member countries co-operate in solving crimes; **they warned Interpol that the criminals might be disguised as women**
NOTE: used without **the**

interpret *verb* **(a)** to say what you think a law *or* precedent means **(b)** to translate what someone has said into another language; **my assistant knows Greek, so he will interpret for us**

◊ **interpretation** *noun* what someone thinks is the meaning of a law *or* precedent; **to put an interpretation on something** = to make something have a different meaning; **his ruling puts quite a different interpretation on the responsibility of trustees; Interpretation Act** = Act of Parliament which rules how words used in other Acts of Parliament are to be understood; **interpretation clause** = clause in a contract stating the meaning to be given to terms in the contract

◊ **interpreter** *noun* person who translates what someone has said into another language; **my secretary will act as interpreter; the witness could not speak English and the court had to appoint an interpreter**

interrogate *verb* to ask questions in a severe manner; **the prisoners were interrogated for three hours**

◊ **interrogation** *noun* severe questioning; **he confessed to the crime during his interrogation; under interrogation, she gave the names of her accomplices**

◊ **interrogator** *noun* person who interrogates

◊ **interrogatories** *plural noun* questions put in writing during a civil action by one side to the other, and which have to be answered on oath

intervene *verb* **(a)** to come between people *or* things so as to make a change; **to intervene in a dispute** = to try to settle a dispute **(b)** to become a party to an action

◊ **intervener** *noun* person who intervenes in an action to which he was not originally a party

◊ **intervention** *noun* acting to make a change; **the government's intervention in the foreign exchange markets; the central bank's intervention in the banking crisis; the association's intervention in the labour dispute; intervention price** = price at which the EEC will buy farm produce which farmers cannot sell, in order to store it

interview *verb* to talk to a person who is applying for a job *or* who may be able to give information; **we interviewed ten candidates for the post of Chief Constable; the police want to interview a man in connection with the burglary; interview room** = room where a person is asked questions *or* is interviewed

inter vivos *Latin phrase meaning* "among living people"; **gift inter vivos** = gift given by a living person to another living person

intestate *adjective* **to die intestate** = to die without having made a will; **intestate succession** = rules which apply when someone dies without having made a will

> COMMENT: when someone dies intestate, the property automatically goes to the surviving partner, unless there are children

◊ **intestacy** *noun* dying without having made a will
NOTE: no plural

intimidate *verb* to frighten someone to make him do something *or* to prevent him from doing something; **the accused was said to have intimidated the witnesses**

◊ **intimidation** *noun* act of frightening someone to make him do something *or* to prevent him from doing something

intoxicated *adjective* drunk *or* under the effects of alcohol

◊ **intoxication** *noun* state of being drunk

in transit *adverb* **goods in transit** = goods being carried from one place to another

intra vires *Latin phrase meaning* "within the permitted powers"; **the minister's action was ruled to be intra vires;** *see* ULTRA VIRES

intrinsic evidence *noun* evidence used to interpret a document which can be found in the document itself; *see also* EXTRINSIC

introduce *verb* to present *or* to put forward; **he is introducing a Bill in Parliament to prevent the sale of drugs; the prosecution has introduced some new evidence**

◇ **introduction** *noun* presenting *or* putting forward; **the introduction of new evidence into the case; introduction of a Bill** = putting forward a Bill for discussion in Parliament

invalid *adjective* not valid *or* not legal; **permit that is invalid; claim which has been declared invalid**

◇ **invalidate** *verb* to make something invalid; **because the company has been taken over, the contract has been invalidated**

◇ **invalidation** *noun* making invalid

◇ **invalidity** *noun* being invalid; **the invalidity of the contract**
NOTE: no plural

invasion of privacy *noun* action (such as being followed by newspaper reporters) which does not allow someone to live a normal private life
NOTE: no plural

invent *verb* to make something which has never been made before; **she invented a new type of computer keyboard; who invented shorthand? the chief accountant has invented a new system of customer filing**

◇ **invention** *noun* thing which has been invented; **she filed a patent application for her invention; he tried to sell his latest invention to a US car company**

◇ **inventor** *noun* person who invents something; **he is the inventor of the all-plastic car**

invest *verb* to put money somewhere (in a bank *or* by buying shares) where it should increase in value; **he invested all his money in a shop; she was advised to invest in real estate**

◇ **investment** *noun* money which has been invested; **he lost all his money in risky investments on the Stock Exchange**

◇ **investor** *noun* person *or* company which invests money

investigate *verb* to examine something which may be wrong

◇ **investigation** *noun* examination to find out what is wrong; **to conduct an investigation into irregularities in share dealings; preliminary investigation** = examining of the details of a case by a magistrate who then has to decide if the case should be committed to a higher court for trial

◇ **investigator** *noun* person who investigates; **a government investigator**

invite *verb* to ask someone to do something; **to invite someone to a meeting; to invite someone to join the board; to invite shareholders to subscribe to a new issue; to invite tenders for a contract**

◇ **invitation** *noun* asking someone to do something; **to issue an invitation to someone to join the board** *or* **an invitation to tender for a contract** *or* **an invitation to subscribe to a new issue; invitation to treat** = asking someone to make an offer to buy (as by putting items for sale in a shop window)

◇ **invitee** *noun* person who has accepted an invitation to go into a property

invoice *noun* note asking for payment of goods *or* services supplied

involuntary *adjective* not done willingly; **involuntary conduct** = conduct beyond a person's control (a defence to a criminal charge); **involuntary manslaughter** = killing someone without having intended to do so

◇ **involuntarily** *adverb* not willingly; **the accused's defence was that he acted involuntarily**

involve *verb* to be concerned with; **there is an increase of crimes involving young girls; his claim involves money spent on trips abroad; deaths involving policemen** *or* **deaths where policemen are involved are always the subject of an inquest**

IOU *noun* = I OWE YOU signed document promising that you will pay back money borrowed; **to pay a pile of IOUs**

ipso facto *Latin phrase meaning* "by this very fact" *or* "the fact itself shows"; **the writing of the letter was ipso facto an admission of guilt; he was found in the vehicle at the time of the accident and ipso facto was deemed to be in charge of it**

irreconcilable *adjective* (differences between husband and wife) which cannot be reconciled, usually leading to a divorce

irrecoverable *adjective* which cannot be recovered; **irrecoverable debt** = debt which will never be paid

irredeemable *adjective* which cannot be redeemed; **irredeemable bond** = bond which has no date of maturity and which therefore provides interest but can never be redeemed at full value

irregular *adjective* not correct *or* not done in the correct way; **irregular documentation; this procedure is highly irregular**
◊ **irregularity** *noun* **(a)** not being regular *or* not being on time; **the irregularity of the postal deliveries (b)** irregularities = things which are not done in the correct way and which are possibly illegal; **to investigate irregularities in the share dealings**

irresistible *adjective* which cannot be resisted; **irresistible impulse** = impulse to do something which you cannot resist due to insanity; **his irresistible impulse to set fire to shoe shops**

irresponsible *adjective* not responsible *or* wild (behaviour)
◊ **irresponsibility** *noun* lack of responsibility *or* not acting in a responsible way

irretrievable *adjective* which cannot be brought back to its former state; **irretrievable breakdown of a marriage** = situation where a marriage cannot be saved, and therefore divorce proceedings can be started
◊ **irretrievably** *adverb* in an irretrievable way; **it was agreed that the marriage had broken down irretrievably**

irrevocable *adjective* which cannot be changed; **irrevocable acceptance** = acceptance which cannot be withdrawn; **irrevocable letter of credit** = letter of credit which cannot be cancelled or changed

Islam *noun* the religion of the Muslims, based on the teachings of the prophet Mohammed
◊ **Islamic** *adjective* referring to Islam; **Islamic Law** = law of Muslim countries set out in the Koran and the teachings of the prophet Mohammed; the law itself cannot be changed, but it can be interpreted in different ways

issue 1 *noun* **(a)** child *or* children of a parent; **he had issue two sons and one daughter; she died without issue; they have no issue** (NOTE: in this meaning issue is either singular or plural and is not used with **the)** **(b)** subject of a dispute; **collateral issue** = issue which arises from a plea in a criminal court; **point at issue** = the point which is being disputed; **the point at issue is the ownership of the property (c)** giving out new shares; **bonus issue** *or* **scrip issue** = new shares given free to shareholders; **issue of debentures** *or* **debenture issue** = borrowing money against the security of the company's assets; **issue of new shares** *or* **share issue** = selling new shares in a company to the public; **rights issue** = giving shareholders the right to buy more shares 2 *verb* to put out *or* to give out; **to issue a letter of credit; to issue shares in a new company; to issue a writ against someone; the government issued a report on London's traffic; the Secretary of State issued guidelines for expenditure; he issued writs for libel in connection with allegations made in a Sunday newspaper**
◊ **issuance** *noun* act of issuing; **upon issuance of the order, the bailiffs seized the property**
◊ **issued** *adjective* **issued capital** = amount of capital which is given out as shares to shareholders; **issued price** = price of shares in a new company when they are offered for sale for the first time
◊ **issuing** *noun* which organizes an issue of shares; **issuing bank** *or* **issuing house** = bank which organizes the selling of shares in a new company

item *noun* **(a)** thing for sale; **cash items** = goods sold for cash **(b)** piece of information; **extraordinary items** = items in accounts which do not appear each year and need to be noted; **item of expenditure** = goods or services which have been paid for and appear in the accounts **(c)** point on a list; **we will now take item four on the agenda** = we will now discuss the fourth point on the agenda

◊ **itemize** *verb* to make a detailed list of things; **itemizing the sales figures will take about two days; itemized account** = detailed record of money paid or owed

Jj

J *abbreviation* Justice: often put after the name of a High Court judge; **Smith J said he was not laying down guidelines for sentencing**
NOTE: **Smith J** is spoken as "Mr Justice Smith"

jactitation *noun* boasting *or* saying proudly that something is true when it is not; **jactitation of marriage** = boasting that you are married to someone when you are not

jail *or* **gaol** **1** *noun* prison *or* place where criminals are kept; **he spent ten years in jail** **2** *verb* to put someone in prison; **she was jailed for three years; he was jailed for manslaughter**

◊ **jailbird** *noun* person who is in prison *or* who has often been sent to prison

◊ **jailbreak** *noun* escape from prison; **mass jailbreak** = escape from prison of several prisoners at the same time

◊ **jailer** *noun* person who works in a jail *or* who is in charge of a jail

jaywalker *noun* person who walks across a street at a place which is not a proper crossing place

◊ **jaywalking** *noun* offence of walking across a street at a place which is not a proper crossing point for pedestrians

jeopardy *noun* **to be in jeopardy** = to be in danger of punishment *or* of harm; **his driving licence is in jeopardy** = he may lose

his driving licence; *see also* DOUBLE JEOPARDY

◊ **jeopardize** *verb* to be likely to harm; **her arrest for drunken driving may jeopardize her work as a doctor specializing in child care**

jetsam *noun* cargo which is thrown off a sinking ship; **flotsam and jetsam** = rubbish floating in the water after a ship has been wrecked and rubbish washed on to the land

jettison *verb* to throw cargo from a ship into the sea to make the ship lighter

jobber *noun* **(stock) jobber** = person who buys and sells shares from other traders on the Stock Exchange

join *verb* **(a)** to put things together; **the offices were joined together by making a door in the wall; the appendix is joined to the contract; to join someone to an action** = to attach someone's name as one of the parties to an action **(b) to join a firm of solicitors** = to start work with a firm; **he joined on January 1st** = he started work on January 1st; **to join an association** *or* **a group** = to become a member of an association *or* a group; **all the staff have joined the company pension plan; he was asked to join the board; Smith Ltd has applied to join the trade association**

◊ **joinder** *noun* bringing together several actions *or* several parties in one action; *see also* MISJOINDER, NONJOINDER

joint **1** *adjective* **(a)** with two or more organizations or people linked together; **joint account** = bank account for two people; **joint commission of inquiry** *or* **joint committee** = commission *or* committee with representatives of various organizations on it; **joint discussions** = discussions between management and workers before something is done; **joint management** = management done by two or more people; **joint ownership** = situation where two or more persons own the same property; *US* **joint resolution** = Bill which has been passed by both House and Senate, and is sent to the President for signature; **joint-stock bank** = bank which is a public company quoted on the Stock Exchange; **joint-stock company** = public company whose shares are owned by many people; **joint venture** *or* *US* **joint adventure**

= very large business partnership where two or more companies join together as partners for a limited period **(b)** one of two or more people who work together *or* who are linked; **joint beneficiary; joint managing director; joint owner; joint signatory; joint heir** = person who is an heir with someone else; **joint tortfeasors** = two or more people who are responsible and liable for a tort **2** *noun slang* place *or* building; **to case a joint** = to investigate a building carefully before breaking into it

◊ **joint and several** *adjective* as a group together and also separately; **joint and several liability** = situation where someone who has a claim against a group of people can sue them separately or together as a group

◊ **jointly** *adverb* together with one or more other people; **to own a property jointly; to manage a company jointly; they are jointly liable for damages; jointly and severally liable** = liable both as a group and as individuals

◊ **joint tenancy** *noun* situation where two or more persons acquire an interest in a property together, where if one of the joint tenants dies, his share goes to the others who survive him; *see also* TENANCY IN COMMON

joy riding *noun* offence of taking a car without the permission of the owner and using it to drive about

JP *noun* = JUSTICE OF THE PEACE
NOTE: the plural is **JPs**

judge 1 *noun* official who presides over a court and in civil cases decides which party is in the right; **a County Court judge; a judge in the Divorce Court; the judge sent him to prison for embezzlement; judge in chambers** = judge who hears a case in his private room without the public being present and not in open court; **Judges' Rules** = informal set of rules governing how the police may question a suspect **2** *verb* to decide; **he judged it was time to call an end to the discussions**

◊ **Judge Advocate-General** *noun* lawyer appointed by the state to advise on all legal matters concerning the Army

◊ **Judge Advocate of the Fleet** *noun* lawyer appointed by the state to advise on all legal matters concerning the Royal Navy

COMMENT: In England, judges are appointed by the Lord Chancellor. The minimum requirement is that one should be a barrister or solicitor of ten years' standing. The majority of judges are barristers, but they cannot practise as barristers. Recorders are practising barristers who act as judges on a part-time basis
The appointment of judges is not a political appointment, and judges remain in office unless they are found guilty of gross misconduct
In the USA, state judges can be appointed by the state governor or can be elected; in the federal courts and the Supreme Court, judges are appointed by the President, but the appointment has to be approved by Congress

judgment *or* **judgement** *noun* legal decision *or* official decision of a court; **certificate of judgment** = official document showing the decision of a court; **judgment by default** *or* **default judgment** = judgment against a defendant who fails to defend his case; **final judgment** = judgment which is given at the end of an action after trial; **interlocutory judgment** = judgment given during the course of an action before full trial; **to pronounce judgment** *or* **to give one's judgment on something** = to give an official or legal decision about something; **to enter judgement** *or* **to take judgment** = to record an official judgment on a case; **to enter judgment for** *or* **against the plaintiff** = to make a legal judgment that the plaintiff's claim is accepted *or* not accepted; **the plaintiff entered judgment in default** = the plaintiff took judgment (because the defendant failed to defend the case); **entry of judgment** = recording the judgment of the court in the official records; **judgment creditor** = person who has been given a court order making a debtor pay him a debt; **judgment debtor** = debtor who has been ordered by a court to pay a debt; **judgment summons** = summons by a court to enforce a court order, such as ordering a judgment debtor to pay or to go to prison
NOTE: the spelling **judgment** is used by lawyers

judicata *see* RES

judicature *noun* administration of justice; **judicature paper** = thick heavy paper on which court documents are engrossed; *see also* SUPREME COURT

judice *see* SUB JUDICE

judicial *adjective* referring to a judge *or* the law; done in a court *or* by a judge; **the Judicial Committee of the House of Lords** = the highest appeal court in England and Wales; **the Judicial Committee of the Privy Council** = the appeal court for appeals from some Commonwealth countries and colonies; **judicial immunity** = safety from prosecution granted to a judge when acting in a judicial capacity; **judicial notice** = facts and matters which a judge is presumed to know, so that evidence does not have to be produced to prove them (such as that New Year's Day is January 1st, that a small baby is not capable of walking); **judicial precedent** = precedent set by a court decision, which can be reversed only by a higher court; **judicial processes** = the ways in which the law works; **judicial review** = (i) examination of a case a second time by a higher court because a lower court has acted wrongly; (ii) examination of administrative decisions by a court; **judicial separation** = legal separation of man and wife, ordered by the court, where each becomes separated, but neither is allowed to marry again

judiciary *noun* **the judiciary** = all judges
NOTE: no plural

junior 1 *adjective* younger *or* lower in rank; **junior clerk** = clerk, usually young, who has lower status than a senior clerk; **junior executive** *or* **junior manager** = less important manager in a company; **junior partner** = person who has a small part of the shares in a partnership; **John Smith, Junior** = the younger John Smith (i.e. the son of John Smith, Senior) **2** *noun* **(a)** (i) barrister who is not a Queen's Counsel; (ii) barrister appearing with a leader **(b)** **office junior** = young man or woman who does all types of work in an office

jurat *noun* words at the end of an affidavit, showing the details of when and by whom it was sworn

juridical *adjective* referring to the law *or* to judges

jurisdiction *noun* legal power over someone *or* something; **within the jurisdiction of the court** = in the legal power of a court; **outside the jurisdiction of the court** = not covered by the legal power of the court; **the prisoner refused to recognize the jurisdiction of the court** = the prisoner said that he did not believe that the court had the legal right to try him; **equitable jurisdiction** = power of a court to enforce a person's rights

jurisprudence *noun* study of the law and the legal system
NOTE: no plural

jurist *noun* person who has specialized in the study and practice of law

◊ **juristic** *adjective* according to the practice of law; **juristic person** = ARTIFICIAL PERSON

juror *noun* member of a jury

> COMMENT: jurors can be selected from registered electors who are between eighteen and sixty-five years old and who have been resident in the UK for five years. Barristers, solicitors, judges, priests, doctors, Members of Parliament, people who are insane are among the categories of people disqualified from being jurors

jury *noun* group of twelve citizens who are sworn to decide whether someone is guilty or not guilty on the basis of the evidence they hear in court; **trial by jury** *or* **jury trial** = proceedings where an accused is tried by a jury and judge; **he has been called for jury service** *or* *US* **for jury duty** = he has been asked to do his duty as a citizen and serve on a jury; **"Members of the jury"** = way of speaking to a jury in court; **the foreman of the jury** = the chief juror, elected by the other jurors, who chairs the discussions of the jury and pronounces the verdict in court afterwards; **jury vetting** = examination of each of the proposed members of a jury to see if he is qualified to be a juror; *US* **grand jury** = group of between twelve and twenty-four jurors who meet as a preliminary to a trial to decide if an indictment should be issued to start criminal proceedings
NOTE: the word jury can take a plural verb

◊ **jury box** *noun* place where the jury sit in the courtroom

◇ **juryman** *noun* member of a jury
NOTE: plural is **jurymen**

◇ **jury room** *noun* room where a jury meet to discuss the trial and reach a verdict

jus *Latin word meaning* "law" *or* "right"

just *adjective* fair *or* right; **to show just cause** = to show a reason which is fair and acceptable in law

justice *noun* (a) fair treatment (in law); **to administer justice** = to make sure that the laws are correctly and fairly applied; **to bring a criminal to justice** = to find a criminal and charge him with an offence; **natural justice** = the general principles of justice; *US* **Department of Justice** *or* **Justice Department** = department of the US government responsible for federal legal cases, headed by the Attorney-General *see also note at* MINISTRY (b) magistrate; **chairman of the justices** = chief magistrate in a magistrates' court; **justices' clerk** *or* **clerk to the justices** = official of a Magistrates' Court who gives advice to the justices on law *or* practice *or* procedure; **Lord Chief Justice** = chief judge of the Queen's Bench Division of the High Court, and second most senior judge after the Lord Chancellor; *US* **Chief Justice** = senior judge in a court (c) title given to a High Court judge; **Mr Justice Adams; Lord Justice** = title given to a judge who is a member of the House of Lords
NOTE: usually written as **J** or **LJ** after the name: **Adams J; Smith LJ**

◇ **justice of the peace** *noun* magistrate *or* local judge

justicia *see* FIAT

justiciary *noun* all judges; **High Court of Justiciary** = supreme criminal court in Scotland

justify *verb* to give an excuse for; **the end justifies the means** = if the result is right, the means used to reach it are acceptable

◇ **justifiable** *adjective* which can be excused; **justifiable homicide** = killing of a person for an acceptable reason (such as in self-defence)

◇ **justification** *noun* showing an acceptable reason for an act; **in justification** = as an acceptable excuse; **in justification, the accused claimed that the burglar had attacked him with an axe; the defendant entered defence of justification**

juvenile *noun & adjective* young person under seventeen years of age; **juvenile court** = court which tries young offenders; **the appeal court quashed the care order made by the juvenile court; juvenile delinquent** = young criminal who commits minor crimes, especially against property; **juvenile offender** = person under the age of sixteen, tried in a juvenile court

Kk

kangaroo court *noun* unofficial and illegal court set up by a group of people

KC = KING'S COUNSEL

keep *verb* (a) to go on doing something; **they kept working, even when the boss told them to stop; the other secretaries complain that she keeps singing when she is typing** (b) to do what is necessary; **to keep an appointment** = to be there when you said you would be; **to keep the books of a company** *or* **to keep a company's books** = to note the accounts of a company; **to keep the law** = to make sure the law is obeyed; **to keep the peace** = to obey the law, to behave well and not to create a disturbance; **he was bound over to keep the peace** (c) to hold items for sale *or* for information; **we always keep this item in stock** = we always have this item in our warehouse *or* shop; **to keep someone's name on file** = to have someone's name on a list for reference (d) to hold things at a certain level; **we must keep our mailing list up to date; to keep spending to a minimum; the price of oil has kept the pound at a high level; the government is encouraging firms to keep prices low; lack of demand for typewriters has kept prices down**
NOTE: **keeping - kept**

◇ **keeper** *noun* person who keeps something; **Keeper of the Great Seal** = the Lord Chancellor

◇ **keeping** *noun* **safe keeping** = being looked after carefully; **we put the documents into the bank for safe keeping; keeping a disorderly house** = offence of being the proprietor *or* manager of a brothel

key *noun* (a) piece of metal used to open a lock; **he has taken the office keys home with him, so no one can get in; we have lost the keys to the computer room; key money** = premium paid when taking over the keys of a flat or office which you are renting (b) part of a computer *or* typewriter which you press with your fingers; **there are sixty-four keys on the keyboard; control key** = key on a computer which works part of a program; **shift key** = key which makes a typewriter *or* computer move to capital letters (c) important; **a key witness has disappeared**

◇ **keyboard** *noun* part of a computer *or* typewriter with a series of keys which are pressed to make letters or figures

kickback *noun* illegal commission paid to someone (especially a government official) who helps in a business deal

kidnap *verb* to take away (a child *or* a person) and keep him alone by force (usually asking for money to be paid before he is released)

◇ **kidnapper** *noun* person who kidnaps someone

◇ **kidnapping** *noun* notifiable offence of taking away a person by force

kill *verb* to make someone die; **he was accused of killing his girl friend with a knife**

◇ **killer** *noun* person who kills; **the police are searching for the girl's killer**

kin *plural noun* relatives *or* close members of the family; *see also* NEXT OF KIN

kind *noun* sort *or* type; **the printer produces two kinds of printout; the law distinguishes several kinds of crime against the person; payment in kind** = payment made by giving goods but not money

kite mark *noun* mark put on British goods to show that they meet official standards

kleptomania *noun* mental illness which makes someone steal things
NOTE: no plural

◇ **kleptomaniac** *noun* person who steals things because he suffers from kleptomania

knock *verb* (a) to hit something; **he knocked on the door and went in; she knocked her head on the filing cabinet** (b) **to knock the competition** = to hit competing firms hard by vigorous selling; **knocking copy** = advertising material which criticizes competing products

◇ **knock down** *verb* **to knock something down to a bidder** = to sell something at an auction; **the stock was knocked down to him for £10,000**

◇ **knockdown** *noun* **knockdown prices** = very low prices; **he sold me the car at a knockdown price**

◇ **knock-for-knock agreement** *noun* agreement between two insurance companies that they will not take legal action against each other, and that each will pay the claims of their own clients

◇ **knock off** *verb* (a) to stop work (b) to reduce a price by an amount; **he knocked £10 off the price for cash** (c) *slang* to steal

◇ **knock-on effect** *noun* effect which an action will have on other situations; **the strike by customs officers has had a knock-on effect on car production by slowing down exports of cars**

know *verb* (a) to learn *or* to have information about something; **I do not know how a computer works; does he know how long it takes to get to the airport? the senior partner's secretary does not know where he is** (b) to have met someone; **do you know Mr Jones, our new sales director?**
NOTE: knowing - known

◇ **know-how** *noun* knowledge about how something works *or* how something is made; **you need some legal know-how to do this job; he needs to acquire computer know-how**
NOTE: no plural

◇ **knowingly** *adverb* deliberately *or* on purpose; **it was charged that he knowingly broke the Official Secrets Act by publishing the document in his newspaper**

◇ **knowledge** *noun* what is known to be true; **he had no knowledge of the contract** = he did not know that the contract existed; **to the best of my knowledge** = I am reasonable certain of the fact; **the witness said that to the best of his knowledge the accused had never left the room; constructive knowledge** = knowledge of a fact *or* matter which the law says a person has whether or not that person actually has such knowledge
NOTE: no plural

LI

labour or US **labor** noun **(a)** heavy work; **manual labour** = work done by hand; **to charge for materials and labour** = to charge for both the materials used in a job and also the hours of work involved; **hard labour** = punishment of sending someone to prison to do hard manual work **(b)** workers in general; **casual labour** = workers who are hired for a short period; **cheap labour** = workers who do not earn much money; **local labour** = workers recruited near a factory, not brought in from somewhere else; **organized labour** = workers who are members of trade unions; **skilled labour** = workers who have special knowledge or qualifications; **labour-intensive industry** = industry which needs large numbers of workers or where labour costs are high in relation to turnover **(c) labour disputes** = arguments between management and workers; **labour law** or **labour laws** or **labour legislation** = laws relating to the employment of workers; **labour relations** = relations between management and workers; US **labor union** = organization which represents workers who are its members in discussions about wages and conditions of work with management **(d) International Labour Organization** = section of the United Nations which tries to improve working conditions and workers' pay in member countries

◊ **labourer** noun person who does unskilled work; **casual labourer** = worker who can be hired for a short period; **manual labourer** = person who does work with his hands

laches noun long delay or neglect in asserting a legal right; see also STATUTE OF LIMITATIONS

lack 1 noun not having enough; **the investigation has been held up by lack of information; charges cannot be brought for lack of evidence; lack of data** or **lack of information** = not having enough information; **the decision has been put back for lack of up-to-date information; lack of funds** = not enough money; **the project was cancelled because of lack of funds 2** verb not to have enough of something; **the police lack any clues to the murder; the fraud squad lacks the necessary staff to undertake the investigation**

lading see BILL

Lady Day noun 25th March, one of the quarter days when rent is paid for land

lag noun **old lag** = criminal who has served many (short) prison sentences or who will never go straight

land 1 noun **(a)** area of earth; **land agent** = person who manages a farm or a large area of land for someone; **land certificate** = document which shows who owns a piece of land, and whether there are any charges on it; **land charges** = covenants, mortgages, etc. which are attached to a piece of land; **land register** = register of land, showing who owns it and what buildings are on it; **land registration** = system of registering land and its owners; **Land Registry** = British government office where land is registered; **land taxes** = taxes on the amount of land owned by someone **(b) lands** = estate or large area of land owned by one owner; **Crown Lands** = estates belonging to the King or Queen **2** verb **(a)** to put goods or passengers on to land after a voyage by sea or by air; **landed costs** = costs of goods which are delivered to a port or airport, unloaded and passed through customs **(b)** to come down to earth after a flight; **the plane landed ten minutes late**

COMMENT: under English law, the ownership of all land is vested in the Crown; individuals or other legal persons may however hold estates in land, the most important of which are freehold estates (which amount to absolute ownership) and leasehold estates (which last for a fixed period of time). Ownership of land usually confers ownership of everything above and below the land. The process of buying and selling land is "conveyancing". Any contract transferring land or any interest in land must be in writing. Interests in land can be disposed of by a will

◇ **landing** *noun* **landing card** = card given to passengers who have passed customs and can land from a ship *or* an aircraft; **landing charges** = payment for putting goods on land and for customs duties; **landing order** = permit which allows goods to be unloaded into a bonded warehouse without paying customs duty

◇ **landlady** *noun* woman who owns a property which she lets

◇ **landlord** *noun* person *or* company which owns a property which is let; **ground landlord** = person *or* company which owns the freehold of a property which is then let and sublet; **our ground landlord is an insurance company; the Landlord and Tenant Act** = Act of Parliament which regulates the letting of property

◇ **landmark decision** *noun* legal *or* legislative decision which creates an important legal precedent

◇ **landowner** *noun* person who owns large areas of land

◇ **Lands Tribunal** *noun* court which deals with compensation claims relating to land

language *noun* words spoken or written by people in a certain country; **he was accused of using offensive language to a policeman** = he was accused of saying rude words; **computer language *or* programming language** = system of signs, letters and words used to instruct a computer

lapse **1** *noun* **(a) a lapse of time** = a period of time which has passed **(b)** ending of a right *or* a privilege *or* an offer (such as the termination of an insurance policy because the premiums have not been paid) **(c)** failure of a legacy because the beneficiary has died before the testator **2** *verb* to stop being valid *or* to stop being active; **to let an offer lapse** = to allow time to pass so that an offer is no longer valid; **lapsed legacy** = legacy which cannot be put into effect because the person who should have received it died before the person who made the will; **lapsed passport** = passport which is out of date; **lapsed (insurance) policy** = insurance which is no longer valid because the premiums have not been paid

larceny *noun* crime of stealing goods which belong to another person; **he was convicted of larceny; petty larceny *or* grand larceny** = minor thefts *or* very large thefts (NOTE: no plural)

> COMMENT: larceny no longer exists in English law, having been replaced by the crime of theft

large *adjective* **(a)** very big *or* important; **our company is one of the largest suppliers of computers to the government; he is our largest customer; why has she got an office which is larger than mine? (b) at large** = not in prison; **three prisoners escaped - two were recaptured, but one is still at large**

◇ **largely** *adverb* mainly *or* mostly; **our sales are largely in the home market; they have largely pulled out of the American market**

last **1** *adjective & adverb* **(a)** coming at the end of a series; **out of a queue of twenty people, I was served last; this is our last board meeting before we move to our new offices; this is the last case which the magistrates will hear before lunch; last quarter** = period of three months to the end of the financial year; **court of last resort** = highest court from which no appeals are allowed; **lender of the last resort** = central bank which lends money to commercial banks **(b)** most recent *or* most recently; **the last case was one of attempted murder, this one is for theft; last week *or* last month *or* last year** = the week *or* month *or* year before this one; **last year's accounts have to be ready by the AGM; last will and testament** = statement written by a person of what he wants to be done with his property after he dies **(c) the week *or* month *or* year before last** = the week *or* month *or* year before the one before this **2** *verb* to go on *or* to continue; **the hearing started in December and lasted until the second week of January**

◇ **last in first out** *phrase* **(a)** redundancy policy, where the people who have been most recently appointed are the first to be made redundant **(b)** accounting method where stock is valued at the price of the latest purchases

late **1** *adjective* **(a)** after the time stated or agreed; **we apologize for the late arrival of the plane from Amsterdam; there is a**

penalty for late delivery = if delivery is later than the agreed date, the supplier has to pay a fine **(b)** at the end of a period of time; **latest date for signature of the contract** = the last acceptable date for signing the contract **(c) latest** = most recent; **he always drives the latest model of car; here are the latest accident figures 2** *adverb* after the time stated or agreed; **the hearing started late; the shipment was landed late; the plane was two hours late**

◊ **late-night** *adjective* happening late at night; **they had a late-night meeting at the airport; their late-night negotiations ended in an agreement which was signed at 3 a.m.**

latent *adjective* hidden *or* which cannot immediately be seen; **latent ambiguity** = words in a contract which can mean two or more things, but which do not at first sight seem to be misleading

Latin *noun* language used by the Romans

COMMENT: Latin was used as the language of the law courts for centuries, and its use still exists in many common legal phrases, such as **habeas corpus, in flagrante delicto, de jure** and **de facto**

---

launch *verb* to begin *or* to start; **the police have launched a campaign against drunken drivers**

launder *verb* *slang* to transfer illegal *or* stolen money into an ordinary bank account, usually by a complex process to avoid detection; **the proceeds of the robbery were laundered through a bank in the Caribbean**

law *noun* **(a)** rule (which may be written or unwritten) by which a country is governed and the activities of people and organizations controlled; **a law has to be passed by Parliament; the government has proposed a new law to regulate the sale of goods on Sundays; conflict of laws** = section in a country's statutes which deals with disputes between that country's laws and those of another country; **labour laws** = laws concerning the employment of workers **(b) law** = all the statutes of a country taken together; **case law** = law as established by precedents, that is by decisions of courts in earlier cases; **civil law** = laws relating to people's rights, and agreements between individuals; **commercial law** = laws regarding business; **company law** = laws which refer to the way companies work; **constitutional law** = laws under which a country is ruled *or* laws relating to government and its function; **contract law** *or* **the law of contract** = laws relating to agreements; **copyright law** = laws concerning the protection of copyright; **criminal law** = laws relating to acts committed against the laws of the land and which are punishable by the state; **international law** = laws referring to the way countries deal with each other; **maritime law** *or* **the law of the sea** = laws referring to ships, ports, etc.; **mercantile law** *or* **law merchant** = law relating to commerce; **private law** = law relating to relations between individual persons (such as the law of contract); **public law** = law which refers to people in general (such as administrative and constitutional law); **law and order** = situation where the laws of a country are being obeyed by most people; **there was a breakdown of law and order following the assassination of the president; law reform** = continuing process of revising laws to make them better suited to the needs of society; **to take someone to law** = to sue someone; **inside the law** *or* **within the law** = obeying the laws of a country; **against the law** *or* **outside the law** = not according to the laws of a country; **dismissing a worker without reason is against the law; the company is operating outside the law; in law** = according to the law; **what are the duties in law of a guardian?; to break the law** = to do something which is not allowed by law; **he is breaking the law by selling goods on Sunday; you will be breaking the law if you try to take that computer out of the country without an export licence (c)** general rule; **law of supply and demand** = general rule that the amount of a product which is available is related to the needs of the possible customers **(d)** *informal* **the law** = the police and the courts; **the law will catch up with him in the end; if you don't stop making that noise I'll have the law on you; the strong** *or* **long arm of the law** = ability of the police to catch criminals and deal with crime

◊ **lawbreaker** *noun* person who breaks the law

◇ **law-breaking** *noun* act of doing something which is against the law

◇ **Law Centre** *noun* local office (mainly in London) with full-time staff who advise and represent clients free of charge

◇ **Law Commission** *noun* permanent committee which reviews English law and recommends changes to it

◇ **law court** *noun* place where a trial is held *or* place where a judge listens to cases

COMMENT: in civil cases he decides which party is right legally; in criminal cases the decision is made by a jury

◇ **lawful** *adjective* acting within the law; **lawful practice** = action which is permitted by the law; **lawful trade** = trade which is allowed by law

◇ **lawfully** *adverb* acting within the law

◇ **lawless** *adjective* not controlled by the law *or* by the police; **the magistrates criticized the lawless behaviour of the football crowd**

◇ **lawlessness** *noun* being lawless; **the government is trying to fight lawlessness in large cities**
NOTE: no plural

◇ **Law List** *noun* annual published list of barristers and solicitors

◇ **Law Lords** *plural noun* members of the House of Lords who are judges

◇ **law-making** *noun* making of laws; **Parliament is the law-making body in Great Britain**

◇ **lawman** *noun* US policeman
NOTE: plural is **lawmen**

◇ **Law Officers** *plural noun* British government posts: the Attorney-General and Solicitor-General in England and Wales, and the Lord Advocate and Solicitor-General in Scotland

◇ **Law Reports** *plural noun* regular reports of new cases and legislation

◇ **law school** *noun* school where lawyers are trained

◇ **Law Society** *noun* organization of solicitors in England and Wales, which represents and regulates the profession

◇ **Laws of Oleron** *plural noun* the first maritime laws, drawn up in 1216 and used as a base for subsequent international laws

◇ **lawsuit** *noun* case brought to a court by a private person; **to bring a lawsuit against someone** = to tell someone to appear in court to settle an argument; **to defend a lawsuit** = to appear in court to state your case

◇ **lawyer** *noun* person who has studied law and can act for people on legal business; **commercial lawyer** *or* **company lawyer** = person who specializes in company law *or* who advises companies on legal problems; **constitutional lawyer** = lawyer who specializes in constitutional law *or* in interpreting constitutions; **international lawyer** = person who specializes in international law; **maritime lawyer** = person who specializes in laws concerning ships

lay 1 *verb* **(a)** to put *or* to place; **to lay an embargo on trade with a country** = to forbid trade with a country; **to lay (an) information** = to start criminal proceedings in a magistrates' court by informing the magistrate of the offence; **to lay a proposal before the House** = to introduce a new Bill before Parliament for discussion **(b) to lay down** = to state clearly; **the conditions are laid down in the document; the guidelines lay down rules for dealing with traffic offences** (NOTE: **laying - laid - has laid**) **2** *adjective* not belonging to a certain profession; **lay assessor** = person (not a lawyer) with technical knowledge who advises a court on specialized matters; **lay magistrate** = magistrate who is not usually a qualified lawyer (as opposed to a stipendiary magistrate)

◇ **layman** *noun* person who does not belong to the legal profession
NOTE: plural is **laymen**

LC = LORD CHANCELLOR

LCJ = LORD CHIEF JUSTICE

lead 1 *noun* clue *or* piece of information which may help solve a crime; **the police are following up several leads in the murder investigation 2** *verb* **(a)** to be the first *or* to be in front; **the company leads the market in cheap computers (b)** to be the main person in a group (especially in a team of barristers appearing for one side in a case); **the prosecution is led by J.M. Jones, QC; Mr Smith is leading for the Crown (c)** to start to do something (especially to start to

present a case in court); **Mr Jones led for the prosecution; the Home Secretary will lead for the Government in the emergency debate (d)** to bring evidence before a court **(e)** to try to make a witness answer a question in court in a certain way; **counsel must not lead the witness**
NOTE: **leading - led - has led**

◊ **leader** *noun* **(a)** person who manages *or* directs others; **the leader of the construction workers' union** *or* **the construction workers' leader; an employers' leader; she is the leader of the trade delegation to Nigeria; the minister was the leader of the party of lawyers on a tour of American courts (b)** main barrister (usually a QC) in a team appearing for one side in a case **(c)** product which sells best; **a market leader** = product which sells most in a market *or* company which has the largest share of a market; **loss-leader** = article which is sold very cheaply to attract customers **(d)** important share *or* share which is often bought or sold on the Stock Exchange

◊ **Leader of the House** *noun* main government minister and member of the cabinet, who is responsible for the administration of legislation in the House of Commons

◊ **Leader of the Opposition** *noun* head of the largest party opposing the government

◊ **leading** *adjective* **(a)** most important; **leading businessmen feel the end of the recession is near; leading shares rose on the Stock Exchange; leading shareholders in the company forced a change in management policy; they are the leading company in the field; leading cases** = important cases which have set precedents; **leading counsel** = main barrister (usually a QC) in a team appearing for one side in a case **(b) leading question** = question put by a barrister to a witness which suggests to the witness what his answer ought to be *or* which can only be answered "Yes" or "No"

> COMMENT: leading questions may be asked during cross-examination or during examination in chief

◊ **lead time** *noun* time between placing an order and receiving the goods; **the lead time on this item is more than six weeks**

◊ **lead (up) to** *verb* to be the cause of; **the discussions led to a big argument**

between the management and the union; **we received a series of approaches leading up to the takeover bid**

leak 1 *noun* passing secret information (to the newspapers *or* TV stations, etc.); **the government is investigating the latest leak of documents relating to the spy trial 2** *verb* to pass secret information (to the newspapers *or* TV stations, etc.); **information about the government plans has been leaked to the Sunday papers**

lease 1 *noun* **(a)** written contract for letting or renting a building *or* a piece of land *or* a piece of equipment for a period of time, against payment of a fee; **long lease** *or* **short lease** = lease which runs for fifty years or more *or* for up to two or three years; **to take an office building on a long lease; we have a short lease on our current premises; to rent office space on a twenty-year lease; full repairing lease** = lease where the tenant has to pay for all repairs to the property; **head lease** = lease from the freeholder to a tenant; **sublease** *or* **underlease** = lease from a tenant to another tenant; **the lease expires** *or* **runs out in 1995** = the lease comes to an end in 1995; **on expiration of the lease** = when the lease comes to an end; *see also* DEMISE **(b) to hold a lease in the North Sea** = to have a lease on a section of the North Sea to explore for oil **2** *verb* **(a)** to let or rent offices *or* land *or* machinery for a period; **to lease offices to small firms; to lease equipment (b)** to use an office *or* land *or* machinery for a time and pay a fee to the landlord *or* lessee; **to lease an office from an insurance company; all our company cars are leased**

◊ **lease back** *verb* to sell a property *or* machinery to a company and then take it back on a lease; **they sold the office building to raise cash, and then leased it back for twenty-five years**

◊ **lease-back** *noun* arrangement where property is sold and then taken back on a lease; **they sold the office building and then took it back under a lease-back arrangement**

◊ **leasehold** *noun & adjective & adverb* possessing property on a lease, for a fixed time; **leasehold property; the company has some valuable leaseholds; to purchase a**

property leasehold; **leasehold enfranchisement** = right of a leaseholder to buy the
freehold of the property he is leasing

◇ **leaseholder** *noun* person who holds a
property on a lease

◇ **leasing** *noun* which leases *or* working
under a lease; **the company has branched
out into car leasing; a computer-leasing
company; to run a copier under a leasing
arrangement**

leave 1 *noun* **(a)** permission to do
something; **counsel asked leave of the court
to show a film taken of the accident; "by
your leave"** = with your permission **(b)** to
be away from work; **leave of absence** =
being allowed to be away from work;
maternity leave = period when a woman is
away from work to have a baby; **sick leave**
= period when a worker is away from
work because of illness; **to go on leave *or* to
be on leave** = to be away from work; **she is
away on sick leave *or* on maternity leave 2**
verb **(a)** to go away from; **he left his office
early to go to the meeting; the next plane
leaves at 10.20** **(b)** to give property to
someone when you die; **he left his house to
his wife; I was left £5,000 by my grand-
mother in her will** **(c)** to resign; **he left his
job and bought a farm**
NOTE: leaving - left - has left

◇ **leave out** *verb* not to include; **she left
out the date on the letter; the contract leaves
out all details of marketing arrangements**

legacy *noun* money or personal property
(but not land) given by someone to
someone else in his will; **she received a
small legacy in her uncle's will**

COMMENT: freehold land left to
someone in a will is a **devise**

legal *adjective* **(a)** according to the law *or*
allowed by the law; **the company's action
was completely legal** **(b)** referring to the
law; **to take legal action *or* to start legal
proceedings** = to sue someone *or* to take
someone to court; **to take legal advice** = to
ask a lawyer to advise about a problem in
law; **legal adviser** = person who advises
clients about problems in law; *US* **legal
age** = age at which a person can sue *or* can
be sued *or* can undertake business; **Legal
Aid scheme** = British government scheme
where a person with very little money can
have legal representation and advice paid

for by the state; **Legal Aid Centre** = local
office giving advice to clients about applications for Legal Aid and recommending clients to solicitors; **legal charge** =
charge created over property by a legal
mortgage (as opposed to an equitable
charge); **legal claim** = statement that
someone owns something legally; **he has no
legal claim to the property; legal costs *or*
legal charges *or* legal expenses** = money
spent on fees to lawyers; **legal currency** =
money which is legally used in a country;
legal department *or* legal section = section
of a company dealing with legal matters;
legal executive = clerk in a solicitor's
office who is not a solicitor and is not
articled to become one but has passed the
examinations of the Institute of Legal
Executives; **legal expert** = person who has
a wide knowledge of the law; **legal fiction**
= assuming something to be true, even if
it is not proved to be so (a procedural
device used by courts to get round problems caused by statute); **legal holiday** =
day when banks and other businesses are
closed; **legal personality** = existence as a
body and so ability to be affected by the
law; **legal separation** = legal separation of
man and wife, ordered by the court, where
each becomes separated, but neither is
allowed to marry; **legal tender** = coins or
notes which can be legally used to pay a
debt (small denominations cannot be used
to pay large debts); **legal writer** = person
who writes and publishes commentaries
on legal problems

◇ **legality** *noun* being allowed by law;
**there is doubt about the legality of the
company's action in dismissing him**
NOTE: no plural

◇ **legalize** *verb* to make something legal

◇ **legalization** *noun* making something
legal; **the campaign for the legalization of
abortion**

◇ **legally** *adverb* according to the law;
the contract is legally binding = according
to the law, the contract has to be obeyed;
the directors are legally responsible = the
law says that the directors are responsible

◇ **legal memory** *noun* time when things
are supposed to be remembered in law,
taken to be 1189; **this practice has existed
from before the time of legal memory;** *see
also* IMMEMORIAL

legatee *noun* person who receives a
legacy from someone who has died

legis *see* CORPUS

legislate *verb* to make a law; **Parliament has legislated against the sale of drugs**

◇ **legislation** *noun* laws *or* written rules which are passed by Parliament and implemented by the courts; **labour legislation** = laws concerning the employment of workers
NOTE: no plural

◇ **legislative** *adjective* used to make laws; **the legislative processes; Parliament has a legislative function**

◇ **legislature** *noun* group of people (such as a Parliament) which makes laws

legitimate 1 *adjective* (a) allowed by law; **he has a legitimate claim to the property** (b) born to parents who are married to each other; **he left his property to his legitimate offspring;** *see also* IL-LEGITIMATE 2 *verb* to make (a child) legitimate

◇ **legitimacy** *noun* (a) state of being legitimate; **the court doubted the legitimacy of his claim** (b) court case to make someone legitimate

◇ **legitimation** *or* **legitimization** *noun* making a person legitimate (as by the marriage of the parents)

lend *verb* to allow someone to use something for a period; **to lend something to someone** *or* **to lend someone something; he lent the company money** *or* **he lent money to the company; she lent the company car to her daughter; to lend money against security; the bank lent him £50,000 to start his business**

◇ **lender** *noun* person who lends money; **lender of the last resort** = central bank which lends money to commercial banks

◇ **lending** *noun* act of letting someone use money for a time; **lending limit** = limit on the amount of money a bank can lend

lenient *adjective* not severe *or* kind (sentence); **the judge took a lenient view of the offence; because of the accused's age, the court passed a lenient sentence**

◇ **leniently** *adverb* in a kind way; **the accused were treated leniently by the military tribunal**

lessee *noun* person who has a lease *or* who pays money for a property he leases

lessen *verb* to make less *or* to make smaller; **the government is taking steps to lessen the overcrowding in prisons**

lesser *adjective* smaller *or* less important (of two things); **he pleaded guilty to the lesser charge of manslaughter**

lessor *noun* person who grants a lease on a property

let 1 *verb* (a) to allow someone to do something; **the magistrate let the prisoner speak to his wife** (b) to lend a house *or* an office *or* a farm to someone for a payment; **to let an office** = to allow someone to use an office for a time in return for payment of rent; **offices to let** = offices which are available to be leased by companies (NOTE: **letting - let - has let**) 2 *noun* (a) period of the lease of a property; **they took the office on a short let** (b) **without let or hindrance** = without any obstruction

◇ **let off** *verb* not to punish someone; **the magistrate let the boys off with a warning**

◇ **let-out clause** *noun* clause which allows someone to avoid doing something in a contract; **he added a let-out clause to the effect that the payments would be revised if the exchange rate fell by more than 5%**

letter *noun* (a) piece of writing sent from one person *or* company to another to give information; **business letter** = letter which deals with business matters; **circular letter** = letter sent to many people; **covering letter** = letter sent with documents to say why they are being sent; **follow-up letter** = letter sent to someone after a previous letter *or* after a visit; **private letter** = letter which deals with personal matters; **standard (form) letter** = letter which is sent without change to various correspondents (b) **letter before action** = letter written by a lawyer to give a party the chance to pay his client before he sues; **letter of acknowledgement** = letter which says that something has been received; **letters of administration** = document given by a court to allow someone to deal with the estate of someone who has died without leaving a will *or* where the executor appointed under the will cannot act; **letter of allotment** *or* **allotment letter** = letter which tells someone how many shares in a new company he has been allotted; **letter of application** = letter in which someone applies for a job *or* applies for shares in a new company; **letter of appointment** = letter in which someone is appointed to a job; **letter of attorney** = document showing that someone has power of attorney; **letter of comfort** *or* **comfort letter** = letter supporting someone who is trying to get a loan *or* letter which reassures someone on a certain point; **letter of complaint** = letter in which someone complains; **letter of credit** = letter from a bank allowing someone credit and promising to repay at a later date; **letter of demand** = letter issued by a party *or* by a lawyer demanding payment before taking legal action; **letter of indemnity** = letter promising payment of compensation for a loss; **letter of intent** = letter which states what someone intends to do if something happens; **letters patent** = official document from the Crown, which gives someone the exclusive right to do something (such as becoming a lord *or* making and selling an invention); **letter of reference** = letter in which an employer or former employer recommends someone for a new job **(c) air letter** = special thin blue paper which when folded can be sent by air without an envelope; **airmail letter** = letter sent by air; **registered letter** = letter which is noted by the Post Office before it is sent, so that compensation can be claimed if it is lost **(d) to acknowledge receipt by letter** = to write a letter to say that something has been received **(e)** written or printed sign (such as A, B, C); **write your name and address in block letters** *or* **in capital letters**

◇ **letterhead** *noun* name and address of a company printed at the top of a piece of notepaper

letting *noun* **letting agency** = agency which deals in property to let; **furnished lettings** = furnished property to let; *see also* LET

levy **1** *noun* money which is demanded and collected by the government *or* by an agency *or* by an official body; **capital levy** = tax on the value of a person's property and possessions; **import levy** = tax on imports, especially in the EEC a tax on imports of farm produce from outside the EEC; **training levy** = tax to be paid by companies to fund the government's training schemes **2** *verb* to demand payment of a tax *or* an extra payment and to collect it;

the government has decided to levy a tax on imported cars; to levy a duty on the import of computer parts

lex *Latin word meaning* "law"; **lex fori** = law of the place where the case is being heard; **lex loci actus** = law of the place where the act took place; **lex loci contractus** = law of the place where the contract was made; **lex loci delicti** = law of the place where the crime was committed

liability *noun* **(a)** being legally responsible for paying for damage *or* loss, etc.; **his insurers have admitted liability but the amount of damages has not yet been agreed; to accept** *or* **to admit liability for something** = to agree that you are responsible for something; **to refuse liability for something** = to refuse to agree that you are responsible for something; **contractual liability** = legal responsibility for something as stated in a contract; **limited liability** = principle that by forming a limited liability company, individual members are liable for that company's debts only to the value of their shares; **limited liability company** = company where a member is responsible for repaying the company's debts only up to the face value of the shares he owns; **liability clause** = clause in the articles of association of a company which states that the liability of its members is limited; **vicarious liability** = liability of one person for torts committed by another, especially the liability of an employer for acts committed by an employee in the course of his work **(b) liabilities** = debts of a business; **the balance sheet shows the company's assets and liabilities; current liabilities** = debts which a company should pay within the next accounting period; **long-term liabilities** = debts which are not due to be repaid for some years; **he was not able to meet his liabilities** = he could not pay his debts; **to discharge one's liabilities in full** = to repay all debts

◇ **liable** *adjective* **(a) liable (for)** = legally responsible (for); **the customer is liable for breakages; the chairman was personally liable for the company's debts; he was found by the judge to be liable for the accident; he will be found liable if he assists a trustee to commit a dishonest breach of trust (b) liable to** = which is officially due to be paid; **sales which are liable to stamp duty; such an act renders him liable to a fine**

libel 1 *noun* **(a)** untrue written and published or broadcast statement which damages someone's character; **he claimed that the newspaper report was a libel; criminal libel** = serious libel which might cause a breach of the peace; *see also* DEFAMATION, SLANDER **(b)** act of making a libel; **action for libel** *or* **libel action** = case in a law court where someone says that another person has written a libel about him (NOTE: no plural for (b)) **2** *verb* to damage someone's character in writing or in a broadcast
NOTE: **libelling - libelled** but US **libeling - libeled**

◊ **libeller** *noun* person who has libelled someone

◊ **libellous** *adjective* which libels someone's character; **he said that the report was libellous**

liberate *verb* to set free; **three prisoners were liberated**

liberty *noun* being free; **at liberty** = free *or* not in prison; **they are still at liberty while waiting for charges to be brought; civil liberties** = freedom for people to work *or* write *or* speak as they want, providing they keep within the law; **liberty of the individual** = freedom for each person to act within the law; **liberty of the press** = freedom of newspapers to publish what they want within the law without censorship; **liberty of the subject** = right of a citizen to be free unless convicted of a crime which is punishable by imprisonment

licence *or* US **license** *noun* **(a)** official document which allows someone to do something *or* to use something; permission given by someone to another person to do something which would otherwise be illegal; **he granted his neighbour a licence to use his field; driving licence** = document which shows that you have passed a driving test and can legally drive a car *or* truck, etc.; **applicants for the police force should hold a valid driving licence; gaming licence** = document which allows someone *or* a club to organize games of chance, such as roulette; **import licence** *or* **export licence** = document which allows goods to be imported *or* exported; **licence to sell liquor** *or* **liquor licence** = document given by the Magistrates' Court allowing someone to sell alcohol; *GB* **off licence** = (i) licence to

sell alcohol to be drunk away from the place where it is bought; (ii) shop which sells alcohol to be taken away for drinking elsewhere; **on licence** = licence to sell alcohol for drinking on the premises (as in a bar *or* restaurant); **occasional licence** = licence to sell alcohol at a certain place and time only **(b)** permission for someone to leave prison before the end of his sentence; **release on licence** = being allowed to leave prison on parole; **the appellant will be released on licence after eight months (c) goods manufactured under licence** = goods made with the permission of the owner of the copyright *or* patent

◊ **license 1** *noun* US = LICENCE **2** *verb* to give someone official permission to do something; **licensed to sell beers, wines and spirits; to license a company to produce spare parts; he is licensed to drive a lorry; she is licensed to run an employment agency; licensed premises** = inn *or* restaurant *or* bar *or* shop which has a licence to sell alcohol

◊ **licensee** *noun* person who has a licence, especially a licence to sell alcohol *or* to manufacture something

◊ **licensing** *noun* which refers to licences; **licensing agreement** = agreement where a person is granted a licence to manufacture something *or* to use something, but not an outright sale; *GB* **licensing hours** = hours of the day where alcohol can be bought to be drunk on the premises; **licensing magistrates** = magistrates who grant licences to persons *or* premises for the sale of alcohol

licit *adjective* legal

lien *noun* legal right to hold someone's goods and keep them until a debt has been paid; **the garage had a lien on her car until she paid the repair bill; lien on shares** = right of a company to sell shares which have not been fully paid up, and where the shareholder refuses to pay for them fully; **carrier's lien** = right of a carrier to hold goods until he has been paid for carrying them; **equitable lien** = right of someone to hold property (which legally he does not own) until the owner pays money due; **general lien** = holding goods *or* property until a debt has been paid; **maritime lien** = right to seize a ship against an unpaid debt; **particular lien** = right of a person to keep possession of another person's property until debts relating to that property have been paid; **repairer's lien** = right of someone who has been carrying out repairs to keep the goods until the repair bill has been paid

NOTE: you have a lien **on** an item

lieu *noun* **in lieu of** = instead of; **to give someone two months' salary in lieu of notice** = to give an employee money equivalent to the salary for two months' work and ask him to leave immediately

life *noun* **(a)** time when a person is alive; **for life** = for as long as someone is alive; **his pension gives him a comfortable income for life**; **life annuity** *or* **annuity for life** = annual payments made to someone as long as he is alive; **life assurance** *or* **life insurance** = insurance which pays a sum of money when someone dies, or at a certain date if he is still alive then; **the life assured** *or* **the life insured** = the person whose life has been covered by the life assurance; **life expectancy** = number of years a person is likely to live; **life imprisonment** *or* **life sentence** = being sent to prison as a punishment for a serious crime, but not necessarily for the whole of your life (the penalty for murder)

> COMMENT: life imprisonment lasts on average ten years

life interest = interest in a property which comes to an end when a person dies; **life peer** = member of the House of Lords who is appointed for life; *slang* **life preserver** = heavy club *or* cosh **(b)** period of time when something is in existence; **the life of a loan; during the life of the agreement; shelf life of a product** = length of time when a product can stay in the shop and still be good to use

◊ **lifer** *noun* *slang* person serving a life sentence

lift *verb* **(a)** to take away *or* to remove; **the government has lifted the ban on imports of technical equipment; the minister has lifted the embargo on the export of firearms (b)** *informal* to steal

light *noun* **ancient lights** = claim by the owner of a property that he has the right to enjoy light in his windows, which must not be blocked by a neighbour's buildings

likelihood *noun* being probable *or* being likely; **likelihood of bias** = being probable that bias will occur

likewise *adverb* in a similar way; **the principal agrees to reimburse the agent, and likewise the agent agrees to reimburse his principal**

limit **1** *noun* point at which something ends *or* point where you can go no further; **to set limits to imports** *or* **to impose limits on imports** = to allow only a certain amount of goods to be imported; **age limit** = top age at which you are permitted to do something; **credit limit** = fixed amount of money which is the most a client can owe; **he has exceeded his credit limit** = he has borrowed more money than is allowed; **lending limit** = restriction on the amount of money a bank can lend; **time limit** = maximum time which can be taken to do something; **weight limit** = maximum permitted weight **2** *verb* to stop something from going beyond a certain point; **the court limited damages to £100; the banks have limited their credit** = the banks have allowed their customers only a certain amount of credit

◊ **limitation** *noun* **(a)** act of allowing only a certain amount of something; **the contract imposes limitations on the number of cars which can be imported; limitation of liability** = (i) making someone liable for only a part of the damage *or* loss; (ii) making shareholders in a limited company liable for the debts of the company only in proportion to their shareholding; **time limitation** = amount of time which is available **(b)** **limitation of actions** *or* **statute of limitations** = law which allows only a certain amount of time (usually six years) for someone to start legal proceedings to claim property *or* compensation for damage, etc.

◊ **limited** *adjective* restricted *or* not open; **limited liability** = principle that by forming a limited liability company, individual members are liable for that company's debts only to the value of their shares; **limited market** = market which can take only a certain quantity of goods; **limited partnership** = partnership where the liability of some of the partners is limited to the amount of capital they have each provided to the business, and where these partners may not take part in the

running of the business, while other working partners are fully liable for all the obligations of the partnership; **limited liability company** = company where a shareholder is responsible for repaying the company's debts only to the face value of the shares he owns; **private limited company** = company with a small number of shareholders, whose shares are not traded on the Stock Exchange; **Public Limited Company** = company whose shares can be bought on the Stock Exchange
NOTE: a private limited company is called **Ltd** or **Limited**; a Public Limited Company is called **Plc** or **PLC** or **plc**

◊ **limiting** *adjective* which limits; **a limiting clause in a contract; the short holiday season is a limiting factor on the hotel trade**

Lincoln's Inn *noun* one of the four Inns of Court in London

lineal descent *noun* direct descent from parent to child

liquid assets *noun* cash, or bills which can be quickly converted into cash

◊ **liquidate** *verb* **to liquidate a company** = to wind up a company *or* to close down a company and sell its assets; **to liquidate a debt** = to pay a debt in full; **to liquidate assets** *or* **stock** = to sell assets *or* stock to raise cash; **liquidated damages** = specific amount which has been calculated as the loss suffered

◊ **liquidation** *noun* **(a) liquidation of a debt** = payment of a debt in full **(b)** winding up *or* closing of a company and selling of its assets; **the company went into liquidation** = the company was closed and its assets sold; **compulsory liquidation** = liquidation which is ordered by a court; **voluntary liquidation** = situation where a company itself decides to close down

◊ **liquidator** *noun* person who administers the assets and supervises the winding up of a company

◊ **liquidity** *noun* having cash *or* assets which can easily be sold to raise cash

lis *Latin word meaning* "lawsuit"; **lis alibi pendens** = legal action has been started in another place; **lis pendens** = pending suit; *see also* AD LITEM

list 1 *noun* **(a)** several items written one after the other; **list of debtors; list of**

products *or* **product list; to add an item to a list; to cross someone's name off a list; list of cases to be heard; list of members** = annual return made by a company listing its shareholders; **address list** *or* **mailing list** = list of names and addresses of people and companies; **black list** = list of goods *or* companies *or* countries which are banned for trade; **Law List** = annual published list of barristers and solicitors **(b)** catalogue; **list price** = price as shown in a catalogue **2** *verb* **(a)** to write a series of items one after the other; **the catalogue lists products by category; the case is listed to be heard next week (b) listed building** = building of special interest (usually because it is old), which the owners cannot alter or demolish; **listed company** = company whose shares can be bought *or* sold on the Stock Exchange; **listed securities** = shares which can be bought on the Stock Exchange *or* shares which appear on the official Stock Exchange list

litem *see* AD LITEM

litigate *verb* to go to law *or* to bring a lawsuit against someone to have a dispute settled

◊ **litigant** *noun* person who brings a lawsuit against someone; **litigant in person** = person bringing a lawsuit who also speaks on his own behalf in court without the help of a lawyer

◊ **litigation** *noun* going to law *or* bringing of a lawsuit against someone to have a dispute settled; **he has got into litigation with the county council**

◊ **litigious** *adjective* (person) who likes to bring lawsuits against people

LJ = LORD JUSTICE
NOTE: written after the surname of the judge in legal reports. **Smith LJ said he was not laying down any guidelines for sentencing** but **Smith LJ** is spoken as "Lord Justice Smith"

◊ **LJJ** = LORD JUSTICES

LL.B. *or* **LL.M.** *or* **LL.D.** letters written after someone's name, showing that he has the degree of Bachelor of Laws *or* Master of Laws *or* Doctor of Laws

Lloyd's *noun* central London market for underwriting insurances; **Lloyd's Register** = classified list showing details of all the ships in the world; **ship which is A1 at Lloyd's** = ship in very good condition

loan 1 *noun* money which has been lent; **loan capital** = part of a company's capital which is a loan to be repaid at a later date, and is not equity or preference shares; **loan stock** = money lent to a company at a fixed rate of interest; **convertible loan stock** = money which can be exchanged for shares at a later date; **bank loan** = money lent by a bank; **bridging loan** = short-term loan to help someone buy a new house when he has not yet sold his old one; **short-term loan** *or* **long-term loan** = loans which have to be repaid within a few weeks or some years; **soft loan** = loan (from a company to an employee *or* from one government to another) with no interest payable; **unsecured loan** = loan made with no security **2** *verb* to lend

lobby 1 *noun* part of the House of Commons, where MPs go to vote **2** *verb* to ask someone (such as an MP, local official) to do something on your behalf; **a group of local businessmen has gone to London to lobby their MPs on the problems of unemployment in the area**

local *adjective* relating to a certain area *or* place; **local authority** = section of elected government which runs a certain area (such as a district council); **local court** = court (such as a magistrates' court) which hears cases coming from a certain area; **a court can give instructions to a local authority as to the exercise of its powers in relation to children in care; a decision of the local authority pursuant to the powers and duties imposed on it by the Act**

loc. cit. *Latin phrase meaning* "in the place which has been mentioned" NOTE: used when referring to a point in a legal text: **"see also Smith J in** *Jones* v. *Associated Steel Ltd* **loc. cit. line 26"**

lock 1 *noun* device for closing a door *or* box so that it can be opened only with a key; **the lock is broken on the petty cash box; I have forgotten the combination of the lock of the safe; time lock** = lock which will open only at a certain time of day (such as in a bank vault) **2** *verb* to close a door with a key, so that it cannot be opened; **the manager forgot to lock the door of the computer room; the petty cash box was not locked**
◇ **lock out** *verb* **to lock out workers** = to shut the factory door so that workers

cannot get in and so make them unable to work until the conditions imposed by the management are met
◇ **lockout** *noun* industrial dispute where the management will not let the workers into the factory until they have agreed to the management's conditions
◇ **lock up** *verb* **(a)** to put (someone) in prison *or* in a psychiatric hospital **(b) to lock up a shop** *or* **an office** = to close and lock the door at the end of the day's work; **to lock up capital** = to have capital invested in such a way that it cannot be used for other investments
◇ **locking up** *noun* **the locking up of money in stock** = investing money in stock so that it cannot be used for other, possibly more profitable, investments
◇ **lock-up 1** *adjective* **lock-up shop** = shop which has no living accommodation which the proprietor locks at night when it is closed **2** *noun informal* prison

loco *see* IN LOCO PARENTIS

locum (tenens) *noun* person who takes the place of another person for a time; **locums wanted in South London**

locus *Latin word meaning* "place"
◇ **locus standi** *Latin phrase meaning* "place to stand": right to be heard in a court; **the taxpayer does not have locus standi in this court**

lodge *verb* to put *or* to deposit (officially); **to lodge caution** = to deposit a document with the Land Registry which prevents land *or* property being sold without notice; **to lodge a complaint against someone** = to make an official complaint about someone; **to lodge money with someone** = to deposit money with someone; **to lodge securities as collateral** = to put securities into a bank to be used as collateral for a loan

loitering *noun* **loitering (with intent)** = offence of walking slowly, stopping frequently, especially to solicit sexual relations

long 1 *adjective* for a large period of time; **long credit** = credit terms which allow the borrower a long time to pay; **in the long term** = over a long period of time; **to take the long view** = to plan for a long period before current investment becomes profitable **2** *noun* **longs** = government stocks which mature in over fifteen years' time

◇ **long-dated** *adjective* **long-dated bills or paper** = bills of exchange which are payable in more than three months' time

◇ **longhand** *noun* handwriting where the words are written out in full and not typed or in shorthand; **applications should be written in longhand and sent to the recruitment officer**

◇ **long-standing** *adjective* (agreement) which has been arranged for a long time

◇ **long-term** *adjective* **on a long-term basis** = for a long period of time; **long-term debts** = debts which will be repaid many years later; **long-term forecast** = forecast for a period of over three years; **long-term loan** = loan to be repaid many years later; **long-term objectives** = aims which will take years to fulfil

◇ **Long Vacation** *noun* summer holiday of the law courts and universities

loophole *noun* **to find a loophole in the law** = to find a means of doing what you want to do, by finding a way of getting round a law which otherwise would prevent you from acting; **to find a tax loophole** = to find a means of legally not paying tax

loot 1 *noun* valuables which have been stolen (by gangs of rioters *or* soldiers, etc.) (NOTE: no plural) **2** *verb* to steal valuable goods from shops *or* warehouse *or* homes (especially during a riot); **the stores were looted by a mob of hooligans**

◇ **looter** *noun* person who steals valuables from shops *or* warehouses *or* homes during a riot

◇ **looting** *noun* act of stealing valuable goods; **the police cordoned off the area to prevent looting**
NOTE: no plural

lord *noun* member of the House of Lords; **Lord of Appeal in Ordinary** = one of eleven lords who are paid to sit as members of the House of Lords when it acts as a court of appeal; **Lord Chancellor** = member of the government and cabinet who presides over the debates in the House of Lords and is responsible for the administration of justice and the appointment of judges; **Lord Chief Justice** = chief judge of the Queen's Bench Division of the High Court who is also a member of the Court of

Appeal; **Lord Justice** = title given to a judge who is a member of the Court of Appeal
NOTE: written **LJ** after the name: **Smith LJ** = Lord Justice Smith

◇ **Lords** *plural noun* **(a)** the House of Lords; **the Lords voted to amend the Bill (b)** members of the House of Lords; **Lords Spiritual** = archbishops and bishops who are members of the House of Lords; **Lords Temporal** = members of the House of Lords who are not bishops; **the Law Lords** = members of the House of Lords who are *or* were judges, and are entitled to sit on the Court of Appeal

◇ **Lord Advocate** *noun* member of the government who is one of the two Law Officers in Scotland

◇ **Lord Ordinary** *noun* judge of first instance in the outer house of the Scottish Court of Session

◇ **Lord President** *noun* judge of the Scottish Court of Session

lose *verb* **(a)** not to win (in legal proceedings); **he lost his appeal to the House of Lords; she lost her case for compensation (b)** not to have something any more; **to lose an order** = not to get an order which you were hoping to get; **during the strike, the company lost six orders to American competitors; to lose control of a company** = to find that you have less than 50% of the shares and so are no longer able to direct the company; **she lost her job when the factory closed** = she was made redundant; **lost profits** = profits which would have been made from a transaction which is the subject of an action for breach of contract **(c)** to have less money; **he lost £25,000 in his father's computer company; the pound has lost value** = the pound is worth less **(d)** to drop to a lower price; **the dollar lost two cents against the pound; gold shares lost 5% on the market yesterday**
NOTE: **losing - lost - has lost**

◇ **lose out** *verb* to suffer as a result of something; **the company has lost out in the rush to make cheap computers**

loss *noun* **(a)** not having something which was had before; **compensation for loss of earnings** = payment to someone who has stopped earning money *or* who is not able to earn money; **compensation for loss of office** = payment to a director who is asked to leave a company before his contract ends **(b)** having less money than before *or* not making a profit; **the company suffered a loss** = the company did not make a profit; **to report a loss** = not to show a profit in the accounts at the end of the year; **capital loss** = loss made by selling assets; **the car was written off as a dead loss *or* a total loss** = the car was so badly damaged that the insurers said it had no value; **trading loss** = situation where the company's receipts are less than its expenditure; **at a loss** = making a loss *or* not making any profit; **the company is trading at a loss; he sold the shop at a loss; to cut one's losses** = to stop doing something which was losing money **(c) loss in weight** = goods which weigh less than when they were packed; **loss in transport** = amount of weight which is lost while goods are being shipped

◊ **loss-leader** *noun* article which is sold at a loss to attract customers

lot *noun* **(a)** large quantity; **a lot of people** *or* **lots of people are out of work (b)** group of items sold together at an auction; **he put in a bid for lot 23; at the end of the auction half the lots had not been sold (c)** group of shares which are sold; **to sell shares in small lots (d)** *US* piece of land, especially one to be used for development

lottery *noun* game of chance, where numbered tickets are sold and prizes given for certain numbers

lucrative *adjective* which makes a lot of money; **there is a lucrative black market in car spare parts; he signed a lucrative contract with a TV company**

lump sum *noun* money paid in one single payment, not in several small amounts; **he received a lump sum payment of £500; the company offer a lump sum of £1,000 as an out-of-court settlement**

lynch *verb* to catch an accused person and kill him (usually by hanging) without a trial

◊ **lynch law** *noun* killing of accused persons by a mob without a trial

Mm

machine *noun* **(a)** device which works with power from a motor; **copying machine** *or* **duplicating machine** = machine which makes copies of documents; **dictating machine** = machine which records what someone dictates, which a typist can then play back and type out **(b) machine code** *or* **machine language** = instructions and information shown as a series of figures (0 and 1) which can be read by a computer; **machine-readable codes** = sets of signs or letters (such as bar codes *or* post codes) which a computer can read

◊ **machinery** *noun* **(a)** machines; **the inspector found that the machinery in the factory was dangerous (b)** organization *or* system *or* method of organizing; **the local government machinery** *or* **the machinery of local government; administrative machinery; the machinery for awarding government contracts**

Madam *noun* formal way of addressing a woman, especially one whom you do not know; **Dear Madam** = beginning of a letter to a woman whom you do not know; **Madam Chairman** = way of addressing a woman who is in the chair at the meeting

Mafia *noun* **the Mafia** = Italian secret society, working on criminal activities in Italy and the USA

magistrate *noun* usually unpaid official who tries cases in a police court; **magistrates' clerk** = official of a magistrates' court who gives advice to the magistrates on law *or* practice *or* procedure; **magistrates' court** = (i) building where magistrates try cases; (ii) court presided over by magistrates; **lay magistrate** = unpaid magistrate who is usually not a qualified lawyer; **stipendiary magistrate** = magistrate who is a qualified lawyer and receives a salary (NOTE: unpaid magistrates are also called **Justices of the Peace** or **JPs**)

COMMENT: the Magistrates' Court hears cases of petty crime, adoption, affiliation, maintenance and violence in the home; it can commit someone for trial or for sentence in the Crown Court. A stipendiary magistrate is a qualified lawyer who usually sits alone; lay magistrates usually sit as a bench of three

Magna Carta *noun* the Great Charter, granted by King John in 1215, which gave his subjects certain political and personal freedoms

magnetic tape *or informal*

mag tape *noun* plastic tape for recording information on a large computer

mail 1 *noun* **(a)** system of sending letters and parcels from one place to another; **by mail** = using the postal services, not sending something by hand or by messenger; **by surface mail** = by land or sea, not by air; **by sea mail** = sent by post abroad, using a ship; **by air mail** = by post using a plane; **electronic mail** = system of sending messages from one computer to another, using the telephone lines **(b)** letters sent or received; **your cheque arrived in yesterday's mail; my secretary opens my mail as soon as it arrives; the receipt was in this morning's mail (c)** direct mail = selling a product by sending advertising material to possible buyers through the post; **mail shot** = advertising material sent by mail to possible customers **2** *verb* to send something by post

◇ **mailing** *noun* sending something in the post; **direct mailing** = sending of advertising material by post to possible buyers; **mailing list** = list of names and addresses of people who might be interested in a product *or* list of names and addresses of members of a society; **to buy a mailing list** = to pay a society, etc. money to buy the list of members so that you can use it to mail advertising material; **mailing piece** = leaflet suitable for sending by direct mail; **mailing shot** = advertising material sent by mail to possible customers

◇ **mail-order** *noun* system of buying and selling from a catalogue, placing orders and sending goods by mail; **mail-order business** *or* **mail-order firm** *or* **mail-order house** = company which sells a product by mail; **mail-order catalogue** = catalogue from which a customer can order items to be sent by mail

maintain *verb* **(a)** to keep something going *or* working; **to maintain good relations with one's customers; to maintain contact with an overseas market; mounted police were brought in to maintain law and order (b)** to keep something working at the same level; **the company has maintained the same volume of business in spite of the recession; to maintain an interest rate at 5%; to maintain a dividend** = to pay the same dividend as in the previous year **(c)** to pay for the food and clothing, etc., for a child *or* a person; **the ex-husband was ordered to maintain his wife and three children**

◇ **maintenance** *noun* **(a)** keeping things going *or* working; **the maintenance of law and order is in the hands of the local police force (b)** keeping a machine in good working order; **maintenance contract** = contract by which a company keeps a piece of equipment in good working order **(c)** payment made by a divorced or separated husband *or* wife to the former spouse, to help pay for living expenses and the cost of bringing up the children; **maintenance order** = court order which orders a divorced or separated husband *or* wife to pay maintenance to the former spouse; **maintenance pending suit** = maintenance obtained by a spouse in matrimonial proceedings until there is a full hearing to deal with the couple's financial affairs (NOTE: US English is **alimony**) **(d)** formerly, the crime *or* tort of unlawfully providing someone with money to help that person to pay the costs of suing a third party

Majesty *see* HER MAJESTY'S PLEASURE

majeure *see* FORCE MAJEURE

major *adjective* important; **major shareholder** = shareholder with a large number of shares

◇ **majority** *noun* **(a)** larger group than any other; **majority of the shareholders** = more than 50% of the shareholders; **the board accepted the proposal by a majority of three to two** = three members of the board voted to accept and two voted against; **majority vote** *or* **majority decision** = decision made after a vote according to the wishes of the larger group; **majority shareholding** *or* **majority interest** = group of shares which is more than 50% of the total; **a majority shareholder** = person who owns more than half the shares in a company; **majority verdict** = verdict reached by a jury where at least ten jurors vote for the verdict **(b)** age at which someone becomes responsible for his actions *or* can sue *or* can be sued *or* can undertake business transactions

> COMMENT: the age of majority in the UK and US is eighteen

maladministration *noun* incompetent *or* illegal administration

mala in se *Latin phrase meaning* "wrongs in themselves": acts (such as murder) which are in themselves crimes

◊ **mala prohibita** *Latin phrase meaning* "forbidden wrongs": acts (such as walking on the grass in a park) which are not crimes in themselves, but which are forbidden

malfeasance *noun* unlawful act

malice *noun* intentionally committing an act from wrong motives *or* intention to commit a crime; **with malice aforethought** = with the intention of committing a crime (especially murder or grievous bodily harm); **express malice** = intention to kill someone; **implied malice** = intention to cause grievous bodily harm to someone

◊ **malicious** *adjective* without a lawful reason *or* with an improper motive; **malicious damage** = deliberate and intentional damage to property; **malicious falsehood** = lie which is said with the intention of harming someone's business interests; **malicious prosecution** = tort of charging someone with a crime out of malice and without proper reason

◊ **maliciously** *adverb* in a malicious way *or* with the intention of causing harm; **he claimed that he had been prosecuted maliciously**

malpractice *noun* acting in an unprofessional *or* illegal way (by a doctor *or* lawyer *or* accountant, etc.)

manage *verb* **(a)** to direct *or* to be in charge of; **to manage a department; to manage a branch office (b)** to **manage property** = to look after rented property for the owner **(c) to manage to** = to

succeed (with some difficulty) in doing something; **did you manage to see the solicitor? counsel managed to have the hearing adjourned; she managed to write six orders and take three phone calls all in two minutes**

◊ **manageable** *adjective* which can be dealt with easily

◊ **management** *noun* **(a)** directing *or* running a business; **to study management; good management** *or* **efficient management; line management** = organization of a business where each manager is directly responsible for a stage in the operation of the business; **management accountant** = accountant who prepares specialized information (especially budgets) for managers so that they can make decisions; **management accounts** = financial information (on sales, costs, credit, profitability) prepared for a manager *or* director of a company; **management consultant** = person who gives advice on how to manage a business; **management course** = training course for managers; **management by objectives** = way of managing a business by planning work for the managers and testing to see if it is completed correctly and on time; **management team** = a group of managers working together; **management training** = training managers by making them study problems and work out ways of solving them; **management trainee** = young person being trained to be a manager **(b)** group of managers or directors; **top management** = the main directors of a company; **middle management** = the department managers of a company who carry out the policy set by the directors and organize the work of a group of workers; **junior management** = managers of small departments *or* deputies to departmental managers

◊ **manager** *noun* **(a)** head of a department in a company; **accounts manager** = head of the accounts department; **area manager** = manager who is responsible for the company's work (usually sales) in an area; **general manager** = manager in charge of the administration in a large company **(b)** person in charge of a branch or shop; **bank manager** = person in charge of a branch of a bank; **branch manager** = person in charge of a branch of a company

◇ **manageress** *noun* woman who runs a shop, or a department

◇ **managerial** *adjective* referring to managers *or* to management; **to be appointed to a managerial position** = to be appointed a manager; **decisions taken at managerial level** = decisions taken by managers

◇ **managing** *adjective* **managing clerk** = former term for a legal executive; **managing director** = director who is in charge of a whole company; **chairman and managing director** = managing director who is also chairman of the board of directors

mandamus *Latin word meaning* "we command": court order from the Divisional Court of the Queen's Bench Division, ordering a body (such as a lower court *or* tribunal) to do a certain legal duty; **the Chief Constable applied for an order of mandamus directing the justices to rehear the case**

mandate *noun* written authority given to a person authorizing and requiring him to act on behalf of the writer; **bank mandate** = written order allowing someone to sign cheques on behalf of a company

mandatory *adjective* which has to be done *or* to take place; **mandatory injunction** = order from a court which compels someone to do something; **mandatory meeting** = meeting which must be held *or* which all members have to attend

manendi *see* ANIMUS

manifest 1 *adjective* obvious; **a manifest injustice** 2 *noun* list of goods in a shipment; **passenger manifest** = list of passengers on a ship or plane

manipulate *verb* **to manipulate the accounts** = to make false accounts so that the company seems profitable; **to manipulate the market** = to work to influence share prices in your favour

◇ **manipulation** *noun* **stock market manipulation** = trying to influence the price of shares

◇ **manipulator** *noun* **stock market manipulator** = person who tries to influence the price of shares in his own favour

manslaughter *noun* notifiable offence of killing someone without having intended to do so *or* of killing someone intentionally but with mitigating circumstances; **he was accused of manslaughter; she was convicted of the manslaughter of her husband; involuntary manslaughter** = killing someone without having intended to do so; **voluntary manslaughter** = killing someone intentionally, but under mitigating circumstances (such as provocation *or* diminished responsibility)
NOTE: no plural

Maria *see* BLACK

Mareva injunction *noun* court order to freeze the assets of a person who has gone overseas *or* of a company based overseas to prevent them being taken out of the country

COMMENT: called after the case of *Mareva Compania Naviera SA* v. *International Bulk-Carriers SA*

margin *noun* difference between the money received from selling a product and the money paid for it; **gross margin** = percentage difference between sales income and cost of sales

marine 1 *adjective* referring to the sea *or* ships; **marine insurance** = insurance of ships and their cargoes; **marine underwriter** = person who insures ships and their cargoes 2 *noun* **the merchant marine** = all the commercial ships of a country

◇ **maritime** *adjective* referring to the sea *or* ships; **maritime law** = laws referring to ships, ports, etc.; **maritime lawyer** = lawyer who specializes in legal matters concerning ships and cargoes; **maritime lien** = right to seize a ship against an unpaid debt; **maritime perils** = PERILS OF THE SEA; **maritime trade** = carrying commercial goods by sea

marital *adjective* referring to a marriage; **marital privileges** = privilege of a spouse not to give evidence against the other spouse in certain criminal proceedings

mark 1 *noun* (a) sign put on an item to show something; **assay mark** = hallmark *or* mark put on gold or silver items to show that the metal is of the correct quality; **kite**

mark = mark on British goods to show that they meet official standards **(b)** cross ("X") put on a document in place of a signature by someone who cannot write **2** *verb* to put a sign on something; **to mark a product "for export only"; article marked at £1.50; to mark the price on something; because he could not write he marked an "X" in place of his signature**

◊ **marksman** *noun* (i) person who can shoot a gun very accurately; (ii) person who cannot write, and who has to put an "X" in place of a signature

market 1 *noun* **(a)** place (often in the open air) where farm produce is sold; **market day** = day when a market is regularly held; **market dues** = rent for a place in a market **(b) the Common Market** = the European Economic Community; **the Common Market policy on trade restrictions; the Common Market ministers (c)** place where a product might be sold *or* group of people who might buy a product; **home** *or* **domestic market** = market in the country where the selling company is based **(d)** possible sales of a certain type of product *or* demand for a certain type of product; **a growth market** = market where sales are likely to rise rapidly **(e) the black market** = buying and selling goods in a way which is not allowed by law; **to pay black market prices** = to pay high prices to obtain items which are not easily available; **there is a lucrative black market in spare parts for cars; he bought gold coins on the black market (f) a buyer's market** = market where goods are sold cheaply because there is little demand; **a seller's market** = market where the seller can ask high prices because there is a large demand for the product **(g) closed market** = market where a supplier deals with only one agent and does not supply any others direct; **free market economy** = system where the government does not interfere in business activity in any way; **open market** = market where anyone can buy and sell; **market overt** = market which is open to all, in which a sale gives good title to a buyer, even though the seller's title may be defective **(h) capital market** = place where companies can look for investment capital; **the foreign exchange markets** = places where currencies are bought or sold; **forward markets** = places where foreign currency or commodities can be bought or sold for delivery at a later

date **(i) stock market** = place where shares are bought and sold; **to buy shares in the open market** = to buy shares on the Stock Exchange, not privately; **over-the-counter market** = secondary market in shares which are not listed on the main Stock Exchange; **market capitalization** = value of a company calculated by multiplying the price of its shares on the Stock Exchange by the number of shares issued; **market maker** = person who trades in stocks and shares on the Stock Exchange; **market price** = price at which a product can be sold **2** *verb* to sell (products); **this product is being marketed in all European countries**

marriage *noun* act *or* state of being joined together as husband and wife; **by marriage** = because of being married; **she became a British citizen by marriage; marriage settlement** = agreement which is made before marriage where money *or* property is given on trust for the benefit of the future spouse; **sham marriage** *or* **marriage of convenience** = form of marriage arranged for the purpose of acquiring the nationality of a spouse *or* for some other financial reason

marshal *noun* **(a) Marshal of the Admiralty Court** = official in charge of the Admiralty Court **(b)** *US* official who carries out the orders of a court

martial *adjective* relating to the armed services; **martial law** = rule of a country *or* part of a country by the army on the orders of the main government, the ordinary civil law having been suspended; **the president imposed** *or* **declared martial law in two provinces; the government lifted martial law;** *see also* COURT-MARTIAL

master *noun* **(a)** official in the Queen's Bench Division or Chancery Division of the High Court whose work is to examine and decide on preliminary matters before trial; **Practice Master** = master on duty in the High Court, who will hear solicitors without appointment and give directions in relation to the general conduct of proceedings; **Taxing Master** = official of the Supreme Court who assesses the costs of a court action **(b) Masters of the Bench** = senior members of one of the Inns of Court **(c) master and servant** = employer and employee; **the law of master and servant** = employment law **(d)** main *or* original; **master copy of a file** = main copy of a computer file, kept for security purposes

◇ **Master of the Rolls** *noun* judge who presides over the Court of Appeal and is responsible for admitting solicitors to the Roll of Solicitors

material 1 *noun* **(a) materials** = substances which can be used to make a finished product; **building materials** = bricks, cement, etc., used in building; **raw materials** = substances which have not been made in a factory (such as wool, wood, sand) **(b) display material** = advertisements, photographs, etc., which can be used to attract attention to goods which are for sale (NOTE: no plural for (b)) 2 *adjective* important *or* relevant; **material alteration** = change made to a legal document which alters the rights *or* duties in it; **material evidence** = evidence which has important relevance to a case; **material witness** = witness whose evidence is important to the case

matricide *noun* murder of one's mother

matrimony *noun* marriage *or* state of being joined together as husband and wife

◇ **matrimonial** *adjective* referring to marriage; **matrimonial causes** = proceedings concerned with rights of partners in a marriage (such as divorce or separation proceedings); **matrimonial home** = place where a husband and wife live together

matter 1 *noun* **(a)** problem; **it is a matter of concern to the members of the committee** = the members of the committee are worried about it **(b) printed matter** = printed books, newspapers, advertising material, etc. (NOTE: no plural) **(c)** question *or* problem to be discussed; **the most important matter on the agenda; we shall consider first the matter of last month's fall in prices; interlocutory matter** = subsidiary dispute which is dealt with before a full trial; **matter of fact** = question of fact which has to be decided; **matters of fact** = facts relevant to a case which is tried at court; **matters of law** = law relevant to a case which is tried at court; **it is a matter of fact whether the parties entered into the contract, but it is a matter of law whether or not the contract is legal** 2 *verb* to be important; **does it matter if one month's sales are down?**

mature *verb* to be due for payment; **bill which will mature in three months**

◇ **maturity** *noun* time when a bill *or* government stock *or* insurance is due for payment

maxim *noun* short phrase which formulates a principle, such as "let the buyer beware"

maximum 1 *noun* largest possible number *or* price *or* quantity; **up to a maximum of £10** = no more than £10 (NOTE: plural is **maxima**) 2 *adjective* largest possible; **maximum income tax rate** *or* **maximum rate of tax; he was sentenced to the maximum sentence of imprisonment; to increase production to the maximum level** = as much as possible

mayhem *noun* (i) general riot *or* disturbance; (ii) violent removal of a person's arm or leg

McNaghten *see* M'NAGHTEN

means *plural noun* money which is available; **statement of means** = statement attached to an application for Legal Aid which shows the financial position of the claimant

measure 1 *noun* **(a)** way of calculating size *or* quantity; **cubic measure** = volume in cubic feet or metres, calculated by multiplying height, width and length; **dry measure** = way of calculating the quantity of loose dry goods (such as corn); **square measure** = area in square feet or metres, calculated by multiplying width and length; **inspector of weights and measures** = government inspector who inspects weighing machines and goods sold in shops to see if the quantities and weights are correct; **measure of damages** = calculation of how much money a court should order one party to pay another to compensate for a tort or breach **(b)** type of action, especially a law passed by Parliament or statutory instrument; **a government measure to reduce crime in the inner cities; to take measures to prevent something happening** = to act to stop something happening; **to take emergency measures** = to act rapidly to stop a dangerous situation developing; **an economy measure** = an action to save money; **fiscal measures** = tax changes made by the government to improve the working of the economy; **as a precautionary measure** = to prevent something taking place; **safety measures** = actions to make sure that something is *or* will be safe **2** *verb* **(a)** to find out the size *or* quantity of something; to be of a certain size *or* quantity; **to measure the size of a package; a package which measures 10cm by 25cm** *or* **a package measuring 10cm by 25cm (b) to measure the government's performance** = to judge how well the government is doing

◊ **measurement** *noun* **(a)** measurements = size (in inches, centimetres, etc.); **to write down the measurements of a package (b)** way of judging something; **performance measurement** *or* **measurement of performance; measurement of profitability** = way of calculating how profitable something is

mechanical reproduction rights *plural noun* right to make a recording of a piece of music *or* to make a copy of something by photographing it, etc. (usually against payment of a fee)

mediate *verb* to try to make the two sides in an argument come to an agreement; **to mediate between the manager and his staff; the government offered to mediate in the dispute**

◊ **mediation** *noun* attempt by a third party to make the two sides in an argument agree; **the employers refused an offer of government mediation; the dispute was ended through the mediation of union officials**

◊ **mediator** *noun* official mediator = government official who tries to make the two sides in an industrial dispute agree

medical *noun* referring to the study or treatment of illness; **medical certificate** = certificate from a doctor to show that a worker has been ill; **medical inspection** = examining a place of work to see if the conditions are safe; **medical insurance** = insurance which pays the cost of medical treatment especially when travelling abroad; **medical officer of health (MOH)** = person responsible for the health services in a town; **he resigned for medical reasons** = he resigned because he was too ill to work

◊ **medicine** *noun* scientific study of diseases and health; **forensic medicine** =

medical science concerned with solving crimes against people (such as autopsies of murdered persons, taking blood samples from clothes)

meet *verb* **(a)** to come together with someone; **to meet a negotiating committee; to meet an agent at his hotel; the two sides met in the lawyer's office (b)** to be satisfactory for; **to meet a customer's requirements; he failed to meet the conditions of the court order; to meet the demand for a new product** = to fill the demand for a product; **we will try to meet your price** = we will try to offer a price which is acceptable to you; **they failed to meet the deadline** = they were not able to complete in time **(c)** to pay for; **to meet someone's expenses; the company will meet your expenses; he was unable to meet his mortgage repayments; to meet your obligations** = to pay your debts
NOTE: **meeting - met - has met**

◊ **meeting** *noun* **(a)** coming together of a group of people; **management meeting; staff meeting; board meeting** = meeting of the directors of a company; **general meeting** *or* **meeting of shareholders** *or* **shareholders' meeting** = meeting of all the shareholders of a company *or* meeting of all the members of a society; **Annual General Meeting** = meeting of all the shareholders of a company which takes place once a year to agree the accounts; **Extraordinary General Meeting** = special meeting of shareholders to discuss an important matter which cannot wait until the next Annual General Meeting **(b) freedom of meeting** = being able to meet as a group without being afraid of prosecution; **to hold a meeting** = to organize a meeting of a group of people; **the meeting will be held in the committee room; to open a meeting** = to start a meeting; **to conduct a meeting** = to be in the chair for a meeting; **to close a meeting** = to end a meeting; **to put a resolution to a meeting** = to ask a meeting to vote on a proposal

member *noun* **(a)** person who belongs to a group *or* a society; **ordinary member** = person who pays a subscription to belong to a club *or* group; **honorary member** = special person who does not have to pay a subscription **(b)** shareholder *or* person who owns shares in a company **(c)** organization which belongs to a society; **the member countries** *or* **the member states**

of the EEC; **the members of the United Nations; the member companies of a trade association**

◇ **Member of Parliament** *noun* person elected to represent a constituency in Parliament
NOTE: often abbreviated to **MP**. The plural is **MPs**

◇ **membership** *noun* **(a)** belonging to a group; **membership qualifications; conditions of membership; to pay your membership *or* your membership fees; is Austria going to apply for membership of the Common Market? (b)** all the members of a group; **the membership was asked to vote for the new president; the club's membership secretary** = committee member who deals with the ordinary members of a society; **the club has a membership of five hundred** = the club has five hundred members

memorandum *noun* short note; **memorandum of association** = legal document setting up a limited company and giving details of its aims, capital structure, and registered office; **memorandum of satisfaction** = document showing that a company has repaid a mortgage *or* charge
NOTE: plural is **memoranda**

menace *noun* threat *or* action which frightens someone; **demanding money with menaces** = crime of getting money by threatening another person

mens rea *Latin phrase meaning* "guilty mind": mental state required to be guilty of committing a crime (intention *or* recklessness *or* guilty knowledge); *see note at* CRIME *and compare* ACTUS REUS

mental *adjective* referring to the mind; **mental disorder** = sickness of the mind

◇ **mentally** *adverb* in the mind; **mentally ill criminals are committed to special establishments**

mention **1** *noun* short hearing at court **2** *verb* to talk about something for a short time; **the judge mentioned the need for the jury to examine all the documents; can you mention to the secretary that the date of the next meeting has been changed?**

mentis *see* COMPOS MENTIS

mercantile law *or* **law merchant** *noun* law relating to commerce

mercy *noun* showing that you forgive; **prerogative of mercy** = power (used by the Home Secretary) to commute or remit a sentence

◇ **mercy killing** *noun* euthanasia *or* killing of someone who is ill to put an end to his suffering

merge *verb* to join together; **the two companies have merged; the firm merged with its main competitor**

◇ **merger** *noun* (i) joining of a small estate to a large one; (ii) joining together of two or more companies; **as a result of the merger, the company is the largest in the field**

meridiem *see* A.M., P.M.

merit *noun* being good or efficient; **merit award** *or* **merit bonus** = extra money given to a worker because he has worked well; **merit increase** = increase in pay given to someone because his work is good; **merit rating** = judging how well a worker does his work, so that he can be paid according to merit

◇ **merits of the case** *plural noun* main question which is at issue in an action

mesne *adjective* in the middle; **mesne process** = process in a legal action, which comes after the first writ but before the outcome of the action has been decided; **action for mesne profits** = action to recover money that should be paid to a landowner in place of rent by a person who is in wrongful possession

messenger *noun* person who brings a message; **he sent the package by special messenger** *or* **by motorcycle messenger; office messenger** = person who carries messages from one person to another in a large office; **messenger boy** = young man who carries messages

Messrs *noun* plural form of Mr, used in names of firms; **Messrs White, White & Smith**

messuage *noun* house where people live, and the land and buildings attached to it

Met *noun* *informal* the Met = the Metropolitan Police

metropolitan *adjective* referring to a large city; **the Metropolitan Police** = the police force of Greater London, which is directly responsible to the Home Secretary; **the Metropolitan Police Commissioner** = the head of the Metropolitan Police, appointed directly by the Home Secretary; **solicitor for the Metropolitan Police** = solicitor responsible for prosecutions brought by the Metropolitan Police

COMMENT: the higher ranks in the Metropolitan Police are Deputy Assistant Commissioner, Assistant Commissioner, and Commissioner. See also DETECTIVE, POLICE

Michaelmas *noun* **(a)** 29th September: one of the quarter days when rent is payable on land **(b)** one of the four sittings of the law courts; one of the four law terms

microfiche *noun* index sheet, made of several microfilm photographs; **we hold our records on microfiche**

◇ **microfilm 1** *noun* roll of film on which a document is photographed in very small scale; **we hold our records on microfilm 2** *verb* to make a very small scale photograph; **send the 1980 correspondence to be microfilmed** *or* **for microfilming**

middle *adjective* in the centre *or* between two points; **middle management** = department managers in a company, who carry out the policy set by the directors and organize the work of a group of workers

◇ **Middle Temple** *noun* one of the four Inns of Court in London

Midland and Oxford Circuit *noun* one of the six circuits of the Crown Court, to which barristers belong, with its centre in Birmingham

Midsummer day *noun* 24th June: one of the four quarter days when rent is payable on land

minder *noun* *slang* bodyguard *or* person employed to protect someone

minimal *adjective* the smallest possible; **there was a minimal quantity of imperfections in the new stock; the head office exercises minimal control over the branch offices**

◇ **minimis** *see* DE MINIMIS

◇ **minimize** *verb* to make something seem to be very small and not very

important; **do not minimize the risks involved; he always minimizes the difficulty of the project**

◇ **minimum 1** *noun* smallest possible quantity *or* price *or* number; **to keep expenses to a minimum; to reduce the risk of a loss to a minimum 2** *adjective* smallest possible; **minimum dividend** = smallest dividend which is legal and accepted by the shareholders; **minimum payment** = smallest payment necessary; **minimum sentence** = shortest possible sentence allowed in law for a certain offence; **minimum wage** = lowest hourly wage which a company can legally pay its workers

minister *noun* member of a government who is in charge of a ministry; **a government minister; the Minister of Information** *or* **the Information Minister; the Minister of Foreign Affairs** *or* **the Foreign Minister; the Minister of Justice** *or* **the Justice Minister; Minister of State** = person who is in charge of a section of a government department

COMMENT: in the USA, heads of government departments are called secretary: the **Secretary for Commerce**; in the UK, heads of government departments (see below) are called **Secretary of State: the Secretary of State for Defence**

◇ **ministerial** *adjective* referring to a minister; **ministerial tribunal** = tribunal set up by a government minister to hear appeals from local tribunals

◇ **ministry** *noun* **(a)** department in the government; **he works in the Ministry of Finance** *or* **the Finance Ministry; he is in charge of the Ministry of Information** *or* **of the Information Ministry; a ministry official** *or* **an official from the ministry (b)** government; **during the Wilson ministry** = when the government headed by Prime Minister Wilson was in office

COMMENT: in Britain and the USA, important ministries are called departments: the **Department of Trade and Industry; the Commerce Department**
Note also that the UK does not have a government department called the "Ministry of Justice", and the duties of supervising the administration of

justice fall to the Lord Chancellor's office and the Home Office

minor 1 *adjective* less important; **minor expenditure; minor shareholders; a loss of minor importance** = not a very serious loss **2** *noun* person less than eighteen years old

◇ **minority** *noun* **(a)** being less than eighteen years old *or* time when someone is less than eighteen years old; **a person is not liable for debts contracted during his minority (b)** number *or* quantity which is less than half of the total; **a minority of board members opposed the chairman; minority shareholding** *or* **minority interest** = group of shares which are less than one half of the shares in a company; **minority shareholder** = person who owns a group of shares but less than half of the shares in a company; **in the minority** = being fewer than half; **the small parties are in the minority on the local council**

minute 1 *noun* **(a)** one sixtieth part of an hour; **counsel cross-examined the witness for fifty minutes (b) minutes** = the record of what happened at a meeting, especially the record of a general meeting of a company; **to take the minutes** = to write notes of what happened at a meeting; **the chairman signed the minutes of the last meeting** = he signed them to show that they were a correct record of what was said and what decisions were taken; **this will not appear in the minutes of the meeting** = this is unofficial and will not be noted as having been said **(c) minutes of order** = a draft order submitted to a court when a party wishes the court to make an order **2** *verb* to put something into the minutes of a meeting; **the chairman's remarks about the auditors were minuted; I do not want that to be minuted** *or* **I want that not to be minuted** = do not put that remark into the minutes of the meeting

◇ **minutebook** *noun* book in which the minutes of a meeting are kept

misadventure *noun* accident; **death by misadventure** = accidental death; **the coroner's verdict was death by misadventure**

misappropriate *verb* to steal *or* to use illegally money which is not yours, but with which you have been trusted

◇ **misappropriation** *noun* illegal use of money by someone who is not the owner but who has been trusted to look after it

misbehaviour *noun* bad behaviour, especially a criminal offence committed by a public official

miscalculate *verb* to calculate wrongly; **the salesman miscalculated the discount, so we hardly broke even on the deal**

◇ **miscalculation** *noun* mistake in calculating

miscarriage of justice *noun* decision wrongly *or* unjustly reached by a court *or* decision which goes against the rights of a party in a case, in such a way that the decision may be reversed on appeal

miscellaneous *adjective* various *or* mixed *or* not all of the same sort; **miscellaneous items; a box of miscellaneous pieces of equipment; miscellaneous expenditure**

misconduct *noun* illegal action *or* action which can harm someone; **professional misconduct** = behaviour by a member of a profession (such as a lawyer *or* accountant *or* doctor) which the body which regulates that profession considers to be wrong; **wilful misconduct** = doing something which harms someone while knowing it is wrong
NOTE: no plural

miscount 1 *noun* mistake in counting **2** *verb* to count wrongly; **the votes were miscounted, so the ballot had to be taken again**

misdeed *noun* crime

misdemeanour *noun* minor crime; **he was charged with several misdemeanours, including driving without a valid licence and creating a disturbance**

misdirect *verb* to give wrong directions to a jury on a point of law

◇ **misdirection** *noun* giving wrong directions to a jury on a point of law

misfeasance *noun* doing something improperly
NOTE: no plural

misinterpret *verb* to understand something wrongly; **the rioters misinterpreted the instructions of the police**

◊ **misinterpretation** *noun* wrong interpretation *or* understanding of something; **clause which is open to misinterpretation** = clause which can be wrongly interpreted

misjoinder *noun* wrongly joining someone as a party to an action

mislead *verb* to make someone understand something wrongly; **the instructions in the document are quite misleading; the wording of the will is misleading and needs to be clarified; the judge misled the jury in his summing up** NOTE: **misleading - misled**

mismanage *verb* to manage badly

◊ **mismanagement** *noun* bad management; **the company failed because of the chairman's mismanagement**

misprision *noun* generally, a mistake in doing something; **misprision of treason** = crime of knowing that treason has been committed

misrepresent *verb* to report facts wrongly

◊ **misrepresentation** *noun* making a wrong statement with the intention of persuading someone to enter into a contract; **fraudulent misrepresentation** = false statement made wilfully to trick someone *or* to persuade someone to enter into a contract

mistake *noun* wrong action *or* wrong decision; **to make a mistake** = to do something wrong; **the shop made a mistake and sent the wrong items; there was a mistake in the address; she made a mistake in addressing the letter; by mistake** = in error *or* wrongly; **they sent the wrong items by mistake; she put my letter into an envelope for the chairman by mistake; mistake in venue** = starting legal proceedings in the wrong court

◊ **mistaken identity** *noun* situation where someone is wrongly thought to be another person; **he was arrested for burglary, but released after it had been established that it was a case of mistaken identity**

mistrial *noun* trial which is not valid

misunderstanding *noun* lack of agreement *or* mistake; **there was a misunderstanding over my tickets**

misuse *noun* wrong use; **misuse of funds** *or* **of assets**

mitigate *verb* to make (a crime) less serious; **mitigating circumstances** *or* **factors** = things which make a crime less serious *or* which can excuse a crime

◊ **mitigation** *noun* reduction of a sentence *or* of the seriousness of a crime; **in mitigation, counsel submitted evidence of his client's work for charity; defence counsel made a speech in mitigation; plea in mitigation** = things said in court on behalf of a guilty party to persuade the court to impose a lenient sentence; **mitigation of damages** = reduction in the extent of damages awarded NOTE: used in the construction **in mitigation of**

M'Naghten Rules *noun* rules which a judge applies in deciding if a person charged with a crime is insane

> COMMENT: to prove insanity, it has to be shown that because of a diseased mind, the accused did not know what he was doing *or* did not know that his action was wrong. Based on the case of *R* v. *M'Naghten* (1843) in which the House of Lords considered and ruled on the defence of insanity

mob *noun* *US* the Mafia

◊ **mobster** *noun* *US* member of the mob

modify *verb* to change *or* to make something fit a different use; **the chairman modified the reporting system; this is the new modified agreement; the car will have to be modified to pass the government tests**

◊ **modification** *noun* change; **to make** *or* **to carry out modifications to the plan; we asked for modifications to the contract**

modus operandi *Latin phrase meaning* "way of working": especially a particular way of committing crimes which can identify a criminal

MOH = MEDICAL OFFICER OF HEALTH

moiety *noun* half

molest *verb* to threaten violent behaviour against (a child *or* a woman, especially a spouse) in a sexual way; **he was accused of molesting children in the park**

◊ **molestation** *noun* act of threatening violent behaviour towards a child *or* a woman, especially a spouse; **non-molestation order** = order made by a court in matrimonial proceedings to prevent one spouse from molesting the other

◊ **molester** *noun* person who molests; **a convicted child molester**

money *noun* **(a)** coins and notes used for buying and selling; **cheap money** = money which can be borrowed at a low rate of interest; **danger money** = extra salary paid to workers in dangerous jobs; **dear money** = money which has to be borrowed at a high rate of interest; **hot money** = (i) money which is moved from country to country to get the best returns; (ii) illegal money; **paper money** = money in notes, not coins; **ready money** = cash *or* money which is immediately available; **money had and received** = cause of action where one party has had money which really belongs to someone else **(b)** **money supply** = amount of money which exists in a country; **money markets** = markets for buying and selling short-term loans; **money rates** = rates of interest for borrowers or lenders **(c)** **money order** = document which can be bought for sending money through the post; **foreign money order** *or* **international money order** *or* **overseas money order** = money order in a foreign currency which is payable to someone living in a foreign country **(d)** **monies** = sums of money; **monies owing to the company; to collect monies due**

◊ **moneylender** *noun* person who lends money at interest

monitor **1** *noun* screen (like a TV screen) on a computer **2** *verb* to check *or* to examine how something is working; **they are monitoring the new system of dealing with young offenders**

monogamy *noun* system of society where a man is married to one woman at a time

monopoly *noun* situation where one person *or* company controls all the market in the supply of a product *or* right given to one person *or* company to control all the market in the supply of a product; **to have the monopoly of alcohol sales *or* to have the alcohol monopoly; the company has the absolute monopoly of imports of French wine; public monopoly *or* state monopoly** = situation where the state is the only suppliers of a product or service (such as the Post Office, the Coal Board); **the Monopolies (and Mergers) Commission** = British body which examines takeovers and mergers to make sure that a monopoly is not being created
NOTE: American English uses **trust** more often

◊ **monopolize** *verb* to create a monopoly *or* to get control of all the supply of a product

◊ **monopolization** *noun* making a monopoly

monopsony *noun* situation where one person *or* company controls all the purchasing in a certain market

Monroe doctrine *noun* *US* principle that the USA has an interest in preventing outside interference in the internal affairs of other American states

> COMMENT: so called because it was first proposed by President Monroe in 1823

monthly *adjective* happening every month; **she paid off the debt in monthly instalments; he was ordered to pay a sum of money to his wife monthly**

moonlight *verb* *informal* to do a second job for cash (often in the evening) as well as a regular job, and usually not declaring the money earned to the income tax authorities

◊ **moonlighter** *noun* person who moonlights

◊ **moonlighting** *noun* doing a second job; **he makes thousands a year from moonlighting**

mooring *noun* place where boats can be tied up in a harbour

moral *adjective* referring to the difference between what is right and what is wrong; **the high moral standard which should be set by judges**

◇ **morals** *plural noun* standards of behaviour; **to corrupt someone's morals =** to make someone behave in a way which goes against the normal standard of behaviour

moratorium *noun* temporary stop to repayments of money owed; **the banks called for a moratorium on payments** NOTE: plural is **moratoria**

mortality *noun* **mortality tables =** chart, used by insurers, which shows how long a person of a certain age can be expected to live, on average

mortgage 1 *noun* (i) agreement where someone lends money to another person so that he can buy a property, the property being used as the security; (ii) money lent in this way; **to take out a mortgage on a house; to buy a house with a £20,000 mortgage; mortgage (re)payments =** money paid each month as interest on a mortgage, together with repayment of a small part of the capital borrowed; **endowment mortgage =** mortgage backed by an endowment policy; **equitable mortgage =** mortgage which does not give the mortgagee a legal estate in the land mortgaged; **first mortgage =** main mortgage on a property; **puisne mortgage =** mortgage where the deeds of the property have not been deposited with the lender; **second mortgage =** further mortgage on a property which is already mortgaged, the first mortgage always having a prior claim; **to foreclose on a mortgaged property =** to take possession of a property because the owner cannot repay money which he has borrowed, using the property as security; **to pay off a mortgage =** to pay back the principal and all the interest on a loan to buy a property; **mortgage bond =** certificate showing that a mortgage exists and that property is security for it; **mortgage debenture =** debenture where the lender can be repaid by selling the company's property 2 *verb* to accept a loan with a property as security; **the house is mortgaged to the bank; he mortgaged his house to set up in business**

◇ **mortgagee** *noun* person or company which lends money for someone to buy a property and takes a mortgage of the property as security

◇ **mortgagor** *noun* person who borrows money, giving a property as security

mortem *see* POST MORTEM

mortis *see* DONATIO, RIGOR

most favoured nation *noun* country which has the best trade terms; **most-favoured-nation clause =** agreement between two countries that each will offer the best possible terms in commercial contracts

motion *noun* **(a)** moving about; **time and motion study =** study in an office *or* factory of the time taken to do certain jobs and the movements workers have to make to do them **(b)** proposal which will be put to a meeting for that meeting to vote on; **to propose *or* to move a motion; the meeting voted on the motion; to speak against *or* for a motion; the motion was carried *or* was defeated by 220 votes to 196 =** the motion was approved *or* not approved; **to table a motion =** to put forward a proposal for discussion by putting details of it on the table at a meeting **(c)** application to a judge in court, asking for an order in favour of the person making the application; **notice of motion =** document telling the other party to a case that an application will be made to the court

motive *noun* reason for doing something

mounted *adjective* riding a horse; **mounted police were brought in to control the crowd**

◇ **mounting** *adjective* which is going up *or* rising; **there is mounting pressure on the police to solve the murder *or* to combat inner city crime**

move *verb* **(a)** to go from one place to another; **the company is moving from London Road to the centre of town; we have decided to move our factory to a site near the airport (b)** to propose formally that a motion be accepted by a meeting; **he moved that the accounts be agreed; I move that the meeting should adjourn for ten minutes (c)** to make an application to the court

◇ **movable** *or* **moveable** 1 *adjective* which can be moved; **movable property =** chattels and other objects which can be moved (as opposed to land) 2 *plural noun* **movables =** movable property

◇ **movement** *noun* **(a)** changing position *or* going up or down; **movements in** the money markets; **cyclical movements of trade; movements of capital** = changes of investments from one country to another; **free movement of capital** = ability to transfer capital from one EEC country to another without any restrictions; **stock movements** = passing of stock into or out of the warehouse **(b)** group of people working towards the same aim

◊ **mover** *noun* person who proposes a motion

MP = MEMBER OF PARLIAMENT, MILITARY POLICE

MR = MASTER OF THE ROLLS
NOTE: usually written after the surname: **Lord Smith, MR** but spoken as "the Master of the Rolls, Lord Smith"

Mr Big *noun informal* important criminal whose name is not known, but who is supposed to be in control of a large criminal operation

mug 1 *noun informal* **(a)** person who is easily cheated **(b)** face; **mug shot** = photograph of a criminal taken, after he has been detained, for the police records 2 *verb* to attack and rob someone; **the tourists were mugged in the station; he was accused of mugging an old lady in the street** NOTE: **mugging - mugged**

◊ **mugger** *noun* person who attacks and robs someone

◊ **mugging** *noun* attacking and robbing someone; **the number of muggings has increased sharply over the last few years**

multiple *adjective* many; **multiple entry visa** = visa which allows a visitor to enter a country many times; **multiple ownership** = situation where something is owned by several parties

municipal *adjective* **(a)** referring to a town; **municipal taxes; municipal offices (b) municipal law** = law which is in operation within a state, as opposed to international law

◊ **municipality** *noun* corporation of a town

murder 1 *noun* **(a)** notifiable offence of killing someone illegally and intentionally; **he was charged with murder** *or* **he was found guilty of murder; the murder rate has fallen over the last year** (NOTE: no plural) **(b)** an act of killing someone illegally and

intentionally; **three murders have been committed during the last week** 2 *verb* to kill someone illegally and intentionally

◊ **murderer** *noun* person who commits a murder

◊ **murderess** *noun* woman who commits a murder

Muslim *adjective* relating to religion and law following the commands of the prophet Mohammed

mutiny 1 *noun* agreement between two or more members of the armed forces to disobey commands of superior officers and to try to take command themselves 2 *verb* to carry out a mutiny

◊ **mutineer** *noun* person who takes part in a mutiny

mutual *adjective* belonging to two or more people; **mutual (insurance) company** = company which belongs to insurance policy holders; *US* **mutual funds** = organizations which take money from small investors and invest it in stocks and shares for them, the investment being in the form of shares in the fund; **mutual wills** = wills made by two people, where each leaves his property to the other

◊ **mutuality** *noun* state where two parties are bound contractually to each other

Nn

name 1 *noun* word used to call a thing *or* a person; **brand name** = name of a particular make of product; **corporate name** = name of a large corporation; **under the name of** = using a particular name; **trading under the name of "Best Foods"** = using the name "Best Foods" as a commercial name for selling a product, but not as the name of the company 2 *verb* to give someone a name *or* to mention someone's name; **the Chief Constable was named in the divorce case;** (*of the speaker*) **to name a Member of Parliament** = to say that an MP has been guilty of misconduct

◇ **named** *adjective* **person named in the policy** = person whose name is given on an insurance policy as the person insured

nark *noun slang* informer *or* person who gives information to the police

nation *noun* country and the people living in it

◇ **national** 1 *adjective* referring to a particular country; **National Insurance** = state insurance which pays for medical care, hospitals, unemployment benefits, etc.; **National Insurance contributions** = money paid into the National Insurance scheme by the employer and the worker; **gross national product** = annual value of goods and services in a country including income from other countries; **National Savings** = savings scheme for small investors run by the Post Office (including a savings bank, savings certificates and premium bonds) 2 *noun* person who is a citizen of a state; **the government ordered the deportation of all foreign nationals**

◇ **nationality** *noun* being the citizen of a state; **he is of United Kingdom nationality** = he is a citizen of the United Kingdom; **he has dual nationality** = he is a citizen of two countries at the same time

◇ **nationalize** *verb* to put a privately-owned industry under state ownership and control; **nationalized industry** = industry which was once privately owned, but now belongs to the state

◇ **nationalization** *noun* taking over of a private industry by the state; *compare* NATURALIZATION

nature *noun* kind *or* type; **what is the nature of the contents of the parcel? the nature of his business is not known**

◇ **natural** *adjective* **(a)** found in the earth; **natural resources** = raw materials (such as coal, gas, iron) which are found in the earth **(b)** not made by people; **natural fibre** = fibre made from animal hair *or* plants, etc. **(c)** normal; **natural child** = child (especially an illegitimate child) of a particular parent; **natural justice** = the general principles of justice; **natural parents** = actual mother and father of a child (as opposed to step-parents, adoptive parents, foster parents, etc.); **natural person** = human being (as opposed to an artificial person such as a company); **natural right** = general right which people

have to live freely, usually stated in a written constitution; **natural wastage** = losing workers because they resign or retire, not through redundancy or dismissals

◇ **natural-born subject** *noun* term formerly applied to a person born in the UK or a Commonwealth country who was a British citizen by birth

◇ **naturalization** *noun* granting of citizenship of a state to a foreigner; **she has applied for naturalization; you must fill in the naturalization papers;** *compare* NATIONALIZATION

◇ **naturalized** *adjective* (person) who has become a citizen of another country; **he is a naturalized American citizen**

necessary *adjective* which has to be done *or* which is needed; **it is necessary to fill in the form correctly; you must have all the necessary documentation before you apply for a subsidy**

◇ **necessaries** *plural noun* things which are needed by a child *or* mentally ill person to live on

◇ **necessarily** *adverb* in an unavoidable way; **the imposition of a fine is not necessarily the only course open to the court**

◇ **necessity** *noun* **(a)** thing which is absolutely important, without which nothing can be done; **the necessities of life** = things which every person needs to live **(b)** situation which makes it impossible not to do something; **of necessity** = unavoidably; **a judge must of necessity be impartial**

negative *adjective* meaning "no"; **the answer was in the negative** = the answer was "no"; **the breathalyser test was negative** = the test showed that there was not an excessive amount of alcohol in the blood

neglect 1 *noun* (i) not doing a duty; (ii) lack of care towards someone *or* something; **the children had suffered from neglect; wilful neglect** = intentionally not doing something which it is your duty to do (NOTE: no plural) 2 *verb* **(a)** to fail to take care of someone; **he neglected his three children (b) to neglect to do something** = to forget *or* omit to do something which has to be done; **he neglected to return his income tax form**

◇ **neglected** *adjective* not well looked after; **the local authority applied for a care order for the family of neglected children**

negligence *noun* lack of proper care *or* not doing a duty (with the result that a person *or* property is harmed) *or* tort of acting carelessly towards others so as to cause harm entitling the injured party to claim damages; **contributory negligence** = negligence partly caused by the plaintiff and partly by the defendant, resulting in harm done to the plaintiff; **criminal negligence** = acting recklessly with the result that harm is done to other people; **culpable negligence** = negligence which is so bad that it amounts to an offence; **gross negligence** = act showing very serious neglect of duty towards other people
NOTE: no plural

◇ **negligent** *adjective* showing negligence *or* not taking proper care; **the defendant was negligent in carrying out his duties as a trustee**

◇ **negligently** *adverb* in a way which shows negligence; **the guardian acted negligently towards his ward**

◇ **negligible** *adjective* very small *or* not worth bothering about; **not negligible** = quite large

negotiable *adjective* **not negotiable** = which cannot be exchanged for cash; **"not negotiable"** = words written on a cheque to show that it can be paid only to a certain person; **negotiable cheque** = cheque made payable to bearer (i.e. to anyone who holds it); **negotiable instrument** = document (such as a bill of exchange *or* cheque) which can be legally transferred to another owner simply by passing it to him or by endorsing it *or* which can be exchanged for cash

◇ **negotiability** *noun* ability of a document to be legally transferred to a person simply by passing it to him

◇ **negotiate** *verb* **to negotiate with someone** = to discuss a problem formally with someone, so as to reach an agreement; **the management refused to negotiate with the union; to negotiate terms and conditions** *or* **to negotiate a contract** = to discuss and agree the terms of a contract; **negotiating committee** = group of representatives of management or unions who negotiate a wage settlement

◇ **negotiation** *noun* discussion of terms and conditions to reach an agreement; **contract under negotiation** = contract which is being discussed; **a matter for negotiation** = something which must be discussed before a decision is reached; **to enter into negotiations** *or* **to start negotiations** = to start discussing a problem; **to resume negotiations** = to start discussing a problem again, after talks have stopped for a time; **to break off negotiations** = to refuse to go on discussing a problem; **to conduct negotiations** = to negotiate

◇ **negotiator** *noun* person who discusses with the aim of reaching an agreement

neighbour *noun* person who lives near to someone; **he was accused of setting fire to his neighbour's car; she sued her next door neighbour for damages**

◇ **neighbourhood** *noun* district and the people living in it; **we live in a very quiet neighbourhood; in the neighbourhood of** = near to; **the factory is in the neighbourhood of the prison; neighbourhood watch** = system where the people living in an area are encouraged to look out for criminals *or* to report any breakdown of law and order

◇ **neighbouring** *adjective* placed next to something; **he lives in the neighbouring street; the factory is in the neighbouring town**

nemine contradicente *or* **nem con** *Latin phrase meaning* "with no one contradicting": phrase used to show that no one voted against the proposal; **the motion was adopted nem con**

nemo dat quod non habet *Latin phrase meaning* "no one can give what he does not have": rule that no one can pass *or* sell to another person something to which he has no title (such as stolen goods)

new *adjective* recent *or* not old; **under new management** = with a new owner; **new for old policy** = insurance policy which covers the cost of buying a new item to replace an old one which has been stolen *or* damaged; **new issue** = issues of new shares; **new trial** = trial which can be ordered to take place in civil cases, when the first trial was improper in some way

◇ **news** *noun* information about things which have happened; **news agency** = office which distributes news to newspapers and television companies; **news release** = sheet giving information about a new event which is sent to newspapers and TV and radio stations so that they can use it

next *adjective & adverb* **(a)** coming afterwards in time; **on Wednesday he arrived in London and the next day tried to assassinate the Prime Minister; the first case this morning was one of murder, the next of attempted murder; the court's next decision was judged to be unconstitutional (b)** nearest (in place); **the trial was adjourned to the next courtroom; the plaintiff sat next to his solicitor**

◊ **next friend** *noun* person who brings an action on behalf of a minor

◊ **next of kin** *noun* person *or* persons who are most closely related to someone; **his only next of kin is an aunt living in Scotland; the police have informed the next of kin of the people killed in the accident** NOTE: can be singular or plural

nick *slang* **1** *noun* police station **2** *verb* **(a)** to steal **(b)** to arrest

nil *noun* zero *or* nothing; **to make a nil return** = to report the figure zero on a form

nisi *see* DECREE, FORECLOSURE

nobble *verb slang* to interfere with *or* to bribe *or* to influence (a jury); **he tried to nobble one of the jurors**

no-claims bonus *noun* reduction of premiums paid because no claims have been made against an insurance policy

nolle prosequi *Latin phrase meaning* "do not pursue": power used by the Attorney-General to stop a criminal trial

nominal *adjective* **(a)** very small (payment); **we make a nominal charge for our services; they are paying a nominal rent; nominal damages** = very small damages, awarded to show that the loss *or* harm suffered was technical rather than actual **(b) nominal capital** = the total of the face value of all the shares which a company is allowed to issue according to its memorandum and articles of association; **nominal value** = face value *or* value written on a share *or* a coin *or* a banknote

nominate *verb* to suggest someone *or* to name someone for a job; **to nominate someone to a post** = to appoint someone to a post without an election; **to nominate someone as proxy** = to name someone as your proxy

◊ **nomination** *noun* act of nominating

◊ **nominee** *noun* person who is nominated, especially someone who is appointed to deal with financial matters on behalf of a person; **nominee account** = account held on behalf of someone; **nominee shareholder** = person named as the owner of shares, when the shares are in fact owned by another person

non- *prefix* not

◊ **non-acceptance** *noun* situation where the person who should pay a bill of exchange does not accept it

◊ **non-arrestable offence** *noun* crime for which a person cannot be arrested without a warrant

> COMMENT: non-arrestable offences are usually crimes which carry a sentence of less than five years imprisonment

◊ **non-capital crime** *or* **offence** *noun* crime *or* offence for which the punishment is not death

◊ **non compos mentis** *Latin phrase meaning* "mad" *or* "not fully sane"

◊ **non-conformance** *noun* act of not conforming; **he was criticized for non-conformance with the regulations**

◊ **non-consummation** *noun* **non-consummation of marriage** = not having sexual intercourse (between husband and wife)

◊ **non-contributory** *adjective* **non-contributory pension scheme** = pension scheme where the employee does not make any contributions and the company pays everything

◊ **non-direction** *noun* (*of a judge*) not giving direction to a jury

◊ **non-executive director** *noun* director who attends board meetings and gives advice, but does not work full time for the company

◊ **nonfeasance** *noun* not doing something which should be done by law

◇ **nonjoinder** *noun* plea that a plaintiff has not joined all the necessary parties to his action

◇ **non-molestation order** *noun* order made by a court in matrimonial proceedings to prevent one spouse from molesting the other

◇ **non-negotiable instrument** *noun* document (such as a crossed cheque) which is not payable to bearer and so cannot be exchanged for cash

◇ **non-payment** *noun* **non-payment of a debt** = not paying a debt due

◇ **non profit-making organization** *or US* **non-profit corporation** *noun* organization (such as a club) which is not allowed by law to make a profit

◇ **non-recurring items** *noun* special items in a set of accounts which appear only once

◇ **non-refundable** *adjective* which will not be refunded

◇ **non-resident** *noun* person who is not considered a resident of a country for tax purposes

◇ **non-returnable** *adjective* which cannot be returned; **non-returnable packing** = packing which is to be thrown away when it has been used and not returned to the person who sent it

◇ **nonsuit** *or* **nonsuited** *adjective* **to be nonsuit** *or* **nonsuited** = (i) situation in civil proceedings where a plaintiff fails to establish a cause of action and is forced to abandon his proceedings; (ii) situation in criminal proceedings where a judge directs a jury to find the defendant not guilty

◇ **non-taxable** *adjective* which is not subject to tax

◇ **non-voting shares** *plural noun* shares which do not allow the shareholder to vote at meetings

normal *adjective* usual *or* which happens regularly; **normal deliveries are made on Tuesdays and Fridays; now that the strike is over we hope to resume normal service as soon as possible; under normal conditions** = if things work in the usual way

North-Eastern Circuit, Northern Circuit *noun* two of the six circuits of the Crown Court to which barristers belong, with centres in Leeds and Manchester

noscitur a sociis *Latin phrase meaning* "the meaning of the words can be understood from the words around them": ambiguous words *or* phrases can be clarified by referring to the context in which they are used

notary public *noun* lawyer (usually but not necessarily a solicitor) who has the authority to witness and draw up certain documents, and so make them official NOTE: plural is **notaries public**

◇ **notarial** *adjective* referring to notaries; **notarial act** = act which can be carried out only by a notary public

note 1 *noun* **(a)** short document *or* short piece of information; **advice note** = written notice to a customer giving details of goods ordered and shipped but not yet delivered; **contract note** = note showing that shares have been bought *or* sold but not yet paid for; **cover note** = letter from an insurance company giving details of an insurance policy and confirming that the policy exists; **covering note** = letter sent with documents to explain why you are sending them; **credit note** = note showing that money is owed to a customer; **debit note** = note showing that a customer owes money; **note of costs** = bill *or* invoice; **note of hand** *or* **promissory note** = document stating that someone promises to pay an amount of money on a certain date **(b)** short letter *or* short piece of information; **the foreman of the jury passed a note to the judge; to make a note of something** = to write something down in a few words; **to take notes of a meeting** = to write down details of a meeting in a few words, so that the details can be remembered later **(c) to take note of something** = to pay attention to something *or* to take something into account; **the jury was asked to take note of the evidence given by the pathologist (d) bank note** *or* **currency note** = piece of printed paper money **2** *verb* **(a)** to pay attention to something; **members of the jury will note that the defendant does not say he was at home on the night of the crime (b)** to write down details of something and remember them; **the policeman noted the number of the car in his notebook; your complaint has been noted (c)** to note a bill = to attach a note to a dishonoured bill of exchange, explaining why it has not been honoured

◇ **notebook** *noun* book for writing notes

◇ **notepad** *noun* pad of paper for writing short notes

notice *noun* **(a)** piece of written information; **the company secretary pinned up a notice about the pension scheme; copyright notice** = note in a book showing who owns the copyright and the date of ownership **(b)** official passing of information to someone (such as a warning that a contract is going to end *or* that terms are going to be changed *or* that an employee will leave his job at a certain date *or* that a tenant must leave the property he is occupying); **to give someone notice *or* to serve notice on someone** = to give someone a legal notice; **to give a tenant notice to quit *or* to serve a tenant with notice to quit** = to inform a tenant officially that he has to leave the premises by a certain date; **she has handed in *or* given her notice** = she has said she will quit her job at a certain date; **period of notice** = time stated in the contract of employment which the worker or company has to allow between resigning or being fired and the worker actually leaving his job; **until further notice** = until different instructions are given; **at short notice** = with very little warning; **you must give seven days' notice of withdrawal** = you must ask to take money out of the account seven days before you want it; **notice of motion** = document telling the other party to a case that an application will be made to the court; **to give notice of appeal** = to start official proceedings for an appeal to be heard; **notice of opposition** = document opposing a patent application **(c)** knowledge of a fact; **actual notice** = real knowledge which a person has of something; **constructive notice** = knowledge which the law says a person has of something (whether or not the person actually has it) because the information is available to him if he asks for it; **judicial notice** = facts and matters which a judge is presumed to know, so that evidence does not have to be provided for them

◇ **noticeboard** *noun* board fixed to a wall where notices can be put up; **the list of electors is put up on the noticeboard in the local offices**

notify *verb* **to notify someone of something** = to tell someone something formally; **they were notified of the impending court action**

◇ **notifiable** *adjective* which must be notified; **notifiable offence** = serious offence which can be tried in the Crown Court

◇ **notification** *noun* informing someone

not proven *adjective* (*in Scotland*) (verdict) that the prosecution has not produced sufficient evidence to prove the accused to be guilty

notwithstanding *adverb & preposition* in spite of; **the case proceeded notwithstanding the objections of the defendant *or* the defendant's objections notwithstanding**
NOTE: can be used before or after the phrase

novation *noun* transaction in which a new contract is agreed by all parties to replace an existing contract (as where one of the parties to the old contract is released from his liability under the old contract, and this liability is assumed by a third party)

noxious *adjective* unpleasant *or* which offends; **noxious substance; noxious smell**

nuisance *noun* something which causes harm *or* inconvenience to someone *or* to property; **public nuisance *or* common nuisance** = criminal act which causes harm *or* damage to members of the public in general *or* their rights; **private nuisance** = nuisance which causes harm *or* damage to a particular person *or* his rights

null *adjective* with no meaning *or* which cannot legally be enforced; **the contract was declared null and void** = the contract was said to be no longer valid; **to render a decision null** = to make a decision useless *or* to cancel a decision

◇ **nullification** *noun* act of making something invalid

◇ **nullify** *verb* to make something invalid *or* to cancel something

◇ **nullity** *noun* situation where a marriage is ruled never to have been in effective existence

numerical order *noun* arrangement (of records) in order of their numbers; **the documents are filed in numerical order**

nuncupative will *noun* will made orally in the presence of a witness (as by a soldier in time of war)

Oo

oath *noun* solemn legal promise that someone will say *or* write only what is true; **he was on oath** *or* **under oath** = he had promised in court to say what was true; **to administer an oath to someone** = to make someone swear an oath; **commissioner for oaths** = solicitor appointed by the Lord Chancellor to administer affidavits which will be used in court

obey *verb* to do what someone asks you to do; **the crowd refused to obey the police instructions; he was asked to give an undertaking that he would obey the court order**

◇ **obedience** *noun* doing what someone asks you to do; **the army swore obedience to the president; every citizen should show obedience to the laws of the state**

obiter dicta *Latin phrase meaning* "things which are said in passing": part of a judgment which is not essential to the decision of the judge and does not create a precedent; *see also* RATIO DECIDENDI
NOTE: the singular is **obiter dictum**

object 1 *noun* purpose; **objects clause** = section in a company's memorandum of association which says what work the company will do **2** *verb* to refuse to do something *or* to say that you do not accept something; **to object to a clause in a contract; to object to a juror** = to ask for a juror not to be appointed because he or she may be biased
NOTE: you object **to** something or someone

◇ **objection** *noun* **to raise an objection to something** = to object to something; **the union delegates raised an objection to the wording of the agreement**

objective 1 *noun* something which you try to do; **long-term objective** *or* **short-term objective** = aim which you hope to achieve within a few years or a few months; **management by objectives** = way of managing a business by planning work for the managers to do and testing if it is completed correctly and on time **2** *adjective* considered from a general point of view and not from that of the person involved; **the judge asked the jury to be objective in considering the evidence put before them; you must be objective in assessing the performance of the staff; to carry out an objective review of current legislation**

obligate *verb especially US* **to be obligated to do something** = to have a legal duty to do something

◇ **obligation** *noun* **(a)** duty to do something; **to be under an obligation to do something** = to feel it is your duty to do something; **he is under no contractual obligation to buy** = he has signed no contract to buy; **to fulfil one's contractual obligations** = to do what is stated in a contract; **two weeks' free trial without obligation** = situation where the customer can try the item at home for two weeks without having to buy it at the end of the test **(b)** debt; **to meet one's obligations** = to pay one's debts

◇ **obligatory** *adjective* necessary according to the law or rules; **each person has to pass an obligatory medical examination**

◇ **oblige** *verb* **to oblige someone to do something** = to make someone feel he must do something; **he felt obliged to cancel the contract**

◇ **obligee** *noun* person who is owed a duty

◇ **obligor** *noun* person who owes a duty to someone

obscene *adjective* (play, book, etc.) which is likely to deprave *or* corrupt someone who sees or reads it *or* offend public morals and decency; **the magazine was classed as an obscene publication; the police seized a number of obscene films**

◇ **obscenity** *noun* being obscene; **the magistrate commented on the obscenity of some parts of the film; obscenity laws** = law relating to obscene publications *or* films

observe *verb* **(a)** to obey (a rule *or* a law); **failure to observe the correct procedure; all members of the association should observe the code of practice (b)** to watch *or* to notice what is happening; **officials have been instructed to observe the conduct of the election**

◇ **observance** *noun* doing what is required by a law; **the government's observance of international agreements**

◇ **observation** *noun* **(a)** noticing what is happening **(b)** remark; **the judge made some observations about the conduct of the accused during the trial**

◇ **observer** *noun* person who observes; **two official observers attended the meeting**

obsolete *adjective* no longer used *or* no longer in force; **the law has been made obsolete by new developments in forensic science**

obstruct *verb* to get in the way *or* to stop something progressing; **the parked cars are obstructing the traffic; obstructing the police** = offence of doing something which prevents a policeman carrying out his duty

◇ **obstruction (a)** thing which gets in the way; **the car caused an obstruction to the traffic (b)** act of obstructing someone; **obstruction of the police is an offence**

obtain *verb* **(a)** to get; **to obtain supplies from abroad; we find these items very difficult to obtain; to obtain an injunction against a company; he obtained control by buying the family shareholding; obtaining by deception** = acquiring money *or* property by tricking someone into handing it over; **obtaining credit** = offence whereby an undischarged bankrupt obtains credit above a limit of £50; **to obtain a property by fraud** *or* **by deception** = to trick someone into handing over possession of property; **obtaining a pecuniary advantage by deception** = crime of tricking someone into handing over money **(b)** to be a rule *or* to have a legal status; **this right does not obtain in judicial proceedings; a rule obtaining in international law**

◇ **obtainable** *adjective* which can be got; **prices fall when raw materials are easily obtainable; our products are obtainable in all computer shops**

occasion **1** *noun* time when something takes place; **the opening of the trial was the occasion of protests by the family of the accused** **2** *verb* to make something happen; **he pleaded guilty to assault occasioning actual bodily harm**

◇ **occasional** *adjective* which happens from time to time; **occasional licence** = licence to sell alcohol at a certain place and time

◇ **occasionally** *adverb* from time to time; **he admitted that he occasionally visited the house**

occupancy *noun* **(a)** act of occupying a property (such as a house, an office, a room in a hotel); **with immediate occupancy** = empty and available to be occupied immediately **(b)** occupying a property which has no owner, and so acquiring title to the property
NOTE: no plural

◇ **occupant** *noun* person *or* company which occupies a property

◇ **occupation** *noun* **(a) occupation of a building** = act of occupying a building **(b)** job *or* work; **what is her occupation? his main occupation is house building; occupations** = types of work; **people in professional occupations**

◇ **occupational** *adjective* referring to a job; **occupational accident** = accident which takes place at work; **occupational disease** = disease which affects people in certain jobs; **occupational hazards** = dangers which apply to certain jobs; **occupational pension scheme** = pension scheme where the worker gets a pension from the company he has worked for

◇ **occupier** *noun* person who lives in a property; **beneficial occupier** = person who occupies a property but does not own it; **occupier's liability** = duty of an occupier to make sure that visitors to a property are not harmed; **owner-occupier** = person who owns the property which he occupies

COMMENT: the occupier has the right to stay in or on a property, but is not necessarily an owner

◇ **occupy** *verb* **(a)** to live *or* work in a property (such as a house *or* office *or* hotel room); **all the rooms in the hotel are occupied; the company occupies three floors of an office block (b)** to enter and stay in a property illegally; **the rebels occupied the Post Office; squatters are occupying the building (c) to occupy a post** = to be employed in a job

occur *verb* to happen *or* to take place; **the witness described how the argument occurred; no infringements have occurred since the court order was made**

off 1 *adverb* **(a)** not working *or* not in operation; **the agreement is off; they called the strike off (b)** taken away from a price; **these carpets are sold at £25 off the marked price; we give 5% off for quick settlement 2** *preposition* **(a)** away from a price; **to take £25 off the price; we give 10% off our normal prices (b)** away from work; **to take time off work; to take three days off; we give the staff four days off at Christmas; it is the secretary's day off tomorrow**

offence *or* *US* **offense** *noun* crime *or* act which is against the law; **he was charged with three serious offences; the minister was arrested and charged with offences against the Official Secrets Act; offence against the person** = criminal act which harms a person physically (such as murder *or* manslaughter); **offence against property** = criminal act which damages *or* destroys property (such as theft *or* forgery *or* criminal damage); **offence against public order** = criminal act which disturbs the general calm of society (such as riot *or* affray); **offence against the state** = act of attacking the lawful government of a country (such as sedition *or* treason); **first offence** = committing an illegal act for the first time; **as it was a first offence, he was fined and not sent to prison; inchoate offences** = offences (such as incitement *or* attempt *or* conspiracy to commit a crime) which are offences even though the substantive offence may not have been committed; **notifiable offence** = serious offence which can be tried in the Crown Court; **offence triable either way** = offence which can be tried before the Magistrates' Court *or* before the Crown Court

◇ **offend** *verb* to commit a crime

◇ **offender** *noun* person who commits a crime; **first offender** = person who has been charged with an offence for the first time; **fugitive offender** = criminal running away from the police who, if he is caught, is sent back to the place where the offence was committed; **persistent offender** = person who has been convicted of a crime several times before; **young offenders** = young persons who commit crimes

◇ **offensive weapon** *noun* object which can be used to harm a person *or* property; **carrying offensive weapons** = offence of holding a weapon or something (such as a bottle) which could be used as a weapon

COMMENT: many things can be considered as offensive weapons if they are used as such: a brick *or* a bottle *or* a piece of wire

offer 1 *noun* **(a)** statement by one party to a contract that he proposes to do something

COMMENT: the offer (and acceptance by the other party) is one of the essential elements of a contract

(b) offer to buy = statement that you are willing to pay a certain amount of money to buy something; **to make an offer for a company; he made an offer of £10 a share; £1,000 is the best offer I can make; to accept an offer of £1,000 for the car; the house is under offer** = someone has made an offer to buy the house and the offer has been accepted provisionally; **we are open to offers** = we are ready to discuss the price which we are asking; **cash offer** = being ready to pay in cash; **or near offer (o.n.o.)** = or an offer of a price which is slightly less than the price asked; **asking price: £200 o.n.o. (c) offer to sell** = statement that you are willing to sell something; **offer for sale** = situation where a company advertises new shares for sale; **offer price** = price at which new shares are put on sale; **bargain offer** = sale of a particular type of goods at a cheap price; **special offer** = goods put on sale at a specially low price **(d) he received six offers of jobs** *or* **six job offers** = six companies told him he could have a job with them **2** *verb* **(a)** to propose something to someone *or* to propose to do something; **he offered to buy the house; to offer someone £100,000 for his house; he offered £10 a share; to offer someone a job** = to tell someone that he can have a job in your company **(b)** to say that you are willing to sell something; **we offered the house for sale**

◇ **offeree** *noun* person who receives an offer

◇ **offeror** *noun* person who makes an offer

office *noun* **(a)** set of rooms where a company works *or* where business is done; **branch office** = less important office, usually in a different town or country from the main office; **head office** *or* **main office** = office building where the board of directors works and meets; **registered office** = in Britain, the office address of a company which is officially registered with the Companies' Registrar and to which certain legal documents must normally be sent **(b) office block** *or* **a block of offices** = building which contains only offices; **office hours** = time when an office is open; **office junior** = young man or woman who does all types of work in an office; **office space** *or* **office accommodation** = space available for offices or occupied by offices; **office staff** = people who work in offices **(c)** room where someone works and does business; **come into my office; she has a pleasant office which looks out over the park; the senior partner's office is on the third floor (d) booking office** = office where you can book seats at a theatre *or* tickets for the railway; **box office** = office at a theatre where tickets can be bought; **general office** = main administrative office in a company; **information office** *or* **inquiry office** = office where someone can answer questions from members of the public; **ticket office** = office where tickets can be bought **(e)** British government department; **the Foreign Office** = ministry dealing with foreign affairs; **the Home Office** = ministry dealing with the internal affairs of the country, including the police and the prisons; **Office of Fair Trading** = government body which protects consumers against unfair *or* illegal business **(f)** post *or* position; **he holds** *or* **performs the office of treasurer; high office** = important position or job; **office of profit (under the Crown)** = government post which disqualifies someone from being a Member of Parliament; **compensation for loss of office** = payment to a director who is asked to leave a company before his contract ends

officer *noun* **(a) police officer** = policeman *or* member of a police force (NOTE: used in US English with a name: **Officers Smith and Jones went to the scene of the accident**; GB English is **constable**) **(b)** person who has an official position; **customs officer** = person working for the customs; **fire safety officer** = person responsible for fire safety in a building; **information officer** = person who gives information about a company *or* about a government

department to the public; **personnel officer** = person who deals with the staff and their conditions of employment, especially interviewing new workers; **training officer** = person who deals with the training of staff; **the company officers** *or* **the officers of a company** = the main executives or directors of a company **(c)** official (usually unpaid) of a club *or* society, etc.; **the election of officers of an association**

◊ **Law Officers** *plural noun* the posts of Attorney-General and Solicitor-General (in England and Wales) and Lord Advocate and Solicitor-General (in Scotland)

official 1 *adjective* **(a)** done because it has been authorized by a government department *or* organization; **on official business; he left official documents in his car; she received an official letter of explanation; official secret** = piece of information which is classified as important to the state and which it is a crime to reveal; **Official Secrets Act** = Act of Parliament which governs the publication of secret information relating to the state; **speaking in an official capacity** = speaking officially; **to go through official channels** = to deal with officials, especially when making a request **(b)** done or approved by a director *or* by a person in authority; **this must be an official order - it is written on the company's notepaper; the strike was made official** = the local strike was approved by the main trade union office **(c) Official Journal** = publication which lists the regulations, statutory instruments and directives of the EEC; **the Official Receiver** = government official who is appointed to close down a company which is in liquidation *or* to deal with affairs of bankrupts; **official referee** = expert judge appointed by the High Court to try complicated. usually technical, cases where specialist knowledge is required; **Official Solicitor** = solicitor who acts in the High Court for parties who have no one to act for them, usually because they are under a legal disability **2** *noun* person working in a government department; **airport officials inspected the shipment; government officials stopped the import licence; customs official** = person working for the customs; **high official** = important person in a government department; **minor official** = person in a low position in a government department

◇ **officialese** *noun* language used in government documents and which can be difficult to understand

◇ **officially** *adverb* in an official way; **officially he knows nothing about the problem, but unofficially he has given us a lot of advice about it**

officio *see* EX OFFICIO, FUNCTUS OFFICIO

off-licence *noun* (a) licence to sell alcohol for drinking away from the place where you buy it (b) shop which sells alcohol for drinking at home

offspring *noun* child *or* children of a parent; **his offspring inherited the estate; they had two offspring**
NOTE: offspring is both singular and plural

old *adjective* having existed for a long time; **the company is 125 years old next year; we have decided to get rid of our old computer system and put in a new one**

◇ **old age** *noun* period when a person is old; **old age pension** = state pension given to a man who is 65 or a woman who is 60; **old age pensioner** = person who receives the old age pension

◇ **Old Bailey** *noun* Central Criminal Court in London

Oleron *noun* **Laws of Oleron** = first international maritime laws, drawn up in 1216

ombudsman *noun* official who investigates complaints by the public against government departments *or* other large organizations

> COMMENT: although the ombudsman may make his recommendations public, he has no power to enforce them

omit *verb* (a) to leave something out *or* not to put something in; **the secretary omitted the date when typing the contract** (b) not to do something; **he omitted to tell the managing director that he had lost the documents**
NOTE: omitting - omitted

◇ **omission** *noun* thing which has been omitted; **errors and omissions excepted** = words written on an invoice to show that

the company has no responsibility for mistakes in the invoice

onerous *adjective* heavy *or* needing a lot of effort or money; **the repayment terms are particularly onerous** = the loan is particularly difficult to pay back

o.n.o. = OR NEAR OFFER

onus *noun* responsibility for doing something difficult; **onus of proof *or* onus probandi** = duty to prove that what has been alleged in court is correct; **the onus of proof is on the plaintiff; if there is a prosecution the onus will normally be on the prosecutor to prove the case;** *see also* BURDEN

op. cit. *Latin phrase meaning* "in the work mentioned"
NOTE: used when referring to a legal text: **"see Smith LJ in** *Jones* v. *Amalgamated Steel Ltd* **op. cit. p. 260"**

open **1** *adjective* (a) at work *or* not closed; **the store is open on Sunday mornings; our offices are open from 9 to 6; they are open for business every day of the week** (b) ready to accept something; **the job is open to all applicants** = anyone can apply for the job; **open to offers** = ready to accept a reasonable offer; **the company is open to offers for the empty factory** = the company is ready to discuss an offer which is lower than the suggested price (c) **open account** = unsecured credit *or* amount owed with no security; **open cheque** = cheque which is not crossed and can be exchanged for cash anywhere; **open court** = court where the hearings are open to the public; **in open court** = in a courtroom with members of the public present; **open credit** = bank credit given to good customers without security up to a certain maximum sum; **open market** = market where anyone can buy or sell; **open policy** = marine insurance policy, where the value of what is insured is not stated; **open prison** = prison with minimum security where category "D" prisoners can be kept; **open ticket** = ticket which can be used on any date; **open verdict** = verdict in a coroner's court which does not decide how the dead person died; **the court recorded an open verdict on the two policemen 2** *verb* (a) to start a new business working; **she has opened a shop in the High Street; we have opened an office in London** (b) to start work *or* to be at work; **the office opens at 9 a.m.; we open for business on Sundays (c)** to begin speaking; **counsel for the prosecution opened with a description of the accused's family background; to open negotiations** = to begin negotiating; **he opened the discussions with a description of the product; the chairman opened the meeting at 10.30 (d)** to start *or* to allow something to start; **to open a bank account; to open a line of credit; to open a loan**

◊ **open-ended** *or* US **open-end** *adjective* with no fixed limit *or* with some items not specified; **an open-ended agreement**

◊ **opening** 1 *noun* (a) act of starting a new business; **the opening of a new branch** *or* **of a new market** *or* **of a new office (b) opening hours** = hours when a shop *or* business is open **(c) job openings** = jobs which are empty and need filling; **a market opening** = possibility of starting to do business in a new market **2** *adjective* at the beginning *or* first; **the judge's opening remarks; the opening speech from the defence counsel** *or* **from the Home Secretary; opening balance** = balance at the beginning of an accounting period; **opening bid** = first bid at an auction; **opening entry** = first entry in an account

◊ **openly** *adverb* in an open way; **he openly admitted that he had sold drugs**

operandi *see* MODUS

operate *verb* (a) to work; **the new terms of service will operate from January 1st; the rules operate on inland postal services (b) to operate a machine** = to make a machine work

◊ **operating** *noun* general running of a business *or* of a machine; **operating budget** = income and expenditure which is expected to be incurred over a period of time; **operating costs** *or* **operating expenses** = costs of the day-to-day organization of a company; **operating profit** *or* **operating loss** = profit *or* loss made by a company in its usual business; **operating system** = the main program which operates a computer

◊ **operation** *noun* (a) business organization and work; **the company's operations in West Africa; he heads up the operations in Northern Europe; operations review** = examining the way in which a company or department works to see how it can be made more efficient and

profitable; **a franchising operation** = selling licences to trade as a franchise **(b) Stock Exchange operation** = buying *or* selling of shares on the Stock Exchange **(c) in operation** = working *or* being used; **the system will be in operation by June; the new system came into operation on June 1st**

◊ **operational** *adjective* (a) referring to how something works; **operational budget** = expenditure which is expected to be made in running a business *or* an office *or* a police force; **operational costs** = costs of running a business *or* a police force; **operational planning** = planning how something is to be run; **operational research** = study of a method of working to see if it can be made more efficient and cost-effective **(b) the system became operational on June 1st** = the system began working on June 1st

◊ **operative** 1 *adjective* referring to the working of a system; **to become operative** = to start working; **operative words** = words in a conveyancing document which transfer the land *or* create an interest in the land **2** *noun* person who operates a machine which makes a product

opinion *noun* (a) **public opinion** = what people think about something; **opinion poll** *or* **opinion research** = asking a sample group of people what their opinion is, so as to guess the opinion of the whole population; **to be of the opinion** = to believe *or* to think; **the judge was of the opinion that if the evidence was doubtful the claim should be dismissed (b)** piece of expert advice; **the lawyers gave their opinion; to ask an adviser for his opinion on a case; counsel prepared a written opinion; counsel's opinion** = a barrister's written advice about a case

opponent *noun* person who is against you *or* who votes against what you propose; **the prosecution tried to discredit their opponents in the case**

oppose *verb* to try to stop something happening; to vote against something; **a minority of board members opposed the motion; we are all opposed to the takeover; counsel for the plaintiff opposed the defendant's application for an adjournment; the police opposed bail** *or* **opposed the granting of bail** = the police said that bail should not be granted to the accused

◇ **opposition** *noun* **(a)** action of trying to stop something *or* of not agreeing to something; **there was considerable opposition to the plan for reorganizing the divorce courts; the voters showed their opposition to the government by voting against the proposal in the referendum; notice of opposition** = document opposing a patent application **(b)** (i) the largest political party which opposes the government; (ii) group of parties which oppose the government; **the opposition tried to propose a vote of censure on the Prime Minister; Leader of the Opposition** = head of the largest political party opposing the government

optimal *adjective* best

◇ **optimum** *adjective* best; **the market offers optimum conditions for sales**

option *noun* **(a)** offer to someone of the right to enter into a contract at a later date; **option to purchase** *or* **to sell** = giving someone the possibility to buy or sell something within a period of time *or* when a certain event happens; **first option** = allowing someone to be the first to have the possibility of deciding something; **to grant someone a six-month option on a product** = to allow someone six months to decide if he wants to be the agent *or* if he wants to make the product; **to take up an option** *or* **to exercise an option** = to accept the option which has been offered and to put it into action; **he exercised his option** *or* **he took up his option to acquire sole marketing rights to the product; I want to leave my options open** = I want to be able to decide what to do when the time is right; **to take the soft option** = to decide to do something which involves the least risk, effort or problems **(b)** (*Stock Exchange*) **call option** = option to buy shares at a certain price; **put option** = option to sell shares at a certain price; **share option** = right to buy or sell shares at a certain price at a time in the future; **stock option** = right to buy shares at a cheap price given by a company to its employees; **option contract** = right to buy or sell shares at a fixed price; **option dealing** *or* **option trading** = buying and selling share options

◇ **optional** *adjective* which can be added if the customer wants; **the insurance cover is optional**

oral *adjective* spoken; **oral evidence** = spoken evidence (as opposed to written)

◇ **orally** *adverb* in speaking, not writing

order 1 *noun* **(a)** general state of calm, where everything is working as planned and ruled; **there was a serious breakdown of law and order; public order** = situation were the general public is calm *or* where there are no riots; **offence against public order** *or* **public order offence** = riot *or* street fight, etc. **(b) court order** = command (which has no bearing on the final decision in a case) made by a court for someone to do something; **the prisoner was removed by order of the court; the factory was sold by order of the receiver; committal order** = order sending someone to prison for contempt of court; **compensation order** = order made by a criminal court which forces a criminal to pay compensation to his victim; **delivery order** = instructions given by the customer to the person holding his goods, telling him to deliver them; **order of discharge** = court order releasing a person from bankruptcy; **interim order** = order of a court which has effect while a case is still being heard; **preservation order** = court order which prevents a building from being knocked down *or* a tree from being cut down **(c) orders** = legislation made by ministers, under powers delegated to them by Act of Parliament, but which still have to be ratified by Parliament before coming into force; **Order in Council** = legislation made by the Queen in Council, which is allowed by an Act of Parliament and which does not have to be ratified by Parliament **(d)** arrangement of records (filing cards, invoices, etc.); **alphabetical order** = arrangement by the letters of the alphabet (A, B, C, etc.); **chronological order** = arrangement by the order of the dates; **numerical order** = arrangement by numbers **(e)** arrangement of business in the House of Commons; **order book** = list showing the House of Commons business for the term of Parliament; **order paper** = agenda of business to be discussed each day in the House of Commons **(f) standing orders** = rules *or* regulations governing the way in which a meeting *or* a debate in Parliament is conducted; **to call a meeting to order** = to start proceedings officially; **to bring a meeting to order** = to get a meeting back to discussing the agenda again (after an interruption); **order ! order!** = call by the Speaker of the House of Commons to bring the meeting to order; **point of order** = question relating to the way in which a meeting is being conducted; **he raised a point of order; on a point of order, Mr Chairman, can this committee approve its own accounts? the meeting was adjourned on a point of order (g)** working arrangement; **machine in full working order** = machine which is ready and able to work properly; **the telephone is out of order** = the telephone is not working; **is all the documentation in order?** = are all the documents valid and correct? **(h) pay to Mr Smith or order** = pay money to Mr Smith or as he orders; **pay to the order of Mr Smith** = pay money directly into Mr Smith's account **(i)** official request for goods to be supplied; **to give someone an order** or **to place an order with someone for twenty filing cabinets; to fill** or **to fulfil an order** = to supply items which have been ordered; **purchase order** = official paper which places an order for something; **items available to order only** = items which will be made only if someone orders them; **on order** = ordered but not delivered; **back orders** or **outstanding orders** = orders received in the past and not yet supplied; **order book** = record of orders; **telephone orders** = orders received over the telephone **(j)** document which allows money to be paid to someone; **he sent us an order on the Chartered Bank; banker's order** or **standing order** = order written by a customer asking a bank to make a regular payment; **money order** = document which can be bought for sending money through the post **2** *verb* **(a)** to tell someone to do something; **he ordered the police to search the premises; the government ordered the army to occupy the radio station (b)** to ask for goods to be supplied; **to order twenty filing cabinets to be delivered to the warehouse; they ordered a new Rolls Royce for the managing director (c)** to put in a certain way; **the address list is ordered by country; that filing cabinet contains invoices ordered by date**

ordinance *noun* **(a)** special decree of a government **(b)** *US* rule made by a municipal authority, and effective only within the jurisdiction of that authority

ordinary *adjective* normal *or* not special; **ordinary member** = person who pays a

subscription to belong to a club *or* group; **ordinary resolution** = resolution which can be passed by a simple majority of shareholders; **ordinary shares** = normal shares in a company, which have no special benefits or restrictions; **ordinary shareholder** = person who owns ordinary shares in a company

◇ **ordinarily** *adverb* normally *or* usually; **ordinarily resident** = usually resident in a certain country

organize *verb* to arrange (a meeting *or* a business *or* a demonstration) so that it is run properly and efficiently; **organized crime** = crime which is run as a business, with groups of specialist criminals, assistants, security staff, etc., all run by a group of directors or by a boss; **organized labour** = workers who are members of trade unions

◇ **organization** *noun* **(a)** way in which something is arranged; **the organization of a protest meeting; the organization of an appeal to the House of Lords (b)** group which is organized for a purpose; **he runs an organization for the rehabilitation of criminals**

origin *noun* where something comes from; **spare parts of European origin; certificate of origin** = document showing where goods were made *or* produced; **country of origin** = country where certain goods are produced

◇ **original 1** *adjective* which was used *or* made first; **they sent a copy of the original invoice; original evidence** = evidence given by a witness, based on facts which he knows to be true (as opposed to hearsay) **2** *noun* first copy made; **send the original and file two copies**

◇ **originally** *adverb* first *or* at the beginning

◇ **originate** *verb* to start *or* to begin; **originating application** = way of beginning certain types of case in the County Court; **originating summons** = official document which begins certain types of case in the High Court

orphan *noun* child whose parents have died

ostensible *adjective* appearing to be something, but not really so; **ostensible partner** = person who appears to be a partner (by allowing his name to be used as such) but really has no interest in the partnership

OTC = OVER-THE-COUNTER

otherwise *adverb* in another way; **John Smith, otherwise known as "the Butcher";** **except as otherwise stated** = except where it is stated in a different way; **unless otherwise agreed** = unless different terms are agreed

ouster *noun* removal of an occupier from a property so that he has to sue to regain possession (especially used against a violent spouse in matrimonial proceedings); **he had to apply for an ouster order; the judge made an ouster order;** *compare* EJECT

outcome *noun* result; **we are waiting for the outcome of the enquiry; the outcome of the trial was in doubt**

outlaw 1 *noun* old term for a person who was thrown out of society as a punishment 2 *verb* to say that something is unlawful; **the government has proposed a bill to outlaw drinking in public**

outline 1 *noun* general description, without giving many details; **they drew up the outline of a plan** *or* **an outline plan; outline planning permission** = general permission to build a property on a piece of land, but not final because there are no details 2 *verb* to make a general description; **the chairman outlined the company's plans for the coming year**

out of court *adverb & adjective* **a settlement was reached out of court** = a dispute was settled between two parties privately without continuing a court case; **they are hoping to reach an out-of-court settlement**

out of pocket *adjective & adverb* having paid out money personally; **out-of-pocket expenses** = amount of money to pay a worker back for his own money which he has spent on company business

output 1 *noun* (a) amount which a company *or* a person *or* a machine produces; **output has increased by 10%; 25% of our output is exported; output tax** = VAT charged by a company on goods *or* services sold (b) information which is

produced by a computer 2 *verb* to produce (by a computer); **the printer will output colour charts; that is the information outputted from the computer** NOTE: **outputting - outputted**

outright *adverb & adjective* completely; **to purchase something outright** *or* **to make an outright purchase** = to buy something completely, including all rights in it

outside *adjective & adverb* not in a company's office or building; **to send work to be done outside** = to send work to be done in other offices; **outside office hours** = when the office is not open; **outside dealer** = person who is not a member of the Stock Exchange but is allowed to trade; **outside director** = director who is not employed by the company; **outside line** = line from an internal office telephone system to the main telephone exchange; **outside worker** = worker who does not work in a company's offices

outstanding *adjective* not yet paid or completed; **outstanding debts** = debts which are waiting to be paid; **outstanding offences** = offences for which a person has not yet been convicted, which can be considered at the same time as a similar offence for which he faces sentence; **outstanding orders** = orders received but not yet supplied; **matters outstanding from the previous meeting** = questions which were not settled at the previous meeting

outvote *verb* to defeat in a vote; **the chairman was outvoted** = the majority voted against the chairman

overcharge 1 *noun* charge which is higher than it should be; **to pay back an overcharge** 2 *verb* to ask too much money; **the hotel overcharged us for meals; we asked for a refund because we had been overcharged**

overcome *verb* to defeat *or* to win against; **the defendant will have to overcome two hurdles if his appeal is to succeed** NOTE: **overcame - has overcome**

overdue *adjective* which has not been paid on time; **interest payments are three weeks overdue** = interest payments which should have been made three weeks ago

overestimate *verb* to think something is larger *or* worse than it really is; **he**

overestimated the amount of time needed to prepare his case

overlook *verb* (a) to look out over; **his chambers overlook the garden of the Middle Temple** (b) not to pay attention to; **in this instance we will overlook the delay; the court overlooked the fact that the defendant's car was not insured**

overreaching *noun* legal principle where an interest in land is replaced by a direct right to money

override *verb* to pay no attention to *or* to be more important than; **the appeal court overrode the decision of the lower court; overriding interest** = interest which comes before that of another party; **his wife established an overriding interest in the property against the bank's charge on it**
NOTE: overriding - overrode - has overridden

◇ **overrider** *or* **overriding commission** *noun* special extra commission which is above all other commissions

overrule *verb* (*of a higher court*) to set a new precedent by deciding a case on a different principle from one laid down by a lower court

overrun *noun* to go beyond a limit; **the construction company overran the time limit set to complete the factory**
NOTE: overrunning - overran - has overrun

overt *adjective* open *or* obvious (as opposed to covert); **overt act** = act which is obviously aimed at committing a criminal offence; *see also* MARKET OVERT

over-the-counter *adjective* **over-the-counter market** = secondary stock market dealing in shares which are not listed on the Stock Exchange; **over-the-counter sales** = legal selling of shares which are not listed in the official Stock Exchange list

overtime **1** *noun* hours worked more than the normal working time; **to work six hours' overtime; the overtime rate is one and a half times normal pay; overtime ban** = order by a trade union which forbids overtime work by its members; **overtime pay** = pay for extra time worked **2** *adverb* **to work overtime** = to work longer hours than in the contract of employment

owe *verb* to have to pay money; **he owes the company for the stock he purchased** = he has not paid for the stock

◇ **owing** *adjective* (a) which is owed; **money owing to the directors; how much is still owing to the company?** (b) **owing to** = because of; **the plane was late owing to fog; I am sorry that owing to pressure of work, we cannot supply your order on time**

own *verb* to have *or* to possess; **a wholly-owned subsidiary** = a subsidiary which belongs completely to the parent company; **a state-owned industry** = industry which is nationalized

◇ **owner** *noun* person who owns something; **beneficial owner** = true *or* ultimate owner (whose interest may be concealed by a nominee); **sole owner** = person who owns something alone; **owner-occupier** = person who owns and lives in a house; **goods sent at owner's risk** = situation where it is the owner of the goods who has to insure them while they are being shipped

◇ **ownership** *noun* act of owning something; **collective ownership** = situation where a business is owned by the workers who work in it; **common ownership** *or* **ownership in common** = ownership of a company *or* of a property by a group of people who each own a part; **joint ownership** = situation where two or more persons own the same property; **public ownership** *or* **state ownership** = situation where an industry is nationalized; **the company has been put into state ownership; private ownership** = situation where a company is owned by private shareholders; **the ownership of the company has passed to the banks** = the banks have become owners of the company
NOTE: no plural

oyez *French word meaning* "hear!": used at the beginning of some types of official proceedings

Pp

pais *see* ESTOPPEL

palimony *noun* money which a court orders a man to pay regularly to a woman with whom he has been living and from whom he has separated

panel *noun* **(a)** flat surface standing upright; **display panel** = flat area for displaying goods in a shop window; **advertisement panel** = special large advertising space in a newspaper **(b) panel of experts** = group of people who give advice on a problem; *see also* EMPANEL

paper *noun* **(a)** thin material for writing on or for wrapping; **carbon paper** = sheet of paper with a black coating on one side used in a typewriter to make a copy; **duplicating paper** = special paper to be used in a duplicating machine; **headed paper** = notepaper with the name and address of the company printed on it; **engrossment paper** *or* **judicature paper** = thick heavy paper on which court documents are engrossed; **lined paper** = paper with thin lines printed on it; **typing paper** = thin paper for use in a typewriter; **paper feed** = device which puts paper into a printer *or* copying machine (NOTE: no plural) **(b) papers** = documents; **the solicitor sent me the relevant papers on the case; the police have sent the papers on the fraud to the Director of Public Prosecutions; he has lost the customs papers; the office is asking for the VAT papers (c) on paper** = as explained in writing, but not tested in practice; **on paper the system is ideal, but we have to see it working before we will sign the contract; paper loss** = loss made when an asset has fallen in value but has not been sold; **paper profit** = profit made when an asset has increased in value but has not been sold **(d)** documents which can represent money (bills of exchange, promissory notes, etc.); **bankable paper** = document which a bank will accept as security for a loan; **negotiable paper** = document which can be transferred from one owner to another for money **(e) paper money** *or* **paper currency** = banknotes **(f)** newspaper; **trade paper** = newspaper aimed at people working in a certain industry; **free paper** *or* **giveaway paper** = newspaper which is given away free, and which relies for its income on its advertising

◊ **paperwork** *noun* office work, especially writing memoranda and filling in forms

NOTE: no plural

parade *noun* **identification** *or* **identity parade** = arrangement where a group of people (including a suspect) stand in line at a police station so that a witness can point out a person whom he recognizes

paragraph *noun* group of several lines of writing which makes a separate section; **the first paragraph of your letter** *or* **paragraph one of your letter; please refer to the paragraph in the contract on "shipping instructions"**

paralegal 1 *adjective* connected with, but not part of, the law **2** *noun* person with no legal qualifications who works in a lawyer's office

parcel *noun* area of land; **for sale: a parcel of land in the Borough of Richmond**

pardon 1 *noun* official ending of a prison sentence which a criminal is serving for a crime; **free pardon** = pardon given to a convicted person where both the sentence and the conviction are recorded as void **2** *verb* to end the prison sentence which a criminal is serving; **the political prisoners were pardoned by the president**

parent *noun* **parents** = father and mother; **parent company** = company which owns more than 50% of the shares of another company

parentis *see* IN LOCO PARENTIS

pari passu *Latin phrase meaning* "equally" *or* "with no distinction between them"; **the new shares will rank pari passu with the existing ones**

parish *noun* area which surrounds a church and which is served by that church

parity *noun* being equal; **the female staff want parity with the men** = they want to have the same rates of pay and conditions as the men; **the pound fell to parity with the dollar** = the pound fell to a point where one pound equalled one dollar
NOTE: no plural

parliament *noun* elected group of representatives who form the legislative body which votes the laws of a country (in the UK formed of the House of Commons and House of Lords); **Act of Parliament** = decision which has been approved by

Parliament and so becomes law; **contempt of Parliament** = conduct which may bring the authority of Parliament into disrepute; **Member of Parliament** = person elected to represent a constituency in Parliament; **the European Parliament** = parliament made up of delegates elected by each member state of the EEC
NOTE: often used without **"the": Parliament voted to abolish the death penalty; this is one of the Bills which will shortly be coming before Parliament**

◊ **parliamentary** *adjective* referring to parliament; **parliamentary agents** = persons (usually solicitors) who advise private individuals who wish to promote a Bill in Parliament; **Parliamentary Commissioner** = the Ombudsman *or* official who investigates complaints by the public against government departments; **parliamentary draftsman** = lawyer who is responsible for drafting Bills going before Parliament; **Parliamentary privilege** = right of a Member of Parliament to speak freely to the House of Commons without possibility of being sued for defamation

parol *noun* thing done by speaking; **parol agreement** *or* **contract** = simple contract *or* informal or oral contract; **parol evidence** = evidence given orally

parole 1 *noun* (i) allowing a prisoner to leave prison for a short time, on condition that he behaves well; (ii) allowing a prisoner who has behaved well to be released from prison early on condition that he continues to behave well; **he was given a week's parole to visit his mother in hospital; after six month's good conduct in prison she is eligible for parole; he was let out on parole and immediately burgled a house; parole board** = group of people who advise the Home Secretary if a prisoner should be released on parole before the end of his sentence 2 *verb* to let a prisoner out of prison on condition that he behaves well; **if you're lucky you will be paroled before Christmas**

part 1 *noun* (a) piece *or* section; **part of the shipment was damaged; part of the staff is on overtime; part of the expenses will be refunded** (b) **in part** = not completely; **to contribute in part to the costs; to pay the costs in part** (c) **spare part** = small piece of machinery used to take the place of a piece which is broken (d) **part-owner** = person who owns something jointly with

one or more other persons; **part-ownership** = situation where two or more persons own the same property (e) **part exchange** = giving an old product as part of the payment for a new one; **part payment** = paying of part of a whole payment; **part performance** = situation where a party has carried out part of a contract, but not complied with all the terms of it 2 *verb* **to part with something** = to give something which you possess to someone else; **he was tricked into parting with the keys to the safe**

parte *see* EX PARTE, INTER PARTES, AUDI ALTERNAM PARTEM

partial *adjective* (a) not complete; **partial loss** = situation where only part of the insured property has been damaged or lost; **he was awarded partial compensation for the damage to his house** = he was compensated for part of the damage (b) biased *or* showing favour towards on party the defendant complained that the judge was partial

particular 1 *adjective* special *or* different from others; **particular average** = situation where part of a shipment is lost or damaged and the insurance costs are borne by the owner of the lost goods and not shared among all the owners of the shipment; **particular lien** = right of a person to keep possession of another person's property until debts relating to that property have been paid; *compare* GENERAL AVERAGE, GENERAL LIEN 2 *noun* (a) **particulars** = details, especially a statement of the facts of a case made by a party in civil proceedings *or* a County Court pleading setting out the plaintiff's claim; **sheet which gives particulars of the items for sale; the inspector asked for particulars of the missing car; to give full particulars of something** = to list all the known details about something; **request for further and better particulars** = pleading served by one party on another in civil proceedings, asking for information about the other party's claim *or* defence; **particulars of claim** = County Court pleading setting out the plaintiff's claim (b) **in particular** = specially *or* as a special point; **goods which are easily damaged, in particular glasses, need special packing**

partition *noun* dividing up of land which is held by joint tenants *or* tenants in common

partly *adverb* not completely; **partly-paid capital** = capital which represents partly-paid shares; **partly-paid up shares** = shares where the shareholders have not paid the full face value; **partly-secured creditors** = creditors whose debts are not fully covered by the value of the security

partner *noun* person who works in a firm and has a share in it with other partners; **he became a partner in a firm of solicitors; active partner** *or* **working partner** = partner who works in a partnership; **junior partner** *or* **senior partner** = person who has a small *or* large part of the shares in a partnership; **limited partner** = partner who has only limited liability for the partnership debts; **sleeping partner** *or* **dormant partner** = partner who has a share in a business but does not work in it

◊ **partnership** *noun* (a) unregistered business where two or more people share the risks and profits equally; **to go into partnership with someone; to join with someone to form a partnership; articles of partnership** = document which sets up the legal conditions of a partnership; **to offer someone a partnership** *or* **to take someone into partnership with you** = to have a working business and bring someone in to share it with you; **to dissolve a partnership** = to bring a partnership to an end; **partnership at will** = partnership with no fixed time limit stated (b) **limited partnership** = registered business where the liability of some of the partners is limited to the amount of capital they have each provided to the business and where these partners may not take part in the running of the business, while other, working partners, are fully liable for all the obligations of the partnership

party *noun* (a) company *or* person involved in a legal dispute *or* legal agreement *or* crime; **one of the parties to the suit has died; the company is not a party to the agreement; identity of parties** = situation where the parties in different actions are the same; **party and party costs** = normal basis for taxation of costs which includes all costs incurred in the party's case (b) **third party** = any third person, in addition to the two main parties involved in a contract; **third party insurance** *or* **third party policy** = insurance which pays compensation if someone who is not the insured person incurs loss or injury (c)

working party = group of experts who study a problem; **the government has set up a working party to study the problems of industrial waste; Professor Smith is the chairman of the working party on drug abuse** (d) **political party** = organized group of people who believe a country should be run in a certain way

◊ **party wall** *noun* wall which separates two adjoining properties (houses *or* land) and belongs to both owners equally

pass 1 *noun* permit to allow someone to go into a building; **you need a pass to enter the ministry offices; all members of staff must show a pass** 2 *verb* (a) to vote to approve *or* to vote to make a law; **Parliament passed the Bill which has now become law; the finance director has to pass an invoice before it is paid; the loan has been passed by the board; to pass a resolution** = to vote to agree to a resolution; **the meeting passed a proposal that salaries should be frozen** (b) **to pass sentence on someone** = to give a convicted person the official legal punishment; **the jury returned a verdict of guilty, and the judge will pass sentence next week** (c) **to pass a dividend** = to pay no dividend in a certain year (d) to be successful; **he passed his typing test; she has passed all her exams and now is a qualified solicitor**

◊ **pass off** *verb* **to pass something off as something else** = to pretend that it is another thing in order to cheat a customer

◊ **passing off** *noun* tort of pretending that goods are someone else's, using that other person's reputation to make a sale

passport *noun* official document proving that you are a citizen of a country, which you have to show when you travel from one country to another; **we had to show our passports at the customs post; his passport is out of date; the passport officer stamped my passport; passport holder** = person who holds a passport; **she is a British passport holder**

patent 1 *noun* (a) official document showing that a person has the exclusive right to make and sell an invention; **to take out a patent for a new type of light bulb; to apply for a patent for a new invention; he has received a grant of patent for his invention; patent applied for** *or* **patent pending** = words on a product showing that the inventor has applied for a patent for it; **to forfeit a patent** = to lose a patent because payments have not been made; **to infringe a patent** = to make and sell a product which works in the same way as a patented product and not pay a royalty for it; **patent agent** = person who advises on patents and applies for patents on behalf of clients; **to file a patent application** = to apply for a patent; **patent examiner** = official who checks patent applications to see if the inventions are really new; **patent holder** = person who has been granted a patent; **infringement of patent** or **patent infringement** = act of illegally using or making or selling an invention which is patented without the permission of the patentee; **patent number** = reference number given to a patented invention; **patent office** = government office which grants patents and supervises them; **patent rights** = rights which an inventor holds under a patent; **patent specification** = full details of an invention which is the subject of a patent application **(b) letters patent** = official document from the Crown, which gives someone the exclusive right to do something (such as becoming a lord or granting a patent to make and sell an invention) **2** verb **to patent an invention** = to register an invention with the patent office to prevent other people from copying it **3** adjective obvious or clear to see; **the prisoner's statement is a patent lie**

◊ **patented** adjective which is protected by a patent

◊ **patentee** noun person who has been granted a patent

◊ **patently** adverb clearly or obviously; **he made a patently false statement to the court**

paternity noun **paternity leave** = permission for a man to be away from work when his wife is having a baby

◊ **paternity action** or **suit** noun lawsuit brought by the mother of an illegitimate child to force the putative father to maintain the child

pathology noun study of disease

◊ **pathologist** noun doctor who specializes in pathology, especially a doctor who examines corpses to find out the cause of death; **Home Office pathologist** = official government pathologist employed by the Home Office to examine corpses

patrial noun person who has the right to live in the UK because he has close family ties with the country (for example, if his grandfather was British)

patricide noun murder of one's father

patrol 1 noun group of people who walk through an area to see what is happening; **a police patrol** = group of policemen who are patrolling an area; **on patrol** = walking through an area to see what is happening; **we have six squad cars on patrol in the centre of the town; on foot patrol** = patrolling an area on foot, not in a car **2** verb to walk regularly through an area to see what is happening; **groups of riot police were patrolling the centre of the town**

◊ **patrol car** noun car used by police on patrol

◊ **patrolman** noun US lowest rank of policeman; **Patrolman Jones was at the scene of the accident**

pattern noun **(a) pattern book** = book showing examples of design **(b)** general way in which something usually happens; **the pattern of crime in the inner cities is different from the pattern in the country**

pauperis see IN FORMA PAUPERIS

pawn 1 noun transfer of a piece of property to someone as security for a loan; **to put something in pawn** = to leave a valuable object with someone in exchange for a loan which has to be repaid if you want to take back the object; **to take something out of pawn** = to repay the loan and so get back the object; **pawn ticket** = receipt given by the pawnbroker for the object left in pawn (NOTE: no plural) **2** verb **to pawn a watch** = to leave a watch with a pawnbroker who gives a loan against it

◊ **pawnbroker** noun person who lends money against the security of valuable objects

◊ **pawnshop** noun pawnbroker's shop

pay 1 noun **(a)** salary or wage or money given to someone for regular work; **back pay** = salary which has not been paid; **basic pay** = normal salary without extra payments; **take-home pay** = pay left after tax and insurance have been deducted; **unemployment pay** = money given by the government to someone who is unemployed **(b) pay cheque** = monthly cheque which pays a salary to a worker; **pay day** = day on which wages are paid to workers (usually Friday for workers paid once a week, and during the last week of the month for workers who are paid once a month); **pay negotiations** *or* **pay talks** = discussions between management and workers about pay increases **2** *verb* **(a)** to give money to buy an item or a service; **to pay in advance** = to give money before you receive the item bought or before the service has been completed; **to pay in instalments** = to give money for an item by giving small amounts regularly; **to pay cash** = to pay the complete sum in cash; "**pay cash**" = words written on a crossed cheque to show that it can be paid in cash if necessary; **to pay on demand** = to pay money when it is asked for, not after a period of credit; **to pay a dividend** = to give shareholders a part of the profits of a company; **to pay interest** = to give money as interest on money borrowed or invested; **building societies pay interest of 10%**; **pay as you earn** *or* *US* **pay-as-you-go** = tax system, where income tax is deducted from the salary before it is paid to the worker **(b)** to give a worker money for work done; **the workers have not been paid for three weeks; we pay good wages for skilled workers; how much do they pay you per hour?**; **to be paid by the hour** = to get money for each hour worked; **to be paid at piece-work rates** = to get money calculated on the number of pieces of work finished NOTE: **paying - paid - has paid**

◇ **payable** *adjective* which is due to be paid; **payable in advance** = which has to be paid before the goods are delivered; **payable on delivery** = which has to be paid when the goods are delivered; **payable on demand** = which must be paid when payment is asked for; **payable at sixty days** = which has to be paid by sixty days after the date of invoice; **cheque made payable to bearer** = cheque which will be paid to the person who has it, not to any particular name written on it; **shares payable on application** = shares which must be paid for when you apply to buy them; **accounts payable** = money owed to creditors; **bills payable** = bills which a debtor will have to pay; **electricity charges are payable by the tenant** = the tenant (and not the landlord) must pay for the electricity

◇ **pay back** *verb* to give money back to someone; **to pay back a loan; I lent him £50**

and he promised to pay me back in a month; he has never paid me back the money he borrowed

◇ **payback** *noun* paying back money which has been borrowed; **payback clause** = clause in a contract which states the terms for repaying a loan; **payback period** = period of time over which a loan is to be repaid *or* an investment is to pay for itself

◇ **pay cheque** *or* **paycheck** *noun* salary cheque given to an employee

◇ **pay down** *verb* **to pay money down** = to make a deposit; **he paid £50 down and the rest in monthly instalments**

◇ **PAYE** = PAY AS YOU EARN

◇ **payee** *noun* person who receives money from someone *or* person whose name is on a cheque *or* bill of exchange

◇ **payer** *noun* person who gives money to someone; **slow payer** = person *or* company which does not pay debts on time

◇ **pay in** *or* **into** *verb* (*of a defendant*) **to pay in** *or* **to pay money into court** = to deposit money with the court at the beginning of a case, so that if the case is lost you cannot be charged with the plaintiff's costs

COMMENT: if at trial the plaintiff fails to recover more than the amount the defendant has paid in, he will have to pay the defendant's costs from the date of the payment in

◇ **payment** *noun* **(a)** transfer of money from one person to another to satisfy a debt *or* obligation; **payment in cash** *or* **cash payment; payment by cheque; payment of interest** *or* **interest payment; payment on account** = paying part of the money owed before a bill is delivered; **the solicitor asked for a payment of £100 on account; full payment** *or* **payment in full** = paying all money owed; **payment on invoice** = paying money as soon as an invoice is received; **payment in** *or* **payment into court** = depositing money into the court before the case starts, so that if the case is lost, the defendant will not have to pay the plaintiff's costs **(b)** money paid; **back payment** = paying money which is owed; **deferred payments** = money paid later than the agreed date; **down payment** = part of a total payment made in advance; **interim payment** = payment of part of a sum owed; **part payment** = paying part of a whole payment

◊ **pay off** *verb* (a) to finish paying money which is owed; **to pay off a mortgage; to pay off a loan** (b) to pay all the money owed to someone and terminate his employment; **when the company was taken over the factory was closed and all the workers were paid off**

◊ **payoff** *noun* money paid to finish paying something which is owed

◊ **pay up** *verb* to give money which is owed; **the company paid up only when we sent them a letter from our solicitor; he finally paid up six months late**

PC = PERSONAL COMPUTER, POLICE CONSTABLE, PRIVY COUNCIL, PRIVY COUNCILLOR
NOTE: the plural is **PCs**

peace *noun* (a) being quiet *or* calm; calm existence; **breach of the peace** = creating a disturbance which is likely to annoy people (b) state of not being at war; **after six years of civil war, the country is now at peace; the peace treaty was signed yesterday; both sides claimed the other side broke the peace agreement**

pecuniary *adjective* referring to money; **obtaining a pecuniary advantage by deception** = crime of deceiving someone so as to derive a financial benefit from the deception; **he gained no pecuniary advantage** = he made no profit

peer *noun* (a) member of the House of Lords; **hereditary peer** = member of the House of Lords who has inherited his title; **life peer** = member of the House of Lords who is appointed for life (b) person who is in the same group *or* rank as another; **peer group** = group of persons of the same level *or* rank

◊ **peeress** *noun* female peer

penal *adjective* referring to punishment; **penal code** = set of laws governing crime and its punishment; **penal colony** = prison camp in a distant place, where prisoners are sent for long periods; **penal institution** = place (such as a prison) where convicted criminals are kept; **penal laws** *or* **the penal system** = system of punishments relating to different crimes; **penal servitude** = former punishment by imprisonment with hard labour

◊ **penalize** *verb* to punish *or* to fine; **to penalize a supplier for late deliveries; they were penalized for bad service**

penalty *noun* punishment (such as a fine) which is imposed if something is not done *or* if a law is not obeyed; **the penalty for carrying an offensive weapon is a fine of £2,000 and three months in prison; death penalty** = sentence of a criminal to be executed; **the president has introduced the death penalty for certain crimes against the state; penalty clause** = clause which lists the penalties which will be imposed if the terms of the contract are not fulfilled; **the contract contains a penalty clause which fines the company 1% for every week the completion date is late**

> COMMENT: penalty clauses in a contract are sometimes unenforceable

pendens *see* LIS

◊ **pendente lite** *Latin phrase meaning* "during the lawsuit"; *see also* ALIMONY

pending 1 *adjective* waiting; **pending action** = action concerned with land which has not been heard; **pending suit** = while a lawsuit is being heard; **maintenance pending suit** = maintenance obtained by a spouse in matrimonial proceedings until there is a full hearing to deal with the couple's financial affairs; **patent pending** = words printed on a product to show that its inventor has applied for a grant of patent **2** *adverb* **pending advice from our lawyers** = while waiting for advice from our lawyers

penitentiary *noun* *US* large prison; **the Pennsylvania State Penitentiary**

penology *noun* study of sentences in relation to crimes
NOTE: no plural

pension 1 *noun* (a) money paid regularly to someone who no longer works; **retirement pension** *or* **old age pension** = state pension given to a man who is over 65 or and woman who is over 60; **occupational pension** = pension which is paid by the company by which a worker has been employed (b) **pension contributions** = money paid by a company or worker into a pension fund; **pension entitlement** =

amount of pension which someone has the right to receive when he retires; **pension fund** = money which provides pensions for retired members of staff; **pension plan** *or* **pension scheme** = plan worked out by an insurance company which arranges for a worker to pay part of his salary over many years and receive a regular payment when he retires; **contributory pension scheme** = scheme where the worker has to pay a proportion of his salary; **graduated pension scheme** = pension scheme where the benefit is calculated as a percentage of the salary of each person in the scheme; **non-contributory pension scheme** = scheme where the employer pays in all the money on behalf of the worker; **personal pension plan** = pension plan which applies to one worker only, usually a self-employed person, not to a group **2** *verb* **to pension someone off** = to ask someone to retire and take a pension

◇ **pensionable** *adjective* able to receive a pension; **pensionable age** = age after which someone can take a pension

◇ **pensioner** *noun* person who receives a pension; **old age pensioner** = person who receives the retirement pension

peppercorn rent *noun* very small *or* nominal rent; **to pay a peppercorn rent; to lease a property for** *or* **at a peppercorn rent**

per *preposition* **(a) as per** = according to; **as per invoice** = as stated in the invoice; **as per sample** = as shown in the sample; **as per previous order** = according to the details given in our previous order **(b)** at a rate of; **per hour** *or* **per day** *or* **per week** *or* **per year** = for each hour *or* day *or* week *or* year; **the rate is £5 per hour; he makes about £2,500 per month; we pay £10 per hour** = we pay £10 for each hour worked; **the earnings per share** = dividend received by each share; **per head** = for each person; **allow £15 per head for expenses; reliable staff cost on average £15,000 per head per annum** = out of; **the rate of imperfect items is about twenty-five per thousand; the birth rate has fallen to twelve per hundred**

◇ **per annum** *adverb* in a year *or* annually; **the rent is £2,500 per annum; what is their turnover per annum?**

◇ **per autre vie** *French phrase meaning* "for the lifetime of another person"

◇ **per capita** *adjective & adverb* **(a)** divided among beneficiaries individually;

(b) per head *or* for each person; **average income per capita** *or* **per capita income** = average income of one person; **per capita expenditure** = total money spent divided by the number of people involved

◇ **per curiam** *Latin phrase meaning* "by a court": decision correctly made by a court, which can be used as a precedent

◇ **per diem** *Latin phrase meaning* "for each day"

◇ **per incuriam** *Latin phrase meaning* "because of lack of care": decision wrongly made by a court (which does not therefore set a precedent)

◇ **per my et per tout** *French phrase meaning* "by half and by all": used to indicate the relationship between joint tenants

◇ **per procurantionem** *Latin phrase meaning* "with the authority of"

◇ **per quod** *Latin phrase meaning* "by which" *or* "whereby"

◇ **per se** *Latin phrase meaning* "on its own" *or* "alone"; **actionable per se** = which is in itself sufficient grounds for bringing an action

◇ **per stirpes** *Latin phrase meaning* "by branches": phrase used in wills where the entitlement is divided among branches of a family rather than among individuals

per cent *adjective & adverb* out of each hundred *or* for each hundred; **eighty per cent (80%) of crimes are solved**
NOTE: usually written % after figures

◇ **percentage** *noun* amount shown as a proportion of one hundred; **percentage increase** = increase calculated on the basis of a rate per hundred; **a percentage point** = one per cent; **what is the percentage of crimes committed at night? the number of crimes of violence has fallen by two percentage points over the last three years**

peremptory challenge *noun* objecting to a juror without stating any reason

perfect 1 *adjective* completely correct *or* with no mistakes; **we check each shipment to make sure it is perfect; she did a perfect typing test; perfect right** = correct and legally acceptable right **2** *verb* to make something which is completely correct; **he perfected the process for making high quality steel**

◇ **perfectly** *adverb* with no mistakes *or* correctly; **she typed the letter perfectly**

perform *verb* (a) to do well *or* badly; **the company *or* the shares performed badly** = the company's share price fell (b) to do (a duty) *or* to do what one is obliged to do by a contract

◊ **performance** *noun* (a) way in which someone *or* something acts; **the poor performance of the shares on the stock market** = the fall in the share price on the stock market; **as a measure of the company's performance** = as a way of judging if the company's results are good or bad; **performance of personnel against objectives** = how personnel have worked, measured against the objectives set; **performance review** = yearly interview between a manager and each worker to discuss how the worker has worked during the year (b) carrying out of something, such as a duty *or* the terms of a contract; **they were asked to put up a £1m performance bond** = they were asked to deposit £1m as a guarantee that they would carry out the terms of the contract; **discharge by performance** = situation where the terms of a contract have been fulfilled; **impossibility of performance** = situation where a party to a contract is unable to perform his part of the contract; **part performance** = situation where a party has carried out part of a contract, but not complied with all the terms of it; **specific performance** = court order to a party to carry out his obligations in a contract

◊ **performing right** *noun* right to allow the playing of a copyright piece of music

peril *noun* danger (especially possible accident covered by an insurance policy); **perils of the sea *or* maritime perils** = accidents which can happen at sea

period *noun* (a) length of time; **for a period of time** *or* **for a period of months** *or* **for a six-year period; to deposit money for a fixed period** (b) **accounting period** = period of time at the end of which the firm's accounts are made up

◊ **periodic** *or* **periodical** 1 *adjective* happening regularly from time to time; **periodical payments** = regular payments (such as maintenance paid to a divorced spouse); **periodic tenancy** = tenancy where the tenant rents for several short periods but not for a fixed length of time 2 *noun* **periodical** = magazine which comes out regularly

perjure *verb* **to perjure yourself** = to tell lies when you have made an oath to say what is true

◊ **perjury** *noun* notifiable offence of telling lies when you have made an oath to say what is true in court; **he was sent to prison for perjury; she appeared in court on a charge of perjury** *or* **on a perjury charge** NOTE: no plural

permanent *adjective* which will last for a very long time *or* for ever; **he has found a permanent job; she is in permanent employment; the permanent staff work a thirty-five hour week**

◊ **permanency** *noun* being permanent NOTE: no plural

◊ **permanently** *adverb* for ever; **he was permanently disabled by the accident**

permission *noun* being allowed to do something; **written permission** = document which allows someone to do something; **verbal permission** = telling someone that he is allowed to do something; **to give someone permission to do something** = to allow someone to do something

permit 1 *noun* official document which allows someone to do something; **building permit** = official document which allows someone to build on a piece of land; **entry permit** = document allowing someone to enter a country; **export permit** *or* **import permit** = official document which allows goods to be exported or imported; **work permit** = official document which allows someone who is not a citizen to work in a country 2 *verb* to allow someone to do something; **this document permits the export of twenty-five computer systems; the ticket permits three people to go into the exhibition**

perpetrate *verb* to commit (a crime)

◊ **perpetrator** *noun* person who does something (especially person who commits a crime)

per pro = PER PROCURANTIONEM; with the authority of; **the secretary signed per pro the manager** = the secretary signed on behalf of, and with the authority of, the manager

persistent offender *noun* person who has been convicted of a crime at least three times before, and is likely to commit the crime again

person *noun* **(a)** someone *or* man or woman; **insurance policy which covers a named person; the persons named in the contract** = people whose names are given in the contract; **the document should be witnessed by a third person** = someone who is not named in the document should witness it; **in person** = someone himself *or* herself; **this important package is to be delivered to the chairman in person** = the package has to be given to the chairman himself (and not to his secretary, assistant, etc.); **he came to see me in person** = he himself came to see me; **litigant in person** = person bringing a lawsuit who also speaks on his own behalf in court without the help of a lawyer **(b) legal person** *or* **artificial person** = company *or* corporation considered as a legal body

◊ **persona** *noun* **(a)** thing (such as a company) which has personality **(b) persona non grata** = foreign person who is not acceptable to a government (used especially of diplomats)

◊ **personal** *adjective* **(a)** referring to one person; **personal action** = (i) legal action brought by a person himself; (ii) common law term for an action against a person arising out of a contract *or* tort; (iii) = ACTION IN PERSONAM; **personal allowances** = part of a person's income which is not taxed; **personal assets** = moveable assets which belong to a person; **personal chattels** *or* **chattels personal** = things (furniture, clothes, cars) which belong to a person and which are not land; **personal computer** = small computer which can be used at home; **personal estate** *or* **personal property** = things which belong to someone (excluding land) which can be inherited by his heirs; **personal income** = income received by an individual person before tax is paid; **personal injury** = injury to the body suffered by the victim of an accident; **personal representative** = person who is the executor of a will *or* the administrator of the estate of a deceased person; **personal service** = act of giving legal documents to someone as part of a legal action (such as serving someone with a writ) **(b)** private; **I want to see the director on a personal matter; personal assistant** = secretary who can take on responsibility in various

ways when the boss is not there

◊ **personally** *adverb* in person; **he personally opened the envelope; she wrote to me personally**

◊ **personality** *noun* **legal personality** = legal existence *or* status of a person; **corporate personality** = legal existence of an incorporated company which can be treated as a person

◊ **personalty** *noun* personal property *or* chattels (as opposed to land)

◊ **personam** *see* ACTION

◊ **personation** *noun* crime of fraudulently pretending to be someone else

personnel *noun* staff *or* people who work in an office *or* company *or* department; **all the personnel have to sign the Official Secrets Act; personnel officer** = manager who deals with the staff and their conditions of employment

NOTE: no plural; personnel usually takes a plural verb

persuade *verb* to talk to someone and get him to do what you want; **after ten hours of discussion, they persuaded the plaintiff to accept an out-of-court settlement; we could not persuade the French company to sign the contract**

◊ **persuasive precedent** *or* **authority** *noun* precedent which a judge is not obliged to follow but is of importance in reaching a judgment, as opposed to a binding precedent

pertain *verb* **to pertain to** = to refer to *or* to relate to; **the law pertaining to public order**

perverse *adjective* strange *or* odd; **perverse verdict** = verdict by a jury which goes against what anyone would normally feel to be the right decision *or* which goes against the direction of the judge

pervert *verb* to change *or* to interfere; **to attempt to pervert the course of justice** = to try to influence the outcome of a trial by tampering with the evidence *or* bribing the jurors, etc.

COMMENT: perverting the course of justice is a notifiable offence

petition 1 *noun* **(a)** written application to a court; **bankruptcy petition** = application to a court asking for an order making someone bankrupt; **to file a petition in bankruptcy** = to apply to the court to be made bankrupt *or* to ask for someone else to be made bankrupt; **divorce petition** = application to a court to end a marriage; **winding up petition** = application to a court for an order that a company be put into liquidation **(b)** written request accompanied by a list of signatures of people supporting it; **they presented a petition with a million signatures to Parliament, asking for the law to be repealed** 2 *verb* to make an official request; **he petitioned the government for a special pension; the marriage had broken down and the wife petitioned for divorce**

◇ **petitioner** *noun* person who puts forward a petition

petty *adjective* small *or* not important; **petty cash** = small amount of money kept in an office to make small purchases; **petty crime** = small crimes which are not very serious; **petty sessions** = magistrates' court; **petty theft** = stealing small items *or* small amounts of money

◇ **petty-sessional division** *noun* area of the country covered by a magistrates' court

physical *adjective* referring to objects *or* to the body, as opposed to ideas; **the court was told of acts of physical violence committed against the police**

◇ **physically** *adverb* referring to the body *or* to the laws of nature; **the testator was physically fit, but mentally incapable of understanding the terms of the will**

pick 1 *noun* thing which is chosen; **take your pick** = choose what you want; **the pick of the group** = the best item *or* person in the group 2 *verb* **(a)** to choose; **the government has picked a leading QC to be the new chairman of the tribunal; the board picked the finance director to succeed the retiring managing director; the Association has picked Paris for its next meeting (b)** to **pick someone's pocket** = to steal something from someone's pocket; **to pick a**

lock = to open a lock using a piece of wire, etc.

◇ **pickpocket** *noun* person who steals things from people's pockets

◇ **picker** *noun* *slang* one of a group of pickpockets, who actually picks the victim's pocket *compare* RUNNER

◇ **pick up** *verb* **(a)** to get better *or* to improve; **business or trade is picking up (b)** *informal* to arrest; **he was picked up by the police at the airport**

picket 1 *noun* striking worker who stands at the gate of a factory to try to persuade other workers not to go to work; **picket line** = line of pickets at the gate of a factory 2 *verb* **to picket a factory** = to put pickets at the gate of a factory to try to prevent other workers from going to work

◇ **picketing** *noun* action of standing at the gates of a factory to prevent workers going to work; **lawful or peaceful picketing** = picketing which is allowed by law; **mass picketing** = picketing by large numbers of pickets who try to frighten workers who want to work; **secondary picketing** = picketing of another factory *or* place of work, not directly connected with the strike, to prevent it supplying the striking factory *or* receiving supplies from it
NOTE: no plural

pilfer *verb* to steal small objects *or* small amounts of money

◇ **pilferage** *or* **pilfering** *noun* stealing small amounts of money *or* small items
NOTE: no plural

◇ **pilferer** *noun* person who steals small objects *or* small amounts of money

pimp *noun* man who organizes prostitutes and lives off their earnings

pinch *verb* *informal* **(a)** to steal **(b)** to arrest

pirate 1 *noun* **(a)** person who attacks a ship at sea to steal cargo **(b)** person who copies a patented invention *or* a copyright work and sells it; **a pirate copy of a book; pirate radio station** = radio station which broadcasts without a licence from outside a country's territorial waters 2 *verb* to copy a copyright work; **a pirated book** *or* a **pirated design; the drawings for the new dress collection were pirated in the Far East**

◇ **piracy** *noun* **(a)** robbery at sea, by attacking ships **(b)** copying of patented inventions *or* copyright works; **laws to ban book piracy**
NOTE: no plural

place 1 *noun* **(a)** where something is *or* where something happens; **to take place =** to happen; **the meeting will take place in our offices; meeting place =** room *or* area where people can meet; **place of performance =** place where a contract is to be performed; **place of work =** office *or* factory, etc., where people work; **public place =** place (such as a road *or* park) where the public in general have a right to be **(b)** job; **he was offered a place with an insurance company; she turned down three places before accepting the one we offered (c)** position (in a text); **she marked her place in the text with a red pen; I have lost my place and cannot remember where I have reached in my filing** 2 *verb* to put; **to place money in an account =** to deposit money; **to place a block of shares =** to find a buyer for a block of shares; **to place a contract with a company =** to decide that a certain company shall have the contract to do work; **to place an order =** to order something; **to place something on file =** to file something **(b) to place staff =** to find jobs for staff
◇ **placement** *noun* finding work for someone
◇ **placing** *noun* **the placing of a line of shares =** finding a buyer for a large number of shares in a new company *or* a company which is going public

plagiarism *noun* copying the text of a work created by someone else and passing it off as your own
NOTE: no plural
◇ **plagiarize** *verb* to copy the text of a work created by someone else and pass it off as your own

plainclothes *adjective* (person) who is working in ordinary clothes, not in uniform; **a group of plainclothes police went into the house; a plainclothes detective travelled on the train**

plain cover *noun* **to send something under plain cover =** to send something in an ordinary envelope with no company name printed on it

plaint *noun* claim brought by one party (the plaintiff) against another party (the defendant); **plaint note =** note issued by a County Court at the beginning of a County Court action
◇ **plaintiff** *noun* person who starts an action against someone in the civil courts; *compare* DEFENDANT

plan 1 *noun* **(a)** organized way of doing something; **contingency plan =** plan which will be put into action if something happens which is expected to happen; **the government's economic plans =** the government's proposals for running the country's economy; **a Five-Year Plan =** proposals for running a country's economy over a five-year period **(b)** drawing which shows how something is arranged *or* how something will be built; **floor plan =** drawing of a floor in a building, showing where different departments are; **street plan** *or* **town plan =** map of a town showing streets and buildings 2 *verb* to organize carefully how something should be done; **the bank robbery was carefully planned in advance; he plans to disguise himself as a policeman; to plan for an increase in bank interest charges =** to change a way of doing things because you think there will be an increase in bank interest charges; **to plan investments =** to propose how investments should be made
◇ **planned** *adjective* **planned economy =** system where the government plans all business activity
◇ **planner** *noun* **(a)** person who plans; **the government's economic planners =** people who plan the future economy of the country for the government; **town planner =** person who supervises the design of a new town *or* the way the streets and buildings in a new town are laid out **(b) desk planner** *or* **wall planner =** book or chart which shows days *or* weeks *or* months so that the work of an office can be shown by coloured lines
◇ **planning** *noun* **(a)** organizing how something should be done, especially how a company should be run to make increased profits; **economic planning =** planning the future financial state of the country for the government **(b)** organizing how land and buildings are to be used; **planning authority =** local body which gives permission for changes to be made to existing buildings or for new use

of land; **planning department** = section of a local government office which deals with requests for planning permission; **planning inquiry** = hearing before a government inspector relating to the decision of a local authority in planning matters; **planning permission** = official document allowing a person or company to plan new buildings on empty land *or* to alter existing buildings; **outline planning permission** = general permission to build a property on a piece of land, but not the final approval because there are no details given; **to be refused planning permission; we are waiting for planning permission before we can start building; the land is to be sold with outline planning permission for four houses**

plant 1 *noun* machinery *or* goods and chattels needed for a business **2** *verb* **to plant evidence** = to put items at the scene of a crime after the crime has been discovered, so that a person can be incriminated and arrested

plc *or* **PLC** *or* **Plc** = PUBLIC LIMITED COMPANY

plea *noun* (i) in civil law, answer made by a defendant to the case presented by the plaintiff; (ii) in criminal law, statement made by a person accused in court in answer to the charge; **to enter a plea of not guilty** = to answer the charge by stating that you are not guilty; **plea in mitigation** = things said in court on behalf of a guilty party to persuade the court to impose a lenient sentence

◊ **plea bargaining** *noun* arrangement where the accused pleads guilty to some charges and the prosecution drop other charges *or* ask for a lighter sentence

plead *verb* **(a)** (i) to make *or* answer an allegation in legal proceedings; (ii) to answer a charge in a criminal court; **fit *or* unfit to plead** = mentally capable *or* not capable of being tried; **to plead guilty *or* not guilty** = to say at the beginning of a trial that you did *or* did not commit the crime of which you are accused **(b)** to speak on behalf of a client in court

◊ **pleading** *noun* **(a) pleadings** = documents setting out the claim of the plaintiff or the defence of the defendant *or* giving the arguments which the two sides will use in proceedings; **the damage is itemized in the pleading; the judge found that the** plaintiff's pleadings disclosed no cause of action; pleadings must be submitted to the court when the action is set down for trial **(b)** action of speaking in court on someone's behalf
NOTE: no plural for (b)

pleasure *see* HER MAJESTY'S PLEASURE

pledge 1 *noun* **(a)** transfer of objects *or* documents to someone as security for a loan **(b)** object given by someone (especially to a pawnbroker) as security for a loan; **to redeem a pledge** = to pay back a loan and interest and so get back the security; **unredeemed pledge** = pledge which the borrower has not claimed back by paying back his loan **2** *verb* **to pledge share certificates** = to deposit share certificates with the lender as security for money borrowed

◊ **pledgee** *noun* person who receives objects or documents as security for money lent

◊ **pledger** *noun* person who gives objects or documents as security for money borrowed

plenipotentiary *noun* official person acting on behalf of a government in international affairs

plunder 1 *noun* valuable things taken when a place is attacked (NOTE: no plural) **2** *verb* to attack and rob (a place), taking valuable things away

p.m. *or* **post meridiem** *Latin phrase meaning* "after 12 o'clock midday"; **the train leaves at 6.50 p.m.; if you phone New York after 6 p.m. the calls are at a cheaper rate**

PM = POST MORTEM, PRIME MINISTER

PO = POST OFFICE

poaching *noun* (i) crime of killing game which belongs to another person *or* trespassing on someone's land to kill game; (ii) enticing workers to work for another company *or* enticing workers to leave one trade union and join another

point *noun* question relating to a matter; **point of fact** = question which has to be decided regarding the facts of a case; **in point of fact** = really *or* actually; **point of law** = question relating to the law as applied to a case; **counsel raised a point of law; the case illustrates an interesting point of legal principle; point of order =** question regarding the way in which a meeting is conducted; **he raised an interesting point of order; on a point of order, Mr Smith asked the chairman to give a ruling on whether the committee could approve its own accounts**

poison 1 *noun* substance which can kill if eaten or drunk; **she killed the old lady by putting poison in her tea 2** *verb* to kill someone using poison; **he was not shot, he was poisoned**

police 1 *noun* group of people who keep law and order in a country *or* town; **the police have cordoned off the town centre; the government is relying on the police to keep law and order during the elections; the bank robbers were picked up by the police at the railway station; military police =** soldiers who act as policemen to keep order among other soldiers; **secret police =** policemen who work in secret, especially dealing with people working against the state; **police cordon =** barriers and policemen put round an area to prevent anyone moving in or out of the area; **police court =** magistrates' court (NOTE: no plural. **Police** is usually followed by a plural verb) **2** *verb* **(a)** to keep law and order in a place; **the meeting was policed by plainclothes men; the council is debating the Chief Constable's policing policy (b)** to make sure that regulations *or* guidelines are carried out

COMMENT: under English law, a policeman is primarily an ordinary citizen who has certain powers at common law and by statute
The police are organized by area, each area functioning independently with its own police force. London, and the area round London, is policed by the Metropolitan Police Force under the direct supervision of the Home Secretary
Outside London, each police force is answerable to a local police authority, although day-to-day control of operations is vested entirely in the Chief Constable

◇ **police authority** *noun* local committee which supervises a local police force

◇ **Police Commissioner** *noun* highest rank in certain police forces; **Metropolitan Police Commissioner =** person in charge of the Metropolitan Police in London

◇ **Police Complaints Board** *noun* group which investigates complaints made by members of the public against the police

◇ **police constable** *noun* ordinary member of the police; **Police Constables Smith and Jones are on patrol; Woman Police Constable MacIntosh was at the scene of the accident**
NOTE: usually abbreviated to **PC** and **WPC**

◇ **police force** *noun* group of policemen organized in a certain area; **the members of several local police forces have collaborated in the murder hunt; the London police force is looking for more recruits**
see also DETECTIVE, METROPOLITAN

COMMENT: the ranks in a British police force are: **Police Constable, Police Sergeant, Inspector, Chief Inspector, Superintendent, Chief Superintendent, Assistant Chief Constable, Deputy Chief Constable and Chief Constable**

◇ **police headquarters** *noun* main offices of a police force

◇ **police inspector** *noun* rank in the police force above a sergeant

◇ **policeman** *noun* man who is a member of the police
NOTE: the plural is **policemen**

◇ **police officer** *noun* member of the police

◇ **police precinct** *noun* *US* section of a town with its own police station

◇ **police sergeant** *noun* rank in the police force above constable and below inspector

◇ **police station** *noun* local office of a police force

◇ **policewoman** *noun* woman member of a police force
NOTE: the plural is **policewomen**

◇ **policing** *noun* keeping law and order in a place, using the police force; **community policing =** way of policing a section of a town, where the members of the local community and the local police force act together to prevent crime and disorder,

with policemen on foot patrol, rather than in patrol cars
NOTE: no plural

policy *noun* **(a)** decisions on the general way of doing something; **government policy on wages** *or* **government wages policy; the government's prices policy; the country's economic policy; our policy is to submit all contracts to the legal department; the government made a policy statement** *or* **made a statement of policy** = the government declared in public what its plans were; **budgetary policy** = policy of expected income and expenditure; *see also* PUBLIC POLICY **(b) insurance policy** = document which shows the conditions of an insurance contract; **accident policy** = insurance against accidents; **comprehensive** *or* **all-risks policy** = insurance policy which covers risks of any kind, with no exclusions; **contingent policy** = policy which pays out only if something happens (as if the person named in the policy dies before the person due to benefit); **endowment policy** = policy where a sum of money is paid to the insured person on a certain date, or to his estate if he dies earlier; **open policy** = marine insurance policy where the value of what is insured is not stated; **policy holder** = person who is insured by an insurance company

political *adjective* referring to a certain idea of how a country should be run; **political crime** = crime (such as assassination) committed for a political reason; **political fund** = part of the funds of a trade union which is allocated to subsidize a political party; **political levy** = part of the subscription of a member of a trade union which the union then pays to support a political party; **political party** = group of people who believe a country should be run in a certain way; **political prisoner** = person kept in prison because he is an opponent of the political party in power

poll 1 *noun* **(a)** voting to choose something; **to go to the polls** = to vote to choose a Member of Parliament *or* a local councillor **(b) opinion poll** = asking a sample group of people what they feel about something, so as to guess the opinion of the whole population **(c) deed poll** = legal agreement which refers only to one

party; **she changed her name by deed poll** = she executed a legal document to change her name **2** *verb* **(a)** to receive a certain number of votes in an election; **he polled only 123 votes in the general election (b)** to **poll a sample of the population** = to ask a sample group of people what they feel about something; **to poll the members of the club on an issue** = to ask the members for their opinion on an issue

◊ **pollster** *noun* expert in understanding what polls mean

◊ **poll tax** *noun* tax levied equally on each member of the population

polygamy *noun* state of having more than one wife
NOTE: no plural

◊ **polygamous** *adjective* referring to polygamy; **a polygamous society** = a society where men are allowed to be married to more than one wife at the same time

popular *adjective* liked by many people; **this is our most popular model; the South Coast is the most popular area for holidays; popular prices** = prices which are low and therefore liked; **popular vote** = vote of the people; **the president is elected by popular vote** = the president is elected by a majority of all the voters in the country (as opposed to being elected by parliament)

pornography *noun* obscene publications *or* films
NOTE: no plural

porridge *noun slang* imprisonment; **to do porridge** = to serve a term of imprisonment

portfolio *noun* **(a)** all the shares owned by someone; **his portfolio contains shares in the major oil companies (b)** office of a minister in the government; **Minister without Portfolio** = minister who does not have responsibility for any particular department

portion *noun* money *or* property given to a young person to provide money for him *or* her as income

position *noun* **(a)** situation *or* state of affairs; **bargaining position** = statement of position by one group during negotiations; **to cover a position** = to have enough money to pay for a forward purchase **(b)**

job *or* paid work in a company; **to apply for a position as manager; we have several positions vacant; all the vacant positions have been filled; she retired from her position in the accounts department; position of trust** = job where the employee is trusted with money *or* confidential documents, etc.

positive *adjective* meaning "yes"; **the board gave a positive reply; the breath test was positive** = the breath test showed that he had too much alcohol in his blood; **positive vetting** = discovery after examination that a person working with classified information may not be reliable

possess *verb* to own *or* to be in occupation of *or* to be in control of; **the company possesses property in the centre of the town; he lost all he possessed when his company was put into liquidation**

◇ **possession** *noun* **(a)** control over property; **actual possession** = occupying and controlling land and buildings; **chose in possession** = physical thing which can be owned; **possession in law** = ownership of land *or* buildings without actually occupying them; **adverse possession** = occupation of property (such as by a squatter) contrary to the rights of the real owner; **vacant possession** = being able to occupy a property immediately after buying it because it is empty; **the property is to be sold with vacant possession (b)** physically holding something (which does not necessarily belong to you); **the documents are in his possession** = he is holding the documents; **how did it come into his possession *or* how did he get possession of it?** = how did he acquire it?; **possession of drugs** = offence of having drugs **(c) possessions** = property *or* things owned; **they lost all their possessions in the fire** NOTE: no plural for (a) and (b)

◇ **possessive action** *noun* action to regain possession of land *or* buildings

◇ **possessory** *adjective* referring to possession of property; **possessory title** = title to land acquired by occupying it continuously, usually for twelve years

post 1 *noun* **(a)** system of sending letters and parcels from one place to another; **to send an invoice by post; he put the letter in the post; the cheque was lost in the post; to send a reply by return of post** = to reply to a letter immediately; **letter post *or* parcel**

post = service for sending letters or parcels; **post room** = room in an office where the post is sorted and sent to each department or collected from each department for sending **(b)** letters sent or received; **has the post arrived yet? my secretary opens the post as soon as it arrives; the receipt was in this morning's post; the letter did not arrive by first post this morning (c)** job *or* paid work in a firm *or* company; **to apply for a post as legal executive; we have three posts vacant; all our posts have been filled; we advertised three posts in "The Times"** 2 *verb* **(a)** to send something by post; **to post a letter *or* to post a parcel (b) to post an entry** = to transfer an entry to an account **(c) to post up a notice** = to put a notice on a wall *or* on a noticeboard; **to post an increase** = to let people know that an increase has taken place

post- *prefix* later

postage *noun* payment for sending a letter or parcel by post

postal *adjective* referring to the post; **postal packet** = small parcel sent by post; **postal service** = (i) sending letters by post; (ii) service of legal documents by post

post code *noun* letters and numbers used to indicate a town or street in an address on an envelope
NOTE: US English is **zip code**

postdate *verb* to put a later date on a document; **he sent us a postdated cheque; his cheque was postdated to June**

poste restante *noun* system where letters can be addressed to someone at a post office, where they can be collected; **send any messages to "Poste Restante, Athens"**

posteriori *see* A POSTERIORI

post free *adverb* without having to pay any postage; **the leaflet is obtainable post free from the Law Society**

posthumous *adjective* (child) born after the death of its father

post mortem *noun* examination of the body of a dead person to see how he died; **the post mortem was carried out *or* was conducted by the police pathologist**

post obit bond *noun* agreement where a borrower will repay a loan when he receives money as a legacy from someone

post office *noun* (a) building where the postal services are based; shop where you can buy stamps, send parcels, etc.; **sub-post office** = small post office, usually part of a general store (b) the Post Office = national organization which deals with sending letters and parcels; **Post Office officials** *or* **officials of the Post Office; Post Office box number** = reference number given for delivering mail to a post office, so as not to give the actual address of the person who will receive it

postpone *verb* to arrange for something to take place later than planned; **he postponed the meeting until tomorrow; they asked if they could postpone payment until the cash situation was better**

◊ **postponement** *noun* arranging for something to take place later than planned; **I had to change my appointments because of the postponement of the board meeting**

post scriptum *see* P.S.

power *noun* (a) strength *or* ability *or* capacity; **bargaining power** = strength of one person or group when discussing prices *or* wages *or* contracts; **borrowing power** = amount of money which a company can borrow; **earning power** = amount of money someone should be able to earn (b) authority *or* legal right; **the powers of a local authority in relation to children in care; the powers and duties conferred on the tribunal by the statutory code; the president was granted wide powers under the constitution; executive power** = right to act as director *or* to put decisions into action; **power of attorney** = official power which gives someone the right to act on someone's behalf in legal matters; **the full power of the law** = the full force of the law when applied; **we will apply the full power of the law to regain possession of our property**

p.p. *verb* to p.p. a receipt *or* a letter = to sign a receipt *or* a letter on behalf of someone; **the secretary p.p.'d the letter while the manager was at lunch;** *see also* PER PROCURATIONEM

PR = PROPORTIONAL REPRESENTATION, PUBLIC RELATIONS

practice *noun* (a) way of doing things; **his practice was to arrive at work at 7.30 and start counting the cash; business practices** *or* **industrial practices** *or* **trade practices** = ways of managing or working in business, industry or trade; **restrictive practices** = ways of working which exclude free competition in relation to the supply of goods or labour in order to maintain prices or wages; **sharp practice** = way of doing business which is not honest, but is not illegal; **code of practice** = rules drawn up by an association which the members must follow when doing business; **practice direction** = notes made by judges as to how certain procedures *or* formalities should be carried out (b) **in practice** = when actually done; **the scheme for dealing with young offenders seems very interesting, but what will it cost in practice?** (c) office and clients (of a professional person); **he has set up in practice as a solicitor** *or* **a patent agent; he is a partner in a country solicitor's practice** (d) carrying on of a profession; **he has been in practice for twenty years**

◊ **Practice Master** *noun* Master on duty in the High Court, who will hear solicitors without appointment and give directions in relation to the general conduct of proceedings

practise *verb* to work (in a profession); **he is a practising solicitor; practising certificate** = certificate from the Law Society allowing someone to work as a solicitor

praecipe *noun* written request addressed to a court, asking that court to prepare and issue a document (such as a writ of execution *or* a subpoena)

pray *verb* to ask; **to pray in aid** = to rely on something in pleading a case; **I pray in aid the Statute of Frauds**

◊ **prayer** *noun* words at the end of a petition *or* pleading, which summarize what the litigant is asking the court to do

pre- *prefix* before; **pre-contract discussion; a pre-stocktaking sale; there will be a pre-AGM board meeting**

preamble *noun* first words in an official document (such as a Bill before Parliament *or* contract) introducing the document and setting out the main points in it

precatory *adjective* which requests; **precatory words** = words (such as in a will) which ask for something to be done

precautionary *adjective* as a **precautionary measure** = in case something takes place

◊ **precautions** *plural noun* care taken to avoid something unpleasant; **to take precautions to prevent thefts in the office; the company did not take proper fire precautions; safety precautions** = actions to try to make sure that something is safe

precede *verb* to go before *or* to come earlier; **see the preceding paragraph of my letter; the preceding clause gives details of the agency arrangements**

precedent 1 *noun* something (such as a judgment) which has happened earlier than the present, and which can be a guide as to what should be done in the present case; **to set a precedent** = to make a decision in court which will show other courts how to act in future; **to follow a precedent** = to decide in the same way as an earlier decision in the same type of case; **the judge's decision sets a precedent for future cases of contempt of court; the tribunal's ruling has established a precedent; the court followed the precedent set in 1926; binding precedent** = decision of a higher court which has to be followed by a judge in a lower court; **judicial precedent** = precedent set by a court decision which can be reversed only by a higher court; **persuasive precedent** = precedent which a judge does not have to follow but which is of importance in reaching a decision **2** *adjective* **condition precedent** = condition which says that a right will not be granted until something is done

> COMMENT: although English law is increasingly governed by statute, the doctrine of precedent still plays a major role. The decisions of higher courts bind lower courts, except in the case of the Court of Appeal, where the court has power to change a previous decision reached per incuriam. Cases can be distinguished by the courts where

> the facts seem to be sufficiently different

precept *noun* order asking for rates to be paid

precinct *noun* **(a) pedestrian precinct** *or* **shopping precinct** = part of a town which is closed to traffic so that people can walk about and shop **(b)** *US* administrative district in a town; **police precinct**

precise *adjective* clear and with correct details; **the will gives precise instructions about the settlement of the estate; the pathologist was unable to give a precise time for the murder**

preclude *verb* to forbid *or* to prevent; **the High Court is precluded by statute from reviewing such a decision; this agreement does not preclude a further agreement between the parties in the future**

predecease *verb* to die before someone; **he predeceased his father; his estate is left to his daughter, but should she predecease him, it will be held in trust for her children**

◊ **predecessor** *noun* person who had a job *or* position before someone else; **he took over from his predecessor last May; she acquired her predecessor's list of clients**

pre-empt *verb* to act before someone else can act

◊ **pre-emption** *noun* right of first refusal to purchase something before it is sold to someone else; **pre-emption clause** = clause in a private company's articles of association which requires any shares offered for sale to be offered first to existing shareholders

prefer *verb* **(a)** to like something better than another thing; **he prefers to deal directly with his clients himself; most people prefer to avoid taking their neighbours to court (b)** to pay one creditor before any others **(c)** to bring something before a court; **to prefer charges** = to charge someone with an offence
NOTE: **preferring-preferred**

◊ **preference** *noun* (i) thing which is preferred; (ii) the payment of one creditor before other creditors; **fraudulent preference** = payment made by an insolvent company to a particular creditor before other creditors; **preference shares** =

shares (often with no voting rights) which receive their dividend before all other shares and which are repaid first (at face value) if the company is liquidated; **preference shareholders** = owners of preference shares; **cumulative preference shares** = preference shares where the dividend will be paid at a later date even if the company cannot pay a dividend in the current year

◊ **preferential** *adjective* showing that something is preferred more than another; **preferential creditor** = creditor who must be paid first if a company is in liquidation; **preferential debt** = debt which is paid before all others; **preferential duty** *or* **preferential tariff** = special low rate of tax; **preferential payment** = payment made to one creditor before others; **preferential terms** *or* **preferential treatment** = terms or way of dealing which is better than usual

◊ **preferment** *noun* **preferment of charges** = act of charging someone with a criminal offence

◊ **preferred** *adjective* **preferred creditor** = creditor who must be paid first if a company is in liquidation; **preferred shares** *or* *US* **preferred stock** = shares which receive their dividend before all other shares, and which are repaid first (at face value) if the company is in liquidation; *US* **cumulative preferred stock** = preference shares where the dividend will be paid at a later date even if the company cannot pay a dividend in the current year

pregnancy *noun* period when a woman is expecting a baby; **to terminate a pregnancy** = to give a woman an abortion

◊ **pregnant** *adjective* (woman) with an unborn child in her body

prejudge *verb* to judge an issue before having heard the evidence; **do not prejudge the issue - hear what defence counsel has to say**

prejudice 1 *noun* **(a)** bias *or* unjust feelings against someone; **racial prejudice** = feelings against someone because of his race **(b)** harm done to someone; **forgery is the copying of a real document, so that it is accepted as genuine to someone's prejudice; without prejudice** = phrase spoken *or* written in letters when attempting to negotiate a settlement, meaning that the negotiations cannot be referred to in court

or relied upon by the other party if the discussions fail; **to act to the prejudice of a claim** = to do something which may harm a claim **2** *verb* to harm; **to prejudice someone's claim**

◊ **prejudiced** *adjective* biased *or* with unjust feelings against someone; **the judge seemed to be prejudiced against foreigners**

preliminary *adjective* early *or* happening before anything else; **preliminary discussion** *or* **a preliminary meeting** = discussion or meeting which takes place before the main discussion or meeting starts; **preliminary hearing** = court proceedings where the witnesses and the defendant are examined to see if there are sufficient grounds for the case to proceed *or* court proceedings to try a specific issue rather than the whole case; **preliminary inquiries** = investigation by the solicitor for the purchaser addressed to the vendor's solicitor concerning the vendor's title to the property for which the purchaser has made an offer; **preliminary investigation** = first examination of the details of a case by a magistrate who then has to decide if the case should be committed to a higher court for trial; **preliminary ruling** = provisional decision of the European Court

premeditated *adjective* which has been thought about carefully *or* which has been planned; **the crime was premeditated; a premeditated murder**

◊ **premeditation** *noun* thinking about and planning a crime (such as murder)
NOTE: no plural

premises *plural noun* **(a)** building and the land it stands on; **business premises** *or* **commercial premises** = building used for commercial use; **office premises** *or* **shop premises** = building which houses an office or shop; **lock-up premises** = shop which is locked up at night when the owner goes home; **licensed premises** = shop *or* restaurant *or* public house which is licensed to sell alcohol; **on the premises** = in the building; **there is a doctor on the premises at all times (b)** things that have been referred to previously
NOTE: used at the end of a pleading: **in the premises the defendant denies that he is indebted to the plaintiff as alleged or at all**

premium *noun* **(a)** sum of money paid by one person to another, especially one paid regularly; **insurance premium** = annual payment made by the insured person or a company to an insurance company; **additional premium** = extra payment made to cover extra items in an existing insurance; **the annual premium is £150; you pay either an annual premium of £360 or twelve monthly premiums of £32 (b)** amount to be paid to a landlord or a tenant for the right to take over a lease; **flat to let with a premium of £10,000; annual rent: £8,500 - premium: £25,000 (c)** extra charge: **exchange premium** = extra cost above the normal rate for buying foreign currency; **the dollar is at a premium; shares sold at a premium** = (i) shares whose price is higher than their face value; (ii) new shares whose market price is higher than their issue price **(d) premium bonds** = government bonds, part of the national savings scheme, which pay no interest, but give the owner the chance to win a weekly or monthly prize and which can be redeemed at face value

prerogative *noun* special right which someone has; **royal prerogative** = right of the king *or* queen to do something; **prerogative order *or* writ** = writ which requests a body to do its duty *or* not to so some act *or* to conduct an inquiry into its own actions

prescribe *verb* to claim rights which have been enjoyed for a long time

◇ **prescription** *noun* acquiring a right *or* exercising a right over a period of time

presence *noun* being present *or* being at a place when something happens; **the will was signed in the presence of two witnesses**

present 1 *noun* **(a)** thing which is given; **these calculators make good presents; the office gave her a present when she got married (b) these presents** = this document itself; **know all men by these presents** = be informed by this document **2** *adjective* **(a)** happening now; **the shares are too expensive at their present price; what is the present address of the company? (b)** being there when something happens; **two police officers were present when the bailiffs seized the property; only six directors were present at the board meeting 3** *verb* **(a)** to give someone something; **he was presented with a watch on completing twenty-five years' service with the company (b)** to bring *or* send and show a document;

to present a bill for acceptance = to send a bill for payment by the person who has accepted it; **to present a bill for payment** = to send a bill to be paid

◇ **presentation** *noun* **(a)** showing a document; **presentation of a bill of exchange; cheque payable on presentation** = cheque which will be paid when it is presented; **free admission on presentation of this card** = you do not pay to go in if you show this card **(b)** demonstration *or* exhibition of a proposed plan; **the marketing company made a presentation of the services they could offer; we have asked two PR firms to make presentations of proposed advertising campaigns**

◇ **presentment** *noun* showing a document; **presentment of a bill of exchange**

◇ **present value** *noun* the value something has now; **in 1974 the pound was worth five times its present value**

preservation order *noun* court order which prevents a building from being knocked down *or* a tree from being cut down

preside *verb* to be chairman, **to preside over a meeting; the meeting was held in the committee room, Mr Smith presiding**

◇ **president** *noun* **(a)** head of a company *or* a club *or* a court; **he was elected president of the sports club; A.B.Smith has been appointed president of the company; President of the Family Division** = judge who is responsible for the work of the Family Division of the High Court

COMMENT: in Britain "president" is a title sometimes given to a non-executive former chairman of a company; in the USA, the president is the main executive director of a company

(b) head of a republic; **the President of the United States**
NOTE: as a title of a head of state, President can be used with a surname: **President Ford, President Wilson**

COMMENT: the President of the United States is both head of state and head of government. He is elected by an electoral college, and holds the executive power under the United States constitution. The legislative power lies with Congress, and the President cannot force Congress to enact legislation, although he can veto legislation which has been passed by Congress

press 1 *noun* newspapers and magazines; **the local press** = newspapers which are sold in a small area of the country; **the national press** = newspapers which sell in all parts of the country; **press conference** = meeting where reporters from newspapers are invited to hear news of a new product *or* of a court case *or* of a takeover bid, etc.; **Press Council** = body concerned with regulation of the press; **press coverage** = reports about something in the press; **press release** = sheet giving news about something which is sent to newspapers and TV and radio stations so that they can use the information; **freedom of the press** = being able to write and publish in a newspaper what you wish without being afraid of prosecution, provided that you do not break the law 2 *verb* **to press charges against someone** = to say formally that someone has committed a crime; **he was very angry when his neighbour's son set fire to his car, but decided not to press charges**

◇ **pressing** *adjective* urgent; **pressing engagements** = meetings which have to be attended; **pressing bills** = bills which have to be paid

presume *verb* to suppose something is correct; **the court presumes the maintenance payments are being paid on time; the company is presumed to be still solvent; we presume the shipment has been stolen; two sailors are missing, presumed drowned**

COMMENT: in English law, the accused is presumed to be innocent until he is proved to be guilty, and presumed to be sane until he is proved to be insane

◇ **presumption** *noun* thing which is assumed to be correct, because it is assumed from other facts; **presumption of death** = situation where a person has not been seen for seven years, and is legally presumed to be dead; **presumption of innocence** = assuming that someone is innocent, until he has been proved guilty

◇ **presumptive** *adjective* **presumptive evidence** = circumstantial evidence; **heir presumptive** = heir who will inherit if

someone dies at this moment, but whose inheritance may be altered in the future

pretence *noun* **false pretence(s)** = doing *or* saying something to cheat someone; **he was sent to prison for obtaining money by false pretences**

pretend *verb* to act like someone else in order to trick *or* to act as if something is true when it really is not; **he got in by pretending to be a telephone engineer; she pretended she had 'flu and asked to have the day off**

pretrial review *noun* meeting of the parties before a civil action, to examine what is likely to arise during the action, so that ways can be found of making it shorter and so reduce costs

prevail *verb* **to prevail upon someone to do something** = to persuade someone to do something; **counsel prevailed upon the judge to grant an adjournment**

prevaricate *verb* to be evasive *or* not to give a straight answer to a question

prevent *verb* to stop something happening; **we must try to prevent the takeover bid; the police prevented anyone from leaving the building; we have changed the locks on the doors to prevent the former managing director from getting into the building**

◇ **prevention** *noun* stopping something taking place; **prevention of corruption** = stopping corruption taking place; **the prevention of terrorism** = stopping terrorist acts taking place

◇ **preventive** *adjective* which tries to stop something happening; **to take preventive measures against theft** = to try to stop things from being stolen; **preventive detention** = formerly, imprisonment of someone who frequently committed a certain type of crime, so as to prevent him from doing it again

COMMENT: now replaced by **extended sentence**

previous *adjective* which has happened earlier; **he could not accept the invitation because he had a previous engagement** = because he had earlier accepted another invitation to go somewhere; **to ask for six previous convictions to be taken into**

consideration = to ask the court to note that the accused has been convicted earlier of similar crimes; **a person of previous good character** = person with no criminal record

◊ **previously** *adverb* happening earlier

price 1 *noun* money which has to be paid to buy something; **agreed price** = price which has been accepted by both the buyer and seller; **all-in price** = price which covers all items in a purchase (goods, insurance, delivery, etc.); **asking price** = price which the seller is hoping to be paid for the item when it is sold; **fair price** = good price for both buyer and seller; **firm price** = price which will not change; **net price** = price which cannot be reduced by a discount; **retail price** = price at which the retailer sells to the final customer; **spot price** = price for immediate delivery of a commodity; **price controls** = legal measures to stop prices rising too fast; **price fixing** = illegal agreement between companies to charge the same price for competing products **(b)** (*on the Stock Exchange*) **asking price** = price which sellers are asking for shares; **closing price** = price at the end of a day's trading; **opening price** = price at the start of a day's trading; **price/earnings ratio** = ratio between the market price of a share and the current earnings it produces **2** *verb* to give a price to a product; **car priced at £5,000**

◊ **pricing** *noun* giving a price to a product; **pricing policy** = a company's policy in setting prices for its products; **common pricing** = illegal fixing of prices by several businesses so that they all charge the same price

prima facie *Latin phrase meaning* "on the face if it *or* as things seem at first"; **there is a prima facie case to answer** = one side in a case has shown that there is a case to answer, and so the action should be proceeded with

primary *adjective* in the first place; **primary evidence** = best evidence (such as original documents, evidence from eye witnesses)

◊ **primarily** *adverb* in the first place; **he is primarily liable for his debts**; *see also* SECONDARY, SECONDARILY

prime *adjective* **(a)** most important; **prime time** = most expensive advertising time for TV advertisements **(b)** basic; **prime bills** = bills of exchange which do not involve any risk; **prime cost** = cost involved in producing a product, excluding overheads; **prime rate** = best rate of interest at which a bank lends to its customers

◊ **Prime Minister** *noun* head of a government; **the Australian Prime Minister** *or* **the Prime Minister of Australia**

COMMENT: the British Prime Minister is not the head of state, but the head of government. The Prime Minister is usually the leader of the party which has the majority of the seats in the House of Commons, and forms a cabinet of executive ministers who are either MPs or members of the House of Lords

primogeniture *noun* former rule that the oldest son inherits all his father's estate
NOTE: no plural

principal 1 *noun* **(a)** person who is responsible for something (especially person who is in charge of a company *or* person who commits a crime) **(b)** person *or* company which is represented by an agent; **the agent has come to London to see his principals (c)** money invested *or* borrowed on which interest is paid; **to repay principal and interest 2** *adjective* most important; **the principal shareholders asked for a meeting; the country's principal products are paper and wood**; *compare* PRINCIPLE

principle *noun* basic point *or* general rule; **in principle** = in agreement with a general rule; **agreement in principle** = agreement with the basic conditions of a proposal; **it is against his principles** = it goes against what he believes to be the correct way to act; *compare* PRINCIPAL

printout *noun* printed copy of information produced by a computer

prior *adjective* earlier; **prior agreement** = agreement which was reached earlier; **prior charge** = charge which ranks before others; **without prior knowledge** = without knowing before

◊ **priori** *see* A PRIORI

◊ **priority** *noun* right to be first (such as the right to be paid first before other creditors); **to have priority** = to have the right to be first; **to have priority over** *or* **to take priority over something** = to be more important than something; **debenture holders have priority over ordinary shareholders; to give something top priority** = to make something the most important item; **the government has given the maintenance of law and order top priority**

prison *noun* (a) safe building where criminals can be kept locked up after they have been convicted *or* while they await trial; **the government has ordered the construction of six new prisons; the prison was built 150 years ago; prison officer** *or* **prison governor** = member of staff *or* person in charge of a prison; **open prison** = prison with minimum security where category "D" prisoners can be kept; **top security prison** = prison with very strict security where category "A" prisoners are kept (b) place where prisoners are kept as a punishment; **he was sent to prison for six years; they have spent the last six months in prison; he escaped from prison by climbing over the wall**
NOTE: no plural for (b), which is also usually written without the article. **in prison; out of prison; sent to prison**

◊ **prisoner** *noun* person who is in prison; **prisoner of war** = member of the armed forces captured and put in prison by the enemy; **prisoner at the bar** = the accused person in the dock *or* being tried in court

◊ **prison visitor** *noun* *see* VISITOR

privacy *noun* private life; **invasion of privacy** = action (such as being followed by newspaper reporters) which prevents someone from living a normal private life
NOTE: no plural

private *adjective* (a) belonging to a single person, not a company or the state; **letter marked "private and confidential"** = letter which must not be opened by anyone other than the person to whom it is addressed; **Private Bill** = Bill relating to a particular person *or* corporation *or* institution; *see below* PRIVATE MEMBER'S BILL; **private business** = business dealing with the members of a group *or* matters which cannot be discussed in public; **the committee held a special meeting to discuss some**

private business; private client *or* **private customer** = client dealt with by a professional man *or* by a salesman as a person, not as a company; **private effects** = goods which belong to someone and are used by him; **private detective** *or* (*informal*) **private eye** = person who for a fee will try to solve mysteries *or* to find missing persons *or* to keep watch on someone; **private law** = law as it refers to individuals; **Private Member's Bill** = Bill which is drafted and proposed in the House of Commons by an ordinary Member of Parliament, not by a government minister on behalf of the government; **private nuisance** = act which can harm a particular person or his rights; **private property** = property which belongs to a private person, not to the public; **private prosecution** = prosecution for a criminal act, brought by an ordinary member of the public and not by the police (b) **in private** = away from other people; **he asked to see the managing director in private** (c) **private limited company** = company with a small number of shareholders whose shares are not traded on the Stock Exchange; **private enterprise** = economic system where businesses are owned by private shareholders, not by the state; **the private sector** = all companies which are owned by private shareholders, not by the state

◊ **privately** *adverb* away from other people; **the deal was negotiated privately**

privilege *noun* protection from the law given in certain circumstances; **absolute privilege** = privilege which protects a person from being sued for defamation (such as an MP speaking in the House of Commons, a judge *or* a lawyer making a statement during judicial proceedings); **breach of parliamentary privilege** = speaking in a defamatory way about Parliament *or* about a Member of Parliament, **Committee of Privileges** = special committee of the House of Commons which examines cases of breach of privilege; **Crown privilege** = right of the Crown *or* of the government not to have to produce documents in court; **qualified privilege** = protection from being sued for defamation which is given to someone only if it can be proved that the statements were made without malice

◇ **privileged** *adjective* protected by privilege; **privileged communication** = letter which could be libellous but which is protected by privilege (such as a letter from a client to his lawyer); **privileged meeting** = meeting where what is said will not be repeated outside

privity of contract *noun* relationship between the parties to a contract, which makes the contract enforceable as between them

Privy Council *noun* body of senior advisers who advise the Queen on certain matters; **Judicial Committee of the Privy Council** = appeal court for appeals from some Commonwealth countries and the colonies

◇ **Privy Councillor** *noun* member of the Privy Council

prize *noun* enemy ship *or* cargo captured in war

pro for *or* on behalf of; **per pro** = with the authority of

probable *adjective* likely to happen *or* to be true; **he is trying to prevent the probable takeover of the company; a heart attack was the probable cause of death**

◇ **probably** *adverb* likely; **the judge is probably going to retire next year; his death was probably caused by a heart attack**

probate *noun* legal acceptance that a document, especially a will, is valid; **grant of probate** = official document proving that a will is genuine, given to the executors so that they can act on the terms of the will; **the executor was granted probate *or* obtained a grant of probate** = the executor was told officially that the will was valid; **Probate Registry** = court office which deals with the granting of probate
NOTE: no plural

probation *noun* (a) legal system for dealing with criminals (often young offenders) where they are not sent to prison provided that they continue to behave well under the supervision of a probation officer; **she was sentenced to probation for one year; probation officer** = official of the social services who supervises young people on probation; **probation order** = court order putting someone on probation (b) period when a

new worker is being tested before being confirmed as having a permanent job (c) **on probation** = (i) being tested; (ii) being under a probation order from a court; **he is on three months' probation; to take someone on probation**
NOTE: no plural

◇ **probationary** *adjective* while someone is being tested; **a probationary period of three months; after the probationary period the company decided to offer him a full-time contract**

◇ **probationer** *noun* person who has been put on probation

problem *noun* thing to which it is difficult to find an answer; **the company suffers from cash flow problems *or* staff problems; to solve a problem** = to find an answer to a problem; **problem area** = area of work which is difficult to manage; **drug-related crime is a problem area in large cities**

procedure *noun* way in which something is done, especially steps taken to bring an action to the court; **to follow the proper procedure; this procedure is very irregular** = this is not the set way to do something; **disciplinary procedure** = way of warning a worker that he is breaking the rules of a company *or* working badly; **complaints procedure *or* grievance procedure** = agreed way of presenting complaints formally from a trade union *or* from an employee to the management of a company; **dismissal procedures** = correct way of dismissing someone, following the rules in the contract of employment

◇ **procedural** *adjective* referring to legal procedure; **procedural law** = rules governing how the civil *or* criminal law is administered by the courts; **procedural problem *or* question** = question concerning procedure; **the hearing was held up while counsel argued over procedural problems**

proceed *verb* to go on *or* to continue; **the negotiations are proceeding slowly; to proceed against someone** = to start a legal action against someone; **to proceed with something** = to go on doing something; **the hearing proceeded after the protesters were removed from the courtroom**

◇ **proceedings** *plural noun* (a) **conference proceedings** = written report of what has taken place at a conference (b)

legal proceedings = legal action *or* lawsuit; **to take proceedings against someone; the court proceedings were adjourned; to institute** *or* **to start proceedings against someone** = to start a legal action against someone; **committal proceedings** = preliminary hearing of a case before the magistrates' court, to decide if it is serious enough to be tried before a jury in a higher court; **interlocutory proceedings** = hearing that takes place before a court before full trial

◊ **proceeds** *plural noun* **the proceeds of a sale** = money received from a sale after deducting expenses

process 1 *noun* **(a) industrial processes** = processes involved in manufacturing products in factories; **decision-making processes** = ways in which decisions are reached **(b)** (i) way in which a court acts to assert its jurisdiction; (ii) writs issued by a court to summon the defendant to appear in court; (iii) legal procedure; **the due process of the law** = the formal work of a fair legal action; **abuse of process** = suing someone in bad faith *or* without proper justification *or* for malicious reasons **2** *verb* **(a) to process figures** = to sort out information to make it easily understood; **the sales figures are being processed by our accounts department; data is being processed in our computer (b)** to deal with something in the usual routine way; **to process an insurance claim; the incident room is processing information received from the public**

◊ **processing** *noun* **(a)** sorting of information; **processing of information** *or* **of figures; data processing** *or* **information processing** = selecting and examining data in a computer to produce information in a special form; **word processing** *or* **text processing** = working with words, using a computer to produce, check and amend texts, contracts, reports, letters, etc. **(b) the processing of a claim for insurance** = putting a claim for compensation through the usual office routine in the insurance company

◊ **process-server** *noun* person who delivers legal documents (such as a writ *or* summons) to people in person

proctor *noun* (*in a university*) official who is responsible for keeping law and order;

Queen's Proctor = solicitor acting for the Crown in matrimonial and probate cases

procurantionem *see* PER PROCURANTIONEM

Procurator Fiscal *noun* (*in Scotland*) law officer who decides whether an alleged criminal should be prosecuted

procure *verb* to get someone to do something, especially to arrange for a woman to provide sexual intercourse for money

◊ **procuring** *or* **procurement** *noun* notifiable offence of getting a woman to provide sexual intercourse for money

◊ **procurer** *noun* person who procures women

produce *verb* to show *or* to bring out; **the police produced a number of weapons seized during the riot; the summons required him to produce a certain document before the court**

product *noun* **(a)** thing which is made; **basic product** = main product made from a raw material; **end product** *or* **final product** *or* **finished product** = product made at the end of a production process; **product liability** = liability of the maker of a product for negligence in the design or production of the product **(b) gross domestic product** = annual value of goods sold and services paid for inside a country; **gross national product** = annual value of goods and services in a country, including income from other countries

production *noun* **(a)** showing something; **on production of** = when something is shown; **the case will be released by the customs on production of the relevant documents; goods can be exchanged only on production of the sales slip (b)** making *or* manufacturing of goods for sale; **production will probably be held up by industrial action; we are hoping to speed up production by putting in new machinery; domestic production** = production of goods in the home market; **mass production** = manufacturing of large quantities of goods; **rate of production** *or* **production rate** = speed at which items are made

◊ **productive** *adjective* which produces; **productive capital** = capital which is invested to give interest; **productive discussions** = useful discussions which lead to an agreement or decision

◇ **productively** *adverb* in a productive way

proferentem *see* CONTRA

profession *noun* (a) work which needs special learning over a period of time; **the managing director is a lawyer by profession** = he trained as a lawyer (b) group of specialized workers; **the legal profession** = all lawyers; **the medical profession** = all doctors

◇ **professional** 1 *adjective* (a) referring to one of the professions; **the accountant sent in his bill for professional services; we had to ask our lawyer for professional advice on the contract; a professional man** = man who works in one of the professions (such as a lawyer, doctor, accountant); **professional misconduct** = action which is considered wrong by the body which regulates a profession (as an action by a solicitor which is considered wrong by the Law Society); **professional qualifications** = documents showing that someone has successfully finished a course of study which allows him to work in one of the professions (b) expert; **professional witness** = witness who is a specialist in a subject and is asked to give evidence to a court on technical matters 2 *noun* skilled person *or* person who does skilled work for money

profit *noun* money gained from a sale which is more than the money spent on making the item sold; **clear profit** = profit after all expenses have been paid; **gross profit** = profit calculated as sales income less the cost of the goods sold; **net profit** = result where income from sales is larger than all expenditure; **operating profit** = result where sales from normal business activities are higher than the costs; **trading profit** = result where the company' receipts are higher than its expenditure; **profit and loss account** = accounts for a company which show expenditure and income balanced to show a final profit or loss; **profit before tax** *or* **pretax profit** = profit before any tax has been paid; **profit after tax** = profit after tax has been paid

◇ **profitability** *noun* (a) ability to make a profit (b) amount of profit made as a percentage of costs; **measurement of profitability** = way of calculating how profitable something is

◇ **profitable** *adjective* which makes a profit

◇ **profitably** *adverb* making a profit

◇ **profit à prendre** *noun* right to take something from land (such as game, or fish from a river passing through the land)

◇ **profiteer** *noun* person who makes too much profit, especially when goods are rationed or in short supply

◇ **profiteering** *noun* making too much profit

pro forma *Latin phrase meaning* "for the sake of form"; **pro forma (invoice)** = invoice sent to a buyer before the goods are sent, so that payment can be made or that business documents can be produced; **pro forma letter** = formal letter which informs a court of a decision of another court

program 1 *noun* computer program = instructions to a computer telling it to do a particular piece of work 2 *verb* to write a program for a computer; **the computer is programmed to search the police records for a certain type of fingerprint; programming language** = system of signs, letters and words used to instruct a computer

progress 1 *noun* movement of work forward; **the superintendent briefed the press on the progress of the investigation; the fraud squad is making progress in the false insurance case** 2 *verb* to move forward; **the investigation progressed rapidly once the details were put onto the police computer**

prohibit *verb* to forbid *or* to say that something must not happen; **parking is prohibited in front of the garage; the law prohibits the sale of alcohol to minors; prohibited degrees** = relationships which make it illegal for a man and woman to marry (such as father and daughter); **prohibited goods** = goods which are not allowed to be imported

◇ **prohibition** *noun* (a) act of forbidding something (b) High Court order forbidding a lower court from doing something which exceeds its jurisdiction

◇ **prohibitive** *adjective* with a price so high that you cannot afford to pay it

◇ **prohibitory injunction** *noun* order from a court preventing someone from doing an illegal act

promise 1 *noun* statement that you will do something *or* not do something; **to keep a promise** = to do what you said you would do; **to go back on a promise** = not to do what you said you would do; **a promise to pay** = a promissory note; **breach of promise** = formerly, a complaint in court that someone had promised to marry the plaintiff and then had not done so; **gratuitous promise** = promise that cannot be enforced because no money has been involved 2 *verb* to say that you will do something; **they promised to pay the last instalment next week; the personnel manager promised to look into the grievances of the office staff**

◇ **promisee** *noun* person to whom a promise is made

◇ **promisor** *noun* person who makes a promise

◇ **promissory** *adjective* which promises; **promissory estoppel** = promise made by one person to another, so that the second person relies on the promise and acts to his detriment, and the first person is stopped from denying the validity of the promise; **promissory note** = document stating that someone promises to pay an amount of money on a certain date

promote *verb* (a) to introduce a new Bill into Parliament (b) to give someone a more important job; **he was promoted from salesman to sales manager** (c) to advertise; **to promote a new product** = to increase the sales of a new product by a sales campaign *or* TV advertising *or* free gifts (d) to encourage something to grow; **to promote a new company** = to organize the setting up of a new company

◇ **promoter** *noun* person who introduces a new Bill into Parliament; **company promoter** = person who organizes the setting up of a new company

◇ **promotion** *noun* (a) moving up to a more important job; **to earn promotion** = to work hard and efficiently and so be promoted (b) **promotion of a company** = setting up a new company (c) **promotion of a product** = selling a new product by advertising *or* sales campaigns *or* free gifts

◇ **promotional** *adjective* used in an advertising campaign; **promotional budget** = expected cost of promoting a new product

prompt 1 *adjective* rapid *or* done immediately; **the minister issued a prompt denial of the allegations against him; failing prompt payment** = if the payment is not made on time 2 *verb* to tell someone what to say; **the judge warned counsel not to prompt the witness**

◇ **promptly** *adverb* rapidly; **the defendant promptly counterclaimed against the plaintiff**

proof *noun* (a) thing *or* evidence which shows that something is true; **documentary proof** = proof in the form of a document; **burden of proof** *or* **onus of proof** = duty to prove that what has been alleged in court is correct; **the onus of proof is on the plaintiff** (b) statement *or* evidence of a creditor to show that he is owed money by a bankrupt *or* by a company in liquidation; **proof of debt** = proceedings for a creditor to claim payment from a bankrupt's assets; **proof of evidence** = written statement of what a witness intends to say in court; **proof of service** = showing that legal documents have been delivered to someone

◇ **-proof** *suffix* which prevents something getting in or out *or* harming; **burglarproof door; inflation-proof pension; escape-proof prison**

proper *adjective* correct *or* appropriate; **proper law of the contract** = law which the parties signing a contract agree should govern that contract *or* its formation

property *noun* (a) ownership *or* right to own something; **law of property** = branch of the law dealing with the rights of ownership (b) anything which can be owned; **industrial property** = intangible property owned by a company (such as copyrights *or* patents *or* trademarks); **intellectual property** = ownership of something (such as a copyright *or* patent *or* trademark) which is intangible; **personal property** = things (but not land) which belong to a person and can be inherited by his heirs; **the storm caused considerable damage to personal property; the management is not responsible for property left in the hotel rooms** (c) **(real) property** = land and buildings; **property tax** *or* **tax on**

property; damage to property or property damage; the commercial property market is declining; property company = company which buys or constructs buildings to lease them; property developer = person who buys old buildings or empty land and builds new buildings for sale or rent; private property = land or buildings which belong to a private person and not to the public (d) a building; we have several properties for sale in the centre of the town NOTE: no plural for (a), (b) or (c)

proportion noun part (of a total); a proportion of the pretax profit is set aside for contingencies; only a small proportion of our sales comes from retail shops; in proportion to = showing how something is related to something else

◇ **proportional** adjective directly related; proportional representation = system of electing representatives where each political party is allocated a number of places which is directly related to the number of votes cast for the party

◇ **proportionately** adverb in proportion

proposal noun (a) suggestion or thing suggested; to make a proposal or to put forward a proposal; to lay a proposal before the House = to introduce a new Bill before Parliament; the committee turned down the proposal = the committee refused to accept what had been suggested (b) proposal form = official document with details of a property or person to be insured which is sent to the insurance company when asking for an insurance

◇ **propose** verb (a) to suggest that something should be done; the Bill proposes that any party to the proceedings may appeal; to propose a motion = to ask a meeting to vote for a motion and explain the reasons for this; to propose someone as president = to ask a group to vote for someone to become president (b) to propose to = to say that you intend to do something; I propose to repay the loan at £20 a month

proprietary adjective (a) product (such as a medicine) which is made and owned by a company; proprietary drug = drug which is made by a particular company and marketed under a brand name; proprietary right = right of someone who owns a property (b) (in South Africa and Australia) proprietary company (Pty) = private limited company

◇ **proprietor** noun owner of a property; the proprietor of a hotel or a hotel proprietor

◇ **proprietorship** noun act of being the proprietor of land; proprietorship register = land register which shows the details of owners of land

◇ **proprietress** noun woman owner; the proprietress of an advertising consultancy

pro rata adjective & adverb at a rate which changes according to the importance of something; a pro rata payment; to pay someone pro rata

prorogation noun end of a session of Parliament

◇ **prorogue** verb to end a session of Parliament; Parliament was prorogued for the summer recess

proscribe verb to ban; a proscribed political party = political party which has been banned

prosecute verb (a) to bring (someone) to court to answer a criminal charge; he was prosecuted for embezzlement (b) to speak against the accused person on behalf of the party bringing the charge; Mr Smith is prosecuting, and Mr Jones is appearing for the defence

◇ **prosecution** noun (a) act of bringing someone to court to answer a charge; his prosecution for embezzlement; Director of Public Prosecutions = government official in charge of a group of lawyers (working under the Attorney-General), who prosecutes in important cases and advises other government departments if prosecutions should be started (b) (i) party who brings a criminal charge against someone; (ii) lawyers representing the party who brings a criminal charge against someone; the costs of the case will be borne by the prosecution; prosecution counsel or counsel for the prosecution = lawyer acting for the prosecution; see also DEFENCE

◇ **prosecutor** noun person who brings criminal charges against someone; Crown prosecutor = official of the Director of Public Prosecutions' department who is responsible for prosecuting criminals in a local area; public prosecutor = government official who brings charges against alleged criminals (in the UK, the Director of Public Prosecutions)

prosequi *see* NOLLE

prospectus *noun* **(a)** document which gives information to attract buyers *or* customers; **the restaurant has girls handing out prospectuses in the street (b)** document which gives information about a company whose shares are being sold to the public for the first time
NOTE: plural is **prospectuses**

prostitution *noun* providing sexual intercourse in return for payment
◊ **prostitute** *noun* person who provides sexual intercourse in return for payment

protect *verb* to defend something against harm; **the workers are protected from unfair dismissal by government legislation; the computer is protected by a plastic cover; the cover protects the machine from dust; to protect an industry by imposing tariff barriers** = to stop a local industry from being hit by foreign competition by stopping foreign products from being imported; **protected tenancy** = tenancy where the tenant is protected from eviction
NOTE: you protect someone **from** something or **from having** something done to him

◊ **protection** *noun* thing which protects; **consumer protection** = protecting consumers against unfair *or* illegal traders; **Court of Protection** = court which administers the property of people suffering from a disability; **data protection** = protecting information (such as records about private people) in a computer from being copied or used wrongly; **police protection** = services of the police to protect someone who might be harmed; **the minister was given police protection; protection racket** = illegal organization where people demand money from someone (such as a small businessman) to pay for "protection" against criminal attacks
NOTE: no plural

◊ **protective** *adjective* which protects; **protective tariff** = tariff which tries to ban imports to stop them competing with local products

pro tem *or* **pro tempore** *adverb* temporarily *or* for a time

protest 1 *noun* **(a)** statement *or* action to show that you do not approve of something; **to make a protest against high prices; sit-down protest** = action by members of the staff who occupy their place of work and refuse to leave; **protest march** = demonstration where protesters march through the streets; **in protest at** = showing that you do not approve of something; **the staff occupied the offices in protest at the low pay offer; to do something under protest** = to do something, but say that you do not approve of it **(b)** official document from a notary public which notes that a bill of exchange has not been paid 2 *verb* **(a) to protest against something** = to say that you do not approve of something; **the retailers are protesting against the ban on imported goods** (NOTE: in this meaning GB English is **protest against something**, but US English is **to protest something**) **(b) to protest a bill** = to draw up a document to prove that a bill of exchange has not been paid

◊ **protester** *noun* person who protests

protocol *noun* **(a)** (i) draft memorandum; (ii) list of things which have been agreed **(b)** correct diplomatic behaviour

prove *verb* to show that something is true; **the tickets proved that he was lying; dispatch of the packet was proved by the Post Office receipt; the claim was proved to be false; to prove a debt** = to show that a bankrupt owes you money; **to prove a will** = to show that a will is valid and obtain a grant of probate

◊ **provable** *adjective* which can be proved; **provable debts** = debts which a creditor can prove against a bankrupt estate

◊ **proven** *adjective* (*in Scotland*) **not proven** = verdict that the prosecution has not produced sufficient evidence to prove the accused to be guilty

provide *verb* **(a) to provide for something** = to allow for something which may happen in the future; **the contract provides for an annual increase in charges; £10,000 has been provided for in the budget; these expenses have not been provided for; payments as provided in schedule 6 attached; to provide for someone** = to put aside money to give someone enough to live on; **he provided for his daughter in his will (b)** to put money aside in accounts to cover expenditure or loss in the future; **£25,000 is provided against bad debts (c) to provide someone with something** = to supply something to someone; **the defendant provided the court with a detailed account of his movements; duress provides no defence to a charge of murder**

◊ **provided that** *or* **providing** *conjunction* on condition that; **the judge will sentence the convicted man next week provided (that)** *or* **providing the psychiatrist's report is received in time** NOTE: in deeds, the form **provided always that** is often used

provision *noun* **(a) to make provision for** = to see that something is allowed for in the future; **to make financial provision for someone** = to give someone enough money to live on; **there is no provision for** *or* **no provision has been made for car parking in the plans for the office block** = the plans do not include space for cars to park **(b)** money put aside in accounts in case it is needed in the future; **the company has made a £2m provision for bad debts (c)** legal condition; **the provisions of a Bill** = conditions listed in a Bill before Parliament; **we have made provision to this effect** = we have put into the contract terms which will make this work

◊ **provisional** *adjective* temporary *or* not final or permanent; **provisional budget; they wrote to give their provisional acceptance of the contract; provisional liquidator** = official appointed by a court to protect the assets of a company which is the subject of a winding up order; **provisional injunction** = temporary injunction granted until a full court hearing can take place

◊ **provisionally** *adverb* not finally; **the contract has been accepted provisionally; he was provisionally appointed director**

proviso *noun* condition in a contract *or* deed; **we are signing the contract with the proviso that the terms can be discussed again in six months' time** NOTE: the proviso usually begins with the phrase **"provided always that"**

provocation *noun* being provoked to commit a crime *or* to carry out an action which you had not intended; **he acted under provocation** NOTE: no plural

◊ **provoke** *verb* to make someone do something *or* to make something happen; **the strikers provoked the police to retaliate; the murders provoked a campaign to increase police protection for politicians** NOTE: you provoke someone **to do** something

◊ **provocateur** *see* AGENT PROVOCATEUR

proxy *noun* **(a)** document which gives someone the power to act on behalf of someone else; **to sign by proxy; proxy vote** = votes made by proxy **(b)** person who acts on behalf of someone else, especially a person appointed by a shareholder to vote on his behalf at a company meeting; **to act as proxy for someone**

P.S. = POST SCRIPTUM; additional note at the end of a letter; **did you read the P.S. at the end of the letter?**

psychiatry *noun* study of diseases of the mind

◊ **psychiatric** *adjective* referring to psychiatry; **psychiatric hospital** = hospital where mentally ill people are treated; **he was sent to hospital for psychiatric treatment; the court was shown a psychiatric report**

◊ **psychiatrist** *noun* doctor specializing in diseases of the mind

Pty = PROPRIETARY COMPANY

public 1 *adjective* **(a)** referring to all the people in general; **Public Bill** = Bill referring to a matter applying to the public in general which is introduced in Parliament by a government minister; **public domain** = land *or* property *or* information which belongs to and is available to the public; **work in the public domain** = written work which is no longer in copyright; **public holiday** = day when all workers rest and enjoy themselves instead of working; **public house** = building which has been licensed for the sale of alcohol to be drunk on the premises; **public image** = idea which the people have of a company *or* a person; **the police are trying to improve their public image; public law** = law which affects the people *or* the public as a whole (such as administrative and constitutional law); **public nuisance** = criminal act which can harm members of the public *or* their rights; **public order** = situation where the general public is calm *or* where there are no riots; **offence against the public order** *or* **public order offence** =

riot *or* street fight *or* looting, etc.; **public place** = place (such as a road *or* park *or* pavement) where the public in general have a right to be; **public policy** = general good of all the people; **public transport** = transport (such as buses, trains) which is used by any member of the public; **Public Trustee** = official who is appointed as a trustee of an individual's property **(b)** referring to the government *or* the state; **Public Accounts Committee** = committee of the House of Commons which examines the spending of each department and ministry; **public administration** = (i) means whereby government policy is carried out; (ii) people responsible for carrying out government policy; **public expenditure** = spending of money by the local or central government; **public finance** = the raising of money by governments (by taxes or borrowing) and the spending of it; **public funds** = government money available for expenditure; **public ownership** = situation where an industry is nationalized **(c) public limited company (plc)** = company whose shares can be bought on the Stock Exchange; **the company is going public** = the company is going to place some of its shares for sale on the Stock Exchange so that anyone can buy them **2** *noun* **the public** *or* **the general public** = the people in general; **in public** = in front of everyone

◊ **publication** *noun* **(a)** (i) making something public (either in speech or writing); (ii) making a libel known to people other than the person libelled; **publication of Cabinet papers takes place after thirty years (b)** printed work shown to the public; **obscene publication** = book *or* magazine which is liable to deprave *or* corrupt someone who sees or reads it; **the magazine was classed as an obscene publication and seized by the customs**

◊ **public relations (PR)** *noun* keeping good links between an organization *or* a company *or* a group and the public so that people know what the organization is doing and approve of it; **public relations department** = section of an organization which deals with relations with the public; **public relations officer** = official who deals with relations with the public

◊ **public sector** *noun* nationalized industries and services; **a report on wage rises in the public sector** *or* **on public sector wage settlements; public sector borrowing**

requirement = amount of money which a government has to borrow to pay for its own spending

publish *verb* to have a document (such as a catalogue *or* book *or* magazine *or* newspaper *or* piece of music) written and printed and then sell or give it to the public; **the society publishes its list of members annually; the government has not published the figures on which its proposals are based; the company publishes six magazines for the business market**

◊ **publisher** *noun* person or company which publishes

puisne *adjective* lesser *or* less important; **puisne judge** = High Court judge; **puisne mortgage** = mortgage where the deeds of the property have not been deposited with the lender

punish *verb* to make (someone) suffer for a crime which he has committed; **you will be punished for hitting the policeman**

◊ **punishable** *adjective* (crime) which can be punished; **crimes punishable by imprisonment**

◊ **punishment** *noun* **(a)** act of punishing someone; **corporal punishment** = punishing someone by hitting him; **capital punishment** = punishing someone by execution **(b)** treatment of someone as a way of making him suffer for a crime; **the punishment for treason is death**

pupillage *noun* training period of one year after completing studies at university and passing all examinations which a person has to serve before he can practise independently as a barrister
NOTE: no plural

purchase 1 *noun* (i) action of buying something; (ii) thing which has been bought; **purchase order** = official order made out by a purchasing department for goods which a company wants to buy; **purchase price** = price paid for something; **purchase tax** = tax paid on things which are bought; **compulsory purchase** = buying of a property by a local authority *or* by the government, even if the owner does not wish to sell; **compulsory purchase order** = official order from a local authority *or* from the government ordering an owner to sell his property; **hire purchase** = system of buying something by paying a sum regularly each month; **hire purchase agreement** = contract to pay for something by instalments **2** *verb* to buy; **to purchase something for cash** = to pay cash for something

◊ **purchaser** *noun* person *or* company which purchases something

purge *verb* **to purge one's contempt** *or* **to purge a contempt of court** = to do something (such as make an apology) to show that you are sorry for the lack of respect you have shown

purpose *noun* aim *or* plan *or* intention; **on purpose** = intentionally; **she hid the knife on purpose; we need the invoice for tax purposes** *or* **for the purpose of declaration to the tax authorities** = in order for it to be declared to the tax authorities; **fitness for purpose** = implied contractual term that goods sold will be of the necessary standard to be used for the purpose for which they were bought

pursue *verb* to continue with (proceedings in court *or* debate in Parliament, etc.)

◊ **pursuant to** *adverb* relating to *or* concerning; **matters pursuant to Article 124 of the EEC treaty; pursuant to the powers conferred on the local authority**

pursuit *noun* **in pursuit** = following *or* chasing; **the bank robbers escaped in a car with the police in pursuit;** *see also* FRESH, HOT

purview *noun* general scope of an Act of Parliament

put 1 *noun* **put option** = right to sell shares at a certain price at a certain date **2** *verb* to place *or* to fix; **to put a proposal to the vote** = to ask a meeting to vote for or against the proposal; **to put a proposal to the board** = to ask the board to consider a suggestion
NOTE: **putting - put - has put**

◊ **put away** *verb* to send to prison; **he was put away for ten years**

◊ **put down** *verb* **(a)** to make a deposit; **to put down money on a house (b)** to write an item in an account book; **to put down a figure for expenses**

◊ **put in** *verb* **to put an ad in a paper** = to have an ad printed in a newspaper; **to put in a bid for something** = to offer (usually in

writing) to buy something; **to put in an estimate for something** = to give someone a written calculation of the probable costs of carrying out a job; **to put in a claim for damage** *or* **loss** = to ask an insurance company to pay for damage *or* loss

◊ **put into** *verb* to put money into a **business** = to invest money in a business

◊ **put off** *verb* to arrange for something to take place later than planned; **the hearing was put off for two weeks; he asked if we could put the visit off until tomorrow**

◊ **put on** *verb* **to put an item on the agenda** = to list an item for discussion at a meeting; **to put an embargo on trade** = to forbid trade

◊ **put out** *verb* to send out; **to put work out to freelance workers; we put all our typing out to a bureau; to put work out to contract** = to decide that work should be done by a company on a contract, rather than employ members of staff to do it

putative *adjective* **putative father** = man who is supposed to be *or* who a court decides must be the father of an illegitimate child

Qq

QB *or* **QBD** = QUEEN'S BENCH DIVISION

QC = QUEEN'S COUNSEL
NOTE: written after the surname of the lawyer: **W. Smith QC.** Note also that the plural is written **QCs**

qua *conjunction* as *or* acting in the capacity of; **a decision of the Lord Chancellor qua head of the judiciary**

quadruplicate *noun* **in quadruplicate** = with the original and three copies; **the invoices are printed in quadruplicate**
NOTE: no plural

qualification *noun* **(a)** proof that you have completed a specialized course of study; **to have the right qualifications for the job; professional qualifications** = documents which show that someone has

successfully finished a course of study which allows him to work in one of the professions **(b) period of qualification** = time which has to pass before something qualifies for something; **qualification shares** = number of shares which a person has to hold to be a director of a company
◇ **qualify** *verb* **(a) to qualify for** = to be in the right position for *or* to be entitled to; **he does not qualify for Legal Aid; she qualifies for unemployment pay (b) to qualify as** = to follow a specialized course and pass examinations so that you can do a certain job; **she has qualified as an accountant; he will qualify as a solicitor next year (c)** to change *or* to amend; **the auditors have qualified the accounts** = the auditors have found something in the accounts of the company which they do not agree with, and have noted it
◇ **qualified** *adjective* **(a)** having passed special examinations in a subject; **she is a qualified solicitor; highly qualified** = with very good results in examinations; **all our staff are highly qualified; they employ twenty-six highly qualified legal assistants (b)** with some reservations *or* conditions; **qualified acceptance of a bill of exchange; the plan received qualified approval from the board; qualified privilege** = protection from being sued for defamation given to someone only if it can be proved that the statements were made without malice; **qualified title** = title to a property which is not absolute because there is some defect **(c) qualified accounts** = accounts which have been noted by the auditors because they contain something with which the auditors do not agree
◇ **qualifying** *adjective* **(a) qualifying period** = time which has to pass before something qualifies for a grant *or* subsidy, etc.; **there is a six month qualifying period before you can get a grant from the local authority (b) qualifying shares** = number of shares which you need to own to get a free issue *or* to be a director of a company

quantify *verb* **to quantify the effect of something** = to show the effect of something in figures; **it is impossible to quantify the effect of the new legislation on the crime rate**
◇ **quantifiable** *adjective* which can be quantified; **the effect of the change on the prison population is not quantifiable**

quantity *adjective* **(a)** amount *or* number of items; **a small quantity of illegal drugs; he bought a large quantity of spare parts (b)** large amount; **the company offers a discount for quantity purchase**

quantum *noun* amount (of damages); **liability was admitted by the defendants, but the case went to trial because they could not agree the quantum of damages**
◇ **quantum meruit** *Latin phrase* meaning "as much as he has deserved": rule that, when claiming for breach of contract, a party is entitled to payment for work done

quarantine **1** *noun* period (originally forty days) when a ship *or* animal *or* person newly arrived in a country has to be kept away from others in case there is danger of carrying diseases; **the animals were put in quarantine on arrival at the port; quarantine restrictions have been lifted on imported animals from that country** NOTE: used without **the: the dog was put in quarantine** *or* **was held in quarantine** *or* **was released from quarantine** **2** *verb* to put in quarantine; **the ship was searched and all the animals on it were quarantined**

quarter *noun* **(a)** period of three months; **first quarter** *or* **second quarter** *or* **third quarter** *or* **fourth quarter** *or* **last quarter** = periods of three months from January to the end of March *or* from April to the end of June *or* from July to the end of September *or* from October to the end of the year; **the instalments are payable at the end of each quarter; the first quarter's rent is payable in advance; quarter day** = day at the end of a quarter, when rents should be paid

> COMMENT: in England the quarter days are 25th March (Lady Day), 24th June (Midsummer Day), 29th September (Michaelmas Day) and 25th December (Christmas Day)

(b) Quarter Sessions = old name for the criminal court replaced by the Crown Court
◇ **quarterly** *adjective & adverb* happening every three months *or* happening four times a year; **there is a quarterly charge for electricity; the bank sends us a quarterly statement; we agreed to pay the rent quarterly** *or* **on a quarterly basis**

quash *verb* to annul *or* to make something not exist; **the appeal court quashed the verdict; he applied for judicial review to quash the order; a conviction obtained by fraud or perjury by a witness will be quashed**

quasi- *prefix* almost *or* which seems like; **a quasi-official body; a quasi-judicial investigation**

◇ **quasi-contract** *noun* = IMPLIED CONTRACT

Queen's Bench Division (QBD) *noun* one of the main divisions of the High Court

Queen's Counsel *noun* senior British barrister, appointed by the Lord Chancellor
NOTE: abbreviated to **QC**

Queen's evidence *noun* **to turn Queen's evidence** = to confess to a crime and then act as witness against the other criminals involved, in the hope of getting a lighter sentence

Queen's Proctor *noun* solicitor acting for the Crown in matrimonial and probate cases

Queen's Speech *noun* speech made by the Queen at the opening of a session of Parliament, which outlines the government's plans for legislation

query 1 *noun* question; **the chief accountant had to answer a mass of queries from the auditors** 2 *verb* to ask a question about something *or* to suggest that something may be wrong; **counsel queried the statements of the police witnesses**

question 1 *noun* **(a)** words which need an answer; **counsel asked the witness questions about his bank accounts; counsel for the prosecution put three questions to the police inspector; the managing director refused to answer questions about redundancies; the market research team prepared a series of questions to test the public's attitude to problems of law and order; Question Time** = period in the House of Commons when Members of Parliament can put questions to ministers about the work of their departments **(b)** problem; **he raised the question of the cost of the lawsuit; the main question is that of time; the tribunal discussed the question of**

redundancy payments (c) question of fact = fact relevant to a case which is tried at court; **question of law** = law relevant to a case which is tried at court 2 *verb* **(a)** to ask questions; **the police questioned the accounts staff for four hours; she questioned the chairman about the company's investment policy (b)** to query *or* to suggest that something may be wrong; **counsel questioned the reliability of the witness' evidence; the accused questioned the result of the breathalyser test**

◇ **questioning** *noun* action of asking someone questions; **the man was taken to the police station for questioning; during questioning by the police, she confessed to the crime; the witness became confused during questioning by counsel for the prosecution**

◇ **questionnaire** *noun* printed list of questions, especially used in market research; **to send out a questionnaire to test the opinions of users of the system; to answer** *or* **to fill in a questionnaire about problems of inner city violence**

queue 1 *noun* **(a)** line of people waiting one behind the other; **to form a queue** *or* **to join a queue; queues formed at the doors of the Crown Court on the morning of the murder trial (b)** series of documents (such as orders, application forms) which are dealt with in order; **mortgage queue** = list of people waiting for mortgages 2 *verb* to form a line one after the other for something; **when food was in short supply, people had to queue for bread; we queued for hours to get into the courtroom**

quick *adjective* fast *or* not taking any time; **the company made a quick recovery; he is hoping for a quick trial**

◇ **quickie (divorce)** *noun* divorce which is processed rapidly through the court by use of the special procedure

◇ **quickly** *adverb* without taking much time; **the divorce case went through the courts quickly; the accountant quickly looked through the pile of invoices**

quid pro quo *Latin phrase meaning* "one thing for another": action done in return for something done or promised

quiet *adjective* calm *or* not excited; **the prisoner seemed very quiet when the clerk read out the charges; on the quiet** = in secret; **he transferred his bank account to**

Switzerland on the quiet; **quiet enjoyment** = right of an occupier to occupy property peacefully under a tenancy without the landlord or anyone else interfering with that right

quit *verb* to leave a job *or* to leave rented accommodation; **he quit after an argument with the managing director; several of the managers are quitting to set up their own company; notice to quit** = formal notice served by a landlord on a tenant before proceedings are started for possession; **to serve a tenant with notice to quit** = to inform a tenant that he has to leave premises by a certain date
NOTE: **quitting - quit - has quit**

quo *see* STATUS QUO

quorum *noun* minimum number of people who have to be present at a meeting to make it valid; **to have a quorum** = to have enough people present for a meeting to go ahead; **do we have a quorum? the meeting was adjourned since there was no quorum**
◇ **quorate** *adjective* having a quorum; **the resolution was invalid because the shareholders' meeting was not quorate;** *see also* INQUORATE

quota *noun* fixed amount of something which is allowed to be sold *or* bought *or* obtained; **import quota** = fixed quantity of a particular type of goods which the government allows to be imported; **the government has imposed a quota on the import of cars; the quota on imported cars has been lifted; quota system** = system where imports *or* exports *or* supplies are regulated by fixing maximum amounts

quote *verb* **(a)** to repeat words used by someone else; to repeat a reference number; **counsel quoted from the statement made by the witness at the police station; she quoted figures from the annual report; in reply please quote this number: PC 1234 (b)** to estimate *or* to say what costs may be; to quote a price for supplying stationery; **to quote a price in dollars; their prices are always quoted in dollars; he quoted me a price of £1,026; can you quote for supplying 20,000 envelopes?; quoted company** = company whose shares are listed on the Stock Exchange
◇ **quotation** *noun* **(a)** estimate of how much something will cost; **they sent in their** quotation for the job; to ask for quotations for building a new courtroom; his quotation was much lower than all the others; we accepted the lowest quotation **(b)** quotation on the Stock Exchange *or* Stock Exchange quotation = listing of the price of a share on the Stock Exchange; **the company is going for a quotation on the Stock Exchange** = the company has applied to the Stock Exchange to have its shares listed

quo warranto *Latin phrase meaning* "by what authority": action which questions the authority of someone

q.v. *or* **quod vide** *Latin phrase meaning* "which see"

Rr

R = REGINA, REX
NOTE: used in reports of cases where the Crown is a party: *R. v. Smith Ltd*

race *noun* group of human beings with similar physical characteristics; **race relations** = relations between different racial groups in a country
◇ **racial** *adjective* referring to race; **racial hatred** = violent dislike of someone *or* of a group of people because of race; **incitement to racial hatred** = offence of encouraging (by words *or* actions *or* writing) people to attack others because of their race; **racial prejudice** *or* **racial discrimination** = treating people in different ways because of differences in race

rack rent *noun* (i) full yearly rent of a property let on a normal lease; (ii) very high rent

racket *noun* illegal deal *or* business which makes a lot of money by fraud; **he runs a cheap ticket racket;** *see also* PROTECTION
◇ **racketeer** *noun* person who runs a racket
◇ **racketeering** *noun* running a racket

raid 1 *noun* sudden attack *or* search; **six people were arrested in the police raid on the club 2** *verb* to make a sudden attack *or* search; **the police have raided several houses in the town; drugs were found when the police raided the club**

raise 1 *noun US* increase in salary; **he asked the boss for a raise; she is pleased - she has had her raise** (NOTE: British English is **rise**) 2 *verb* **(a)** to ask a meeting to discuss a question; **to raise a question** *or* **a point at a meeting; in answer to the point of order raised by Mr Smith; to raise an objection** = to object to something; **the union representatives raised a series of objections to the wording of the agreement (b)** to increase *or* to make higher; **the government has raised the penalties for drug smuggling; the company raised its dividend by 10% (c)** to obtain (money) *or* to organize (a loan); **the company is trying to raise the capital to fund its expansion programme; the government raises money by taxation; where will he raise the money from to start up his business?**

rank 1 level *or* grade in the police force *or* armed services; **he was promoted to the rank of Chief Superintendent; to reduce someone to the ranks** = to punish an officer reducing him to the rank of ordinary soldier 2 *verb* to be level with; **the new shares will rank pari passu with the existing ones**

ransom 1 *noun* money paid to abductors to get back someone who has been abducted; **the daughter of the banker was held by kidnappers who asked for a ransom of £1m; to hold someone to ransom** = to keep someone secretly until a ransom is paid; **ransom note** = message sent by kidnappers asking for a ransom to be paid 2 *verb* to pay money so that someone is released; **she was ransomed by her family**

rape 1 *noun* notifiable offence of forcing a woman (other than one's wife) to have sexual intercourse without her consent; **he was brought to court and charged with rape; the incidence of cases of rape has increased over the last years** 2 *verb* to force (a woman other than one's wife) to have sexual intercourse without her consent

rata *see* = PRO RATA

rate 1 *noun* **(a)** money charged for time worked *or* work completed; **all-in rate** = price which covers all items in a purchase (such as delivery, tax and insurance, as well as the goods themselves); **fixed rate** = charge which cannot be changed; **flat rate** = charge which always stays the same; **full rate** = full charge, with no reductions; **reduced rate** = specially cheap charge **(b) insurance rates** = amount of premium which has to be paid per £1,000 of insurance; **interest rate** *or* **rate of interest** = percentage charge for borrowing money; **rate of return** = amount of interest *or* dividend which comes from an investment, shown as a percentage of the money invested **(c) exchange rate** *or* **rate of exchange** = rate at which one currency is exchanged for another; **forward rate** = rate for purchase of foreign currency at a fixed price for delivery at a later date; **freight rates** = charges for carrying goods; **letter rate** *or* **parcel rate** = postage (calculated by weight) for sending a letter *or* a parcel; **night rate** = cheap telephone calls at night **(d)** amount *or* number *or* speed compared with something else; **birth rate** = number of children born per 1,000 of the population; **error rate** = number of mistakes per thousand entries *or* per page **(e)** *GB* (*usually plural*) local tax on property; **the local authority has fixed** *or* **has set the rate for next year; our rates have gone up by 25% this year; to set a legal rate** = to fix a rate which is within the limits approved by Parliament 2 *verb* **(a) to rate someone highly** = to value someone *or* to think someone is very good **(b) highly-rated part of London** = part of London with high local taxes

◇ **rateable** *adjective* **rateable value** = value of a property as a basis for calculating local taxes

◇ **ratepayer** *noun* **domestic ratepayer** = person who pays local taxes on a house *or* flat; **business ratepayer** = business which pays local taxes on a shop *or* factory, etc.

ratify *verb* to approve officially (something which has already been agreed); **the treaty was ratified by Congress; the agreement has to be ratified by the board; although the directors had acted without due authority, the company ratified their actions**

◇ **ratification** *noun* official approval of something which then becomes legally binding

ratio decidendi *Latin phrase meaning* "reason for deciding": main part of a court judgment setting out the legal principles applicable to the case and forming the binding part of the judgment to which other courts must pay regard; *see also* OBITER DICTA

RD = REFER TO DRAWER

re *preposition* about *or* concerning *or* referring to; **re your inquiry of May 29th; re: Smith's memorandum of yesterday; re: the agenda for the AGM; in re** = concerning *or* in the case of; **in re** *Jones & Co. Ltd*

re- *prefix* again

rea *see* MENS REA

reach *verb* to come to *or* to arrive at; **to reach an agreement; the jury was unable to reach a unanimous decision**

reading *noun* **First Reading** *or* **Second Reading** *or* **Third Reading** = the three stages of discussion of a Bill in Parliament

COMMENT: First Reading is the formal presentation of the Bill; Second Reading is the stage when the Bill is explained by the Minister proposing it and a vote is taken; the Bill is then discussed in Committee and at the Report Stage; Third Reading is the final discussion of the Bill in the whole House of Commons

real *adjective* **(a)** true *or* not an imitation; **his case is made of real leather** *or* **he has a real leather case; that car is a real bargain at £300; real income** *or* **real wages** = income which is available for spending after tax, etc. has been deducted; **in real terms** = actually *or* really; **sales have gone up by 3% but with inflation running at 5% that is a fall in real terms (b) real time** = time when a computer is working on the processing of data while the problem to which the data refers is actually taking place; **real-time system** = computer system where data is inputted directly into the computer which automatically processes it to produce information which can be used immediately **(c)** referring to things as opposed to persons; **chattels real** = leaseholds **(d)** referring to land (especially freehold land); **real estate** *or* **real property** = land or buildings considered from a legal point of view

realize *verb* **(a)** to understand clearly; **counsel realized the defendant was making a bad impression on the jury; the small shopkeepers realized that the supermarket would take away some of their trade; when he went into the police station he did not realize he was going to be arrested (b)** to make something become real; **to realize a project** *or* **a plan** = to put a project *or* a plan into action **(c)** to sell something to produce money; **to realize property** *or* **assets; the sale realized £100,000**

◊ **realizable** *adjective* **realizable assets** = assets which can be sold for money

◊ **realization** *noun* **(a)** gradual understanding; **the chairman's realization that he was going to be outvoted (b)** making real; **the realization of a project** = putting a plan into action; **the plan moved a stage nearer realization when the contracts were signed (c) realization of assets** = selling of assets for money

realty *noun* property *or* real estate *or* legal rights to land
NOTE: no plural

reapply *verb* to apply again; **the company reapplied for an injunction against the union; she reapplied for a maintenance order; when he saw that the job had still not been filled, he reapplied for it**

◊ **reapplication** *noun* second application

reason *noun* thing which explains why something has happened; **the defence gave no reason for their objections to the juror; the chairman of the magistrates asked him for the reason why he was late again; the witness was asked for his reasons for returning to the fire**

◊ **reasonable** *adjective* **(a)** sensible *or* not annoyed; **the magistrates were very reasonable when she explained that the driving licence was necessary for her work; beyond reasonable doubt** = so that no reasonable person could doubt it (proof needed to convict a person in a criminal case); **the prosecution in a criminal case has to establish beyond reasonable doubt that the accused committed the crime; no reasonable offer refused** = we will accept any offer which is not too low **(b)** not expensive; **the restaurant offers good food at reasonable prices**

◇ **reasoned** *adjective* carefully thought out and explained; **after three months, the judge delivered a reasoned judgment**

◇ **reasoning** *noun* thinking which produces a decision; **it is difficult to understand the reasoning behind the judge's decision**

rebate *noun* money returned; **rent rebate** = state subsidy paid to poor people who do not have enough income to pay their rents

rebel 1 *noun* person who fights against the government *or* against people in authority; **anti-government rebels have taken six towns; rebel ratepayers have occupied the town hall 2** *verb* to fight against authority
NOTE: **rebelling - rebelled**

◇ **rebellion** *noun* fight against the government *or* against those in authority; **the army has crushed the rebellion in the southern province**

rebut *verb* to contradict *or* to go against; **he attempted to rebut the assertions made by the prosecution witness**
NOTE: **rebutting - rebutted**

◇ **rebuttal** *noun* act of rebutting

recall *verb* **(a)** to ask someone to come back; **the witness was recalled to the witness box (b)** to remember; **the witness could not recall having seen the accused**

recapture *verb* to capture again; **six prisoners escaped, but they were all quickly recaptured**

recd = RECEIVED

receipt 1 *noun* **(a)** paper showing that money has been paid *or* that something has been received; **customs receipt; rent receipt; receipt for items purchased; please produce your receipt if you want to exchange items; receipt book** *or* **book of receipts** = book of blank receipts to be filled in when purchases are made **(b)** act of receiving something; **goods will be supplied within thirty days of receipt of order; invoices are payable within thirty days of receipt; on receipt of the notification, the company lodged an appeal; to acknowledge receipt of a letter** = to write to say that you have received a letter; **we acknowledge receipt of your letter of the 15th; in receipt of** = having receipt; **we are in receipt of a letter of complaint; he was accused of being in receipt of stolen cheques (c) receipts** = money taken in sales; **to itemize receipts and expenditure; receipts are down against the same period of last year** (NOTE: no plural for (b)) **2** *verb* to stamp *or* to sign a document to show that it has been received *or* to stamp an invoice to show that it has been paid

receive *verb* **(a)** to get something which has been delivered; **we received the payment ten days ago; the workers have not received any salary for six months; the goods were received in good condition; "received with thanks"** = words put on an invoice to show that a sum has been paid **(b) to receive stolen goods** = crime of taking in and disposing of property which you know to be stolen

◇ **receivable** *adjective* which can be received; **accounts receivable** = money owed by debtors

◇ **receivables** *plural noun* money which is owed by debtors

◇ **receiver** *noun* **(a)** person who receives something; **receiver of wrecks** = official of the Department of Trade who deals with legal problems of wrecked ships within his area **(b) Official Receiver** = (i) person who is appointed to administer a company for a period until the person who has appointed him has been paid money due; (ii) government official who is appointed to administer the liquidation of a limited company after a winding up by the court *or* the affairs of a bankrupt after a receiving order has been made; **the court appointed a receiver for the company; the company is in the hands of the receiver; the Court of Protection appointed a receiver to administer the client's affairs (c)** person who receives stolen goods and disposes of them

◇ **receivership** *noun* administration by a receiver; **the company went into receivership** = the company was put into the hands of a receiver
NOTE: no plural

◇ **receiving** *noun* **(a)** act of taking something which has been delivered; **receiving clerk** = official who works in a receiving office; **receiving department** = section of a company which deals with goods *or* payments which are received by the company; **receiving office** = office where goods *or* payments are received; **receiving stolen property** = crime of taking in and disposing of goods which are known to be stolen **(b) receiving order** = court order made placing the Official Receiver in charge of a person's assets before a bankruptcy order is made

recess *noun* period when Parliament is not sitting

recession *noun* fall in general trade *or* the economy; **the recession has put many people out of work; he lost all his money in the recession**

recidivist *noun* criminal who commits a crime again

recipient *noun* person who receives something; **the recipient of an allowance from the company**

reciprocal *adjective* given by one country *or* person *or* company to another and vice versa; (arrangement) where each party agrees to benefit the other in the same way; **reciprocal holdings** = situation where two companies own shares in each other to prevent takeover bids; **reciprocal trade** = trade between two countries; **reciprocal wills** = wills where two people (usually man and wife) leave their property to each other

◊ **reciprocate** *verb* to do the same thing to someone as he has just done to you; **they offered us an exclusive agency for their cars and we reciprocated with an offer of the agency for our buses**

◊ **reciprocity** *noun* arrangement which applies from one party to another and vice versa

recitals *plural noun* introduction to a deed *or* conveyance which sets out the main purpose and the parties to it

reckless *adjective* (person) who takes a risk even if he knows that what he does may be dangerous; **reckless driving** = offence of driving a car in a wild way where the driver does not think he is causing a risk to other people

> COMMENT: causing death by reckless driving is a notifiable offence

◊ **recklessly** *adverb* taking risks, and not caring about the effect on other people; **the company recklessly spent millions of pounds on a new factory; he was accused of driving recklessly**

◊ **recklessness** *noun* (act of) taking risks, without caring if other people may be harmed

reclaim *verb* to claim back money which has been paid earlier

recognize *verb* **(a)** to know someone *or* something because you have seen *or* heard them before; **she recognized the man who attacked her; I recognized his voice before he said who he was; do you recognize the handwriting on the letter? (b)** to approve something as being legal; **to recognize a government** = to say that a government which has taken power in a foreign country is the legal government of that country; **the prisoner refused to recognize the jurisdiction of the court** = the prisoner said that he did not believe that the court had the legal right to try him; **to recognize a union** = to accept that a union can act on behalf of staff; **although all the staff had joined the union, the management refused to recognize it; recognized agent** = agent who is approved by the company for which he acts

◊ **recognition** *noun* act of recognizing; **to grant a trade union recognition** = to recognize a trade union

◊ **recognizance** *noun* obligation undertaken by someone to a court that he *or* someone else will appear in court at a later date to answer charges, or if not, he will pay a penalty; **he was remanded on his own recognizance of £4,000; estreated recognizance** = recognizance which is forfeited because the person making it has not come to court

recommend *verb* **(a)** to suggest that something should be done; **the legal adviser recommended applying for an injunction against the directors of the company; we do not recommend bank shares as a safe investment; the Parole Board recommended him for parole; he was sentenced to life imprisonment, the judge recommending that he should serve a minimum of twenty years (b)** to say that someone *or* something is good; **I certainly would not recommend Miss Smith for the job; the board meeting recommended a dividend of 10p a share; can you recommend a good hotel in Amsterdam?**
NOTE: you recommend someone **for** a job or you recommend something **to** someone or that someone **should do something**

◇ **recommendation** *noun* **(a)** advising that something should be done; **he was sentenced to life imprisonment, with a recommendation that he should serve at least twenty years; he was released on the recommendation of the Parole Board** *or* **on the Parole Board's recommendation (b)** saying that someone *or* something is good; **we appointed him on the recommendation of his former employer**

reconcile *verb* to make two accounts *or* statements agree; **to reconcile one account with another; to reconcile the accounts**

◇ **reconciliation** *noun* making two accounts *or* parties *or* statements agree; **reconciliation statement** = statement which explains why two accounts do not agree

reconstruction *noun* new way of organizing; **the reconstruction of a company** = restructuring the finances of a company by transferring the assets to a new company

re-convict *verb* to convict someone again who has previously been convicted of a crime

◇ **re-conviction** *noun* conviction of someone who has been previously convicted of a crime; **the re-conviction rate is rising**

record **1** *noun* **(a)** report of something which has happened, especially an official transcript of a court action; **the chairman signed the minutes as a true record of the last meeting; a matter of record** = something which has been written down and can be confirmed; **for the record** *or* **to keep the record straight** = to note something which has been done; **on record** = (fact) which has been noted; **the chairman is on record as saying that profits are set to rise; off the record** = unofficially *or* in private; **he made some remarks off the record about the rising crime figures (b) records** = documents which give information; **the names of customers are kept in the company's records; we find from our records that our invoice number 1234 has not been paid (c)** description of what has happened in the past; **the clerk's record of service** *or* **service record; the company's record in industrial relations; criminal record** = note of previous crimes for which someone has been convicted; **he has a criminal record stretching back twenty years; the court was told she had no previous criminal record; track record** = success or failure of someone in the past; **he has a good track record as a detective; the company has no track record in the computer market (d)** result which is better *or* higher than anything before; **record crime figures** *or* **record losses** *or* **record profits** = crime figures *or* losses *or* profits which are higher than ever before; **1985 was a record year for bankruptcies; road accidents in 1983 equalled the record of 1980; the figure for muggings has set a new record** *or* **has broken all previous records 2** *verb* to note *or* to report; **the company has recorded another year of increased sales; your complaint has been recorded and will be investigated; the court recorded a plea of not guilty; the coroner recorded a verdict of death by misadventure; recorded delivery** = mail service where a receipt for the letter is signed by the person receiving it

◇ **recorder** *noun* part-time judge of the Crown Court; **Recorder of London** = chief judge of the Central Criminal Court; *see comment at* JUDGE

◇ **recording** *noun* making of a note; **the recording of an order** *or* **of a complaint**

recours *see* SANS

recourse *noun* **to decide to have recourse to the courts** = to decide in the end to start legal proceedings

recover *verb* **(a)** to get back something which has been lost; **he never recovered his money; the initial investment was never recovered; to recover damages from the driver of the car; to start a court action to recover property (b)** to get better *or* to rise; **the market has not recovered from the rise in oil prices; the stock market fell in the morning, but recovered during the afternoon**

◇ **recoverable** *adjective* which can be got back

◇ **recovery** *noun* **(a)** getting back something which has been lost *or* stolen; **we are aiming for the complete recovery of the money invested; to start an action for recovery of property (b)** movement upwards of shares *or* of the economy; **the economy showed signs of a recovery; the recovery of the economy after a recession**

recruit **1** *noun* new member of a police force *or* other organization; **new recruits**

have to take a special training course **2** *verb* to get people to join an organization; **twenty-five women were recruited into the local police force**

◇ **recruitment** *noun* action of recruiting; **the recruitment rate is rising** NOTE: no plural

rectify *verb* to make changes to a document to make it correct *or* to make something correct; **the court rectified its mistake**

◇ **rectification** *noun* making changes to a document *or* register to make it correct

red bag *noun* bag in which a barrister carries his gown, given him by a QC; *see also* BLUE BAG

redeem *verb* **(a)** to pay back all the principal and interest on a loan *or* a debt *or* a mortgage **(b) to redeem a bond** = to sell a bond for cash

◇ **redeemable** *adjective* which can be sold for cash; **redeemable preference shares** = preference shares which the company may buy back from the shareholder for cash

redemption *noun* **(a)** repayment of a loan; **redemption date** = date on which a loan, etc., is due to be repaid; **redemption before due date** = paying back a loan before the date when repayment is due; **redemption value** = value of a security when redeemed **(b)** repayment of a debt *or* a mortgage; **equity of redemption** = right of a mortgagor to redeem the estate by paying off the principal and interest

red tape *noun* (i) red ribbon used to tie up a pile of legal documents; (ii) rules which slow down administrative work; **the application has been held up by red tape**

reduce *verb* to make smaller *or* lower; **to reduce expenditure on prisons** *or* **on crime detection; the Appeal Court reduced the fine imposed by the magistrates** *or* **reduced the sentence to seven years' imprisonment; we have made some staff redundant to reduce costs; the government's policy is to reduce inflation to 5%**

◇ **reduced** *adjective* lower; **he received a reduced sentence on appeal; prices have fallen due to a reduced demand for the goods**

◇ **reduction** *noun* lowering of prices, etc.; **price reductions; tax reductions; staff**

reductions; reduction of expenditure; reduction in demand; a reduction in the nominal capital of a limited company requires the leave of the court

redundancy *noun* **(a)** state where someone is no longer employed, because the job is no longer necessary; **redundancy payment** = payment made to a worker to compensate for losing his job; **voluntary redundancy** = situation where the worker asks to be made redundant, usually in return for a payment **(b)** person who has lost a job because he is not needed any more; **the takeover caused 250 redundancies**

◇ **redundant** *adjective* **(a)** more than is needed *or* useless; something which is no longer needed; **this law is now redundant; a redundant clause in a contract; the new legislation has made clause 6 redundant (b) to make someone redundant** = to decide that a worker is not needed any more; **redundant staff** = staff who have lost their jobs because they are not needed any more

re-entry *noun* going back into a property; **right of re-entry** = (i) right of a landlord to take back possession of the property if the tenant breaks his agreement; (ii) right of a person resident in a country to go back into that country after leaving it for a time

re-examine *verb* (*of counsel*) to ask his own witness more questions after the witness has been cross-examined by counsel for the other party

◇ **re-examination** *noun* asking a witness more questions after cross-examination by counsel for the other party

refer *verb* **(a)** to mention *or* to deal with *or* to write about something; **we refer to your letter of May 26th; he referred to an article which he had seen in "The Times"; referring to the court order dated June 4th; the schedule before referred to** = the schedule which has been mentioned earlier **(b)** to pass a problem on to someone else to decide; **to refer a question to a committee; we have referred your complaint to the tribunal (c) the bank referred the cheque to drawer** = the bank returned the cheque to person who wrote it because there was not enough money in the account to pay it; **"refer to drawer"** = words written on a cheque which a bank refuses to pay

NOTE: **referring - referred**

◇ **referee** *noun* **(a)** person who can give a report on someone's character *or* ability *or* speed of work, etc.; **to give someone's name as referee; she gave the name of her boss as a referee; when applying please give the names of three referees (b)** person to whom a problem is passed for a decision; **the question of maintenance payments is with a court-appointed referee; official refereee** = expert judge appointed by the High Court to try complicated, usually technical, cases where specialist knowledge is required

◇ **reference** *noun* **(a)** passing a problem to a referee for his opinion; **terms of reference** = areas which a committee *or* an inspector can deal with; **under the terms of reference of the committee, it cannot investigate complaints from the public; the tribunal's terms of reference do not cover traffic offences (b)** mentioning *or* dealing with; **with reference to your letter of May 25th (c)** numbers or letters which make it possible to find a document which has been filed; **our reference: PC/MS 1234; thank you for your letter (reference 1234); please quote this reference in all correspondence; when replying please quote reference 1234 (d)** written report on someone's character *or* ability, etc.; **to write someone a reference** *or* **to give someone a reference; to ask applicants to supply references; to ask a company for trade references** *or* **for bank references** = to ask for reports from traders or a bank on the company's financial status and reputation; **letter of reference** = letter in which an employer or former employer recommends someone for a job **(e)** person who reports on someone's character *or* ability, etc.; **to give someone's name as reference; please use me as a reference if you wish**

referendum *noun* type of vote, where a whole population is asked to vote on a single question; **the government decided to hold a referendum on the abolition of capital punishment**
NOTE: plural is **referenda**

reform 1 *noun* change made to something to make it better; **they have signed an appeal for the reform of the remand system; the reform in the legislation was intended to make the court procedure more straightforward; law reform** = continuing process of revising laws to make them better suited to the needs of society 2 *verb* to change something to make it better; **the group is pressing for the prison system to be reformed; the prisoner has committed so many crimes of violence that he will never be reformed**

refrain *verb* **to refrain from something** = to agree not to do something which you were doing previously; **he was asked to give an undertaking to refrain from political activity**

refresher *noun* fee paid to counsel for the second and subsequent days of a hearing; **counsel's brief fee was £1,000 with refreshers of £250**

refund 1 *noun* money paid back; **full refund** *or* **refund in full** = refund of all the money paid 2 *verb* to pay back money; **to refund the cost of postage; travelling expenses will be refunded to witnesses giving evidence to the tribunal; all money will be refunded if the goods are not satisfactory**

refuse *verb* to say that you will not do something *or* will not accept something; **the court refused to allow the witness to speak; the accused refused to take the oath; the bank refused to lend the company any more money; he asked for a rise but it was refused; the loan was refused by the bank; the customer refused the goods** *or* **refused to accept the goods**
NOTE: you **refuse to do something** or **refuse something**

◇ **refusal** *noun* saying "No"; **his request met with a refusal** = his request was refused; **to give someone first refusal of something** = to allow someone to be the first to decide if they want something or not; **blanket refusal** = refusal to accept many different items

regard *noun* **having regard to** *or* **as regards** *or* **regarding** = concerning *or* referring to something; **having regard to the opinion of the European Parliament; as regards** *or* **regarding the second of the accused, the jury was unable to reach a majority verdict**

◇ **regardless** *adverb* **regardless of** = without concerning; **such conduct constitutes contempt of court regardless of intent; the court takes a serious view of such crimes, regardless of the age of the accused**

Regina *Latin word meaning* "the Queen": the Crown *or* state, as a party in legal proceedings
NOTE: in written reports, usually abbreviated to **R: the case of** *R.* v. *Smith*

register 1 *noun* **(a)** official list; **to enter something in a register; to keep a register up to date; companies' register** *or* **register of companies** = list of companies, showing their directors and registered addresses, and statutory information kept at Companies House for public inspection; **register of charges** = index of charges affecting land; **register of debentures** *or* **debenture register** = list of debentures over a company's assets; **register of directors** = official list of the directors of a company which has to be sent to the Registrar of Companies; **register of electors** = list of names and addresses of all people in an area who are entitled to vote in local or national elections; **land register** = list of land, showing who owns it and what buildings are on it; **Lloyd's register** = classified list showing details of all the ships in the world; **register of members** *or* **of shareholders** *or* **share register** = list of shareholders in a company with their addresses **(b)** large book for recording details (as in a hotel, where guests sign in, or in a registry where deaths are recorded) 2 *verb* **(a)** to write something in an official list *or* record; **to register a company; to register a sale; to register a property; to register a trademark; to register a marriage** *or* **a death (b)** to arrive at a hotel *or* at a conference, sign your name and write your address on a list; **they registered at the hotel under the name of MacDonald (c)** to send (a letter) by registered post; **I registered the letter, because it contained some money**

◇ **registered** *adjective* **(a)** which has been noted on an official list; **registered company** = company which has been properly formed and incorporated; **registered land** = land which has been registered with the land registry; **a company's registered office** = the address of a company which is officially registered with the Registrar of Companies and to which certain legal documents must normally be sent; **registered trademark** = trademark which has been officially recorded; **registered user** = person *or* company which has been officially given a licence to use a registered trademark **(b) registered letter** *or* **registered parcel** = letter *or* parcel which is noted by the post office before it is sent, so that compensation can be claimed if it is lost; **to send documents by registered mail** *or* **registered post**

◇ **registrar** *noun* **(a)** person who keeps official records; **Registrar of Companies** = official who keeps a record of all companies which have been incorporated, with details of directors and turnover; **registrar of trademarks** = official who keeps a record of all trademarks **(b)** official of a court who can hear preliminary arguments in civil cases **(c) district registrar** = official who registers births, marriages and deaths in a certain area

◇ **Registrar-General** *noun* official who is responsible for registry offices and the registering of births, marriages and deaths

◇ **registration** *noun* **(a)** act of having something noted on an official list; **registration of a trademark** *or* **of a share transaction; certificate of registration** *or* **registration certificate** = document showing that an item has been registered; **registration fee** = money paid to have something registered *or* money paid to attend a conference; **registration number** = official number of something which has been registered (such as the number of a car) **(b) land registration** = system of registering land and its owners

◇ **registry** *noun* **(a)** place where official records are kept; **Land Registry** = British government office where details of land are kept; **probate registry** = court office which deals with the granting of probate; **district registry** *or* **registry office** = office where records of births, marriages and deaths are kept **(b)** registering of a ship; **certificate of registry** = document showing that a ship has been officially registered; **port of registry** *or* **registry port** = port where a ship is registered

regulate *verb* **(a)** to adjust something so that it works well *or* is correct **(b)** to change *or* maintain something by law; **prices are regulated by supply and demand** = prices are increased *or* lowered according to supply and demand; **government-regulated price** = price which is imposed by the government; **regulated tenancy** = PROTECTED TENANCY

◇ **regulation** *noun* act of making sure that something will work well; **the regulation of trading practices**

◇ **regulations** *plural noun* **(a)** laws *or* rules made by ministers, which then have to be submitted to Parliament for approval; **the new government regulations on standards for electrical goods; safety regulations which apply to places of work; regulations concerning imports and exports; fire regulations** = local or national regulations which owners of buildings used by the public have to obey in order to be granted a fire certificate **(b)** rules laid down by the Commission of the European Communities, which do not have legal force in member countries

rehabilitate *verb* to make (a criminal) fit to become a member of society again

◇ **rehabilitation** *noun* making someone fit to be a member of society again; **rehabilitation of offenders** = principle whereby a person convicted of a crime and being of good character after a period of time is treated

> COMMENT: by the Rehabilitation of Offenders Act, 1974, a person who is convicted of an offence, and then spends a period of time without committing any other offence, is not required to reveal that he has a previous conviction

rehear *verb* to hear a case again (such as when the first hearing was in some way invalid)

◇ **rehearing** *noun* hearing of a case again

reign 1 *noun* period of time when someone is King or Queen; **an Act dating back to the reign of Queen Victoria 2** *verb* **(a)** to be King or Queen **(b)** to exist; **chaos reigned in the centre of town until the police arrived**

reimburse *verb* to pay someone back money which has been spent; **witnesses' travelling expenses will be reimbursed**

reinsurance *noun* insurance taken out by one insurer to protect himself in relation to insurance cover he has extended to an insured party

reject 1 *noun* thing which has been thrown out because it is not of the usual standard; **sale of rejects** *or* **of reject items; to sell off reject stock 2** *verb* to refuse to accept *or* to say that something is not satisfactory; **the appeal was rejected by the House of Lords; the union rejected the management's proposals; the magistrate rejected a request from the defendant; the company rejected the takeover bid** = the directors recommended that the shareholders should not accept the bid

◇ **rejection** *noun* refusal to accept; **the rejection of the defendant's request; the rejection of the appeal by the tribunal**

rejoinder *noun* pleading served in answer to a plaintiff's reply

relate *verb* **to relate to** = to refer to *or* to have a connection with something

◇ **related** *adjective* connected *or* linked *or* being of the same family; **offences related to drugs** *or* **drug-related offences; the law which relates to drunken driving; related company** = company which is partly owned by another company; **earnings-related pension** = pension which is linked to the size of the salary

◇ **relating to** *adverb* referring to *or* connected with; **documents relating to the case**

relation *noun* **(a) in relation to** = referring to *or* connected with; **documents in relation to the case; the court's powers in relation to children in care (b) relations** = links (with other people *or* other companies); **to enter into relations with someone** = to start discussing a business deal with someone; **to break off relations with someone** = to stop dealing with someone; **industrial relations** *or* **labour relations** = relations between management and workers; **public relations** = keeping good links between a company *or* a group and the public so that people know what the company is doing and approve of it; **public relations department** = section of a company which deals with relations with the public; **public relations officer** = official who deals with relations with the public

◇ **relationship** *noun* connection *or* link with another person *or* company; **what is the relationship between the accused and** witness?; **there is no relationship between the two crimes**

◊ **relatives** *or* **relations** *plural noun* members of a family *or* people with close family links to a certain person

◊ **relator** *noun* private person who suggests to the Attorney-General that proceedings should be brought (usually against a public body)

release 1 *noun* (a) setting (someone) free *or* allowing someone to leave prison; **release on licence** = allowing a prisoner to leave prison on parole; **day release** = arrangement whereby a company allows a worker to go to college to study for one day each week (b) abandoning of rights by someone in favour of someone else (c) **press release** = sheet giving news about something which is sent to newspapers and TV and radio stations so that they can use the information in it; **the company sent out** *or* **issued a press release about the launch of the new car** 2 *verb* (a) to free (someone *or* something) *or* to allow (someone) to leave prison; **the president released the opposition leader from prison; to release goods from customs; the customs released the goods against payment of a fine; to release someone from a debt** *or* **from a contract** = to make someone no longer liable for the debt *or* for the obligations under the contract (b) to make something public; **the company released information about the new mine in Australia; the government has refused to release figures for the number of unemployed women**

relevance *noun* connection with a subject being discussed; **counsel argued with the judge over the relevance of the documents to the case**

◊ **relevant** *adjective* which has to do with what is being discussed; **the question is not relevant to the case; which is the relevant government department? can you give me the relevant papers?**

reliable *adjective* which can be trusted; **he is a reliable witness** *or* **the witness is completely reliable; the police have reliable information about the gang's movements**

◊ **reliability** *noun* being reliable; **the court has to decide on the reliability of the witnesses**
NOTE: no plural

relief *noun* (a) remedy sought by a plaintiff in a legal action; **the relief the plaintiff sought was an injunction and damages** (b) help; **ancillary relief** = financial provision *or* adjustment of property rights ordered by a court for a spouse *or* child in divorce proceedings; **mortgage relief** = allowing someone to pay no tax on the interest payments on a mortgage; **tax relief** = allowing someone to pay less tax on certain parts of his income

rem *see* ACTION

remain *verb* (a) to be left; **half the stock remained on the shelves; we will sell off the old stock at half price and anything remaining will be thrown away** (b) to stay; **she remained behind at the office after 6.30 to finish her work**

◊ **remainder** 1 *noun* (a) things left behind; **the remainder of the stock will be sold off at half price; remainders** = new books sold cheaply (b) right to an estate which will return to the owner at the end of a lease; **contingent remainder** = remainder which is contingent upon something happening in the future; **interest in remainder** = interest in land which will come into someone's possession when another person's interest ends; **vested remainder** = remainder which is vested in someone because the identity of that person has been established; *see also* REVERSION 2 *verb* **to remainder books** = to sell new books off cheaply

remand 1 *noun* sending a prisoner away for a time when a case is adjourned to be heard at a later date; **prisoner on remand** *or* **remand prisoner** = prisoner who has been told to reappear in court at a later date; **remand centre** = special prison for keeping young persons who have been remanded in custody 2 *verb* (a) to send (a prisoner) away to reappear later to answer a case which has been adjourned; **he was remanded in custody** *or* **remanded on bail for two weeks** = he was sent to prison *or* allowed to go free on payment of bail while waiting to return to court two weeks later (b) *US* to send a case back to a lower court after a higher court has given an opinion on it

remedy 1 *noun* way of repairing harm *or* damage suffered; **the plaintiff is seeking**

remedy through the courts 2 *verb* to help repair harm *or* damage

remember *verb* to bring back into your mind something which you have seen *or* heard *or* read before; **do you remember seeing the defendant in the house?** she cannot remember where she left the jewels; he remembered the registration number of the car; the last thing he remembered was the sound of the police siren; I remember locking the door of the safe; did you remember to sign the statement?
NOTE: you **remember doing something** which you did in the past; you **remember to do something** in the future

remind *verb* to make someone remember; **I must remind the court of the details of the defendant's relationship with the plaintiff; can you remind me to lock the safe?**

◇ **reminder** *noun* letter to make a person remember to pay; **he paid the maintenance after several reminders**

remission *noun* reduction of a prison sentence; **he was sentenced to five years, but should serve only three with remission; she got six months' remission for good behaviour**
NOTE: no plural

remit *verb* **(a)** to reduce (a prison sentence) **(b)** to send (money); **to remit by cheque**
NOTE: **remitting - remitted**

◇ **remittance** *noun* money which is sent; **please send remittances to the treasurer; the family lives on a weekly remittance from their father in the USA**

remote *adjective* too far to be connected; **the court decided that the damage was too remote to be recoverable by the plaintiff**

◇ **remoteness** *noun* being too far to be connected; **remoteness of damage** = legal principle that damage that is insufficiently connected *or* foreseeable by a defendant should not make the defendant liable to the plaintiff

remove *verb* to take something away; **we can remove his name from the mailing list; the government has removed the ban on imports from Japan; the minister has removed the embargo on the sale of computer equipment; two directors were removed from the board at the AGM** = two directors were dismissed from the board

◇ **removal** *noun* **(a)** moving to a new house *or* office; **removal company** = company which specializes in moving the contents of a house *or* an office to a new building **(b)** moving an action from one court to another **(c)** sacking someone (usually a director) from a job; **the removal of the managing director is going to be very difficult**

remuneration *noun* payment for a service; **he receives no remuneration for his work as honorary secretary of the football club**
NOTE: no plural

render *verb* to make (someone *or* something) be; **failure to observe the conditions of bail renders the accused liable to arrest; the state of health of the witness renders his appearance in court impossible**

renew *verb* to grant something again so that it continues for a further period of time; **to renew a bill of exchange** *or* **to renew a lease; to renew a subscription** = to pay a subscription for another year; **to renew an insurance policy** = to pay the premium for another year's insurance

◇ **renewal** *noun* act of renewing; **renewal of a lease** *or* **of a subscription** *or* **of a bill; the lease is up for renewal next month; when is the renewal date of the bill?; renewal notice** = note sent by an insurance company asking the insured person to renew the insurance; **renewal premium** = premium to be paid to renew an insurance

renounce *verb* to give up a right *or* a planned action; **the government has renounced the use of force in dealing with international terrorists**

rent 1 *noun* money paid (or occasionally a service provided) for the use of an office *or* house *or* factory for a period of time; **high rent** *or* **low rent** = expensive *or* cheap rent; **to pay three months' rent in advance; back rent** = rent owed; **ground rent** = rent paid by the lessee to the ground landlord; **nominal rent** = very small rent; **rent action** = proceedings to obtain payment of rent owing; **rent controls** = government regulation of rents charged by landlords; **income from rents** *or* **rent income** = income from letting office *or* houses, etc.; **rent allowance** *or* **rent rebate** = state subsidy paid to poor people who do not have enough income to pay their rents; **rent**

tribunal = court which adjudicates in disputes about rents and awards fair rents **2** *verb* **(a)** to pay money to hire an office *or* house *or* factory *or* piece of equipment for a period of time; **to rent an office *or* a car; he rents an office in the centre of town; they were driving a rented car when they were stopped by the police (b) to rent (out)** = to own a car *or* office, etc. and let it to someone for money; **we rented part of the building to an American company**

◇ **rental** *noun* money paid to use an office *or* house *or* factory *or* car *or* piece of equipment, etc., for a period of time; **the telephone rental bill comes to over £500 a quarter; rental income *or* income from rentals** = income from letting offices *or* houses, etc.

◇ **rentcharge** *noun* payment of rental on freehold land

> COMMENT: rare except in the case of covenants involving land

renunciation *noun* act of giving up a right, especially the ownership of shares; **letter of renunciation** = form sent with new shares, which allows the person who has been allotted the shares to refuse to accept them and so sell them to someone else

reopen *verb* to start investigating (a case) again; to start (a hearing) again; **after receiving new evidence, the police have reopened the murder inquiry; the hearing reopened on Monday afternoon**

reorganize *verb* to organize in a new way

◇ **reorganization** *noun* new way of organizing; **the reorganization of a company *or* a company reorganization** = restructuring the finances of a company

repair 1 *noun* **(a)** mending something which is damaged; **the landlord carried out repairs to the roof; the bill for repairs to the car came to £250 (b)** state of repair = physical condition of something; **the house was in a bad state of repair when he bought it 2** *verb* to mend something which is damaged *or* broken; **full repairing lease** = lease where the tenant has to pay for all repairs to the property

◇ **repairer** *noun* person who repairs; **repairer's lien** = right of someone who has

been carrying out repairs to keep the goods until the repair bill has been paid

repatriate *verb* to force someone to leave the country he is living in and go back to his own country

◇ **repatriation** *noun* forcing someone to return to his own country

repay *verb* to pay back money borrowed *or* interest on a loan; **the loan is to be repaid at the rate of £50 a month**

◇ **repayable** *adjective* which can be repaid; **the loan is repayable over five years**

◇ **repayment** *noun* paying back a loan; **he was unable to meet *or* to keep up with his mortgage repayments**

repeal 1 *noun* abolishing a law so that it is no longer valid; **MPs are pressing for the repeal of the Immigration Act 2** *verb* to abolish *or* to do away with (a law); **the Bill seeks to repeal the existing legislation**

repeat *verb* **(a)** to say something again; **he repeated his evidence slowly so that the police officer could write it down; when asked what he planned to do, the chairman of the magistrates repeated "Nothing" (b) to repeat an offence** = to commit an offence again

◇ **repetition** *noun* act of repeating something; **repetition of a libel is an offence**

replevin *noun* action brought to obtain possession of goods which have been seized, by paying off a judgment debt

reply 1 *noun* **(a)** answer; **there was no reply to my letter *or* to my phone call; in reply to your letter of the 24th; the company's reply to the takeover bid; international postal reply coupon** = coupon which can be used in another country to pay the postage of replying to a letter; **reply paid card *or* letter** = card or letter to be sent back to the sender with a reply, the sender having already paid for the return postage **(b)** (i) written statement by a plaintiff in a civil case in answer to the defendant's defence; (ii) speech by prosecution counsel *or* counsel for the plaintiff which answers claims made by the defence; **right of reply** = right of someone to answer claims made by an opponent; **he demanded the right of reply to the newspaper allegations 2** *verb* **(a)** to answer; **to reply to a letter; the company has replied to**

the takeover bid by offering the shareholders higher dividends **(b)** to answer claims made by an opponent; to give an opposing view in a discussion

report 1 *noun* **(a)** statement describing what has happened *or* describing a state of affairs; **to make a report** *or* **to present a report** *or* **to send in a report; the court heard a report from the probation officer; the chairman has received a report from the insurance company; the company's annual report** *or* **the chairman's report** *or* **the directors' report** = document sent each year by the chairman of a company or the directors to the shareholders, explaining what the company has done during the year; **confidential report** = secret document which must not be shown to other than a few named persons; **Law Reports** = collection of reports of cases which are legal precedents; **progress report** = document which describes what progress has been made; **the treasurer's report** = document from the honorary treasurer of a society to explain the financial state of the society to its members **(b) a report in a newspaper** *or* **a newspaper report** = article *or* news item; **can you confirm the report that charges are likely to be brought? (c)** official document from a government committee; **the government has issued a report on the problems of inner city violence 2** *verb* **(a)** to make a statement describing something; **the probation officer reported on the progress of the two young criminals; he reported the damage to the insurance company; we asked the bank to report on his financial status; reporting restrictions** = restrictions on information about a case which can be reported in newspapers; **reporting restrictions were lifted** = journalists were allowed to report details of the case **(b) to report to someone** = to be responsible to *or* to be under someone; **he reports direct to the managing director (c)** to go to a place *or* to attend; **to report for an interview; please report to our London office for training; a condition of bail is that he has to report to the police station once a week**

◇ **reported case** *noun* case which has been reported in the Law Reports because of its importance as a precedent

◇ **Report Stage** *noun* stage in the discussion of a Bill in the House of Commons, where the amendments proposed at Committee Stage are debated by the whole House of Commons

repossess *verb* to take back an item which someone is buying under a hire-purchase agreement, because the purchaser cannot continue the payments

represent *verb* **(a)** to state *or* to show; **he was represented as a man of great honour (b)** to act on behalf of someone; **the defendant is represented by his solicitor (c)** to be the elected representative of an area (in Parliament *or* on a council); **he represents one of the Northern industrial constituencies**

◇ **representation** *noun* **(a)** statement, especially a statement made to persuade someone to enter into a contract; **false representation** = offence of making a wrong statement which misleads someone **(b) to make representations** = to complain **(c)** being represented by a lawyer; **the applicant had no legal representation** = he had no lawyer to represent him in court **(d)** system where the people of a country elect representatives to a Parliament which governs the country; **the Representation of the People Act** = Act of Parliament which states how elections must be organized; **proportional representation** = system of electing representatives where each political party is allocated a number of places which is directly related to the number of votes cast for each party

◇ **representative** *noun* **(a)** person who represents another person; **the court heard the representative of the insurance company; personal representative** = person who is the executor of a will *or* who is the administrator of the estate of a deceased person **(b)** *US* member of the lower house of Congress; **House of Representatives** = lower house of the American Congress
NOTE: a Representative is also referred to as **Congressman**

reprieve 1 *noun* temporarily stopping the carrying out of a sentence *or* court order **2** *verb* to stop a sentence *or* order being carried out; **he was sentenced to death but was reprieved by the president**

reprimand 1 *noun* official criticism; **the police officer received an official reprimand**

after the inquiry into the accident **2** *verb* to criticize someone officially; **he was reprimanded by the magistrate**

reproduce *verb* to make a copy of something; **the documents relating to the hearings are reproduced in the back of the report**

◊ **reproduction** *noun* making a copy of something; **the reproduction of copyright material without the permission of the copyright holder is banned by law; mechanical reproduction rights** = right to make a recording of a piece of music *or* right to make a copy of a printed document by photographing it (against payment of a fee)

repudiate *verb* to refuse to accept; **to repudiate an agreement** *or* **a contract** = to refuse to perform one's obligations under an agreement *or* contract

◊ **repudiation** *noun* refusal to accept; refusal to perform one's obligations under an agreement *or* contract

reputable *adjective* with a good reputation; **we use only reputable carriers; a reputable firm of accountants**

◊ **reputation** *noun* opinion of someone *or* something held by other people; **company with a reputation for quality; he has a reputation for being difficult to negotiate with**

request 1 *noun* asking for something; **they put in a request for a government subsidy; his request for an adjournment was turned down by the coroner; on request** = if asked for; **we will send samples on request** *or* **"samples available on request" 2** *verb* to ask for; **to request assistance from the government; the witness requested permission to give evidence sitting down**

require *verb* **(a)** to ask for *or* to demand something; **to require a full explanation of expenditure; the law requires you to submit all income to the tax authorities; the Bill requires social workers to seek the permission of the juvenile court before taking action (b)** to need; **the document requires careful study; to write the program requires a computer specialist**

◊ **requirement** *noun* what is needed; **public sector borrowing requirement** = amount of money which a government has to borrow to pay for its own spending

requisition 1 *noun* **requisition on title** = asking the vendor of a property for details of his title to the property **2** *verb* to take (private property) into the ownership of the state for the state to use; **the army requisitioned all the trucks to carry supplies**

res *Latin word meaning* "thing" *or* "matter"

◊ **res ipsa loquitur** *Latin phrase meaning* "the matter speaks for itself": situation where the facts seem so obvious, that it is for the defendant to prove he was not negligent, rather than for the plaintiff to prove his claim

◊ **res judicata** *Latin phrase meaning* "matter on which a judgment has been given"

rescind *verb* to annul *or* to cancel; **to rescind a contract** *or* **an agreement**

◊ **rescinding** *or* **rescission** *noun* cancellation of a contract

reserve 1 *noun* **(a)** money from profits not paid as dividend, but kept back by a company in case it is needed for a special purpose; **bank reserves** = cash and securities held by a bank to cover deposits; **cash reserves** = a company's reserves in cash deposits *or* bills kept in case of urgent need; **contingency reserve** *or* **emergency reserve** = money set aside in case it is needed urgently; **reserve for bad debts** = money kept by a company to cover debts which may not be paid; **hidden reserves** = illegal reserves which are not declared in the company's balance sheet; **reserve fund** = profits in a business which have not been paid out as dividend but which have been ploughed back into the business **(b) reserve currency** = strong currency held by other countries to support their own weaker currencies; **currency reserves** = foreign money held by a government to support its own currency and to pay its debts; **a country's foreign currency reserves** = a country's reserves in currencies of other countries **(c) in reserve** = kept to be used at a later date **(d) reserve (price)** = lowest price which a seller will accept at an auction; **the painting was withdrawn when it did not reach its reserve 2** *verb* **(a)** to reserve a room *or* a table *or* a seat = to book a room *or* table *or* seat to ask for a room *or* table *or* seat to be kept free for you; **I want to reserve a table for four**

people; can your secretary reserve a seat for me on the train to Glasgow? **(b)** to keep back; **to reserve one's defence** = not to present any defence at a preliminary hearing, but to wait until full trial; **to reserve judgment** = not to pass judgment immediately, but keep it back until later so that the judge has time to consider the case; **to reserve the right to do something** = to indicate that you consider that you have the right to do something, and intend to use that right in the future; **he reserved the right to cross-examine witnesses; we reserve the right to appeal against the tribunal's decision**

◇ **reservation** *noun* **(a)** booking a room *or* table *or* seat; **he phoned reservations and asked to book a room for four nights (b)** doubt; **he expressed reservations about the legality of the action; the plan was accepted by the committee with some reservations (c)** keeping something back; **reservation of title clause** = clause in a contract whereby the seller provides that title to the goods does not pass to the buyer until the buyer has paid for them; *see also* ROMALPA CLAUSE

residence *noun* **(a)** place where someone lives; **he has a country residence where he spends his weekends (b)** act of living *or* operating officially in a country; **residence permit** = official document allowing a foreigner to live in a country; **he has applied for a residence permit; she was granted a residence permit for one year**

◇ **resident** *noun* person *or* company living or operating in a country; **the company is resident in France; person ordinarily resident in the UK** = person who normally lives in the UK; **non-resident** = person *or* company which is not officially resident in a country; **he has a non-resident account with a French bank; she was granted a non-resident visa**

residue *noun* what is left over, especially what is left of an estate after debts and bequests have been made; **after paying various bequests the residue of his estate was split between his children**

◇ **residual** *adjective* remaining after everything else has gone

◇ **residuary** *adjective* referring to what is left; **residuary devisee** = person who receives the rest of the land when the other bequests have been made; **residuary estate**

= (i) estate of a dead person which has not been bequeathed in his will; (ii) what remains of an estate after the debts have been paid and bequests have been made; **residuary legatee** = person who receives the rest of the personal property after specific legacies have been made

resign *verb* to leave a job; **he resigned from his post as treasurer; he has resigned with effect from July 1st; she resigned as finance director**

◇ **resignation** *noun* act of giving up a job; **he wrote his letter of resignation to the chairman; to hand in *or* to give in *or* to send in one's resignation** = to resign from a job

resist *verb* to fight against something *or* not to give in to something; **the accused resisted all attempts to make him confess; the company is resisting the takeover bid; resisting arrest** = offence of refusing to allow oneself to be arrested

◇ **resistance** *noun* showing that people are opposed to something; **there was a lot of resistance from the prison officers to the new plan; the Home Secretary's proposal met with strong resistance from the probation service**

resolution *noun* decision taken at a meeting, especially a meeting of shareholders; **to put a resolution to a meeting** = to ask a meeting to approve a resolution; **ordinary resolution** = decision which is taken by a majority vote of shareholders; **extraordinary *or* special resolution** = resolution (such as a change to the articles of a company) which requires the holders of 75% of the shares to vote for it; *US* **joint resolution** = Bill passed by both House and Senate, sent to the President for signature to become law

resort 1 *noun* **court of last resort** = highest court from which no appeals are allowed; **lender of the last resort** = central bank which lends money to commercial banks **2** *verb* **to resort to** = to come to use; **he had to resort to threats of court action to get repayment of the money owing; workers must not resort to violence in industrial disputes**

respect 1 *noun* **with respect to** *or* **in respect of** = concerning; **his right to an indemnity in respect of earlier disbursements; the defendant**

counterclaimed for loss and damage in respect of a machine sold to him by the plaintiff **2** *verb* to pay attention to; **to respect a clause in an agreement; the company has not respected the terms of the contract**

◇ **respectively** *adverb* referring to each one separately

respondeat superior *Latin phrase meaning* "let the superior be responsible": rule that a principal is responsible for actions of the agent *or* the employer for actions of the employee

respondent *noun* (i) the other side in a case which is the subject of an appeal; (ii) person who answers a petition, especially one who is being sued for divorce; *see also* CO-RESPONDENT

responsibility *noun* (a) duty *or* thing which you are responsible for doing; **he finds the responsibilities of being managing director too heavy; keeping the interior of the building in good order is the responsibility of the tenant** (b) being responsible; **there is no responsibility on the company's part for loss of customers' property; the management accepts full responsibility for loss of goods in storage; collective responsibility** = doctrine that all members of a group (such as the British cabinet) are responsible together for the actions of that group; **age of criminal responsibility** = age at which a person is considered to be capable of committing a crime; **diminished responsibility** = state of mind of a criminal (inherited *or* caused by illness or injury) which means that he cannot be held responsible for a crime he has committed

◇ **responsible** *adjective* (a) **responsible for** = directing *or* being in charge of *or* being in control of; **the tenant is responsible for all repairs to the building; the consignee is held responsible for the goods he has received on consignment; she was responsible for a series of thefts from offices** (b) **responsible to someone** = being under someone's authority; **magistrates are responsible to the Lord Chancellor** (c) **a responsible job** = job where important decisions have to be taken *or* where the employee has many responsibilities

◇ **responsibly** *adverb* in a responsible way; **the judge congratulated the jury on acting responsibly**

restante *see* POSTE RESTANTE

restitutio in integrum *Latin phrase meaning* "returning everything to the state as it was before"

restitution *noun* (a) giving back *or* return (of property) which has been illegally obtained; **the court ordered the restitution of assets to the company; restitution order** = court order asking for property to be returned to someone (b) compensation *or* payment for damage or loss (c) (*in the EEC*) **export restitution** = subsidies to European food exporters

restrain *verb* (a) to control *or* to hold someone back; **the prisoner fought and had to be restrained by two policemen** (b) to tell someone not to do something; **the court granted the plaintiff an injunction restraining the defendant from breaching copyright**

◇ **restraining order** *noun* court order which tells a defendant not to do something while the court is still taking a decision

◇ **restraint** *noun* control; **pay restraint** *or* **wage restraint** = keeping increases in wages under control; **restraint of trade** = (i) situation where a worker is not allowed to use his knowledge in another company if he changes jobs; (ii) attempt by companies to fix prices *or* create monopolies *or* reduce competition, which could affect free trade

restrict *verb* to limit *or* to impose controls on; **the agreement restricts the company's ability to sell its products; we are restricted to twenty staff by the size of our offices; to restrict the flow of trade** *or* **to restrict imports**

◇ **restriction** *noun* limit *or* act of controlling; **import restrictions** *or* **restrictions on imports; to impose restrictions on imports** *or* **on credit** = to start limiting imports *or* credit; **to lift credit restrictions** = to allow credit to be given freely; **reporting restrictions** = restrictions on information about a case which can be reported in newspapers; **reporting restrictions were lifted** = journalists were allowed to report details of the case

◇ **restrictive** *adjective* which limits; **restrictive covenant** = clause in a contract which prevents someone from doing something; **restrictive practices** = ways of working which exclude free competition in relation to the supply of goods or labour in order to maintain prices or wages; **Restrictive Practices Court** = court which decides in cases of restrictive practices

resume *verb* to start again; **the discussions resumed after a two hour break**

résumé *noun* *US* summary of a person's life story with details of education and work experience
NOTE: GB English is **curriculum vitae**

resumption *noun* starting again; **we expect an early resumption of negotiations** = we expect negotiations will start again soon
NOTE: no plural

retail *noun* sale of small quantities of goods to individual customers; **retail price** = price to the individual customer

◊ **retailer** *noun* person who runs a retail business, selling goods to the public; *see also* WHOLESALE

retain *verb* (a) to keep; **out of the profits, the company has retained £50,000 as provision against bad debts; retained income** = profit not distributed to the shareholders as dividend (b) **to retain a lawyer to act for you** = to agree with a lawyer that he will act for you (and pay him a fee in advance)

◊ **retainer** *noun* (a) fee paid to a barrister (b) money paid in advance to someone so that he will work for you when required, and not for someone else; **we pay him a retainer of £1,000 per annum**

retaliate *verb* to act against someone who has acted against you; **the court granted an injunction to the workers, and the management retaliated by locking the office doors**

◊ **retaliation** *noun* acting against someone; **the robbers fired at the bank staff, and the police fired back in retaliation**

retire *verb* (a) to stop work and take a pension; **she retired with a £6,000 pension; the chairman of the company retired at the age of 65; the shop is owned by a retired policeman; retiring age** = age at which people retire (in the UK usually 65 for men and 60 for women) (b) to make a worker stop work and take a pension; **they decided to retire all staff over 50 years of age** (c) to come to the end of an elected term of

office; **the treasurer retires after six years; two retiring directors offer themselves for re-election** (d) to go away from a court for a period of time; **the magistrates retired to consider their verdict; the jury retired for four hours**

◊ **retiral** *noun* *US & Scottish* = RETIREMENT

◊ **retirement** *noun* (a) act of retiring from work; **to take early retirement** = to leave work before the usual age; **retirement age** = age at which people retire (in the UK usually 65 for men and 60 for women); **retirement pension** = pension which someone receives when he retires (b) (*of a jury*) going out of the courtroom to consider their verdict

retrial *noun* new trial; **the Court of Appeal ordered a retrial**

retroactive *adjective* which takes effect from a time in the past; **they received a pay rise retroactive to last January**

◊ **retroactively** *adverb* going back to a time in the past

retrospective *adjective* going back in time; **retrospective legislation** = Act of Parliament which applies to the period before the Act was passed; **with retrospective effect** = applying to a past period; **the tax ruling has retrospective effect**

◊ **retrospectively** *adverb* in a retrospective way; **the ruling is applied retrospectively**

retry *verb* to try a case a second time; **the court ordered the case to be retried**

return 1 *noun* (a) going back *or* coming back; **return journey** = journey back to where you came from; **return fare** = fare for a journey from one place to another and back again (b) sending back; **he replied by return of post** = he replied by the next post service back; **return address** = address to send back something; **these goods are all on sale or return** = if the retailer does not sell them, he sends them back to the supplier, and pays only for the items sold (c) profit *or* income from money invested; **return on investment** *or* **on capital** = profit shown as a percentage of money invested; **rate of return** = amount of interest *or* dividend produced by an investment, shown as a percentage (d) **official return** = official report *or* statement; **to make a return to the tax office** *or* **to make an income tax return** = to send a statement of income to the tax office; **to fill in a VAT return** = to complete the form showing VAT income and expenditure; **annual return** = form to be completed by each company once a year, giving details of the directors and the financial state of the company; **nil return** = report showing no sales *or* no income *or* no tax etc. **(e)** election of an MP **2** *verb* **(a)** to send back; **to return damaged stock to the wholesaler; to return a letter to sender (b)** to make a statement; **to return income of £15,000 to the tax authorities** = to notify the tax authorities that you have an income of £15,000; **returning officer** = official (usually a High Sheriff *or* mayor) who superintends a parliamentary election in a constituency and announces the result; (*of a jury*) **to return a verdict** = to state the verdict at the end of a trial; **the jury returned a verdict of not guilty (c)** to elect an MP for a constituency; **he was returned with an increased majority**

reus *see* ACTUS REUS

reveal *verb* to show something which was hidden before; **examination of the bank account revealed that large sums had been drawn out in August; the garden revealed several clues to the murder**

revenue *noun* money earned *or* income; **Inland Revenue** *or* *US* **Internal Revenue Service** = government department dealing with tax; **to make a declaration to the Inland Revenue; revenue officer** = person working in a government tax office

reversal *noun* **(a)** change of a decision; **the reversal of the High Court ruling by the Court of Appeal (b)** change from being profitable to unprofitable; **the company suffered a reversal in the Far East**

reverse 1 *adjective* opposite *or* in the opposite direction; **reverse takeover** = takeover of a large company by a small company; **reverse charge call** = telephone call where the person receiving the call agrees to pay for it **2** *verb* **(a)** to change a decision to the opposite one; **the Appeal Court reversed the decision of the High Court (b) to reverse the charges** = to make a phone call, asking the person receiving it to pay for it

revert *verb* to go back to the previous state *or* owner; **the property reverts to its original owner in 1998**

◊ **reversion** *noun* return of property to an original owner when a lease expires; **he has the reversion of the estate** = he will receive the estate when the present lease ends

◊ **reversionary** *adjective* (property) which passes to another owner on the death of the present one; **reversionary annuity** = annuity paid to someone on the death of another person; **reversionary right** = right of an writer's heir to his copyrights after his death; *see also* REMAINDER

review 1 *noun* **(a)** general examination of something again; **to conduct a review of sentencing policy; the coroner asked for a review of police procedures; financial review** = examination of an organization's finances; **judicial review** = review by a higher court of the actions of a lower court *or* of an administrative body; **wage review** *or* **salary review** = examination of salaries *or* wages in a company to see if the workers should earn more **(b)** magazine *or* monthly or weekly journal **2** *verb* to examine something generally; **a committee has been appointed to review judicial salaries; the High Court has reviewed the decision**

revise *verb* to change (a text *or* a decision) after considerable thought; **the revised examination procedures have been published; the judge revised his earlier decision not to consider a submission from defence counsel**

◊ **revision** *noun* act of changing something; **the Lord Chancellor has proposed a revision of the divorce procedures**

revocandi *see* ANIMUS

revoke *verb* to cancel *or* to annul (a permission *or* right *or* agreement *or* offer *or* will); **to revoke a clause in an agreement; the treaty on fishing rights has been revoked**

◊ **revocable** *adjective* which can be revoked

◊ **revocation** *noun* cancelling *or* annulment (of permission *or* right *or* agreement *or* offer *or* will)

revolution *noun* armed rising against a government; **the government was**

overthrown by a revolution led by the head of the army

reward *noun* payment given to someone who does a service (especially someone who finds something which has been lost *or* who gives information about something); **she offered a £50 reward to anyone who found her watch; the police have offered a reward for information about the man seen at the bank**

Rex *Latin word meaning* "the King": the Crown *or* state, as a party in legal proceedings
NOTE: in written reports, usually abbreviated to **R: the case of** *R*. v. *Smith*

rider *noun* additional clause; **to add a rider to a contract**

right *noun* **(a)** legal entitlement to something; **right of renewal of a contract; she has a right to the property; he has no right to the patent; the staff have a right to know what the company is doing; civil rights** = rights and privileges of each individual according to the law; **conjugal rights** = rights of a husband and wife in relation to each other; **constitutional right** = right which is guaranteed by the constitution of a country; **foreign rights** = legal entitlement to sell something in a foreign country; **human rights** = rights of individual men and women to basic freedoms, such as freedom of speech, freedom of association; **right to strike** = general right of workers to stop working if they have a good reason for it; **right of way** = legal title to go across someone else's property; *see also* BILL OF RIGHTS **(b) rights issue** = giving shareholders the right to buy more shares at a lower price than the current market price

◊ **rightful** *adjective* legally correct; **rightful claimant** = person who has a legal claim to something; **rightful owner** = legal owner

rigor mortis *Latin phrase meaning* "stiffening of the dead": state where a dead body becomes stiff some time after death, and which can allow a pathologist to estimate the time of death in some cases

ring *noun* group of people who try to fix the prices paid at an auction so as not to compete with each other, so making a large profit by holding a secret auction

afterwards with only the members of the group as bidders

riot 1 *noun* notifiable offence when three or more people meet illegally and plan to use force to achieve their aims *or* to frighten the public **2** *verb* to form an illegal group to use force

◊ **rioter** *noun* person who takes part in a riot; **rioters attacked the banks and post offices**

◊ **riotous assembly** *noun* meeting of people who have come together to use force to achieve their aims *or* to frighten other people

riparian *adjective* referring to the bank of a river; **riparian rights** = rights of people who own land on the bank of a river (usually the right to fish in the river)

rise 1 *noun* **(a)** increase *or* growing high; **a rise in the crime rate** *or* **in interest rates (b)** increase in salary (NOTE: US English is **raise**) **2** *verb* to move upwards *or* to become higher; **prices are rising faster than inflation; the clear-up rate for crimes of violence has risen by 15%**
NOTE: **rising - rose - has risen**

risk 1 *noun* **(a)** possible harm *or* loss *or* chance of danger; **to run a risk** = to be likely to suffer harm; **in allowing him to retain his passport, the court runs the risk that the accused may try to escape to the USA; at owner's risk** = situation where goods shipped *or* stored are the responsibility of the owner, not of the shipping company or storage company **(b)** loss *or* damage against which you are insured; **fire risk** = situation *or* goods which could start a fire; **he is a bad risk** = it is likely that an insurance company will have to pay out compensation as far as he is concerned; **he is likely to die soon, so is a bad risk for an insurance company 2** *verb* to put something in danger; **he is risking his job by complaining to the police; he risked being arrested** *or* **he risked arrest by throwing an egg at the Prime Minister**

rob *verb* to steal something from (someone), usually in a violent way; **they robbed a bank in London and stole a car to make their getaway; the gang robbed shopkeepers in the centre of the town**
NOTE: **robbing - robbed.** Note also that you rob someone **of** something

◊ **robber** *noun* person who robs people

◊ **robbery** *noun* (a) offence of stealing something from someone (usually in a violent way); **robbery with violence** = stealing goods and harming someone at the same time (b) act of stealing something with violence; **he committed three petrol station robberies in two days**
NOTE: no plural for (a)

roll *noun* (a) something which has been turned over and over to wrap round itself; **the desk calculator uses a roll of paper** (b) list of names (which used to be written on a long roll); **Roll of Solicitors** = list of admitted solicitors; **he was struck off the roll** = he was banned from practising as a solicitor; **Master of the Rolls** = judge who presides over the Court of Appeal, and is also responsible for admitting solicitors to the Roll of Solicitors

◊ **roll over** *verb* **to roll over credit** = to make credit available over a continuing period

Romalpa clause *noun* clause in a contract, whereby the seller provides that title to the goods does not pass to the buyer until the buyer has paid for them

> COMMENT: called after the case of *Aluminium Industrie Vaassen BV* v. *Romalpa Ltd*

Roman law *noun* laws which existed in the Roman Empire

> COMMENT: Roman law is the basis of the laws of many European countries but has had only negligible and indirect influence on the development of English law

root of title *noun* basic title deed which proves that the vendor has the right to sell the property

rotation *noun* taking turns; **to fill the post of chairman by rotation** = each member of the group is chairman for a period then gives the post to another member; **two directors retire by rotation** = two directors retire because they have been directors longer than any others, but can offer themselves for re-election

rough *adjective* (a) not very accurate; **rough calculation** *or* **rough estimate** = approximate answer; **rough justice** = legal processes which are not always very fair (b) not finished; **rough copy** = draft of a document which, it is expected, will have changes made to it before it is complete

◊ **roughly** *adverb* more or less; **the turnover is roughly twice last year's; the development cost of the project will be roughly £25,000**

◊ **rough out** *verb* to make a draft *or* a general design; **the finance director roughed out a plan of investment**

rout *noun* offence of gathering together of people to do some unlawful act

royal *adjective* referring to a King *or* Queen; **Royal Assent** = signing of a Bill by the Queen, confirming that the Bill is to become law as an Act of Parliament; **by Royal Command** = by order of the Queen *or* King; **Royal Commission** = group of people specially appointed by a minister to examine and report on a major problem; **Royal pardon** = pardon whereby a person convicted of a crime is forgiven and need not serve a sentence

royalty *noun* money paid to an inventor *or* writer *or* the owner of land for the right to use his property (usually a certain percentage of sales, or a certain amount per sale); **oil royalties make up a large proportion of the country's revenue; he is receiving royalties from his invention**

RSVP = REPONDEZ S'IL VOUS PLAIT; letters on an invitation showing that a reply is asked for

rule 1 *noun* (a) general order of conduct which says how things should be done; **company rules (and regulations)** = general way of working in a company; **to work to rule** = to work strictly according to the rules agreed by the company and union, and therefore to work very slowly; **Judges' Rules** = informal set of rules governing how the police should act in questioning suspects; **Rules of the Supreme Court** = rules governing practice and procedure in the Supreme Court; *see also* WHITE BOOK (b) way in which a country is governed; **the country has had ten years of military rule; the rule of law** = principle of government that all persons and bodies and the government itself are equal before and answerable to the law and that no person shall be punished without trial decision made by a court; **Rule in Rylands v. Fletcher** = rule that when a person brings a dangerous thing (substance *or* animal) to his own land, and the dangerous thing escapes and causes harm, then that person is absolutely liable for the damage caused 2 *verb* (a) to give an official decision; **we are waiting for the judge to rule on the admissibility of the defence evidence; the commission of inquiry ruled that the company was in breach of contract** (b) to be in force *or* to be current; **prices which are ruling at the moment** (c) to govern (a country); **the country is ruled by a group of army officers**

◊ **ruling** 1 *adjective* in operation at the moment *or* current; **we will invoice at ruling prices** 2 *noun* decision (made by a judge *or* magistrate *or* arbitrator, etc.); **the inquiry gave a ruling on the case; according to the ruling of the court, the contract was illegal**

run 1 *noun* (a) making a machine work; **a cheque run** = series of cheques processed through a computer; **a computer run** = period of work of a computer; **test run** = trial made of a machine *or* a work process (b) rush to buy something; **a run on the bank** = rush by customers to take deposits out of a bank which they think may close down; **a run on the pound** = rush to sell pounds and buy other currencies 2 *verb* (a) to be in force; **the lease runs for twenty years; the lease has only six months to run; a covenant which runs with the land** = covenant which is attached to an estate and has to be obeyed by each new owner of the estate when it changes hands (b) to amount to; **the costs ran into thousands of pounds** (c) to manage *or* to organize; **to run a business; she runs a mail-order business from home; they run a staff sports club; he is running a multimillion-pound company** (d) to work on a machine; **do not run the copying machine for more than four hours at a time; the computer was running invoices all night** (e) (*of buses, trains etc.*) to be working; **there is an evening plane running between London and Paris; this train runs on weekdays**
NOTE: running - ran - has run

◊ **runner** *noun* *slang* member of a gang of pickpockets who takes the items stolen and runs away with them to a safe place

rustle *verb* to steal livestock (especially cows and horses)

◊ **rustler** *noun* person who steals livestock; **a cattle rustler**

◊ **rustling** *noun* crime of stealing cattle *or* horses

Ss

sabotage *noun* malicious damage done to machines *or* equipment; **several acts of sabotage were committed against radio stations**
NOTE: no plural

sack 1 *noun* (a) large bag made of strong cloth or plastic; **the burglars carried a sack of clocks from the shop** (b) **to get the sack** = to be dismissed from a job 2 *verb* **to sack someone** = to dismiss someone from a job; **he was sacked after being late for work**

◊ **sacking** *noun* dismissal from a job; **the union protested against the sackings**

safe 1 *noun* heavy metal box which cannot be opened easily, in which valuable documents, money, etc. can be kept; **put the documents in the safe; we keep the petty cash in the safe; fire-proof safe** = safe which cannot be harmed by fire; **night safe** = safe in the outside wall of a bank, where money and documents can be deposited at night, using a special door; **wall safe** = safe fixed in a wall 2 *adjective* (a) out of danger; **keep the documents in a safe place** = in a place where they cannot be stolen or destroyed; **safe keeping** = being looked after carefully; **we put the documents into the bank for safe keeping** (b) **safe investments** = shares, etc., which are not likely to fall in value

◊ **safe deposit** *noun* safe in a bank vault where you can leave jewellery or documents

◊ **safe deposit box** *noun* small box which you can rent to keep jewellery or documents in a bank's safe

◊ **safely** *adverb* without being harmed; **the cargo was unloaded safely from the sinking ship**

◇ **safeguard** 1 *noun* protection; **the proposed legislation will provide a safeguard against illegal traders** 2 *verb* to protect; **the court acted to safeguard the interests of the shareholders**

◇ **safety** *noun* **(a)** being free from danger or risk; **Health and Safety at Work Act** = Act of Parliament which regulates what employers must do to make sure that their employees are kept healthy and safe at work; **safety margin** = time *or* space allowed for something to be safe; **to take safety precautions** *or* **safety measures** = to act to make sure something is safe; **safety regulations** = rules to make a place of work safe for the workers **(b) fire safety** = making a place of work safe for the workers in case of fire; **fire safety officer** = person in a company responsible for seeing that the workers are safe if a fire breaks out **(c) for safety** = to make something safe *or* to be safe; **put the documents in the cupboard for safety; take a copy of the disk for safety**
NOTE: no plural

sale *noun* **(a)** act of selling *or* of transferring an item *or* a property from one owner to another in exchange for a consideration, usually in the form of money; **forced sale** = selling something because a court orders it *or* because it is the only way to avoid insolvency; **sale and lease-back** = situation where a company sells a property to raise cash and then leases it back from the purchaser; **sale or return** = system where the retailer sends goods back if they are not sold, and pays the supplier only for goods sold; **bill of sale** = (i) document which the seller gives to the buyer to show that a sale has taken place; (ii) document given to a lender by a borrower to show that the lender owns a property as security for a loan; **conditions of sale** *or* **terms of sale** = list of terms under which a sale takes place (such as discounts and credit terms); **Sale of Goods Act** = Act of Parliament which regulates the selling of goods (but not land, copyrights, patents, etc.); **the law relating to the sale of goods is governed by the Sale of Goods Act 1979 (b) for sale** = ready to be sold; **to offer something for sale** *or* **to put something up for sale** = to announce that something is ready to be sold; **they put the factory up for sale; his shop is for sale; these items are not for sale to the general public (c) sales** = money received for selling something *or*

number of items sold; **sales conference** *or* **sales meeting** = meeting of sales managers, representatives, advertising staff, etc, to discuss results and plan future sales; **sales department** = section of a company which deals in selling the company's products or services; **domestic sales** *or* **home sales** = sales in the home market; **sales figures** = total sales, or sales broken down by category; **forward sales** = sales (of shares *or* commodities *or* foreign exchange) for delivery at a later date; **sales tax** = tax to be paid on each item sold **(d)** selling of goods at specially low prices; **the shop is having a sale to clear old stock; the sale price is 50% of the normal price; half-price sale** = sale of items at half the usual price; **the sales** = period when major stores sell many items at specially low prices

salvage 1 *noun* **(a)** right of a person who saves a ship from being wrecked *or* cargo from a ship which has been wrecked, to receive compensation; **salvage agreement** = agreement between the captain of a sinking ship and a salvage crew, giving the terms on which the ship will be saved; **salvage (money)** = payment made by the owner of a ship *or* a cargo to the person who has saved it from being destroyed or wrecked; **salvage vessel** = ship which specializes in saving other ships and their cargoes **(b)** goods saved from a wrecked ship *or* from a fire, etc.; **a sale of flood salvage items** (NOTE: no plural) 2 *verb* **(a)** to save goods *or* a ship from being wrecked; **we are selling off a warehouse full of salvaged goods (b)** to save something from loss; **the company is trying to salvage its reputation after the managing director was sent to prison for fraud; the receiver managed to salvage something from the failure of the company**

sample 1 *noun* small part of something taken to show what the whole is like; **they polled a sample group of voters; blood sample** *or* **urine sample** = small amount of blood *or* urine taken from someone to be tested 2 *noun* to take a small part of something and examine it; **the suspect's breath was sampled and the test proved positive**

sanction 1 *noun* **(a)** official permission to do something; **you will need the sanction of the local authorities before you can knock**

down the office block; **the payment was made without official sanction (b)** punishment for an act which goes against what is normally accepted behaviour; **(economic) sanctions** = restrictions on trade with a country in order to influence its political situation *or* in order to make its government change its policy; **to impose sanctions on a country** *or* **to lift sanctions 2** *verb* to approve *or* to permit (officially); **the board sanctioned the expenditure of £1.2m on the development plan**

sane *adjective* mentally well; **was he sane when he made the will?**

◊ **sanity** *noun* being mentally well

sans recours *French phrase meaning* "with no recourse": used to show that the endorser of a bill (as an agent acting for a principal) is not responsible for paying it

satisfaction *noun* **(a)** (i) acceptance of money *or* goods by an injured party who then cannot make any further claim; (ii) payment *or* giving of goods to someone in exchange for that person's agreement to stop a claim; **accord and satisfaction** = payment by a debtor of (part of) a debt *or* performing by a debtor of some act or service which is accepted by the creditor in full settlement, so that the debtor can no longer be sued; **memorandum of satisfaction** = document showing that a company has repaid a mortgage *or* charge **(b)** feeling of being happy *or* good feeling; **job satisfaction** = a worker's feeling that he is happy in his place of work and pleased with the work he does
NOTE: no plural

◊ **satisfy** *verb* **(a)** to convince someone that something is correct; **when opposing bail the police had to satisfy the court that the prisoner was likely to try to leave the country (b)** to make someone pleased; **to satisfy a client** = to make a client pleased with what he has purchased; **a satisfied customer** = a customer who has got what he wanted **(c)** to fulfil *or* to carry out fully; **has he satisfied all the conditions for parole? the company has not satisfied all the conditions laid down in the agreement; we cannot produce enough to satisfy the demand for the product**

save *verb* **(a)** to keep (money) *or* not to spend (money); **he is trying to save money by walking to work; she is saving to buy a house (b)** not to waste *or* to use less; **to save time, let us continue the discussion in the taxi to the airport; the government is encouraging companies to save energy (c)** to store data on a computer disk; **do not forget to save your files when you have finished correcting them**

scaffold *noun* raised platform on which executions take place

scale 1 *noun* **(a)** system which is classified into various levels; **scale of charges** *or* **scale of prices** = list showing various prices; **fixed scale of charges** = rate of charging which does not change; **scale of salaries** *or* **salary scale** = list of salaries showing different levels of pay in different jobs in the same company **(b) large scale** *or* **small scale** = working with large or small amounts of investment *or* staff, etc.; **to start in business on a small scale** = to start in business with a small staff *or* few products *or* little investment; **economies of scale** = making a product more cheaply by producing it or buying it in large quantities **2** *verb* **to scale down** *or* **to scale up** = to lower *or* to increase in proportion

scam *noun US informal* case of fraud

schedule 1 *noun* **(a)** timetable *or* plan of time drawn up in advance; **to be ahead of schedule** = to be early; **to be on schedule** = to be on time; **to be behind schedule** = to be late; **the Bill is on schedule; the Second Reading was completed ahead of schedule; I am sorry to say that we are three months behind schedule; the managing director has a busy schedule of appointments; his secretary tried to fit me into his schedule (b)** additional documents attached to a contract; **schedule of markets to which a contract applies; see the attached schedule** *or* **as per the attached schedule; the schedule before referred to (c)** list; **schedule of charges (d) tax schedules** = six types of income as classified in the Finance Acts for British tax; **Schedule A** = schedule under which tax is charged on income from land *or* buildings; **Schedule B** = schedule under which tax is charged on income from woodlands; **Schedule C** = schedule under which tax is charged on profits from government stock; **Schedule D** = schedule under which tax is charged on income from trades *or* professions, interest and other earnings not derived

scheme 252 **secondarily**

from being employed; **Schedule E =** schedule under which tax is charged on income from salaries *or* wages *or* pensions; **Schedule F =** schedule under which tax is charged on income from dividends **2** *verb* **(a)** to list officially; **scheduled prices** *or* **scheduled charges (b)** to plan the time when something will happen; **the building is scheduled for completion in May**

scheme of arrangement *noun* agreement between a company and its creditors, whereby the creditors accept an agreed sum in settlement of their claim rather than force the company into insolvency

scope *noun* limits covered by something; **the question does not come within the scope of the authority's powers; the Bill plans to increase the scope of the tribunal's authority**

screen 1 *noun* glass surface on which computer information *or* TV pictures, etc., can be shown **2** *verb* **to screen candidates** = to examine candidates to see if they are completely suitable
◊ **screening** *noun* **the screening of candidates** = examining candidates to see if they are suitable

screw *noun* *slang* prison warder

scrip *noun* certificate showing that someone owns shares in a company; **scrip issue** = new shares given free to shareholders
NOTE: no plural

seal 1 *noun* **(a)** piece of wax *or* red paper attached to a document to show that it is legally valid; stamp printed *or* marked on a document to show that it is valid; **common seal** *or* **company's seal** = metal stamp which every company must possess, used to stamp documents with the name of the company to show they have been approved officially; **to attach the company's seal to a document; contract under seal** = contract which has been signed and legally approved with the seal of the company *or* the person entering into it **(b)** piece of paper *or* metal *or* wax attached to close something, so that it can be opened only if the paper *or* metal *or* wax is removed *or* broken; **the seals on the ballot box had been tampered with; customs seal** = seal attached by customs officers to a box, to show that the contents have passed through the customs **2** *verb*

(a) to close something tightly; **the computer disks were sent in a sealed container; sealed envelope** = envelope where the back has been stuck down to close it; **the information was sent in a sealed envelope; sealed tenders** = tenders sent in sealed envelopes, which will all be opened together at a certain time; **the company has asked for sealed bids for the warehouse (b)** to attach a seal *or* to stamp something with a seal; **the customs sealed the shipment; sealed instrument** = document which has been signed and sealed
◊ **seal off** *verb* to put barriers across a street *or* an entrance to prevent people from going in or out; **police sealed off all roads leading to the town**

search 1 *noun* **(a)** examining a place to try to find something; **search warrant** = official document signed by a magistrate allowing the police to enter premises and look for persons suspected of being criminals *or* objects which are believed to have been stolen *or* dangerous or illegal substances **(b) searches** = examination of records by the lawyer acting for someone who wants to buy a property, to make sure that the vendor has the right to sell it **2** *verb* to examine a place *or* a person to try to find something *or* to look inside something to see what is there; **the agent searched his files for a record of the sale; all drivers and their cars are searched at the customs post; the police searched the area round the house for clues**

secondary *adjective* second in importance; **secondary banks** = companies which provide money for hire-purchase deals; **secondary evidence** = evidence which is not the main proof (such as copies of documents, not the original documents themselves)

COMMENT: secondary evidence can be admitted if there is no primary evidence available

secondary action *or* **secondary picketing** = picketing of another factory *or* place of work, which is not directly connected with a strike, to prevent it supplying a striking factory *or* receiving supplies from it
◊ **secondarily** *adverb* in second place; **the person making a guarantee is secondarily liable if the person who is primarily liable defaults;** *see also* PRIMARY, PRIMARILY

second degree murder *noun* *US* murder without premeditation and not committed at the same time as rape *or* robbery

second mortgage *noun* further mortgage on a property which is already mortgaged (the first mortgage still has prior claim)

Second Reading *noun* detailed presentation of a Bill in the House of Commons by the responsible minister, followed by a discussion and vote; *US* detailed examination of a Bill in the House, before it is passed to the Senate

secret *noun & adjective* (something) hidden *or* not known by many people; **the Chief Constable kept the report secret from the rest of the force; they signed a secret deal with their main competitor; to keep a secret** = not to tell someone a secret which you know; **in secret** = without telling anyone; **the gang leader met the detective inspector in secret; he photographed the plan of the bank vault in secret; official secret** = piece of information which is classified as important to the state, and which it is a crime to reveal; **Official Secrets Act** = Act of Parliament governing the publication of secrets relating to the state

◊ **secretly** *adverb* without telling anyone; **the treaty was signed secretly by the Prime Minister and the President; he offered to copy the plans secretly and sell them to another firm**

secretary *noun* (a) person who types letters *or* files documents *or* arranges meetings, etc. for someone; **secretary and personal assistant; my secretary deals with visitors; his secretary phoned to say he would be late; legal secretary** = secretary in a firm of solicitors *or* in the legal department of a company, etc. (b) official of a company *or* society; **company secretary** = person who is responsible for a company's legal and financial affairs; **honorary secretary** = person who keeps the minutes and official documents of a committee *or* club, but is not paid a salary (c) member of the British government in charge of a department; **Education Secretary; Foreign Secretary;** *US* **Secretary of the Treasury** = senior member of the government in charge of financial affairs

◊ **Secretary of State** *noun* (a) *GB* member of the government in charge of a department (b) *US* senior member of the government in charge of foreign affairs; *see also notes at* FOREIGN, MINISTER

◊ **secretarial** *adjective* referring to the work of a secretary; **she is taking a secretarial course; he is looking for secretarial work; we need extra secretarial help to deal with the mailings; secretarial college** = college which teaches typing, shorthand and word-processing

◊ **secretariat** *noun* important office and the officials who work in it; **the United Nations secretariat**

section *noun* (a) part; **legal section** = department dealing with legal matters in a company (b) part of an Act of Parliament *or* bylaw; **he does not qualify for a grant under section 2 of the Act**

sector *noun* general area of business; **private sector** = all companies which are owned by private shareholders, not by the state; **public sector** = nationalized industries and services; **public sector borrowing requirement** = amount of money which a government has to borrow to pay for its own spending

secure **1** *adjective* (a) safe *or* which cannot change; **secure job** = job from which you are not likely to be made redundant; **secure investment** = investment where you are not likely to lose money; **secure tenant** = tenant of a local authority who has the right to buy the freehold of the property he rents at a discount (b) safe *or* not likely to be opened; **the documents should be kept in a secure place; the police and army have made the border secure** **2** *verb* (a) to secure a loan = to pledge a property *or* other assets as a security for a loan (b) to make sure that (something) is done; **they secured the release of the hostages**

◊ **secured** *adjective* **secured loan** = loan which is guaranteed by the borrower giving valuable property as security; **secured creditor** = person who is owed money by someone, and holds a mortgage *or* charge on that person's property as security; **secured debts** = debts which are guaranteed by assets

◊ **securities** *plural noun* (i) investments in stocks and shares; (ii) certificates to show that someone owns stock; **gilt-edged securities** *or* **government securities** = British government stock; **the securities market** = Stock Exchange *or* place where stocks and shares can be bought or sold; **securities trader** = person whose business is buying and selling stocks and shares

◊ **security** *noun* **(a)** being safe *or* not likely to change; **security of employment** = feeling by a worker that he has the right to keep his job until he retires; **security for costs** = guarantee that a party in a dispute will pay costs; **the master ordered that the plaintiff should deposit £2,000 as security for the defendant's costs**

> COMMENT: where a foreign plaintiff or a company which may become insolvent brings proceedings against a defendant, the defendant is entitled to apply to the court for an order that the proceedings be stayed unless the plaintiff deposits money to secure the defendant's costs if the plaintiff fails in his action

security of tenure = right to keep a position *or* rented accommodation, provided that certain conditions are met **(b)** being protected; **airport security** = actions taken to protect aircraft and passengers against attack; **security guard** = person whose job is to protect money *or* valuables *or* an office against possible theft or damage; **office security** = protecting an office against theft of equipment *or* personal property *or* information; **top security prison** = prison with very strict security where category "A" prisoners are kept **(c)** being secret; **security in this office is nil** = nothing can be kept secret in this office; **security printer** = printer who prints paper money, secret government documents, etc. **(d)** social security = money *or* help provided by the government to people who need it; **he lives on social security payments (e)** guarantee that someone will repay money borrowed; **to stand security for someone** = to guarantee that if the person does not repay a loan, you will repay it for him; **to give something as security for a debt; to use a house as security for a loan; the bank lent him £20,000 without security**

◊ **Security Council** *noun* permanent ruling body of the United Nations

sedition *noun* crime of doing acts *or* speaking or publishing words which bring

the royal family or the government into hatred or contempt and encourage civil disorder (NOTE: no plural)

> COMMENT: sedition is a lesser crime than treason

◊ **seditious** *adjective* which provokes sedition; **seditious libel** = offence of publishing a libel with seditious intent

seek *verb* **(a)** to ask for; **they are seeking damages for loss of revenue; the applicant sought judicial review to quash the order; the Bill requires a social worker to seek permission of the Juvenile Court; a creditor seeking a receiving order under the Bankruptcy Act; to seek an interview** = to ask if you can see someone; **she sought an interview with the minister (b)** to look for someone *or* something; **the police are seeking a tall man who was seen near the scene of the crime; two men are being sought by the police (c)** to try to do something; **the local authority is seeking to place the ward of court in accommodation**
NOTE: **seeking - sought - has sought**

seised *adjective* **seised of a property** = being legally in possession of property

◊ **seisin** *noun* possession of land

seize *verb* to take hold of something *or* to take possession of something; **the customs seized the shipment of books; his case was seized at the airport; the court ordered the company's funds to be seized**

◊ **seizure** *noun* taking possession of something; **the court ordered the seizure of the shipment *or* of the company's funds**
NOTE: no plural

select 1 *adjective* of top quality *or* specially chosen; **our customers are very select; a select group of clients;** (*in the House of Commons*) **select committee** = special committee (with members representing various political parties) which examines the work of a ministry; **the Select Committee on Defence *or* the Defence Select Committee 2** *verb* to choose; **three members of the committee have been selected to speak at the AGM; he has been selected as a candidate for a Northern constituency**

◊ **selection** *noun* (i) choice; (ii) thing which has been chosen; **selection board *or* selection committee** = committee which chooses a candidate for a job; **selection procedure** = general method of choosing a candidate for a job

self-defence *noun* trying to protect yourself when attacked; **he pleaded that he had acted in self-defence when he had hit the mugger**
NOTE: no plural

> COMMENT: this can be used as a defence to a charge of a crime of violence, where the defendant pleads that his actions were attributable to defending himself rather than to a desire to commit violence

◊ **self-incrimination** *noun* act of incriminating yourself *or* of saying something which shows you are guilty; **right against self-incrimination** = right not to say anything, when questioned by the police, in case you may say something which could incriminate you

sell *verb* to transfer the ownership of property to another person in exchange for money; **to sell cars** *or* **to sell refrigerators; they have decided to sell their house; they tried to sell their house for £100,000; to sell something on credit; her house is difficult to sell; their products are easy to sell; to sell forward** = to sell foreign currency, commodities, etc., for delivery at a later date
NOTE: **selling - sold - has sold**

◊ **seller** *noun* **(a)** person who sells; **there were few sellers in the market, so prices remained high; seller's market** = market where the seller can ask high prices because there is a large demand for the product **(b)** thing which sells; **this book is a good seller; best-seller** = item (especially a book) which sells very well

◊ **selling** *noun* **direct selling** = selling a product direct to the customer without going through a shop; **mail-order selling** = selling by taking orders and supplying a product by post; **selling price** = price at which someone is willing to sell

semble *French word meaning* "it appears": word used in discussing a court judgment where there is some uncertainty about what the court intended

senate *noun* upper house of a parliament; **the Senate of the USA; the Senate Foreign Relations Committee**

◊ **senator** *noun* member of a senate

sender *noun* person who sends a letter *or* parcel *or* message

senior *adjective* older; more important; (worker) who has been employed longer than another; **senior manager** *or* **senior executive** = manager *or* director who has a higher rank than others; **senior partner** = partner who has a large part of the shares in a partnership; **John Smith, Senior** = the older John Smith (i.e. the father of John Smith, Junior)

◊ **seniority** *noun* being older *or* more important; being an employee of the company longer; **the managers were listed in order of seniority** = the manager who had been an employee the longest *or* the manager with the most important job was put at the top of the list

sentence 1 *noun* legal punishment given by a court to a convicted person; **he received a three-year jail sentence; the two men accused of rape face sentences of up to six years in prison; to pass sentence on someone** = to give someone the official legal punishment; **the jury returned a verdict of manslaughter and the judge will pass sentence next week; concurrent sentence** = sentence which takes place at the same time as another; **consecutive sentences** = two sentences which follow one after the other; **custodial sentence** = sentence which involves sending someone to prison **2** *verb* to give (someone) the official legal punishment; **the judge sentenced him to six months in prison** *or* **he was sentenced to six months' imprisonment; the accused was convicted of murder and will be sentenced next week;** *compare* CONVICT

◊ **sentencer** *noun* person (such as a judge) who can pass a sentence on someone

separate 1 *adjective* not together; **to send something under separate cover** = to send something in a different envelope **2** *verb* to divide; **the personnel are separated into part-timers and full-time staff**

◊ **separately** *adverb* not together; **the two brothers were charged separately**

◊ **separation** *noun* **(a)** agreement between a man and his wife to live apart from each other; **judicial** *or* **legal separation** = legal separation of man and wife, ordered by the court, where each becomes separated, but neither is allowed to marry again because they are not divorced **(b)** *US* leaving a job (resigning, retiring, or being fired or made redundant)

seq *or* **sequenter** *see* ET SEQ

sequester *or* **sequestrate** *verb* to take and keep (property) because a court has ordered it

◊ **sequestration** *noun* taking and keeping of property on the order of a court, especially seizing property from someone who is in contempt of court; **his property has been kept under sequestration**

◊ **sequestrator** *noun* person who takes and keeps property on the order of a court

sergeant *noun* **(police) sergeant** = rank in the police force above constable and below inspector

seriatim *Latin word meaning* "one after the other in order"

serious *adjective* bad *or* important; **he faces six serious charges; she claims there has been a serious miscarriage of justice**

◊ **seriousness** *noun* being serious; **the length of the prison sentence depends on the seriousness of the crime; the Police Commissioner asked for a report on the seriousness of the situation in the centre of town**

Serjeant *see* COMMON SERJEANT

servant *noun* **(a)** person who is employed by someone; **civil servant** = person who works in the civil service; **master and servant** = employer and employee; **the law of master and servant** = employment law **(b)** person who is paid to work in someone's house

serve *verb* **(a)** to spend time in prison following being sentenced to imprisonment; **he served six months in a local jail; she still has half her sentence to serve (b)** to deal with (a customer) *or* to do a type of work; **to serve articles** = to work as an articled clerk in a solicitor's office; **to serve a customer** = to take a customer's order and provide what he wants; **to serve in a shop** *or* **in a restaurant** = to deal with customers' orders; **to serve on a jury** = to be a juror **(c) to serve someone with a writ** *or* **to serve a writ on someone** = to give

someone a writ officially, so that he has to obey it

◊ **server** *noun* **process-server** = person employed to serve legal documents

service *noun* **(a) service (of process)** *or* **personal service** = delivery of a document (such as a writ *or* summons) to someone in person *or* to his solicitor; **address for service** = address where court documents (such as pleadings) can be sent to a party in a case; **to acknowledge service** = to confirm that a legal document (such as a writ) has been received; **acknowledgement of service** = document in which a defendant confirms that a writ *or* legal document has been received **(b)** duty to do work for someone; **contract of service** *or* **service contract** = contract between employer and employee showing all conditions of work; **community service order** = punishment where a convicted person is sentenced to do unpaid work in the local community; **jury service** = duty which each citizen has of serving on a jury if asked to do so; **service charge** = charge made by a landlord to cover general work done to the property (cleaning of the stairs, collection of rubbish, etc.) *or* charge made in a restaurant for serving the customer **(c) civil service** = organization and personnel which administers a country under the direction of the government

servient tenement *noun* land over which the owner grants an easement to the owner of another property

COMMENT: the grantee of the easement is the **dominant tenement**

servitude *noun* **penal servitude** = former punishment by imprisonment with hard labour

session *noun* **(a)** meeting *or* period when a group of people meets; **the morning session** *or* **the afternoon session will be held in the conference room; opening session** *or* **closing session** = first part *or* last part of a conference; **closed session** = meeting which is not open to the public or to newspaper reporters **(b)** period when Parliament is meeting; **the government is planning to introduce the Bill at the next session of Parliament (c) Court of Session** = highest civil court in Scotland

◇ **sessions** *plural noun* court; **petty sessions** = Magistrates' Court; **special sessions** = Magistrates' Court for a district which is held for a special reason (such as to deal with terrorists)

set *verb* to put

◇ **set aside** *verb* to decide not to apply a decision; **the arbitrator's award was set aside on appeal**

◇ **set down** *verb* to arrange for a trial to take place by putting it on one of the lists of trials; **pleadings must be submitted to the court when the action is set down for trial**

◇ **set forth** *verb* to put down in writing; **the argument is set forth in the document from the European Court**

◇ **set-off** *noun* counterclaim by a defendant which should be deducted from the sum being claimed by the plaintiff

◇ **set out** *verb* **(a)** to put down in writing; **the claim is set out in the enclosed document; the figures are set out in the tables at the back of the book (b)** to try to do something; **counsel for the prosecution has set out to discredit the defence witness**

settle *verb* **(a) to settle an account** = to pay what is owed; **to settle a claim** = to agree to pay what is asked for; **the insurance company refused to settle his claim for storm damage; the two parties settled out of court** = the two parties reached an agreement privately without continuing the court case **(b)** to settle **property on someone** = to arrange for land to be passed to trustees to keep for the benefit of future owners **(c)** to write out in final form; **counsel is instructed to settle the defence**

◇ **settled land** *noun* land which is subject of a settlement

◇ **settlement** *noun* **(a)** payment of an account; **settlement day** = day when accounts have to be settled; **our basic discount is 20% but we offer an extra 5% for rapid settlement** = we take a further 5% off the price if the customer pays quickly; **settlement in cash** *or* **cash settlement** = payment of an invoice in cash, not by cheque **(b)** agreement after an argument; **to effect a settlement between two parties** = to bring two parties together to make them agree; **to accept something in full settlement** = to accept money *or* service from a debtor and agree that it covers all the claim

(c) arrangement where land is passed to trustees to keep for the benefit of future owners; **marriage settlement** = arranging for property to be passed to a person who is getting married **(d)** convict settlement = prison camp where convicts are sent

◇ **settle on** *verb* to leave property to someone when you die; **he settled his property on his children**

◇ **settlor** *noun* person who settles property on someone

several *adjective* **(a)** more than a few *or* some; **several judges are retiring this year; several of our clients have received long prison sentences (b)** separate; **joint and several liability** = situation where someone who has a claim against a group of people may sue them separately or as a group

◇ **severally** *adverb* separately *or* not jointly; **they are jointly and severally liable** = they are liable both together as a group and as individuals

severance *noun* **(a)** ending of a joint tenancy **(b)** ending of a contract of employment; **severance pay** = money paid as compensation to someone who is losing his job

severe *adjective* strict *or* not kind; **the judge passed severe sentences on the rapists**

◇ **severely** *adverb* **(a)** in a strict way; **the police has asked for the gang to be treated severely (b)** strongly *or* badly; **he was severely wounded in the battle with the rebel army**

◇ **severity** *noun* being severe; **the law treats convicted rapists with great severity; the press commented on the severity of the sentences**

sexual *adjective* relating to the two sexes; **sexual intercourse** = sexual act between man and woman; **it is an offence to have sexual intercourse with a girl under sixteen years of age; sexual offences** = criminal acts where sexual intercourse takes place (such as rape, incest)

shady *adjective* not honest; **shady deal**

sham *adjective* false *or* not true; **sham marriage** = form of marriage arranged for the purpose of acquiring the nationality of the spouse *or* for other financial reasons

share 1 *noun* one of many parts into which a company's capital is divided, owned by shareholders; **he bought a block of shares in Marks and Spencer; shares fell on the London market; the company offered 1.8m shares on the market; "A" shares** = ordinary shares with limited voting rights; **"B" shares** = ordinary shares with special voting rights; **deferred shares** = shares which receive a dividend only after all other dividends have been paid; **ordinary shares** = normal shares in a company, which have no special benefits or restrictions; **preference shares** = shares (often with no voting rights) which receive their dividend before all other shares and are repaid first (at face value) if the company is liquidated; **share capital** = value of the assets of a company held as shares; **share certificate** = document proving that someone owns shares; **share issue** = selling new shares in a company to the public 2 *verb* **(a)** to own *or* use something together with someone else; **to share a telephone; to share an office (b)** to divide something among several people; **three companies share the market; to share computer time; to share the profits among the senior executives; to share information** *or* **to share data** = to give someone information which you have

◊ **shareholder** *noun* person who owns shares in a company; **shareholders' equity** = ordinary shares owned by shareholders in a company; **majority** *or* **minority shareholder** = person who owns more than *or* less than half the shares in a company; **the solicitor acting on behalf of the minority shareholders**

◊ **shareholding** *noun* group of shares in a company owned by one person; **a majority shareholding** *or* **a minority shareholding** = group of shares which are more *or* less than half the total

sharp *adjective* **(a)** sudden; **sharp rise in crimes of violence; sharp drop in prices (b) sharp practice** = way of doing business which is not honest, but not illegal

◊ **sharper** *noun* **card sharper** = person who makes a living by cheating at cards

◊ **sharply** *adverb* suddenly; **the number of mugging cases has risen sharply over the last few years**

sheriff *noun* **(a)** *US* official in charge of justice in a county **(b) (High) Sheriff** = official appointed as the government's representative in a county, responsible for executing court decisions, such as sending in bailiffs to seize property and acting as returning officer in parliamentary elections **(c)** (*in Scotland*) chief judge in a district; **Sheriff Court** = court presided over by a sheriff

ship 1 *noun* large boat for carrying passengers and cargo on the sea; **to jump ship** = to leave the ship on which you are working and not come back 2 *verb* to send goods (but not necessarily on a ship); **to ship goods to the USA; we ship all our goods by rail; the consignment of cars was shipped abroad last week**

◊ **shipment** *noun* sending of goods *or* goods sent; **consolidated shipment** = goods from different companies grouped together into a single shipment; **drop shipment** = delivery of a large order from a producer direct to a customer's shop or warehouse, without going through an agent

◊ **shipper** *noun* person who sends goods *or* who organizes the sending of goods for other customers

◊ **shipping** *noun* sending of goods; **shipping agent** = company which specializes in the sending of goods; **shipping company** *or* **shipping line** = company which owns ships; **shipping instructions** = details of how goods are to be shipped and delivered; **shipping note** = note which gives details of goods being shipped
NOTE: no plural

◊ **shipwreck** *noun* action of sinking *or* badly damaging a ship

shop 1 *noun* **(a)** place where goods are stored and sold (usually to the general public); **a bookshop; a computer shop; an electrical goods shop; he has bought a shoe shop in the centre of town; she opened a women's wear shop; all the shops in the centre of town close on Sundays; retail shop** = shop where goods are sold only to the public **(b)** place where goods are made; **machine shop** = place where working machines are kept; **repair shop** = small factory where machines are repaired **(c) closed shop** = system where a company agrees to employ only union members in certain jobs 2 *verb* **(a)** to shop (for) something = to look for thing in shops **(b)** *slang* to give information about someone to the police; **he was shopped to the police by**

the leader of the other gang
NOTE: shopping - shopped

◇ **shoplifter** *noun* person who steals goods from shops

◇ **shoplifting** *noun* offence of stealing goods from shops, by taking them when the shop is open and not paying for them

Short Cause List *noun* cases to be heard in the Queen's Bench Division which the judge thinks are not likely to take very long to hear

shorthand *noun* system of taking notes quickly by writing signs instead of letters; **the court proceedings were taken down in shorthand; the reporters could take notes in shorthand; shorthand writer** = person who takes down in shorthand evidence *or* a judgment given in court

shorthold tenancy *noun* protected tenancy for a limited period of less than five years

short sharp shock *noun* type of treatment for young offenders where they are subjected to harsh discipline for a short period in a detention centre

short title *noun* usual name by which an Act of Parliament is known

show 1 *noun* **(a)** exhibition *or* display of goods or services for sale; **motor show; computer show (b) show of hands** = way of casting votes where people show how they vote by raising their hands; **the motion was carried on a show of hands 2** *verb* to make something be seen; **to show a gain *or* a fall; to show a profit *or* a loss; to show cause** = to appear before a court to show why an order nisi should not be made absolute

SI = STATUTORY INSTRUMENT

sic *noun* used to show that this was the way a word was actually written in the document in question; **the letter stated : "my legal adviser intends to apply for attack (sic) of earnings"**

sign 1 *noun* advertising board *or* notice which advertises something **2** *verb* to write your name in a special personal way on a document to show that you have written it or approved it; **to sign a letter *or* a contract *or* a document *or* a cheque; the letter is signed by the managing director; the cheque is not valid if has not been signed by the finance director**

◇ **signatory** *noun* person who signs a contract, etc.; **you have to get the permission of all the signatories to the agreement if you want to change the terms**

◇ **signature** *noun* name written in a special way by someone, which identifies that person; **the contract has been engrossed ready for signature; a pile of letters waiting for the managing director's signature; a will needs the signature of the testator and two witnesses; all the company's cheques need two signatures**

silence *noun* not speaking; **the accused maintained silence throughout the trial; right of silence** = right of an accused not to say anything when charged with a criminal offence

silk *noun* **(a)** expensive soft material made from threads made by an insect; **to take silk** = to become a Queen's Counsel **(b)** *informal* **a silk** = a QC

similiter *Latin word meaning* "similarly" *or* "in a similar way"

simple *adjective* not complicated *or* not difficult to understand; **the case appears to be a simple one; it was a simple misunderstanding of the government regulations; simple interest** = interest calculated on the capital only, and not added to it; **simple contract** = contract which is not under seal, but is made orally *or* in writing; *see also* FEE

sincerely *adverb* **yours sincerely** *or* *US* **sincerely yours** = words used as an ending to a business letter addressed to a named person

sine die *Latin phrase meaning* "with no day"; **the hearing was adjourned sine die** = the hearing was put off to a later date without saying when it would start again

sine qua non *Latin phrase meaning* "without which nothing": condition without which something cannot work; **agreement by the management is a sine qua non of all employment contracts**

sit *verb* **(a)** to take place; **the court sat from eleven to five o'clock (b) to sit on the bench** = to be a magistrate

◇ **sitting** *noun* **(a)** meeting of a court *or* of a tribunal **(b) sittings** = periods when courts sit

> COMMENT: there are four sittings in the legal year: **Michaelmas, Hilary, Easter** and **Trinity**

site *noun* place where something is *or* where something took place; **the judge and jury visited the site of the crime; the planning application includes a photograph of the site**

situation *noun* **(a)** state of affairs; **financial situation of a company; the general situation of the economy (b)** job; **situations vacant** *or* **situations wanted** = list in a newspaper of vacancies for workers *or* of people wanting work **(c)** place where something is; **the factory is in a very pleasant situation by the sea**

◇ **situate** *or* **situated** *adjective* in a certain place; **a freehold property situate in the borough of Richmond**

slander 1 *noun* untrue spoken statement which damages someone's character; **action for slander** *or* **slander action** = case in a law court where someone says that another person had slandered him **2** *verb* **to slander someone** = to damage someone's character by saying untrue things about him; *compare* LIBEL

◇ **slanderous** *adjective* which could be slander; **he made slanderous statements about the Prime Minister on television**

sleeping partner *noun* partner who has shares in a business but does not work in it

slip *noun* **(a)** small piece of paper, especially a note of the details of a marine insurance policy; **compliments slip** = piece of paper with the name of the company printed on it, sent with documents, gifts, etc., instead of a letter **(b)** mistake; **he made a couple of slips in calculating the discount; slip rule** = name for one of the Rules of the Supreme Court allowing minor errors to be corrected on pleadings

◇ **slip up** *verb* to make a mistake; **we slipped up badly in not signing the agreement with the Chinese company**

◇ **slip-up** *noun* mistake

small *adjective* not large; **small ads** = short private advertisements in a newspaper (selling small items, asking for jobs, etc.); **small claim** = claim for less than £500 in the County Court; **small claims court** = a court which deals with disputes over small amounts of money

◇ **small-scale** *adjective* (business) working in a small way, with few staff and not much money

smuggle *verb* to take goods into *or* out of a country without declaring them to the customs; **they had to smuggle the spare parts into the country**

◇ **smuggler** *noun* person who smuggles

◇ **smuggling** *noun* offence of taking goods illegally into *or* out of a country, without paying any tax; **he made his money in arms smuggling**
NOTE: no plural

social *adjective* referring to society in general; **social security** = money *or* help provided by the government to people who need it; **social services** = department of a local *or* national government which provides a service for people who need it; **social worker** = person who works in a social services department, visiting and looking after people who need help

soft *adjective* not hard; **soft currency** = currency of a country with a weak economy, which is cheap to buy and difficult to exchange for other currencies; **soft loan** = loan (from a company *or* a government) with no interest payable

sole *adjective* only; **sole owner** *or* **sole proprietor** = person who owns a business on his own, with no partners; **sole trader** = person who runs a business by himself; *see also* FEME

solemn *adjective* **solemn and binding agreement** = agreement which is not legally binding, but which all parties are supposed to obey

solicit *verb* **(a) to solicit orders** = to ask for orders *or* to try to get people to order goods **(b)** to ask for something immoral, especially to offer to provide sexual intercourse for money

◇ **soliciting** *noun* offence of offering to provide sexual intercourse for money

◊ **solicitor** *noun* (*in England and Wales*) lawyer who has passed the examinations of the Law Society and has a valid certificate to practise and who gives advice to members of the public and acts for them in legal matters; **to instruct a solicitor** = to give orders to a solicitor to act on your behalf; **duty solicitor** = local solicitor who is on duty at a magistrates' court and can be contacted at any time by a party who is appearing in that court *or* who has been taken to a police station under arrest *or* for questioning; **the Official Solicitor** = solicitor who acts in the High Court for parties who have no one to act for them, usually because they are under an official disability

◊ **Solicitor-General** *noun* one of the law officers, a Member of the House of Commons and deputy to the Attorney-General; **Solicitor-General for Scotland** = junior law officer in Scotland

solitary confinement *noun* being kept alone in a cell, without being able to see *or* speak to other prisoners; **he was kept in solitary confinement for six months**

solus agreement *noun* agreement where one party is linked only to the other party, especially an agreement where a retailer buys all his stock from a single supplier

solve *verb* to find the answer to something; **to solve a crime** = to find out who committed a crime; **to solve a problem** = to find an answer to a problem; **the loan will solve some of our short-term problems**

solvent *adjective* having enough money to pay debts; **when he bought the company it was barely solvent**

◊ **solvency** *noun* being able to pay all debts
NOTE: no plural

sought *see* SEEK

sound *adjective* reasonable *or* which can be trusted; **the company's financial situation is very sound; the solicitor gave us some very sound advice; the evidence brought forward by the police is not very sound; of sound mind** = sane *or* mentally well; **he was of sound mind when he wrote the will**

◊ **soundness** *noun* being reasonable

source *noun* place where something comes from; **source of income; you must declare income from all sources to the Inland Revenue; income which is taxed at source** = where the tax is removed before the income is paid

South-Eastern Circuit *noun* one of the six circuits of the Crown Court to which barristers belong, with its centre in London

sovereign *noun* King *or* Queen

◊ **sovereign state** *noun* independent country which governs itself

◊ **sovereignty** *noun* power to govern; **to have sovereignty over a territory** = to have power to govern a territory
NOTE: no plural

speaker *noun* person who presides over a meeting of a parliament

COMMENT: in the House of Commons, the speaker is an ordinary Member of Parliament chosen by the other members; the equivalent in the House of Lords is the Lord Chancellor. In the US Congress, the speaker of the House of Representatives is an ordinary congressman, elected by the other congressmen; the person presiding over meetings of the Senate is the Vice-President

special *adjective* different *or* not normal *or* referring to one particular thing; **he offered us special terms; the car is being offered at a special price; special agent** = (i) person who represents someone in a particular matter; (ii) person who does secret work for a government; **special constable** = part-time policeman who works mainly at weekends or on important occasions; **special damages** = damages awarded by a court to compensate for a quantifiable loss (such as the expense of repairing something); **special deposits** = large sums of money which banks have to deposit with the Bank of England; **special procedure** = special system for dealing quickly with undefended divorce cases whereby the parties can obtain a divorce without the necessity of a full trial; **special resolution** = resolution to change the articles of a company, which has to be passed by 75% of the shareholders; **special**

sessions = magistrates' courts held for a particular reason (such as to deal with terrorists)

◇ **specialist** *noun* person *or* company which deals with one particular type of product or one subject; **you should go to a specialist in divorce cases *or* to a divorce specialist for advice**

◇ **specialize** *verb* to specialize in something = to be particularly interested *or* expert in a certain subject; **this firm of solicitors specializes in divorce cases; a QC who specializes in international contract cases**

◇ **specialty contract** *noun* contract made under seal

specific *adjective* particular *or* relating to one particular thing; **specific performance** = court order to a party to carry out his obligations in a contract

◇ **specifically** *adverb* referring to a particular thing; **the contract specifically excludes the USA; he drafted the will specifically to benefit his grandchildren**

specify *verb* to state clearly what is needed; **to specify full details of the grounds for complaint; the contract specifies that the goods have to be delivered to London**

◇ **specification** *noun* details of what is needed *or* of what is to be supplied; **patent specification** = full details of an invention which is the subject of a patent application

specimen *noun* thing which is given as a sample; **to give specimen signatures on a bank mandate** = to write the signatures of all people who can sign cheques on an account so that the bank can recognize them

speech *noun* **(a)** speaking *or* ability to talk; **freedom of speech** = being able to say what you want without being afraid of prosecution, provided that you do not break the law **(b)** talk given in public; **to make a speech in Parliament; counsel's closing speech to the jury; Queen's Speech** = speech made by the Queen at the opening of a session of Parliament which outlines the government's plans for legislation

spend *verb* **(a)** to pay money; **they spent all their savings on buying the shop; the company spends thousands of pounds on research (b)** to use time; **the tribunal spent weeks on hearing evidence; the chairman spent yesterday afternoon with the auditors; spent conviction** = previous conviction for which an accused person has been sentenced in the past and which must not be referred to in open court

NOTE: **spending - spent - has spent**

spiritual *adjective* **Lords Spiritual** = archbishops and bishops sitting in the House of Lords

spoil *verb* to ruin *or* to make something bad; **half the shipment was spoiled by water; the company's results were spoiled by the last quarter; spoilt ballot paper** = voting paper which has not been filled in correctly by the voter

NOTE: **spoiling - spoiled *or* spoilt**

◇ **spoils of war** *plural noun* goods *or* valuables taken by an army from an enemy

spouse *noun* husband *or* wife; person who is married to another person

spy 1 *noun* person who tries to find out secrets about another country; **he spent many years as a spy for the enemy; he was arrested as a spy 2** *verb* to try to find out secrets about another country; **she was accused of spying for the enemy**

squad *noun* **(a)** special group of police; **the Fraud Squad** = department of a police force which deals with cases of fraud; **the Homicide Squad** *or* **Murder Squad** = department of a police force which deals with cases of murder **(b)** special group of soldiers *or* workers; **firing squad** = group of soldiers who execute someone by shooting

◇ **squad car** *noun* police patrol car

squat *verb* to occupy premises belonging to another person unlawfully and without title *or* without paying rent

NOTE: **squatting - squatted**

◇ **squatter** *noun* person who squats in someone else's property; **squatter's rights** = rights of a person who is squatting in another person's property to remain in unlawful possession of premises until ordered to leave by a court

squeal *verb* *slang* to inform the police about other criminals

squire *noun* *US* local legal official, such as a magistrate

stakeholder *noun* person who holds money impartially (such as money deposited by one of the parties to a wager) until he has to give it up to another party

stamp 1 *noun* (a) (i) device for making marks on documents; (ii) mark made in this way; **the invoice has the stamp "Received with thanks" on it; the customs officer looked at the stamps in his passport; date stamp** = stamp with rubber figures which can be moved, used for marking the date on documents; **rubber stamp** = stamp made of hard rubber cut to form words **(b)** small piece of gummed paper which you buy from a post office and stick on a letter *or* parcel to pay for the postage; **a postage stamp; a £1 stamp (c) stamp duty** = tax on legal documents (such as the conveyance of a property to a new owner *or* the contract for the purchase of shares) 2 *verb* **(a)** to mark a document with a stamp; **to stamp an invoice "Paid"; the documents were stamped by the customs officials (b)** to put a postage stamp on (an envelope, etc.); **stamped addressed envelope** = envelope with your own address written on it and a stamp stuck on it to pay for the return postage

stand down *verb* to withdraw your name from an election; **the wife of one of the candidates is ill and he has stood down**

◇ **stand in for** *verb* to take the place of someone; **Mr Smith is standing in for the chairman who is away on holiday**

◇ **stand over** *verb* to adjourn; **the case has been stood over to next month**

standard 1 *noun* normal quality *or* normal conditions against which other things are judged; **standard of living** *or* **living standards** = quality of personal home life (such as amount of food or clothes bought, size of family car); **production standards** = quality of production; **up to standard** = of acceptable quality; **gold standard** = attaching of the value of a currency to value of a quantity of gold 2 *adjective* normal *or* usual; **the standard charge for consultation is £50; we have a standard charge of £25 for a thirty minute session; standard agreement** *or* **standard contract** = normal printed contract form; **standard form contract** = contract which states the conditions of carrying out a common commercial arrangement (such as

chartering a ship); **standard letter** = letter which is sent with only minor changes to various correspondents; **standard rate** = basic rate of income tax which is paid by most taxpayers *or* basic rate of VAT which is levied on most goods and services

standi *see* LOCUS

standing 1 *adjective* permanent; **standing committee** = (i) permanent committee which always examines the same problem; (ii) committee of Members of Parliament which examines in detail Bills which are not passed to other committees; *see also* AD HOC 2 *noun* **(a) long-standing customer** *or* **customer of long standing** = person who has been a customer for many years **(b)** good reputation; **the financial standing of a company; company of good standing** = very reputable company

◇ **standing order** *noun* **(a)** order written by a customer asking a bank to pay money regularly to an account; **I pay my subscription by standing order;** *compare* DIRECT DEBIT **(b) standing orders** = rules *or* regulations which regulate conduct in any body, such as the House of Commons *or* an army camp *or* a police station

Star Chamber *noun* **(a)** formerly, a royal court which tried cases without a jury **(b)** cabinet committee which examines the spending proposals of government departments

stare decisis *Latin phrase meaning* "stand by preceding decisions": principle that courts must abide by precedents set by judgments made in higher courts

state 1 *noun* **(a)** independent country; semi-independent section of a federal country (such as the USA); **to turn state's evidence** = to confess to a crime and then act as a witness against the other criminals involved in the hope of getting a lighter sentence; *see also* SECRETARY OF STATE **(b)** government of a country; **offence against the state** = act of attacking the lawful government of a country; **state enterprise** = company run by the state; **the bosses of state industries are appointed by the government; state ownership** = situation where an industry is nationalized 2 *verb* to say clearly; **the document states that all revenue has to be declared to the tax office; case stated** = statement of the facts of a case which has been heard in a lower court, drawn up so that a higher court can decide on an appeal

◇ **state-controlled** *adjective* run by the state; **state-controlled television**

◇ **State Department** *noun* US government department dealing with relations between the USA and other countries; *see note at* FOREIGN

◇ **stateless person** *noun* person who is not a citizen of any state

◇ **state-owned** *adjective* owned by the state

statement *noun* (a) saying something clearly; **to make a statement** = to give details of something to the press *or* to the police; **to make a false statement** = to give wrong details; **statement of affairs** = official statement made by a bankrupt *or* an insolvent company, listing its assets and liabilities; **statement of claim** = pleading containing details of a plaintiff's case and the relief sought against the defendant; **Statement of Means** = statement showing the financial position of the claimant, attached to an application for Legal Aid; **bank statement** = written document from a bank showing the balance of an account; **monthly *or* quarterly statement** = statement which is sent every month *or* every quarter by the bank (b) **financial statement** = document which shows the financial situation of a company; **the accounts department have prepared a financial statement for the shareholders (c) statement of account** = list of invoices and credits and debits sent by a supplier to a customer at the end of each month

station 1 *noun* (a) **police station** = building where the police have their local offices; **six demonstrators were arrested and taken to the police station; he spent the night in the station cells** (b) place where trains stop for passengers; **the train leaves the Central Station at 14.15 (c)** TV station *or* radio station = building where TV or radio programmes are produced 2 *verb* to place someone on duty; **six police officers were stationed at the door of the courtroom**

stationer *noun* person who makes *or* supplies paper, pens, typewriter ribbons, etc.; **law stationer** = person who specializes in supplying stationery to legal firms

◇ **stationery** *noun* office supplies for writing, such as paper, typewriter ribbons,

pens, etc.; **legal stationery supplier; shop selling office stationery; continuous stationery** = paper made as a long sheet used in computer printers; **Her Majesty's Stationery Office (HMSO)** = government office which produces state documents and government stationery
NOTE: no plural

status *noun* (a) importance *or* position in society; **loss of status** = becoming less important in a group; **status inquiry** = checking on a customer's credit rating (b) **legal status** = legal identity of a person *or* body (such as a company *or* partnership)
NOTE: no plural

◇ **status quo** *noun* state of things as they are now; **the contract does not alter the status quo; status quo ante** = the situation as it was before

statute *noun* established written law, especially an Act of Parliament; **statute book** = all laws passed by Parliament which are still in force; **statute of limitations** = law which prevents a plaintiff from bringing proceedings after a certain period of time (usually six years)

◇ **statute-barred** *adjective* which cannot take place because the time laid down in the statute of limitations has expired

◇ **statutorily** *adverb* by statute; **a statutorily protected tenant**

◇ **statutory** *adjective* fixed by law *or* by a statute; **there is a statutory period of probation of thirteen weeks; the authority has a statutory obligation to provide free education to all children; powers conferred on an authority by the statutory code; statutory books** = official registers which a company must keep; **statutory declaration** = (i) statement made to the Registrar of Companies that a company has complied with certain legal conditions; (ii) declaration signed and witnessed for official purposes; **statutory duty** = duty which someone must perform and which is laid down by statute; **statutory holiday** = holiday which is fixed by law; **statutory instrument** = order (which has the force of law) made under authority granted to a minister by an Act of Parliament; **statutory undertakers** = bodies formed by statute and having legal duties to provide services (such as gas, electricity, water)

stay 1 *noun* (a) length of time spent in one place; **the tourists were in town only for**

a short stay **(b)** temporary stopping of an order made by a court; **stay of execution =** temporary prevention of someone from enforcing a judgment; **the court granted the company a two-week stay of execution; stay of proceedings =** stopping of a case which is being heard **2** *verb* **(a)** to stop at a place; **the chairman is staying at the Hotel London; inflation has stayed high in spite of the government's efforts to bring it down (b)** to stop (an action) temporarily; **the defendant made an application to stay the proceedings until the plaintiff gave security for costs**

steal *verb* to take something which does not belong to you; **two burglars broke into the office and stole the petty cash; one of our managers left to form his own company and stole the list of our clients' addresses; one of our biggest problems is stealing in the wine department; stolen goods =** goods which have been stolen; **handling** *or* **receiving stolen goods =** offence of dealing with goods (receiving them *or* selling them) which you know to have been stolen
NOTE: **stealing - stole - has stolen.** Note also that you steal things **from** a person *or* company

◊ **stealing** *noun* crime of taking property which belongs to someone else; **going equipped for stealing =** notifiable offence of carrying tools which could be used for burglary

stenographer *noun* official person who can write in shorthand and so take records of what is said in court

step- *prefix* showing a family relationship through a parent who has married again; **step-father =** man who has married a child's mother, but is not the natural father of the child

stiff *adjective* strong *or* difficult; **he received a stiff prison sentence; he had to take a stiff test before he qualified**

stipendiary magistrate *noun* magistrate who is a qualified lawyer and who receives a salary (as opposed to an unpaid Justice of the Peace)

> COMMENT: a stipendiary magistrate usually sits alone

stipulate *verb* to demand that a condition be put into a contract; **to stipulate that the contract should run for five years;**

to pay the stipulated charges; the company failed to pay on the stipulated date *or* **on the date stipulated in the contract; the contract stipulates that the seller pays the buyer's legal costs**

◊ **stipulation** *noun* condition in a contract

stirpes *see* PER STIRPES

stock **1** *noun* **(a)** quantity of raw materials; **we have large stocks of oil** *or* **coal; the country's stocks of butter** *or* **sugar (b)** quantity of goods for sale; **opening stock =** details of stock at the beginning of an accounting period; **closing stock =** details of stock at the end of an accounting period; **stock control =** making sure that enough stock is kept and that quantities and movements of stock are noted; **stock valuation =** estimating the value of stock at the end of an accounting period; **to buy a shop with stock at valuation =** to pay for the stock the same amount as its value, as estimated by an independent valuer **(c) in stock** *or* **out of stock =** available *or* not available in the warehouse *or* store **(d) stocks and shares =** shares in ordinary companies; **stock certificate =** document proving that someone owns shares in a company; **debenture stock =** capital borrowed by a company, using its fixed assets as security; **dollar stocks =** shares in American companies; **government stocks =** government securities; **loan stock =** money lent to a company at a fixed rate of interest; *US* **common stock =** ordinary shares in a company giving the shareholders the right to vote at meetings and receive a dividend **2** *verb* to hold goods for sale in a warehouse *or* store

◊ **stockbroker** *noun* person who buys or sells stocks and shares for clients; **stockbroker's commission =** payment to a broker for a deal carried out on behalf of a client

◊ **stockbroking** *noun* trade of dealing in shares for clients; **a stockbroking firm**

◊ **Stock Exchange** *noun* place where stocks and shares are bought and sold; **he works on the Stock Exchange; shares in the company are traded on the Stock Exchange; Stock Exchange listing =** official list of shares which can be bought or sold on the Stock Exchange

◊ **stockholder** *noun* person who holds shares in a company

◊ **stockholding** *noun* shares in a company held by someone

◊ **stock jobber** *noun* person who buys and sells shares from other traders on the Stock Exchange

> COMMENT: stock jobbers are now being replaced by **market makers**

◊ **stock jobbing** *noun* buying and selling shares from other traders on the Stock Exchange
NOTE: no plural

◊ **stock market** *noun* place where shares are bought and sold; **stock market price** *or* **price on the stock market; stock market valuation** = value of shares based on the current market price

straight *adjective* direct *or* not dishonest; **to play straight** *or* **to act straight with someone** = to act honestly with someone; **to go straight** = to stop criminal activities

strict *adjective* exact; **in strict order of seniority; to follow a strict interpretation of the rules; strict liability** = total liability for an offence which has been committed (whether you are at fault or not)

◊ **strictly** *adverb* exactly; **the police ask all drivers to follow strictly the new highway code**

strife *noun* violent public arguments and disorder; **civil strife** = trouble when gangs of people fight each other

strike 1 *noun* **(a)** stopping of work by the workers (because of lack of agreement with management *or* because of orders from a union); **general strike** = strike of all the workers in a country; **official strike** = strike which has been approved by the union; **protest strike** = strike in protest at a particular grievance; **token strike** = short strike to show that workers have a grievance; **unofficial strike** = strike by local workers, which has not been approved by the union as a whole **(b) to take strike action** = to go on strike; **strike ballot** *or* **strike vote** = vote by workers to decide if a strike should be held; **strike call** = demand by a union for a strike; **no-strike agreement** *or* **no-strike clause** = (clause in an) agreement where the workers say that they will never strike; **strike fund** = money collected by a trade union from its members, used to pay strike pay; **strike**

pay = money paid to striking workers by their trade union during a strike **(c) to come out on strike** *or* **to go on strike** = to stop work; **the office workers are on strike for higher pay; to call the workers out on strike** = to tell the workers to stop work 2 *verb* **(a)** to stop working because there is no agreement with management; **to strike for higher wages** *or* **for shorter working hours; to strike in protest against bad working conditions; to strike in sympathy with the postal workers** = to strike to show that you agree with the postal workers who are on strike **(b)** to hit (someone); **two policemen were struck by bottles; he was struck on the head by a cosh**
NOTE: **striking - struck**

◊ **strike off** *verb* to cross off (a name from a list); **to strike someone off the rolls** = to stop a solicitor from practising by removing his name from the list of solicitors

◊ **strike out** *verb* to cancel an action which has started, because the plaintiff has not appeared or for some other reason; **the statement of claim was struck out because it disclosed no cause of action**

strong *adjective* with a lot of force *or* strength; **a strong demand for the abolition of capital punishment; the country needs a strong police force**

◊ **strongbox** *noun* safe *or* heavy metal box which cannot be opened easily, in which valuable documents, money, etc., can be kept

◊ **strongroom** *noun* special room (in a bank) where valuable documents, money, gold, etc., can be kept

study 1 *noun* report which examines something carefully; **the government has asked the commission to prepare a study of prison systems in other countries; he has read the government study on inner city crime; to carry out a feasibility study on a project** = to examine the costs and possible profits to see if the project should be started 2 *verb* to examine (something) carefully; **we are studying the possibility of setting up an office in New York; the government studied the committee's proposals for two months**

sub- *prefix* under *or* less important; **sub-agency** = small agency which is part of a large agency; **sub-agent** = person who is in charge of a sub-agency; **sub-committee** = small committee which reports on a special subject to a main committee; **he is chairman of the Finance Sub-Committee; sub-post office** = small post office which is usually on the same premises as a general store

subcontract 1 *noun* contract between the main contractor for a whole project and another firm who will do part of the work; **they have been awarded the subcontract for all the electrical work in the new building; we will put the electrical work out to subcontract** 2 *verb* to agree with a company that they will do part of the work for a project; **the electrical work has been subcontracted to Smith Ltd**

◊ **subcontractor** *noun* company which has a contract to do work for a main contractor

subject *noun* (a) what something is concerned with; **the subject of the action was the liability of the defendant for the plaintiff's injuries** (b) person who is a citizen of a country and bound by its laws; **he is a British subject; British subjects do not need visas to visit Common Market countries; liberty of the subject** = right of a citizen to be free unless convicted of a crime which is punishable by imprisonment

◊ **subject to** 1 *adjective* (a) depending on; **the contract is subject to government approval** = the contract will be valid only if it is approved by the government; **agreement *or* sale subject to contract** = agreement *or* sale which is not legal until a proper contract has been signed; **offer subject to availability** = the offer is valid only if the goods are available (b) which can receive; **these articles are subject to import tax** = import tax has to be paid on these articles 2 *verb* to make someone suffer something; **he was subjected to torture; she subjected her husband to bad treatment**

sub judice *Latin phrase meaning* "under the law": being considered by a court (and so not to be mentioned in the media or in Parliament); **the papers cannot report the case because it is still sub judice**

sublease 1 *noun* lease from a tenant to another tenant 2 *verb* to lease a leased property from another tenant; **they subleased a small office in the centre of town**

◊ **sublessee** *noun* person *or* company which holds a property on a sublease

◊ **sublessor** *noun* tenant who lets a leased property to another tenant

◊ **sublet** *verb* to let a leased property to another tenant; **we have sublet part of our office to a financial consultancy**
NOTE: **subletting - sublet - has sublet**

submit *verb* (a) to put (something) forward to be examined; **to submit a proposal to the committee; he submitted a claim to the insurers** (b) to plead an argument in court; **counsel submitted that the defendant had no case to answer; it was submitted that the right of self-defence can be available only against unlawful attack** (c) to agree to be ruled by something; **he refused to submit to the jurisdiction of the court**
NOTE: **submitting - submitted**

◊ **submission** *noun* pleading an argument in court; **the court heard the submission of defence counsel that there was no case to answer *or* in the submission of defence counsel there was no case to answer**

subordinate 1 *adjective* less important; **subordinate to** = governed by *or* which depends on 2 *noun* member of staff who is directed by someone; **his subordinates find him difficult to work with**

subornation of perjury *noun* offence of getting someone to commit perjury

subpoena 1 *noun* court order requiring someone to appear in court; **subpoena ad testificandum** = court order requiring someone to appear as a witness; **subpoena duces tecum** = court order requiring someone to appear as a witness and bring with him documents relevant to the case 2 *verb* to order someone to appear in court; **the finance director was subpoenaed by the prosecution**

subrogation *noun* legal principle whereby someone stands in the place of another person and acquires that person's rights and is responsible for that person's liabilities

subscribe *verb* (a) **to subscribe to a magazine** = to pay for a series of issues of a magazine **(b) to subscribe for shares** = to apply to buy shares in a new company

◇ **subscriber** *noun* person who subscribes (to a magazine *or* for shares in a new company); **subscriber shares** = the first shares issued when a new company is formed

subsequent *adjective* which follows because of something; **condition subsequent** = condition which says that a contract will be modified *or* annulled if something is not done

subsidiary *adjective* less important than *or* depending on (something); **he faces one serious charge and several subsidiary charges arising out of the main charge; subsidiary company** = company which is owned by a parent company

subsidize *verb* to help by giving money; **the government has refused to subsidize the car industry; subsidized accommodation** = cheap accommodation which is partly paid for by an employer *or* a local authority, etc.

◇ **subsidy** *noun* **(a)** money given to help something which is not profitable; **the industry exists on government subsidies; the government has increased its subsidy to the car industry (b)** money given by a government to make a product cheaper

substance *noun* **(a)** material; **dangerous substance** = material which may cause harm to someone **(b)** real basis of a report *or* argument; **there is no substance to the stories about his resignation**

substandard *adjective* not of the necessary quality to meet a standard

substantial *adjective* large *or* important; **she was awarded substantial damages** = she received a large sum of money as damages; **to acquire a substantial interest in a company** = to buy a large number of shares in a company

substantive *adjective* real *or* actual; **substantive law** = all laws including common law and statute law which deal with legal principles (as opposed to procedural law which refers to the procedure for putting law into practice); **substantive offence** = offence which has actually taken place

substitute 1 *noun* person *or* thing which takes the place of someone *or* something else **2** *verb* to take the place of something else; **substituted service** = serving a legal document on someone other than by the legally prescribed method, for example by posting it to the last known address *or* by advertising

subtenancy *noun* agreement to sublet a property

◇ **subtenant** *noun* person *or* company to which a property has been sublet

subversive *adjective* which acts secretly against the government; **the police is investigating subversive groups in the student organizations**

succeed *verb* to follow, especially to take the place of someone who has retired *or* died; **to succeed to a property** = to become the owner of a property by inheriting it from someone who has died

◇ **succession** *noun* acquiring property *or* title from someone who has died; **law of succession** = laws relating to how property shall pass to others when the owner dies; **intestate succession** = rules which apply when someone dies without having made a will

◇ **successor** *noun* person who takes over from someone; **Mr Smith's successor as chairman will be Mr Jones**

sue *verb* to take someone to court *or* to start legal proceedings against someone to get compensation for a wrong; **to sue someone for damages; he is suing the company for £50,000 compensation**

sufferance *noun* agreement to something which is not stated, but assumed because no objection has been raised; **he has been allowed to live in the house on sufferance; tenancy at sufferance** = situation where a previously lawful tenant is still in possession of property after the termination of the lease

sufficient *adjective* enough; **the company has sufficient funds to pay for its expansion programme**

suffrage *noun* right to vote in elections; **universal suffrage** = right of all citizens to vote
NOTE: no plural

suggest *verb* to put forward a proposal; **the chairman suggested (that) the next meeting should be held in October; we suggested Mr Smith for the post of treasurer**

◇ **suggestion** *noun* proposal *or* idea which is put forward; **suggestion box** = place in a company where members of staff can put forward their ideas for making the company more efficient and profitable

suicide *noun* **(a)** act of killing yourself; **after shooting his wife, he committed suicide in the bedroom; the police are treating the death as suicide, not murder; to commit suicide** = to kill yourself; **suicide pact** = agreement between two or more people that they will all commit suicide at the same time **(b)** person who has committed suicide

COMMENT: aiding suicide is a notifiable offence

◇ **suicidal** *adjective* likely to commit suicide; **the warders should keep close watch on that prisoner - we think he may be suicidal**

sui generis *Latin phrase meaning* "of its own right": (thing) which is in a class of its own

sui juris *Latin phrase meaning* "in one's own right": (person) who is able to make contracts and sue others *or* be sued himself

suit *noun* civil legal proceedings *or* lawsuit; *US* **class suit** = legal action brought on behalf of several people

suitable *adjective* convenient *or* which fits; **Wednesday is the most suitable day for the hearing; we had to advertise the job again because there were no suitable candidates**

sum 1 *noun* **(a)** quantity of money; **a sum of money was stolen from the personnel office; he lost large sums on the Stock Exchange; she received the sum of £500 in compensation; the sum insured** = the largest amount which an insurer will pay under the terms of an insurance; **lump sum** = money paid in one payment, not in several small payments **(b)** 2 *verb* (*of a judge*) **to sum up** = to speak at the end of a

trial and review all the evidence and arguments for the benefit of the jury
NOTE: **summing - summed**

◇ **summing up** *noun* speech by the judge at the end of a trial, where he reviews all the evidence and arguments and notes important points of law for the benefit of the jury
NOTE: US English is **instructions**

summary 1 *noun* short account of what has happened *or* of what has been written; **the chairman gave a summary of his discussions with the German delegation; the police inspector gave a summary of events leading to the raid on the house** 2 *adjective* which happens immediately; **summary arrest** = arrest without a warrant; **summary conviction** = conviction by a magistrate sitting without a jury; **summary dismissal** = dismissal of an employee without giving the notice stated in the contract of employment; **summary judgment** = immediate judgment of a case which is applied for by a plaintiff when he believes the defendant cannot put forward any sensible defence; **summary jurisdiction** = power of a magistrates' court to try a case without a jury *or* to try a case immediately without referring it to the Crown Court; **summary offence** = minor crime which can be tried only in a magistrates' court

◇ **summarily** *adverb* immediately; **magistrates can try a case summarily or refer it to the Crown Court**

◇ **summarize** *verb* to make a short account of something; **the case was summarized in the evening papers**

summon *verb* to call someone to come; **he was summoned to appear before the committee**

◇ **summons** *noun* official command from a court requiring someone to appear in court to be tried for a criminal offence *or* to defend a civil action; **he tore up the summons and went on holiday to Spain; judgment summons** = summons by a court ordering a judgment debtor to pay or to go to prison; **originating summons** = summons whereby a legal action is commenced (usually in the Chancery Division of the High Court in cases relating to land or the administration of an estate) **writ of summons** = document which starts a legal action in the High Court

sundry *adjective & noun* various; **sundry items** *or* **sundries** = small items which are not listed in detail

supergrass *noun slang* person (usually a criminal) who gives information to the police about a large number of criminals

superintend *verb* to be in charge of; **he superintends the company's overseas sales**

◊ **superintendent** *noun* person in charge; **(police) superintendent** = high rank in a police force, above Chief Inspector and below Chief Superintendent

superior 1 *adjective* **(a)** better *or* of better quality; **our product is superior to all competing products; their sales are higher because of their superior service (b)** higher *or* more important; **the case will be heard in a superior court; he tried to blackmail a superior officer** 2 *noun* more important person; **each manager is responsible to his superior for accurate reporting of sales**

supersede *verb* to take the place of; **the government has published a Bill to supersede the current legislation**

supervise *verb* to watch work carefully to see if it is well done; **the move to the new offices was supervised by the administrative manager; she supervises six girls in the legal department**

◊ **supervision** *noun* being supervised *or* orders given to someone who is supervised; **new staff work under supervision for the first three months; she is very experienced and can be left to work without any supervision; the cash was counted under the supervision of the finance director; supervision order** = court order for a young offender to be placed under the supervision of the probation service
NOTE: no plural

◊ **supervisor** *noun* person who supervises

◊ **supervisory** *adjective* as a supervisor; **supervisory staff; he works in a supervisory capacity**

supply 1 *noun* **(a)** providing something which is needed; **money supply** = amount of money which exists in a country; **Supply Bill** = Bill for providing money for government requirements; **supply price** = price at which something is provided; **supply and demand** = amount of a product

which is available at a certain price and the amount which is wanted by customers at that price; **the law of supply and demand** = general rule that the amount of a product which is available is related to the needs of the possible customers **(b) in short supply** = not available in large enough quantities to meet the demand; **spare parts are in short supply because of the strike (c)** stock of something which is needed; **the factory is running short of supplies of coal; supplies of coal have been reduced; office supplies** = goods needed to run an office (such as paper, pens, type-writers) **(d) supplies** = goods *or* services provided; **exempt supplies** = sales of goods *or* services which are exempt from VAT 2 *verb* to provide something which is needed; **to supply a factory with spare parts; the prosecution supplied the court with a detailed map of the area where the crime took place; details of staff addresses and phone numbers can be supplied by the personnel department**

◊ **supplier** *noun* person *or* company which supplies something

support 1 *noun* **(a)** giving money to help; **the government has provided support to the computer industry; we have no financial support from the banks (b)** agreement *or* encouragement; **the chairman has the support of the committee; support price** = price (in the EEC) at which a government will buy farm produce to stop the price from falling 2 *verb* **(a)** to give money to help; **the government is supporting the computer industry to the tune of $2m per annum; we hope the banks will support us during the expansion period (b)** to encourage *or* to agree with; **she hopes the other members of the committee will support her; the market will not support another price increase**

suppress *verb* to stop something from being made public; **the government tried to suppress the news about the prison riot**

◊ **suppression** *noun* act of suppressing; **the suppression of the truth about the case**

suppressio veri *Latin phrase meaning* "suppressing the truth": act of not mentioning some important fact

supra *adverb* above *or* see above

supreme court *noun* **(a) Supreme Court (of Judicature)** = highest court in England and Wales, consisting of the Court of Appeal and the High Court of Justice **(b)** *US* highest federal court

surety *noun* **(a)** person who guarantees that someone will do something, especially by paying to guarantee that someone will keep the peace; **to stand surety for someone (b)** money *or* deeds *or* share certificates, etc., deposited as security for a loan

surname *noun* family name; **a woman usually takes the surname of her husband when she marries**

surrender 1 *noun* giving up of an insurance policy before the contracted date for maturity; **the contract becomes null and void when these documents are surrendered; surrender value** = money which an insurer will pay if an insurance policy is given up before it matures **2** *verb* **(a)** to give in a document *or* to give up a right; **the court ordered him to surrender his passport; to surrender a policy** = to give up an insurance **(b)** to give oneself up to be arrested by the police; **the hijackers surrendered to the airport security guards**

surveillance *noun* watching someone carefully to get information about what he is doing; **the diplomats were placed under police surveillance; surveillance at international airports has been increased; surveillance device** = bugging device; **electronic surveillance** = surveillance using hidden microphones, etc. NOTE: no plural

survive *verb* to live longer than another person; **he survived his wife; she is survived by her husband and three children; he left his estate to his surviving relatives** = to the relatives who were still alive

◊ **survivor** *noun* someone who lives longer than another person

◊ **survivorship** *noun* right of the survivor of a joint tenancy to the estate, rather than the heirs of the deceased tenant

SUS law *noun* law which allows the police to stop and arrest a person whom they suspect of having committed an offence

suspect 1 *noun* person whom the police think has committed a crime; **the police**

have taken six suspects into custody; the police are questioning the suspect about his movements at the time the crime was committed 2** *verb* to believe that someone has done something; **he was arrested as a suspected spy; the police suspect that the thefts were committed by a member of the shop's staff** NOTE: you suspect someone **of** committing a crime

suspend *verb* **(a)** to stop (something) for a time; **we have suspended payments while we are waiting for news from our agent; the hearings have been suspended for two weeks; work on the preparation of the case has been suspended; the management decided to suspend negotiations; suspended sentence** = sentence of imprisonment which a court orders shall not take effect unless the offender commits another crime **(b)** to stop (someone) working for a time; **he was suspended on full pay while the police investigations were proceeding**

◊ **suspension** *noun* stopping something for a time; **suspension of payments; suspension of deliveries**

suspicion *noun* feeling that someone has committed a crime; **he was arrested on suspicion of being an accessory after the fact**

◊ **suspicious** *adjective* which makes someone suspect; **the police are dealing with the suspicious package found in the car; suspicious substances were found in the man's pocket**

swear *verb* to make an oath *or* to promise that what you will say will be the truth; **he swore to tell the truth; "I swear to tell the truth, the whole truth and nothing but the truth"** = words used when a witness takes the oath in court NOTE: **swearing - swore - has sworn**

◊ **swear in** *verb* to make someone take an oath before taking up a position; **he was sworn in as a Privy Councillor; swearing-in** = act of making someone take an oath before taking up a position

swindle 1 *noun* illegal deal in which someone is cheated out of his money **2** *verb* to cheat someone out of his money; **he made £50,000 by swindling small shopkeepers; the gang swindled the bank out of £1.5m**

◊ **swindler** *noun* person who swindles

system *noun* **(a)** arrangement *or* organization of things which work together; **the British legal system has been taken as the standard for many other legal systems; filing system** = way of putting documents in order for easy reference; **to operate a quota system** = to regulate supplies by fixing quantities which are allowed **(b) computer system** = set of programs, commands, etc., which make a computer work; **control system** = system used to check that a computer system is working correctly **(c) systems analysis** = using a computer to suggest how a company should work by analyzing the way in which it works at present; **systems analyst** = person who specializes in systems analysis

◊ **systematic** *adjective* in order *or* using method; **he ordered a systematic report on the probation service**

Tt

table 1 *noun* list of figures *or* facts set out in lists; **table of contents** = list of contents in a book; **actuarial tables** = lists showing how long people of certain ages are likely to live, used to calculate life assurance premiums; **Table A, B, C, D, E** = specimen forms for setting up companies, set out in the Companies Act; *see* A, B, C, D, E **2** *verb* to put items of information on the table before a meeting; **the report of the finance committee was tabled; to table a motion** = to put forward a proposal for discussion by putting details of it on the table at a meeting

tacit *adjective* agreed but not stated; **he gave the proposal his tacit approval; the committee gave its tacit agreement to the proposal**

tack *noun* (*in Scotland*) lease

tail *see* FEE

take 1 *noun* money received in a shop **2** *verb* **(a)** to receive *or* to get; (*of a lawyer*) **to take instructions** = to ask one's client how he wishes the lawyer to deal with something; **when the defence offered**

£1,000, the plaintiff's solicitor said he would take his client's instructions **(b)** to do a certain action; **to take action** = to do something; **you must take immediate action if you want to stop thefts; to take the chair** = to be chairman of a meeting; **in the absence of the chairman his deputy took the chair; to take someone to court** = to sue someone *or* to start civil proceedings against someone **(c)** to need (a time *or* a quantity); **it took the jury six hours to reach a verdict** *or* **the jury took six hours to reach a verdict; it will take her all morning to type my letters; it took six policemen to hold the burglar**

NOTE: **taking - took - has taken**

◊ **take in** *verb* to trick *or* to swindle (someone); **we were taken in by his promise of quick profits**

◊ **take out** *verb* **to take out a patent for an invention** = to apply for and receive a patent; **to take out insurance against theft** = to pay a premium to an insurance company, so that if a theft takes place the company will pay compensation

◊ **take over** *verb* **(a)** to start to do something in place of someone else; **Miss Black took over from Mr Jones on May 1st; the new chairman takes over on July 1st; the take-over period is always difficult** = the period when one person is taking over work from another **(b) to take over a company** = to buy (a business) by offering to buy most of its shares; **the buyer takes over the company's liabilities; the company was taken over by a large international corporation**

◊ **takeover** *noun* buying a business; **takeover bid** *or* **offer** = offer to buy all or a majority of the shares in a company so as to control it; **to make a takeover bid for a company** = to offer to buy most of the shares in a company; **to withdraw a takeover bid** = to say that you no longer offer to buy most of the shares in a company; **the company rejected the takeover bid** = the directors recommended that the shareholders should not accept the offer; **the disclosure of the takeover bid raised share prices; Takeover Panel** = body which supervises and regulates takeovers; **contested takeover** = takeover where the board of the company being bought do not recommend the bid, and try to fight it

talaq *noun* Islamic form of divorce, where the husband may divorce his wife unilaterally by an oral declaration made three times

tamper *verb* **to tamper with something** = to change something *or* to act in such a way that something does not work; **the police were accused of tampering with the evidence; the charges state that he tampered with the wheels of the victim's car**

tangible *adjective* **tangible assets** *or* **property** = property *or* assets which are solid (such as furniture *or* jewels *or* cash)

tariff *noun* **(a) customs tariffs** = tax to be paid for importing *or* exporting goods; **tariff barriers** = customs duty intended to make imports more difficult; **to impose tariff barriers on** *or* **to lift tariff barriers from a product; General Agreement on Tariffs and Trade (GATT)** = international treaty which aims to try to reduce restrictions in trade between countries; **protective tariff** = tariff which aims to ban imports to prevent competition with local products **(b)** rate of charging for electricity, hotel rooms, train tickets, etc.

tax 1 *noun* **(a)** money taken compulsorily by the government *or* by an official body to pay for government services; **capital gains tax** = tax on capital gains; **capital transfer tax** = tax on the transfer of capital *or* assets from one person to another; **excess profits tax** = tax on profits which are higher than what is thought to be normal; **income tax** = tax on salaries and wages; **land tax** = tax on the amount of land owned; **sales tax** = tax paid on each item sold; **Value Added Tax (VAT)** = tax on goods and services, added as a percentage to the invoiced sales price **(b) ad valorem tax** = tax calculated according to the value of the goods taxed; **back tax** = tax which is owed; **basic rate tax** = lowest rate of income tax; **to levy a tax** *or* **to impose a tax** = to make a tax payable; **the government has imposed a 15% tax on petrol; to lift a tax** = to remove a tax; **tax adviser** *or* **tax consultant** = person who gives advice on tax problems; **tax allowances** *or* **allowances against tax** = part of one's income which a person is allowed to earn and not pay tax on; **tax avoidance** = trying (legally) to minimize the amount of tax to be paid; **tax code** =

number given to indicate the amount of tax allowances a person has; **tax concession** = allowing less tax to be paid; **tax credit** = part of a dividend on which the company has already paid tax, so that the shareholder is not taxed on it again; **tax deductions** = (i) money removed from a salary to pay tax; (ii) *US* business expenses which can be claimed against tax; **tax deducted at source** = tax which is removed from a salary, interest payment or dividend payment before the money is paid out; **tax evasion** = illegally trying not to pay tax; **tax exemption** = (i) being free from payment of tax; (ii) *US* part of income which a person is allowed to earn and not pay tax on; **tax haven** = country where taxes levied on foreigners *or* foreign companies are low; **tax holiday** = period when a new business is exempted from paying tax; **tax inspector** *or* **inspector of taxes** = official of the Inland Revenue who examines tax returns and decides how much tax someone should pay; **tax loophole** = legal means of not paying tax; **tax planning** = planning one's financial affairs so that one pays as little tax as possible; **tax relief** = allowing someone not to pay tax on certain parts of his income; **tax return** *or* **tax declaration** = completed tax form, with details of income and allowances; **double tax treaty** = treaty between two countries so that citizens pay tax in one country only; **tax year** = twelve month period on which taxes are calculated (in the UK, 6th April to 5th April of the following year) **2** *verb* **(a)** to make someone pay a tax *or* to impose a tax on something; **to tax businesses at 50%; income is taxed at 29%; these items are heavily taxed (b)** to have the costs of a legal action assessed by the court; **the court ordered the costs to be taxed if not agreed; taxed costs** = variable amount of costs awarded in legal proceedings by the Taxing Master

◊ **taxable** *adjective* which can be taxed; **taxable items** = items on which a tax has to be paid; **taxable income** = income on which a person has to pay tax

◊ **taxation** *noun* **(a)** act of taxing; **direct taxation** = taxes (such as income tax) which are paid direct to the government out of earnings *or* profit; **double taxation** = taxing the same income twice; **double taxation treaty** = treaty between two countries that citizens pay tax in one

country only **(b) taxation of costs** = assessment of the costs of a legal action by the Taxing Master
NOTE: no plural

◊ **tax-deductible** *adjective* which can be deducted from an income before tax is calculated; **these expenses are not tax-deductible** = tax has to be paid on these expenses

◊ **tax-exempt** *adjective* (person *or* organization) not required to pay tax; (income *or* goods) which are not subject to tax

◊ **tax-free** *adjective* on which tax does not have to be paid

◊ **Taxing Master** *noun* official of the Supreme Court who assesses the costs of a court action

◊ **taxpayer** *noun* person *or* company which has to pay tax; **basic taxpayer** *or* **taxpayer at the basic rate; corporate taxpayers**

◊ **tax point** *noun* (i) time when goods are supplied and VAT is charged; (ii) time at which a tax begins to be applied

technical *adjective* referring to a specific legal point *or* using a strictly legal interpretation; **nominal damages were awarded as the harm was judged to be technical rather than actual**

◊ **technicality** *noun* special interpretation of a legal point; **the Appeal Court rejected the appeal on a technicality**

teller *noun* **(a)** MP who counts the votes in the House of Commons **(b)** bank clerk

tem *see* PRO TEM

Temple *see* INNER TEMPLE, MIDDLE TEMPLE

temporary *adjective* which lasts only a short time; **he was granted a temporary injunction; the police took temporary measures to close the street to traffic; she has a temporary job** *or* **temporary post with a firm of solicitors; he has a temporary job as a filing clerk** *or* **he has a job as a temporary filing clerk; temporary employment** = full-time work which does not last for more than a few days or months; **temporary injunction** = injunction which is granted until a case comes to court; **temporary staff** = staff who are appointed for a short time

◊ **temporarily** *adverb* lasting only for a short time

tenancy *noun* (i) agreement by which a person can occupy a property; (ii) period during which a person has an agreement to occupy a property; **joint tenancy** = situation where two or more persons acquire interests in a property together where, if one of the joint tenants dies, his share goes to the others who survive him; **several tenancy** = holding of property by several persons, each separately and not jointly with any other person; **protected tenancy** = tenancy where the tenant is protected from eviction; **tenancy in common** = situation where two or more persons jointly hold a property and each can leave his interest to his heirs when he dies; **tenancy at will** = situation where the owner of a property allows a tenant to hold it for as long as either party wishes

◊ **tenant** *noun* person *or* company which rents a house *or* flat *or* office in which to live or work; **the tenant is liable for repairs; tenant at will** = tenant who holds a property at the will of the owner; **tenant for life** = person who can occupy a property for life; **secure tenant** = tenant of a local authority who has the right to buy the freehold of the property he rents at a discount; **sitting tenant** = tenant who is living in a house when the freehold or lease is sold

tender **1** *noun* **(a)** offer to work for a certain price; **to put a project out to tender** *or* **to ask for** *or* **to invite tenders for a project** = to ask contractors to give written estimates for a job; **to put in a tender** *or* **to submit a tender** = to make an estimate for a job; **to sell shares by tender** = to ask people to offer in writing a price for shares; **sealed tenders** = tenders sent in sealed envelopes which will all be opened together at a certain time **(b) legal tender** = coins or notes which can be legally used to pay a debt (small denominations cannot be used to pay large debts) NOTE: no plural for (b) **2** *verb* **(a) to tender for a contract** = to put forward an estimate of cost for work to be carried out under contract; **to tender for the construction of a hospital (b) to tender one's resignation** = to give in one's resignation

◊ **tenderer** *noun* person *or* company which tenders for work; **the company was the successful tenderer for the project**

tenement *noun* property which is held by a tenant; (*in Scotland*) building which is divided into rented flats; **dominant tenement** = land which has been granted an easement over another property; **servient tenement** = land whose owner grants an easement to the owner of the dominant tenement

tenens *see* LOCUM

tentative *adjective* not certain; **they reached a tentative agreement over the proposal; we suggested Wednesday May 10th as a tentative date for the next meeting** ◊ **tentatively** *adverb* not sure; **we tentatively suggested Wednesday as the date for our next meeting**

tenure *noun* **(a)** right to hold property *or* a position; **security of tenure** = right to keep a job *or* rented accommodation provided certain conditions are met; **land tenure** = way in which land is held (such as leasehold) **(b)** time when a position is held; **during his tenure of the office of chairman** NOTE: no plural

term *noun* **(a)** period of time; **the term of a lease; the term of the loan is fifteen years; to have a loan for a term of fifteen years; during his term of office as chairman; term deposit** = money invested for a fixed period which gives a higher rate of interest than normal; **term insurance** = life assurance which covers a person's life for a fixed period of time; **term loan** = loan for a fixed period of time; **term of years** = fixed period of several years (of a lease); **term shares** = type of building society deposit for a fixed period of time at a higher rate of interest; **fixed term** = period which is fixed when a contract is signed and which cannot be changed afterwards; **short-term** = for a period of months; **long-term** = for a long period of time; **medium-term** = for a period of one or two years **(b)** **term** *or* **terms** = conditions *or* duties which have to be carried out as part of a contract *or* arrangements which have to be agreed before a contract is valid; **he refused to agree to some of the terms of the contract; by** *or* **under the terms of the contract, the company is responsible for all damage to the property; terms of payment** *or* **payment terms** = conditions for paying something; **terms of sale** = agreed ways in which a sale takes place (such as discounts and credit terms); **cash terms** = lower terms which

apply if the customer pays cash; **implied terms and conditions** = terms and conditions which are not written in a contract, but which are legally taken to be present in the contract; **trade terms** = special discount for people in the same trade **(c)** part of a legal *or* university year; **the autumn** *or* **winter term starts in September**

COMMENT: the four law terms are Easter, Hilary, Michaelmas and Trinity

(d) **terms of employment** = conditions set out in a contract of employment; **terms of reference** = areas which a committee *or* an inspector can deal with; **under the terms of reference of the committee it can only investigate complaints from the public; the tribunal's terms of reference do not cover traffic offences**

terminate *verb* to end (something) *or* to bring (something) to an end *or* to come to an end; **to terminate an agreement; his employment was terminated; an offer terminates on the death of the offeror** ◊ **terminable** *adjective* which can be terminated ◊ **termination** *noun* **(a)** bringing to an end; **the termination of an offer** *or* **of a lease; to appeal against the termination of a foster order; termination clause** = clause which explains how and when a contract can be terminated **(b)** *US* leaving a job (resigning, retiring, or being fired or made redundant)

territory *noun* area of land (ruled by a government); **their government has laid claim to part of our territory** ◊ **territorial** *adjective* referring to land; **territorial claims** = claims to own land which is part of another country; **territorial waters** = sea waters near the coast of a country, which is part of the country and governed by the laws of that country; **outside territorial waters** = in international waters, where a single country's jurisdiction does not run

terrorism *noun* violent action (such as assassination *or* bombing) taken for political reasons; **the act of terrorism was condemned by the Minister of Justice** ◊ **terrorist** *noun* person who commits a violent act for political reasons; **the bomb**

was planted by a terrorist group *or* by a group of terrorists; six people were killed in the terrorist attack on the airport

test 1 *noun* **(a)** examination to see if something works well *or* is possible; **test certificate** = certificate to show that something has passed a test; **control test** = test to decide if someone is an employee *or* is self-employed (used for the purposes of tax assessment); **feasibility test** = test to see if something is possible **(b) test case** = legal action where the decision will fix a principle which other cases can follow **2** *verb* to examine something to see if it is working well; **to test a computer system**

testament *noun* **last will and testament** = will *or* document by which a person says what he wants to happen to his property when he dies

◊ **testamentary** *adjective* referring to a will; **testamentary capacity** = legal ability of someone to make a will; **testamentary disposition** = passing of property to someone in a will

testate *adjective* having made a will; **did he die testate?** *see also* INTESTATE

◊ **testator** *noun* man who has made a will

◊ **testatrix** *noun* woman who has made a will

testify *verb* to give evidence in court

testimonium clause *noun* last section of a will *or* conveyance, etc., which shows how it has been witnessed

COMMENT: the testimonium clause usually begins with the words: "in witness whereof I have set my hand"

testimony *noun* oral statement given by a witness in court about what happened; **she gave her testimony in a low voice**
NOTE: no plural

text *noun* written part of something; **he wrote notes at the side of the text of the agreement**; **text processing** = working with words, using a computer to produce, check and change documents, contracts, reports, letters, etc.

◊ **textbook** *noun* book of legal commentary which can be cited in court

theft *noun* **(a)** crime of stealing *or* of taking of property which belongs to someone else with the intention of depriving that person of it; **we have brought in security guards to protect the store against theft; the company is trying to reduce losses caused by theft; to take out insurance against theft; petty theft** = stealing small items *or* small amounts of money **(b)** act of stealing; **there has been a wave of thefts from newsagents**
NOTE: no plural for (a)

COMMENT: types of theft which are notifiable offences are theft from the person of another; theft in a dwelling; theft by an employee; theft of mail *or* pedal cycle *or* motor vehicle; theft from vehicles *or* from a shop *or* from an automatic machine or meter

there- *prefix* that thing
NOTE: the following words formed from **there-** are frequently used in legal documents

◊ **thereafter** *adverb* after that

◊ **thereby** *adverb* by that

◊ **therefor** *adverb* for that

◊ **therefrom** *adverb* from that

◊ **therein** *adverb* in that

◊ **thereinafter** *adverb* afterwards listed in that document

◊ **thereinbefore** *adverb* before mentioned in that document

◊ **thereinunder** *adverb* mentioned under that heading

◊ **thereof** *adverb* of that; **in respect thereof** = regarding that thing

◊ **thereto** *adverb* to that

◊ **theretofore** *adverb* before that time

◊ **therewith** *adverb* with that

thief *noun* person who steals *or* who takes property which belongs to someone else; **thieves broke into the office and stole the petty cash; petty thief** = person who steals small items *or* small amounts of money
NOTE: plural is **thieves**

third *noun* part of something which is divided into three equal parts; **to sell everything at one third off** = to sell everything at a discount of 33%

◊ **third party** *noun* any person other than the two main parties involved in proceedings *or* contract; the other person involved in an accident; **third-party insurance** = insurance which pays compensation if someone who is not the insured person incurs loss or injury; **third party notice** = pleading served by a defendant on another party joining that party to an existing court action; **third party proceedings** = introduction of a third party into a case by the defendant; **the case is in the hands of a third party** = the case is being dealt with by someone who is not one of the main interested parties

◊ **Third Reading** *noun* final discussion and vote on a Bill in Parliament

threat *noun* words (spoken *or* written) which say that something unpleasant may happen to someone, and which frighten that person

◊ **threaten** *verb* to warn someone that unpleasant things may happen to him; **he threatened to take the tenant to court** *or* **to have the tenant evicted; she complained that her husband threatened her with a knife**

throne *noun* special chair for a King *or* Queen; **speech from the throne** = QUEEN'S SPEECH

throw out *verb* (a) to reject *or* to refuse to accept; **the proposal was thrown out by the planning committee; the board threw out the draft contract submitted by the union** (b) to get rid of (something which is not wanted); **we threw out the old telephones and put in a computerized system; the AGM threw out the old board of directors**
NOTE: throwing - threw - has thrown

thug *noun* man who attacks people; **a group of teenage thugs attacked the couple as they left the shop**

◊ **thuggery** *noun* attacking people
NOTE: no plural

time *noun* (a) period when something takes place (such as one hour, two days, fifty minutes); **computer time** = time when a computer is being used (paid for at an hourly rate); **real time** = time when a computer is working on the processing of data while the problem to which the data refers is actually taking place; **time charter** = agreement to charter a ship for a fixed period; **time policy** = marine insurance policy which runs for a fixed period of time; **time immemorial** = from before

1189, the date from which events are supposed to be remembered; **time summons** = summons issued to apply to the court for more time in which to serve a pleading; **extension of time** = extra time allowed in which to serve a pleading *or* to take a step in a court action (b) hour of the day (such as 9.00, 12.15, ten o'clock at night); **the time of arrival** *or* **the arrival time is indicated on the screen; departure times are delayed by up to fifteen minutes because of the volume of traffic; on time** = at the right time; **the plane was on time; you will have to hurry if you want to get to the hearing on time** *or* **if you want to be on time for the hearing** (c) system of hours on the clock; **Summer Time** *or* **Daylight Saving Time** = system where clocks are set back one hour in the summer to take advantage of the longer hours of daylight; **Standard Time** = normal time as in the winter months (d) hours worked; **he is paid time and a half on Sundays** = he is paid the normal rate with an extra 50% when he works on Sundays (e) period before something happens; **time limit** = period during which something should be done; **to keep within the time limits** *or* **within the time schedule** = to complete work by the time stated; **time lock** = lock which will open only at a certain time of day (as in a bank vault)

◊ **timetable** 1 *noun* (a) list showing times of arrivals *or* departures of buses *or* trains *or* planes, etc.; **according to the timetable, there should be a train to London at 10.22; the bus company has brought out its new timetable for the next twelve months** (b) list of appointments *or* events; **Mr Smith has a very full timetable, so I doubt if he will be able to see you today; conference timetable** = list of speakers *or* events at a conference 2 *verb* to make a list of times

tipstaff *noun* official of the Supreme Court who is responsible for arresting persons in contempt of court

title *noun* (a) (i) right to hold goods *or* property; (ii) document proving a right to hold a property; **she has no title to the property; he has a good title to the property; title deeds** = document showing who is the owner of a property; **to have a clear title to something** = to have a right to something with no limitations *or* charges; **good title** = title to a property which gives the owner full rights of ownership; **possessory title** =

title to land acquired by occupying it continuously (usually for a period of twelve years); **qualified title** = title to a property which is not absolute as there is some defect **(b)** name given to a person in a certain job; **he has the title "Chief Executive" (c)** honourable name given to some (such as Lord Smith, Mr Justice Jones) **(d)** name of a bill which comes before Parliament *or* name of an Act of Parliament; **full title** *or* **long title** = complete title of an Act of Parliament; **short title** = usual title of an Act of Parliament

token *noun* thing which acts as a sign; **token charge** = small charge which does not cover the real costs; **a token charge is made for heating; token payment** = small payment to show that a payment is being made; **token rent** = very low rent payment to show that a rent is being asked; **token strike** = short strike to show that workers have a grievance

toll *noun* payment made for using a road *or* bridge *or* ferry

tort *noun* civil wrong done by one person to another and entitling the victim to claim damages; **action in tort** = action brought by a plaintiff who has suffered damage *or* harm caused by the defendant; **proceedings in tort** = court action for damages for a tort

◇ **tortfeasor** *noun* person who has committed a tort; **joint tortfeasors** = two people who together commit a tort

◇ **tortious** *adjective* referring to a tort; **tortious act** = a tort; **tortious liability** = liability for harm caused by a breach of duty

torture *verb* to hurt someone badly so as to force him to give information

◇ **torturer** *noun* person who tortures

total **1** *adjective* complete *or* with everything added together; **total amount; total assets; total cost; total expenditure; total income; total output; total revenue; the cargo was written off as a total loss** = the cargo was so badly damaged that the insurers said it had no value **2** *noun* amount which is complete *or* with everything added up; **the total of the charges comes to more than £1,000; he was**

sentenced to a total of twelve years' imprisonment; **grand total** = final total made by adding several smaller totals **3** *verb* to add up to; **costs totalling more than £25,000** NOTE: **totalling - totalled** but US English **totaling - totaled**

◇ **totally** *adverb* completely; **the factory was totally destroyed in the fire; the cargo was totally ruined by water**

toties quoties *Latin phrase meaning* "as often as necessary"

town *noun* large group of houses and other buildings which is the place where many people live and work; **Town Clerk** = formerly the title of the person appointed as chief administrator of a town; **town planner** = person who supervises the design of a town *or* the way the streets and buildings in a town are laid out and the land in a town used; **town planning** = supervising the design of a town *or* the use of land in a town

trace *verb* to follow *or* to look for someone *or* something; **we have traced the missing documents; the police traced the two men to a hotel in London; tracing action** = court action begun to trace money *or* proceeds of a sale

trade **1** *noun* **(a)** business of buying and selling; **export trade** *or* **import trade** = the business of selling to other countries *or* buying from other countries; **home trade** = trade in the country where a company is based **(b) fair trade** = international business system where countries agree not to charge import duties on certain items imported from their trading partners; **free trade** = system where goods can go from one country to another without any restrictions; **free trade area** = group of countries practising free trade; **trade agreement** = international agreement between countries over general terms of trade; **trade description** = description of a product to attract customers; **Trade Descriptions Act** = Act of Parliament which limits the way in which products can be described so as to protect customers from wrong descriptions made by the makers of the products; **trade directory** = book which lists all the businesses and business people in a town; **to ask a company to supply trade references** = to ask a company to give names of traders who can report on the company's financial situation and reputation **(c)**

people *or* companies dealing in the same type of product; **he is in the secondhand car trade; she is very well known in the clothing trade; trade association** = group which joins together companies in the same type of business (NOTE: no plural) **2** *verb* to buy and sell *or* to carry on a business; **to trade with another country; to trade on the Stock Exchange; the company has stopped trading; he trades under the name *or* as "Eeziphitt"**

◇ **trademark** *or* **trade mark** *or* **trade name** *noun* particular name, design, etc., which identifies the product, has been registered by the maker, and which cannot be used by other makers; **you cannot call your beds "Softn'kumfi" - it is a registered trademark**

◇ **trader** *noun* person who does business; **commodity trader** = person whose business is buying and selling commodities; **free trader** = person who is in favour of free trade; **sole trader** = person who runs a business, usually by himself, but has not registered it as a company

◇ **trade union** *or* **trades union** *noun* organization which represents workers, who are its members, in discussions about wages and conditions of employment with employers; **they are members of a trade union *or* they are trade union members; he has applied for trade union membership *or* he has applied to join a trade union; Trades Union Congress** = central organization for all British trade unions
NOTE: although **Trades Union Congress** is the official name for the organization, **trade union** is commoner than **trades union**

◇ **trading** *noun* carrying on a business; **fair trading** = way of doing business which is reasonable and does not harm the consumer; **Office of Fair Trading** = government department which protects consumers against unfair *or* illegal business practices; **fraudulent trading** = carrying on the business of a company while knowing that the company is insolvent

traffic 1 *noun* cars *or* vehicles on the road; **traffic offences** = offences committed by drivers of vehicles; **traffic police** = section of the police concerned with problems on the roads; **traffic warden** = official whose duty is to regulate the traffic under the supervision of the police, especially to deal with cars which are illegally parked **2** *verb* **to traffic in some-**

thing = to buy and sell something illegally; **he was charged with trafficking in drugs *or* with drug trafficking**

train *verb* to teach someone a skill *or* a profession; **he is a trained accountant; the director is American-trained; day training centre** = centre where young offenders attend courses as part of their probation

◇ **trainee** *noun* young person who is learning a skill; young person who is contracted to work in a solicitor's office for some years to learn the law

transact *verb* **to transact business** = to carry out a piece of business

◇ **transaction** *noun* **business transaction** = piece of business *or* buying or selling; **cash transaction** = transaction paid for in cash; **a transaction on the Stock Exchange** = purchase *or* sale of shares on the Stock Exchange; **the paper publishes a daily list of Stock Exchange transactions; exchange transaction** = purchase *or* sale of foreign currency; **fraudulent transaction** = transaction which aims to cheat someone

transcript *noun* record (written out in full) of something noted in shorthand; **the judge asked for a full transcript of the evidence; transcripts of cases are available in the Supreme Court Library**

transfer 1 *noun* moving someone *or* something to a new place; **transfer of property *or* transfer of shares** = moving the ownership of property *or* shares from one person to another; **bank transfer** = moving money from a bank account to an account in another country; **capital transfer tax** = tax on the transfer of capital *or* assets from one owner to another; **credit transfer *or* transfer of funds** = moving money from one account to another; **deed of transfer** = agreement which transfers the ownership of shares; **stock transfer form** = form to be signed by the person transferring shares to another **2** *verb* **(a)** to move someone *or* something to a new place; **the accountant was transferred to our Scottish branch; he transferred his shares to a family trust; she transferred her money to a deposit account; transferred charge call** = phone call where the person receiving the call agrees to pay for it **(b)** to change from one type of travel to another; **when you get to London airport, you have to transfer onto an internal flight**
NOTE: **transferring - transferred**

◊ **transferable** *adjective* which can be passed to someone else; **the season ticket is not transferable** = the ticket cannot be given or lent to someone else to use; **single transferable vote** = voting system in proportional representation where each voter votes for the candidates in order of preference, and his vote is transferred to the next candidate if his first choice is not elected

◊ **transferee** *noun* person to whom property *or* goods are transferred

◊ **transferor** *noun* person who transfers goods *or* property to another

transit *see* IN TRANSIT

traverse *noun* denial in a pleading by one side in a case that the facts alleged by the other side are correct

treason *noun* notifiable offence *or* crime of betraying one's country, usually by helping the enemy in time of war; **he was accused of treason; three men were executed for treason; the treason trial lasted three weeks; high treason** = formal way of referring to treason; **misprision of treason** = crime of knowing that treason has been committed and not reporting it; **treason felony** = notifiable offence of planning to remove a King *or* Queen *or* of planning to start a war against the United Kingdom NOTE: no plural

◊ **treasonable** *adjective* which may be considered as treason; **he was accused of making treasonable remarks**

treasure *noun* gold *or* silver *or* jewels, especially when found or stolen; **thieves broke into the palace and stole the king's treasure; treasure trove** = treasure which has been hidden by someone in the past and is now discovered

> COMMENT: treasure which has been found is declared to the coroner, who decides if it is treasure trove. If it is declared treasure trove, it belongs to the state, though the person who finds it will usually get a reward equal to its market value

◊ **treasurer** *noun* (a) person who looks after the money *or* finances of a club or society, etc.; **honorary treasurer** = treasurer who does not receive any fee (b) main financial manager of a large company

◊ **treasury** *noun* **the Treasury** = government department which deals with the country's finance; **the Treasury Benches** = front benches in the House of Commons where the government ministers sit; **Treasury Bill** = bill of exchange which does not give any interest and is sold by the government at a discount; **treasury bonds** = bonds issued by the Treasury of the USA; **Treasury counsel** = barrister who pleads in the Central Criminal Court on behalf of the Director of Public Prosecutions; **Treasury Solicitor** = in England, the solicitor who is head of the government's legal department

treaty *noun* (a) written legal agreement between countries; **commercial treaty; cultural treaty; Treaty of Accession** = treaty whereby the UK joined the EEC; **Treaty of Rome** = treaty which established the EEC in 1957 (b) agreement between individual persons; **to sell (a house) by private treaty** = to sell (a house) to another person not by auction

treble *verb* to increase three times; **the company's borrowings have trebled**

trend *noun* general way things are going; **there is a trend away from old-style policing methods; a downward trend in investment; we notice a general trend to sell to the student market; the report points to upwards trends in reported crimes of violence; economic trends** = way in which a country's economy is moving

trespass 1 *noun* tort of interfering with the land *or* goods of another person; **trespass to goods** = tort of harming *or* stealing *or* interfering with goods which belong to someone else; **trespass to land** = tort of interfering with *or* going on someone's property *or* putting things *or* animals on someone's property without permission; **trespass to the person** = tort of harming someone by assault *or* false imprisonment (NOTE: no plural)

> COMMENT: trespass on someone's property is not a criminal offence

2 *verb* to offend by going on to property without the permission of the owner

◊ **trespasser** *noun* person who commits trespass by going on to land without the permission of the owner

triable *adjective* (offence) for which a person can be tried in a court; **offence triable either way** = offence which can be tried before the Magistrates' Court or before the Crown Court

trial *noun* **(a)** criminal *or* civil court case heard before a judge; **the trial lasted six days; the judge ordered a new trial when one of the jurors was found to be the accused's brother; he is on trial *or* is standing trial for embezzlement** = he is being tried for embezzlement; **to commit someone for trial** = to send someone to a court to be tried; **trial judge** = judge who is hearing a trial **(b)** test to see if something is good; **on trial** = (i) being tested; (ii) before a court; **the product is on trial in our laboratories; trial period** = time when a customer can test a product before buying it; **trial sample** = small piece of a product used for testing; **free trial** = testing of a machine *or* product with no payment involved **(c) trial balance** = draft adding of debits and credits to see if they balance

tribunal *noun* a court; especially a specialist court outside the judicial system which examines special problems and makes judgments; **industrial tribunal** = court which can decide in disputes between employers and employees; **Lands Tribunal** = court which deals with compensation claims relating to land; **military tribunal** = court made up of army officers; **rent tribunal** = court which adjudicates in disputes about rents, and can award a fair rent

trick 1 *noun* clever act to make someone believe something which is not true; **confidence trick** = business where someone gains another person's confidence and then tricks him 2 *verb* to get money *or* property by making someone believe something which is not true; **the gang tricked the bank manager into giving them the keys of the vault; they tricked the old lady out of £25,000**

◊ **trickster** *noun* **confidence trickster** = person who carries out a confidence trick on someone

Trinity *noun* one of the four sittings of the law courts; one of the four law terms

◊ **Trinity House** *noun* body which superintends lighthouses and pilots in some areas of the British coast

trip *noun* journey; **business trip** = journey to discuss business matters with people who live a long way away or overseas

triplicate *noun* **in triplicate** = with an original and two copies; **to print an invoice in triplicate; invoicing in triplicate** = preparing three copies of invoices

trouble *noun* problem *or* difficult situation; **the police are expecting trouble at the football match; there was some trouble in the courtroom after the verdict was announced**

◊ **troubleshooter** *noun* person whose job is to solve problems

trough *noun* low point in the economic cycle

trove *see* TREASURE

trover *noun* action to recover property which has been converted *or* goods which have been taken *or* passed to other parties

true *adjective* correct *or* accurate; **true bill** = verdict by a grand jury that an indictment should proceed; **true copy** = exact copy; **I certify that this is a true copy; certified as a true copy**

truly *adverb* **Yours truly** *or* *US* **Truly yours** = ending to a formal business letter where you do not know the person to whom you are writing

trust 1 *noun* **(a)** being confident that something is correct, will work, etc.; **we took his statement on trust** = we accepted his statement without examining it to see if it was correct **(b)** duty of looking after goods *or* money *or* property which someone (the beneficiary) has passed to you (the trustee); **he left his property in trust for his grandchildren; breach of trust** = failure on the part of a trustee to act properly in regard to a trust; **position of trust** = job where an employee is trusted by his employer to look after money *or* confidential information, etc.; **constructive trust** = trust arising by reason of a person's behaviour; **implied trust** = trust which is implied by the intentions of the parties; **trust for sale** = trust whereby property is held but can be sold and the money passed to the beneficiaries **(c)** management of money *or* property for someone; **they set up a family trust for their grandchildren;** *US* **trust company** = organization which supervises the financial affairs of private trusts, executes wills, and acts as a bank to a limited number of customers; **trust deed** *or* **instrument** = document which sets out the details of a trust; **trust fund** = assets (money, securities, property) held in trust for someone; **discretionary trust** = trust where the trustees decide when and how much money is to be paid to the beneficiaries; **investment trust** = company whose shares can be bought on the Stock Exchange and whose business is to make money by buying and selling stocks and shares; **unit trust** = organization which takes money from investors and invests it in stocks and shares for them under a trust deed **(d)** *US* small group of companies which control the supply of a product NOTE: no plural for (a) and (b) **2** *verb* **to trust someone with something** = to give something to someone to look after; **can he be trusted with all that cash?**

◇ **trustee** *noun* person who has charge of money *or* property in trust *or* person who is responsible for a family trust; **the trustees of the pension fund; trustee in bankruptcy** = person who is appointed by a court to run the affairs of a bankrupt and pay his creditors; **Public Trustee** = official who is appointed as a trustee of a person's property; **Trustee Savings Bank** = bank which takes savings from small savers, and is guaranteed by the government

◇ **trusteeship** *noun* position of being a trustee

◇ **trustworthy** *adjective* (person) who can be trusted; **the staff who deal with cash are completely trustworthy**

◇ **trusty** *noun slang* prisoner who is trusted by the prison warders

truth *noun* what is true *or* not false; **the court is trying to find out the truth about the payments; counsel for the defence said that the plaintiff was not telling the truth; witnesses have to swear to tell the truth**

◇ **truthful** *adjective* true (statement)

try *verb* to hear a civil *or* criminal trial; **he was tried for murder and sentenced to life imprisonment; the court is not competent to try the case**

TUC = TRADES UNION CONGRESS

turn 1 *noun* **(a)** movement in a circle *or* change of direction **(b)** profit *or* commission; **jobber's turn** = profit made by a stock jobber **2** *verb* to change direction *or* to go round in a circle; **to turn Queen's evidence** *or* *US* **to turn state's evidence** = to confess to a crime and then act as witness against the other criminals involved in the the hope of getting a lighter sentence

◇ **turn down** *verb* to refuse; **the court turned down his petition; the bank turned down their request for a loan; the application for a licence was turned down**

◇ **turnkey operation** *noun* contract where a company takes all responsibility for building, fitting and employing staff for a building (such as a school *or* hospital *or* factory) so that it is completely ready for the purchaser to take over

◇ **turn over** *verb* to have a certain amount of sales; **we turn over £2,000 a week**

◇ **turnover** *noun* **(a)** *GB* amount of sales; **the company's turnover has increased by 235%; we based our calculations on last year's turnover (b) staff turnover** *or* **turnover of staff** = changes in staff, when some leave and others join **(c)** *US* number of times something is used *or* sold in a period (usually one year), expressed as a percentage of a total

type 1 *noun* sort *or* kind; **a new type of drug; several types of murder 2** *verb* to write with a typewriter; **he can type quite fast; all his reports are typed on his typewriter**

◇ **typewriter** *noun* machine which prints letters *or* figures on a piece of paper when a key is pressed; **electronic typewriter**

◇ **typewritten** *adjective* written using a typewriter; **he sent in a typewritten job application**

◇ **typing** *noun* writing letters with a typewriter; **typing error** = mistake made when using a typewriter; **copy typing** = typing documents from handwritten or typed originals, not from dictation
NOTE: no plural

◇ **typist** *noun* person whose job is to write letters using a typewriter; **copy typist** = person who types documents from handwritten or typed originals, and not from dictation; **shorthand typist** = typist who takes dictation in shorthand and then types it

Uu

uberrimae fidei *Latin phrase meaning* "of total good faith": state which should exist between parties to certain types of legal relationship (such as partnerships or insurance); **an insurance contract is uberrimae fidei**

ulterior motive *noun* reason for doing something which is not immediately connected with the action, but is done in anticipation of its result, and so is an act of bad faith

ultimate *adjective* last *or* final; **ultimate consumer** = the person who actually uses the product; **ultimate owner** = real *or* true owner

◇ **ultimatum** *noun* final demand *or* proposal to someone that unless he does something within a period of time, action will be taken against him; **the union officials argued among themselves over the best way to deal with the ultimatum from the management**
NOTE: plural is **ultimatums** or **ultimata**

ultra vires *Latin phrase meaning* "beyond powers"; **their action was ultra vires** = they acted in a way which exceeded their legal powers; *see* INTRA VIRES

umpire *noun* person called in to decide when two arbitrators cannot agree

unable *adjective* not able; **the court was unable to adjudicate because one side had not finished presenting its evidence**

unanimous *adjective* where everyone votes in the same way; **there was a unanimous vote against the proposal; they reached unanimous agreement; unanimous**

verdict = verdict agreed by all the jurors; **the jury reached a unanimous verdict of not guilty**

◇ **unanimously** *adverb* with everyone agreeing; **the proposals were adopted unanimously; the appeal court decided unanimously in favour of the defendant**

unascertained *adjective* not identified; **title to unascertained goods cannot pass to the buyer until the goods have been ascertained**

unavoidable *adjective* which cannot be avoided; **planes are subject to unavoidable delays**

◇ **unavoidably** *adverb* in a way which cannot be avoided; **the hearing was unavoidably delayed**

unbecoming *adjective* (behaviour *or* dress) which is not as decent as it should be

unborn *adjective* (child) which is still in its mother's body and has not yet been born

unchallenged *adjective* (evidence) which has not been challenged

unconditional *adjective* with no conditions attached; **unconditional acceptance of the offer by the board; on the plaintiff's application for summary judgment the master gave the defendant unconditional leave to defend; the offer went unconditional last Thursday** = the takeover bid was accepted by the majority of the shareholders and therefore the conditions attached to it no longer apply

◇ **unconditionally** *adverb* without imposing any conditions; **the offer was accepted unconditionally**

unconfirmed *adjective* which has not been confirmed; **there are unconfirmed reports that our agent has been arrested**

unconstitutional *adjective* which is in conflict with a constitution *or* which is not allowed by the rules *or* laws of a country *or* organization; **the chairman ruled that the meeting was unconstitutional; the Appeal Court ruled that the action of the Attorney-General was unconstitutional**

uncontested *adjective* which is not contested *or* defended; **an uncontested divorce case *or* election**

uncontrollable *adjective* which cannot be controlled; **uncontrollable inflation; he had an uncontrollable impulse to steal**

uncrossed cheque *noun* cheque which may be exchanged for cash anywhere

undefended *adjective* (case) where the defendant does not acknowledge service and does not appear at the court to defend the case; **an undefended divorce case**

under *preposition* **(a)** lower than or less than; **the interest rate is under 10%; under 50% of reported crimes are solved (b)** controlled by or according to; **regulations under the Police Act; under the terms of the agreement, the goods should be delivered in October; he is acting under rule 23 of the union constitution; she does not qualify under section 2 of the 1979 Act; a creditor seeking a receiving order under the Bankruptcy Act 1974**

◊ **undercover agent** *noun* secret agent or agent acting in disguise

◊ **underestimate 1** *noun* estimate which is less than the actual figure; **the figure of £50,000 in legal costs was a considerable underestimate 2** *verb* to think that something is smaller or not as bad as it really is; **they underestimated the effects of the sanctions on their sales; he underestimated the amount of time needed to finish the work**

◊ **underlease** *noun* lease from a tenant to another tenant

◊ **underlet** *verb* to let a property which is held on a lease

◊ **undermentioned** *adjective* mentioned lower down in a document

◊ **undersheriff** *noun* person who is second to a High Sheriff and deputizes for him

◊ **undersigned** *noun* person who has signed a letter; **we, the undersigned =** we, the people who have signed below
NOTE: can be singular or plural

◊ **understanding** *noun* private agreement; **the two parties came to an understanding about the division of the estate; on the understanding that =** on condition that or provided that; **we accept the terms of the contract, on the understanding that it has to be ratified by the full board**

◊ **undertake** *verb* to promise to do something; **to undertake an investigation of the fraud; the members of the jury have undertaken not to read the newspapers; he undertook to report to the probation office once a month**
NOTE: **undertaking - undertook - has undertaken**

◊ **undertaking** *noun* **(a)** business; **a commercial undertaking (b)** (legally binding) promise; **they have given us a written undertaking that they will not infringe our patent; the judge accepted the defendant's undertaking not to harass the plaintiff**

◊ **undertenant** *noun* person who holds a property on an underlease

◊ **underworld** *noun* world of criminals; **the police has informers in the London underworld; the indications are that it is an underworld killing**

◊ **underwrite** *verb* **(a)** to accept responsibility for; **to underwrite a share issue =** to guarantee that a share issue will be sold by agreeing to buy all shares which are not subscribed; **the issue was underwritten by three underwriting companies; to underwrite an insurance policy =** to accept liability for the payment of compensation according to the policy **(b)** to agree to pay for costs; **the government has underwritten the development costs of the building**
NOTE: **underwriting - underwrote - has underwritten**

◊ **underwriter** *noun* **(a)** person who underwrites a share issue **(b)** person who accepts liability for an insurance; **Lloyd's underwriter =** member of an insurance group at Lloyd's who accepts to underwrite insurances; **marine underwriter =** person who insures ships and their cargoes

undischarged bankrupt *noun* person who has been declared bankrupt and has not been released from that state

undisclosed *adjective* not identified; **undisclosed principal =** principal who has not been identified by his agent

> COMMENT: the doctrine of the undisclosed principal means that the agent may be sued as well as the principal if his identity is discovered

undue influence *noun* wrong pressure put on someone which prevents that person from acting independently

unemployed *adjective & noun* (person) with no work; **the unemployed** = people with no work

◊ **unemployment** *noun* absence of work; **the unemployment figures** *or* **the figures for unemployment are rising; unemployment benefit** = money paid by the government to someone who is unemployed

unenforceable *adjective* (contract *or* right) which cannot be enforced

unequivocal *adjective* clear *or* not ambiguous

unfair *adjective* **unfair competition** = trying to do better than another company by using methods such as importing foreign goods at very low prices or by wrongly criticizing a competitor's products; **unfair contract term** = term in a contract which is held by law to be unjust; **unfair dismissal** = removing someone from a job for reasons which are not fair

COMMENT: an employee can complain of unfair dismissal to an industrial tribunal

unfit *adjective* **unfit to plead** = not mentally capable of standing trial

unilateral *adjective* on one side only *or* done by one party only; **they took the unilateral decision to cancel the contract**

◊ **unilaterally** *adverb* by one party only; **they cancelled the contract unilaterally**

unincorporated association *noun* group of people (such as a club *or* partnership) which is not legally incorporated

uninsured *adjective* with no valid insurance; **the driver of the car was uninsured**

union *noun* (a) state of being linked together, as the linking of independent states into a federation; **the Soviet Union** *or* **the Union of Soviet Socialist Republics; the States of the Union** = the states joined together to form the United States of America; **State of the Union message** = annual speech by the President of the USA

which summarizes the political situation in the country (b) **trade union** *or* **trades union** *or* *US* **labor union** = organization which represents workers who are its members in discussions with management about wages and conditions of work; **union agreement** = agreement between a management and a trade union over wages and conditions of work; **union dues** *or* **union subscription** = payment made by workers to belong to a union; **union recognition** = act of agreeing that a union can act on behalf of staff in a company (c) **customs union** = agreement between several countries that goods can go between them without paying duty, while goods from other countries have special duties charged on them

◊ **unionist** *noun* member of a trade union

◊ **unionized** *adjective* (company) where the members of staff belong to a trade union

universal *adjective* which applies everywhere *or* to everyone; **universal franchise** *or* **suffrage** = right to vote which is enjoyed by all adult members of the population

unjust *adjective* contrary to law *or* not just *or* not fair

◊ **unjustly** *adverb* not fairly; **she was unjustly accused of wasting police time**

unlawful *adjective* (act) which is against the law; **unlawful trespass on property; unlawful sexual intercourse; unlawful assembly** = notifiable offence when three or more people come together to commit a breach of the peace or other crime

◊ **unlawfully** *adverb* illegally *or* in an unlawful way; **he was charged with unlawfully carrying firearms**

unlimited *adjective* with no limits; **the bank offered him unlimited credit; unlimited company** = company where the shareholders have no limit as regards liability; **unlimited liability** = situation where a sole trader *or* each partner is responsible for all the firm's debts with no limit at the amount each may have to pay

unliquidated claim *noun* claim for unliquidated damages

◊ **unliquidated damages** *plural noun* damages which are not for a fixed amount of money but are awarded by a court as a matter of discretion

> COMMENT: torts give rise to claims for unliquidated damages

unmarried *adjective* (person) who is not married

unofficial *adjective* not official; **unofficial strike** = strike by local workers which has not been approved by the union as a whole

◊ **unofficially** *adverb* not officially; **the tax office told the company, unofficially, that it would be prosecuted**

unopposed *adjective* (motion) with no one voting against; (proceedings) which have not been opposed; **the Bill had an unopposed second reading in the House**

unpaid *adjective* (person) who does not receive a salary; (debt *or* bill) which has not been paid

unprecedented *adjective* which has no precedent *or* which has not happened before; **in an unprecedented move, the tribunal asked the witness to sing a song**

unprofessional conduct *noun* way of behaving which is not suitable for a professional person *or* which goes against the code of practice of a profession

unquantifiable *adjective* (damage *or* loss) which cannot be quantified

unreasonable *adjective* (behaviour) which is not reasonable in a normal person; **his answer to our letter consisted of a number of unreasonable demands for money**

◊ **unreasonably** *adverb* in a way which is not reasonable *or* which cannot be explained; **approval shall not unreasonably be withheld**

unredeemed pledge *noun* pledge which the borrower has not claimed back by paying back his loan

unregistered *adjective* (land) which has not been registered

unreliable *adjective* which cannot be relied on; **the prosecution tried to show that the driver's evidence was unreliable; the**

defence called two witnesses and both were unreliable

unreported *adjective* **(a)** not reported to the police; **there are thousands of unreported cases of theft (b)** not reported in the Law Reports; **counsel referred the judge to a number of relevant unreported cases**

unsecured *adjective* **unsecured creditor** = creditor who is owed money, but has no mortgage *or* charge over the debtor's property as security; **unsecured debt** = debt which is not guaranteed by assets; **unsecured loan** = loan made with no security

unsolicited *adjective* which has not been asked for; **an unsolicited gift; unsolicited goods** = goods which are sent to someone who has not asked for them, suggesting that he might like to buy them

unsolved *adjective* (crime) which has not been solved

unsound *adjective* **persons of unsound mind** = people who are not sane

unsuccessful *adjective* without any success; **the police carried out an unsuccessful search for the suspect**

unsworn *adjective* which has not been made on oath; **an unsworn statement**

untrue *adjective* not true; **he made an untrue statement in court**

unwritten *adjective* **unwritten agreement** = agreement which has been reached orally (such as in a telephone conversation) but has not been written down; **unwritten law** = rule which is established by precedent

uphold *verb* to keep in good order; **to uphold the law** = to make sure that laws are obeyed; **to uphold a sentence** = to reject an appeal against a sentence; **the Appeal Court upheld the sentence** NOTE: **upholding - upheld**

urgent *adjective* which has to be done quickly

◊ **urgently** *adverb* immediately

urine *noun* waste water from the body;
urine test = test of a sample of a person's
urine to see if it contains drugs *or* alcohol

usage *noun* **(a)** custom *or* way in which
something is usually done **(b)** how something is used

use 1 *noun* **(a)** land held by the legal
owner on trust for a beneficiary; **change of
use** = order allowing a property to be used
in a different way (such as a dwelling
house to be used as a business office, a
shop to be used as a factory); **land zoned for
industrial use** = land where planning
permission has been given to build factories **(b)** way in which something can be
used; **directions for use** = instructions how
to run a machine; **to make use of something**
= to use something; **items for personal use**
= items which a person will use for
himself, not on behalf of the company; **he
has the use of a company car** = he has a
company car which he uses privately **2**
verb to take a machine *or* a company *or* a
process, etc., and work with it; **he used the
courts to evict his tenants; we use second-
class mail for all our correspondence; the
office computer is being used all the time;
they use freelance typists for most of their
work**

◊ **user** *noun* person who uses something;
end user = person who actually uses a
product; **user's guide** *or* **handbook** = book
showing someone how to use something;
registered user = person *or* company
which has been given official permission
to use a registered trademark

◊ **user-friendly** *adjective* which a computer user finds easy to work; **these
programs are really user-friendly**

usher *noun* person who guards the door
leading into a courtroom and maintains
order in court

usual *adjective* normal *or* ordinary; **our
usual terms** *or* **usual conditions are thirty
days' credit; the usual practice is to have the
contract signed by a director of the
company; the usual hours of work are from
9.30 to 5.30**

usufruct *noun* right to enjoy the use *or* the
profit of the property *or* land of another
person

usurp *verb* to take and use a right which is
not yours (especially to take the throne
from a rightful king)

◊ **usurpation** *noun* taking and using a
right which is not yours

usury *noun* lending money at very high
interest
NOTE: no plural

utter *verb* **(a)** to say; **the prisoner did not
utter a word when the sentence was read out
(b)** to use a forged document criminally;
forgery and uttering = notifiable offence
of forging and then using an official
document (such as a prescription for
drugs)

Vv

v. = VERSUS against
NOTE: titles of cases are quoted as *Hills* v. *The
Amalgamated Company Ltd*; *R.* v. *Smith*

vacant *adjective* empty *or* not occupied;
vacant possession = being able to occupy a
property immediately after buying it
because it is empty; **the house is for sale
with vacant possession; situations vacant** *or*
appointments vacant = list (in a newspaper) of jobs which are available

vacantia *see* BONA VACANTIA

vacate *verb* **to vacate the premises** = to
leave premises, so that they become empty

◊ **vacation** *noun* **(a)** *GB* period when
the courts are closed between sittings *or*
period of university holidays **(b)** *US*
holiday *or* period when people are not
working

vagrant *noun* person who goes about with
no place to live

◊ **vagrancy** *noun* being a vagrant; **he
was charged with vagrancy**
NOTE: no plural

valid *adjective* **(a)** which is acceptable
because it is true; **that is not a valid
argument** *or* **excuse (b)** which can be used
lawfully; **the contract is not valid if it has**

not been witnessed; **ticket which is valid for three months; he was carrying a valid passport**

◇ **validate** *verb* **(a)** to check to see if something is correct; **the document was validated by the bank (b)** to make (something) valid; **the import documents have to be validated by the customs officials**

◇ **validation** *noun* act of making something valid

◇ **validity** *noun* being valid; **period of validity** = length of time for which a document is valid
NOTE: no plural

valorem *see* AD VALOREM

valuable *adjective* which is worth a lot of money; **valuable consideration** = something of value (such as money) which is passed from one party (the promisee) to another (the promisor) as payment for what is promised; **valuable property** *or* **valuables** = personal items which are worth a lot of money

◇ **valuation** *noun* estimate of how much something is worth; **to ask for a valuation of a property before making an offer for it; stock valuation** = estimating the value of stock at the end of an accounting period

◇ **value** 1 *noun* amount of money which something is worth; **he imported goods to the value of £250; the fall in the value of the dollar; the valuer put the value of the stock at £25,000; asset value** = value of a company calculated by adding together all its assets; **book value** = value as recorded in the company's accounts; **declared value** = value of goods entered on a customs declaration form; **face value** *or* **nominal value** = value written on a coin *or* banknote *or* share; **market value** = value of an asset *or* of a product *or* of a company, if sold today; **surrender value** = money which an insurer will pay if an insurance policy is given up before maturity date **2** *verb* to estimate how much money something is worth; **goods valued at £250; he valued the stock at £25,000; we are having the jewellery valued for insurance; valued policy** = marine insurance policy where the value of what is insured is stated

◇ **Value Added Tax (VAT)** *noun* tax imposed as a percentage of the invoice value of goods and services

◇ **valuer** *noun* person who values property for insurance purposes

vandal *noun* person who destroys property, especially public property, wilfully; **vandals have pulled the telephones out of the call boxes**

◇ **vandalism** *noun* wilful destruction of property
NOTE: no plural

◇ **vandalize** *verb* to destroy property wilfully; **none of the call boxes work because they have all been vandalized**

vary *verb* to change (the conditions of an order)

◇ **variation** *noun* change in conditions; **the petitioner asked for a variation in her maintenance order**

VAT = VALUE ADDED TAX

vault *noun* underground strongroom usually built under a bank

VC = VICE CHANCELLOR

vendor *noun* **(a)** person who sells; **the solicitor acting on behalf of the vendor (b) street vendor** = person who sells food or small items in the street

venue *noun* place where a meeting *or* hearing is held; **mistake in venue** = starting legal proceedings in the wrong court

verbal *adjective* using spoken words, not writing; **verbal agreement** = agreement which is spoken (such as over the telephone); **verbal warning** = stage in warning a worker that his work is not satisfactory (followed by a written warning, if his work does not improve)

◇ **verbally** *adverb* using spoken words, not writing; **they agreed to the terms verbally, and then started to draft the contract**

verbatim *adjective & adverb* in the exact words; **a verbatim transcript of the trial**

verdict *noun* **(a)** decision of a jury *or* magistrate; **to bring in** *or* **to return a verdict** = to state a verdict at the end of a trial; **the jury brought in** *or* **returned a verdict of not guilty; to come to a verdict** *or* **to reach a verdict** = to decide whether the accused is guilty or not; **the jury took two hours to reach their verdict; majority verdict** =

verdict agreed by at least ten of the jurors **(b)** decision reached by a coroner's court; **the court returned a verdict of death by misadventure; open verdict** = verdict in a coroner's court which does not decide how a person died; **the court recorded an open verdict on the dead policeman**

verify *verb* to check to see if something is correct

◇ **verification** *noun* checking if something is correct; **the shipment was allowed into the country after verification of the documents by the customs**

versa *see* VICE VERSA

version *noun* description of what happened; **she disputed the policeman's version of events** = she argued that the policeman's story of what happened was wrong

versus *preposition* against
NOTE: usually abbreviated to **v.** as in **the case of** *Smith* v. *Williams*

vest *verb* to transfer to someone the legal ownership and possession of land *or* of a right; **the property was vested in the trustees**
NOTE: you vest something **in** *or* **on** someone

◇ **vested interest** *noun* **(a)** interest in a property which will come into a person's possession when the interest of another person ends **(b)** special interest in keeping an existing state of affairs; **she has a vested interest in keeping the business working** = she wants to keep the business working because she will make more money if it does

◇ **vested remainder** *noun* remainder which is absolutely vested in a person

◇ **vesting assent** *noun* document which vests settled land on a tenant for life

◇ **vesting order** *noun* court order which transfers property

vet *verb* to examine someone *or* a document carefully to see if there is any breach of security; **all applications are vetted by the Home Office; positive vetting** = discovery after examination that a person working with classified information may after all not be reliable
NOTE: **vetting - vetted**

veto **1** *noun* ban *or* order not to allow something to become law, even if it has been passed by a parliament; **the President**

has the power of veto over Bills passed by Congress; the UK used its veto in the Security Council** **2** *verb* to ban something *or* to order something not to become law; **the resolution was vetoed by the president; the council has vetoed all plans to hold protest marches in the centre of town**

vexatious *adjective* annoying *or* done in order to annoy; **vexatious action** *or* **litigation** = case brought in order to annoy the defendant; **vexatious litigant** = person who frequently starts legal actions to annoy people and who is barred from bringing actions without leave of the court

viable *adjective* which can work; **not commercially viable** = not likely to make a profit; **viable alternative** = different proposal which may work

vicarious *adjective* not direct *or* not personally interested; **vicarious performance** = performance of a contract where the work has been done by a third party; **vicarious liability** = liability of one person for torts committed by someone else, especially the liability of an employer for acts committed by an employee in the course of his work

> COMMENT: if the employee is on a frolic of his own, the employer may not be liable

◇ **vicariously** *adverb* not directly

vice- *prefix* deputy *or* second in command; **he is the vice-chairman of an industrial group; she was appointed to the vice-chairmanship of the committee**

◇ **Vice Chancellor** *noun* senior judge in charge of the Chancery Division of the High Court

◇ **Vice-President** *noun* deputy to a president

vice versa *Latin phrase meaning* "reverse position": in the opposite way; **the responsibilities of the employer towards the employee and vice versa**

victim *noun* person who suffers a crime *or* a wrong; **the mugger left his victim lying in the road; he was the victim of a con trick; the accident victims** *or* **victims of the accident were taken to hospital**

vide *Latin word meaning* "see": used in written texts to refer to another reference

videlicet *Latin word meaning* "that is" NOTE: usually abbreviated to **viz**

view 1 *noun* way of thinking about something; **to take a view on something** = to have an opinion about something; **to take the view that** = to decide that *or* to have the opinion that; **the court takes the view that the defendant did not publish the defamation maliciously; to take the long view** = to plan for a long period before your current investment will become profitable; **in view of** = because of; **in view of the age of the accused the magistrates gave him a suspended sentence 2** *verb* to look at; **viewing the scene** = visit by a judge and jury to the place where a crime was committed

villain *noun GB informal* criminal; **the job of the policeman is to catch villains**
◊ **villainy** *noun* wilful illegal act

violate *verb* to break a rule *or* a law; **the council has violated the planning regulations; the action of the government violates the international treaty on commercial shipping**
◊ **violation** *noun* act of breaking a rule; **the number of traffic violations has increased; the court criticized the violations of the treaty on human rights; in violation of a rule** = breaking a rule; **the government has acted in violation of its agreement**

violent *adjective* using force; **a violent attack on the police; the prisoner became violent** = the prisoner tried to attack
◊ **violence** *noun* action using force; **robbery with violence** = robbery where force is used against people *or* property; **violence against the person** = one of the types of notifiable offence (such as murder *or* assault) against people
◊ **violently** *adverb* in a violent way

vires *see* INTRA VIRES, ULTRA VIRES

virtute officii *Latin phrase meaning* "because of his office"

vis major *Latin words meaning* "superior force": force of people *or* of nature (such as a revolution *or* an earthquake) which cannot be stopped

visa *noun* special document *or* special stamp in a passport which allows someone to enter a country; **you will need a visa before you go to the USA; he filled in his visa application form; entry visa** = visa allowing someone to enter a country; **multiple entry visa** = visa allowing someone to enter a country many times; **tourist visa** = visa which allows a person to visit a country for a short time on holiday; **transit visa** = visa which allows someone to spend a short time in one country while travelling to another country

visitor *noun* person who goes to see someone for a short time; **prison visitor** = member of a board of visitors appointed by the Home Secretary to visit, inspect and report on conditions in a prison

viva voce *Latin phrase meaning* "orally *or* by speaking"

vivos *Latin word meaning* "living people"; **gift inter vivos** = present given by one living person to another

viz *see* VIDELICET

void 1 *adjective* not legally valid *or* not having any legal effect; **void marriage** = marriage which is declared not to have had any legal existence; **the contract was declared null and void** = the contract was said to be no longer valid **2** *verb* **to void a contract** = to make a contract invalid
◊ **voidable** *adjective* which can be made void

COMMENT: a contract is void where it never had legal effect, but is voidable if it is apparently of legal effect and remains of legal effect until one or both parties take steps to rescind it

volenti non fit injuria *Latin phrase meaning* "there can be no injury to a person who is willing": rule that if someone has agreed to take the risk of an injury he cannot sue for it (as in the case of someone injured in a boxing match)

volume *noun* large book *or* one book out of a set of books; **Volume 13 of the Law Reports; look in the 1985 volume of the regulations**

voluntary *adjective* **(a)** done without being forced *or* without being paid; **voluntary confession** = confession made by an accused person without being threatened *or* paid; **voluntary disposition** = transfer of property without any valuable consideration; **voluntary liquidation** *or* **winding up** = situation where a company itself decides it must close and sell its assets; **voluntary redundancy** = situation where a worker asks to be made redundant, usually in return for a payment **(b)** without being paid a salary; **voluntary organization** = organization which has no paid staff

◊ **voluntarily** *adverb* without being forced *or* paid; **he voluntarily gave himself up to the police**

volunteer 1 *noun* **(a)** person who gives *or* receives property without consideration **(b)** person who offers to do something without being forced 2 *verb* **(a)** to offer information without being asked; **he volunteered the information that the defendant was not in fact a British subject (b)** to offer to do something without being forced; **six men volunteered to go into the burning house**

vote 1 *noun* marking a paper, holding up your hand, etc., to show your opinion *or* to show who you want to be elected; **to take a vote on a proposal** *or* **to put a proposal to the vote** = to ask people present at a meeting to say if they agree or do not agree with the proposal; **block vote** = casting of a large number of votes at the same time (such as of trade union members) by a person who has been delegated by the holders of the votes to vote for them in this way; **casting vote** = vote used by the chairman in the case where the votes for and against a proposal are equal; **the chairman has the casting vote; he used his casting vote to block the motion; popular vote** = vote of all the people in a country; **the president is elected by popular vote** = the president is elected by a majority of all the people in a country; **postal vote** = election where the voters send in their voting papers by post; **vote of censure** *or* **censure vote** = vote which criticizes someone, especially a vote which criticizes the government in the House of Commons; **vote of no confidence** = vote to show that a person *or* group is not trusted; **the chairman resigned after the vote of no confidence in him was passed by the AGM** 2 *verb* to show an opinion by marking a paper *or* by holding up your hand at a meeting; **the meeting voted to close the factory; 52% of the members voted for Mr Smith as chairman; to vote for a proposal** *or* **to vote against a proposal** = to say that you agree or do not agree with a proposal; **two directors were voted off the board at the AGM** = the AGM voted to dismiss two directors; **she was voted on to the committee** = she was elected a member of the committee

◊ **voter** *noun* person who votes

◊ **voting** *noun* act of making a vote; **voting paper** = paper on which the voter puts a cross to show for whom he wants to vote; **voting rights** = rights of shareholders to voting at company meetings; **non-voting shares** = shares which do not allow the shareholder to vote at company meetings

vouch for *verb* to state that you believe something is correct *or* to say that you take responsibility for something; **I cannot vouch for the correctness of the transcript of proceedings**

voucher *noun* paper which entitles the bearer to receive something

Ww

wager 1 *noun* bet *or* amount deposited when you risk money on the result of a race *or* a game *or* an election 2 *verb* to bet *or* to risk money on the possibility of something happening; **he wagered £100 on the result of the election**

> COMMENT: a wager will not normally be enforced by a court under English law

waive *verb* to give up (a right); **he waived his claim to the estate; to waive a payment** = to say that payment is not necessary

◊ **waiver** *noun* voluntarily giving up (a right) *or* removing the conditions (of a rule); **if you want to work without a permit, you will have to apply for a waiver; waiver clause** = clause in a contract giving the conditions under which the rights in the contract can be given up

Wales and Chester Circuit *noun* one of the six circuits of the Crown Court to which barristers belong, with its centre in Cardiff

walking possession *noun* temporary possession of a debtor's goods taken by a bailiff *or* sheriff until they can be sold to satisfy execution

war *noun* situation where one country fights another; **the two countries are at war; to declare war on a country** = to state officially that a state of war exists between the two countries; **civil war** = situation inside a country where groups of armed people fight against each other *or* fight against the government; **prisoner of war** = member of the armed forces captured by the enemy in time of war

ward 1 *noun* (a) minor protected by a guardian; **Mr Jones acting on behalf of his ward, Miss Smith** (b) minor protected by a court; **ward of court** = minor under the protection of the High Court; **the High Court declared the girl ward of court, to protect her from her uncle who wanted to take her out of the country** 2 *verb* to make a child a ward; **the court warded the girl**

◊ **wardship** *noun* being in charge of a ward *or* the power of a court to take on itself the rights and responsibilites of parents in the interests of a child; **the judge has discretion to exercise the wardship jurisdiction**
NOTE: no plural

warden *noun* (i) person who is in charge of an institution; (ii) person who sees that rules are obeyed; **traffic warden** = official whose duty is to regulate the traffic under the supervision of the police, especially to deal with cars which are illegally parked

warder *noun* guard in a prison

warehouse 1 *noun* large building where goods are stored; **bonded warehouse** = warehouse where goods are stored until excise duty has been paid 2 *verb* to store (goods) in a warehouse

◊ **warehousing** *noun* act of storing goods; **warehousing costs are rising rapidly; warehousing in bond** = keeping imported goods in a warehouse without payment of

duty, either to be exported again, or for sale into the country when the duty has been paid
NOTE: no plural

warn *verb* to say that there is a possible danger; **the judge warned the jury that the trial would be long and complicated; the policeman warned the motorist not to exceed the speed limit; he warned the shareholders that the dividend might be cut; the government warned of possible import duties**
NOTE: you warn someone **of** something, or **that** something may happen

◊ **warning** *noun* notice of possible danger; **to issue a warning about pickpockets; warning notices were put up around the construction site; he received a warning from the magistrates that for the next offence he might be sent to prison; drivers paid no attention to the warning signs**

warrant 1 *noun* official document from a court which allows someone to do something; **to issue a warrant for the arrest of someone** *or* **to issue an arrest warrant for someone** = to make out and sign an official document which authorizes the police to arrest someone; **bench warrant** = warrant issued by a court for the arrest of an accused person who has not appeared to answer charges; **search warrant** = official document signed by a magistrate allowing the police to enter and search premises; **warrant of committal** *or* **committal warrant** = court order sending a convicted person to prison; **warrant of execution** = warrant issued by a court which gives the bailiffs *or* sheriffs the power to seize goods from a debtor in order to pay his debts 2 *verb* to guarantee; **all the spare parts are warranted; the car is warranted in perfect condition**

◊ **warrantee** *noun* person who is given a warranty

◊ **warrantor** *noun* person who gives a warranty

◊ **warranty** *noun* (a) guarantee; **the car is sold with a twelve-month warranty; the warranty covers spare parts but not labour costs** (b) contractual term which is secondary to the main purpose of the contract; **breach of warranty** = failing to do something which is a part of a contract (c) statement made by an insured person which declares that the facts stated by him are true

wastage *noun* things which have been wasted; **natural wastage** = losing workers because they resign or retire, not through redundancies or dismissals

waste 1 *noun* permanent damage done to land which diminishes its value **2** *verb* to use something wrongly *or* to make bad use of something; **to waste time** = to spend too much time doing something *or* to use time for purposes which are not relevant; **he was accused of wasting the court's time** *or* **of wasting police time**

watch *noun* group of people who patrol the streets to maintain law and order; **watch committee** = committee of a local authority which supervises the policing of an area; **neighbourhood watch** = system where the residents in an area are encouraged to look out for criminals and help the police

◇ **watchdog body** *noun* body which watches something (especially government departments *or* commercial firms) to see that regulations are not being abused

way *noun* **(a)** act of going; **right of way** = right to go lawfully along a path on another person's land (NOTE: no plural) **(b)** manner of doing something; **Committee of Ways and Means** = committee of the whole House of Commons which examines the Supply Bill

weak *adjective* not strong; **weak case** = criminal case where the evidence against the accused is not strong

◇ **weakness** *noun* being weak; **the hearing was abandoned because of the weakness of the prosecution case**

weapon *noun* **dangerous** *or* **offensive weapon** = item (such as a gun *or* knife) which can be used to harm someone physically; **carrying offensive weapons** = offence of holding a weapon *or* something (such as a bottle) which could be used as a weapon

wear and tear *noun* **fair wear and tear** = acceptable damage caused by normal use; **the insurance policy covers most damage but not fair wear and tear to the machine**
NOTE: no plural

Weekly Law Reports (WLR) *plural noun* regular reports of cases published by the Council of Law Reporting

welfare *noun* comfort *or* being well cared for; **it is the duty of the juvenile court to see to the welfare of children in care; welfare state** = state which spends a large amount of money to make sure that its citizens are well looked after

Western Circuit *noun* one of the six circuits of the Crown Court to which barristers belong, with its centre in Bristol

whatsoever *adjective* of any sort; **there is no substance whatsoever in the report; the police found no suspicious documents whatsoever**
NOTE: always used after a noun and after a negative

where- *prefix* which thing
NOTE: the following words formed from **where-** are frequently used in legal documents

◇ **whereas** *conjunction* as the situation is stated *or* taking the following fact into consideration; **whereas the property is held in trust for the appellant; whereas the contract between the two parties stipulated that either party may withdraw at six months' notice**

◇ **whereby** *adverb* by which; **a deed whereby ownership of the property is transferred**

◇ **wherein** *adverb* in which; **a document wherein the regulations are listed**

◇ **whereof** *adverb* of which; **in witness whereof I sign my hand** = I sign as a witness that this is correct

◇ **whereon** *adverb* on which; **land whereon a dwelling is constructed**

◇ **wheresoever** *adverb* in any place where; **the insurance covering jewels wheresoever they may be kept**

whip 1 *noun* **(a)** long thin piece of leather, used for beating animals to make them work **(b)** MP who controls the attendance of other MPs of his party at the House of Commons, who makes sure that all MPs vote **(c)** instruction given by a whip to other MPs; **three line whip** = strict instructions to MPs to vote as the whips tell them **2** *verb* to beat with a whip

White Book *noun* book containing the Rules of the Supreme Court and a commentary on them

◊ **white collar crime** *noun* crimes committed by business people *or* office workers (such as embezzlement, computer fraud, insider dealings)

◊ **White Paper** *noun* *GB* report from the government on a particular problem

whole *adjective* complete *or* total; **of the whole blood** = relationship whereby a person is related to someone by two common ancestors

whole-life insurance *or* **whole-life policy** *noun* insurance *or* policy where the insured person pays a fixed premium each year and the insurance company pays a sum when he dies

wholesale *noun & adverb* buying goods direct from the producers and selling in large quantities to traders who then sell in smaller quantities to the general public; **wholesale dealer** = person who buys in bulk from producers and sells to retailers NOTE: no plural

◊ **wholesaler** *noun* person who buys goods in bulk from producers and sells them to retailers

wholly-owned subsidiary *noun* company which is owned completely by another company

widow *noun* woman whose husband has died

◊ **widower** *noun* man whose wife has died

wife *noun* female spouse *or* woman married to a husband

wilful *adjective* (person) who is determined to do what he wants *or* (act) which is done because someone wants to do it, regardless of the effect it may have on others; **wilful misconduct** = behaviour which may harm someone and which is known to be wrong; **wilful murder** = murder which is premeditated; **wilful neglect** = intentionally not doing something which it is your duty to do

◊ **wilfully** *adverb* done because someone wants to do it, regardless of the effect on others; **he wilfully set fire to the building**

will *noun* (a) **will** *or* (*formal*) **last will and testament** = legal document by which a person gives instructions to his executors as to how his property should be disposed of after he dies; **he wrote his will in 1964; according to her will, all her property is left to her children; holograph will** = will, written out by hand, and not necessarily witnessed; **nuncupative will** = unwritten will stated in the presence of a witness (such as by a soldier in time of war); *see also* BEQUEST, DEVISE, LEGACY

COMMENT: to make a valid will, a person must be of age and of sound mind; normally a will must be signed and witnessed in the presence of two witnesses who are not interested in the will. In English law there is complete freedom to dispose of one's property after death as one wishes. However, any dependant may apply for provision to be made out of the estate of a deceased under the Inheritance (Provision for Family and Dependants) Act

(b) wishing *or* wanting to do something; **tenancy at will** = situation where the owner of a property allows a tenant to occupy it as long as either party wishes

wind up *verb* (a) to end (a meeting); **he wound up the meeting with a vote of thanks to the committee** (b) **to wind up a company** = to put a company into liquidation; **the court ordered the company to be wound up** NOTE: **winding - wound - has wound**

◊ **winding up** *noun* liquidation *or* closing of a company and selling its assets; **compulsory winding up order** = order from a court saying that a company must be wound up; **voluntary winding up** = situation where a company itself decides it must close down; **winding up petition** = application to a court for an order that a company be put into liquidation

with costs *adverb* **judgment for someone with costs** = judgment that the party's plea was correct and that all the costs of the case should be paid by the other party

withdraw *verb* (a) to take (money) out of an account; **to withdraw money from the bank** *or* **from your account; you can withdraw up to £50 from any bank on presentation of a banker's card** (b) to take back (an offer); **one of the company's**

backers has withdrawn = he stopped supporting the company financially; **to withdraw a takeover bid (c)** to take back a charge *or* an accusation *or* a statement; **the prosecution has withdrawn the charges against him; the opposition MPs forced the minister to withdraw his statement; the chairman asked him to withdraw the remarks he had made about the finance director**
NOTE: **withdrawing - withdrew - has withdrawn**

◊ **withdrawal** *noun* removing money from an account; **withdrawal without penalty at seven days' notice** = money can be taken out of a deposit account, without losing any interest, provided that seven days' notice has been given

withhold *verb* to keep back *or* not to give (information); **he was charged with withholding information from the police; approval of any loan will not be unreasonably withheld**

within *preposition* inside; **the case falls within the jurisdiction of the court; he was within his rights when he challenged the statement made by the police officer**

without *preposition* **without prejudice** = phrase spoken *or* written in letters when attempting to negotiate a settlement, meaning that the negotiations cannot be referred to in court *or* relied upon by the other party if the discussions fail; **without reserve** = sale at an auction where an item has no reserve price

witness 1 *noun* **(a)** person who sees something happen *or* who is present when something happens; **to act as a witness to a document** *or* **a signature** = to sign a document to show that you have watched the main signatory sign it; **the contract has to be signed in the presence of two witnesses; in witness whereof** = first words of the testimonium clause, where the signatory of the will *or* contract signs **(b)** person who appears in court to give evidence; **defence witness** *or* **witness for the defence** = person who is called to court to give evidence which helps the case of the defendant *or* of the accused; **prosecution witness** *or* **witness for the prosecution** = person called by the prosecution side to give evidence against the defendant *or* the accused; **adverse witness** = witness whose evidence is not favourable to the side which has called

him; **expert** *or* **professional** *or* **skilled witness** = witness who is a specialist in a subject and is asked to give his opinion on technical matters **2** *verb* to sign (a document) to show that you guarantee that the other signatures on it are genuine; **to witness an agreement** *or* **a signature; "now this deed witnesseth"** = words indicating that the details of the agreement follow

WLR = WEEKLY LAW REPORTS

Woolsack *noun* seat of the Lord Chancellor in the House of Lords

word 1 *noun* separate item of speech *or* writing; **word processing** = working with words, using a computer to produce, check and change texts, letters, contracts, etc.; **to give one's word** = to promise; **he gave his word that the matter would remain confidential 2** *verb* to put something into words; **the contract was incorrectly worded**

◊ **wording** *noun* series of words; **did you understand the wording of the contract?**
NOTE: no plural

wound 1 *noun* cut done to the skin of a person; **she has a knife wound in her leg 2** *verb* to injure *or* to hurt someone in such a way that his skin is cut; **he was wounded in the fight**

WPC = WOMAN POLICE CONSTABLE

wreck 1 *noun* **(a)** (i) action of sinking *or* badly damaging a ship; (ii) ship which has sunk *or* which has been badly damaged and cannot float; **they saved the cargo from the wreck; oil poured out of the wreck of the ship (b)** company which has become insolvent; **he managed to save some of his investment from the wreck of the company; investors lost thousands of pounds in the wreck of the investment company 2** *verb* to damage badly *or* to ruin; **they are trying to salvage the wrecked ship; the defence case was wrecked by the defendant's behaviour in court**

writ *noun* **(a) writ (of summons)** = legal document which begins an action in the High Court; **the company issued a writ to prevent the trade union from going on strike; he issued writs for libel in connection with allegations made in a Sunday newspaper; to serve someone with a writ** = to give someone a writ officially, so that he has to defend it *or* allow judgment to be taken against him; **writ of habeas corpus =** writ to obtain the release of someone who has been unlawfully held in prison or in police custody *or* to make the person holding a prisoner appear in court to explain why he is being held **(b)** legal action to hold a by-election; **to move a writ** = to propose in the House of Commons that a by-election should be held

wrong 1 *adjective* not right *or* not correct *or* not legal; **copying computer data is wrong; the total in the last column is wrong; the driver gave the wrong address to the policeman; I tried to phone you, but I got the wrong number 2** *noun* act against natural justice *or* act which infringes someone else's right; **civil wrongs against persons or property are called "torts"**

◊ **wrongdoer** *noun* person who commits an offence

◊ **wrongdoing** *noun* bad behaviour *or* actions which are against the law
NOTE: no plural

◊ **wrongful** *adjective* unlawful; **wrongful dismissal =** removing someone from a job for a reason which does not justify dismissal and which is in breach of the contract of employment

> COMMENT: an employee can complain of wrongful dismissal to the County Court

◊ **wrongfully** *adverb* in an unlawful way; **he claimed he was wrongfully dismissed; she was accused of wrongfully holding her clients' money**

◊ **wrongly** *adverb* not correctly *or* badly; **he wrongly invoiced Smith Ltd for £250, when he should have credited them with the same amount**

Xx Yy Zz

Yard *noun* **Scotland Yard** *or* **the Yard =** headquarters of the Metropolitan Police in London

year *noun* period of twelve months; **calendar year =** year from January 1st to December 31st; **financial year =** the twelve month period for a firm's accounts; **fiscal year** *or* **tax year =** twelve month period on which taxes are calculated (in the UK it is April 6th to April 5th of the following year); **year end =** the end of the financial year, when a company's accounts are prepared; **the accounts department has started work on the year-end accounts**

yellow dog contract *noun US* contract of employment where the employee is forbidden to join a trade union

yield 1 *noun* money produced as a return on an investment **2** *verb* to produce interest *or* dividend; **the bonds yield 8%**

young offender *noun* person aged between seventeen and twenty years of age who has committed an offence

◊ **young person** *noun* person over fourteen years of age, but less than seventeen

youth *noun* young man *or* young person; **youth custody order =** sentence sending a young person to detention in a special centre

zebra crossing *noun* place in a street marked with white lines, where pedestrians can cross and have right of way

zero *noun* nought *or* number 0; **the code for international calls is zero one zero (010); zero inflation =** inflation at 0%

◊ **zero-rated** *adjective* (item) which has a VAT rate of 0%

◊ **zero-rating** *noun* rating an item at 0% VAT

zip code *noun US* letters and numbers used to indicate a town *or* street in an address on an envelope
NOTE: GB English is **post code**

zone *verb* to order that land in a district shall be used only for one type of building; **the land is zoned for industrial use**

◊ **zoning** *noun* order by a local council that land shall be used only for one type of building
NOTE: no plural

SUPPLEMENT

c. 29   1

ELIZABETH II

Enduring Powers of Attorney Act 1985

1985 CHAPTER 29

An Act to enable powers of attorney to be created which will survive any subsequent mental incapacity of the donor and to make provision in connection with such powers.   [26th June 1985]

BE IT ENACTED by the Queen's most Excellent Majesty, by and with the advice and consent of the Lords Spiritual and Temporal, and Commons, in this present Parliament assembled, and by the authority of the same, as follows:—

Enduring powers of attorney

1.—(1) Where an individual creates a power of attorney which is an enduring power within the meaning of this Act then—

> (a) the power shall not be revoked by any subsequent mental incapacity of his; but
>
> (b) upon such incapacity supervening the donee of the power may not do anything under the authority of the power except as provided by subsection (2) below or as directed or authorised by the court under section 5 unless or, as the case may be, until the instrument creating the power is registered by the court under section 6; and

Enduring power of attorney to survive mental incapacity of donor.

A 2

1986 No. 636 (L.3)

COUNTY COURTS

PROCEDURE

The County Court (Amendment) Rules 1986

Made - - - -	26*th March* 1986
Coming into force	28*th April* 1986

Citation and interpretation

1.—(1) These Rules may be cited as the County Court (Amendment) Rules 1986.

(2) In these Rules, unless the context otherwise requires, an Order referred to by number means the Order so numbered in the County Court Rules 1981**(a)** and Appendix A, B or C means Appendix A, B or C to those Rules.

Service of documents through document exchanges

2. After the definition of "defendant" in Order 1, rule 3, there shall be inserted the following definition:—

" 'document exchange' means any document exchange for the time being approved by the Lord Chancellor;".

3. After Order 2, rule 5(1), there shall be inserted the following new paragraph:—

"(1A) References in paragraph (1) to the conduct of business by post and to the sending of documents by prepaid post shall include in any case where the court is a member of a document exchange and the party is represented by a solicitor references to the conduct of business and to the sending of documents through a document exchange.".

4. For Order 7, rule 1(1)(*b*), there shall be substituted the following sub-paragraph:—

"(*b*) if the person to be served is acting by a solicitor:—

(i) by delivering the document at, or sending it by first-class post to, the solicitor's address for service, or

(ii) where the solicitor's address for service includes a numbered box at a document exchange, by leaving the document at that document exchange or at a document exchange which transmits documents daily to that document exchange.".

(a) S.I. 1981/1687; the relevant amending instruments are S.I. 1982/436, 1140, 1794, 1983/1716, 1984/576, 878, 1985/566 and 1269.

A

B I L L

T O

Establish a legally enforceable right to interest on late payment of debts.

BE IT ENACTED by the Queen's most Excellent Majesty, by and with the advice and consent of the Lords Spiritual and Temporal, and Commons, in this present Parliament assembled, and by the authority of the same, as follows:— A.D. 1986.

5 **1.** The High Court or the County Court is empowered to award simple interest on late payment of debts subject to the provisions of section 2 below. Right to Interest.

2.—(1) Subject to the Rules of Court, in proceedings (whenever instituted) before the High Court or a County Court for the 10 recovery of simple interest, the Court shall give judgement, at such rate as the Court thinks fit, or the rules of Court may provide, for the period between the date when the cause of action arose and the date of payment. Conditions relating to right to Interest.

(2) The cause of action shall arise 30 days after notice in 15 writing is given of the intention to claim simple interest on a debt.

(3) The Rules of Court may provide for a rate of interest by reference to the rate specified in section 17 of the Judgements Act 1838 as that section has effect from time to time or by reference to a rate for which any other enactment provides. 1838 c. 110.

[Bill 127] 49/3

2   *Right to Interest*

(4) Interest in respect of a debt shall not be awarded under this section for a period during which, for whatever reason, interest on the debt already runs.

(5) Interest under this section may be calculated at different rates in respect of different periods.   5

Short title
and
commence-
ment.

3.—(1) This Act may be cited as the Right to Interest Act 1986.

(2) This Act shall come into force at the end of the period of two months beginning with the day on which it is passed.

[Bill 127]

Printed and published by
Her Majesty's Stationery Office
Printed in England at St Stephen's
Parliamentary Press

LONDON

(312767)

45p net

49/3

*Ordered by The House of Commons,
to be Printed, 8 April 1986.*

*Ordered to be brought in by
Mr. Richard Ottaway, Mr. Patrick Nicholls,
Mr. Andrew Rowe, Mr. Michael Grylls,
Mr. Michael Fallon, Mr. Michael Forsyth
and Mr. Michael Knowles*

A

B I L L

To establish a legally enforceable right to
interest on late payment of debts.

Right to Interest

ISBN 0 10 312786 0

Notice of the European Parliament

III

(Notices)

EUROPEAN PARLIAMENT

NOTICE

(86/C 116/03)

GENERAL PROVISIONS GOVERNING OPEN COMPETITIONS

Open competitions organized for the recruitment of officials of the European Communities shall, in accordance with the provisions of the Staff Regulations, be preceded by a notice of competition published in the *Official Journal of the European Communities*. Competitions may be organized both to fill a certain number of vacancies and to draw up a reserve list.

I. General conditions

To be eligible for appointment as an official in an institution of the European Communities, the candidate shall, pursuant to the provisions of the Staff Regulations:

1. be a national of one of the Member States of the Communities (¹), unless an exception is authorized by the appointing authority, and enjoy his full rights as citizen;

2. have fulfilled any obligations imposed on him by the laws concerning military service;

3. produce the appropriate character references as to his suitability for the performance of his duties;

4. have passed a competition based on either qualifications or tests, or both qualifications and tests;

5. be physically fit to perform his duties;

6. have a thorough knowledge of one of the official languages of the Communities (²) and a satisfactory knowledge of another official language of the Communities to the extent necessary for the performance of his duties.

(¹) The Member States are Belgium, Denmark, France, the Federal Republic of Germany, Greece, Ireland, Italy, Luxembourg, the Netherlands, Portugal, Spain and the United Kingdom.

(²) The official Community languages are Danish, Dutch, English, French, German, Greek, Italian, Portuguese and Spanish.

Regulation of the Commission of the European Communities

13. 5. 86   Official Journal of the European Communities   No L 125/15

COMMISSION REGULATION (EEC) No 1399/86

of 12 May 1986

amending Regulation (EEC) No 1146/86 laying down protective measures, in respect of imports of sweet potatoes

THE COMMISSION OF THE EUROPEAN COMMUNITIES,

Having regard to the Treaty establishing the European Economic Community,

Having regard to Council Regulation (EEC) No 2727/75 of 29 October 1975 on the common organization of the market in cereals [1], as last amended by Regulation (EEC) No 3793/85 [2], and in particular Article 20 (2) thereof,

Whereas, in accordance with Commission Regulation (EEC) No 1146/86 [3], the issue of import licences for sweet potatoes falling within subheading 07.06 B of the Common Customs Tariff has been suspended since 19 April 1986 ;

Whereas this is the first time that the issue of import licences has been suspended for such products and this has occured in the middle of a period of shipment ; whereas the special situation of products which were being loaded or shipped by sea on 19 April 1986 should be taken into account ;

Whereas, with a view to control and administrative management, the term of validity of licences issued in compliance with this Regulation should be limited,

HAS ADOPTED THIS REGULATION :

Article 1

The following three subparagraphs are added to Article 1 of Regulation (EEC) No 1146/86 :

'This Regulation shall not apply to products which are shown to be in shipment on the date of publication of this Regulation, or to have left the supplying country by that date.

The parties concerned shall prove to the satisfaction of the competent authority that the conditions laid down in the second subparagraph are fulfilled.

The term of validity of licences issued in compliance with this Article shall be limited to 30 June 1986.'

Article 2

This Regulation shall enter into force on the day of its publication in the *Official Journal of the European Communities.*

It shall apply from 19 April 1986.

This Regulation shall be binding in its entirety and directly applicable in all Member States.

Done at Brussels, 12 May 1986.

For the Commission
Frans ANDRIESSEN
Vice-President

---

[1] OJ No L 281, 1. 11. 1973, p. 1.
[2] OJ No L 367, 31. 12. 1985, p. 19.
[3] OJ No L 103, 19. 4. 1986, p. 58.

BRITISH COURT SYSTEM

CIVIL	*Appeals*	CRIMINAL
County Court (minor cases)	*from* County Court *to* Court of Appeal	Magistrates' Court (minor cases, or cases for committal to Crown Court)
	from Magistrates' Court *to* Crown Court *or to* Queen's Bench Divisional Court	
High Court (major cases)	*from* High Court *to* Court of Appeal	Crown Court (major cases)
	from Crown Court *to* Queen's Bench Divisional Court *or to* Court of Appeal	
	from Court of Appeal *to* House of Lords	
	from Court of Appeal *and* Queen's Bench Divisional Court *to* House of Lords	
	from House of Lords *to* European Court of Justice	

Action in the High Court: a Writ

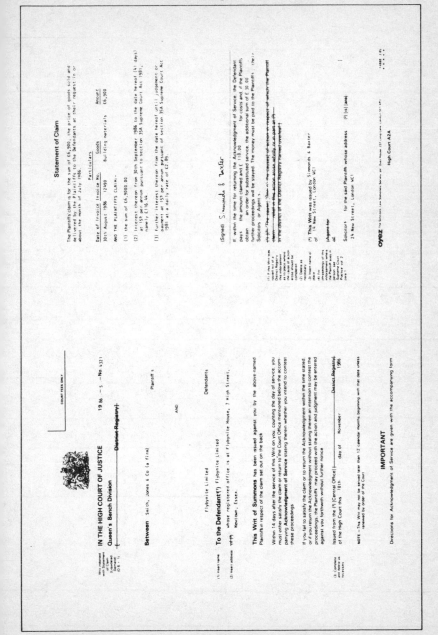

Acknowledgement
of Service of Writ
of Summons
(Queen's Bench)

The addition
heading should
be completed by
the Plaintiff

IN THE HIGH COURT OF JUSTICE   198⎯ ⎯ 5 ⎯ No. 432 ı

Queen's Bench Division   District Registry ı

Between   Smith, Jones & Co. (a firm)   Plaintiff s

AND

Flybynite Limited   Defendant s

If you intend to instruct a Solicitor to act for you, give him this form IMMEDIATELY. Please complete in black ink.

IMPORTANT Read the accompanying directions and notes for guidance carefully before completing this form. If any information requested is omitted or given wrongly, THIS FORM MAY HAVE TO BE RETURNED. Delay may result in judge ors being entered against a Defendant whereby he or his solicitor may have to pay the costs of applying to set it aside

See Notes 3, 4
and 5

1   State the full name of the Defendant by whom or on whose behalf the service of the Writ is being acknowledged

FLYBYNITE LIMITED

2   State whether the Defendant intends to contest the proceedings (tick
appropriate box)   X yes   no

See Direction 3

3   If the claim against the Defendant is for a debt or liquidated demand AND he does not intend to contest the proceedings, state if the Defendant intends to apply for a stay of execution against any judgment entered by the Plaintiff
(tick box)   yes

See Direction 4

4   If the Writ of Summons was issued out of a District Registry and
    (a)   the Defendant's residence, place of business or registered office of a limited company is NOT within the district of that District Registry
       AND
    (b)   there is no endorsement on the Writ that the Plaintiff's cause of action arose wholly or in part within that district
    state if the Defendant applies for the transfer of the action (tick box)   yes

State which
Registry

If YES state⎯   to the Royal Courts of Justice, London
                OR
                to me   District Registry

Service of the Writ is acknowledged accordingly

(Where words
appear between
square brackets
delete if
inapplicable
Insert Defendant
or Person
appropriate

(Signed)   [signature]
1 (Solicitor) (Agent)

Address for service **(See notes overleaf)**

9 Court Road, Liverpool

Please complete overleaf

Non applicable
if the Defendant
is a Company
served at its
Registered Office

Notes for Guidance

1   Each Defendant (if there are more than one) is required to complete an Acknowledgment of Service and return it to the appropriate Court Office

*2   For the purpose of calculating the period of 14 days for acknowledging service a writ served on the Defendant personally is treated as having been served on the day it was delivered to him and a writ served by post or by insertion through the Defendant's letter box is treated as having been served on the seventh day after the date of posting or insertion.)

3   Where the Defendant is sued in a name different from his own the form must be completed by him with the addition in paragraph 1 of the words sued as (the name stated on the Writ of Summons)

4   Where the Defendant is a FIRM and a Solicitor is not instructed, the form must be completed by a PARTNER by name with the addition in paragraph 1 of the description partner in the form of ( ) after his name

5   Where the Defendant is sued as an individual **TRADING IN A NAME OTHER THAN HIS OWN**, the form must be completed by him with the addition in paragraph 1 of the description trading as ( )
after his name

6   Where the Defendant is a LIMITED COMPANY the form must be completed by a Solicitor or by someone authorised to act on behalf of the Company, but the Company can take no further step in the proceedings without a Solicitor acting on its behalf

7   Where the Defendant is a MINOR or a MENTAL Patient, the form must be completed by a Solicitor acting for a guardian and litem

8   A Defendant acting in person may obtain help in completing the form either at the Central Office of the Royal Courts of Justice or at any District Registry of the High Court or at any Citizens Advice Bureau

9   A Defendant who is NOT a Limited Company or a Corporation may be entitled to legal aid. Information about the Legal Aid Scheme may be obtained from any Citizens Advice Bureau and from most firms of Solicitors

10   These notes deal only with the more usual cases in case of difficulty a Defendant in person should refer to paragraphs 8 and 9 above

Action in the High Court: Acknowledgement of Service

Acknowledgement
of Service
of Writ
of Summons
(Queen's Bench)
No 12 - 3)

(Insert address)

Directions for Acknowledgment of Service

1. The accompanying form of **ACKNOWLEDGMENT OF SERVICE** should be detached and completed by the Defendant acting on behalf of the Defendant or by the Defendant if acting in person. After completion it must be delivered or sent by post to the District Registrar (*)

2. A Defendant who states in his Acknowledgment of Service that he intends to contest the proceedings **MUST ALSO SERVE A DEFENCE** on the Solicitor for the Plaintiff (or on the Plaintiff if acting in person)

If a Statement of Claim is endorsed on the Writ (i e the words 'Statement of Claim' appear at the top of the back of the first page), the Defence must be served within 14 days after the time for acknowledging service of the Writ, unless in the meantime a summons for judgment is served on the Defendant

If a Statement of Claim is not endorsed on the Writ, the Defence need not be served until 14 days after a Statement of Claim has been served on the Defendant. If the Defendant fails to serve his defence within the appropriate time, the Plaintiff may enter judgment against him without further notice

3. **A STAY OF EXECUTION** against the Defendant's goods may be applied for where the Defendant is unable to pay the money for which any judgment is entered. If a Defendant to an action for a debt or liquidated demand (i e a fixed sum) who does not intend to contest the proceedings states, in answer to Question 3 in the Acknowledgment of Service, that he intends to apply for a stay execution will be stayed for 14 days after his Acknowledgment. But he must within that time, **ISSUE A SUMMONS** for a stay of execution, supported by an affidavit of his means. The affidavit should state any offer which the Defendant desires to make for payment of the money by instalments or otherwise

4. **IF THE WRIT IS ISSUED OUT OF A DISTRICT REGISTRY** but the Defendant does not reside or carry on business within the district of the registry and the writ is not indorsed with a statement that the Plaintiff's cause of action arose in that district, the Defendant may, in answer to Question 4, in the Acknowledgment of Service, apply for the transfer of the action to some other District Registry or to the Royal Courts of Justice

See over for Notes for Guidance

Indorsement by Plaintiff's solicitor (or by Plaintiff if suing in person) of his name, address and reference, if any, in the box below

Simmonds & Baxter

24 New Street

London WC1

Tel: 01-999 0022 Ref: 58

Notes as to Address for Service

Solicitor Where the Defendant is represented by a Solicitor, state the Solicitor's place of business in England or Wales. If the Solicitor is the Agent of another Solicitor, state the name and the place of business of the Solicitor for whom he is acting

Defendant in person Where the Defendant is acting in person, he must give his residence OR if he does not reside in England or Wales, he must give an address in England or Wales where communications for him should be sent. In the case of a limited company, residence means its registered or principal office

Indorsement by Defendant's solicitor (or by Defendant if suing in person) of his name, address and reference, if any, in the box below.

HAXBYS

9 COURT ROAD

LIVERPOOL

Tel: 051-232 9876 Ref: H/2

Summons
under Order 14
for Whole Claim

IN THE HIGH COURT OF JUSTICE   19 86 __ S __ No. 4321
Queen's Bench Division

Master Archer   Master in Chambers

Between Smith, Jones & Co (a firm)

AND

Plaintiffs

Flybynite Limited   Defendant s

(1) The Defendant
or if appeal one
or some of several
Defendants insert
names

Let all parties concerned attend the Master in Chambers, in Room No. 96,
Central Office, Royal Courts of Justice, Strand, London, on   the   day
the   10th   day of   January   1991, at   11 : 00   o'clock in
the   fore   noon on the hearing of an application on the part of the Plaintiff for final
judgment in this action against(1)   the defendants

(2) Or as the case
may be setting
out the nature of
the claim

for the amount claimed in the statement of claim with interest if any (²)

and costs

Take Notice that a party intending to oppose this application or to apply for a stay of
execution should send to the opposite party or his solicitor, to reach him not less than
three days before the date above-mentioned, a copy of any affidavit intended to be
used

Dated the   28th   day of   November   1986

This Summons was taken out by Simmonds & Baxter
of 14 New Street, London WC1
[Agent for
of

Solicitor for the Plaintiff s

To M essrs Maxbys

Solicitor s or Agent for the Defendants

---

19 86 __ S __ No. 4321

IN THE HIGH COURT OF JUSTICE
Queen's Bench Division

Dated 28th November   19 86

Returnable 10th January   19 87

Smith, Jones & Co (a firm)

v

Flybynite Ltd

Summons
Under Order 14 for Whole Claim

Simmonds & Baxter
14 New Street,
London WC1

Agent   for the

of

Solicitor for the Plaintiff s

oyez The Solicitors' Law Stationery Society plc Oyez House
        27 Crimscott Street, London SE1
High Court S3 (PR)

IN THE HIGH COURT OF JUSTICE
Queen's Bench Division

1986 — S — No. 432

Between

Smith, Jones & Co (a firm)   Plaintiffs

AND

Flybynite Limited   Defendants

I, John Jones, builder,
of 24 New Street, London WC1
make oath and say as follows:—

1. The Defendants, Flybynite Limited
(*) were, and (*) are at the commencement of this action,
justly and truly indebted to (*) the Plaintiffs

in the sum of £ 6,960.00, the   for the price of building materials
supplied by the Plaintiffs to the Defendants at their request.

The particulars of the said claim appear by the indorsement on the Writ of Summons in this action.

2. It is within my own knowledge that the said debt was incurred and is still due and owing as aforesaid.

or

~~I am informed by (*)~~
~~and/or I verily believe (*)~~
~~that the said debt was incurred and is still due and owing as aforesaid.~~

3. I verily believe that there is no defence to this action.

4. I am duly authorised by the Plaintiff to make this affidavit. (*)

Sworn at 41 Old Street, London WC2

the 30th day of November, 19 86.

Before me,   John Jones

                                   A Commissioner for Oaths

This affidavit is filed on behalf of the Plaintiff

IN THE HIGH COURT OF JUSTICE
Queen's Bench Division

1986 — S — No. 432

Sworn the 30th day of November, 19 86.

Smith, Jones & Co
(a firm)
v
Flybynite Ltd

Affidavit
under Order 14,
Rule 2.
by or on behalf
of Plaintiff

Filed on behalf of the Plaintiff

Simmonds & Baxter,
14 New Street,
London WC1

Plaintiffs Solicitors

oyez   The Solicitors' Law Stationery Society plc, Oyez House,
237 Long Lane, London SE1 4PU.
High Court B34 (PRI)

IN THE HIGH COURT OF JUSTICE

Queen's Bench Division

1986 — S — No. 4321

Dated 10th January 1986

Smith, Jones & Co (a Firm)

v

Flybynite Ltd

Judgment

Under Order 14 Rule 3

Plaintiff's Solicitors

Simmonds & Baxter
14 New Street,
London WC1

OYEZ The Solicitors' Law Stationery Society plc, Oyez House

High Court D5

Judgment under Order 14 Rule 3 or sections O 14 3 O 42 1

IN THE HIGH COURT OF JUSTICE

Queen's Bench Division

1986 — S — No. 4321

Between

Smith, Jones & Co (a Firm)   Plaintiffs

AND

Flybynite Limited   Defendants

The 10th day of January 1987

The Defendant having given notice of intention to defend herein and the Court having under Order 14 Rule 3 ordered that judgment as hereinafter provided be entered for the Plaintiff against the Defendant

IT IS THIS DAY ADJUDGED that the Defendant

do pay the Plaintiffs £6,900.00 together with interest from the due date of payment to the date of issue of the writ at 15% per annum pursuant to section 35A Supreme Court Act 1981 namely £116.44 and further interest from the date of issue to the date hereof at 15% per annum pursuant to section 35A Supreme Court Act 1981 amounting to £176.08 a total of £7,192.52

and £178.50   costs [or costs to be taxed]

The above costs have been taxed and allowed at £   as appears by a taxing officer's certificate dated the   day of

19

Plaintiff's Solicitor

IN THE HIGH COURT OF JUSTICE
QUEEN'S BENCH DIVISION   1986 -A- No. 1390

The Honourable Mr Justice Good   Judge in Chambers

BETWEEN

ACME ADVERTISING LIMITED   Plaintiffs
              and
SIMON SLY   Defendant

            ORDER

UPON HEARING Counsel for the Plaintiffs and the Defendant in person and upon reading the affidavit of Adrian Acme sworn herein

And the Plaintiffs by their said Counsel undertaking to abide by any Order this Court may make as to damages in case this Court shall hereafter be of opinion that the Defendant shall have sustained any by reason of this Order which the Plaintiffs ought to pay

IT IS ORDERED and directed that the Defendant be restrained and an injunction is hereby granted restraining him until 15th October 1987, directly or indirectly, whether for himself, any other person, firm, company or otherwise from soliciting or seeking orders for advertising from any person, firm or company within the Greater London area who were customers of the Plaintiffs on 16th October 1986

AND IT IS ORDERED that the Defendant do deliver up forthwith to the Plaintiffs' solicitors any books, records, customer lists or other documents, the property of the Plaintiffs, or any copies thereof which are in his possession or control

AND IT IS ORDERED that the costs of this application be costs in the cause.

DATED the 30th day of October 1986

To:
XYZ (Supplies) Limited.
9 Old Street,
London EC7.

Dear Sirs,

In consideration of your agreeing at my request to refrain from taking proceedings to recover payment of the debt of £6,497.50 owed to you by Simon Baxter Ltd, we jointly and severally guarantee payment of it (or of such part of it as remains unpaid after 2nd December 1986) on the understanding that all sums received by you from Simon Baxter Ltd, or for the credit of their account with you shall be first applied by you in reduction of that debt.

This guarantee is not to be impaired by any time or indulgence which you may grant. Moreover, our right to be subrogated to you in respect of payments received from, or from the resources of, Simon Baxter Ltd is not to attach until you have received the full amount of your claim to which this guarantee relates.

Yours faithfully,

Simon Baxter
John Baxter

Simon Baxter

John Baxter

CONTRACT OF SALE

The National Conditions of Sale, Twentieth Edition

Vendor JOHN PETER SMITH and MAUREEN ANNE SMITH both of
12 Sherborne Avenue Norwood Green Southall Middlesex

Purchaser ROBERT FRANK GREEN and LINDA GREEN both of
291 Finchley Road London NW3

Registered Land	Purchase price	£ 100,000	00
District Land Registry HARROW	Deposit	£ 10,000	00
Title Number NGL 227147	Balance payable	£ 90,000	00
Agreed rate of interest	Price fixed for chattels or valuation money (if any)	£ 7,000	00
4½ per annum above base rate at Midland Bank plc for the time being in force.	Total	£ 97,000	00

Property and interest therein sold

ALL THAT freehold property situate at and known as
12 Sherborne Avenue Southall in the London
Borough of Ealing as the same is registered
at H M Land Registry with Title Absolute.

Vendor sells as   Beneficial Owners   Completion date

AGREED that the Vendor sells and the Purchaser buys as above subject to the Special Conditions
endorsed hereon and to the National Conditions of Sale Twentieth Edition so far as the latter Conditions
are not inconsistent with the Special Conditions

* Signed

Date   19

* This is a form of legal document. Neither the form nor the National Conditions of Sale which the form embodies
were produced or drafted for use without technical assistance by r   infamiliar with the law and practice of
conveyancing.

SPECIAL CONDITIONS OF SALE

A   The sale is with vacant possession on completion.

B   The deposit shall be paid by way of bankers draft, Building Society cheque or
Solicitors' client account cheque to the Vendors Solicitors as Stakeholders.

C   The Purchaser hereby acknowledges that, save for replies to enquiries made of
the Vendors Solicitors by the Purchasers Solicitors :-

i.   No statement or representation made to the Purchaser or to anyone concerned
on his behalf by or on behalf of the Vendors whether orally or in writing induced
him to enter into this contract.

ii.   Any such statement or representation does not form part of this contract.

iii. Any liability of the Vendors and any remedy of the Purchaser at law or in
equity in respect of any such statement or representation is excluded to the
extent authorised by the Unfair Contract Terms Act 1977.

D   If the Vendors Solicitors receive the monies due on completion after 2.30pm the
following working day shall be deemed the date of actual completion And where
completion is by post, all deeds and documents shall be posted at the Purchasers
risk.

E   On completion the Vendors will sell and the Purchaser will buy the following
additional items for the price of Seven thousand pounds (£7,000):

All carpets   Wardrobes in bedroom 2 and small bedroom
All curtains   Tumbledryer
All blinds   Fridge/Freezer
Chandeliers   Cooker

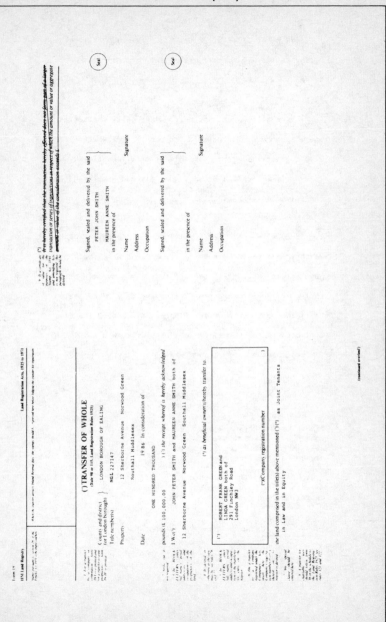

Form 19

HM Land Registry

Land Registration Acts, 1925 to 1971

( ) TRANSFER OF WHOLE

(Rule 98 or 115, Land Registration Rules 1925)

County and district
(or London borough) } LONDON BOROUGH OF EALING

Title number(s) NGL 227147

Property 12 Sherborne Avenue Norwood Green
Southall Middlesex

Date 19 86 In consideration of

ONE HUNDRED THOUSAND

pounds (£ 100,000.00) ( ) the receipt whereof is hereby acknowledged

I We( ) JOHN PETER SMITH and MAUREEN ANNE SMITH both of
12 Sherborne Avenue Norwood Green Southall Middlesex

( ) as beneficial owner( ) hereby transfer to

( ) ROBERT FRANK GREEN and
LINDA GREEN both of
291 Finchley Road
London NW3

( )(Company, registration number   )

the land comprised in the title(s) above mentioned ( )( ) as Joint Tenants

in Law and in Equity

(continued overleaf)

It is hereby certified that the transaction hereby effected does not form part of a larger
transaction or series of transactions in respect of which the amount or value or aggregate
amount or value of the consideration exceeds £

Signed, sealed and delivered by the said

PETER JOHN SMITH

MAUREEN ANNE SMITH

in the presence of

Signature

Name

Address

Occupation

Seal

Signed, sealed and delivered by the said

in the presence of

Signature

Name

Address

Occupation

Seal

313

Will

I, <u>JOHN HENRY BROWN</u> of 22 New Grove, Wincham, Suffolk,
hereby revoke all former testamentary dispositions made
by me.

1. I give all my real and personal property whatsoever
and wheresoever (including any property over which I may
have a general power of appointment or disposition by will)
to my wife Emily Jane Brown absolutely and appoint her
the sole executrix of this my will.

2. If my wife shall not survive me for the period of one
month then I declare that the foregoing clause shall not
have effect and in lieu thereof I give all my said property
including the income accruing from the date of my death
until the death of my wife to Robert Black of 9 The Elms
Littleton in the County of Kent absolutely and appoint him
the sole executor of this my will.

IN WITNESS whereof I have hereunto set my hand this 10th day
of October 1972

SIGNED by the above-named)
John Henry Brown as his last)
will in the presence of us)
present at the same time) *John H. Brown.*
who at his request in his)
presence and in the presence)
of each other have hereunto)
subscribed our names as)
witnesses   )

Nigel Day
Accountant
10 Oak Way
Wincham
Suffolk

Ronald Henderson
Teacher
16 New Grove
Wincham
Suffolk.

Particulars of Claim in the County Court

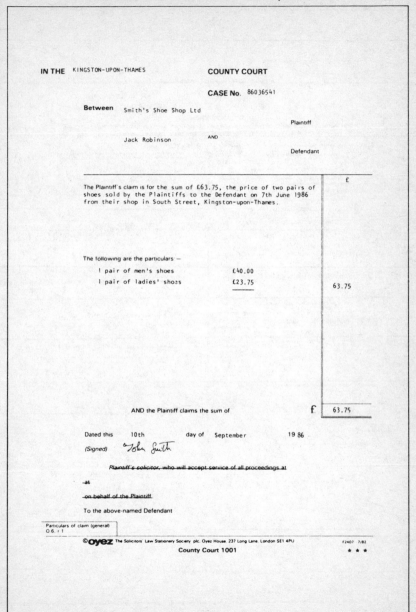

IN THE KINGSTON-UPON-THAMES   **COUNTY COURT**

CASE No. 86036541

Between   Smith's Shoe Shop Ltd

                                       Plaintiff

           Jack Robinson   AND

                                       Defendant

	£
The Plaintiff's claim is for the sum of £63.75, the price of two pairs of shoes sold by the Plaintiffs to the Defendant on 7th June 1986 from their shop in South Street, Kingston-upon-Thames.	
The following are the particulars —	
1 pair of men's shoes £40.00	
1 pair of ladies' shoes £23.75	63.75
AND the Plaintiff claims the sum of £	63.75

Dated this   10th   day of   September   19 86

(Signed)   *John Smith*

~~Plaintiff's solicitor, who will accept service of all proceedings at~~

~~at~~

~~on behalf of the Plaintiff~~

To the above-named Defendant

Particulars of claim (general)
O 6. 1

Defence to Claim in the County Court

In the KINGSTON-UPON-THAMES County Court

CASE No. 86036541

SMITH'S SHOE SHOP LTD v JACK ROBINSON

ADMISSION

Read the instructions on the back of the summons carefully before completing this form. Immediately after you have filled in this form send it by post or take it to the Court Office as stated on the summons. PLEASE USE BLACK INK.

1. Do you admit the plaintiff's claim in full YES/**NO**

2. Do you admit part of the plaintiff's claim YES/**NO**

   If so, how much do you admit? £ 40.00
   (Put your reasons for disputing the balance overleaf)

3. If you wish the court to consider whether to make an instalment order answer the following questions:—

PAY AND MEANS

(a) What is your occupation lorry driver

(b) What is the name and address of your employer?

   H.G.V. LORRY COMPANY
   RICHMOND ROAD
   KINGSTON ON THAMES

(c) What is your pay before deductions? £ 120.00 per week/month

(d) What overtime, bonuses, fees, allowances, or commissions do you receive? £ 20.00 per week/month

(e) What is your usual take home pay? £ 113.00 per week/month

(f) Do you receive
   (i) a pension? £ No per week/month
   (ii) any state benefits? £ No per week/month
   (iii) any other income? £ No per week/month

(g) What contributions, if any, are made by any member of your household?

   NONE

LIABILITIES

(a) What persons, if any, are financially dependent on you? Please give details including the ages of any dependent children:—

   My wife and 2 children ages 4 and 7

(b) What rent or mortgage instalments are you liable to pay? £ 25.00 per week/month

   What amount do you actually pay? £ 25.00 per week/month

(c) What rates are you liable to pay? £ 12.00 per week/month

   What amount do you actually pay? £ 12.00 per week/month

(d) Do you have to pay under any Court Orders? Please give details including name of court and case number, the amount still owing and the instalments you are paying.

   Judgement for arrears of rates in this court which I am paying at £5 per month. I still have £25 to pay.

(e) What other regular payments do you have to make?:

   H.P. on car £30 per month. Maintenance to my former wife and children £10 per month.

(f) Have you any other liabilities which you would like the Court to take into account? Please give details:—

   No.

WHAT OFFER OF PAYMENT DO YOU MAKE?

Payment in full on the ____ day of ____ 19__   OR by instalments of £ 3.00 per month

Address to which notices about this case should be sent to you:
13 Black Street
Kingston on Thames

SIGN HERE J. Robinson

DATE 14th September 1986

NB Form of Admission, Defence and Counterclaim to accompany form N1, 2, 3 and 4
Order 3 Rule 3(2)(c)

MCR 341637/1/F24336 9m 3/85 TL

Defence to Claim in the County Court

In the KINGSTON-UPON-THAMES County Court

CASE No. 86036541

SMITH'S SHOE SHOP LTD   v   JACK ROBINSON

DEFENCE	COUNTERCLAIM
1. Do you dispute the plaintiff's claim or any part of it? YES/NO	1. Do you wish to make a claim against the plaintiff? YES/NO
2. If so, how much do you dispute and what are your reasons?	2. If so, for how much? £
	3. What is the nature of the claim?

I returned the shoes I
bought for £23.75 2 days
after I bought them
because they fell apart.

TO BE COMPLETED WHERE THE SUM CLAIMED OR AMOUNT INVOLVED EXCEEDS £500

If you dispute the plaintiff's claim or wish to make a claim against him do you want the proceedings referred to arbitration?   YES/NO

NOTES:

1. Any claim for £500 or less which is defended will be referred to arbitration automatically, but the reference may be rescinded on application.

2. When a defended claim is arbitrated the right of appeal against the arbitrator's award is very limited.

3. If your claim against the plaintiff is bigger than his claim against you, you may have to pay a fee before it can be dealt with. You can find out whether a fee is payable by enquiring at any county court office.

Address to which notices about this case should be sent to you: 17 Black Street Kingston on thames

SIGN HERE J. Robinson

DATE 14th September 1986

N9   Form of Admission, Defence and Counterclaim to accompany forms N1, 2, 3 and 4
Order 3 Rule 3(2)(c)

317

In the _____ County Court*

Divorce Registry

No of matter 1472 of 1986

IN THE MATTER of the Petition of

JEAN BROOKS Petitioner

and

JOHN BROOKS Respondent

Divorce Petition

(Wife against Husband)

(Behaviour)

Note 22

Simmonds & Baxter
14 New Street,
London WC1

OYEZ The Solicitors' Law Stationery Society plc, Oyez House
237 Long Lane, London SE1 4PU

Divorce 2W

(Wife—Petition—Behaviour)

MATRIMONIAL
CAUSES RULES*

Rule 9
Appendix 2

IN THE

No of matter 1472 of 1986

The Petition of Jean Brooks (née Smith)

Shows that

Note 1

1   On the 10th   day of June   19 72   the Petitioner
was lawfully

married to John Brooks

(hereinafter called the Respondent) at St. John's Church in Oldham in the
County of Sussex.

Note 2   2   The Petitioner and the Respondent last lived together as husband and
wife at 14 Chaucer Crescent, London N2

Note 3   3   The Petitioner is domiciled in England and Wales

Note 4   The Petitioner is a   dress designer   and resides at
14 Chaucer Crescent, London N2
and the Respondent is a   unemployed   and resides
at 9 Acacia Grove, Bromley, Kent.

Note 5   4   There is (are) two   children of the family now living
James Brooks born on 14th February 1974.
Sarah Brooks born on 9th July 1977

Note 6   5   No other child now living has been born to the Petitioner during the
marriage

Note 7   6   There are or have been no other proceedings in any court in England
and Wales or elsewhere with reference to the marriage (or to any children of the
family) or between the Petitioner and the Respondent with reference to any

property of either or both of them

Note 8

7 There are no proceedings continuing in any country outside England and Wales which relate to the marriage or are capable of affecting its validity or subsistence

Note 9

Note 10

8 The said marriage has broken down irretrievably

Note 11

9 The Respondent has behaved in such a way that the Petitioner cannot reasonably be expected to live with the Respondent

10 (a) The Respondent throughout the marriage has drunk to excess and **Note 13** in spite of the Petitioner's requests refuses to seek medical or other assistance.

(b) when drunk the Respondent is abusive to the Petitioner and the children of the family causing them distress.

(c) As a result of the Respondent's excessive drinking the Respondent has failed to keep any employment and thus has been unable adequately or at all to contribute to the maintenance of the family, the full burden of which has fallen on the Petitioner.

Note 14
Note 15
Note 16

The Petitioner therefore prays –

(1) That the said marriage may be dissolved

Note 17
(2) That she may be granted the custody of James Brooks and Sarah Brooks.

Note 18
Note 19
(3) That the Respondent may be ordered to pay the costs of this suit

Note 20
(4) That she may be granted the following ancillary relief

(i) an order for maintenance pending suit

(ii) a periodical payments order

(iii) a secured periodical payments order } for herself

(iv) a lump sum order

(v) a periodical payments order

(vi) a secured periodical payments order } for the children of the family

(vii) a lump sum order

(viii) a property adjustment order

Note 21

Simmonds & Baxter (Signed)

Note 22
The names and addresses of the persons who are to be served with this Petition are –

John Brooks,
9 Acacia Grove, Bromley, Kent

Note 23
The Petitioner's address for service is c/o Messrs Simmonds & Baxter, 4 New Street, London WC1

Dated this 14th day of September 1986

Address all communications for the court to "The Registrar, County Court".....